HISTORY

OF THE

REBELLION OF 1745-6

HISTORY OF THE

REBELLION OF 1745-6

BY

ROBERT CHAMBERS.

NEW EDITION.

Raising the Standard in Glenfinnin.

Page 48.

W. & R. CHAMBERS.

LIMITED.

EDINBURGH AND LONDON

TO

SIR PETER MURRAY THREIPLAND,

OF FINGASK, BARONET,

REPRESENTATIVE OF A FAMILY WHICH

CAN STILL VIEW WITH GENEROUS REGRET

THE CAUSE FOR WHICH FORMER GENERATIONS

GLADLY SUFFERED,

THIS

WORK IS RESPECTFULLY

AND AFFECTIONATELY INSCRIBED.

PREFACE TO THE FIFTH EDITION.

THE present work appeared originally in *Constable's Miscellany* in 1827. The principal sources of information which then existed for a history of the civil war of 1745, were the contemporary public journals, Mr Home's work (valuable at least for its reports of what the author himself witnessed), the Lockhart and Culloden Papers, the Chevalier Johnstone's *Memoirs*, and the still fresh traditions of the people. Since from these documents the author constructed the first edition of his narrative, a greater quantity of valuable materials has become accessible than during eighty preceding years. The personal narratives of two distinguished actors, Lord Elcho and Mr Maxwell of Kirkconnel, have been in part or wholly given to the world. In Dr James Browne's *History of the Highlands and Highland Clans*, there appeared extensive and very important excerpts from the great collection in the possession of the British sovereign, styled 'The Stuart Papers.' To this valuable set of excerpts, Lord Mahon has made additions in his *History of Great Britain between the Peace of Utrecht and that of Aix-la-Chapelle.* I was myself so fortunate, in 1832, as to become possessed of an extensive collection of papers which had been gathered, early in the present century, by the late Sir Henry Steuart of Allanton, with a view to his composing a History of the Efforts in behalf of the House of Stuart from the Revolution downwards. Amongst these was an assemblage of memoirs, notes, letters, and other memorabilia respecting the insurrection of 1745 and its actors, which had been formed with great labour, during the twenty years ensuing upon the event, by the Rev. Robert

Forbes, Episcopal minister at Leith, and ultimately (titular) Bishop of Orkney. From Sir Henry's collection, which eventually became mine, I published a selection in 1834, under the title of *Jacobite Memoirs of the Rebellion of* 1745-6; but by far the greater part of the more valuable documents still remained in manuscript.

In the present edition of my own narrative, advantage has been taken of the abundance of new materials thus placed at command. So ample were these, and so great were the changes consequently required in the fabric of the narrative, that the present might almost be described as a new work. That part, in particular, which records the singular adventures of the Prince after the battle of Culloden, is much more copious, and also more strictly correct, than it was before, chiefly in consequence of the special pains which Bishop Forbes took to ascertain all the particulars of those adventures from the gentlemen and others who had been concerned in them. The work is now submitted, in its extended and corrected form, not without a hope that it will be found to contain sufficient information to satisfy all reasonable curiosity upon the subject.

EDINBURGH, *February* 24, 1840.

PREFACE TO THE SEVENTH EDITION.

A FEW words as to the *feeling* manifested in this narrative.

It has been customary to call it a Jacobite history. To this let me demur. Of the whole attempt of 1745 I disapprove, as most men do. I think its authors were under a grave mistake in preferring a supposed right of One to the interest of the entire body of the people; and, undoubtedly, it was a crime to disturb with war, and to some extent with rapine, a nation enjoying internal peace under a settled government.

But, on the other hand, those who followed Charles Edward in his hazardous enterprise, acted according to their lights, with heroic self-devotion. They were not fairly liable to the vulgar ridicule and vituperations thrown upon them by those whose duty it was to resist and punish them. Even the sovereigns succeeding him whom Charles Edward strove to displace, came to feel for the exiled dynasty, and to wish for no better friends than it had had. Knowing how these men did all in honour, I deem it but just that their adventures should be detailed with impartiality, and their unavoidable misfortunes be spoken of with humane feeling.

There is no other Jacobitism in the book that I am aware of.

R. C.

EDINBURGH, 1869.

GENEALOGICAL AND HISTORICAL INTRODUCTION.

JAMES, sixth of Scotland and first of England, was the common progenitor of the two families whose contentions for the throne of Great Britain form the subject of this work. He was succeeded, at his death in 1625, by his eldest surviving son Charles.

Charles I., after a reign of twenty-three years, the latter portion of which had been spent in war with a party of his subjects, perished on the scaffold in 1649.

Charles II., eldest son of Charles I., lived in exile for eleven years after the death of his father, during which time the government was vested first in a Parliament, and afterwards in a Protectorate. He was at length placed upon the throne, May 1660. This event is known in British history by the title of 'the Restoration.' Charles died without legitimate issue in 1685, and was succeeded by his brother James, who had previously been entitled Duke of York.

James II. was fifty-three years of age when he mounted the throne. In his youth he had, as Admiral of England, shewn some talent for business, and considerable skill in naval affairs ; but during his reign he manifested a want of judgment which would almost indicate premature dotage. Having been converted to the Roman Catholic faith, he entered into the spirit of it with the zeal natural to a weak mind, and ventured upon some steps which impressed his subjects with the conviction that he wished to place this religion on a par with Protestantism, if not to restore it to its ancient supremacy. Thus he alienated the affections of the people, but more especially of the clergy, who were otherwise disposed to have been his most zealous friends. The compliance of bad judges, and some imperfections of the British constitution, left it in his power to take the most arbitrary measures for the accomplishment of his designs; and he attempted to establish as a maxim, that he could do whatever he pleased by a proclamation of his own, without the consent of Parliament. Finally, his obstinacy and infatuation rendered it necessary for all parties of the state to seek his deposition. A secret coalition of Whigs and Tories resolved to call in the assistance of William, Prince of Orange, nephew and son-in-law to the king. William landed upon the south coast of England with an army of sixteen thousand men, partly his own native subjects, and partly English refugees, November 5, 1688. As he proceeded to London, James was deserted by his army, his friends, and even his own children; and in a confusion of mind, the result of fear and offended feelings, he retired to France. William, at the head of a powerful force, took possession of London. A Convention-Parliament then declared that James had abdicated the throne, and resolved to offer the crown to William and his consort Mary. In British history, this event is termed 'the Revolution.'

William III., son of Mary, eldest daughter of Charles I., and who had married his cousin Mary, eldest daughter of James II., thus assumed the crown, in company with his consort; while King James remained in exile in France. Mary died in 1695, and King William then became sole monarch. In consequence of a fall from his horse, he died in 1701, leaving no issue.

Anne, second daughter of King James II., was then placed upon the throne. James meanwhile died in France, leaving a son, James, born in England, June 10, 1688, the heir of his unhappy fortunes. This personage, known in history by the epithet of the Pretender, and less invidiously by his *incognito* title, the Chevalier St George, continued an exile in France, supported by his cousin Louis XIV., and by the subsidies of his English adherents. Anne, after a reign of thirteen years, distinguished by military and literary glory, died without surviving issue, August 1, 1714. During the life of this sovereign, the crown had been destined, by act of Parliament, to the nearest Protestant heir, Sophia, Electress of Hanover, daughter of Elizabeth, Queen of Bohemia, the daughter of King James VI. Sophia having predeceased Queen Anne, it descended of course to her son George, Elector of Hanover, who accordingly came over to England and assumed the sovereignty, to the exclusion of his cousin the Chevalier.

George I. was scarcely seated on the throne, when (1715) an insurrection was raised against him by the friends of his rival, now generally known as the Jacobite party. This rebellion was suppressed; and George I. continued to reign, almost without further disturbance, till his death in 1727.

George II. acceded to the crown on the death of his father. Meanwhile the Chevalier St George had married Clementina, grand-daughter of John Sobieski, the heroic king of Poland; by this lady he had two sons—1st, Charles Edward Lewis Casimir, born December 31, 1720, and, 2d, Henry Benedict, born 1725, afterwards well known by the name of Cardinal de York. James was himself a man of weak, though mild and virtuous character; but the blood of Sobieski seems to have descended to his eldest son, whose boldness, as displayed in 1745-6, did everything but retrieve the fortunes of his family.

CONTENTS.

CONTENTS.

HISTORY

REBELLION OF 1745-6.

CHAPTER I.

PRINCE CHARLES'S VOYAGE AND LANDING.

'*Guard.* Qui est là?
Pucelle. Païsans, pauvres gens de France.'
King Henry VI.

THE idea of an insurrection in favour of the exiled house
of Stuart, though, from the Revolution, it had never been
for a moment out of the thoughts of the Jacobite party,
remained, during the long peace which preceded 1739, in that
state of dormancy which usually befalls the most deeply
cherished schemes, when there is no hope of their being
immediately carried into execution. When, however, Britain
became engaged in war with Spain, and not long after mingled
in the general conflict of European powers which took place in
consequence of the exclusion of the house of Austria from the
imperial dignity, the friends of the Stuarts eagerly embraced the
belief that a fitting time had at length arrived for striking a blow

in behalf of legitimacy.   They had every reason to believe that France, in particular, if not also Spain, would grant them the assistance of an invading armament, under favour of which they might themselves take up arms.   What made their prospects the more cheerful was, that a new promise had sprung up in the exiled family, in the person of the old Chevalier's eldest son, Charles Edward, whose character was understood to comprehend all that was graceful in a prince, united with the spirit of one destined to be a military hero.   In this respect they stood in a better position than they had ever done before ; for the two preceding generations of the dethroned family had possessed no personal qualities that could afford much aid to the cause.

So early, therefore, as 1740, associations had begun to be formed by the Scottish partisans of the Stuarts, engaging to rise in arms, provided that competent assistance should be sent from abroad.[1]   At the end of 1743, the French court actually entered into the design of an invasion of Britain in behalf of the Stuarts, and sent to Rome for the young Chevalier, that he might be ready to accompany it, the chief command of the troops being designed for the celebrated Marshal Saxe.   Charles instantly proceeded to Paris, and in the latter part of February 1744, a fleet was ready to sail, with an army of 15,000 men on board. The British government was thrown into great alarm, for their shores were comparatively unprotected, and the people were in a state of violent discontent.   A small fleet was mustered under Sir John Norris, and sent to watch the French at Dunkirk. What this aged admiral could scarcely have done, was done by a storm, which drove the French vessels from their moorings, destroying some, and irretrievably damaging others.   This, with the attacks of the British vessels, so far deranged the scheme, that the French ministry determined on abandoning it.   The

---

[1] In the year 1740, seven persons of rank entered into an association of this kind— namely, the Earl of Traquair ; his brother, John Stuart : Lord Lovat ; James Drummond, commonly called Duke of Perth ; Lord John Drummond, uncle of James Drummond ; Sir James Campbell of Auchinbreck ; and Cameron, younger of Locheil—most of these being persons possessing influence in the Highlands.   Many others afterwards entered into similar engagements.

mortification of Charles was great ; and with his characteristic boldness he actually proposed to his father's veteran partisan, Earl Marischal, to set sail in a herring-boat for Scotland, in order to put himself at the head of his friends—believing, apparently, that his own presence as their leader was alone wanting for success.   The earl of course refused to sanction such a scheme ; and Charles, after an ineffectual endeavour to be allowed by his father to serve in the French army, retired to an obscure part of France, to wait for better times.

At the end of the year, and in the early part of 1745, he used every exertion, by means of his emissaries, and by personal solicitations, to induce the French court to renew the enterprise ; but without success.   It appears that some of the Protestant powers in alliance with Louis had remonstrated against his giving aid to the Catholic party in Britain : every effort, they said, ought to be concentrated on the seat of war in Flanders.[1] Charles, therefore, found himself coldly treated in Paris.   It is remarkable that he was not even introduced to the king—nor had he ever this honour until after his return from Scotland. Yet, for the sake of an object to which he had devoted his whole affections, he patiently endured this contumely, and all the other distresses of his situation, among which the low intrigues of some of his immediate followers were not the least. Writing to his father, January 3, 1745, when about to retire, for reasons of policy, to a dull place in the country, he says : ' This I do not regret in the least, as long as I think it of service to our cause.   I would put myself in a tub, like Diogenes, if necessary.' [2]   Afterwards (March 7), when contemplating some preparations for the expedition with his own means, he writes to the same person : ' I wish you would pawn all my jewels, for on *this* side of the water I should wear them with a very sore heart, thinking that there might be a better use for them ; so that, in an urgent necessity, I may have a sum which can be of use for the cause.'   Of another sum which he had obtained from his

[1] *Mémoires de Noailles*, vi. 22, quoted in Lord Mahon's *History of England*, iii. 335.
[2] Extracts from Stuart Papers, in Lord Mahon's *History*.

father, and expended in the purchase of broadswords, he says in the same letter : ' Rather than want it, I would have pawned my shirt : it is but for such uses that I shall ever trouble you with requests for money ; *it will never be for plate or fine clothes, but for arms and ammunition, or other things which tend to what I am come about to this country.*' [1]   It is generally believed that the victory, such as it was, gained by the French over the British army at Fontenoy in May, completed the resolution of France not to fit out a new armament for the young Chevalier, a diversion of the enemy by such means being now considered unnecessary.

When Charles was at length despairing of aid from this source, the very sense of resentment seems to have acted as an additional stimulus to throw him back upon the romantic design first propounded to Lord Marischal.   He had great confidence in the enthusiasm of his British, and more particularly his Scottish partisans, some of whom had requested him to come to them, if he only could bring a sufficiency of arms and money. He thought if he could once raise his standard in Scotland, his friends would flock to it, and that at this particular juncture, when the British army had just sustained a notable defeat, and the country was drained of troops, he should be able at least to keep his ground until foreign aid should arrive, if not to do something which should make that aid more likely to come. The loud discontents expressed in Britain respecting the war and the existing ministry, held out additional encouragement. He therefore determined upon a secret voyage to Scotland, no matter how few might share in the danger, or how slenderly provided he might be with money or with military stores.   Early in June, we find him at the Château de Navarre, near Evreux, writing a letter to his father, not to ask his sanction for the projected enterprise, but to inform him that, before the writing could be in his hands, that enterprise would be commenced.   ' I am to tell you,' says he, ' what will be a great surprise to you.

---

[1] Extracts from Stuart Papers, in Lord Mahon's *History.*

I have been, above six months ago, invited by our friends to go to Scotland, and carry what money and arms I could conveniently get ; this being, they are fully persuaded, the only way of restoring you to the crown, and them to their liberties. . . . . After such scandalous usage as I have received from the French court, even had I not given my word to do so, or got so many encouragements from time to time as I have had, I should have been obliged, in honour and for my own reputation, to have flung myself into the hands of my friends, and die with them, rather than live longer in such a miserable way here, or be obliged to return to Rome, which would be just giving up all hopes.   I cannot but mention a parable here, which is : a horse that is to be sold, if [when] spurred, [he] does not skip, or shew some sign of life, nobody would care to have him even for nothing ; just so my friends would care very little to have me, if, after such usage, which all the world is sensible of, I should not shew that I have life in me.   Your majesty cannot disapprove a son's following the example of his father.   You yourself did the like in the year 1715 ; but the circumstances now are indeed very different, by being much more encouraging. . . . .   I have been obliged to steal off, without letting the king of France so much as suspect it ; for which I make a proper excuse in my letter to him, by saying it was a great mortification to me never to be able to speak and open my heart to him ; that this thing was of such a nature that it could not be communicated by any of the ministers, but to himself alone, in whom, after God Almighty, my resting lies, and that the least help would make my affair infallible.   If I had let the French court know this beforehand, it might have had all these bad effects : *1st*, It is possible they might have stopped me, having a mind to keep measures with the elector ;[1] and then, to cover it over, they would have made a merit of it to you, by saying they had hindered me from doing a wild and desperate thing : *2dly*, My being invited by my friends would not be believed, or

---

[1] The king of Great Britain was, by the Stuarts and their partisans, only allowed to be Elector of Hanover.

at least would have made little impression on the French court.

'I have,' he continues, 'sent Stafford to Spain, and appointed Sir Thomas Geraldine to demand succours in my name, to complete the work, to whom I sent letters for the king and queen, written in the most engaging terms to the same purpose. Let what will happen, the stroke is struck, and *I have taken a firm resolution to conquer or to die, and to stand my ground as long as I shall have a man remaining with me.* . . . . Whatever happens unfortunate to me, cannot but be the strongest engagement to the French court to pursue your cause. Now, if I were sure they were capable of any sensation of this kind, if I did not succeed, I would perish, as Curtius did, to save my country and make it happy; it being an indispensable duty on me as far as lies in my power. . . . . I write this from Navarre, but it will not be sent off till I am on shipboard. . . . . I should think it proper (if your majesty pleases) to put myself at his holiness's feet, asking his blessing on this occasion; but what I chiefly ask is your own, which I hope will procure me that of God Almighty, upon my endeavours to serve you, my family, and my country.'[1]

One Waters, a banker in Paris, had lent Charles 60,000 livres, which he had employed in paying off the debts he incurred at Paris during the past winter. The younger Waters, also a banker, now advanced to him 120,000 livres, with which he bought 1500 fusees, 1800 broadswords, and a considerable quantity of gunpowder, ball, flints, dirks, and other articles, including 20 small field-pieces. Mr Walsh, a merchant in Nantes, agreed to convey him to the coast of Scotland in a brig of 18 guns, which he had fitted out to cruise against the British trade; at the same time Mr Rutledge, a friend of Walsh, obtained from the French court the services of the *Elizabeth*, a vessel of 68 guns and 700 men, which was to cruise on the coast of Scotland. Some obscurity rests on the point; yet it is

[1] This remarkable letter is printed in the appendix to Lord Mahon's *History*, from the Stuart Papers.

clear that the Prince had the use of this latter vessel, to carry his stores, and convoy his own ship, without the knowledge of the French government. While the preparations were making at Nantes, the few gentlemen who had agreed to accompany the Prince lodged in different parts of the town, and when they met in public, took no notice of each other, the better to conceal their design.[1] They were seven in number; the most important being the Marquis of Tullibardine, who, having been concerned in the affair of 1715, was attainted, and thus prevented from succeeding to his father's title and estates as Duke of Athole, which were now enjoyed by his next younger brother. The rest were—Sir Thomas Sheridan, who had been the Prince's preceptor; Sir John Macdonald, an officer in the Spanish service; Mr Kelly, an English clergyman, who had been concerned in the Bishop of Rochester's plot in 1722; O'Sullivan, an Irish officer in the French service; Francis Strickland, an English gentleman; and Mr Æneas Macdonald, banker in Paris, a younger brother of Macdonald of Kinlochmoidart.   Lord Mahon says very justly, 'that the charm of this romantic enterprise seems singularly heightened, when we find, from the secret papers now disclosed, that it was undertaken not only against the British government, but without, and in spite of, the French.'

At seven of the evening of the 22d of June, old style,[2] the Prince embarked at St Nazaire, in the mouth of the Loire, on board Walsh's little vessel, named the *Doutelle*, attended by his seven friends, besides one Buchanan, a messenger.   Proceeding to Belleisle, he was there detained for some days, in expectation of the *Elizabeth*.   Since the letter to his father before quoted, he had written again: 'I made my devotions,' he says, 'on Pentecost day, recommending myself particularly to the Almighty on this occasion to guide and direct me, and to continue to me always the same sentiments; which are, *rather to*

---

1 *Jacobite Memoirs*, from the papers of Bishop Forbes, p. 2.
2 Such was the day in British reckoning, old style being still used there.   In France, the day was esteemed as the 3d of July.   Old style is here preferred, as that used throughout the whole of the ensuing narrative.

suffer anything than fail in any of my duties.' He afterwards wrote to his father's secretary, Mr Edgar: 'I hope in God we shall soon meet, which I am resolved shall not be but at *home;'* meaning in the seat of his father's government.[1] His last words to the same gentleman in a postscript, dated the 12th July (N.S.), were: 'After having waited a week here, not without a little anxiety, we have at last got the escort I expected, which is just arrived—namely, a ship of 68 guns, and 700 men aboard. I am, thank God, in perfect health, but have been a little sea-sick, and expect to be more so; but it does not keep me much abed, for I find the more I struggle against it the better.' None of these letters were sent off till after he had finally quitted the shores of France. He had acted in like manner by his Scottish friends, sending Mr Murray of Broughton to apprise them of his intention of sailing, but too late to allow of their sending any answer that could be expected to reach him before he should have set sail. The Scottish gentlemen consequently met in great anxiety, to deliberate on the message, when it was agreed by all, excepting the Duke of Perth, that the scheme was the extreme of rashness, and Mr Murray was appointed by them to watch for the Prince in the West Highlands, and warn him off the coast. It would thus appear that Charles was, in some measure, under a false impression as to the eagerness of his Scottish friends for the undertaking. Probably only a very few had invited him to come, no matter how attended or provided. Murray actually waited during the whole month of June upon the west coast, when, finding that the Prince did not arrive, and conceiving that the scheme had been given up, he returned to his house in Peeblesshire. To the friends of the cause in England, it does not appear that any message was sent by the Prince before his voyage.

---

[1] After all that is here related of the Prince's proceedings, it seems scarcely necessary to allude to a letter of David Hume, in which that generally acute person relates an absurd story, communicated to him by Helvetius the philosopher, to the effect that Charles became faint-hearted at the point of commencing his enterprise, and had to be carried on board by his followers. The utter inconsistency of the tale with the above unquestionable facts, must be at once apparent.

All things being in readiness, the expedition sailed from Belleisle on the 2d July. Four days after, in latitude 47° 57′ north, and 39 leagues to the west of the Lizard Point, an English man-of-war appeared in sight. D'Eau, the captain of the *Elizabeth*, came on board the *Doutelle*, and asked Mr Walsh to aid in attacking this vessel, representing that an immediate engagement might be the best course, as the English ship, if joined by any other of the same nation, would become more than a match for both of theirs. Mr Walsh, feeling a great responsibility as to the Prince's person, declined this proposal. Captain D'Eau then resolved to make the attack singly. The British vessel proved to be the *Lion*, of 58 guns, commanded by Captain Brett, an officer who had distinguished himself in Anson's expedition by storming Paita. The engagement between the two vessels lasted five hours, during which the *Doutelle* looked on from a little distance. While the fight continued, the Prince several times represented to Mr Walsh what a small assistance would serve to give the *Elizabeth* the advantage, and importuned him to engage in the action; but Mr Walsh positively refused, and at last desired the Prince not to insist any more, otherwise he would order him down to his cabin.[1] At the close of the action, the *Lion* sheered off like a tub upon the water, but the *Elizabeth* was unable to give it any further annoyance. The vessel was much damaged in the rigging, and between thirty and forty of the officers and men were wounded or killed, the captain himself being amongst the former. It therefore returned to France to refit, carrying with it the Prince's too slender stores. Charles, nevertheless, continued his voyage, cheering himself up with the hopes he entertained from the ardour of his Scottish partisans.

In this voyage the Prince and his friends maintained a strict incognito, as may have been surmised from the liberty which Mr Walsh has just been represented as taking with one who

---

[1] *Jacobite Memoirs.*

considered himself as rightfully Prince Regent of the British
dominions.   Charles wore the dress of a student of the Scotch
College at Paris, and, to conceal his person still more, he had
allowed his beard to grow from the day he embarked.   The
vessel sailed by night without a light, the better to escape
observation.   On one occasion it was chased, and prepared
for an action; but escaped by fast sailing.   After some days'
sailing, it approached that remotest range of the Hebrides which
—comprehending Lewis, Uist, Barra, and many others—is commonly called the Long Island, from its appearing at a distance
to form a single continent.   A large Hebridean eagle came and
hovered over the vessel.   It was first observed by the Marquis
of Tullibardine, who did not at first choose to make any remark
upon it, lest his doing so might have been considered superstitious; but, some hours later, on returning upon deck after
dinner, seeing the eagle still following their course, the marquis
pointed it out to the Prince, saying: 'Sir, this is a happy omen:
the king of birds is come to welcome your royal highness on
your arrival in Scotland.'[1]

They now sailed into a strait between the islands of Eriska
and South Uist, and, observing some doubtful sails at a
distance, made haste to land on the former island, carrying on
shore their money, arms, and ammunition.   The Prince was
conducted to the house of the *tacksman*, or tenant, and learned
that Macdonald of Clanranald, chief of a branch of that great
clan, and who held extensive possessions in the West Highlands
and Hebrides, was upon South Uist, with his brother Boisdale,[2]
while young Clanranald,[3] the son of the chief, and a person in
whom he had great confidence, was at Moidart upon the mainland.   A messenger was despatched to desire an interview with

[1] *Jacobite Memoirs*, p. 9.
[2] Throughout this narrative, the custom of the country has been conformed to, in
designating the Scottish chiefs and landed proprietors by their family and territorial titles.
[3] The eldest son of a Highland chief always receives his father's title, with the additional
epithet of *young*; thus, for instance, young Glengarry, young Locheil, &c. In the Lowlands,
something like the same custom did lately, and perhaps still does exist, though it is more
common to call him the *young laird*.   Ludicrous instances sometimes occur of a man
being called the young laird, when he is in reality far advanced in life.

Boisdale, and in the meantime Charles spent the night in the house of the tacksman.

He returned on board his vessel next morning, and Boisdale soon after came to visit him. This gentleman was supposed to have great influence over the mind of his elder brother the chief, who, on account of his advanced age and bad health, did not take an active part in the management of his own affairs.[1] Charles knew that, if Boisdale could be brought over to his views, the rising of the clan would be a matter of course. Here, however, he experienced a disappointment. Mr Macdonald seems to have been well affected to the cause, but strongly impressed with its hopelessness at the present moment. He spoke in a very discouraging manner, and advised the Prince to return home. 'I am *come* home, sir,' said Charles, 'and can entertain no notion of returning to the place whence I came. I am persuaded that my faithful Highlanders will stand by me.' Boisdale said he was afraid that the contrary would be found the case. Charles instanced Macleod of Macleod and Sir Alexander Macdonald of Sleat as chieftains upon whom he could depend. These were men who could bring twelve hundred broadswords to the field. Boisdale now gave him the unwelcome intelligence that these gentlemen had not only resolved to abandon his cause, but might be found to act against it. To prove this, he said a messenger might be sent to ask them to join the proposed expedition. As might be expected, Charles in vain exerted his eloquence to induce Boisdale to engage his brother's clan. He plainly told the Prince that he would rather use any influence he had with his brother and the clan to prevent them from taking arms.

Charles was greatly disconcerted at Boisdale's coldness, but he took care to shew no symptom of depression. He ordered his ship to be unmoored, and set sail for the mainland, expressing a resolution to pursue the enterprise he had commenced. He carried Boisdale along with him for several miles, and

---

[1] *Historical and Genealogical Account of the Clan or Family of Macdonald,* p. 159.

endeavoured, with all his eloquence, to make him relent and give a better answer.   But Mr Macdonald continued to express the same unfavourable sentiments; and finally descending into his boat, which hung astern, he left the Prince to follow his own apparently hopeless course.[1]

Continuing his voyage to the mainland, it was with a still resolute heart that, on the 19th of July,[2] Charles cast anchor in Lochnanuagh, a small arm of the sea, partly dividing the countries of Moidart and Arisaig.   The place which he thus chose for his disembarkation was as wild and desolate a scene as he could have found throughout the dominions of his fathers. Yet it was scarcely more unpromising than the reception he at first met with from its people.

The first thing he did, after casting anchor, was to send a boat ashore with a letter for young Clanranald, whom he knew to be inspired with the most enthusiastic affection to his cause. The young chief did not permit him to remain long in suspense. Next day (the 20th) he came to Forsy, a small village on the shore of the estuary in which the Prince's vessel lay, accompanied by his kinsmen, the Lairds of Glenaladale and Dalily, and by another gentleman of his clan, who has left an intelligent journal of the subsequent events.[3] 'Calling for the ship's boat,' says this writer, 'we were immediately carried on board, our hearts bounding at the idea of being at length so near our long-wished-for Prince. We found a large tent erected with poles upon the ship's deck, the interior of which was furnished with a variety of wines and spirits.   On entering this pavilion, we were warmly welcomed by the Duke of Athole, to whom most of us had been known in the year 1715.[4] While we were conversing with the duke, Clanranald was called away to see the Prince, and we were given to understand that we should not

---

[1] *History of the Rebellion*, by the Rev. John Home; Home's Works, ii. 427.—*Jacobite Memoirs*, pp. 11, 12.

[2] Lockhart Papers, ii. 479.   [3] Printed in the Lockhart Papers.

[4] The person here meant was the Marquis of Tullibardine, whom the Jacobites considered as rightfully the Duke of Athole.

probably see his royal highness that evening.' Clanranald, being introduced into Charles's presence, proceeded to assure him that there was no possibility, under the circumstances, of taking up arms with any chance of success. In this he was joined by his relation, Macdonald of Kinlochmoidart, whom Mr Home has associated with him in the following romantic anecdote, though the journalist does not allude to his presence. Charles is said, by the historian, to have addressed the two Highlanders with great emotion; to have summed up, with much eloquence, all the reasons for now beginning the war; and, finally, to have conjured them, in the warmest terms, to assist their Prince, their friend, in this his utmost need. With eloquence scarcely less warm, the brave young men entreated him to desist from his enterprise for the present, representing to him that now to take up arms, without regular forces, without officers of credit, without concert, and almost without arms, would but draw down certain destruction upon the heads of all concerned.   Charles persisted, argued, and implored; and they still as positively adhered to their opinion. During this conversation, the parties walked hurriedly backwards and forwards upon the deck, using all the gesticulations appropriate to their various arguments.   A Highlander stood near them, armed at all points, as was then the fashion of his country.   He was a younger brother of Kinlochmoidart, and had come off to the ship to inquire for news, not knowing who was on board.   When he gathered from their discourse that the stranger was the heir of Britain, when he heard his chief and brother refuse to take up arms for their Prince, his colour went and came, his eyes sparkled, he shifted his place, and grasped his sword.   Charles observed his demeanour, and turning suddenly round, appealed to him: 'Will *you* not assist me?' 'I will! I will!' exclaimed Ranald, 'though not another man in the Highlands should draw a sword; I am ready to die for you!' With tears and thanks Charles acknowledged the loyalty of the youth, and said he wished that all the Highlanders were like him.   The two obdurate chieftains were overpowered by this incident, and no longer expressed any reluctance to make an appearance in the cause.[1]

The Prince's interview with Clanranald, according to the journalist, who was on board at the same time, occupied no less than three hours. The young chief then returned to his friends, who had spent that space of time in the pavilion. 'About half an hour after,' says the journalist, 'there entered the tent a TALL YOUTH of a most agreeable aspect, dressed in a plain black coat, with a plain shirt, a cambric stock fixed with a plain silver buckle, a fair round wig out of the buckle, a plain hat with a canvas string, one end of which was fixed to one of his coat-buttons, black stockings, and brass buckles in his shoes. At the first appearance of this pleasing youth I felt my heart swell to my throat. But one O'Brien, a churchman, immediately told us that he was only an English clergyman, who had long been possessed with a desire to see and converse with the Highlanders.'

'At his entry,' continues the same writer, 'O'Brien forbade any of those who were sitting to rise; he saluted none of us, and we only made a low bow at a distance. I chanced to be one of those who were standing when he came in, and he took his seat near me; but he immediately started up again, and desired me to sit down by him upon a chest. Taking him at this time for only a passenger and a clergyman, I presumed to speak to him with perfect familiarity, though I could not suppress a suspicion that he might turn out some greater man. One of the questions which he put to me, in the course of conversation, regarded my Highland dress. He inquired if I did not feel cold in that habit, to which I answered that I believed I should only feel cold in any other.[2] At this he laughed heartily; and he next desired to know how I lay with it at night. I replied

---

[1] Home's Works, ii. 427.

[2] This is a common Highlandman's answer to a very common question. The fact is, that the philabeg, while exposing the knees, invests the haunches and middle with such dense folds, as to give great general warmth. I believe it has been found that the private men of the Highland regiments have nowhere complained of their dress so much as in the West Indies.

that the plaid served me for a blanket when sleeping, and I
shewed him how I wrapped it about my person for that purpose.
At this he remarked that I must be unprepared for defence
in case of a sudden surprise; but I informed him that, during
war or any time of danger, we arranged the garment in such
a way as to enable us to start at once to our feet, with a drawn
sword in one hand and a cocked pistol in the other.   After
a little more conversation of this sort, the mysterious youth rose
from his seat and called for a dram, when O'Brien whispered
to me to pledge the stranger, but not to drink to him, which
confirmed me in my suspicions as to his real quality.   Having
taken a glass of wine in his hand, he drank to us all round, and
soon after left the tent.' [1]

During this and the succeeding day, Clanranald remained
close in council with Charles, the Marquis of Tullibardine, and
Sir Thomas Sheridan, devising means for raising the rest of the
well-affected clans, who were at this time reckoned to number
12,000 men.   On the 22d (July), young Clanranald proceeded
with Allan Macdonald, a younger brother of Kinlochmoidart,
on an embassy to Sir Alexander Macdonald of Sleat and the
Laird of Macleod, whom Charles was most unwilling to suppose
unfaithful to his cause.   During the absence of these emissaries,
Mr Hugh Macdonald, a younger brother of the Laird of Morar,
was brought on board the *Doutelle* to visit the Prince.   This
gentleman, after a short complimentary conversation, took leave
to caution him as to the necessity of keeping strictly incognito
for the present, as the garrison of Fort William was not far off,
and the neighbouring clan Campbell might be very glad to
obtain possession of his person.   Charles answered: ' I have no
fear about that at all.'   With reference to the proposed expedition, Mr Macdonald said he had great fears of the event, and,
like Boisdale, he recommended the Prince to return to France.
Charles said 'he did not choose to owe his restoration to
foreigners, but to his own friends, to whom he was now come

to put it into their power to have the glory of that event.   And
as to returning to France, foreigners should never have it to say
that he had thrown himself upon his friends, that they turned
their backs upon him, and that he had been forced to return
from them to foreign parts.   In a word, if he could get but six
trusty men to join him, *he would choose far rather to skulk with
them among the mountains of Scotland, than to return to France.*'

On the 25th he came on shore from the *Doutelle*, accompanied by only the seven gentlemen formerly mentioned.   He
first set his foot upon Scottish ground at Borodale, a farm
belonging to Clanranald, close by the south shore of Lochnanuagh.   Borodale is a wild piece of country, forming a
mountainous tongue of land betwixt two bays.   It was a place
suitable above all others for the circumstances and designs of
the Prince, being remote and difficult of access, and in the
centre of that country where Charles's surest friends resided.
It belongs to a tract of stern mountain land, serrated by deep
narrow firths, forming the western coast of Inverness-shire.
Although in the very centre of the Highland territory, it is not
above one hundred and eighty miles from the capital.   The
Macdonalds and the Stuarts, who possessed the adjacent territories, had been, since the time of Montrose, inviolably attached
to the elder line of the royal family ; had proved themselves
irresistible at Kilsyth, Killiecrankie, and Sheriffmuir ; and were
now, from their resistance to the Disarming Act, perhaps the
fittest of all the clans to take the field.

During the absence of young Clanranald, into whose arms
Charles had thus thrown himself, several gentlemen of the
family collected a guard for his person, and he remained a
welcome and honoured guest in the house of Borodale.[1]   Considering that no other chief had yet declared for him, and that,
indeed, the enterprise might never advance another step, it
must be acknowledged that the Clanranald family acted with no
small share of gallantry ; for there can be little doubt that if he

had retired, they must have been exposed to the vengeance of government. 'We encountered this hazard,' says the journalist, 'with the greatest cheerfulness, determined to risk everything, life itself, in behalf of our beloved Prince.' Charles, his company, and about one hundred men constituting his guard, were entertained with the best cheer which it was in the power of Mr Macdonald, tenant of Borodale, to purvey. He sat in a large room, where he could see all his adherents at once, and where the multitudes of people who flocked from the country around, 'without distinction of age or sex,'[1] to see him, might also have an opportunity of gratifying their curiosity. At the first meal which took place under these circumstances, Charles drank the *grace*-drink in English, a language which all the gentlemen present understood; but for a toast of more extensive application, our friend the journalist rose and gave the king's[2] health in Gaelic—'*Deoch slaint an Righ.*' This of course produced universal satisfaction; and Charles desired to know what was meant. On its being explained to him, he requested to hear the words pronounced again, that he might learn them himself. He then gave the king's health in Gaelic, uttering the words as correctly and distinctly as he could. 'The company,' adds the journalist, 'then mentioning my skill in Gaelic, his royal highness said I should be his master in that language; and I was then desired to ask the healths of the prince and duke.'[3] It may be scarcely possible to conceive the effect which Charles's flattering attention to their language had upon the hearts of this brave and simple people.

[1] Lockhart Papers, ii. 482.　　[2] Charles's father.
[3] Charles's younger brother, styled the Duke of York.

CHAPTER II.

THE HIGHLANDERS.

> ' *Belarius.* 'Tis wonderful,
> That an invisible instinct should frame them
> To loyalty unlearned ; honour untaught ;
> Civility not seen from other ; valour,
> That wildly grows in them, but yields a crop
> As if it had been sowed.'
>
> *Cymbeline.*

THE people amidst whom Charles Stuart had cast his fate, were then regarded as the rudest and least civilised portion of the nation of which he conceived himself the rightful ruler. Occupying the most remote and mountainous section of Britain, and holding little intercourse with the rest of the community, they were distinguished by peculiar language, dress, and manners ; had as yet yielded a very imperfect obedience to government ; and formed a society not only distinct from their immediate neighbours, but which had probably no exact parallel in Europe.

The country possessed by this people, forming the north-west portion of Scotland, comprehends a large surface; but being of a mountainous and rugged character, it has never maintained a large population.   In numbers, the Highlanders did not now exceed 100,000, or a twelfth of the whole population of Scotland.   The community was divided into about forty different tribes, denominated *clans*, each of which dwelt upon its own portion of the territory.

At the period of this history, the Highlanders displayed, in a state almost entire, what has been called the patriarchal form of society.   This extreme corner of Europe had the fortune to shelter nearly the last unmixed remnants of the Celts, that early race of people whom the dawn of history shews in possession of the ancient continent, but who were gradually dispelled to the extremities by others which we are now accustomed to call ancient. As they retained their primitive manners with almost unmixed purity, there was to be seen in the Highlanders of Scotland nearly a distinct picture of a state of society compared with which that of Rome might be considered as modern.

Owing to the circumstances of their country, the Highlanders were, however, by no means that simple and quiescent people who are described as content to dwell each under his own vine and fig-tree, any more than their land was one flowing with milk and honey. A perpetual state of war with the neighbours who had driven them to their northern fastnesses, and their disinclination to submit to the laws of the country in which they nominally lived, caused them, on the contrary, to make arms a sort of profession, and even to despise in some measure all peaceful modes of acquiring a subsistence. Entertaining, moreover, a belief that the Lowlands had been originally theirs, many of them, even at this period, practised a regular system of reprisal upon the frontier of that civilised region, for which of course the use of arms was indispensably necessary. What still more tended to induce military habits, many of the tribes maintained a sort of hereditary enmity against each other, and therefore required to be in perpetual readiness, either to seize or repel opportunities of vengeance.

The Highlanders, in the earlier periods of history, appear to have possessed no superiority over the Lowlanders in the use of arms. At the battle of the Harlaw in 1410 (till which period they had been quite independent of the kings of Scotland), the largest army that ever left the Highlands was checked by an inferior number of Lowlanders. They proved not more invincible at the battles of Corrichie, Glenlivat, and others, fought during the sixteenth century.

But the lapse of half a century after this last period, during which the Border spear had been converted into a shepherd's crook, and the patriot steel of Lothian and Clydesdale into

penknives and weavers' shears, permitted the mountaineers at
length to assert a decided superiority in arms.   When they were
called into action, therefore, by Montrose, they proved invariably
victorious in that short but brilliant campaign, which almost
retrieved a kingdom for their unfortunate monarch.   Amidst the
exploits of that time, the victory of Kilsyth (1645) was attended
with some circumstances displaying their superiority in a
remarkable degree.   The army arrayed against them, almost
doubling theirs in number, consisted chiefly of the townsmen
of Fife, which county has been described, in a publication of
the time,[1] as remarkable for the enthusiasm of its inhabitants
in regard to the cause of this quarrel—the National Covenant.
Religious fervour proved nothing in this case when opposed to
the more exalted enthusiasm of ' loyalty unlearned,' and the
hardihood of an education among the hills.   The Whig militia
scarcely stood a minute before the impetuous charge of the
Highlanders, but running off in a shameful rout, were killed in
great numbers by their pursuers.[2]

Though the Highlanders were nominally subjugated by
Cromwell, they regained at the Restoration their former privileges and vigour.   They were kept in arms, during the reigns
of the last two Stuarts, by their occasional employment as a
militia, for the harassment of the west-country Presbyterians.
At the Revolution, therefore, when roused by the voice of
Dundee, they were equally ready to take the field in behalf of
King James, as they had been fifty years before to rise up
for his father.   The patriarchal system of laws upon which
Highland society was constituted, disposed them to look upon
these unfortunate princes as the general fathers or *chiefs* of the
nation, whose natural and unquestionable power had been

---

[1] *Montrose Redivivus*, 1650.

[2] Sir John Sinclair of Longformacus reported to the late Bishop Low, his having in
early life met an aged Highlander who had been at the battle of Kilsyth.   The man
spoke with savage glee of his performances amongst the hen-hearted Fife men.   ' It was
a braw day Kilsyth; at every stroke of my sword I cut an ell o' breeks !'   The people
of Fife are said to have consequently got a distaste for the army, which had not ceased at
the close of the ensuing century.   See *Statistical Account of Scotland*, xii. 86.

rebelliously disputed by their children ; and there can be little doubt that, both on these occasions and the subsequent attempts in behalf of the Stuart family, they fought with precisely the same ardour which would induce a man of humanity to ward off the blow which an unnatural son had aimed at a parent. On the field of Killiecrankie, where they were chiefly opposed by regular and even veteran troops, they fought with signal bravery.[1] Their victory was, however, unavailing, owing to the death of their favourite leader, *Ian Dhu nan Cath*, as they descriptively termed him—Dark John of the Battles—without whose commanding genius their energies could not be directed, nor even their bands kept together.

The submission which was nominally paid throughout Britain to the '*parliamentary*' sovereigns, William and Anne, was in no degree participated by the children of the mountains, whose simple ideas of government did not comprehend either a second or a third estate, and who could perceive no reasons for preferring a sovereign on account of any peculiarity in his religion. In the meantime, moreover, the progress of civilisation, encouraged in the low countries by the Union, affected but slightly the warlike habits of the clans. Their military ardour is said to have been, if possible, increased during this period, by the injudicious policy of King William, who, in distributing £20,000 amongst them to bribe their forbearance, only inspired an idea that arms were their best means of acquiring wealth and importance. The call, therefore, which was made upon them by the exiled Prince in 1715, found them as willing and ready as ever to commence a civil war.

---

[1] The battle of Killiecrankie was fought upon a field immediately beyond a narrow and difficult pass into the Highlands. The royal troops, under General Mackay, on emerging from this pass, found Dundee's army, which was not half so numerous, posted in columns or clusters upon the face of an opposite hill. Both lay upon their arms, looking at each other, till sunset, when the Highland troops came down with their customary impetuosity, and, charging through Mackay's lines, soon put them to the rout. Mackay retreated in the utmost disorder, and reached Stirling next day with only two hundred men. His whole army must have been cut to pieces in retreating through the pass, but for the death of Dundee, and the greater eagerness of the Highlanders to secure the baggage than to pursue their enemies.

C

The accession of the house of Hanover was at this period so recent, and the rival candidate shared so largely in the affections of the people, that very little was wanting to achieve the restoration of the house of Stuart. That little *was* wanting—a general of military talent, with some degree of resolution on the part of the candidate. The expedition was commanded in Scotland by the Earl of Mar, who had signalised himself by some dexterity in the slippery politics of the time, but possessed no other abilities to fit him for the important station he held. In England, the reigning sovereign had even less to dread, in the ill concerted proceedings of a band of debauched young noblemen, who displayed this remarkable difference from the Scottish insurgents—that they could not fight at all. Mar permitted himself to be cooped up on the north of the Forth, with an army of 8000 or 9000 men, by the Duke of Argyll, who occupied Stirling with a force not half so numerous. An action at length took place on Sheriffmuir, in which it is impossible to say whether the bravery of the Highlanders, the pusillanimity of their leader, or the military genius of Argyll, was most signally distinguished.

The Duke of Argyll learning, on the 11th of November, that Mar had at length formed the resolution to fight him, and was marching for that purpose from Perth, set forward from Stirling ; and next day the armies came within sight of each other upon the plain of Sheriffmuir, a mile north-east from Dumblane. They both lay upon their arms all night ; and a stone is still shewn upon the site of the Highlanders' bivouac, indented all round with marks occasioned by the broadswords of these warriors, who here sharpened their weapons for the next day's conflict. The battle commenced on Sunday morning, when Argyll himself, leading his dragoons over a morass which had frozen during the night, and which the insurgents expected to protect them, almost immediately routed their whole left wing, consisting of the Lowland cavaliers, and drove them to the river Allan, two or three miles from the field. His left wing, which was beyond the scope of his command, did not meet the same success against the right of the insurgents, which consisted entirely of Highlanders.

Those warriors had come down from their fastnesses with a resolution to fight as their ancestors had fought at Kilsyth and Killiecrankie. They appeared before the Lowlanders of Perthshire, who had not seen them since the days of Montrose, in the wild Irish shirt or plaid, which, covering only the body and haunches, leaves the arms and most of the limbs exposed in all their shaggy strength.[1] Their enthusiasm may be guessed from a simple anecdote. A Lowland gentleman, observing amongst their bands a man of ninety, from the upper part of Aberdeenshire, had the curiosity to ask how so aged a creature as he, and one who seemed so extremely feeble, had thought of joining their enterprise. 'I have sons here, sir,' replied the man, 'and I have grandsons; if they fail to do their duty, cannot I shoot them?'—laying his hand upon a pistol which he carried in his bosom.[2]

The attack of these resolute soldiers upon the left wing of the royal army was, to use language similar to their own, like the storm which strews a lee-shore with wrecks. The chief of Clanranald was killed as they were advancing; but that circumstance, which might have been expected to damp their ardour, only served to inspire them with greater fury. 'Tomorrow for lamentation!' cried the young chieftain of Glengarry; 'to-day for revenge!' and the Macdonalds rushed on the foe with irresistible force. Instantly put to rout, this portion of the royal army retired to Stirling, leaving hundreds a prey to the Highland broadsword. Thus each of the two armies was partially successful and partially defeated.

The battle was by no means indecisive in its results. Mar, as he deserved none of the credit of his partial victory, reaped no profit from it, but was obliged to retire to Perth. Argyll remained upon the field, in possession of the enemy's cannon and many of his standards. The conduct of this celebrated

---

[1] Preface to Pinkerton's *Select Old Scottish Poems.*

[2] 'Can I no *sheet* them?'—these were the exact words.

warrior and patriot was in every respect the reverse of that of
Mar.   He had won a victory, so far as it could be won, by
his own personal exertions, and that with every advantage of
numbers against him.   The humanity he displayed was also
such as seldom marks the details of a civil war.   He offered
quarter to all he met, in the very hottest of the fight, and he
granted it to all who desired it.   With his own sword he
parried three different blows which one of his dragoons
aimed at a wounded cavalier who had refused to ask his
life.[1]

In January, James himself, the weak though amiable man
for whom all this blood was shed, landed at Peterhead, and
immediately proceeded *incognito* to join the Earl of Mar at
Perth.   His presence might inspire some enthusiasm, but it
could not give strength or consistency to the army.   Some
preparations were made for his coronation in the great hall of
Scoon, where his ancestors had been invested with the emblems
of sovereignty so many centuries ago.   But the total ruin of
his English adherents conspired with his own imbecility and
that of his officers to prevent the ceremony from taking place.
In February, he retired before the advance of the royal army.
The Tay was frozen at the time, and thus he and all his army
were fortunately enabled to cross without the difficulty which
must otherwise have attended so sudden a retreat; directing
their march towards the seaports of Aberdeenshire and Angus.
I have heard that, as the good-natured prince was passing over,
the misery or his circumstances prompted a slight sally of wit,
as a dark evening will sometimes produce lightning; and
he remarked to his lieutenant-general, in allusion to the
delusive prospects by which he had been induced to come
over: ' Ah, John, you see how you have brought me on the
ice.'[2]

The Chevalier embarked with Mar and other officers at
Montrose; and the body of the army dispersed with so much

---

[1] Printed *broadside* of the battle.   [2] Information by Bishop Low.

rapidity, that Argyll, who traversed the country only a day's march behind, reached Aberdeen without ever getting a glimpse of it. We may safely suppose that the humanity of this general, if not the secret leaning to Jacobitism of which he was suspected, induced him to favour the dispersion and escape of the unfortunate cavaliers. The Lowland gentlemen and noblemen who had been concerned in the campaign suffered attainder, proscription, and in some cases death; but the Highlanders returned to their mountains unconquered and unchanged.

In 1719, a plan of invasion and insurrection in favour of the Stuarts was formed by Spain. A fleet of ten ships of the line, with several frigates, having on board 6000 troops and 12,000 stand of arms, sailed from Cadiz to England; and while this fleet was preparing, the Earl Marischal left St Sebastian with two Spanish frigates, having on board 300 Spanish soldiers, ammunition, arms, and money, and landed in the island of Lewis. The Spanish fleet was completely dispersed by a storm off Cape Finisterre; and as everything remained quiet in England, very few Highlanders rose. General Wightman came up with the Spanish and Highland force in Glenshiel, a wild vale in the west of Ross-shire. The Highlanders, favoured by the ground, withdrew to the hills without having suffered much; and the Spaniards laid down their arms, and were made prisoners.

During the ensuing twenty years, the state of the Highlands was often under the consideration of government, and some steps were taken with a view to render the people less dangerous, but none with the design of making them more friendly. Three forts—one at Inverness; a second, named Fort Augustus, at Killiewhimmen; and a third, named Fort William, at Inverlochy, in Lochaber—were kept in full garrison, as a means of overawing the disaffected clans. Under the care of General Wade, the soldiers were employed in forming lines of road, for the purpose of connecting these forts with the low country. An act was also passed to deprive the people of their arms. It was obeyed to some extent by such clans as the Campbells, Suther-lands, and Mackays, whose superiors were, from whatever cause, well affected to the government; but was generally evaded by the Macdonalds, Stuarts, Camerons, and others, who maintained their zeal for the house of Stuart. Thus the measure was rather favourable to the Jacobite cause in the Highlands than other-wise.

Such had been the history, and such was the warlike condi-tion of the Scottish mountaineers at the time when Prince Charles landed amongst them in July 1745. If anything else were required to make the reader understand the motives of the subsequent insurrection, it might be said that Charles's father and himself had always maintained, from their residence in Italy, a correspondence with the chiefs who were friendly to them. For the service of these unhappy princes, their unlimited power over their clans gave them an advantage which the richest English partisans did not possess. At the same time, as suffi-ciently appears from the preceding and following chapter, the idea of taking the field for the Stuarts without foreign assistance was not agreeable to the Jacobite chiefs, though, in most instances, their ardour of character ultimately overcame their scruples on that point.

The constitution of Highland society, as already remarked, was strictly and simply patriarchal. The clans were families, each of which, bearing one name, occupied a well-defined tract of country, the property of which had been acquired long before the introduction of writs. Every clan was governed by its chief, whose native designation—*Kean-Kinnhe* (' The Head of the Family ')—sufficiently indicated the grounds and nature of his power. In almost every clan there were some subordinate chiefs called chieftains, being cadets of the principal family, who had acquired a distinct territory, and founded separate septs. In every clan, moreover, there were two ranks of people—the *Doaine-uailse*, or gentlemen, persons who could clearly trace their derivation from the chiefs of former times, and assert their kinsmanship to the present ; and a race of commoners, who could not tell how they came to belong to the clan, and who always acted in inferior offices.

There is a very common notion among the Lowlanders that their northern neighbours, with, perhaps, the exception of the chiefs, were all alike barbarians, and distinguished by no shades of comparative worth. Nothing could be further from the truth. The *Doaine-uailse* were, in every sense of the word, gentlemen—*poor* gentlemen, perhaps, but yet fully entitled, by their feelings and acquirements, to that appellation. On the contrary, the commoners, who yet generally believed themselves related to the chiefs, were a race of mere serfs, having no certain idea of a noble ancestry to nerve their exertions or elevate their conduct. The *Doaine-uailse* invariably formed the body upon which the chief depended in war; for they were inspired with notions of the most exalted heroism by the well-remembered deeds of their forefathers, and always acted upon the supposi tion that their honour was a precious gift, which it was incum- bent upon them to deliver down unsullied to posterity. The commoners, on the contrary, were often left behind to perform the humble duties of agriculture and cow-driving ; or, if admitted into the array of the clan, were put into the rear rank, and armed in an inferior manner.

With such a sentiment of heroism, the Highland gentleman of the year 1745 must have been a person of no mean order. His mind was further exalted, if possible, by a devoted attach- ment to his chief, for whose interests he was at all times ready to fight, and for whose life he was even prepared to lay down his own. His politics were of the same abstract and disinter- ested sort. Despising the commercial Presbyterians of the low country, and regarding with a better-founded disgust the dark system of parliamentary corruption which characterised the government of the *de facto* sovereign of England, he at once threw himself into the opposite scale, and espoused the cause of an exiled and injured prince, whom he looked upon as in some measure a general and higher sort of chief. Charles's cause was the cause of justice, of filial affection, and even, in his estimation, of *patriotism;* and with all his prepossessions, it was scarcely possible that he should fail to espouse it.[1]

CHAPTER III.

THE GATHERING.

'Oh, high-minded Murray, the exiled, the dear,
In the blush of the dawning the standard uprear;
Wide, wide on the winds of the north let it fly,
Like the sun's latest flash when the tempest is nigh!'
Waverley.

AT Borodale, the Prince received a reply to the message which he had sent to Sir Alexander Macdonald and the Laird of Macleod. What Boisdale had said of these chiefs proved exactly true. Originally well affected to the Stuart family, they had recently been tampered with by Duncan Forbes, president of the Court of Session, so distinguished as a virtuous and enlightened friend of the Hanover succession, as well as by the genuine love he bore for his native country. Being now disposed to remain on good terms with the government, the two insular chiefs returned for answer, that although they had promised to support his royal highness if he came with a foreign force, they did not conceive themselves to be under any obligation since he came so ill provided. They likewise offered the advice, that he should immediately return to France. It was

---

[1] In this chapter notice might also have been taken of the effect which their popular native poetry had upon the minds of the Highlanders. Throughout nearly the whole country, but especially in Athole and the adjacent territories, *there were innumerable songs and ballads tending to advance the cause of the Stuarts, while there was not one to depreciate them.* A Lowlander and a modern cannot easily comprehend, nor can he set forth, the power of this simple but energetic engine. It has been described to me as something overpowering. Most of the ballads were founded upon the wars of Montrose and Dundee, and aimed at rousing the audience to imitate the actions of their ancestors in these glorious campaigns.

not known at the time, but has since been made manifest, that these chiefs at this crisis did active service for the government, in sending intelligence of the Prince's arrival. Their answer to Charles was so disheartening, that now even those who had come with him joined with his Highland friends in counselling him to give up the enterprise.[1] The example of the two Skye chiefs would, they said, be fatal, as many others would follow it. Nevertheless, Charles adhered to his design, repeating, in reply to all their representations, the same words he had used to Mr Hugh Macdonald. With six good trusty followers, he said, he would skulk in Scotland rather than return to France.

From Borodale, where he lived in the manner described for several days, he despatched messengers to all the chiefs from whom he had any expectation of assistance. The first that came to see him was Donald Cameron, younger of Locheil; a man in middle age, of great bravery, and universally respected character. Young Locheil, as he was generally called, was the son of the chief of the clan Cameron, one of the most numerous and warlike of all the Highland tribes. His father had been engaged in the insurrection of 1715, for which he was attainted and in exile; and his grandfather, Sir Evan Cameron, the fellow-soldier of Montrose and Dundee, had died in 1719, after three-fourths of a century of military partisanship in behalf of the house of Stuart. Young Locheil had been much in confidence with the exiled family, whose chief agent in the north of Scotland he might be considered; an office for which he was peculiarly well qualified, on account of his talents, his integrity, and the veneration in which he was held by his countrymen. He was one of the seven gentlemen who, in 1740, entered into an association to procure the restoration of King James; and he

1 Young Clanranald was himself shaken in his resolution of arming for the Prince by the conversation he had with Sir Alexander Macdonald, and returned to his own country with a decided disinclination to the enterprise. But when he arrived, he found his clan determined to go out at all hazards, *whether he should head them or not*, having probably been much gained upon in the interval by the Prince's address. The young chieftain was thus ultimately brought back to his former resolution. These facts are stated by Bishop Forbes (*Lyon in Mourning*, MS. in my possession), on the concurring testimony of Ranald Macdonald, a son of Borodale, and Mr Macdonald of Bellfinlay.

had long wished for the concerted time when he should bring the Highlands to aid an invading party in that cause. When he now learned that Charles had landed without troops and arms, and with only seven followers, he determined to abstain from the enterprise ; but thought himself bound, as a friend, to visit the Prince in person, and endeavour to make him withdraw from the country.

In passing from his own house to Borodale, Locheil called at Fassefern, the residence of his brother, John Cameron, who, in some surprise at the earliness of his visit, hastily inquired its reason. Locheil informed his relative that the Prince of Wales had landed at Borodale, and sent for him. Fassefern asked what troops his royal highness had brought with him ?—what money ?—what arms ? Locheil answered that he believed the Prince had brought with him neither troops, nor money, nor arms ; and that, resolved not to be concerned in the affair, he designed to do his utmost to prevent it from going any further. Fassefern approved of his brother's sentiments, and applauded his resolution, advising him at the same time not to go any farther on the way to Borodale, but to come into the house, and impart his mind to the Prince by a letter. ' No,' said Locheil ; ' although my reasons admit of no reply, I ought at least to wait upon his royal highness.' ' Brother,' said Fassefern, ' I know you better than you know yourself ; if this Prince once sets his eyes upon you, he will make you do whatever he pleases.' [1]

On arriving at Borodale, Locheil had a private interview with the Prince, in which the probabilities of the enterprise were anxiously debated. Charles used every argument to excite the loyalty of Locheil, and the chief exerted all his eloquence to persuade the Prince to withdraw till a better opportunity. Charles represented the present as the best possible opportunity, seeing that the French general kept the British army completely engaged abroad, while at home there were no troops but one or two newly raised regiments. He expressed his confidence that a small body of Highlanders would be sufficient to gain a victory

[1] Home's Works, iii. 7.

over all the force that could now be brought against him; and he was equally sure that such an advantage was all that was required to make his friends at home declare in his favour, and cause those abroad to send assistance. All he wanted was, that the Highlanders should begin the war. Locheil still resisted, entreating Charles to be more temperate, and consent to remain concealed where he was, till his friends should meet together, and concert what was best to be done. Charles, whose mind was wound up to the utmost pitch of impatience, paid no regard to this proposal, but answered that he was determined to put all to the hazard. 'In a few days,' said he, 'with the few friends I have, I will raise the royal standard, and proclaim to the people of Britain that Charles Stuart is come over to claim the crown of his ancestors—to win it, or to perish in the attempt! Locheil, who my father has often told me was our firmest friend, may stay at home, and learn from the newspapers the fate of his Prince!' 'No!' said Locheil, stung by so poignant a reproach, and hurried away by the enthusiasm of the moment; 'I will share the fate of my Prince; and so shall every man over whom nature or fortune has given me any power.' Such was the juncture upon which depended the civil war of 1745; for it is a point agreed, says Mr Home, who narrates this conversation, that if Locheil had persisted in his refusal to take arms, no other chief would have joined the standard, and 'the spark of rebellion must have been instantly extinguished.'[1]

Locheil immediately returned home, and proceeded to raise

[1] Mr Home's account of this affair harmonises with all besides that we know of the reckless ardour of the young Prince, and the cautious reluctance of the principal chiefs. We may therefore receive it as in the main true. Perhaps, however, the ultimate consent of Locheil was less sudden than is here represented. In the volume entitled *Jacobite Memoirs*, compiled by the present author from the papers of Bishop Forbes (p. 22, note), it is stated that Locheil, before agreeing to *come out*, took full security for the value of his estates from the Prince, and that it was to fulfil this engagement that Charles, after the unfortunate conclusion of the enterprise, obtained a French regiment for Locheil. It is scarcely necessary to remark, that the presence of generous feelings does not necessarily forbid that some attention should be paid to the dictates of prudence and caution. Locheil might feel that he had a right to peril his life and connection with his country, but not the fortune on which the comfort of others besides himself depended, especially in an enterprise of which he had a bad opinion, and which he only acceded to from a romantic deference to the wishes of another person.

his clan, as did some other gentlemen whom Charles then prevailed upon to join him. It being now settled that he was to erect his standard at Glenfinnin on the 19th of August, he despatched letters on the 6th of the month to all the friendly chiefs, informing them of his resolution, and desiring them to meet him at the time and place mentioned. In the meantime Clanranald, returned from his unsuccessful mission to Skye, actively set about raising his own clan.

Charles removed, about the 11th of August, from the farm-house of Borodale to the mansion of Kinlochmoidart, situated seven miles off. While he and his company went by sea, with the baggage and artillery, the guard of Clanranald Macdonalds, which had been already appointed about his person, marched by the more circuitous route along the shore of the intervening bays. At Kinlochmoidart[1] he was joined by Mr John Murray of Broughton, who has already been mentioned as an emissary of the Prince to his Scottish friends, and who, after waiting during June to warn him from the west coast, had afterwards returned to his house in Peeblesshire. Mr Murray, who was a man of good talents and education, had now once more come to the Highlands, in order to join an enterprise which it was too late to think of stopping. From this time he acted throughout the campaign as the Prince's secretary. Charles remained at Kinlochmoidart till the 18th, when he went by water to Glenala-dale, the seat of another chieftain of the clan Macdonald, upon the brink of Loch Shiel. He was here joined by Gordon of Glenbucket, a veteran partisan, who had figured in the affair of 1715, and who brought with him a prisoner of the opposite party, in the person of Captain Sweetenham, of Guise's regiment, who had been taken by the Keppoch Macdonalds, while travelling from Ruthven barracks, in Badenoch, to Fort William.

[1] 'As the Prince was setting out for Glenfinnin, I was detached to Ardnamurchan to recruit, and soon returned with fifty clever fellows, who pleased the Prince; and upon review, his royal highness was pleased to honour me with the command of them, telling me I was *the first officer he had made in Scotland*. This compliment delighted me exceedingly, and we all vowed to the Almighty that we should live and die with our noble Prince, though all Britain should forsake him but our little regiment alone.'—*Macdonald's Journal; Lockhart Papers*, ii. 483.

From Glenaladale the Prince proceeded next morning, with a company of about five-and-twenty persons, in three boats, to the eastern extremity of Loch Shiel, near which was the place where he designed to raise his standard.

Meanwhile an incident had occurred which tended not a little to foment the rising flame of insurrection. The governor of Fort Augustus (a military post, at the distance of forty or fifty miles from Charles's landing-place) concluding, from reports he heard, that the Moidart people were hatching some mischief, thought proper, on the 16th of August, to despatch two companies of the Scots Royals to Fort William, as a reinforcement to awe that rebellious district. The distance between the two forts is twenty-eight miles, and the road runs chiefly along the edge of a mountain, which forms one side of the Great Glen, having the sheer height of the hill on one side, and the long narrow lakes, out of which the Caledonian Canal has since been formed, on the other. The men were newly raised, and, besides being inexperienced in military affairs, were unused to the alarming circumstances of an expedition in the Highlands. When they had travelled twenty out of the eight-and-twenty miles, and were approaching High Bridge, a lofty arch over a mountain torrent, they were surprised to hear the sound of a bagpipe, and to discover the appearance of a large party of Highlanders, who were already in possession of the bridge. The object of their alarm was in reality a band of only ten or twelve Macdonalds of Keppoch's clan; but by skipping and leaping about, displaying their swords and firelocks, and by holding out their plaids between each other, they contrived to make a very formidable appearance. Captain (afterwards General) Scott, who commanded the two companies, ordered an immediate halt, and sent forward a sergeant with his own servant to reconnoitre. These two persons no sooner approached the bridge, than two nimble Highlanders darted out and seized them. Ignorant of the number of the Highlanders, and knowing he was in a disaffected part of the country, Captain Scott thought it would be better to retreat than enter into hostilities.

Accordingly, he ordered his men to face about, and march back again. The Highlanders did not follow immediately, lest they should expose the smallness of their number, but permitted the soldiers to get two miles away (the ground being so far plain and open) before leaving their post. As soon as the retreating party had passed the west end of Loch Lochy, and were entering upon the narrow road between the lake and the hill, out darted the mountaineers, and ascending the rocky precipices above the road, where there was shelter from both bush and stone, began to fire down upon the soldiers, who only retreated with the greater expedition.

The party of Macdonalds who attempted this daring exploit was commanded by Macdonald of Tiendrish, who, having early observed the march of the soldiers, had sent expresses to Locheil and Keppoch, whose houses were only a few miles distant on both sides of High Bridge, for supplies of men. They did not arrive in time, but he resolved to attack the party with the few men he had; and he had thus far succeeded, when the noise of his pieces causing friends in all quarters to fly to arms, he now found himself at the head of a party almost sufficient to encounter the two companies in the open field.

When Captain Scott reached the east end of Loch Lochy, he perceived some Highlanders near the west end of Loch Oich, directly in the way before him; and not liking their appearance, he crossed the isthmus between the lakes, intending to take possession of Invergarry Castle, the seat of Macdonell of Glengarry. This movement only increased his difficulties. He had not marched far, when he discovered the Macdonells of Glengarry coming down the opposite hill in full force against him. He formed the hollow square, however, and marched on. Presently after, his pursuers were reinforced by the Macdonalds of Keppoch, and increased their pace to such a degree as almost to overtake him. Keppoch himself then advanced alone towards the distressed party, and offered good terms of surrender; assuring them that any attempt at resistance, in the midst of so many enemies, would only be the signal for their being cut in pieces. The soldiers, by this time fatigued with a march of thirty miles, had no alternative but to surrender. They had scarcely laid down their arms, when Locheil came up with a body of Camerons from another quarter, and took them under his charge. Two soldiers were slain, and Captain Scott himself was wounded in this scuffle, which had no small effect in raising the spirits of the Highlanders, and encouraging them to commence the war.[1]

The *gathering of the clans* was therefore proceeding with great activity, and armed bodies were seen everywhere crossing the country to Glenfinnin, at the time when Charles landed at that place to erect his standard. Glenfinnin is a narrow vale, surrounded on both sides by lofty and craggy mountains, about twenty miles north from Fort William, and as far east from Borodale, forming, in fact, the outlet from Moidart into Lochaber. The place gets its name from the little river Finnin, which runs through it, and falls into Loch Shiel at its extremity. Charles disembarked with his company from the three boats which had brought them from Glenaladale, at the place where the river discharges itself into the lake. It was eleven in the forenoon, and he expected to find the whole vale alive with the assembled bands which he had appointed to meet him. In this he was disappointed. Only a few natives, the inhabitants of a little village, were there to say ' *God save him !* ' Some accident, it was concluded, had prevented the arrival of the clans, and he went into one of the neighbouring hovels to spend the anxious hours which should intervene before they appeared.

At length, about an hour after noon, the sound of a pibroch was heard over the top of an opposite hill, and immediately after the adventurer was cheered by the sight of a large band of Highlanders in full march down the slope. It was the Camerons, to the amount of 700 or 800,

> ' All plaided and plumed in their tartan array,'

coming forward in two columns of three men abreast, to the

[1] Home's Works, iii. 12.

spirit-stirring notes of the bagpipe, and enclosing the party of soldiers whom they had just taken prisoners. Elevated by the fine appearance of this clan, and by the auspicious result of the little action just described, Charles set about the business of declaring open war against the Elector of Hanover.

The spot selected for the rearing of the standard was a little eminence in the centre of the vale. The Marquis of Tulli-bardine, whose rank entitled him to the honour, pitched himself upon the top of this knoll, supported by two men, on account of his weak state of health. He then flung upon the mountain breeze that flag which, shooting like a streamer from the north, was soon to spread such omens of woe and terror over the peaceful vales of Britain. It was a large banner of red silk, with a white space in the centre, but without the motto of 'TANDEM TRIUMPHANS,' which has been so often assigned to it —as also the significant emblems of a crown and coffin, with which the terror of England at one time adorned it. The appearance of the standard was hailed by a storm of pipe-music, a cloud of skimmering bonnets, and a loud and enduring shout. Tullibardine then read several documents of an important nature, with which the Prince had provided himself. The first was a declaration, or manifesto, in the name of James VIII., dated at Rome, December 23, 1743; containing a view of the public grievances of Britain, and expressing an earnest desire to do the utmost to redress them; calling for this purpose on all his loyal subjects to join his standard as soon as it should be set up; and promising, in the event of his restoration, to respect all existing institutions, rights, and privileges. The second was a commission of the same date, in which James appointed his son Charles to be prince regent. The third was a manifesto by the Prince, dated at Paris, May 16, 1745, declaring that he was now come to execute the will of his father by setting up the royal standard, and asserting his undoubted right to the throne of his ancestors; offering pardon for all treasons to those who should now take up arms in his behalf, or at the least abjure allegiance to the usurper; calling on the officers of the army

...vy to come over to his service, in which case he should pay all their arrears, and reappointing as his servants all public officers whatever who should henceforth act in his name; commanding payment of all public moneys to officers authorised by him; promising the same respect to existing institutions and privileges as his father; and, finally, calling on all his father's subjects 'to be assisting to him in the recovery of his just rights and of their own liberties.' The standard was carried back to the Prince's quarters by a guard of fifty Camerons.[1]

About two hours after this solemnity was concluded, Macdonald of Keppoch arrived with 300 of his hardy and warlike clan; and in the evening, some gentlemen of the name of Macleod came to offer their services, expressing great indignation at the defection of their chief, and proposing to return to Skye and raise all the men they could. The army, amounting to about 1200 men, was encamped that evening in Glenfinnin, Sullivan being appointed quartermaster-general.

The insurrection was thus fairly commenced; and it will now be necessary to advert to the means taken by government for its suppression, as well as to the state of the country upon which Charles was about to descend.

CHAPTER IV.

PROCEEDINGS OF GOVERNMENT.

'*Duke Frederick.* Come on; since the youth will not be entreated, his own peril on his forwardness.'   *As You Like It.*

AT the time when the insurrection broke out, George II. was absent in Hanover, on one of those frequent visits to his paternal dominions which, with great appearance of truth,

---

[1] Amongst the spectators on this occasion was a lady named Miss Jeany Cameron, who afterwards became the subject of many unfounded popular rumours. She was, in reality, a middle-aged lady, of perfect propriety of deportment, and after this occasion did not see the Prince any more, except when she met him in public during his stay in Edinburgh,

caused his British subjects to accuse him of being more de
to the interests of his electorate, than he was to those of the
more important empire over which his family had been called to
reign. The government was intrusted, during his absence, to a
regency composed of his principal ministers. So far as the
northern section of the island was concerned in the affairs of
government, it was then managed by a minister called Secretary
of State for Scotland; and the Marquis of Tweeddale held the
office in 1745.

The negotiations which the exiled family had constantly
carried on with their adherents in Britain, and their incessant
menaces of invasion, rendered the event which had now taken
place by no means unexpected on the part of government, and
indeed scarcely alarming. During the whole summer, a report
had been flying about the Highlands that Prince Charles was to
come over before the end of the season; but the king's servants
at Edinburgh heard nothing of it till the 2d of July, when the
President of the Court of Session came to Sir John Cope,
commander-in-chief of the forces in Scotland, and shewed him a
letter which he had just received from a Highland gentleman,
informing him of the rumour, though affecting to give it little
credit. Cope instantly sent notice of what he heard to the
Marquis of Tweeddale, expressing disbelief in the report, but
yet advising that arms should be transmitted to the forts in
Scotland, for the use of the well-affected clans, in anticipation of
any attempt which might be made. The marquis answered
General Cope upon the 9th, ordering him to keep a vigilant eye
upon the north, but mentioning that the lords of the regency
seemed to decline so alarming a measure as sending arms.
Cope replied immediately that he would take all the measures
which seemed necessary for his majesty's service, avoiding as
much as possible the raising of unnecessary alarm. Some
further correspondence took place before the end of the month,
in which the zeal and promptitude of this much-ridiculed general
appear very conspicuous, while the supineness and security of
the regency are just as remarkable.

John Cope, whose fortune it was to be Charles's first opponent, and who was regarded by President Forbes as a good officer of his standing, had at present under his command in Scotland two regiments of dragoons,[1] three full regiments of infantry,[2] and fourteen odd companies,[3] together with the standing garrisons of invalids in the various castles and forts. The most of these troops were newly raised, being, indeed, intended for immediate transportation to Flanders; and it was impossible to place much confidence in them, especially as forming an entire army, without the support of more experienced troops.

With this little army, nevertheless, Cope found himself obliged to undertake a campaign against the formidable bands of the north.   He received a letter from the Scottish secretary on the 3d of August, announcing that the young Chevalier, as Charles was called, had really left France in order to invade Scotland, and was even said to have already landed there; commanding him to make such a disposition of his forces as to be ready at a moment's notice; and promising immediately to send him down the supply of arms he formerly requested.   On the 8th, he received a letter from the Lord Justice-clerk (Milton), then residing at Roseneath, enclosing another letter, dated the 5th instant, which had just been transmitted to Mr Campbell of Stonefield, sheriff of Argyle, by Mr Campbell of Aird (factor in Mull to the Duke of Argyll); which letter gave him almost certain intelligence of the Prince's landing.   Next morning, the 9th, Cope was shewn by the Lord President another letter, confirming the news; and he sent all these papers to London, as the best means of rousing the slumbering energies of government.

---

[1] Gardiner's, lying at Stirling, Linlithgow, Musselburgh, Kelso, and Dunse; and Hamilton's, quartered at Haddington, Dunse, and adjacent places.   Their horses, as was then the custom, were placed at grass in the parks near the quarters of the men.

[2] Guise's regiment of foot at Aberdeen, Murray's in the Highland forts, and Lascelles's at Edinburgh and Leith.

[3] Five of Lees's at Dumfries, Stranraer, Glasgow, and Stirling; two of the Scots Royals (taken by Keppoch's men); two of the Scots Fusiliers at Glasgow; two of Lord Semple's at Cupar, in Fife; and three of Lord John Murray's at Crieff.

Without waiting for this communication, the Lords Re...
published on the 6th of August a proclamation, offering £30,000
for the person of the young Chevalier, whom they announced
to have sailed from France for the purpose of invading Britain.
This proclamation proceeded upon an act of George I., by
which the blood of James Stuart and of his children was
attainted, and themselves outlawed.   Charles, on learning the
price offered for his life, issued from his camp at Kinlocheil
(August 20) a proclamation expressing great indignation at ' so
insolent an attempt,' and offering a like sum for the *person* of
the Elector of Hanover.   Charles's first idea is said to have
been to propose only £30 for the latter object; but ultimately
he was induced to offer the same sum which the government
had placed upon his own head.

It is amusing to observe, in the newspapers of the period,
the various reports which agitated the public mind, and, above
all, the uncertainty and meagreness of the intelligence which
reached Edinburgh regarding Charles's transactions in Lochaber.
On the 5th of August, it is mentioned in the *Edinburgh Courant*
that the Prince had left France.   Next day, it is reported, as a
quotation from some foreign journal, that he had actually landed
in the Highlands, and was sure of 30,000 men and ten ships
of war.   No other intelligence of note is observable till the
22d, when it is stated that two Glasgow vessels, in their way
home from Virginia, had touched somewhere in the north-west
Highlands, and learned that the dreaded Pretender was actually
there, with 10,000 men, and had sent word to the governor of
Fort William ' *that he would give him his breakfast that morning.*'
The uncertainty which long prevailed in Edinburgh regarding
the proceedings in Lochaber, shews, in a striking manner, how
difficult it was to obtain correct intelligence in those days from
a district which now would be considered as distant little more
than a day's journey.

In projecting measures against the threatened insurrection,
Sir John Cope had all along held council with those civil officers
who, ever since the Union, have exercised influence over the

...s of Scotland—the Lord President of the Court of Session, the Lord Justice-clerk, the Lord Advocate, and the Solicitor-general. The gentlemen who held the first two of these offices —Duncan Forbes and Andrew Fletcher—were men of not only the purest patriotism and loyalty, but of good understanding and attainments. Duncan Forbes, in particular, from his intimate acquaintance with the Highlanders, of whom he had previously converted many to government, seemed well qualified to direct the operations of a campaign against that people.

The advice of all these gentlemen tended to this effect—that Sir John Cope should march as fast as possible into the Highlands, in order to crush the insurrection before it reached any height. It is very probable[1] that this advice was dictated by a feeling of humanity towards the insurgents, many of whom were the intimate friends and associates of the advisers. Forbes seems to have wished, by this means, at once to repress those who *had* risen, before government should become exasperated against them, and to prevent as many as possible from joining, who, he was sure, would soon do so if the enterprise was not immediately checked. The counsel was more honourable in its motive than prudent in policy. The royal army was not only inferior in numbers to that which Charles was believed to have drawn together, but had to contend with all the disadvantages of a campaign in an enemy's country, and on ground unsuitable for its evolutions : would first have to drag its way slowly over rugged wildernesses, with a clog of baggage and provisions behind it, and then perhaps fight in a defile, where it would be gradually cut to pieces, or, what was as bad, permit the enemy to slip past and descend upon the low country, which it ought to have protected. The advice was even given in defiance of experience. The Duke of Argyll, in 1715, by guarding the pass into the Lowlands at Stirling, prevented the much superior army of Mar from disturbing the valuable part of the kingdom, and eventually was able to paralyse and confound the whole of that enterprise.

1 Probable from the tenor of their letters.—See Culloden Papers.

Cope is conjectured by Mr Home,[1] though the fact is ι.
obvious, to have been confirmed in his desire of prompt measures
by a piece of address on the part of the Jacobites.   These
gentlemen, who were very numerous in Edinburgh, remembering
perhaps the precedent alluded to, and knowing that Charles,
with a small supply of money, would not be able to keep the
Highlanders long together in their own country, conceived it to be
their best policy to precipitate a meeting between the two armies.
They therefore contrived, it is said, that Sir John Cope, who
seemed to have no opinions of his own, but consulted everybody
he met, should be urged to perform the march he proposed, as
the measure most likely to quell the insurrection, which, it was
hinted by these insidious advisers, wanted nothing but a little
time to become formidable.

Thus advised, and thus perhaps deluded, Sir John Cope
rendezvoused his raw troops at Stirling, and sent off a letter to
the Scottish secretary, requesting permission to march immediately against the rebels.   The reasons which he gave for his
proposal seemed so strong in the eyes of the Lords Regent,
that they not only agreed to it, but expressly ordered him to
march to the north and engage the enemy, whatever might be
his strength, or wherever he might be found.   This order
reached Sir John at Edinburgh on the 19th of August, the
very day when Charles reared his standard; and Cope set
out that day for Stirling, to put himself at the head of his
little army.

Next day, the commander-in-chief commenced his fatal
march.   His force consisted of twenty-five companies of foot,
amounting in all to 1400 men; for he had left the two regiments
of dragoons behind, on account of their presumed unfitness
for a Highland campaign.   He carried with him four pieces
of cannon (one-and-a-half pounders), as many cohorns, and
a thousand stand of arms, to be given to the native troops
which he expected to join him as he went along.   Besides a

[1] Works, iii. 28. Mr Home adds, that he was assured of the fact by the Jacobites
themselves.

⌐quantity of baggage, he was followed by a train of black-cattle, with butchers to kill them as required; and he had as much bread and biscuit as would serve for twenty-one days; for the production of which, all the bakers in Edinburgh, Leith, and Stirling had been working for a week.[1]

It was Sir John's intention to march to Fort Augustus, the central fort of the three which are pitched along the Great Glen. He considered this the most advantageous post that could be occupied by the king's army, because it was in the centre of the disaffected country, and admitted of a ready communication with the adjacent places of strength. He accordingly adopted that military road through the middle of the Highlands, which, stretching athwart the Grampians, is so remarkable in the memory of all travellers for its lonely desolation in summer, and its dangerous character when the ground is covered with snow. His first day's march was to Crieff, where he was obliged to halt till he should be overtaken by 100 *horse-loads* of bread that had been left at Stirling. He had previously written to the Duke of Athole, Lord Glenorchy (son of the Earl of Breadalbane), and other loyal chiefs, desiring them to raise their men, and the first of these noblemen here visited him; but the chief of Athole, though disposed to preserve his estate by keeping on good terms with the government, was by no means so ardently loyal as to take arms in its defence. Cope was then, for the first time, shaken in his hope of gaining accessions of strength as he went along—the hope which had mainly induced him to go north with so small an army; and he would have gladly returned to Stirling, had not the orders of government, as he afterwards acknowledged,[2] been so peremptory for a contrary course. Lord Glenorchy waited upon the disconcerted general on the afternoon of the same day, and gave him additional pain by the intelligence that he could not gather his men in proper time. He then saw fit to send back 700 of his spare arms to Stirling.

Advancing on the 22d to Amulree, on the 23d to Tay Bridge,

---

1 Report of Cope's Trial.   2 Ibid. 17.

on the 24th to Trinifuir, and on the 25th to Dalnacardoch,
difficulties of a Highland campaign became gradually more and
more apparent to the unhappy general, whose eyes were at the
same time daily opened wider and wider to the secret disaffection of the Highlanders.   His baggage-horses were stolen in the
night from their pastures, so that he was obliged to leave
hundreds of his bread-bags behind him.   Those who took
charge of this important deposit, though they promised to send
it after him, contrived that it should never reach its destination,
or at least not until it was useless.   He was also played upon
and distracted by all sorts of false intelligence; so that he at
last could not trust to the word of a single native, gentleman or
commoner.

When at the lonely inn of Dalnacardoch, he was met by
Captain Sweetenham, the officer already mentioned as having
been taken by the insurgents; who, after witnessing the erection
of the standard, had been discharged upon his parole, and now
brought Cope the first certain intelligence he had received
regarding the real state of the enemy.   Sweetenham had left
them when their numbers were 1400; he had since met many
more who were marching to the rendezvous; and as he passed
Dalwhinnie, the last stage, he had been informed by Macintosh
of Borlum that they were now 3000 strong, and were marching
to take possession of Corriearrack.   Cope soon after received a
letter from President Forbes (now at his house of Culloden,
near Inverness), confirming the latter part of Captain Sweetenham's intelligence.

Corriearrack, of which the insurgents were about to take
possession, is a lofty and wide-spreading mountain, interposed
betwixt Cope's present position and Fort Augustus, and over
which lay the road he was designing to take.   This road, which
had recently been formed under the care of General Wade,
ascends the steep sides of the mountain by seventeen *traverses*,
each of which leads the traveller but a small way forward in the
actual course of his journey.   It was the most dangerous peculiarity of the hill, in the present case, that the deep ditch or

er-course along the side of the road afforded many positions in which an enemy could be intrenched to the teeth, so as to annoy the approaching army without the risk of being annoyed in return ; and that, indeed, a very small body of resolute men could thus entirely cut off and destroy an army, of whatever numbers or appointments, acting upon the offensive. It was reported to Sir John Cope that a party of the Highlanders was to wait for him at the bridge of Snugborough, one of the most dangerous passes in the mountain, and that, while he was there actively opposed, another body, marching round by a path to the west, and coming in behind, should completely enclose him, as between two fires, and in all probability accomplish his destruction.[1]

The royal army had advanced to Dalwhinnie, about twenty miles distant from the summit of Corriearrack, when the general received this intelligence ; and so pressing had his dilemma then become, that he conceived it improper to move farther without calling a council of war. It was on the morning of the 27th of August that this meeting took place, at which various proposals were made and considered for the further conduct of the army. All agreed, in the first place, that their original design of marching over Corriearrack was impracticable. To remain where they were was needless, as the insurgents could slip down into the Lowlands by other roads. Two objections lay against the measure which seemed most obvious, that of *marching back again*—namely, the orders of government, so express in favour of a northward march, and an immediate encounter with the enemy; and the likelihood of the Highlanders intercepting them in their retreat by breaking down the bridges and destroying the roads. The only other course was to turn aside towards Inverness, where they had a prospect of being joined by some loyal clans, and in which case they might expect that the insurgents would scarcely dare to descend upon the Lowlands, as such a course would necessarily leave their own country exposed to the vengeance of an enemy.

1 Report of Cope's Trial, 24.

In reality, as the event shewed, the proper course on
occasion would have been to fall back on some convenient post
near the frontier of the low country, there to make a determined
stand against the clans, as the Duke of Argyll had done in
1715. Yet this expedient was supported by only one voice in
the council. It was at last *unanimously agreed* to turn aside to
Inverness—thus leaving the valuable part of the country completely exposed, and sacrificing a real object for the mere sake
of obeying the letter of an order given, probably, in the contemplation of totally different circumstances. Sir John, having
taken care to get the seals-manual of his companions to the
resolution, issued orders to alter the route of the army. The
van had reached Blairobeg, three and a half miles south of
Garvamore Inn, and ten miles from Corriearrack, and the rear
was at Catlaig, four miles behind, when the troops were ordered
to halt, face about, and, retracing their steps, turn off by the
road which parts to the east at the last-mentioned place, and
proceeds by Ruthven to Inverness.[1] In order to deceive the
enemy, who lay upon the top of Corriearrack expecting his
approach, the general caused a small portion of his army to
advance, with the camp-colours flying, towards the hill, under
the semblance of an advanced guard, with orders to overtake
the main body with all speed, when they had allowed time for it
to get half a day's march upon its new route. He arrived, by
forced marches, at Inverness upon the 29th, without having
rested a single day since he left Crieff.

---

[1] 'Two rowan-trees (mountain-ashes) mark the place where Sir John Cope's army faced
about, and avoided an action with the rebels.'—HOME.

CHAPTER V.

CHARLES'S DESCENT UPON THE LOWLANDS.

> ' Rouse, rouse, ye kilted warriors !
>   Rouse, ye heroes of the north !
> Rouse, and join your chieftains' banners ;
>   'Tis your Prince that leads you forth.'
> *Jacobite Song.*

AT Glenfinnin, where the standard had been raised on the 19th, the Prince spent two happy days. So at least we are assured they were by Major Macdonald of Tiendrish, who, when confined in the castle of Edinburgh, told Bishop Forbes ' that he had never seen the Prince more cheerful at any time, and in higher spirits, than when he had got together four or five hundred men about the standard.' He then removed to Kinlocheil —that is, the head of Loch Eil—in the country of the chief of the Camerons. The retaliatory proclamation, offering £30,000 for the person of the reigning king, was ' given in our camp at Kinlocheil, August the 22d.' He lodged on the night of Friday the 23d at Fassefern, on the side of Loch Eil, the residence of the young chief's brother. Loch Eil is a branch of Loch Linnhe, the arm of the sea on which Fort William is situated : it was therefore liable to a hostile inroad from the nautical craft of the enemy. A war-vessel having actually appeared at Fort William, the Chevalier removed across a hill to Moy, a village on the river Lochy, belonging to the Camerons. He was now daily receiving intelligence of Cope's northern progress from deserters who nightly left the camp of that general, in order to join their respective clans. On the 26th he crossed the Lochy, and advanced to Letterfinlay, a lonely inn on the brink of Loch Lochy ; he was joined on the way (at Low Bridge) by the Stuarts of Appin, 260 in number, under the command of

Stuart of Ardshiel.   About midnight, an express arrived from
Gordon of Glenbucket, informing him that Cope had advanced
into Badenoch, and was designing to cross Corriearrack; immediately on which, though the night was extremely stormy, he
gave orders for his men to go forward and take possession of
the hill, and went himself to Invergarry Castle, where he spent
the remainder of the night.

At Invergarry he was visited by Fraser of Gortuleg, on a
secret embassy from Lord Lovat.   This nobleman, now advanced
to the seventy-eighth year of his age, was chief of the clan Fraser,
and possessed large estates in Inverness-shire : he was able to
bring several hundred men into the field.   Discontented with
the government, and well inclined to the Stuart family, he was
yet disposed to act with great caution.   Gortuleg therefore
excused the personal presence of the chief on account of his
age, but recommended Charles to march into his country of
Stratherrick, and raise the Frasers; at the same time he asked
for a patent which had been promised by the old Chevalier,
creating Lovat a duke, and begged to have an order for seizing
the President Forbes *dead or alive.*   The patent chanced to be
left behind with the baggage, and was therefore not forthcoming:
the Prince so far complied with the other request as to give an
order for seizing the person of the Lord President.   With this
Gortuleg returned to his chief.   He is found, two days after,
writing a friendly letter to the President, in which he only
adverts to his having seen some of the insurgent chiefs at Invergarry, and seems anxious to serve the government by communicating the information he had thus acquired.   We shall see
more of the crooked policy of Lovat in the sequel.

Next day, the 27th, while the royal officers were determining
upon their evasive march to Inverness, Charles and his army,
now augmented by the Macdonells of Glengarry and Grants of
Glenmorriston to 1800 men, proceeded to the foot of Corriearrack, the summit of which was already in possession of the
party which had been sent forward the night before.   The
Prince, always the most eager man of the whole army, is said by

Fraser of Gortuleg, in his letter to the Lord President, to have
'called that morning for his Highland clothes, and, tying the
latchets of his shoes, solemnly declared that he would be up
with Mr Cope before they were unloosed.'   The insurgents were
informed of Cope's evasive movement by a soldier of the clan
Cameron, who deserted in order to convey the intelligence, as
soon as he perceived the army turn off at Catlaig.   They hailed
the news with a loud shout of exultation; and the Prince, calling
for a glass of brandy, and ordering every man one of usquebaugh,
drank : 'To the health of good Mr Cope, and may every general
in the usurper's service prove himself as much our friend as he
has done !' [1]   They then descended the steep traverses upon the
south side of Corriearrack, with the rapid steps and eager countenances of men who give chase.

It was the first wish of the Highland army on this occasion
that Johnny Cope, as they called him, should be pursued, and
he and his men cut to pieces.   However, when they reached
Garvamore, the first stage from the bottom of the hill, it was
determined, by a council of war, that the unfortunate general
should be left to the consequences of his own false step at
Inverness, and that they should proceed in the meantime to
take advantage of his desertion of the Lowlands.   They were
confirmed in this resolution by Mr Murray of Broughton, who
represented that, by the influence of the Jacobites in Edinburgh,
they would gain easy possession of that capital, and thus give as
much *éclat* to their arms as might be expected from the achievement of a victory.   It also appeared that, by this course, if they
left the Frasers, the Macintoshes, and other northern clans,
whom they expected to join them, the Marquis of Tullibardine
would raise the men of Athole before the duke his brother had
time to interest them in the cause of government.

It was more particularly at this juncture that Charles's enterprise assumed that bold and romantic character for which it was
destined to be so remarkable.   Having once made the resolution

---

[1] Henderson's *History of the Rebellion*, 34.

to descend upon the low countries, he did so with spirit and rapidity. Two days sufficed to carry him through the alpine region of Badenoch ; another to open up to his view the pleasant vale of Athole, which might be considered as the avenue into the fertile country he was invading. He seems to have acted entirely like a man who has undertaken a high and hazardous affair, which he is resolved to carry through with all his spirit and address. Nature and education had alike qualified him for such an enterprise. Originally gifted with a healthy and robust constitution, he had taken care to inure himself to a hardy and temperate mode of life ; had instructed himself in all kinds of manly exercises ; and, in particular, had made himself a first-rate pedestrian by hunting afoot over the plains of Italy.[1] The Highlanders were astonished to find themselves overmatched at running, wrestling, leaping, and even at their favourite exercise of the broadsword, by the slender stranger of the distant lands ; but their astonishment gave place to admiration and affection, when they discovered that Charles had adopted all these exercises out of compliment to them, and that he might some day shew himself, as he said, a true Highlander. By walking, moreover, every day's march alongside one or other of their corps, inquiring into their family histories, songs, and legends, he succeeded in completely fascinating the hearts of this simple people, who could conceive no greater merit upon earth than accomplishment in the use of arms, accompanied by a taste for tales of ancient glory. The enthusiastic and devoted attachment with which he succeeded in inspiring them, was such as no subsequent events could ever altogether extinguish. Half a century after, when age might have been supposed to deaden their early feelings, his surviving fellow-adventurers rarely spoke of him without a sigh or a tear.

At Dalwhinnie, where the army cheerfully bivouacked, along

---

[1] Boswell's *Tour to the Hebrides* (2d ed.), 231. In his march through the Highlands to meet Cope, he walked sixteen Scottish miles one day, in boots, fatiguing the hardiest of his companions. The men, hearing that one of his boots had lost a heel, said they were glad of it, as he would now be obliged to walk more at leisure.—*Donald Cameron's Narrative, Lyon in Mourning*.

with their young leader, on the open moor, a party who had gone upon an unsuccessful expedition against the small government fort of Ruthven,[1] brought in Macpherson of Cluny, chief of that clan, and son-in-law of Lord Lovat—a man of vigorous character, and one whose accession to the cause at such a moment would have been of considerable importance. He had accepted a command under government, and only the day before attended Sir John Cope at Dalwhinnie, and received orders to embody his clan, in which there were about 300 fighting men ; but he was in reality a partisan of the Stuart family, though, under the present circumstances, not decided to take up arms in its behalf. He was conducted to Charles as a kind of honourable prisoner, and carried along with the army to Perth, whence he returned to raise his clan for the Chevalier. The same cautious policy which has been attributed to Locheil, is said to have been followed by Cluny. Before consenting to join the Prince, he demanded and obtained from him security for the full value of his estate, lest the expedition should prove unsuccessful.[2] Let not this policy be regarded as detracting too much from any merit of self-sacrifice hitherto attributed to these men. It might appear to them as not only justified, but demanded, in consequence of the failure of the Prince to bring foreign aid. And, after all, the purchase-money of a Highland gentleman's estate was but a small part of what he risked on this occasion, seeing that, in the first place, he took the common hazards of war ; in the second, risked the pains of treason ; and, after these, the loss of his home and country, in which was included all that was enviable in the state and circumstance of one who enjoyed the veneration, and could control the actions, of perhaps a thousand of his fellow-creatures.

[1] 'In this route, Lochgary, Dr Cameron, and O'Sullivan, were sent to Ruthven, in Badenoch, to take the barracks. Neither side had any cannon. The Highland party endeavoured to set fire to the door ; but the soldiers fired through holes in the door, killed one man, and mortally wounded two more ; and then the party retired. This garrison consisted only of twelve men, commanded by Sergeant Molloy.'—*Journal of Æneas Macdonald, Forbes Papers, in possession of the author*.

[2] Young Glengarry communicated this fact, which he said he had from Cluny's own mouth, to Bishop Forbes in April 1752.—*Jacobite Memoirs*, p. 22.

As the mountain host descended upon the plain, they were joined, like one of their own rivers, by accessions of strength at the mouths of all the little glens which they passed. But while many of the people joined, and prepared to join them, a very considerable number of the landed proprietors fled at their approach; among the rest, the Duke of Athole. In the absence of this nobleman from his house at Blair, his brother, the Marquis of Tullibardine, took possession of it as his own; and here Charles spent the night of the 30th of August. Along with Charles, the marquis undertook on this occasion to entertain all the Highland chiefs; and the supper which he gave was suitable to the distinguished character of the guests. During the evening, it is said, the Prince exerted himself to appear cheerful, though the anxiety arising from his circumstances occasionally drew a shade of thoughtfulness over his otherwise sprightly features. He partook only of the dishes which are supposed to be peculiar to Scotland; and, in pursuance of the same line of policy which induced him to walk in tartan at the head of his troops, attempted to drink the healths of the chiefs in the few words of Gaelic which he had already picked up. To the Marquis of Tullibardine, who, as a gentleman of the old school, always talked in broad Scotch, he addressed himself in similar language; and in all his deportment, he shewed an evident anxiety to conciliate and please those among whom his lot was cast.[1] Observing the guard which his host had placed in the lobby to be constantly peeping in, he affected a desire of enjoying the open air; and walking out into the lobby, gratified the poor Highlanders with a view of his person, which they had not previously seen, on account of their recent arrival at the house.[2]

The morning after his arrival at Blair, he reviewed his troops. Some whom he had lately seen around him being now wanting, he despatched a few of his officers to bring them forward to Blair, when it was found that their only reason for lingering behind was, that they had been denied the satisfaction of

[1] Henderson's *History of the Rebellion*. 36.   [2] Tradition in Athole.

pursuing General Cope! At Blair he spent two days, during which he was joined by Lord Nairn, a cadet of the great house of Athole, and by several gentlemen of the country. At Lude, the seat of a chieftain of the clan Robertson, to which he next proceeded, he was very cheerful, and took his share in several dances, including minuets and Highland reels. A faithful chronicler informs us that the first tune he called for was the well-known Jacobite one, 'This is no my ain house'—referring to the alien character of all political arrangements since 1688.[1] Proceeding down the Blair or Plain of Athole, he arrived on the 3d at Dunkeld, and next day he dined at Nairn House, between that town and Perth. Here 'some of the company happened to observe what a thoughtful state his father would now be in, from the consideration of those dangers and difficulties he had to encounter, and that upon this account he was much to be pitied. The Prince replied that he did not half so much pity his father as his brother; "for," said he, "the king has been inured to disappointments and distresses, and has learned to bear up easily under the burdens of life; but poor Harry! his young and tender years make him much to be pitied, for few brothers love as we do."'[2]

This evening he entered Perth, where a party of his troops had already proclaimed his father and himself as respectively king and regent. He rode on this occasion the horse which had been given to him by Major Macdonald of Tiendrish, and was attended by a cavalcade of gentlemen, amongst whom were the Duke of Perth, Oliphant of Gask, and Mercer of Aldie, who joined him as he passed through their estates. Well mounted, and attired in a handsome suit of tartan trimmed with gold lace, he made a very good appearance. The people, dazzled by the novelty of the spectacle, hailed him with acclamations, and conducted him in a kind of triumph to the quarters that had been prepared for him in the house of a gentleman. This was the first town of consequence

[1] Duncan ... arrative, *Jacobite Memoirs*. [2] The same.

E

which Charles had yet arrived at, and he had every reason to be satisfied with his reception; although the magistrates had thought proper to leave their charge, and disappear on the preceding evening. A fair being held at the time in Perth, there were many strangers present, to join in the novel and agitated feelings with which this singular scene was contemplated.

The house appropriated for Charles's residence was that of the Viscount Stormont,[1] elder brother to the elegant William Murray, who afterwards became Chief-justice of the King's Bench and Earl of Mansfield. Stormont, like his brother and all the rest of the family, was a Jacobite at heart, but one who did not feel inclined to risk life and property in the cause. He did not choose to be present on this occasion to entertain the Prince; but no attentions were wanting on the part of his household; and one of his sisters is said to have spread down a bed for Prince Charlie with her own fair hands.[2]

The neighbouring seaport of Dundee, though not in the Prince's line of march, was of too much importance to escape notice on this occasion. That very evening Charles despatched Keppoch and Clanranald with a party of Macdonalds, who, entering the town about daybreak next morning, captured two vessels in the harbour, containing arms and ammunition, which they immediately sent to Perth for the use of the army.

The 'Duke of Perth,' who had joined the Prince before he reached that town, was, strictly speaking, only James

---

1 It was an antique house with a wooden front, standing upon the site of the present Union Bank, near the bottom of the High Street.

2 Information from the late John Young, Esq., W.S., Castle Street, Edinburgh. Mr Young, as the son of a non-jurant clergyman in Fife, was likely to be correctly informed on such matters. The Stormont family relaxed in their Jacobitism as the great men of their family advanced in legal and state honours; for which, it may be supposed, the more faithful of the remnants of the party did not like them the better. One day in the partisan, reign of George III., Hamilton of Kilbrachmont, in Fife, a most determined annoyed and a good deal soured in his temper, calling upon the Misses Murray, was so of the at the ostentation with which the good ladies paraded a few portraits of the royal family, which had been sent to them by their brother. The irritation by their speaking of the great personages represented as 'the people above!' exclaimed old Hamilton—'fient nor they were up the lum' in English. And, thus saying, he flung out of the house.

Drummond, proprietor of large estates in Perthshire, and representative of the Drummonds, Earls of Perth, one of the most
distinguished of the noble families of Scotland.   His grandfather, James, fourth Earl of Perth, had followed the fortunes of
James II., and been created a duke at St Germain.   The son
of this nobleman, joining the insurrection in 1715, was attainted,
so that, at his father's death in 1716, the titles became dormant.
But the estates having been previously transferred to his infant
son, were preserved for the benefit of that person, who now
lived upon them, boldly assuming the title which had been conferred by James II. upon his grandfather.   The so-called duke
was thirty-two years of age, brave, frank, and liberal, but disliked
by many on account of his profession of the Catholic faith, in
which he had been reared by a remarkably enthusiastic mother.
When Charles was in the West Highlands, a warrant was issued
for the seizure of the duke; and two Highland officers, Sir
Patrick Murray of Auchtertyre, and Mr Campbell of Inverary,
undertook to execute it, under circumstances extremely discreditable to them.   Having asked themselves to his house to
dinner, he invited them to come in the kindest terms, as friends
and neighbours, and entertained them hospitably.   Meanwhile
they had ordered a military party to surround the house, and
when all was prepared, they announced their warrant.   The
duke with difficulty restrained his temper, and told them he
would step into a closet off the dining-room, to prepare himself
to go with them.   They, trusting that he could not escape,
assented.   He instantly went down a back stair, through his
gardens, and into the adjoining wood, crawling on hands and
knees to avoid being seen by the sentinels.   Fortunately, he
found a horse, though without a saddle, and only haltered, on
which he rode to the house of his friend Moray of Abercairney.[1]
Having thus escaped the fangs of the government, by which he
should otherwise have been held in restraint till after the insurrection was over, he was now by no means less eager than

---

[1] *Jacobite Memoirs*, 16.

before to promote the cause of the house of Stuart, by personal service, and the aid of his numerous dependants, who of themselves nearly formed a regiment.

Charles received considerable reinforcements at Perth. Viscount Strathallan, a cadet of the Drummond family, Lord Ogilvie, son of the Earl of Airlie, and John Roy Stuart, a gentleman of Speyside, and the *beau idéal* of a clever Highland officer,[1] were amongst the most conspicuous persons of note who here joined him: the last-mentioned gentleman brought with him from abroad some very agreeable letters from persons of importance, promising assistance.[2] He had already been joined by the tenants of Lord Nairn, and the Lairds of Gask and Aldie.   The Robertsons of Struan, Blairfitty, and Cushievale, the Stuarts who inhabited the uplands of Perthshire, and many of the tenants of the Duke of Athole, raised by the Marquis of Tullibardine, now poured themselves into the tide of insurrection.   In raising the men of lower Perthshire, considerable difficulties were experienced by the chiefs and landlords.   The Duke of Perth, having ordered his tenants to contribute a man for every plough, is said, though with extremely little probability, to have shot one refractory person, in order to enforce his orders among the rest.   Tullibardine, from the equivocal nature of his title, found still greater difficulty in raising the tenants upon those estates which he conceived to be his own.   But perhaps no one experienced so much difficulty in his levies as the good Laird of Gask, though he was at the same time perhaps the person of all others the most anxious to provide men for the service of his beloved Prince.   This enthusiastic Jacobite was, it seems, so extremely incensed at

---

[1] John Roy was the son of the Baron of Kincardine on the Spey, and lineally descended from Robert II., the first of the Stuart kings. He was in the prime of life, an excellent soldier, and also a writer of verses, both English and Gaelic, many of which are still traditionally preserved in the Highlands. An old Highland woman, a few years ago (1827), describing John Roy's person, which she had seen, said that his eye in particular was very fine—her expression was, *like the eye of a horse*—of course an exaggeration, yet marking a feature of no common size and brilliancy.

[2] A Mr Johnstone, who afterwards wrote a memoir of the insurrection, also joined the Prince at Perth.

the resistance he received from some of his tenants, that he laid an arrestment or inhibition upon their corn-fields, by way of trying if their interest would not oblige them to comply with his request. The case was still at issue, when Charles, in marching from Perth, observed the corn hanging dead ripe, and inquired the reason. He was informed that Gask had not only prohibited his tenants from cutting their grain, but would not permit their cattle to be fed upon it, so that these creatures were absolutely starving. He instantly leaped from the saddle, exclaiming: 'This will never do,' and began to gather a quantity of the corn. Giving this to his horse, he said to those that were by that he had thus broken Gask's inhibition, and the farmers might now, upon his authority, proceed to put the produce of their fields to its proper use.[1]

When Charles entered Perth, he had only a single guinea in his pocket.[2] During his march hitherto, he had freely given his chiefs what sums they thought necessary for the subsistence of the men; and his purse was now exhausted, but fortunately at a moment when it was in his power to replenish it. By sending detachments of his men to various towns at no great distance, he raised some of the public money; and several of his Edinburgh friends now came in with smaller, but less reluctant subsidies. From the city of Perth he exacted £500.

Perhaps the most important accession to his force which Charles received at Perth was that of Lord George Murray, whom his brother, the Marquis of Tullibardine, brought down from Athole the day after the army entered the city. This gentleman was advanced to middle age, and had been in arms for the Stuarts at the affair of Glenshiel in 1719. Having served abroad since, in the Sardinian service, he possessed considerable military experience; but his talents and enterprising character were such as to render knowledge of his profession comparatively a matter of secondary moment. Charles had so much confidence in his abilities, as immediately to make him

---

[1] Tradition.   [2] Home's Works, iii. 43.

lieutenant-general of his army—a trust for which he soon proved himself admirably qualified.

Charles was compelled to linger eight days at Perth, by the double necessity of providing himself with money, and gathering the Perthshire clans together. He did not, however, spend his time in vain. He seized this opportunity of reducing the ill-assorted elements of his army to some kind of order, and exerted himself to get the men instructed in the various evolutions of military discipline. The sturdy mountaineers were, as may be easily imagined, somewhat intractable, displaying great inaptitude in the conventional rules by which a whole body is to be governed, though, at the same time, every individual evinced a readiness and dexterity in the use of his own arms far beyond what is seen in ordinary soldiers. At a review held on the North Inch, a common near the town (September 7), Charles was observed to smile occasionally at the awkwardness of their general motions; at the same time he complimented their agility and wild elegance by calling them 'his *stags*.'[1] Lord George Murray now took some pains to furnish the men with many things which, though they make but a poor appearance in a romantic narrative, are yet eminently useful during the actual progress of a campaign. Amongst these were provisions, and the means of carrying them. He caused each man to be provided with a sacken knapsack, large enough to carry a peck of oatmeal—the food chiefly depended upon by these hardy soldiers. He also took measures for supplying meal and knapsacks to the clans who were on their march to join the Prince. By no other means could this little army have long been kept together.

It would almost appear that Charles occupied himself so closely in business while at Perth, as to have little time for amusement. Not only did he make a point of rising early every morning to drill his troops, but it is told of him that, being one night invited to a ball by the gentlewomen of Perth, he had no

---

[1] Henderson's *History of the Rebellion*, 37.

sooner danced one measure, than he made his bow, and hastily withdrew, alleging the necessity of visiting his sentry-posts. From a newspaper of the time,[1] it appears that he attended divine service on Sunday the 8th of September, when a Mr Armstrong, probably a clergyman of the Scottish Episcopal Church, preached from the text (Isaiah, xiv. 1, 2) : ' For the Lord will have mercy on Jacob, and will yet choose Israel, and set them in their own land : and the strangers shall be joined with them, and they shall cleave to the house of Jacob. And the people shall take them, and bring them to their place : and the house of Israel shall possess them in the land of the Lord for servants and handmaids : and they shall take them captives, whose captives they were; and they shall rule over their oppressors.' The nature of the discourse may be easily conjectured from the text. It is said that this was the first time the Prince had ever attended a Protestant place of worship.

Many of the strangers whom Charles found at Perth attending the fair procured passports from him, to protect their persons and goods in passing through the country. To all these persons he displayed great courteousness of manner. One of them, a linendraper from London, had some conversation with the youthful adventurer, who desired him to inform his fellow-citizens that he expected to see them at St James's in the course of two months.[2]

[1] The *Caledonian Mercury.*   [2] *Edinburgh Evening Courant.*

CHAPTER VI.

ALARM OF EDINBURGH.

'Can you think to front your enemies' revenges with the easy groans of old women, the virginal palms of your daughters, or with the palsied intercession of such a weak dotard as you seem to be ? Can you think to blow out the intended fire of your city with such weak breath as this ? '—*Coriolanus*.

FOR upwards of a week after Cope's march into the Highlands, the people of Edinburgh had felt all the anxiety which civilians usually entertain regarding an impending action ; but as yet they expressed little alarm about their own particular safety. The common talk of the day amongst the Whigs was, that Cope would soon 'cock up the Pretender's beaver'—that he would speedily 'give a good account of the Highland host'—and other vauntings, indicating great confidence. To speak in another strain was considered treason. Prudence joined with inclination, on the part of the Jacobites, to keep this tone of the public mind undisturbed. They knew it to be Charles's wish that the low countries, and also the government, should be as little alarmed as possible by his proceedings. They therefore conspired with the zealous Whigs to spread a general impression of his weakness.

The better to lull the town, and consequently the whole nation, into security, Charles, or some of his officers, thought proper to despatch a person of gentlemanly rank from their camp in Lochaber, with a report calculated to increase this dangerous confidence. They selected for this purpose James Macgregor, or Drummond, son to the celebrated Rob Roy ; a man of not the purest character, but who seemed eligible on account of his address, and because he enjoyed some confidence amongst the Whig party. By way of making himself as useful

as possible, Macgregor volunteered at the same time to carry
with him to Edinburgh copies of the Prince's proclamations and
manifestos, which he thought he should easily be able to get
printed there, and disseminated amongst the friends of the
cause. He reached Edinburgh on the 26th, and, being immediately admitted into the presence of the civil and civic officers,
reported that the Highlanders, when he left them a day or two
ago, were not above 1500 strong at most. As far as he could
judge of them, they would run at the first onset of the royal
army, being chiefly old men and boys, and very ill armed.
When he had performed this part of his duty, he lost no time
in setting about the other. His papers were printed by one
Drummond, a zealous Jacobite;[1] and so speedily were they
diffused throughout the town, that the magistrates were obliged,
within three or four days after the arrival of this faithful
messenger, to issue a proclamation offering a high reward for
the discovery of the printer.

Macgregor's report, though partially successful in assuring the
citizens, who immediately learned it through the newspapers,
was not so completely effective with the public authorities as to
prevent them from taking a measure next day which they had
for some time contemplated—that of applying to the king for
permission to raise a regiment, to be paid by voluntary subscription of the inhabitants, with which they might at once
defend their property and advance his majesty's interests, in
case of the town being attacked. Their previous security,
however, was about this time slightly disturbed by a piece of
intelligence brought to town by a Highland street-porter, who
had been visiting his friends in the north. This man declared
that when he saw the insurgents in Lochaber, their camp was
as long as the space between Leith and the Calton Hill (at

[1] Drummond, some years afterwards, fell under the anger of the government for similar
proceedings, and had his printing-office shut up; on which occasion the workmen being
thrown idle, and public sympathy, at least with one party, being excited in their behalf, it
was suggested to them to act the drama of the *Gentle Shepherd*, which had not before been
represented on the stage, though many years published. Thus Drummond's men became
the first performers of this celebrated pastoral.

least a mile) ;[1] a local illustration, which inspired a much more respectful idea of the Chevalier's forces than any they had yet entertained.

It was not till the 31st of August that the alarm of the city of Edinburgh became serious. On that day the inhabitants received intelligence of Cope's evasion of the Highland forces at Dalwhinnie, and of the consequent march of the Chevalier upon the low country. They had previously looked upon the insurrection as but a more formidable kind of riot, which would soon be quelled, and no more heard of; but when they saw that a regular army had found it necessary to decline fighting with the insurgents, who were consequently left at liberty to disturb the open country, it began to be looked upon in a much more serious light. Their alarm was, if possible, increased next day (Sunday, the 1st of September), by the Duke of Athole coming suddenly to town on his way from Blair, which, as already mentioned, he had left on the approach of the Highlanders. It was reported that his Grace had been compelled to take this step with greater precipitation than would have otherwise been necessary, by receiving a letter from his brother, the marquis, calling upon him to deliver up the house and estate which he had so long possessed unjustly. But the venerable Thomas Ruddiman, who gave currency to this rumour by means of his paper, the *Caledonian Mercury*, was obliged during the same week to acknowledge it false, beg the duke's pardon, and pay a fine of two guineas, besides being imprisoned for two days.

The friends of government now began to make preparations for the defence of the capital.

'Piled deep and massive, close and high,'

and chiefly situated upon a steep and isolated hill, Edinburgh was then partly surrounded by a wall, and partly by a lake. The wall was of little use but to check smuggling, or evasion of the city customs; it had no embrasures for cannon, and part of

---

[1] *Caledonian Mercury*. Henderson's *History of the Rebellion*, 37.

it was overlooked by lines of lofty houses, forming the suburbs; while the lake was fordable in many places. The friends of the Hanover succession were nevertheless of opinion that the city was capable of making a defence, provided that the inhabitants were determined upon it, and that arms were obtained from government. It was at least possible, they thought, to hold out until Cope's troops should come to their relief. On the other hand, a considerable section of the inhabitants, including the Lord Provost (Mr Archibald Stewart) and others of the magistracy, were Jacobites, though necessarily making no outward demonstration of such politics. Everything which they could safely or plausibly do to discourage the idea of defending the town was done; and doubtless their efforts were attended with some success. Burghal politics came in to add to the difficulties of the time. Opposed to the existing magistracy were the materials of a Whig one, which had been excluded from power for five years; at its head was Mr George Drummond, a man of virtuous and benevolent character, who had fought in behalf of government at Sheriffmuir. The time was approaching when, according to the custom of the burgh, a new election of magistrates should take place; and it was obviously the policy of the Whigs to profess an eagerness for the defence of the town. On the other hand, the existing magistracy, considering this as a mere mode of party warfare, or an appeal to mob feelings, were the more inclined to go upon the opposite side. 'Defend the town,' or 'not defend the town,' thus became party cries for the *ins* and *outs* of burghal office; and it would have been difficult for any cool onlooker to say whether the Whigs, in their profession of a wish to keep out Prince Charles, or the opposite party, in expressing their belief that the town was indefensible, were the least sincere.

The living force available for defence actually appears to have been of no great amount, although many more formidable enemies have been resisted with something much less. Now that Cope, with his infantry, was off the field, the whole of the regular forces in the south of Scotland, besides the invalids who

garrisoned the fortresses, consisted of two regiments of dragoons
—Hamilton's at Edinburgh, and Gardiner's at Stirling, both of
them newly raised.   In Edinburgh there was a body of military
police, or. *gendarmes*, called the Town-guard, generally amounting to 96 men, but now increased to 126 : these were for the
most part elderly men, who had never been active soldiers, but
they had the advantage of being pretty well disciplined.   There
was another body of militia connected with the city, called the
Trained Bands, the members of which, exceeding 1000 in
number, were ordinary citizens possessed of uniforms, in which
they appeared once a year to fire off their pieces in honour of
the king's birthday, but which none of them had adopted with
the prospect of ever becoming active soldiers, or, indeed, with
any other view than to enjoy the civic dinner which was given
to them on that joyous anniversary.   The Trained Bands had,
at their first institution in the reign of King James VI., worn
defensive armour, and carried the long Scottish spear ; but in
these degenerate days they only assumed a simple uniform, and
were provided with firelocks so old as scarcely to be fit for
service.   To give the reader some idea of the military prowess
of these citizen-soldiers, an extract may be made from a pamphlet
of the day.[1]   The author of this tract says that, when a boy, he
used to see the Trained Bands drawn up on the High Street to
honour the natal day of Britain's majesty, on which occasions,
he affirms, it was common for any one who was bolder than the
rest, or who wished to give himself airs before his wife or
mistress, to fire off his piece in the street, without authority of
his officers : and ' I always observed,' says the pamphleteer,
' they took care to shut their eyes before venturing on that
military exploit ;' though he immediately afterwards remarks in
a note, their fear was perhaps better grounded than he imagined,
considering the danger there was of their firelocks bursting about
their ears.

To increase this hopeful force, the state officers had instigated

---

[1] *Account of the Behaviour of Archibald Stewart.* London, 1748.

the magistrates, as already mentioned, to raise a regiment, which was to be paid by public subscription. The royal[1] permission was not procured for this purpose till the 9th of September, on which day a subscription-paper was laid before the citizens, and a drum sent through the town and its neighbourhood to enlist men. But it is unusual to yield to the solicitations of recruiting-sergeants for the direct purpose of fighting a severe action on the succeeding week. As may be easily imagined, more fortune than life was volunteered on the present occasion. The subscription-paper filled almost immediately; but, after a week, only about 200 men had been procured.

Besides this force, which was dignified with the name of the Edinburgh Regiment, a number of the loyal inhabitants associated themselves as volunteers into a separate band or regiment, for which 400 were ultimately collected. The discipline of all these men was wretched, or rather they had no discipline. The members of the Edinburgh Regiment were, in general, desperate persons, to whom the promised pay was a temptation, and who cared nothing for the cause in which they were engaged. The volunteers, on the other hand, were all decent tradesmen, or youths drawn from the counter and desk, inspired no doubt with a love of liberty and the Protestant religion, but little qualified to oppose the approaching Highlanders.

One circumstance may here be mentioned, which seems to have had a great effect in determining the subsequent events; namely, the ignorance which prevailed in the Lowlands regarding the real character of the insurgents. The people were indeed aware that, far in the north, there existed tribes of men living each under the rule of its own chief, wearing a peculiar dress, speaking an unknown language, and going armed even in their most ordinary and peaceful vocations. They occasionally saw specimens of these following the droves of black-cattle which were the sole exportable commodity of their country—

---

[1] The king arrived in great haste from Hanover on the 31st of August.

plaided, bonneted, belted, and brogued — and driving their
bullocks, as Virgil is said to have spread his manure, with an
air of great dignity and consequence.[1]   To their immediate
neighbours they were known by more fierce and frequent causes
of acquaintance; by the forays which they made upon the
inhabitants of the plains, and the tribute or protection-money
which they exacted from those whose possessions they spared.
Yet it might be generally said that little was known of them
either in the Lowlands of Scotland or in England, and that the
little which was known was only calculated to inspire sensations
of fear and dislike.   The idea, therefore, that a band of wild
Highlanders, as they were called, were descending to work their
will upon the peaceful inhabitants of the plains, occasioned a
consternation on the present occasion such as it is now difficult
to conceive, but which must have proved very fatal to the wish
which the friends of government entertained of defending the
country.

CHAPTER VII.

CHARLES'S MARCH UPON EDINBURGH.

'*French Herald.* You men of Angiers, open wide your gates,
And let young Arthur, Duke of Bretagne, in.'

King John.

HAVING recruited both his purse and his muster-roll, and done
something towards the organisation and discipline of his army,
Charles left Perth on Wednesday the 11th of September.   The
direct road from Perth to Edinburgh was by the well-known
passage across the Firth of Forth called the Queen's Ferry,
and the cities were little more than forty miles distant from
each other.   But as all the boats upon that estuary had been

1 Sir Walter Scott ; *Quarterly Review.*

carefully brought to the south side, and as he could not have passed, at anyrate, without being exposed to the fire of a war-vessel lying in the Firth, as well as to whatever danger was to be apprehended from Gardiner's dragoons, who awaited his approach, he was obliged to take a more circuitous and safe route by a fordable part of the river above Stirling. Marching, therefore, to Dunblane, he was joined upon the way by sixty of the Macdonalds of Glencoe, in addition to as many more who had previously come to his standard; and by forty Mac-gregors, the retainers of Macgregor of Glencairnaig, who had deputed their command to James Mor Macgregor or Drummond, the same person who did the service at Edinburgh which has been before mentioned.[1]

The Prince remained a day at Dunblane, waiting till a portion of his army, which he had left at Perth, should come up to join the main body. On the evening of the 12th, the whole encamped about a mile to the south of Dunblane.

Charles proceeded on Friday, the 13th, towards the Ford of Frew. He passed by Doune, where an incident occurred which shewed that he was at least the elected sovereign of the ladies of Scotland. At the house of Mr Edmondstone of Cambus, in the neighbourhood of Doune, the gentlewomen of the district of Monteith had assembled to see him pass; and he was invited to stop and partake of some refreshment. He drew up before the house, and, without alighting from his horse, drank a glass of wine to the healths of all the fair ladies present. The Misses Edmondstone, daughters of the host, acted on this occasion as servitresses, glad to find an opportunity of approaching a person for whom they entertained so much reverence; and when Charles had drunk his wine, and restored his glass to the plate which they held for him, they begged, in respectful terms, the honour of kissing his royal highness's hand. This favour he granted with his usual grace; but Miss Clementina Edmondstone, 'he other young ladies, and then on a visit at Doune,

---

[1] Gartmore MS., quoted in Birt's *Letters* (2d ed.), ii. 351.

thought she might obtain a much more satisfactory taste of royalty, and made bold to ask permission 'to pree his royal highness's mou'.' Charles did not at first understand the homely Scottish phrase in which this last request was made; but it was no sooner explained to him than he took her in his arms and gave her a hearty kiss—to the no small vexation, it is added, of the other ladies, who had contented themselves with so much less liberal a share of princely grace.[1]

At this period of his career Charles lost an expected adherent in a mysterious manner. Stewart of Glenbuckie, the head of a small sept of that family in Balquhidder, and Macgregor of Glencairnaig, chief of his ancient and famous clan, were both passing Leny House (above Callander) with their respective 'followings,' to join the Prince, when Mr Buchanan of Arnprior, proprietor of the house, came out and invited the two gentlemen in to spend the night. Glencairnaig positively refused to stop, and marched on with his retainers; but Glenbuckie consented to accept of Arnprior's hospitality. He supped with his host, apparently in good spirits, and was in due time conducted to his bedroom. According to another account, Mr Buchanan went to meet Mr Stewart and his party in Strathyre, where they had a dispute about the majorship of the Duke of Perth's regiment.[2] In any case, Stewart lodged that night in Leny House, and was found next morning in his bed shot dead, with a discharged pistol in his hand. Mr Buchanan alleged that the unfortunate gentleman was the author of his own death; but was not generally believed. Glenbuckie's men took up the body of their master, carried it home to their own glen, and did not afterwards join the Prince.[3] Arnprior also abstained from joining in the enterprise, though well inclined to it. Notwithstanding practical neutrality, he was seized a short while before the battle of Culloden, and conducted to Carlisle, where an unsigned letter of his, which had been intercepted on its way

1 Nimmo's *History of Stirlingshire*, edited by the Rev. Mr Macgregor Stirling, p. 564.
2 Lyon in Mourning, MS.
3 Information from a daughter of Glenbuckie, who was alive in 1827.

to the Highland army, proved sufficient, with the odium of Glenbuckie's suspected murder, to procure his condemnation. It is but justice to the memory of this gentleman to add, that, immediately before his death, he uttered, in presence of a clergyman, a solemn denial of all share in the death of Mr Stewart.[1]

The Ford of Frew, by which Charles had to cross the Forth, was a shallow part of the river, formed by the efflux of the

The Ford of Frew, from an original drawing.

Boquhan Water, about eight miles above Stirling. It was expected that Gardiner's dragoons would attempt to dispute the passage with the Highlanders; but those doughty heroes, who had hitherto talked of cutting the whole host in pieces as soon as it approached the Lowlands, now thought proper to retire

1 The whole declaration is in the Lyon in Mourning, MS. in my possession.

upon Stirling. Charles, therefore, found no opposition to
prevent him from taking this decisive and intrepid step, which
was, everything considered, much the same to him as the
passage of the Rubicon had been to a greater person. Hitherto
he had been in a land where the Highlanders had a natural
advantage over any troops which might be sent to oppose them ;
but he was now come to the frontier of a country where, if
they fought at all, they must fight on equal, or perhaps inferior
terms. The adventurer's heart was, however, screwed up to
every hazard. Some of his officers had just questioned the
propriety of venturing into a country so open and hostile ; and
various less decisive measures were proposed, and warmly
advocated. But Charles was resolved to make promptitude
and audacity his sole tactics and counsellors. Coming to the
brink of the river, he drew his sword, flourished it in the air, and
pointing to the other side, walked into the stream with an air
of resolution. The river having been somewhat reduced by a
course of dry weather, he found no difficulty in wading across.
When he reached the opposite side, he paused upon the bank,[1]
and congratulated every successive detachment as it reached
the land.

Charles dined in the afternoon of this day at Leckie House,
the seat of a Jacobite gentleman named Moir,[2] who had been
seized on the preceding night in his bed, and hurried to Stirling
Castle by the dragoons, on suspicion that he was preparing to
entertain the Chevalier.[3] The remainder of the day's march
was in a direction due south, to the Moor of Touch ; and it was
for a time uncertain whether Charles designed to attack Edinburgh or Glasgow. The latter presented great temptations, on
account of its being unprotected, and quite as wealthy as
Edinburgh ; and Charles had sufficient reason to owe it a
grudge, on account of its zeal against his family on all occasions

---

[1] Dougal Graham's *Metrical History*, 15.

[2] Mr Moir had married the heiress of Leckie : his own patrimonial estate was a very
small one, at some distance. He would sometimes point out the latter to his friends at
Leckie House, saying slily : ' Yon is my Hanover.'

[3] Lockhart Papers, ii. 487.

when such zeal could be displayed. But the *éclat* of seizing the seat of government, and the assurance of his Edinburgh friends that he would easily be able to do so, proved decisive in confirming his own original wishes to that effect. He, however, sent off a detachment to demand a subsidy of £15,000 from the commercial capital.[1]

The Highland army then moved eastwards, fetching a compass to the south of Stirling, in order to avoid the castle guns. Meanwhile, Colonel Gardiner, who had retreated from Stirling the preceding night, continued to retire before them, designing to fall back upon the other regiment, which was now lying near Edinburgh. In this day's march the Prince passed over the field of Bannockburn, where his illustrious ancestor, Bruce, gained the greatest victory that adorns the Scottish annals. He spent the night succeeding this brief day's march

---

[1] The conduct of the insurgent army on first entering the Lowlands is minutely portrayed by Dougal Graham, the metrical historian of the insurrection, who seems to have been present, and observed their proceedings. The reader will be surprised to find young Locheil, with all his amiable qualities, represented as shooting one of his clan for petty theft:

'Here for a space they took a rest,
And had refreshment of the best
The country round them could afford,
Though many found but empty board.
As sheep and cattle were drove away,
Yet hungry men sought for their prey;
Took milk and butter, kirn and cheese,
On all kinds of eatables they seize:
And he who could not get a share,
Sprang to the hills like dogs for hare;
There shot the sheep and made them fall,
Whirled off the skin, and that was all;
Struck up fires, and boiled the flesh;
With salt and pepper did not fash.
This did enrage the Camerons' chief,
To see his men so play the thief;
And finding one into the act,
He fired, and shot him through the back;
Then to the rest himself addressed:
"This is your lot, I do protest,
Whoe'er amongst you wrongs a man.
Pay what you get, I tell you plain;
For yet we know not friend or foe,
Nor how all things may chance to go." '—P. 16.

in Bannockburn House, the seat of Sir Hugh Paterson, a gentleman attached in the most enthusiastic manner to his cause.   Sir
Hugh was descended from the last Archbishop of Glasgow, and
was married to a sister of the Earl of Mar, who commanded the
insurgent army in 1715.   The army lay upon the neighbouring
field of Sauchie, where King James III., in 1488, was defeated
and slain by his rebellious subjects.[1]   From this place Charles
sent a message to the magistrates of Stirling, who submitted to
him, and sent out provisions to be sold to the army.

On the 14th the Prince proceeded to Falkirk, where his army
lay all night among some broom to the east of Callander House.
He himself lodged in that mansion, where he was kindly entertained, and assured of faithful service, by the Earl of Kilmarnock.   His lordship informing Charles that Gardiner's dragoons
intended next day to dispute the passage of Linlithgow Bridge,
Charles despatched a band of 900 well-armed Highlanders to
attack him, who, without delay, marched during the night on
this expedition.   But the dragoons did not wait to come to
blows.   They retired precipitately to Kirkliston, eight miles
nearer Edinburgh ; and the Highlanders entered Linlithgow
without disturbance before break of day.

Charles brought up the remainder of the army to Linlithgow
about ten o'clock that forenoon, when he was only sixteen miles
from Edinburgh.   It was Sunday, and the people were about to
attend worship in their ancient church ; but the arrival of so
distinguished a visitor suspended their pious duties for at least
one day.   Linlithgow, perhaps on account of its having been so
long a seat of Scottish royalty, was possessed by a Jacobite
spirit ; and on the present occasion, it is said that even some
of the magistrates could not restrain their loyal enthusiasm.
Charles was conducted in triumph to the palace, where a handsome entertainment was prepared for him by Mrs Glen Gordon,
the keeper of the house, who, in honour of the visit, set the
palace well flowing with wine, of which she invited all the

[1] Lockhart Papers, ii. 444.

respectable inhabitants of the burgh to partake. The Prince mingled in their festivities with his usual grace.[1]

The Highland army, at four o'clock in the afternoon, marched to a rising ground between three and four miles to the eastward (near the twelfth milestone from Edinburgh), where they bivouacked, while the Prince slept in a neighbouring house.[2] They proceeded next morning (Monday the 16th) towards Edinburgh, from which they were now distant only four hours' march.

On reaching Corstorphine, Charles thought proper, in order to avoid the guns of Edinburgh Castle, to strike off into a by-road leading in a southerly direction towards the little village of Slateford. His men there bivouacked for the night in a field called Gray's Park, which at that time bore a crop of pease nearly ripe. The tradition of Slateford relates, that the proprietor of the ground applied to Charles at his lodgings for some indemnification for the loss of his crop. He was asked if he would take the Prince Regent's bill for the sum, to be paid when the troubles of the country should be concluded. The man hesitated at the name of the Prince Regent, and said he would prefer a bill from some person whom he knew. Charles

---

1 Mr Bucknay, provost of Linlithgow in 1745, was a keen Jacobite. On the 10th of June preceding the commencement of the insurrection, he had attended a sort of *fête* given in the palace by Mrs Glen Gordon, in honour of the old Chevalier's birthday, when a large bonfire was kindled in the inner court, the fountain in the centre adorned with flowers and green boughs, and King James's health drunk. When the Highland army drew near, the provost fled towards Edinburgh; but his wife and daughters remained, and waited upon the Prince, with tartan gowns and white cockades, and had the honour of kissing his hand at the cross.—See *Jacobitism Triumphant;* a pamphlet dated 1753, which appears to have been occasioned by the following ridiculous circumstance. Some of the Jacobite gentry around Linlithgow suspecting that the postmaster of the town (a notorious loyalist) was in the habit of opening their letters and exposing them to government, Mr James Dundas of Philipstoun wrote a letter to Provost Bucknay, of which the following are the *ipsissima verba:*

'Sir—Is it not very hard that you and I cannot keep up a correspondence for that damned villain of a postmaster?   (Signed)   JA. DUNDAS.'

They expected that the object of their suspicions would open this epistle, and be overwhelmed with shame and rage. To their surprise, the letter passed inviolate. There remained, however, the joke, of which the postmaster became aware some years afterwards; and the pamphlet is a sort of memorial arising out of the process for defamation which he then instituted against Mr Dundas before the Court of Session.

2 Lockhart Papers, ii. 445.

smiled at his caution, and asked if he would take the name of the Duke of Perth, who was his countryman, and at the same time a more credit-worthy man than he could pretend to be. The rustic accepted a promissory-note from the duke.

CHAPTER VIII.

CAPTURE OF EDINBURGH.

'*King Philip.* Now, citizens of Angiers, ope your gates;
Let in that amity which you have made.'

King John.

THE delay of the Highland army at Perth for a time subdued the alarm which had been excited in Edinburgh by the first intelligence of Charles's descent upon the Lowlands. But when he set out from that city, and was understood to be marching upon Edinburgh, all the terrors of the citizens were renewed, at least of that part of them who looked upon the Highland army as a public enemy, or who conceived their entrance into the city to be inconsistent with the safety of private property. On the other hand, the Jacobite part of the population could scarcely conceal their joy at the news of every successive day's march which Charles made towards the city.

The conflicting ferment into which the passions of all ranks of people were thrown by the course of public events, was now increased in a great degree by another agitating matter—the election of heads of incorporations, which began to take place on the 10th of September, as preparatory to the nomination of the magistrates. So engrossing a matter was this, that the magistrates were obliged to discontinue the repairs which they were making upon the city walls, because it was impossible to get workmen to attend to their respective occupations.

Sir John Cope had sent one of his captains from Inverness

early in the month, to order a number of transports to sail from Leith to Aberdeen, in which he might bring back his men to the shores of Lothian. These vessels sailed on the 10th, escorted by a ship of war; and as the weather was excellent, they were expected to return very soon with an army of relief. From that day the people of Edinburgh, according to Mr Home, were continually looking up with anxiety to the vanes and weathercocks, watching the direction of the wind.

As no certain dependence could be placed upon Cope's arrival, the Whigs did not, in the meantime, neglect in aught the training of their civic levies. Drills took place twice a day. Professor Maclaurin, the celebrated mathematician, exerted all his faculties in completing the works of defence which he had designed; and the walls began to bristle with old pieces of cannon, which had been hastily collected from the country around. The various gates or ports of the town were all strongly barricaded, and a guard appointed to each. If we are to believe this party, all their measures were thwarted and clogged by difficulties thrown in their way by the provost. To one proposal, he would object that he had no authority; to another, that it was treasonable—adding, with a sneer, that 'he knew no treason but what the law had made so:' some efforts of zeal he scoffed at; others he held as more productive of danger than safety. Personally, he afforded no active encouragement to any plan of a defensive nature: some were suspiciously blundered in the working: for example, in the digging of a ditch at the Well-house Tower, under the castle, the earth was thrown outwards, so as to be favourable to the assailing, rather than to the defending party. Now, also, he gave countenance and publicity to every rumour which magnified the insurgent forces. The Whigs accused him of having always had a set of Jacobites in his company, from whom he seemed to take counsel. Their own advices were, on the other hand, listened to with reluctance.

No incident of importance occurred in Edinburgh till Sunday the 15th, when, a false alarm reaching the city that the insurgents were advanced within eight miles, it was proposed that

Hamilton's and Gardiner's regiments of dragoons should make a stand at Corstorphine, supported by a body of infantry composed of the volunteers, Edinburgh Regiment, and Town-guard.

Public worship had commenced this day at the usual hour of ten, and the ministers were all preaching with swords by their sides, when the fire-bell was rung as a signal of approaching danger, and the churches were instantly deserted by their congregations. The people found the volunteers ranked up in the Lawnmarket, ready to march out of town; and immediately after, Hamilton's dragoons rode up the street, on their way from Leith to Corstorphine. These heroes clashed their swords against each other as they rode along, and displayed, in their language, the highest symptoms of courage. The volunteers, put into heart by the formidable appearance of these squadrons, uttered a hearty huzza, and the people threw up their hats in the air. But an end was soon put to this affectation of bravery. The mothers and sisters of the volunteers began to take alarm at seeing them about to march out to battle, and with tears, cries, and tender embraces, implored them not to hazard their precious lives. Even their male relations saw fit to advise them against so dangerous a measure, which, they said, staked their valuable persons against a worthless rabble. Many then began to demur, saying that they had engaged to defend the town, but not to march out of it. At this juncture Captain ex-provost Drummond, anxious to stop the spreading murmurs, led off his company down the West Bow towards the West Port, trusting that the rest would follow. His astonishment was great when, on reaching the Port, and looking round, he found that, so far from other companies having followed, his own had melted away in the course of its brief march, and he had only a few of his immediate friends behind him. Some had gone back to the Lawnmarket; others had slipped down *closes*, as lanes are called in Edinburgh, and thus vanished. A city wag afterwards compared their march to the course of the Rhine, which at one place is a majestic river flowing through fertile fields, but, being continually drawn off by little canals, at last becomes a small rivulet, and almost ceases to be distinguishable before reaching the ocean.[1]

Drummond immediately sent back a lieutenant to know what had detained the regiment; and this gentleman, out of all who remained in the Lawnmarket, found one hundred and forty-one who still retained some sense of either shame or courage, and professed to be willing to march out of town. The lieutenant brought these down to the West Port, where, being added to the Town-guard and the half-fledged subscription-regiment, they made up a body of three hundred and sixty-three men, besides officers.

Even this insignificant band was destined to be further reduced before making a movement against the approaching danger. As they were standing within the West Port, before setting out, Dr Wishart, a clergyman of the city, and Principal of the College, came with several other clergymen, and conjured the volunteers to remain within the walls, and reserve themselves for the defence of the city. The words of the reverend man appealed directly to the sentiments of the persons addressed; only a few affected a courage which could listen to no proposals of peace. Happily, their manhood was saved the shame of a direct and point-blank retreat. Drummond having sent a message to the provost, bearing, that unless he gave his final permission for their march, they should not proceed, they were gratified with an answer, in which the provost congratulated them upon their resolution not to march; on which Drummond withdrew, with the air of a man who is balked by malice in a design for the public service; and all the rest of the volunteers dispersed, except a few, chiefly hot-headed college youths, who resolved to continue in arms till the end of the war.[2] Meanwhile the Town-guard and Edinburgh Regiment, in

[1] *True Account of the Conduct and Behaviour of Provost Archibald Stewart*, p. 18.

[2] A story is told of one John Maclure, a writing-master, who, knowing the irresolution of his fellow-volunteers, and that they would never fight, assumed what the reviewer of Mr Home's Works (*Quar. Rev.* No. 71) calls 'a professional cuirass;' namely, a quire of writing-paper, upon which he wrote: 'This is the body of John Maclure—pray, give it a Christian burial.' The same humorist, finding himself jostled in the ranks at the West Port, called out: 'Stand about! *we're all alike burgesses here.*'

number one hundred and eighty men, marched out, by order of
the provost, to support the dragoons at Corstorphine; being the
whole force which the capital of Scotland found it possible on
this occasion to present against the descendant of its ancient
kings.

It was generally expected that an attack would be made
during the succeeding night. The walls were guarded by six or
seven hundred men, consisting of trained bands, volunteers,
armed seceders, and a few of the Duke of Buccleuch's tenants;
but no pains were taken by the magistrates to encourage,
refresh, or duly relieve these men. If a Whig reporter is to be
believed, it was even found that, at eleven at night, one of the
gates—one presented towards the position of the enemy—was
standing wide open, without a sentry![1] In the course of the
night, the two regiments of dragoons retired to a field betwixt
Leith and Edinburgh, and the infantry entered the city.
Brigadier-general Fowkes arrived on the same night from
London, in order to take the command of this little army of
protection. He did so next morning; and by an order from
General Guest, governor of the castle, marched out to Coltbridge, a place two miles to the west of the city, where he was
joined in the course of the forenoon by the civic troops.

A person who saw these soldiers at their post,[2] describes
them as having been drawn up in the open field to the east of
the bridge, in the form of a crescent, with Colonel Gardiner at
their head, who, on account of his age and infirm health, was
muffled in a wide blue surcoat, with a handkerchief drawn round
his hat, and tied under his chin. The Edinburgh Regiment
and Town-guard he describes as looking extremely dismal; but
certainly their hearts could not be fainter than those of the
dragoons. The event shewed that few had escaped the panic
of this momentous day.

[1] This important fact is stated, *from personal knowledge*, by a volunteer, in a paper (now
in my possession) which appears to have been drawn up for the information of the Solicitor-
general. The gate was that called Bristo Port, which might be considered, on this
occasion, as the second in point of importance.
[2] Henderson's *History of the Rebellion*, 43.

On retreating the preceding night to their quarters between Edinburgh and Leith, the dragoons had left a small reconnoitring party at Corstorphine, which is about two miles in advance of Coltbridge. It was with this party that the panic commenced. The insurgents, observing them on their approach to Corstorphine, sent forward one or two of their number on horseback to take a view of them, and bring a report of their number. These gentlemen, riding up pretty near, thought proper to fire their pistols *towards* the party; and the poor dragoons immediately, in the greatest alarm, wheeled about, without returning a shot, and retired upon the main body at Coltbridge, to whom they communicated all their fears. The whole party immediately broke up, and commenced a retreat, not to Edinburgh, with the design of still defending it within the walls, but to the open country beyond it. In this movement, afterwards styled the *Canter of Coltbrigg*, the men rode over the ground now occupied by the New Town, where they were exposed to the view of the citizens. The Jacobites beheld the spectacle with ill-concealed pleasure, while the Whigs were proportionately discouraged.

A clamour immediately rose in the streets, which, till this period, had been crowded with anxious faces; and hundreds ran about, crying that it was madness to think of defending the town after the dragoons had fled, and that if this measure was persisted in, ' they should all be murdered !' A message from the young Chevalier [1] had previously been delivered to them, importing that, if they admitted him peaceably into the town, they should be civilly dealt with, but that resistance would subject them to all the pains of military usage; and the general cry now was, that the town should be surrendered. The provost, in returning from the West Port, where he had been giving orders, in consequence of the retreat of his militia, was assailed

---

[1] Delivered between ten and eleven in the forenoon by Mr Alves, a gentleman of Edinburgh, who had passed the Highland army on the road, and been intrusted with it by the Duke of Perth. Mr Alves was put into prison that afternoon by the provost, for having been so imprudent as to communicate the message to the people on the streets, instead of confining it to his lordship's own ear.

upon the street by multitudes of the alarmed inhabitants, and
implored to call a meeting of the citizens, to determine what
should be done.   He consented with some reluctance to do so,
or rather the people pressed so close around him and his
council in their chamber, that a meeting was constituted without
his consent.   He then sent for the officers of the crown, whose
advice he wished to ask; but it was found, to the still greater
consternation of the people, that all these gentlemen had
deserted the city.   The meeting was then adjourned to a larger
place, the New Church Aisle, where the question of 'Defend,
or not defend, the town' being put, by far the greater part of
those present exclaimed in favour of the latter alternative, and
all who attempted to urge the contrary measure were borne
down by clamour.   Whig reporters of the time call this a packed
assembly; but it appears to have fairly enough represented the
general feeling of the moment.   While the ferment was at its
height, a letter was handed in from the door, addressed to the
Lord Provost, Magistrates, and Town-council of Edinburgh.
Deacon Orrock, a shoemaker, got this document into his hands,
and announced that it was subscribed 'Charles, P. R.'   On this
the provost rose, and saying he could not be present at the
reading of such a letter, left the assembly.   He was, however,
prevailed upon, after some time, to return, and permit the letter
to be read, when it was found to run as follows:

'*From our Camp*, 16*th September* 1745.

'Being now in a condition to make our way into the capital of
his majesty's ancient kingdom of Scotland, we hereby summon
you to receive us, as you are in duty bound to do; and in order
to it, we hereby require you, on receipt of this, to summon the
Town-council, and to take proper measures for securing the
peace of the city, which we are very desirous to protect.   But
if you suffer any of the usurper's troops to enter the town, or
any of the cannon, arms, or ammunition now in it (whether
belonging to the public or to private persons) to be carried
off, we shall take it as a breach of your duty, and a heinous
offence against the king and us, and shall resent it accordingly.

We promise to preserve all the rights and liberties of the city, and the particular property of every one of his majesty's subjects. But if any opposition be made to us, we cannot answer for the consequences, being firmly resolved, at anyrate, to enter the city; and in that case, if any of the inhabitants are found in arms against us, they must not expect to be treated as prisoners of war.   CHARLES, P. R.'

The tenor of this letter decided the meeting in their proposal for a capitulation, and a deputation, headed by Bailie Gavin Hamilton (father of the late ingenious inquirer into the national debt), was despatched to Slateford, where they understood Charles to have taken up his quarters for the night, with power to entreat time for deliberation.

In the course of the afternoon, when the inhabitants were violently debating in the New Church Aisle, a gentleman, whose person was not recognised by any one, rode up the West Bow upon a gray horse, and rushing rapidly along the lines of the volunteers, where they were standing in the Lawnmarket, cried with a loud voice that he had seen the Highlanders, and they were 16,000 strong! Without stopping to be questioned, he was out of sight in a moment; but the impression he made upon the faint-hearted volunteers was decisive. Four companies immediately marched up to the Castle-hill, and surrendered their arms to General Guest, from whom they had received them; and their example was speedily followed by all the different bodies of militia that had been supplied with arms from the castle magazine. When this transaction was completed, Edinburgh might be said to have virtually resigned all hope of defence, though the Trained Bands still continued upon the walls, with their rusty firelocks in their hands, and the gates were still barricaded.

Throughout these scenes of civic pusillanimity, there were not wanting instances of vigorous resolution and consistent loyalty. Mr Joseph Williamson, an advocate (son to the celebrated *Mass David Williamson*, minister of the West Church of

Edinburgh during the reigns of the last Charles and James), who had been intrusted with the keys of the gates, on account of his office of town-clerk, on being asked by the provost to deliver up his charge, absolutely refused to do so; and when commanded peremptorily by his lordship, implored that he might be permitted at least to escape over the walls, so as not to share in what he considered the general disgrace of the city.[1] A similar enthusiast, by name Dr Stevenson, though he had long been bed-rid through age and disease, sat for some days, as one of the guards, at the Netherbow Port, *in his arm-chair!*[2]

The deputies, who had gone out in a carriage to Slateford at eight o'clock, returned at ten, with a letter from Charles, reiterating his demand to be peaceably admitted into the town, and pointing out that his manifesto and his father's declaration were a sufficient guarantee for the protection of the city.[3] By this time the magistrates had been informed, though it after-wards appeared prematurely, that General Cope's transports were arrived off Dunbar (twenty-seven miles east from the city), and felt disposed to hold out, in the hope of speedy relief from a government army. A second deputation of two persons (one of whom was father of the late Mr Coutts, banker) was therefore sent to Slateford about two o'clock in the morning, with a petition for a little longer time.

According to one account, the Prince simply refused to admit

[1] Williamson *did* go over the walls through the night, and was the first man to reach London with the intelligence of the surrender of Edinburgh.

[2] MS. Note to a copy of Lord Hailes's pamphlet against the extension of the city of Edinburgh, 1753.

[3] The letter was as follows:

'His Royal Highness the Prince Regent thinks his manifesto, and the king his father's declaration, already published, are a sufficient capitulation for all his Majesty's subjects to accept of with joy. His present demands are to be received into the city as the son and representative of the king his father, and obeyed as such when he is there.

'His Royal Highness supposes that since the receipt of his letter to the Provost and Magistrates, no arms or ammunition have been suffered to be carried off or concealed, and will expect a particular account of all things of that nature.

'Lastly, he expects a positive answer to this before two o'clock in the morning, otherwise he will find himself obliged to take measures conform.

By his Royal Highness's command,

JOHN MURRAY.

'*At Gray's Mill*, 16th Sept. 1745.'

them to his presence ; but Mr Home says that they prevailed on Lord George Murray to second their application ; and from another source [1] we have the actual words of a reply sent to them : ' His Royal Highness has already given all the assurances he can, that he intends to exact nothing of the city in general, nor of any in particular, but what his character of regent entitles him to. This he repeats, and renews his summons to the magistrates to receive him as such.' Dated at three in the morning. The deputies were then ordered ' to get them gone.' [2]

Charles, during this anxious night, slept only two hours, and that without taking off his clothes. [3] Finding that the inhabitants of Edinburgh were paltering with him, and afraid that the city would soon be relieved, he gave orders, at an early hour in the morning, for an attempt to take the city by surprise. The gentlemen whom he selected for this purpose were Locheil, Keppoch, Ardshiel, and Sullivan. They were commanded to take the best armed of their respective parties, to the amount of about nine hundred, together with a barrel of powder, to blow up one of the gates if necessary. Mr Murray of Broughton, who was well acquainted with the localities, acted as guide. This band mustered by moonlight upon the Borough Moor, where they could hear the watches calling the rounds within the castle. Strict silence and abstinence from intoxicating liquors were enjoined the men. Several plans for breaking into the city were agitated ; but at length it was determined to attempt getting access by stratagem. A select party of twenty-four was planted close to the Netherbow Port ; another party of sixty took station in St Mary's Wynd, close by ; while the remainder hung a little way off, but ready to advance at a moment's notice. Locheil then sent forward one of his men, disguised in a riding-coat and hunting-cap, so as to appear as the servant of an officer of dragoons, in which character he was to knock at the wicket, and request admission, under pretence of being sent by his master to bring something which had been forgot in the city.

---

[1] Lyon in Mourning, MS.   [2] Provost Stewart's Trial.   [3] *Caledonian Mercury.*

The man did as he was bid; but without success, the guard ordering him to retire, under pain of being shot at. The chiefs were now at a loss how to proceed, for morn was breaking, and Locheil was anxious to avoid using violence. Mr Murray of Broughton recommended that they should retire to St Leonard's Crags, and wait for further orders; and they were about to follow this advice, when an accident enabled them to accomplish their object. The hackney-coach which took out the last party of deputies to Slateford, and afterwards brought them back to the city, was now returning to its master's quarters in the Canongate. The port was opened, contrary to orders, to allow it egress; and no sooner had that been done, than the Highlanders, who had not yet retired, rushed in and took possession of the gate.[1] The guard was so slender, that this feat was much more easily performed than they expected; but not knowing what resistance they might meet, they rushed into the High Street, sword in hand, with one of those outcries with which they were accustomed to make an onset in the field of battle.[2] The neighbouring people, roused from their beds, looked over their windows, and beheld in the dusk of the morning their street filled with a thickening troop of those enemies whom they had been so anxious to exclude, while the pipes screamed out a stormy pibroch, such as might have suited a day of fight.[3] A first object of the intruding party was to seize the guard-house in the High Street, and disarm the men posted there. They then went to the different ports of the city, and also to all the posts upon the walls, and relieved the guards, as quietly, says Mr Home, as one guard relieves another in the

---

[1] The first man who entered the city was Captain Evan Macgregor, a younger son of Macgregor of Glencairnaig, and grandfather to Sir Evan Murray Macgregor, Bart., chief of this ancient clan. In consideration of his gallantry, he was that night raised to a majority by the Prince at Holyrood House.—*MS. Account of the Campaign by Duncan Macpharig.*

[2] Lockhart Papers, ii. 488.

[3] The tune was called *We'll awa to Sherramuir to haud the Whigs in order*, according to the report of an aged female, whose mother, servant at the time to Commissioner Cochrane (father of the mechanical Earl of Dundonald), saw from her master's windows in the Netherbow the scene above described.

routine of duty on ordinary occasions.[1] They fixed a strong
guard at the head of the West Bow, to cut off all communication
between the city and the castle, using the Weigh-house as their
court of guard; and the remainder of the body drew themselves
up in two lines upon the street, to await the arrival of the army.
When the inhabitants began to stir at their usual hour of rising,
they found the government of the city transferred from the
magistrates in the name of King George, to the Highlanders in
the name of King James.[2]

[1] Mr Home perhaps adopted this idea from a saying to the same effect which tradition
puts into the mouth of a Highlander. A citizen of Edinburgh, taking a stroll round the
walls on the morning of this momentous day, observed a mountaineer sitting astride upon
a cannon, with an air of great vigilance and solemnity, as if deeply impressed with a sense
of his duty as a sentinel. The citizen accosted him with a remark, that surely these were
not the same troops which mounted guard yesterday. ' Och, no,' said the Highlander,
' she pe relieved.'

[2] At the period of these memorable transactions, there were two newspapers regularly
published in Edinburgh—the *Evening Courant* and the *Caledonian Mercury*. The
former continued throughout all the subsequent campaign to express such violent hostility
to the insurgents, that the editor was burned in effigy at Rome on the 10th of June 1746,
amongst the other festivities with which the birthday of the old Chevalier was there celebrated. The *Mercury*, on the contrary, was so enthusiastic a Jacobite, that it was afterwards very much discountenanced and even persecuted by government. There is something
quite amusing in the conduct of the *Courant* on the occasion of Charles's entry into
Edinburgh. So long as the Highlanders were at a distance, the editor talks of them with
the most dignified contempt. Even when they had pushed their way to Perth, he describes
them as ' a pitiful ignorant crew, good for nothing, and incapable of giving any reason for
their proceedings, but talking only of *snishing, King Jamesh, ta rashant* [the regent],
plunter, and new progues.' At every successive advance, however, which they made
towards Edinburgh, and at every additional symptom of imbecility displayed by the pro-
tectors of the city, this tone is perceptibly decreased, till at last, in the number for Tuesday,
September 17, it is altogether extinguished, and we only find a notice to the following
effect : ' By order of Mr Murray of Broughton, Secretary. Since our last, the Prince,
with his Highland army, has taken possession of this place ; but we must refer you for
particulars to our next.' *Our next*, however, did not come out for a week, instead of
appearing, as it ought to have done, at the distance of two days ; and during the whole
stay of the Prince in Edinburgh, the editor seems fain to say as little on either side as
possible. The *Mercury*, which, as already mentioned, was then under the charge of
Ruddiman, the distinguished grammarian, both talks with more respect of the Highland
army when at a distance, and afterwards becomes more readily its organ of intelligence,
than the *Courant*. In the first publication after the capture of Edinburgh, ' affairs ' are
stated to have ' taken a surprising turn in this city since yesterday, Highlanders and bagpipes being now as common in our streets as formerly were dragoons and drums.' Then
follows an account of the taking of the city, concluding with a statement that ' the
Highlanders behave most civilly to the inhabitants, paying cheerfully for everything they
get,' &c. Both papers are printed without the affix of a printer's or publisher's name—a
circumstance which at once indicated their terror of government, and the compulsion under

CHAPTER IX.

PRINCE CHARLES'S ENTRY INTO EDINBURGH.

'To match this monarch, with strong Arcite came
Emetrius, king of Inde, a mighty name,
On a bay courser goodly to behold—
  *   *   *   *
His amber-coloured locks in ringlets run
With graceful negligence, and shone against the sun ;
His nose was aquiline, his eyes were blue,
Ruddy his lips, and fresh and fair his hue :
Some sprinkled freckles on his face were seen,
Whose dusk set off the whiteness of his skin ;
His awful presence did the crowd surprise,
Nor durst the rash spectator meet his eyes—
Eyes that confessed him born for kingly sway,
So fierce, they flashed intolerable day.'

         Palamon and Arcite.

INTELLIGENCE of the capture of Edinburgh having been conveyed to the Prince, he prepared, at an early hour, to leave his lodgings in Slateford, and lead forward the remainder of his army. This march, though short, was not altogether free of

which the Highland army had laid them. They are also unstamped ; because the Stamp-office, as well as the banks and other public offices, had been removed into the castle before the army approached.

It remains to be stated, that Provost Archibald Stewart was afterwards apprehended, and, being confined for fourteen months, and only liberated on finding bail to the enormous amount of £15,000, was tried by the High Court of Justiciary, upon an obsolete statute of the Scottish James II., 'for neglect of duty, and misbehaviour in the execution of his office.' The trial, which took place in March 1747, lasted for two or three days, and was considered the most solemn ever witnessed in this country. He was acquitted by a unanimous jury. My impression is, that Mr Stewart acted throughout exactly as might have been expected of a Jacobite who wished to keep a fair face towards the government. On the other hand, after the government troops had committed the blunder of leaving the Lowlands exposed, great daring for the repulse of the Highlanders was not to be reasonably expected in Edinburgh ; and the citizens at large most unquestionably betrayed feelings which gave only too good a colour to the actual proceedings of their provost.

danger; for he could see from his present position the flag of defiance flaunting on the battlements of the castle, and apparently daring him to venture within the scope of its guns. The eminent position of that fortress was such as to command nearly the whole country for miles around, and it was a matter of difficulty to discover a path which should conduct him to the city without being exposed to its fire. Some of his train, however, by their acquaintance with the localities, enabled him to obviate this petty danger.

By the direction of his guides, Charles made a circuit to the south of Edinburgh, so as not only to maintain a safe distance from the castle, but to keep some swelling grounds between, which screened him from its view. Debouching upon the open or turnpike road near Morningside, and turning towards the city, he reached a sequestered and almost obsolete cross-road, which turns off to the east by the house of Grange, and completely precludes the view of the city or castle. Charles conducted his army along this road, and soon entered the King's Park near Prestonfield, by a breach which had been made in the wall.[1]

It must have been with elated feelings that Charles traversed this venerable domain, whose recesses had so often sounded to the bugle-horn of his royal ancestors. Leaving his troops about noon in the Hunter's Bog, a deep and sheltered valley betwixt Arthur's Seat and Salisbury Crags, he rode forward, with the Duke of Perth on one hand, and Lord Elcho on the other,[2] some other gentlemen coming up behind. When he reached the eminence under St Anthony's Well, where he for the first time came within sight of the palace, he alighted from his horse,[3] and paused a few moments to survey the scene.

The park and gardens below, intervening betwixt the Prince and the palace, were now filled with the inhabitants of Edinburgh, who, on learning that he approached the city in this

---

[1] Lockhart Papers, ii. 446.
[2] This young nobleman, son of the Earl of Wemyss, had joined him the night before.
[3] *Hist. Reb., with an Account of the Genius and Temper of the Clans.*

quarter, had flocked in great numbers to see him. The crowd consisted of all ranks and persuasions of people, excepting only those who had taken a leading part in opposing his entrance into the city. The Jacobites of course abounded ; and many of these now approached Charles, where he was standing beside his horse, and knelt to kiss his hand. He received their homage and congratulations with smiles, and bowed gracefully to the huzza which immediately after rose from the crowded plain below.[1]

Descending to the Duke's Walk, a footpath through the park, so called from having been the favourite promenade of his grandfather, he stood for a few minutes to shew himself to the people. As it was here that he might be said to have first presented himself to the people of Scotland, it may be necessary to describe his appearance.

The figure and presence of Charles are said by one of his historians, who saw him on this occasion,[2] to have been not ill suited to his lofty pretensions. He was in the prime of youth, tall and handsome, of a fair complexion ; he wore a light-coloured peruke, the ringlets of which descended his back in graceful masses, and over the front of which his own pale hair was neatly combed. His complexion was ruddy, and, from its extreme delicacy, slightly marked with freckles. His visage was a perfect oval, and his brow had all the intellectual but melancholy loftiness so remarkable in the portraits of his ancestors. His neck, which was long, but not ungracefully so, had, according to the fashion of the time, no other covering or encumbrance than a slender stock buckled behind. His eyes were large and rolling, and of a light blue. The fair, but not ill-marked eyebrows which surmounted these features were beautifully arched. His nose was round and high, and his

[1] ' He came to the royal palace, at the abbey of Holyrood House, amidst a vast crowd of spectators, who, from town and country, flocked together to see this uncommon sight, expressing their joy and surprise together by long and loud huzzas. Indeed the whole scene, as I have been told by many, was rather like a dream, so quick and amazing seemed the change, though no doubt wise people saw well enough we had much to do still.'— *Journalist in Lockhart Papers*, ii. 489.

[2] Mr Home.

mouth small in proportion to the rest of his features.   He was above five feet ten in stature, and his body was of that straight and round description which is said to indicate not only perfect

PRINCE CHARLES EDWARD STUART.
From Strange's contemporary engraving.

symmetry, but also the valuable requisites of agility and health. In the language of one of his adherents,[1] he was as 'straight

---

[1] *The Wanderer, or Surprising Escape, &c.*   Glasgow, 1752; p. 17.   It is added by that writer that he 'would fight, run, or leap with any man in the Highlands.'

as a lance, and as round as an egg.' By all ladies who ever saw him, his person was excessively admired; and the powers of fascination which he could exercise over the male sex have been sufficiently attested. On the present occasion he wore a blue velvet bonnet, bound with gold lace, and adorned at top with a white satin cockade, the well-known badge of his party. He had a short tartan coat, on the breast of which hung the star of the order of St Andrew. A blue sash, wrought with gold, came gracefully over his shoulder. He wore small-clothes of red velvet, a pair of military boots, and a silver-hilted broadsword.[1]

After he had stood for a few minutes in the midst of the people, he mounted a fine bay gelding, which had been presented to him by the Duke of Perth, and slowly rode towards the palace. Being an excellent horseman, a murmur of admiration ran at this moment through the crowd, which soon amounted to, and terminated in, a long and loud huzza. Around him, as he rode, there was a small guard of ancient Highlanders,[2] whose outlandish and sunburned faces, as they were occasionally turned up with reverence towards the Prince, and occasionally cast with an air of stupid wonder over the crowd, formed not the least striking feature in this singular scene.

The Jacobites, delighted beyond measure by the gallant aspect of their idol, were now indulging themselves in the most extravagant terms of admiration. With their usual propensity to revert to the more brilliant periods of the Scottish monarchy, they fondly compared Charles to King Robert Bruce, whom they said he resembled in his figure,[3] as they fondly anticipated he would also do in his fortunes. The Whigs, however, though compelled to be cautious in the expression of their sentiments, talked of him in a different style. They acknowledged he was a goodly person, but observed that, even in that triumphant

---

[1] *Hist. Reb., with an Account of the Genius and Temper of the Clans.*

[2] Most of them stooping with age, and imperfectly armed. See *Hist. of the Rise, Progress, and Extinction of the Reb. in Scot.* 8vo. London, sold by R. Thomson, &c., p. 30. (A violent party production.)

[3] Home's Works, iii. 71.

hour, when about to enter the palace of his fathers, the air of his countenance was languid and melancholy; that he looked like a gentleman and man of fashion, but not like a hero or a conqueror.[1]

Charles approached Holyrood House by the same path over which George IV., seventy-seven years after, was drawn thither in his daily progresses from Dalkeith. As he was parading along, the Duke of Perth stopped him a little, while he described the limits and peculiar local characteristics of the King's Park. It was observed on this occasion by an eye-witness, that during the whole five minutes the duke was expatiating, Charles kept his eye bent sideways upon Lord Elcho (who stood aside at a little distance), and seemed lost in a mental speculation about that new adherent. As the procession—for such it might be termed—moved along the Duke's Walk, the crowd greeted the principal personage with two distinct huzzas, which he acknowledged with bows and smiles. The general feeling of the crowd seemed to be a very joyful one, arising in some cases from the influence of political prepossessions, in many others from gratified curiosity, and perhaps in still more from the satisfaction with which they had observed the fate of the city so easily decided that morning. Many had previously conceived Charles to be only the leader of a band of predatory barbarians, at open warfare with property, and prepared to commit any outrage for the accomplishment of his purposes. They now regarded him in the interesting light of an injured prince, seeking, at the risk of life, one single noble object, which did not very obviously concern their personal interests. All, more or less, resigned themselves to the charm with which the presence of royalty is so apt to be attended. Youthful and handsome; gallant and daring; the leader of a brave and hardy band; the commander and object of a most extraordinary enterprise; unfortunate in his birth and prospects, but making apparently one manly effort to retrieve the sorrows of his fate;

[1] Home's Works, iii. 71.

the descendant of those time-honoured persons by whose sides the ancestors of those who saw him had fought at Bannockburn and Flodden ; the representative of a family peculiarly Scottish, but which seemed to have been deprived of its birthright by the machinations of the hated English—Charles was a being calculated to excite the most fervent emotions amongst the people who surrounded him. The modern sovereign, as he went over the same ground in his splendid chariot, was beheld with respect, as the chief magistrate of the nation ; but the boot of Charles was dimmed, as he passed along, with kisses and tears.

A remarkable instance of the effect of these feelings occurred as Charles was entering the palace. When he had proceeded along the piazza within the quadrangle, and was just about to enter the porch of what are called the Hamilton apartments, the door of which stood open to receive him, a gentleman of mature age stepped out of the crowd, drew his sword, and, raising it aloft, marshalled the way before him up-stairs. James Hepburn of Keith, in East Lothian, who adopted this conspicuous mode of enlisting himself, did not act altogether under the influence of a devoted attachment to the Stuart family, but was stimulated by a sense of the injustice of the Union, which he said had ruined his country, and reduced a Scottish gentleman from being a person of some estimation to being the same as nobody. Since the insurrection of 1715, in which he was engaged, he had for thirty years kept himself in constant readiness to strike another blow for what he considered the independence of his country. Learned and intelligent, advanced in life, and honoured by all parties of his countrymen, this man is said by Mr Home, who knew him, to have been a perfect model of ancient simplicity, manliness, and honour. That he was inspired with as pure and noble a sense of patriotism as any Whig that ever breathed, it is impossible to doubt. The Jacobites beheld with pride a person so accomplished set the first example in Edinburgh of joining the Prince ; auguring that his ' silver hairs ' would ' purchase them a good opinion.' The Whigs, on the other hand, by whom he was equally admired, looked with pity upon a brave and worthy gentleman thus offering himself up a sacrifice to the visionary idea of national independence.[1]

The Prince being thus established in his paternal palace, it was the next business of his adherents to proclaim his father at the Cross. The party which entered the city in the morning had taken care to secure the heralds and pursuivants whose business it was to perform such ceremonies. About one o'clock, therefore, an armed body was drawn up around the Cross; and that venerable pile, which, notwithstanding its association with so many romantic events, was soon after removed by the magistrates, had the honour of being covered with carpet for the occasion.[2] The officers were clothed in their fantastic but rich old dresses, in order to give all the usual *éclat* to this disloyal ceremony. David Beatt, a Jacobite teacher of Edinburgh,[3] then proclaimed King James, and read the commission of regency, with the declaration dated at Rome in 1743, and a manifesto in the name of Charles Prince Regent, dated at Paris, May 16, 1745. An immense multitude witnessed the solemnity, which they greeted with hearty but partial huzzas. The ladies, who viewed the scene from their lofty lattices in the High Street, strained their voices in acclamation, and waved white handkerchiefs in honour of the day.[4] The Highland guard looked round the crowd with faces expressing wild joy and triumph, and, with the license and extravagance appropriate to the occasion, fired off their pieces in the air. The bagpipe was not wanting to greet the name of James with a loyal pibroch; and during the ceremony, Mrs Murray of Broughton, whose enthusiasm was only surpassed by her beauty, sat on horseback beside the Cross, with a drawn sword in her hand, and her person profusely decorated with white ribbons, which signified devotion to the house of Stuart.[5]

[1] Home's Works, iii. 72.
[2] *Caledonian Mercury.*
[3] Boyse's *History of the Rebellion.*   [4] Mr Home.   [5] Boyse, 77.

CHAPTER X.

COPE'S PREPARATIONS.

' Cope sent a letter from Dunbar,
  Saying : " Charlie, meet me if ye daur,
  And I 'll learn you the art of war,
      Right early in the morning." '

Jacobite Song.

WHILST the Highlanders were proclaiming King James at the
Cross of Edinburgh, Sir John Cope was landing his troops at
Dunbar.   The evasive movement of this general had been most
unfortunate, as it completely deprived the Lowlands of such
protection as his troops were able to afford.   He shewed, however, all possible anxiety to repair the consequences of his
error, marching his army without delay from Inverness to
Aberdeen, where it was embarked with the design of landing in
some Lowland port, and in the hope of still being in time to
protect the principal parts of the kingdom.

Sir John's infantry was reinforced at Dunbar by the craven
dragoons, who had fled thither as the safest place within their
reach.   Of their flight an amusing, though perhaps highly
coloured account has been given in a pamphlet already quoted.[1]
' Before the rebels,' says the writer, ' came within sight of the
king's forces [then posted at Coltbridge], before they came
within three miles' distance of them, orders were issued to the
dragoons to wheel, which they immediately did with the greatest
order and regularity imaginable.   As it is known that nothing
is more beautiful than the evolutions and movements of cavalry,
the spectators stood in expectation of what fine manœuvre they
might terminate in, when new orders were immediately issued

---

[1] *A True Account of the Behaviour and Conduct of Archibald Stewart, Esq., late
Lord Provost of Edinburgh, in a Letter to a Friend.*   London, 1748.

to retreat; they instantly obeyed, and began to march in the usual pace of cavalry. Orders were repeated every furlong to quicken their pace; and, both precept and example concurring, they quickened it so well, that before they reached Edinburgh, they quickened it to a very smart gallop. They passed in inexpressible hurry and confusion through the narrow lanes at Barefoot's Parks, in the sight of all the north part of Edinburgh, to the infinite joy of the disaffected, and equal grief and consternation of all the other inhabitants. They rushed like a torrent down to Leith, where they endeavoured to draw breath; but some unlucky boy (I suppose a Jacobite in his heart) calling to them that the Highlanders were approaching, they immediately took to their heels again, and galloped to Prestonpans, about five [nine] miles farther. There, in a literal sense, *timor addidit alas*—there fear added wings, I mean to the rebels; for, otherwise, they could not possibly have imagined these formidable enemies to be within several miles of them. But at Prestonpans the same alarm was repeated. The Philistines be upon thee, Samson! They galloped to North Berwick; and being now about twenty miles to the other side of Edinburgh, they thought they might safely dismount from their horses, and look out for victuals. Accordingly, like the ancient Grecian heroes, each began to kill and dress his provisions—*egit amor dapis atque pugnæ*—they were actuated by the desire of supper and of battle. The sheep and turkeys of North Berwick paid for this warlike disposition. But behold the uncertainty of human happiness! When the mutton was just ready to be put upon the table, they heard, or thought they heard, the same cry of Highlanders. Their fear proved stronger than their hunger; they again got on horseback; but were informed of the falseness of the alarm time enough to prevent the spoiling of their meal. By such rudiments as these, the dragoons were so thoroughly initiated in the art of running, that at the battle of Preston they could practise it of themselves, though even there the same good example was not wanting. I have seen an Italian opera called *Cesare in Egitto*—Cæsar in Egypt—where, in the first scene, Cæsar is introduced in a great hurry, giving orders to his soldiers, *Fugge, fugge; allo scampo*—Fly, fly; to your heels! This is a proof that the commander at Coltbridge is not the first hero that gave such orders to his troops.'

The 'Canter of Coltbridge' is related by Mr Home with circumstances somewhat different, but not less ridiculous. After passing through Leith and Musselburgh, they encamped for the evening in a field near Colonel Gardiner's house at Preston. Between ten and eleven at night, one of their number, going in search of forage, fell into a disused coal-pit, which was full of water, and making an outcry for assistance, impressed his companions with a belief that their dreaded enemy was upon them. Not stopping to ascertain the real cause of the noise, or to relieve their unfortunate fellow-soldier, the whole mounted their horses, and with all imaginable speed galloped off to Dunbar. Colonel Gardiner, awaking in the morning, found a silent and deserted camp, and was obliged, with a heavy heart, to follow in the direction which he learned they had taken. There was little danger that he should have missed their track, for, as he passed along, he found the road strewed with swords, pistols, and firelocks, which they had thrown away in their panic. He caused these to be gathered, and conveyed in covered carts to Dunbar, where he arrived in time to greet General Cope as he landed.

The disembarkation of the troops, artillery, and stores was not completed till the 18th of September; when Mr Home, author of the History already quoted, presented himself at the camp, and gave the general all the information he could desire regarding the numbers and condition of the Highland army. The author of *Douglas* had gone to the different posts about the city, and counted the men there stationed; he had then ascended the hill which overlooked the bivouac of the main body, and reckoned them as they sat at food in lines upon the ground. The whole number, in his estimation, did not exceed two thousand; but he had been told that several bodies from the north were on their march to join them. The general asked

his informant what sort of appearance they made, and, in particular, how they were armed; to which the young poet replied,
that most of them seemed to be strong, active, hardy men,
though many were of an ordinary size, and, if clothed like
Lowlanders, would appear inferior to the king's troops. The
Highland garb, he said, favoured them, as it shewed their naked
limbs, which were strong and muscular; while their stern
countenances, and bushy uncombed hair, gave them a fierce,
barbarous, and imposing aspect. As to their arms, he continued, they had no artillery of any sort but one small unmounted
cannon, which he had seen lying upon a cart, drawn by a little
Highland pony. Fourteen or fifteen hundred of them were
armed with firelocks and broadswords, and many others had
only either the one or the other of these weapons. Their
firelocks were of all sorts and sizes—muskets, fusees, and
fowling-pieces; but they must soon provide themselves more
generally with that weapon, as the arsenal of the Trained Bands
had fallen into their hands. In the meantime, he had seen one
or two companies, amounting altogether perhaps to a hundred
men, each of whom had no other weapon than the blade of a
scythe fastened end-long upon a pole.[1] General Cope dismissed
Mr Home, with many compliments for bringing him so accurate
an account of the enemy.

The king's army was joined at Dunbar by several judges and
other civil officers, who, having fled from Edinburgh on the
evening before the Prince had entered it, now resolved to
remain with the royal troops, not as fighting men, but as
anxious and interested spectators of the approaching action.
There also came a few noblemen and gentlemen of the country,
attended by their tenants in arms. Among these was the Earl
of Home, who, being then an officer in the Guards, thought it
his duty to offer his services when the king's troops were in the
field. The retinue which this nobleman brought along with
him was such as to surprise many persons. At the time when

---

[1] Home's Works, iii. 76.

the Lowlands of Scotland were equally warlike, and equally under the influence of the feudal system with the Highlands, his lordship's ancestors could have raised as many men upon their dominions in Berwickshire as would have themselves repelled the Chevalier's little army.   In 1633, the Earl of Home had greeted Charles I., as he crossed the Border to visit Scotland, at the head of six hundred well-mounted gentlemen, his relations and retainers.   The whole force that the present earl could bring, besides himself, to assist his sovereign in opposing a public enemy, consisted of *two body-servants !*[1]

It was not till the day succeeding the disembarkation, Thursday, the 19th of September, that the royal army left Dunbar to meet the insurgents.   It is said to have made a great show upon its march; the infantry, cavalry, cannon, and baggage occupying several miles of road.   The country-people, long unaccustomed to wars and arms, flocked from all quarters to see an army going to fight a battle in Lothian, and with infinite concern and anxiety beheld this uncommon spectacle.[2]

The army halted for the night in a field to the west of Haddington, sixteen miles east of Edinburgh.   In the evening, it was proposed to employ some young people who followed the camp to ride betwixt Haddington and Edinburgh during the dark hours, lest the Highlanders, whose movements were rapid, should march in the night-time and surprise the army.   Accordingly sixteen young men, most of whom had been volunteers at Edinburgh, and among whom the author of *Douglas* was one, offered their services.   About nine at night eight of them set out, in four parties, by four different roads, for Duddingston, where they understood the Highlanders to be encamped.   They returned safe at midnight, reporting that all was quiet; and the other eight then set out in the same manner.[3]

---

[1] Home's Works, iii. 77.   [2] Ibid. iii. 78.

[3] It was the duty of two of this little corps to pursue the coast road towards Musselburgh. Their names were Francis Garden and Robert Cunningham—the one afterwards better known by his judicial title of Lord Gardenstone, and the other by his official designation of General.   On approaching Musselburgh, says Sir Walter Scott in a lively contribution to the *Quarterly Review,* ' they avoided the bridge, to escape observation, and crossed the

On the morning of the succeeding day, Friday the 20th of September, Cope continued his march towards Edinburgh by the ordinary post-road from Haddington. After marching a very few miles, it occurred to him that the defiles and enclosures near the road would, in case of an attack, prove unfavourable to the action of cavalry, and he resolved to adopt a less frequented and more open path. On coming to Huntington, therefore, he turned off to the right, and took what is called the *Low Road;* that is, the road which traverses the low country near the sea, passing by St Germains and Seton. At the same time he sent forward his adjutant-general, the Earl of Loudon, accompanied by the Earl of Home, to mark out a camp for the army near Musselburgh, intending to go no farther that day.

Esk, it being then low water, at a place nigh its junction with the sea. Unluckily, there was at the opposite side a snug thatched tavern kept by a cleanly old woman called Luckie F——, who was eminent for the excellence of her oysters and sherry. The patrol were both *bon vivants;* one of them, whom we remember in the situation of a senator, was unusually so, and a gay, witty, agreeable companion besides. Luckie's sign, and the heap of oyster-shells deposited near her door, proved as great a temptation to this vigilant forlorn-hope as the wine-house to the abbess of Andouillet's muleteer. They had scarcely got settled at some right *pandores,* with a bottle of sherry as an accompaniment, when, as some Jacobite devil would have it, an unlucky north-country lad, a writer's (that is, attorney's) apprentice, who had given his indentures the slip, and taken the white cockade, chanced to pass by on his errand to join Prince Charlie. He saw the two volunteers through the window, knew them, and guessed their business : he saw the tide would make it impossible for them to return along the sands, as they had come. He therefore placed himself in ambush upon the steep, narrow, impracticable bridge, which was then, and for many years afterwards, the only place of crossing the Esk : and how he contrived it I could never learn, but the courage and assurance of his province are proverbial, and the Norland whipper-snapper surrounded and made prisoners of the two unfortunate volunteers before they could draw a trigger.'—*Quarterly Review,* vol. xxxvi. 177.

They were immediately conducted to the camp at Duddingston, and put into the hands of John Roy Stuart, commander of the Prince's bodyguard, who at once pronounced them spies, and proposed to hang them accordingly. Thrown into consternation by this sentence, they luckily recollected that a youthful acquaintance, by name Colquhoun Grant, bore a commission in the very body which John Roy commanded ; and they entreated him to lead them before that person, who was able to attest their innocence. Colquhoun Grant, who lived many years afterwards as a respectable writer to the signet in Edinburgh, used to relate that he never was so much surprised in his life, and at the same time amused, as when his two young friends were brought up to him for his verdict. Stuart introduced them with the following words : 'Here are two fellows who have been caught prowling near the camp. I am certain they are spies, at least this oldest one [Mr Garden] ; and I propose that, to make sure, we should hang them baith.' Mr Grant, of course, interfered in behalf of his friends, and afterwards getting them into his own custody, took it upon him to permit their escape.—Information by the late Henry Mackenzie, author of the *Man of Feeling.*

The soldiers are described as having been in high spirits during the march; the infantry feeling confident in the assistance of the cavalry, and the cavalry acquiring some portion of the same courage by a junction with the infantry.

The first files of the troops were entering the plain betwixt Seton and Preston, when Lord Loudon came back at a round pace with information that the Highlanders were in full march towards the royal army. The general, surprised, but not disconcerted by this intelligence, and thinking the plain which lay before him a very proper place to receive the enemy, called a halt there, and drew up his troops with a front to the west. His right was thus extended to the sea, and his left towards the village of Tranent. Soon after he had taken up his ground, the Chevalier's army came in sight.

CHAPTER XI.

THE PRINCE'S MARCH TO PRESTON.

'When Charlie looked this letter upon,
  He drew his sword the scabbard from,
    Crying : " Follow me, my merry, merry men,
      And we 'll meet Johnnie Cope in the morning."'

Jacobite Song.

THREE days of rest in Edinburgh, where they were supplied with plenty of food, and did not want opportunities of improving their appointments, had meanwhile increased in no inconsiderable degree the efficacy and confidence of the Highland army. Learning that Cope had landed at Dunbar, and was marching to give him battle, the Prince came on Thursday night to Duddingston, where, calling a council of war, he proposed to march next morning and meet the enemy half-way. The council agreed that this was the only thing they could do; and

Charles then asked the Highland chiefs how they thought their
men would behave in meeting a general who had already
avoided them. The chiefs desired Macdonald of Keppoch to
speak for them, as he had served in the French army, and was
thought to know best what the Highlanders could do against
regular troops. Keppoch's speech was brief, but emphatic. He
said that the country having been long at peace, and few or
none of the private men having ever seen a battle, it was
difficult to foretell how they would behave ; but he would
venture to assure his royal highness that the gentlemen would
be in the midst of the enemy, and that the clansmen, devoted to
their chiefs, and loving the cause, would certainly not be far
behind them. Charles, catching the spirit of the moment,
exclaimed he would be the first man to charge the foe ! But
the chiefs discountenanced this imprudent proposal, declaring
that in his life lay the strength of their cause, and that, should
he be slain, they would be undone beyond redemption, whether
victorious or defeated. They even went so far as to declare
that they would go home, and endeavour to make the best terms
they could for themselves, if he persisted in so rash a resolution.
This remonstrance with difficulty repressed the ardour of their
young commander, whose great passion at this moment seems
to have been to strike a decisive blow, and share personally in
its glory.[1]

On the morning of Friday the 20th of September, when the
king's army was commencing its march from Haddington, the
Highlanders roused themselves from their bivouac near Duddingston, and prepared to set forward. They had been
reinforced since daybreak by a party of Grants from Glenmorriston,[2] as they had been the day before by some

---

[1] Home's Works, iii. 81.

[2] Grant of Glenmorriston arrived with his little party in great haste, anxious not to be
too late for the first battle. He had travelled all night, and was of course travel-soiled and
unshaven. When he rushed into the Prince's presence at Holyrood House, his appearance
drew an ill-timed, but probably half-jocular remark from Charles as to his beard. The
chief turned away with kindling wrath, saying : ' Sir, it is not beardless boys who are to
do your business.'—*Information from the late Mr W. Grant, W.S.*

Maclachlans and Athole men.   The Prince, putting himself at the head of his army, thus increased by 250, presented his sword, and said aloud: 'My friends, I have thrown away the scabbard!'[1]   He was answered by a cheerful huzza; and the band then set forward in three files, Charles marching on horseback by their side, along with some of his principal officers.

The army proceeded from Duddingston Park, where they had what was called their camp, by the road which passes Easter Duddingston, and enters the main or post road near Magdalen Bridge.   A lady, who in early youth had seen them pass the last-mentioned village,[2] was able, in 1827, to describe the memorable pageant.   The Highlanders strode on with their squalid clothes and various arms, their rough limbs and uncombed hair, looking around them with an air of fierce resolution. The Prince rode amidst his officers at a little distance from the flank of the column, preferring to amble over the dry stubble-fields beside the road.   My informant remembered, as yesterday, his graceful carriage and comely looks, his long light hair straggling below his neck, and the flap of his tartan coat thrown back by the wind, so as to make the jewelled St Andrew dangle for a moment clear in the air by its silken ribbon.   He was viewed with admiration by the simple villagers; and even those who were ignorant of his claims, or who rejected them, could not help wishing him good fortune, and at least no calamity.

Soon after falling into the post-road, the insurgents continued their march till they entered the Market-gate of Fisherrow—an old narrow street leading to the bridge across the Esk.   One there went up to a new house upon which the tilers were engaged, and took a long slip of wood, technically called a *tile-lath*; from another house he abstracted an ordinary broom, which he tied upon the end of the pole.   This he bore aloft over his head, emblematising what seemed to be the general sentiment of the army, that they would sweep their enemies off the face of the earth.   The shouts with which the symbol was

---

[1] *Caledonian Mercury.*   [2] The late Mrs Handasyde of Fisherrow.

hailed on the present occasion testified the high courage and resolution of the troops, and but too truly presaged the issue of the approaching conflict.   Charles, in passing along the Market-gate, bowed gracefully to the ladies who surveyed him from their windows.[1]

The army now passed along the ancient bridge of Mussel-burgh—a structure supposed to be of Roman origin, and over which the Scottish army had passed, two centuries before, to the field of Pinkie.   Proceeding directly onward, the column traversed, not the town of Musselburgh, but the old post-road which winds to the south, behind the gardens of Pinkie House. When passing these gardens, Lord George Murray, who led the van, received intelligence that Cope was at or near Preston, and was likely to seek the high grounds to the south, so as to obtain an advantage over the Highland army.   Being convinced that the Highlanders could do nothing unless they got above the enemy, he immediately struck off through the fields to the right, with which he was well acquainted, ordering the army to follow him.   By half an hour of quick marching, he reached the height near Falside, and then marched slow, that the rear might close up.   He now became aware that Cope had remained content with his position at Preston, and therefore commenced a slanting march down-hill towards Tranent.   On coming within half a mile of that village, the army halted.   During the last two miles of their march, they had had the enemy within sight.[2]

At this early stage of the campaign, the mode of *forming* the Highland army was extremely simple, on account of the want of horse and artillery.   The column in which it always moved was merely halted at the proper place, and then facing about, became at once a line.   Such was the evolution by which, on the present occasion, Charles brought his men to their first *tête-à-tête* with the devoted host of his antagonist.

When the royal troops first perceived the Highlanders they raised a spirited shout, to which the others readily replied,

1 Tradition in Fisherrow.
2 Lord George Murray's Narrative, *Jacobite Memoirs*, 36.

The two armies were about a mile distant from each other, with a gentle slope and a long strip of marshy ground between. It was a little after noon, and the weather was favourable for immediate combat. Both armies had marched the equal distance of eight miles, and were alike fresh and ardent. It was Charles's wish, as it had been his expectation, to engage the enemy before nightfall; and the ground appeared perfectly favourable for the purpose. The descent towards Cope's position, though gentle, was sufficient to increase the natural speed and impetuosity of the Highlanders, whose ancestors had been always successful in conflicts fought in that manner. But Cope had not the same eager desire of battle; and various considerations, arising from the nature of the ground, interposed to prevent an immediate attack on the part of the Highlanders.

The English general had at first arranged his troops with their front to the west, expecting the enemy to come directly from Musselburgh; but when he saw them appear on the southern heights, he altered his position accordingly, and now lay upon a plain swelling gently up from the coast, with Cockenzie and the sea behind him, the intricate little village of Preston, with its numerous parks and garden-walls, on his right, Seton House at a distance on his left, and a deep ditch or drain traversing the morass before him. On all sides but the east he was inaccessible, except, perhaps, by a column which no enemy could ever have thought of directing against him.

By examining the country-people, who, as usual, flocked about him in great numbers, the Prince soon learned that to attack General Cope across the morass was impracticable, except at a great risk. In order to ascertain the point still more satisfactorily, Lord George Murray despatched Colonel Ker of Graden, an officer of experience, to survey and report upon the ground. Mounted upon a little white pony, Mr Ker descended alone from Tranent, and with great deliberation approached the post of the enemy. When very near it, he rode slowly along the edge of the morass, carefully inspecting the ground on all sides, and scanning the breadth and depth of the ditch. Some of the king's troops moved along the ditches, and shot at him; but he was not in the least discomposed. Coming to a stone fence which he required to cross, he dismounted, pulled down a piece of the dike, and then led his horse through the breach. When he had completely satisfied himself, he returned to the army, and reported his observations to the lieutenant-general. The morass, he said, could not be passed without the troops being exposed to several unreturned fires, and was therefore not to be thought of.[1] When Charles learned this, he moved a considerable part of his army back to Dolphingston, and affected to meditate an attack upon Cope's west or right flank. The English general observing this, resumed his first position, in order to meet the insurgents with the front of his army.

Charles, probably deterred from making an attack in this quarter by the park-dikes, which so effectually screened the enemy's front, now once more shifted his ground, and returned to his first station near Tranent. The king's army faced round at the same time. The whole afternoon was occupied by these evolutions. When evening approached, General Cope found himself still in possession of the advantageous ground he had originally chosen; but it was feared by some unconcerned spectators that he had been perhaps over-cautious in his evolutions; that he had cooped himself up in a narrow place, while the Highlanders were at liberty to move about as they pleased; and that he had disheartened his men by keeping them so carefully on the defensive, while the Highlanders were proportionably animated by feeling themselves in the predicament of an attacking party.[2]

Cope had not acted altogether on the defensive. Sullivan had posted fifty of Locheil's men at the parish church at the bottom of the village, 'for what reason,' says Lord George Murray, 'I could not understand.' The enemy brought their cannon to bear on this post, and fired off a few shots, which

---

1 Home's Works, iii. 84. 'Without risking the loss of the whole army,' is the expression put into Mr Ker's mouth by the author of an account of the young Chevalier's operations, printed in the Lockhart Papers.

2 Home's Works, iii. 85.

they accompanied with huzzas, being under the impression that the Highlanders were very liable to be frightened by cannon. They soon wounded one or two men, when Lord George Murray sent an order for the party to join the main body. Charles, however, posted 500 men under Lord Nairn at Preston, to the west of Cope's position, to prevent him from stealing a march in that direction.

Since the insurgents had first risen in Lochaber, the weather had been generally fine. The nights, however, though calm, were chill, as generally happens in the finest autumn weather under our northern climate. The night of Friday, the 20th of September 1745, set in with a cold mist, which, without doing any particular injury to the hardy children of the north, was annoying to their opponents, less accustomed to bivouacking, and obliged to be more upon the alert, in apprehension of a night attack. General Cope lighted great fires all round his position, to warm and inspirit his men,[1] and threw off a few cohorns during the night, to let the enemy know he was on his guard. At an early period of the evening he had planted pickets, with great care, in every direction around him, especially towards the east; he had also sent his military chest and baggage down to Cockenzie under a strong guard.

The royal army was arranged along the front of the morass in a manner displaying sufficient military skill. The centre consisted of eight companies of Lascelles's regiment, and two of Guise's. On the right were five companies of Lees's; on the left the whole of Sir John Murray's. Besides these, there were a number of recruits for different regiments at present abroad, and a few small parties of volunteers, comprising the gentlemen with their tenants already mentioned, and some persons who had been induced to join by religious considerations. The infantry was protected on the right flank by Gardiner's, on the left by Hamilton's dragoons, who stood each with two troops to the front, and one in the rear, for a reserve. Some

---

[1] Lockhart Papers, ii. 489, 490.

Highland companies composed a second line in the rear. The cannon, six pieces in all, guarded by a company of Lees's regiment, commanded by Captain Cochrane, and under the orders of Lieutenant-colonel Whiteford, were placed on the right of the army, near the wagon-road or railway from Tranent to Cockenzie.

The army of Cope altogether consisted of 2100 men; but a number of these did not fight in the subsequent engagement, being engaged elsewhere as videttes and guards. The artillery corps was by far the most hopeless part of the army. At the time when General Cope marched to the north, there were no gunners or matrosses to be had in Scotland but one old man, who had belonged to the Scots train of artillery before the Union. This person, with three old invalid soldiers, the general carried with him to Inverness; and the hopeful band was afterwards reinforced by a few sailors from the ship of war which escorted the troops to Dunbar. A more miserable troop could hardly have been intrusted with so important a charge.

As soon as it became dark, the Highland army moved from the west to the east side of Tranent, where the morass seemed to be more practicable; and a council of war being called, it was resolved to attack the enemy in that quarter at break of day. The Highlanders, wrapping themselves in their plaids, then laid themselves down to sleep upon the stubble-fields. Charles, whose pleasure it had all along been to share in the fatigues and privations of his men, rejecting the opportunity of an easier couch in the village, also made his lodging upon the ground. During the night not a light was to be seen and not a word to be heard in his bivouac, in obedience to an order which had been issued, for the purpose of concealing their position from Sir John Cope.[1]

1 Home's Works, iii. 92.

CHAPTER XII.

THE BATTLE OF PRESTON.

> '*Brutus.* Slaying is the word ;
> It is a deed in fashion.'
>
> *Julius Cæsar.*

A YOUNG gentleman named Robert Anderson (son of Anderson of Whitburgh, in East Lothian), who joined the insurgents at Edinburgh, had been present at the council which determined the place and mode of attack, but did not take the liberty to speak or give his opinion. After the dismissal of the council, Anderson told his friend, Mr Hepburn of Keith, that he knew the ground well,[1] and thought there was a better way to come at the king's army than that which the council had resolved to follow. 'I could undertake,' he added, 'to shew them a place where they might easily pass the morass without being seen by the enemy, and form without being exposed to their fire.' Hepburn listened attentively to this information, and expressed his opinion of it in such terms, that Anderson desired he would carry him to Lord George Murray. Mr Hepburn advised him to go alone to the lieutenant-general, with whom he was already perfectly well acquainted, and who would like best to receive any information of this kind without the presence of a third party. Anderson immediately sought Lord George, whom he found asleep in a field of cut pease, with the Prince and several of the chiefs lying near him. The young gentleman immediately awoke his lordship, and proceeded to inform him of his project. To Lord George it appeared so eligible that he

---

1 Mr Anderson, while residing occasionally with his relatives, the Andersons of St Germains, had often shot snipes on this ground. Such, I have been informed by his family, was the accident by which he gained this valuable piece of knowledge.

hesitated not a moment to use the same freedom with the Prince which Mr Anderson had used with him. Charles sat up on his bed of pease-straw, and listened to the scheme with great attention. He then caused Locheil and the other leaders to be called and taken into counsel. They all approved of the plan, and a resolution was instantly passed to take advantage of Mr Anderson's offers of service.[1]

Lord Nairn's party being recalled from Preston, the Highland army began to move about three o'clock in the morning (Saturday, 21st September), when the sun was as yet three hours below the horizon. It was thought necessary, on this occasion, to reverse the order of march, by shifting the rear of the column to the van. Colonel Ker managed this evolution with his characteristic skill and prudence. Passing slowly from the head to the other end of the column, desiring the men, as he went along, to observe the strictest silence, he turned the rear forwards, making the men wheel round his own person till they were all on the march.[2] Mr Anderson led the way. Next to him was Macdonald of Glenaladale, major of the Clanranald regiment, with a chosen body of sixty men, appointed to secure Cope's baggage whenever they saw the armies engaged.[3] Close behind came the army, marching, as usual, in a column of three men abreast. They came down by a sort of valley, or hollow, that winds through the farm of Rigganhead. Not a whisper was heard amongst them. At first their march was concealed by darkness, and, when daylight began to appear, by the mist. When they were near the morass, some dragoons, who stood upon the other side as an advanced guard, called out: 'Who's there?' The Highlanders made no answer, but marched on. The dragoons, soon perceiving who they were, fired their pieces, and rode off to give the alarm.[4]

The ditch so often mentioned as traversing the morass became a mill-course at this easterly point, for the service of Seton Mill with water. The Highlanders had therefore not

---

1 Home's Works, iii. 88.   2 Lockhart Papers, ii. 449.
3 Lockhart Papers, ii. 491.   4 Home's Works, iii. 89.

only the difficulty of wading through the bog knee-deep in mud, but also that of crossing a broad deep stream by a narrow wooden bridge. Charles himself jumped across the dam, but fell on the other side, and got his legs and hands beslimed. The column, as it gradually cleared this impediment, moved directly onwards to the sea, till it was thought by those at the head that all would be over the morass; a line was then formed, in the usual manner, upon the firm and level ground.

The arrangement of the Highland army for the battle about to take place was ruled by some fanciful considerations. The great clan Colla, or Macdonalds, formed the right wing, in consequence of a tradition that Robert Bruce had assigned it that station at the battle of Bannockburn, in gratitude for the treatment he had received from its chief when in hiding in the Hebrides, and because it had assumed that station in every battle since, except that of Harlaw, on which occasion the post of honour was voluntarily resigned in favour of the Macleods.[1] The Camerons and Appin Stuarts composed the left wing, perhaps for some similar reason; while the Duke of Perth's regiment and the Macgregors stood in the centre. The Duke of Perth, as oldest lieutenant-general, commanded the right wing, Lord George Murray the left.

Behind the first line a second was arranged, at the distance of fifty yards, consisting of the Athole men, the Robertsons, the Macdonalds of Glencoe, and the Maclachlans, under the command of Lord Nairn. Charles took his place between the two lines. The whole army was rather superior in numbers to that of General Cope, being probably about 2400; but as the second line never came into action, the real number of combatants, as stated by the Prince's authority after the battle, was only 1456.

Surprise being no part of the Prince's plan, no regret was expressed at the alarm which the videttes had carried to the king's army; but it was thought necessary to form the lines as quickly as possible. When this was effected, Charles addressed

---

[1] Lockhart Papers, ii. 510.

his men in these words: 'Follow me, gentlemen, and by the blessing of God I will this day make you a free and happy people!'[1] The Duke of Perth then sent Mr Anderson to inform Lord George Murray that he was ready to march. Anderson met an aide-de-camp sent by Lord George to inform the duke that the left wing was moving. Some time of course elapsing before the right wing was aware of this motion, it was a little behind the left, and the charge was thus made in an oblique manner.[2]

It was just dawn, and the mist was fast retiring before the sun when the Highlanders set out upon their attack. A long uninterrupted series of fields, from which the grain had recently been reaped, lay between them and General Cope's position. Morn was already on the waters of the Forth to their right, and the mist was rolling in large masses over the marsh and the crofts to their left; but it was not yet clear enough to admit of either army seeing the other. An impervious darkness lay between, which was soon, however, to disclose to both the exciting spectacle of an armed enemy. On the part of the Highlanders there was perfect silence, except the rushing sound occasioned by their feet going through the stubble: on that of General Cope, only an occasional drum was to be heard, as it hoarsely pronounced some military signal.

At setting out upon the charge, the Highlanders pulled off their bonnets, and looking upwards, uttered a short prayer.[3] The front-rank men, most of whom were gentlemen, and all of whom had targets, stooped as much as they could in going forward, keeping their shields in front of their heads, so as to protect almost every part of their bodies, except the limbs, from the fire which they expected.[4] The inferior and worse-armed men behind endeavoured to supply the want of defensive weapons by going close in rear of their companions. Every chief charged in the centre of his regiment, supported imme- diately on both sides by his nearest relations and principal

---

[1] The Prince's authorised account of the battle, *Caledonian Mercury.*
[2] Home's Works, iii. 91.　　[3] *Caledonian Mercury.*　　[4] Ibid.

officers;[1] any one of whom, as of the whole clan, would have willingly substituted his person to the blow aimed at that honoured individual.

A little in advance of the second line, Charles himself went on, in the midst of a small guard. His situation was not so dangerous as it would have been if he had persisted in his wish of going foremost into the enemy's lines, but yet such as a gallant man might have been glad to have. As his courage has been most absurdly challenged, it is the more necessary to be particular as to his conduct on this occasion. A Highland gentleman, who wrote a journal of the campaign, relates that, just before the moment of the onset at Preston, he saw the Prince leave his guard, and go forward to the front line to give his last orders to the Duke of Perth and Clanranald. Passing the reporter of the circumstance on his return, and recognising him, he said, with a smile: ' Gres-ort, gres-ort !'—that is, ' Make haste, make haste !'[2]

Not only was the front line, as already mentioned, oblique, but it was soon further weakened from another cause. After commencing the charge, it was found that the marsh retired southwards a little, and left some firm ground unoccupied by that extremity of the army, so that it would have been possible for Cope to turn their flank with a troop of dragoons. In order to obviate this disadvantage, the Camerons were desired by Lord George Murray to incline that way, and fill the open ground. When they had done so, there was an interval in the centre of the line, which was ordered to be filled up from the second line; but it could not be done in time.[3] Some of the Prince's officers afterwards acknowledged that, when they first saw the regular lines of the royal army, and the level rays of the new-risen sun reflected at a thousand points from the long extended series of muskets, they could not help expecting that the wavering, unsteady clusters into which their own line was broken would be defeated in a moment, and

---

[1] Highland tradition.   [2] Lockhart Papers, ii. 491.   [3] Ibid. ii. 449.

swept from the field.[1]   The issue was destined to be far otherwise.

Sir John Cope, who had spent the night at the little village of Cockenzie, where his baggage was disposed under a guard, hastened to join his troops on first receiving intelligence that the Highlanders were moving towards the east.   His first impression regarding their movements seems to have been, that, after finding it impossible to attack him either across the morass or through the defiles of Preston, they were now about to take up a position on the open fields to the east, in order to fight a fair battle when daylight should appear.   It does not seem to have occurred to him that they would make the attack immediately ; and, accordingly, although he thought proper to form his lines, and turn them in the direction of the enemy, he was at last somewhat disconcerted, and his men were not a little surprised, when it was given out by the sentries that the Highlanders were upon them.[2]

The mode of fighting practised at this period by the Highlanders, though as simple as can well be conceived, was well calculated to set at nought and defeat the tactics of a regular soldiery.   It has been thus described by the Chevalier Johnstone, who was engaged in all the actions fought during this campaign : They advanced with the utmost rapidity towards the enemy, gave fire when within a musket-length of the object, and then throwing down their pieces, drew their swords, and holding a dirk in their left hand along with the target, darted with fury on the enemy through the smoke of their fire.   When within reach of the enemy's bayonets, bending their left knee, they contrived to receive the thrust of that weapon on their

---

[1] Home's Works, iii. 92.

[2] The circumstances which lead to this conclusion were the following.   According to the journal-writer already quoted, the advancing mountaineers, on first coming within sight of Cope's army, heard them call out: 'Who is there? Who is there? Cannons! cannons! Get ready the cannons, cannoniers!'   Andrew Henderson, a Whig historian, has also mentioned, in his account of the engagement, that the sentries, on first perceiving the Highland line through the mist, thought it a hedge which was gradually becoming apparent as the light increased.   The event, however, was perhaps the best proof that the royal army was somewhat taken by surprise.

targets; then raising their arm, and with it the enemy's point, they rushed in upon the soldier, now defenceless, killed him at one blow, and were in a moment within the lines, pushing right

A full-armed Highland Gentleman.—From a unique drawing in possession of W. F. Watson, Esq.

and left with sword and dagger, often bringing down two men at once. The battle was thus decided in a moment, and all that followed was mere carnage.

Cope, informed by his retreating sentries that the enemy was

advancing, had only time to ride once along the front of his
lines to encourage the men, and was just returned to his place
on the right of the infantry, when he perceived, through the thin
sunny mist, the dark clumps of the clans rushing swiftly and
silently on towards his troops; those which were directly
opposite to him being most visible, while on the left they faded
away in an interminable line amongst the darkness from which
they seemed gradually emerging.   The numerous clusters in
which they successively burst upon his sight—the rapidity with
which they advanced—the deceptive and indefinite extent given
to their appearance by the mist—all conspired to appal the
royal troops.   Five of the six cannon were discharged against
the left of the advancing host, with such effect as to make that
part of the army hover for a moment upon the advance ; and
one volley of musketry went along the royal lines from right to
left as the clans successively came up.   But all was unavailing
against the ferocious resolution of the Highlanders.

The victory began, as the battle had done, among the
Camerons.   That spirited clan, notwithstanding their exposure
to the cannon, and although received with a discharge of
musketry by the artillery guard, ran on with undaunted speed,
and were first up to the front of the enemy.   Having swept
over the cannon, they found themselves opposed to a squadron
of dragoons under Lieutenant-colonel Whitney, which was
advancing to attack them.   They had only to fire a few shots,
when these dastards, not yet recovered from their former fright,
wheeled about, and fled over the artillery guard, which was
accordingly dispersed.   The posterior squadron of dragoons,
under Colonel Gardiner himself, was then ordered to advance to
the attack.   Their gallant old commander led them forward,
encouraging them as well as he could by the way ; but they had
not proceeded many steps, when, receiving a few shots from the
Highlanders, they reeled, turned, and followed their companions.
Locheil had ordered his men to strike at the noses of the horses,
as the best means of getting the better of their masters ; but
they never found a single opportunity of practising this *ruse*, the

men having chosen to retreat while they were yet some yards distant.

Hamilton's dragoons, at the other extremity of the army, no sooner saw their fellows flying before the Camerons, than they also turned about and fled, without having fired a carabine, and while the Macdonalds were still at a little distance.

The infantry, when deserted by those from whom they were taught to expect support, gave way on all hands, without having reloaded their pieces, or stained a single bayonet with blood. The whole at once threw down their arms, either to lighten them in their flight, or to signify that they surrendered; and many fell upon their knees before the impetuous Highlanders, to beg the quarter which, in the hurry of the moment, could scarcely be given them. One small party alone, out of the army, had the resolution to make any resistance. They fought for a brief space under the command of Colonel Gardiner, who, deserted by his own troop, and observing their gallant behaviour, had put himself at their head. They only fled when they had suffered considerably, and when their brave leader was cut down by numerous wounds. Such was the rapidity with which the Highlanders in general bore the royal soldiers off the field, that their second line, though only fifty yards behind, and though it ran fully as fast as the first, on coming up to the place, found nothing upon the ground but the killed and wounded.[1] The whole battle, indeed, is said to have lasted only four minutes.

In the panic flight which immediately ensued, the Highlanders used their weapons with unsparing vigour, and performed many feats, such as might rather adorn the pages of some ancient romance than the authentic narrative of a modern battle. A small party of Macgregors, in particular, bearing for their only arms the blades of scythes, fastened end-long upon poles, clove heads to the chin, and cut off the legs of horses. With even the broadsword, strength and skill enabled them to do prodigious execution. Men's feet and hands, and also

---

[1] Chevalier Johnstone's *Memoirs*, 37.

the feet of horses, were severed from the limbs by that powerful weapon; and it is a well-authenticated fact, that 'a Highland gentleman, after breaking through Murray's regiment, gave a grenadier a blow which not only severed the arm raised to ward it off, but cut the skull an inch deep, so that the man immediately died.'[1]

While the clans on the right and left behaved with distinguished bravery, a portion of the centre, including some of the Lowland tenantry of the Duke of Perth, acted in a manner resembling the conduct of the royal troops. They are said, on approaching the enemy's lines, to have 'stood stock-still like oxen.'[2] It was to this regiment that the scythe-armed company of Macgregors belonged. These at least evinced all the ardour and bravery which were so generally displayed that day by their countrymen. Disregarding the example of their immediate fellows, they continued to rush forward, under the command of their captain, Malcolm Macgregor. A space being left betwixt them and their clan-regiment, which went on beside the Camerons, under command of Glencairnaig, their chief, they edged obliquely athwart the field in that direction, in order to rank themselves beside their proper banner—an evolution which exposed them in a peculiar manner to the fire coming at that moment from the British regiments. Their captain fell before this fire, pierced with no fewer than five bullets, two of which went quite through his body. Stretched on the field, but unsubdued in spirit, he raised himself upon his elbow, and cried out, as loud as he could: 'Look ye, my lads, I'm not dead; by G—, I shall see if any of you does not do his duty!' This speech, half-whimsical as it was, is said to have communicated an impulse to his men, and perhaps contributed, with other acts of individual heroism, to decide the fate of the day.[3]

The general result of the battle of Preston may be stated as

[1] *Caledonian Mercury*, September 25, 1745.
[2] Manuscript by Duncan Macpharig, temporarily in the possession of the late Rev. Mr Macgregor Stirling.
[3] Chevalier Johnstone's *Memoirs*.

I

having been the total overthrow and almost entire destruction of the royal army. Most of the infantry falling back upon the park-walls of Preston, were there huddled together, without the power of resistance, into a confused drove, and had either to surrender or be cut in pieces. Many, in vainly attempting to climb over the walls, fell an easy prey to the ruthless claymore. Nearly 400, it is said, were thus slain, 700 taken, while only about 170 in all succeeded in effecting their escape.

The dragoons, with worse conduct, were much more fortunate. In falling back, they had the good luck to find outlets from their respective positions by the roads which run along the various extremities of the park-wall, and they thus got clear through the village with little slaughter; after which, as the Highlanders had no horse to pursue them, they were safe. Several officers, among whom were Fowkes and Lascelles, escaped to Cockenzie and along Seton Sands, in a direction contrary to the general flight.

The unfortunate Cope had attempted, at the first break of Gardiner's dragoons, to stop and rally them, but was borne headlong, with the confused bands, through the narrow road to the south of the enclosures, notwithstanding all his efforts to the contrary. On getting beyond the village, where he was joined by the retreating bands of the other regiment, he made one anxious effort, with the Earls of Loudon and Home, to form and bring them back to charge the enemy, now disordered by the pursuit; but in vain. They fled on, ducking their heads along their horses' necks to escape the bullets which the pursuers occasionally sent after them.[1] By using great exertions, and holding pistols to the heads of the troopers, Sir John and a few of his officers induced a small number of them to halt in a field near St Clement's Wells, about two miles from the battle-ground. But, after a momentary delay, the accidental firing of a pistol renewed the panic, and they rode off once more in great disorder. Sir John Cope, with a portion of them, reached

[1] Report of Cope's Examination.

Channelkirk at an early hour in the forenoon, and there halted to breakfast, and to write a brief note to one of the state officers, relating the fate of the day. He then resumed his flight, and reached Coldstream that night. He next morning proceeded to Berwick, whose fortifications seemed competent to give the security he required. He everywhere brought the first tidings of his own defeat.

The number of dragoons who accompanied the general was about 400; besides which, there were perhaps half as many who dispersed themselves in different directions. A small party which made for the castle of Edinburgh permitted themselves to be pursued and galled the whole way by a single cavalier, without ever once having the courage to turn about and face him. Colquhoun Grant, who had the hardihood to perform this feat, was a man of great bodily strength, and was animated by a most heroic zeal for the interests of the Chevalier. After performing some valorous deeds on the field of Preston, he mounted the horse of a British officer, whom he had brought down with his broadsword, and rode after the fugitive dragoons with all possible speed. Within an hour after the battle, the inhabitants of Edinburgh were informed of the result, by seeing these dispirited men galloping up their principal street, followed by a single enemy! The troopers got into the castle in safety, and Grant, when he arrived there, finding the gate closed behind them, stuck into it his bloody poniard, which he left in token of defiance. He then rode back, and was allowed to pass from the town without interruption.[1] Another single pursuer was less fortunate. This was Mr David Threipland, eldest son of Sir David Threipland of Fingask, in Perthshire. He was in delicate health, but animated by great courage and zeal. On his own horse he pursued a party of dragoons till they came to the place where Cope was endeavouring to rally his troopers near St Clement's Wells. Here, pausing a moment,

---

[1] Information by a surviving friend of Mr Grant. Sir Walter Scott gives a somewhat different version of apparently the same story, in which it is stated that the dragoons were refused admission.—See *Tales of a Grandfather*.

they became aware that they were pursued by only a single gentleman, with two servants. They turned, and cut him down with their swords. He was buried on the spot. 'I remember, when a child,' says Sir Walter Scott, 'sitting on his grave, where the grass long grew rank and green, distinguishing it from the rest of the field. A female of the family then residing at St Clement's Wells used to tell me the tragedy, of which she had been an eye-witness, and shewed me, in evidence, one of the silver clasps of the unfortunate gentleman's waistcoat.' It is not unworthy of notice, that so lately as 1824, in the course of some legal proceedings, a lady, who was cousin-german to Mr Threipland, gave evidence of the fact of his death, stating that she remembered being put into mourning on his account.[1]

'The cowardice of the English,' says the Chevalier Johnstone, in allusion to their conduct at Preston, 'surpassed all imagination. They threw down their arms, that they might run with more speed, thus depriving themselves of the only means they had of arresting the vengeance of the Highlanders. Of so many men, in a condition, from their numbers, to preserve order in their retreat, not one thought of defending himself. Terror had taken complete possession of their minds. I saw,' he continues, 'a young Highlander, scarcely formed, who was presented to the Prince as a prodigy, having killed, it was said, fourteen of the enemy. The Prince asked him if this were true. "I do not know," replied he, "if I killed them, but I brought fourteen soldiers to the ground with my broadsword!" Another Highlander brought ten soldiers to the Prince, whom he had made prisoners of war, driving them before him like a flock of sheep. This Highlander, from a rashness without example, having pursued a party to some distance from the field of battle, along the road between the two enclosures, struck down the

[1] The horse on which Mr Threipland rode was observed next year in a fair at Perth, by the *grieve* or land-steward of Fingask, having found its way thither in the possession of a horse-dealer, who had probably obtained it from some marauding Highlander. The animal was purchased with a melancholy pleasure by the family, and kept sacred from work till the end of its days.

hindermost with a blow of his sword, calling at the same time: "Down with your arms!" The soldiers, terror-struck, threw down their arms without looking behind them; and the Highlander, with a pistol in one hand and his sword in the other, made them do just as he pleased.'

From the eagerness of the Highlanders to secure as much plunder as possible, they did not improve their victory by a very eager or long-continued pursuit. A great proportion remained upon the field, investing themselves with the spoils of the slain and wounded, while others busied themselves in ransacking the house of Colonel Gardiner, which happened to be immediately adjacent to the field. A small party, among whom were the brave Macgregors, continued the chase for a mile and a half, when, in the words of Duncan Macpharig, 'the Prince came up, and successively took Glencairnaig and Major Evan in his arms, congratulating them upon the result of the fight. He then commanded the whole of the clan Gregor to be collected in the middle of the field; and a table being covered, he sat down with Glencairnaig and Major Evan to refresh himself, all the rest standing round as a guard, and each receiving a glass of wine and a little bread.' In regard to Charles's conduct after the battle, the report of another eye-witness, Andrew Henderson, author of a historical account of the campaign, is as follows: 'I saw the Chevalier, after the battle, standing by his horse, dressed like an ordinary captain, in a coarse plaid and large blue bonnet, with a narrow plain gold lace about it, his boots and knees much dirtied, the effects of his having fallen in a ditch. He was exceedingly merry, and twice cried out, with a hearty laugh: "My Highlanders have lost their plaids." But his jollity seemed somewhat damped when he looked upon the seven standards which had been taken from the dragoons; at this sight he could not help observing, with a sigh: "We have missed some of them!" After this he refreshed himself upon the field, and with the greatest composure ate a slice of cold beef and drank a glass of wine.' Mr Henderson ought to have mentioned that Charles had, before thus attending to his own personal wants, spent several hours in providing for the relief of the wounded of both armies; preserving (to use the language of Mr Home), from temper or from judgment, every appearance of moderation and humanity. It remains to be stated that, after giving orders for the disposal of the prisoners and for securing the spoils, which comprised the baggage, tents, cannon, and a military chest containing £4000, he left the field, and rode towards Pinkie House, the seat of the Marquis of Tweeddale, where he lodged for the night.

Though the general behaviour of the king's army on this memorable morning was the reverse of soldierly, there were not wanting in it instances of respectable conduct. The venerable Gardiner, whose name has been rendered familiar by the affectionate biography of his friend Doddridge, afforded a noble example of fidelity to duty. On the previous afternoon, though so weak that he had to be carried forward from Haddington in a postchaise, he urged the propriety of instantly attacking the Highlanders, and even, it is said, offered Cope his neighbouring mansion of Bankton as a present, provided he would consent to that measure, which he felt convinced was the only one that could insure victory. When he found this counsel decidedly rejected, he gave all up for lost, and began to prepare his mind by pious exercises for the fate which he expected to meet in the morning. In the battle, notwithstanding his gloomy anticipations, he behaved with the greatest fortitude, making more than one of the insurgents fall around him. Deserted by his dragoons, and severely wounded, he put himself at the head of a small body of foot which still refused to yield; and he only ceased to fight when brought to the ground by severe and repeated wounds. He expired in the manse of Tranent, after having rather breathed than lived a few hours.[1]

[1] Doddridge's *Life of Colonel Gardiner*. A large thorn-tree, in the centre of the battle-ground, marks the spot where Gardiner fell. He was buried in the north-west corner of the church of Tranent, where eight of his children had been previously interred. Some years ago, on the ground being incidentally disturbed, his head was found marked by the stroke of the weapon which despatched him, and still adhered to by his military *club*, which, bound firmly with silk, and dressed with powder and pomatum, seemed as fresh as it could have been on the day he died.

Another redeeming instance of self-devotion was presented by
Captain Brymer of Lees's regiment, the only officer in the army
who had ever before seen the Highlanders attack regular troops.
He had witnessed the wild onset of the Macdonalds at Sheriffmuir, which impressed him with a respect for the instinctive
valour of the race. At Haddington, two nights before, when
all the rest of the officers were talking lightly of the enemy, and
anticipating an easy victory, Brymer retired to solitary meditation, assured that the danger which approached was by no
means inconsiderable. When the dread moment of fight
arrived, he disdained to fly like the rest, but fell at his station,
'with his face to the foe.'

The wounded of the royal army were treated by their con-
querors with a degree of humanity which might have been well
imitated by the regular troops on a subsequent occasion. The
conduct of the Prince has been spoken of: that of his lieutenant-general, Lord George Murray, was not less kind, if we
are to believe his own statement. A party, whose wounds were
not very severe, was conducted by Lord George to Musselburgh,
he walking by their side, and allowing some of them to use his
horses. At Musselburgh he obtained accommodation for them
in an empty house, and slept beside them that night, to protect
them from any violence on the part of his troops.[1] This precaution seems scarcely to have been necessary. The Clanranald
journalist says:[2] 'Whatever notion our Low-country people may
entertain of the Highlanders, I can attest they gave many
proofs this day of their humanity and mercy. Not only did I
often hear our common clansmen ask the soldiers if they wanted
quarter, and not only did we, the officers, exert our utmost
pains to save those who were stubborn, or who could not make
themselves understood, but I saw some of our private men,
after the battle, run to Port Seton for ale and other liquors to
support the wounded. As one proof for all, of my own particular observation, I saw a Highlander carefully, and with patient

---

[1] *Jacobite Memoirs*, 42.　　　[2] Lockhart Papers.

kindness, carry a poor wounded soldier on his back into a house, where he left him, with a sixpence to pay his charges. In all this,' adds the journalist, 'we followed not only the dictates of humanity, but also the orders of our Prince, who acted in everything as the true father of his country.'

Of the Highlanders themselves, only thirty were killed, including three officers, and about seventy or eighty wounded. The greater part of the wounded of both armies were taken into Colonel Gardiner's house, where it was thought possible, a few years ago, to see upon the oaken floors the dark outlines or prints of the tartaned warriors, formed by their bloody garments, where they lay.[1]

Whatever humanity may have been displayed by the common Highlanders towards the wounded, they exhibited quite as much activity in despoiling the slain.   Every article they conceived to be of the least value they eagerly appropriated; often, in their ignorance of civilised life, making the most ludicrous mistakes. One who had got a watch, sold it soon afterwards to some person for a trifle, and remarked, when the bargain was concluded, with an air of great self-congratulation, that he was glad to be quit of it, for it had died last night; the machine having in reality stopped for want of winding up.   Another exchanged a horse for a horse-pistol.   Rough old Highlanders were seen going with the fine shirts of the English officers over the rest of their clothes, while little boys went strutting about with large gold-laced cocked-hats on their heads, and bandoleers dangling down to their heels.   One of the Highlanders was seen soon after passing through Stirling, on his way to the north, carrying

---

[1] The greater part of the slain were interred at the north-east corner of the park-wall so often alluded to, where the ground is still perceptibly elevated in consequence.   A considerable number were also buried round the thorn-tree already mentioned, which is said to have marked the centre of Cope's first line.   The country-people, of whom it might truly be said that

'With more dismay
They saw the fight, than those that made the fray,'

were drawn forth and employed in this disagreeable duty : which they performed by carting quantities of earth, and emptying it upon the bloody heaps.

a military saddle on his back : he probably thought he had secured a competency for life.[1]

When the search for spoil had ceased, the Highlanders began to collect provisions. They fixed their mess-room in one of the houses of Tranent, and, sending abroad through the neighbouring parks, seized such sheep as they could conveniently catch. The

---

[1] Information by a bishop of the Scottish Episcopal Church.—A quantity of chocolate, found in General Cope's carriage, was afterwards sold publicly in the streets of Perth, under the denomination of *Johnnie Cope's saw*—that is, salve. The carriage itself was employed to carry home old Robertson of Struan, who had come down from the Highlands with his clan, but was unable, from age, to accompany the expedition any farther. At that time there was no coach-road to Struan's residence ; but when he had driven as far as he could, the vehicle was carried forward over the remaining tract by the clansmen. After lying in the courtyard at Mount Alexander till almost rotten, it was broken up for firewood.

In the blind eagerness of the Highlanders for spoil, it is said that they plundered many of the inhabitants of Edinburgh and other neighbouring towns who came, during the course of the day, to see the battle-ground. The whimsical Skirving, in his ballad of *Tranent Muir*, says :

> ' That afternoon, when a' was done,
>   I gaed to see the fray, man ;
> But had I wist what after past,
>   I 'd better stayed away, man.
> On Seton sands, wi' nimble hands,
>   They picked my pockets bare, man ;
> But I wish ne'er to dree sic fear,
>   For a' the sum and mair, man.'

In this rude but clever composition, the honest farmer embodies almost the whole talk of the times regarding the actors on both sides. He animadverts in severe terms upon the conduct of the British officers, one of whom betrayed an especial degree of cowardice, and that under circumstances which also disgraced his humanity. This was a Lieutenant Smith, of Hamilton's regiment, and of Hibernian extraction :

> ' When Major Bowle, that worthy soul,
>   Was brought down to the ground, man,
> His horse being shot, it was his lot
>   For to get many a wound, man.
> Lieutenant Smith, of Irish birth,
>   Frae whom he called for aid, man,
> Being full of dread, lap owre his head,
>   And wadna be gainsaid, man.
>
> He made sic haste, sae spurred his beast,
>   'Twas little there he saw, man ;
> To Berwick rade, and falsely said
>   The Scots were rebels a', man.
> But let that end, for weel it 's kenned
>   His use and wont 's to lie, man ;
> The Teague is naught—he never faught
>   When he had room to fly, man.'

So famous did this scandal become in a little time, that an advertisement was inserted in

people of the village have a tradition of their coming straggling in every now and then during the day, each with a sheep upon his back, which he threw down at the general dépôt with the exclamation: 'Tare's mhair o' Cope's paagage!' When men's minds are agitated by any mirthful or triumphant emotion, they are pleased with wonderfully small jokes.

the *Edinburgh Courant* of the 6th of January 1746, to the following effect: 'Whereas there has been a scandalous report spread, to the prejudice of Lieutenant Peter Smith of General Hamilton's dragoons, that he refused to assist Major Bowles, when dismounted at Preston: I, the said Major Bowles, do affirm it to be an infamous falsehood, Lieutenant Smith not being in the same squadron with me; nor did any officer of the corps refuse me his assistance on that occasion. Witness my hand, at Prestonpans, this 1st of January 1746. (Signed) RICHARD BOWLES.' It is needless to say that the lame and limited circulation of this exculpatory evidence went but little way to recover the unfortunate lieutenant's fame. Smith seems, therefore, to have at last aimed at another mode of redress. He is said to have come to Haddington, with the intention of challenging Mr Skirving, and to have sent a friend to the house of that gentleman, in order to settle the preliminaries of a personal combat. Here, however, poor Smith was quite as much at fault as ever. The farmer was busy forking his dunghill when the *friend* approached, whose hostile intentions he no sooner learned, than he proceeded to put that safe barrier between his own person and that of the challenger; after which, he patiently waited till the gentleman disclosed his errand. When he had heard all, and paused a little to consider it, he at last replied with great coolness: 'Gang awa back to Mr Smith; tell him that I hae nae time to come to Haddington to gie him satisfaction; but say, if he likes to come here, I'll tak a look o' him; and if I think I'm fit to fecht him, I'll fecht him; and if no, I'll just do as he did— I'll rin awa!' This Mr Skirving was the father of a very clever artist in the department of crayon portraits, long well known in Edinburgh.

The weapon which slew Colonel Gardiner.

CHAPTER XIII.

PRINCE CHARLES AT HOLYROOD.

'What says King Bolingbroke?'
Richard II.

THE Camerons entered Edinburgh scarcely three hours after the battle, playing their pipes with might and main, and exhibiting, with many marks of triumph, the colours they had taken from Cope's dragoons.[1] But the return of the main body of the army was reserved for the succeeding day (Sunday), when an attempt was made to impress the citizens with as high an idea as possible of the victory they had achieved. The clans marched in one long extended line into the lower gate of the city, with bagpipes exultingly playing the cavalier air, *The king shall enjoy his own again.*[2] They bore, besides their own standards, those which had been taken from the royal army; and they displayed, with equally ostentatious pride, the vast accession of dress and personal ornament which they had derived from the vanquished. In the rear of their own body came the prisoners,[3] at least half as numerous as themselves, and then followed the wounded in carts.[4] At the end of all, were the baggage and cannon under a strong guard. They paraded through the principal streets of the city, as if anxious to leave no one unimpressed with the sight of their good fortune. Charles himself did not accompany the procession, but came in the evening to Holyrood House,

---

[1] *The Wanderer, or Surprising Escape* (Glasgow, 1752), p. 43.

[2] Boyse's *History*, 82.

[3] The prisoners were confined, the officers in Queensberry House, and the privates in the jail and church of the Canongate. The wounded were committed to the Royal Infirmary, where the utmost possible pains was taken to heal them. In the course of a few days after the battle, the officers were liberated on parole, and permitted to lodge in the town. Afterwards, on one person breaking his word by going into the castle, the whole were sent to Cupar-Angus; and the private men were put into custody at Logierait in Athole.

[4] Boyse's *History*.

where, according to the *Caledonian Mercury*, he was 'welcomed
with the loudest acclamations of the people.'

It is difficult to describe the extravagant rejoicings with which
the Jacobites hailed the news of Preston.   They received the
messengers and homeward-bound Highlanders, who everywhere
dispersed the intelligence, with unbounded hospitality; and they
no longer made any scruple to disclose those sentiments in
public which they had hitherto been obliged to conceal as
treasonable.   The gentlemen drank fathom-deep healths to the
Prince, who, in their own language, 'could eat a dry crust, sleep
on pease-straw, take his dinner in four minutes, and win a battle
in five;'[1] whilst the ladies busied themselves in procuring locks
of his hair, miniature portraits of his person, and ribbons on
which he was represented as 'the Highland laddie.'   But
perhaps the most extraordinary instance of individual zeal in
his behalf was one afforded by an old nonjurant clergyman of
the Scottish Episcopal communion, who had attended his camp
before Preston, as some of the violent Presbyterians, on the
other hand, followed that of Cope.   This zealous partisan,
immediately after the battle, set out on foot for his place of
residence beyond Doune in Perthshire; and, having travelled
considerably more than fifty miles, next morning gave out the
news of the victory from his own pulpit, at the ordinary hour of
worship, invoking a thousand blessings on the arms and person
of the Chevalier.[2]

The conduct of the Prince himself was marked by a becoming
moderation.   On Monday the 23d, he issued several proclamations, in one of which he expressed his anxiety that no interruption should be experienced by persons passing to and from
Edinburgh on business, and formally granted protection to the
inhabitants and the country-people around 'from all insults,
seizures, injuries, and abuses of our army against them respectively.'   In another, he alluded to a wish which had been
expressed by many, that his victory should be marked by public

---

[1] *Caledonian Mercury*.   [2] Information by a bishop of the Scottish Episcopal Church.

rejoicings, and added: ' We, reflecting that, however glorious it may have been to us, and however beneficial to the nation in general, as the principal means, under God, for the recovery of their liberty; yet, in so far as it has been obtained by the effusion of the blood of his majesty's subjects, and has involved many unfortunate people in great calamity, we hereby forbid any outward demonstrations of public joy; admonishing all true friends to their king and country to return thanks to God for His goodness towards them, as we hereby do for ourselves.'

An addition to this proclamation was elicited by a circumstance which came into notice on the preceding day. On the Saturday evening Charles sent messengers to the clergy of the city, requesting them to hold public worship as usual, and apprehend no disturbance from him. To his surprise, not one of the regular clergy appeared in his pulpit on the Sunday: it was found that they had all deserted the town. He therefore added to the above proclamation: ' And we hereby repeat, what we have so often declared, that no interruption shall be given to public worship, but, on the contrary, all protection to those concerned in it; and if, notwithstanding hereof, any shall be found neglecting their duty in that particular, let the blame lie entirely at their own door, as we are resolved to inflict no penalty that may possibly look like persecution.' The clergy, as a body, continued absent during the remainder of his stay in Edinburgh. It has been stated [1] 'that they sent a deputation of their number to know whether they would be permitted, in the course of divine service, to pray for King George, when it was answered, on the part of Charles, that to grant the request would be in so far to give the lie to those family pretensions for the assertion of which he was in arms, but that, notwithstanding, he would give them his royal assurance that they should not be called to

[1] *Tales of a Grandfather*, third series, iii. 38. During Charles's stay at Holyrood House, a sermon was preached before him from Joshua xxii. 22: ' The Lord God of gods, the Lord God of gods, he knoweth, and Israel he shall know; if it be in rebellion, or if in transgression against the Lord, save us not this day.'—*Information by the late Mr George Robertson, author of ' Ayrshire Families,'* &c.

account for any imprudent language they might use in the pulpit.' This assurance, if it was ever made, did not induce any of the ministers to return to duty. There was, however, a suburban clergyman, by name Macvicar, who, having some countenance from the guns of the castle, continued to preach as usual, and offer up the ordinary prayers for the king. He also added, though several of the Highland army were present : ' As to this young person who has come among us seeking an earthly crown, do Thou, in thy merciful favour, grant him a heavenly one !' [1]

Amongst other traits of real or affected liberality, the Prince proclaimed immunity to all who might have distinguished themselves by acting against himself, his father, or grandfather, provided they should, within twenty days, formally engage to live inoffensively for the future.

He was at the same time obliged to publish an edict less creditable to his little army. It appears that, in searching for arms, the Highlanders used some license in regard to other matters of property ; though it is also allowed that many persons unconnected with the army assumed the appearance of clansmen, and were the chief perpetrators of the felonies complained of. Whole bands, indeed, went about the country, shewing forged commissions, and affecting to sell protections in Charles's name, for which they exacted considerable sums of money.[2] The Highland army were partly blamable for these misdemeanours, because they had opened the public jails wherever they came, and let loose the culprits ; and because, since their

---

[1] The *ipsissima verba* of this singular prayer, as given in Ray's *History of the Rebellion*, were these : ' Bless the king ; Thou knows what king I mean—may the crown sit long easy upon his head, &c. And for the man that is come among us to seek an earthly crown, we beseech Thee in mercy to take him to thyself, and give him a crown of glory !'

[2] Among the rest, a certain malefactor named Ratcliff, who has been made well known to the public by means of a popular novel, seems to have been by no means the least active. It is mentioned in the *Caledonian Mercury* for October 11, that 'the *very villain* James Ratcliff, who has spent his whole life in pilfering and robbing, and who has escaped twenty several times from jail, particularly twice when under sentence of death in this city, was yesternight apprehended in the Grassmarket, and committed to the Thief's Hold. He had gone about the country since he last got out of jail, at the head of a gang of villains in Highland and Lowland dress, imposing upon and robbing honest people.'

arrival in Edinburgh, the sword of justice had been suspended. Charles, however, who was not personally blamable, made every exertion to suppress practices which tended so much to bring his cause into bad repute ; and his exertions seem to have been not altogether ineffectual.[1] It unfortunately happened that, while he did all he could to prevent small or individual robberies, the necessities of his own exchequer compelled him to authorise others of considerable magnitude upon the public bodies of the kingdom. From the city of Edinburgh he exacted a thousand tents, six thousand pair of shoes, and a vast quantity of smaller articles, for the use of his troops ; the expense of which was so great as to call for an assessment of half-a-crown a pound on the rental of the city. He seized all the goods in the custom-houses of Leith and Borrowstounness, and immediately converted them into money, by selling them back to the smugglers from whom they had been taken. From the city of Glasgow he raised £5500.

Though with 2000 men he had now obtained possession of

---

[1] It is the confident assertion of all who witnessed and have described the transactions of this time, that many persons really belonging to the Highland army *did commit acts of depredation.* It was common, for instance, for well-dressed persons to be stopped in the streets by men who presented their pieces with a threatening aspect, and who, on being asked what they wanted, usually answered : ' A *paapee,*' that is, a halfpenny. Sometimes these persons were contented with a still humbler tribute—a pinch of snuff. When we consider the extreme moderation of these demands, we can scarcely visit the practice with anything but a smile. Even this was only practised by the *canaille* of the clans, or rather perhaps by those loose persons who hang upon the skirts of all armies, and whose only motive for carrying arms is, that they may take advantage, for their own proper profit, of the license which more or less accompanies the presence of all military bodies whatever. The general tradition of the Lowlands is, that the Highlanders behaved with great civility as they were advancing in their expedition, and that it was only when retreating, and when their pride of spirit had been in a great measure destroyed, that their conduct in this respect was to be complained of.

A worthy Quaker in Edinburgh, by name Erskine, and by trade a brewer, called upon Charles at Holyrood House, to complain of a robbery which had been committed upon him by a troop wearing the Highland dress and cognizance, and concluded his remonstrance with these words : ' Verily, friend Charles, thou art harder to deal with than our present ruler : George only takes a part of our substance, but thou takest it all.' It is said that the Prince told this strange expostulator that what he had lost was little enough to compensate for the long arrears of tax and duty which he was owing to the king *de jure.* But he appears, on the contrary, to have taken measures for bringing the perpetrators of the robbery to deserved punishment. There is an advertisement in the *Courant* of the time, proceeding from him, in which he offers a reward for the robbers, and requires all to whom the stolen goods might be offered for sale to restore them to the owner.

Scotland, excepting the fortresses, it was impossible with that small force to take any immediate step for the advancement of his cause. It was necessary to wait for some time, that his forces might be augmented, either by accessions of his Scottish partisans, or by aid from abroad. He therefore encamped his troops at Duddingston, and, taking up his own residence in Holyrood House, enjoyed for a short period the privileges of undisputed sovereignty. Even at this most brilliant part of his career his deportment was generally thought pensive. He nevertheless gave a few balls to the ladies [1] who favoured his cause, and generally dined in public with his officers. On these occasions, if not uniformly cheerful, he at least endeavoured to appear pleased with what he saw of Scotland, its people, and whatever was peculiar to it. He was heard to say at dinner, that, should his enterprise be successful, he would make Scotland his *Hanover*, and Holyrood his *Herrenhausen*—thus conveying at once a compliment to the Scotch, and a sarcasm at the partiality of King George for his native dominions and palace. At his balls, which were held in the picture-gallery, he took care to dress very elegantly, wearing on some occasions ' a habit of fine silk tartan (with crimson-velvet breeches), and at other times an English court dress, with the ribbon, star, and order of the Garter.' Here his affability and great personal grace wrought him high favour with the ladies, who, as we learn from the letters of President Forbes, became generally so zealous in his cause as to have some serious effect in inducing their admirers to declare for the Prince. There was, we know for certain, a Miss Lumsden, who plainly told her lover, a young artist named Robert Strange, that he might think no more of her unless he should immediately join Prince Charles ; and thus actually prevailed upon him to take up arms. It may be added that he survived the enterprise, escaped with great difficulty, and married the lady. He was afterwards the best line-engraver of his time, and received the honour of knighthood from George

[1] A tune to which he danced with Lady Betty Wemyss on one or more of these occasions has been preserved and published.

III.[1] White ribbons and breast-knots became at this time conspicuous articles of female attire in private assemblies. The ladies also shewed considerable zeal in contributing plate and other articles for the use of the Chevalier at the palace, and in raising pecuniary subsidies for him. Many a posset-dish and snuff-box, many a treasured necklace and repeater, many a jewel which had adorned its successive generations of family beauties, was at this time sold or laid in pledge, to raise a little money for the service of Prince Charlie.[2]

The external graces and accomplishments of the Prince have never been denied ; but much doubt has been expressed

[1] Miss Lumsden, who was a most accomplished and high-minded person, was sister of Mr Andrew Lumsden, an adherent of the Prince. Mr Strange had no predilection for the Stuart cause, but solely obeyed the dictates of his lady-love.

[2] One of his officers has given the following account of the Prince's daily life at Holyrood House : ' In the morning, before the council met, the Prince Regent had a levee of his officers, and other people who favoured his cause. Upon the rising of the council, which often sat very long—for his counsellors frequently differed in opinion with one another, and sometimes with him—he dined in public with his principal officers. After dinner, he rode out to Duddingston (where the army lay encamped after their return to Edinburgh). In the evening he returned to Holyrood House, and received the ladies who came to his drawing-room. He then supped in public, and generally there was music at supper, and a ball afterwards.'—*Home's History*.

The following description of Charles was drawn during his stay at Holyrood House by an Englishman, who was sent from York in the middle of October as a spy, to report upon the appearance of himself and his forces : ' I was introduced to him on the 17th, when he asked me several questions as to the number of the troops, and the affections of the people of England. The audience lasted for a quarter of an hour, and took place in the presence of other two persons. The young Chevalier is about five feet eleven inches high, very proportionally made ; wears his own hair, has a full forehead, a small but lively eye, a round brown-complexioned face ; nose and mouth pretty small; full under the chin ; not a long neck ; under his jaw a pretty many pimples. He is always in a Highland habit, as are all about him. When I saw him, he had a short Highland plaid [*tartan*] waistcoat ; breeches of the same ; a blue garter on, and a St Andrew's cross, hanging by a green ribbon, at his button-hole, but no star. He had his boots on, *as he always has*. He dines every day in public. All sorts of people are admitted to see him then. He constantly practises all the arts of condescension and popularity—talks familiarly to the meanest Highlanders, and makes them very fair promises.'—Excerpt from a MS. in the possession of the late George Chalmers, Esq., given in his *Caledonia*, vol. ii. p. 717. That learned antiquary adds, that the description corresponds with a bust by Le Moine, executed after his return to Paris.

The description which the spy gives of the Highlanders is also worthy of quotation, though not flattering. ' They consist,' he says, ' of an odd medley of gray-beards and no-beards—old men fit to drop into the grave, and young boys whose swords are near equal to their weight, and I really believe more than their length. Four or five thousand may be very good determined men ; but the rest are mean, dirty, villainous-looking rascals, who seem more anxious about plunder than their Prince, and would be better pleased with four shillings than a crown.'

J

whether he possessed the genuine qualities of head and heart which would have given him true esteem, had he been established on the throne. Without here entering upon the whole question, it may at least be asserted with confidence, that, throughout the affair of 1745–6, he gave eminent proofs of a merciful and forgiving disposition, insomuch as to offend many adherents, and shewed himself to be superior to all low and cruel arts for advancing his cause. Mr Maxwell of Kirkconnel, who joined him at Edinburgh, and has left a memoir of the campaign,[1] presents the following illustrations of this point : 'Everybody,' says he, 'was mightily taken with the Prince's figure and personal behaviour. There was but one voice about them. Those whom interest or prejudice made a runaway to his cause, could not help acknowledging that they wished him well in all other respects, and could hardly blame him for his present undertaking. Sundry things had concurred to raise his character to the highest pitch, besides the greatness of the enterprise, and the conduct that had hitherto appeared in the execution of it. There were several instances of good nature and humanity that had made a great impression on people's minds. I shall confine myself to two or three. Immediately after the battle, as the Prince was riding along the ground that Cope's army had occupied a few minutes before, one of the officers came up to congratulate him, and said, pointing to the killed : "Sir, there are your enemies at your feet." The Prince, far from exulting, expressed a great deal of compassion for his father's deluded subjects, whom he declared he was heartily sorry to see in that posture. Next day, when the Prince was at Pinkie House, a citizen of Edinburgh came to make some representation to Secretary Murray about the tents that city was ordered to furnish against a certain day. Murray happened to be out of the way, which the Prince hearing of, called to have the gentleman brought to him, saying he would rather despatch the business, whatever it was, himself, than have the gentleman

[1] Printed at Edinburgh, 1841. 4to.

wait, which he did by granting everything that was asked. So much affability in a young prince flushed with victory, drew encomiums even from his enemies. But what gave the people the highest idea of him, was the negative he gave to a thing that very nearly concerned his interest, and upon which the success of his enterprise perhaps depended. It was proposed to send one of the prisoners to London, to demand of that court a cartel for the exchange of prisoners taken, and to be taken, during the war, and to intimate that a refusal would be looked upon as a resolution on their part to give no quarter. It was visible a cartel would be of great advantage to the Prince's affairs; his friends would be more ready to declare for him if they had nothing to fear but the chances of war in the field; and if the court of London refused to settle a cartel, the Prince was authorised to treat his prisoners in the same manner as the Elector of Hanover was determined to treat such of the Prince's friends as fell into his hands. It was urged that a few examples would induce the court of London to comply. It was to be presumed that the officers of the English army would make a point of it. . . . . Though this scheme was plausible, and represented as very important, the Prince could never be brought into it; it was below him, he said, to make empty threats, and he would never put such as those into execution; he would never in cold blood take away lives which he had saved in the heat of action at the peril of his own. These were not the only proofs of good nature the Prince gave about this time. Every day produced something new of this kind.[1] These things

---

[1] Perhaps we are to consider in this light a ceremony which he consented to perform under the following circumstances: When at Perth, he had been petitioned by a poor woman to *touch* her daughter, a child of seven years, who had been afflicted with the king's evil ever since her infancy. He excused himself by pleading want of time, but directed that the girl should be brought to him at Edinburgh; to which she was accordingly despatched, under the care of a sick-nurse, and a day was appointed when she should be introduced to his presence in the palace. When the child was brought in, he was found in the picture-gallery, which served as his ordinary audience-chamber, surrounded by his principal officers and by many ladies. He caused a circle to be cleared, within which the child was admitted, together with her attendant, and a priest in his canonicals. The patient was then stripped, and placed upon her knees in the centre of the circle. The clergyman having pronounced an appropriate prayer, Charles approached the kneeling

softened the rigour of a military government, which was only imputed to the necessity of his affairs, and which he endeavoured to make as gentle and easy as possible.'

As yet, excepting a letter he had addressed to Lord Barrymore from Perth, Charles had had no correspondence with the friends of his family in England. On the day after the battle of Preston, he despatched an agent, named Hickson, with instructions drawn up, probably by himself, in the following brief but forcible terms : 'You are hereby authorised and directed to repair forthwith to England, and there notify to my friends, and particularly to those in the north and north-west, the wonderful success with which it has hitherto pleased God to favour my endeavours for their deliverance. You are to let them know that it is my full intention, in a few days, to move towards them; and that they will be *inexcusable before God and man, if they do not all in their power to assist and support me in such an undertaking.* What I demand and expect is, that as many of them as can, should be ready to join me ; and that they should take care to provide provisions and money, that the country may suffer as little as possible by the march of my troops. Let them know that there is no more time for deliberation; *now or never is the word.* I AM RESOLVED TO CONQUER, OR PERISH. If this last should happen, let them judge what they and their posterity have to expect. C. P. R.' Hickson was apprehended on the 27th at Newcastle, with this document in his cloak-bag. He was put into prison, where he next morning attempted to take away his life by cutting his throat, but without immediately succeeding in his object.[1] What afterwards became of him does not appear.

On the 10th of October, Charles issued a proclamation 'unto

girl, and with great solemnity touched the sores, pronouncing at every different application the words : 'I touch, but God heal !' The ceremony was concluded by another prayer from the priest ; and the patient, being again dressed, was carried round the circle, and presented with little sums of money by all present. The story goes on to say that, precisely twenty-one days from the date of her being submitted to Charles's touch, the ulcers closed and healed, and nothing remained to shew that she had been afflicted except the scars or marks left upon the skin ! These marks my informant had himself touched.

[1] Culloden Papers, 226.

all his majesty's subjects, of what degree soever,' in which he made an earnest appeal to their affections, and took occasion to explain his views on some important points in the political state of the country.[1] He declared that his father's sole intention was ' to reinstate all his subjects in the full enjoyment of their religion, laws, and liberties.' ' Our present attempt,' said he, ' is not undertaken in order to enslave a free people, but to redress and remove the encroachments made upon them ; not to impose upon any a religion which they dislike, but to secure them all in the enjoyment of those which are respectively at present established amongst them either in England, Scotland, or Ireland.' He promised to respect the national debt, but said he could upon no account be induced to ratify the Union.   He alluded to the endeavours which were made by ill-designing men to prejudice the people against himself and his undertaking. ' Do not,' says he, ' the pulpits and congregations of the clergy, as well as your weekly papers, ring with the dreadful threats of popery, slavery, tyranny, and arbitrary power, which are now ready to be imposed upon you by the formidable powers of France and Spain ? Is not my royal father represented as a blood-thirsty tyrant, breathing out nothing but destruction to all who will not immediately embrace an odious religion ? Or have I myself been better used ? But listen only to the naked truth.

' I with my own money, hired a small vessel, ill supplied with money, arms, or friends ; I arrived in Scotland, attended by seven persons ; I publish the king my father's declaration, and proclaim his title, with pardon in one hand, and in the other liberty of conscience, and the most solemn promises to grant whatever a free parliament shall propose for the happiness of a people. I have, I confess, the greatest reason to adore the goodness of Almighty God, who has in so remarkable a manner protected me and my small army through the many dangers to

1 Lord Mahon expresses his opinion that this document was of his own composition, notwithstanding that Mr Murray of Broughton, in his examination, states it to have been drawn up by Sir Thomas Sheridan and Sir James Steuart.

which we were at first exposed, and who has led me in the way to victory, and to the capital of this ancient kingdom, amidst the acclamations of the king my father's subjects. Why, then, is so much pains taken to spirit up the minds of the people against this my undertaking?

'The reason is obvious; it is, lest the real sense of the nation's present sufferings should blot out the remembrance of past misfortunes, and of the outcries formerly raised against the royal family. Whatever miscarriages might have given occasion to them, they have been more than atoned for since; and the nation has now an opportunity of being secured against the like for the future.

'That our family has suffered exile during these fifty-seven years, everybody knows. Has the nation, during that period of time, been the more happy and flourishing for it? Have you found reason to love and cherish your governors, as the fathers of the people of Great Britain and Ireland? Has a family, upon whom a faction unlawfully bestowed the diadem of a rightful prince, retained a due sense of so great a trust and favour? Have you found more humanity and condescension in those who were not born to a crown, than in my royal forefathers? Have their ears been open to the cries of the people? Have they, or do they consider only the interest of these nations? Have you reaped any other benefit from them than an immense load of debts? If I am answered in the affirmative, why has their government been so often railed at in all your public assemblies? Why has the nation been so long crying out in vain for redress against the abuse of parliaments, upon account of their long duration, the multitude of placemen which occasions their venality, the introduction of penal laws, and, in general, against the miserable situation of the kingdom at home and abroad? All these and many more inconveniences must now be removed, unless the people of Great Britain be already so far corrupted that they will not accept of freedom when offered to them, seeing the king, on his restoration, will refuse nothing that a free parliament can ask for the security of the religion, laws, and liberty of his people. . . . .

'It is now time to conclude, and I shall do it with this reflection. Civil wars are ever attended with rancour and ill-will, which party rage never fails to produce in the minds of those whom different interests, principles, or views set in opposition to one another. I therefore earnestly require it of my friends to give as little loose as possible to such passions; this will prove the most effectual means to prevent the same in the enemies of our royal cause. And this my declaration will vindicate to all posterity the nobleness of my undertaking, and the generosity of my intentions.'[1]

[1] This document was burlesqued on the spur of the occasion by Mrs Cockburn, author of the beautiful song, *The Flowers of the Forest*, and whose wit, as here exemplified, may for the future check in some degree the too confident assertion that the Muses were exclusively Jacobite. The verses form a kind of parody of a song called *Clout the Cauldron*:

> 'Have you any laws to mend?
>   Or have you any grievance?
> I am a hero to my trade,
>   And truly a most leal prince.
> Would you have war, would you have peace,
>   Would you be free of taxes,
> Come chapping to my father's door,
>   You need not doubt of access.
>
> Religion, laws, and liberty,
>   Ye ken are bonnie words, sirs;
> They shall be a' made sure to you,
>   If you 'll fecht wi' your swords, sirs.
> The nation's debt we soon shall pay,
>   If ye 'll support our right, boys;
> No sooner we are brought in play,
>   Than all things shall be tight, boys.
>
> Ye ken that by a Union base,
>   Your ancient kingdom's undone,
> That a' your ladies, lords, and lairds,
>   Gang up and live at London.
> Nae langer that we will allow,
>   For, crack—it goes asunder—
> What took sic time and pains to do;
>   And let the warld wonder.
>
> I 'm sure, for seven years and mair,
>   Ye 've heard o' sad oppression;
> And this is all the good ye got
>   By the Hanover succession.

CHAPTER XIV.

GATHERING AT EDINBURGH.

'To wanton me, to wanton me,
　Ken ye what maist wad wanton me?
To see King James at Edinburgh Cross,
　Wi' fifty thousand foot and horse,
And the usurper forced to flee;
Oh, this is what maist wad wanton me!'

Jacobite Song.

THE court of St James's, thoroughly alarmed at Charles's progress and success, were now taking measures to present a large force against him.   About the end of September, the king ordered a strong body of troops, consisting of several battalions of foot and some squadrons of horse, to march directly to Scotland, under the command of Marshal Wade.   They were

'For absolute power and popery,
　Ye ken it's a' but nonsense:
I here swear to secure to you
　Your liberty of conscience.

And, for your mair encouragement,
　Ye shall be pardoned byganes;
Nae mair fight on the continent,
　And leave behind your dry banes.
Then come away, and dinna stay;
　What gars ye look sae landart?
I'd have ye run, and not delay,
　To join my father's standard.'

Sir Walter Scott, in a manuscript note which he communicated to the author of this history, says: 'I remember having heard repeated a parody on Prince Charles's proclamation, in burlesque verse, to the tune of *Clout the Cauldron*.   In the midst of the siege or blockade of the castle of Edinburgh, the carriage in which Mrs Cockburn was returning from a visit to Ravelston was stopped by the Highland guard at the West Port; and as she had a copy of the parody about her person, she was not a little alarmed for the consequences, especially as the officer talked of searching for letters and correspondence with the Whigs in the city.   Fortunately the arms on the coach were recognised as belonging to a gentleman favourable to the cause of the adventurer, so that Mrs Cockburn escaped, with the caution not to carry political squibs about her person in future.'

appointed to assemble at Doncaster, and Wade set out from London on the 6th of October to assume the command. It was not till the 29th of October that this army reached Newcastle, on their way to meet the Highland army, by which time Charles was on the point of marching into England.[1]

This force being still considered too small, the king, besides using every endeavour to enlist new men, ordered home a considerable portion of his veteran army from Flanders, along with its youthful commander, William, Duke of Cumberland, his second son, who had already distinguished himself at the well-fought though unsuccessful battle of Fontenoy. Thirteen regiments of infantry and two of cavalry were also in the course of being raised by the nobility and gentry of England to oppose the insurgents; and the king, the better to carry on the war, was favoured with a loan of £700,000, by the proprietors of two privateer vessels, which had recently taken upwards of that sum in specie from the French. The royal assent was also given, October 21, to a bill for suspending the Habeas Corpus Act; and many persons of importance were arrested on suspicion.

To oppose forces thus leisurely collected, and in such quantities, Charles exerted himself, for six weeks after his victory, to raise the clans which had not at first declared themselves, and to organise his little army as well as time and circumstances would allow. This was the more necessary, as, in addition to the regular forces mustered by the government, President Forbes was exerting himself to raise a loyal force in the Highlands out of the *followings* of the Laird of Grant, the Earl of Sutherland, Monro of Foulis, and a few other well-affected landlords, and for this purpose had obtained from court twenty commissions for an equal number of *independent companies*, as they were called, of 100 men each. On the 24th of September,

---

[1] Wade, on the 30th of October, issued a proclamation, addressed to such as had been forced by their superiors into rebellion, offering them his majesty's free pardon, on condition of their returning to their homes before the 12th of November.

Charles despatched Mr Alexander Macleod of Muiravonside, a cousin of young Clanranald, as a messenger to the Isle of Skye, to assure Sir Alexander Macdonald and the Laird of Macleod, that, not imputing their inactivity to disaffection, he was ready to receive them and their powerful clans as the most favoured of his father's loyal subjects. From Skye, this messenger was commissioned to go to Castle Downie, the residence of Lord Lovat, and to deliver to him the same message. He met with no success in Skye, where Duncan Forbes had been exerting himself to confirm the two recusant chiefs in their loyalty. At Castle Downie he found Lovat still undecided as to which course he should take. This aged chief had been greatly rejoiced by the tidings of Preston. It is said that, momentarily hurried from his prudent course, he pronounced it a victory of unparalleled brilliancy, and descending to his courtyard, and casting his hat upon the ground, drank, in a bumper of wine, 'Success to the White Rose, and confusion to the White Horse and all its adherents!'—the white rose being a badge of the house of Stuart, and the white horse a conspicuous object on the armorial shield of the house of Hanover. Still he was too much in fear of the government, and too closely watched by his neighbour, President Forbes, to commit himself in the character of a declared partisan of the Chevalier. It occurred to Lovat's subtle, but at the same time superficial mind, that he might give the Prince the use of his clan, as a portion of his army, while he himself might keep up a fair face towards the government, and thereby save his person and estates from risk. He therefore caused the clan to be mustered by his subalterns, the chief of whom was Fraser of Gortuleg; and summoning his son, a youth of eighteen, from college at St Andrews, forced him to assume the appearance of a rebellious young chief, determined to muster and lead away the clan for the service of the Chevalier, against the will of an aged father, unable by personal infirmity to prevent him.

The letters addressed by Lovat to President Forbes during the time when these transactions were going on have been preserved and published,[1] and perhaps we have nowhere more faithful illustrations of that mean cunning, the natural language of which Hogarth has so well expressed in his lordship's portrait. On the 7th of October, he speaks with indignation of the 'villainous, malicious, and ridiculous reports' that had been circulated respecting his conduct, and to which Forbes had alluded, assuring the President that 'there was nothing ever out of hell more false.' Forbes replied on the same day, in terms expressing full confidence in his continued prudence and loyalty. On the 11th, Lovat writes again, representing (this was an important part of his system) his health as extremely bad; he could not move without the assistance of three or four men. He is full of intelligence favourable to the Chevalier's object—a French army landed in the south of England—the Duke of Beaufort, Sir Watkins William Wynne, and Morgan of Tredegar, at the head of a native English army of six thousand men—all the gentry of Banff, Aberdeen, Perth, and Stirling, and many of the clans, flocking to the standard at Edinburgh. The contagion of disloyalty has reached his men, and he finds it morally impossible to prevent them from arming in behalf of the 'mad young gentleman.' He really does not know how to act: he wishes he had been in any part out of Britain for these twelve months past. Finally, he craves the Lord President's advice. On the night of the 16th, a large party of Lovat's clan, under some of his subalterns, made an unsuccessful attack on Culloden House, in order to seize the person of the President, for which, it will be recollected, he had obtained a warrant from Prince Charles, not dictated in such unscrupulous terms as he had wished. Apparently, on hearing of this attack, he wrote to the Lord President in condoling terms; but the letter has not been preserved. Of course, he would disclaim all connection with the attempt, though there is no doubt that it was of his own scheming. In the same letter, as we can judge from the President's answer, he must have stated that his son had put

[1] Culloden Papers, 4to.

himself at the head of the clan, and was about to conduct it to
the standard of the Chevalier. On the 20th, he renews this
subject, with many affected complaints as to the distresses of
his situation. 'This Prince's landing,' says he, 'was as great a
surprise to me as it was to any man in Scotland; but who can
prevent accidents, or the designs of Providence? It is certain
that what he has done since he landed seems rather to be a
miracle, than the effects of men's heads or hands; and how far
that favourable providence may follow him, or conduct him,
God alone knows; for *he seems at present in a fair and probable
way of succeeding.*' For this, which probably was his genuine
opinion, he adduces facts; particularly the great number of his
adherents in Scotland, and the succours expected from abroad.
Nevertheless, 'I do solemnly declare to your lordship that
nothing ever vexed my soul so much as the resolution of my
son to go and join the Prince. . . . . This mad resolution
struck him in the head as soon as he heard of the Prince's
landing; and after what Macleod said to him, and what Gortuleg
said to him, and what myself said to him, I know by his answers
to Macleod, Gortuleg, and me, that all the creation will not
keep him from going to live and die with that Prince. I refer
it to your lordship, who has a true sense of the danger of my
family from his going out, what a load and weight of grief must
be upon my soul to see my son, myself, and my family in such
danger and jeopardy. But I cannot help it. I must submit to
the will of God, and there must leave it.'

In this letter he whiningly complains that his son, when he
ventures to remonstrate with him, only 'smiles and laughs:' in
another of the 27th, we have the young man described as flying
in his face 'like a wild-cat' whenever he but speaks of his folly.
The President having, in a reply dated the 29th, plainly intimated
that, in an age of such suspicion, the Master of Lovat's conduct
might be the ruin of his father and family, the old chief, on the
30th, exclaims loudly against the very idea of such a thing, than
which, he says, there never could have been greater injustice
among the Turks or Persians. 'Am I, my lord, the first man

that has had ane undutiful son? Or am I the first man that has made a good estate, and saw it destroyed in his own time by the foolish actings of ane unnatural son, who prefers his own extravagant fancies to the solid advice of ane affectionate old father? I have seen instances of this in my own time; but I never heard till now that the foolishness of a son would take away the liberty and life of a father, that lived peaceably, that was ane honest man, and well inclined to the rest of mankind. But I find the longer a man lives, the more wonders and extraordinary things he sees.' On the 6th of November, he entreats the Lord President to continue his friendship, and to represent his case in the most favourable light in important quarters—adding, with that view, a recital of how his clan had been infected by the general enthusiasm, how they had gone off to the Prince, leaving me 'a contemptible old infirm fellow in my house, and no more notice taken of me than if I was a child'—and finally, how he was, after all, exerting himself to make up a regiment for the government, 'most of them pretty fellows, though some of them are between sixty and seventy years of age' (many of them, he elsewhere says, 'about my own age,' that is, on the borders of eighty!), and at whose head he was to put a set of 'pretty gentlemen.' He was determined to live at home in peace, and, if he should suffer on his son's account, it would be a greater severity than was ever practised to any subject. 'My house and green,' he adds, 'has been like a market-place for some time past; and my son was such a fool, that he entertained, and does entertain, every man he thinks favours his part, and he is ten times [more] master of this house than I am; but I have resolved from the beginning, and still continue firm in my resolution, let them do or say what they will, I will never black paper with them; and as soon as I am able to travel out of this house, I 'll stay no longer in it, for I am downright killed with vexation of heart and spirit, to see my health much hurt, my family in danger, and any money and rent I have foolishly spent and squandered away. There is no help for it; I must submit to Divine Providence.' Then, after a few matters of no importance, he tells how the Earl of Cromarty and Lord Macleod had come to Beaufort, on their way to join the Prince. 'So your lordship sees that the *wise and worldly* people of the Mackenzies are infected; so that it's no wonder that the Frasers, *who never were thought worldly or wise*, should be infected with a contagion, though never so foolish or dangerous.'

It is very remarkable, amidst all these proofs of refined cunning, to observe the want of the simplest wisdom in Lovat. From the magnificent accounts he gives of the Prince's circumstances and prospects, he appears to have been among the most credulous and easily deceived men of his day.

The Master of Lovat—afterwards the well-known General Fraser of the British army—led out the Frasers, it has always been said, with great reluctance, but not in time to join the army before its march into England.

Although the President was generally successful in his negotiations, he could not prevent a considerable number of the clans from marching to join the Prince's standard. As he himself declares in one of his letters, rebels stalked out from families for whose loyalty he could have previously staked his life; and even his own nephew, to his great astonishment and mortification, one day assumed the white cockade, and joined the insurgents. It would indeed appear that he was in some cases, besides that of Lovat, egregiously deceived; and that, by a policy not less fine-spun than his own, many whom he considered his friends had only assured him of their loyalty in order to lull him into security, and that they might be able to circumvent him in their turn. Under these circumstances, it is not surprising that the Independent Companies did not at first muster very quickly. The Earl of Loudoun came to Inverness to take the command on the 11th of October; but only two companies had been gathered at the end of that month, and only four more during the first half of the next.

Edinburgh was in the meantime experiencing some of the miseries of civil war. For a few days after the battle of Preston, the communication between the city and castle continued open.

The Highlanders kept guard at the Weigh-house, an old building situated in the centre of the street leading to the castle, about four hundred yards from the fortress itself; and they at first allowed all kinds of provisions to pass, particularly for the use of the officers. But, the garrison soon beginning to annoy them with cohorns and cannon, orders were issued, on the 29th of September, that no person should be permitted to pass. General Guest then sent a letter to the city, threatening to use his cannon against the stations of the Highland guards, unless they permitted a free communication. As that involved the safety of the town to a great extent, the inhabitants—for there were no magistrates—implored a respite for a single night, which was granted. They then waited upon Prince Charles, and shewed him General Guest's letter. He immediately gave them an answer in writing, that they might shew it to the governor, expressing his surprise at the barbarity of the officer who threatened to bring distress upon the citizens for not doing what was out of their power, and at the extravagance which demanded his renunciation of all the advantages he possessed by the fortune of war. He concluded by threatening to retaliate upon the garrison, in reprisals upon their estates, and also upon those of 'all known abetters of the German government.' Upon presenting this letter to General Guest, and making earnest entreaty for a further respite, the citizens obtained a promise that no shots should be fired till his majesty's pleasure should be known upon the subject, providing that the besiegers should, during that time, offer no annoyance to the garrison.

This condition was broken next day by the levity of the Highlanders, who fired off their pieces, to frighten some people who were carrying provisions up the Castle-hill. The governor then considered himself justified in firing upon the guard. Charles, on learning what had taken place, published a proclamation, prohibiting all intercourse with the castle, upon pain of death, and gave orders to strengthen the blockade, by posting additional guards at several places. The garrison retaliated for this measure, by firing at all the Highlanders they could see. On the 4th of October, they commenced a bombardment of the city. When it grew dark, the cannonading ceased, and a party sallying out, threw up a trench across the Castle-hill, where they planted cannon, and fired balls and small-shot down the street. They also set fire to one or two deserted houses at the head of the street, and on the people running to extinguish the flames, destroyed some innocent lives. The people, then greatly alarmed, began to busy themselves in transporting their aged and infirm friends to the country, along with their most valuable effects; and the streets, on which the bullets were every moment descending, were soon as completely deserted by day as they usually were by night. In running down to Leith for shelter, a great party met the inhabitants of that town hurrying for the same purpose towards Edinburgh, because a British ship of war, lying off in the roads, and whose intercourse with the shore had been cut off by the Highlanders, was firing into their streets with the same fatal effect. All was perplexity and dismay; and the unhappy citizens stood still, wringing their hands, and execrating the cruel necessities of war.

The distress which the blockade of the castle had brought upon the city was now found to be so unfavourable to Charles's cause, that he was obliged, for the sake of that cause, to take it off. He did so by proclamation on the evening of the day succeeding its commencement. The cannonade then ceased on the part of the castle, into which provisions were thenceforth conveyed without molestation.

The prisoners taken at Gladsmuir had meanwhile been sent to distant parts of the country—the officers to Perth, and the private men to Logierait in Athole. Some sergeants, corporals, and private men were prevailed upon to enlist in the victorious army; but most of them afterwards deserted. It will be found that most of the officers, who, besides their parole, had also taken an oath not to serve against the house of Stuart for a twelvemonth, held as little faith with their captors. The Prince not only freed those private soldiers who had been severely wounded (about seventy in number), but, with his usual humanity, gave them money to bear them to their homes. Many travelled into England as beggars, shewing their dreadful gashes wherever they went; by which means the curiosity of the English populace was at once gratified, and their minds impressed with no small terror for the claymore.

The accessions of force which Prince Charles received at Edinburgh were not inconsiderable. The first that joined him was Lord Ogilvie, eldest son of the Earl of Airlie, who arrived in town on the 3d of October with a regiment of 600 men, most of whom were of his own name, and from the county of Forfar. Next day came Gordon of Glenbucket, with 400 men from the head of Aberdeenshire, forming a regiment, of which he and his kinsmen were the officers. Lord Pitsligo arrived on the 9th, with a great body of gentlemen from the counties of Aberdeen and Banff, attended by their servants, all well armed and mounted; as also a small body of infantry. On the 16th, Lord Lewis Gordon, brother of the Duke of Gordon, arrived, and kissed the Chevalier's hand. It was understood that he on this occasion represented his brother, who was not inclined to appear in person.[1] These valuable recruits were from the northern part of the Lowlands of Scotland, where non-jurancy might be said to have its principal citadel, and where the Episcopal and Roman Catholic forms of worship still flourish. Various other gentlemen from the north, along with some inferior septs of Highland families, joined the army before the end of October, when the whole amount was somewhat less than 6000.

[1] Amongst many who declared for the Chevalier a cautious policy was adopted. In cases where the head of a family and proprietor of an estate went out, he would previously make over his property to his eldest son, who remained at home in possession. When the father, on the contrary, was averse to active partisanship, a son went out, along with all the forces, both in the way of men and money, which the house could contribute, assured that, although the youth should fall or be attainted, he had still brothers to inherit the patrimonial property for the behoof of the family. Some of the Highland gentlemen themselves saw fit to adopt this policy. The Macdonalds of Clanranald, and also those of Glengarry, were led out by the sons of their respective chiefs. At a subsequent period of the campaign, the *wife* of the chief of the Mackintoshes raised the clan in behalf of Charles, while Mackintosh himself served as an officer in the militia raised for the defence of government.

K

The Chevalier, notwithstanding the success of Preston, found few adherents in Edinburgh, or in any part of the country south of the Forth. Even when he was in complete possession of the city, only about three hundred of the inhabitants, and those not the most respectable, did him the honour of assuming the white cockade.[1]   In fact, his enterprise was a thing quite foreign to the feelings and ordinary pursuits of the Lowland population. It was also opposed by the stern Presbyterian principle of dislike to his family, originating in the religious persecutions to which his ancestors had subjected a portion of the people of Scotland. It is true that the most rigid sect of Presbyterians had, since the revolution, expressed a strong desire to coalesce with the Jacobites, with the hope, in case the house of Stuart were restored, to obtain what they called a covenanted king; and that 1000 of this sect had assembled in Dumfriesshire, at the first intelligence of the insurrection, bearing arms and colours, and supposed to contemplate a junction with the Chevalier. But these religionists were now almost as violently distinct from the Established Church of Scotland as ever they had been from those of England and Rome, and had long ceased to play a prominent part in the national disputes. The established clergy, and the greater part of their congregations, were averse to Charles upon considerations perfectly moderate, but at the same time not easy to be shaken.

Some instances have been reported which shew the efficacy of these sentiments against Charles's cause, and at the same time prove the disinclination to war which an age of domestic peace and increasing commerce had produced in the Lowlands. When the Earl of Kilmarnock exerted himself in 1715 for the defence of government, he found no difficulty in raising a large regiment among his tenants and dependants, all of whom were at once willing to attend their baronial master, and hearty in the cause for which he desired their services; but on the son of that earl coming to Kilmarnock in 1745, and requesting the

---

[1] *Edinburgh Packet Opened*, 1745. 8vo. P. 12.

inhabitants to arm themselves in behalf of the house of Stuart, there was a very different result. The people were acquiring wealth by the manufacture of carpets and nightcaps, and had got different lights regarding feudal servitude, which, added to their prejudices against the pope and the Pretender, caused them fairly to rebel against their baronial superior. His lordship assembled them in the town-hall, and tried them first with entreaties, and then with threats; but not one man would consent to join his standard. He then confined his demands to their arms; for, weavers as they were, they still retained the old muskets and rusty swords of their covenanting ancestors, and occasionally displayed them at bloodless wapenshaws. But this requisition they were equally prepared to resist; and one of them even told his lordship, that 'if they presented him with their guns, it would be *with the muzzle till him!*' [1] The Earl of Kilmarnock, therefore, brought none but himself and his body-servants to the Prince's army.

The Earl of Kellie was equally unsuccessful in his attempt to raise his dependants. This eccentric nobleman is described in the *Mercury* as going over to Fife, in order to raise a regiment for the Prince's service upon his estates in that well-affected district. He never got above three men—himself as colonel, an old Fife laird for lieutenant-colonel, and a serving-man, who had to represent all the rest of the troop by his own single person!

Several other Lowland gentlemen joined the Prince at this time—amongst the rest William Hamilton of Bangour, an amiable man and pleasing poet, who became the laureate of the enterprise, and seems at one time to have designed being its historian. Another of some note was the Honourable Arthur Elphingstone of Balmerino, who had been an officer in Queen Anne's army, and who, in the ensuing January, while engaged in the enterprise, succeeded to his family title of Lord Balmerino. 'I might easily,' said this brave veteran in his *last*

---

[1] Tradition at Kilmarnock.

speech, 'have excused myself taking arms on account of my age; but *I never could have had peace of conscience* if I had stayed at home, when that brave Prince was exposing himself to all manner of dangers and fatigue both night and day.' An adherent of still greater importance, and one whose becoming so occasioned more surprise, was Sir James Steuart of Goodtrees and Coltness, afterwards distinguished as the author of the first British work of importance on political economy, and unquestionably a man of considerable talents. Descended of a Whig family, Sir James had, nevertheless, allowed himself, in the course of his travels, to form an intimacy with the Stuart princes and some of their principal adherents. He had more lately been piqued at the treatment he had received at an election from one of the officers of the government. He was disposed to join the enterprise of the Prince, but wished that, in doing so, he should not appear quite a free agent. His sister's husband, the Earl of Buchan, a good man, of moderate understanding,[1] was brought by him to the same views, and they agreed with Lady Steuart's brother, Lord Elcho, that they should be seized in a public place, and carried to Holyrood House, as if against their will. Walking next day at the Cross of Edinburgh, Sir James and the earl were seized accordingly, and conducted to the palace. There a message was sent from an anteroom to the Chevalier, mentioning their presence. The Prince, who in the meanwhile had heard of the manner of their visit, returned for answer, that if the Earl of Buchan and Sir James Steuart came as willing partisans to befriend his cause, he should be proud and happy to see them, but not otherwise. This bluntness, though honourable to the Prince's candour, displeased Buchan, whose resolution, perhaps, had already begun to give way. He therefore made a low bow to the officer, and said: 'Please inform his royal highness that I have the honour to be his most obedient humble servant;' after which he instantly left the palace. Sir James, too much offended with the government to

---

[1] Though the father of two uncommonly clever men—the Honourable Henry Erskine and Lord Erskine, Chancellor of England.

retrace his steps, remained to see the Prince upon the terms prescribed.[1]

When the old Chevalier was first informed of Charles's departure for Scotland, he, though disapproving of the enterprise, did all he could to favour its success. Besides remitting 200,000 francs to O'Brien, his chief agent at Paris, to pay off the debts contracted by the Prince, he deposited another sum of 50,000 francs in the hands of Waters, junior, his banker there, to be at O'Brien's disposal for the service of the enterprise, and soon after sent 80,000 Roman crowns for the same purpose, promising soon to follow the same up with a still further remittance of 28,000 crowns, which he said would exhaust his treasury.[2] He likewise wrote a letter (August 5, new style—July 24, old style) to the king of France, pressingly urging him to second the Prince's attempt by an efficient force.[3] He at the same time addressed the Cardinal Tencin, the Maréchal de Noailles, and indeed the whole of the French ministers, to the same effect. Immediately after his taking possession of Edinburgh, the Prince despatched Mr Kelly to France, to give an account of his marvellous success, and urge it as a reason for the government sending him the much-desired aid.[4] He now sent Sir James Steuart, in the more formal character of an ambassador, to enforce the arguments of Kelly. Meanwhile the young Duc de Bouillon, with whom Charles had formed a romantic friendship, was exerting all his eloquence with the king and ministers to the same effect. The various means taken to obtain French aid were in some degree successful. Early in October several ships from France arrived at Montrose, Stonehaven, and other ports in the north with arms and ammunition. The first of these brought £5000 in money, and 2500 stand of arms, besides a Monsieur de Boyer, styled Marquis d'Eguilles, who, on the 10th, was received with

---

[1] The family tradition, communicated by the late Sir Henry Steuart of Allanton.

[2] Stuart Papers, appendix to Browne's *History*.

[3] Stuart Papers, Browne's *History*.

[4] Kelly went by Campvere, in Holland, where he was near being arrested by the Conservator of Scots Privileges, an agent kept by the Scottish merchants at that port.

studious parade at Holyrood House as the French ambassador.
It was given out that this gentleman brought letters from
Louis XV., promising that an armament should be immediately
despatched to the Prince's assistance, under the conduct of his
brother, the Duke of York.   Another vessel, besides some
money and arms, brought a few French-Irish officers.   A third
landed part of a company of artillerymen, with six field-pieces.
A difficulty was experienced in getting these stores transported
to Edinburgh, as the bridge of Stirling was under command of
the castle, and the Firth of Forth was swept by British cruisers.
The expedient adopted was to erect a battery of four or five
guns at Higgins' Nook, near Airth, and a similar one on the
other side of the Forth, to guard that narrow passage from the
boats of the cruisers.   The stores were brought over by this
way in a hundred and eighty-five carts, under the conduct of a
guard, and arrived at Dalkeith just in time to accompany the
army on its southward march.

The account given by Maxwell of Kirkconnel presents a
favourable view of the character and conduct of the Prince, as
both appeared during his residence in Edinburgh.   One less
flattering has been given by Lord Elcho, who likewise left a
memoir respecting the insurrection.   Lord Elcho's account of
the Chevalier's council is peculiarly valuable, because we
nowhere else obtain the same light ; but some allowance must
be made for the bitter personal feeling under which he evidently
writes.   'The Prince,' says he, 'formed a council, which met
regularly every morning in his drawing-room.   The gentlemen
whom he called to it were the Duke of Perth, Lord Lewis
Gordon, Lord George Murray, Lord Elcho, Lord Ogilvie, Lord
Pitsligo, Lord Nairn, Locheil, Keppoch, Clanranald, Glencoe,
Lochgarry, Ardshiel, Sir Thomas Sheridan, Colonel O'Sullivan,
Glenbucket, and Secretary Murray.   The Prince, in this council,
used always first to declare what he himself was for, and then
he asked everybody's opinion in his turn.   There was one-third
of the council whose principles were, that kings and princes can
never either act or think wrong ; so, in consequence, they

always confirmed what the Prince said.   The other two-thirds, who thought that kings and princes thought something like other men, and were not altogether infallible, and that this Prince was no more so than others, begged leave to differ from him, when they could give sufficient reasons for their difference of opinion.   This very often was no difficult matter to do ; for as the Prince and his old governor, Sir Thomas Sheridan, were altogether ignorant of the ways and customs of Great Britain, and both much for the doctrine of absolute monarchy, they would very often, had they not been prevented, have fallen into blunders which might have hurt the cause.   The Prince could not bear to hear anybody differ in sentiment from him, and took a dislike to everybody that did; for he had a notion of commanding the army as any general does a body of mercenaries, and so let them know only what he pleased, and expected them to obey without inquiring further about the matter.   This might have done better had his favourites been people of the country ; but as they were Irish, and had nothing to risk, the people of fashion, that had their all at stake, and consequently ought to be supposed likely to give the best advice of which they were capable, thought they had a title to know and be consulted in what was good for the cause ; and if it had not been for their insisting strongly upon it, the Prince, when he found that his sentiments were not always approved of, would have abolished this council long ere he did.

'There was a very good paper sent one day by a gentleman in Edinburgh, to be perused by his council.   The Prince, when he heard it read, said that it was below his dignity to enter into such a reasoning with subjects, and ordered the paper to be laid aside.   The paper was afterwards printed, under the title of "The Prince's Declaration to the People of England," and is esteemed the best manifesto published in those times, for those that were printed at Rome and Paris were reckoned not well calculated for the present age.

'The Prince created a committee for providing the army with forage.   It was composed of Lord Elcho, president;

Graham of Duntroon, whom they called Lord Dundee; Sir William Gordon of Park; Hunter of Burnside; Haldane of Lanark, and his son; Mr Smith; and Mr Hamilton. They issued out orders, in the Prince's name, to all the gentlemen's houses who had employments under the government, to send in certain quantities of hay, straw, and corn upon such a day, under pain of military execution if not complied with; but their orders were very punctually obeyed.

'There were courts-martial sat every day for the discipline of the army, and some delinquents were punished with death.'

During the stay of the Chevalier in Edinburgh, the newspapers served as organs of intelligence in his favour, and were the chief vehicles of his proclamations. While the *Courant* submitted to this necessity with the reluctance which might have been expected from its principles, the *Mercury* not only complied with promptitude, but rejoiced in the opportunity thus afforded of indulging its natural propensities without constraint. Ruddiman himself had retired to the country, after having only once, as he himself informs us (in the preface to his *Dissertation concerning the Competition between Bruce and Baliol*), seen his Prince *for two minutes.* At the age of seventy-one, he could not promote by any active measures the cause of his heart. During his absence, however, the paper was conducted with sufficient vigour by his partner, James Grant, a young man of more violent political prejudices than himself, and who eventually took arms in behalf of the Chevalier. Grant did all that the command of such a tool put into his power to further the views of the Highland army. Making allowance for the partiality displayed in his paragraphs, many of them contain curious memorabilia of the time.

Friday, September 27.—'Several sergeants and corporals, with a vast many private men, have entered into the Prince's service; so that, with the volunteers who come in, the clerks of the office have not leisure to eat, drink, or sleep, by enlisting. These sergeants and volunteers are now beating for volunteers to serve Prince Charles.

'The poor soldiers who were wounded at the late battle daily die of their wounds, both in town and country; and such of them as have been able to crawl to town, are cheerfully succoured by the inhabitants.

'His Royal Highness, whose robust and hardy constitution supports his natural inclination to fatigue and hardships, lay last night in a soldier's tent at the camp, preferring that tent to the royal palace of Holyrood House.'

Monday, September 30.—'There is now forming, and pretty well advanced, a body of horse life-guards for his Royal Highness the Prince, commanded by the Right Honourable the Lord Elcho. Their uniform is blue, trimmed with red, and laced waistcoats; they are to consist of four squadrons of gentlemen of character.

'The Prince's tent has been erected in the camp near Duddingston, where his Royal Highness lies every night wrapped up in his Highland plaid. He takes the utmost pleasure in reviewing his people, and is highly beloved by them. There was yesterday a general review.

'Several persons of distinction, and a vast number of private gentlemen, have joined the Prince's army since our last.

'A gentleman, a citizen of London, arrived yesterday in the Prince's camp, and offered himself a volunteer.

'Ever since the castle has been blocked up somewhat strictly on the *side of this city*, the friends of the garrison have the night-long conveyed up by ropes to them whatever necessaries they want, by the corner of the West Port side.'

Wednesday, October 2.—'Among the observables of this time, one is, that there is not in the city jail one single prisoner for crime, debt, or otherwise. The like, perhaps, never could have been said before.'

Some of the subsequent publications overflow with flattering accounts of the rising in the north, and intimate the highest hopes regarding the issue of the expedition. The clans are described as descending in thousands from their fastnesses, and every party which really came to the camp is greatly exaggerated. Cheerful accounts are also given of the readiness with which the contributions of the towns and rents of the forfeited estates are paid to the Prince. Altogether, from the magnificence of the reports which the *Mercury* puts into circulation, it is scarcely to be wondered at that so many sober men saw fit to embark in the expedition. I should suppose that Lord Lovat must have been a constant reader of the *Mercury*.

Wednesday, October 16.—'On Monday last, Monseigneur de Boyer, a French person of quality, arrived at the palace of Holyrood House with dispatches from the court of Versailles. He has brought with him a great quantity of arms, ammunition, money, &c.

'Yesternight, the Right Honourable Lord Lewis Gordon, third son of the deceased Alexander, Duke of Gordon, came and kissed the Prince's hand, and joined his Royal Highness's standard. His lordship was some time an officer in the navy. The court, which was very numerous and splendid, seemed in great joy on this occasion, as several gentlemen, not only of the name of Gordon, but many others in the shires of Aberdeen, Banff, and Murray, who had declined joining the Prince's standard, unless some one or other of the sons of the illustrious house of Gordon was to head them, will now readily come up and join the army.'

Monday, October 21.—'Friday last, at one afternoon, a woman was observed by the sentinels on duty at the park of artillery near Holyrood House, carrying, as they believed, dinner to some of the guard; under which colour she actually got past the outer sentinels, and even made an attempt to get by the inner sentinels; but, being pushed back, she stept to the south-east wall of the park, and actually got upon it, though the sentinels called out and fired upon her. She was immediately apprehended, and there were found upon her several combustible affairs. The people asking what business she had within the artillery ground, where so much powder was, with her straw, fagots, &c., she only answered that she believed it was a churchyard, and pretended to be delirious. It is assured that two suspicious-looking fellows were at the same time seen stepping over the easter wall of the park, but that they unhappily escaped by the surprise everybody was in.'

Monday, October 28.—'Saturday last, his Royal Highness the Prince reviewed the Macdonells of Glengarry at Musselburgh; they made a most noble appearance.'

Besides innumerable paragraphs of local news, calculated more or less to favour the Chevalier's enterprise, Grant inserted in his paper a detailed account, compiled from the records of parliament, of the Massacre of Glencoe; also a life of Viscount Dundee, and some letters by the Duke of Berwick, lauding the conduct of Prince Charles at the siege of Gaeta —the whole tending to throw infamy upon the Whigs, and lustre on the Cavaliers. It is worthy of remark, that, after the accession of several Lowland gentlemen, the position of the insurgent army is always termed the *Scots* Camp, probably to give it a more national and respectable appearance in print.

CHAPTER XV.

INVASION OF ENGLAND.

'Cock up your beaver, and cock it fu' sprush,
    We 'll over the Border and gie them a brush ;
    There 's somebody there we 'll teach better behaviour—
    Hey, brave Johnnie lad, cock up your beaver.'

Old Song.

THE closing days of October saw Charles in possession of an army of between 5000 and 6000 men, with a small park of artillery, and abundance of arms and ammunition, while still further reinforcements were preparing for him in the north, though not likely to join immediately. At the same time large bodies of troops were collecting against him in England, and even in the north of Scotland. In such circumstances, it would have been difficult for the most prudent head to say what step ought to be taken. Charles, who had had no maxim in the business but that the nearer he could advance to the seat of government the better, determined for the most vigorous course, and surprised his council one day by the announcement that he designed to march for Newcastle, and give battle to Marshal Wade, who, he was convinced, would fly before him. The proposal was combated by the more cautious of his friends, but ultimately agreed to.

Orders were now therefore given to call in all the various parties which had been posted in different parts of the country, and the Chevalier held a final review of his whole force upon the beach betwixt Leith and Musselburgh,[1] now known by the name of Portobello Sands.

During the latter half of October the army had not lain at

---

[1] Boyse's *History*, 95.

Duddingston, but in more comfortable lodgings within and around the city. On the 26th, the main body left Edinburgh, and pitched a camp a little to the west of Inveresk church, where they had a battery pointing to the south-west. At a still later period of the month they removed to a strong situation above Dalkeith, having that town on their left, the South Esk in front, the North Esk in rear, and an opening on the right towards Polton.[1]

At six o'clock on the evening of Thursday the 31st of October, Prince Charles finally left the palace and capital of his paternal kingdom, and, accompanied by his life-guards, rode to Pinkie House. Having slept there that night, he rode next day at noon to Dalkeith, where he gave orders for the march of his army. In order to deceive Marshal Wade as to the point in which he designed to invade England, he had previously sent orders for quarters to all the towns upon the road to Berwick, and despatched little detachments of his men in various other directions. His actual resolution was to enter England by the western border, at once with the view of eluding the army at Newcastle, and that he might gather the troops which he expected to come to his standard in Lancashire and Wales, which were unusually well affected. He now also appointed his principal officers—the Duke of Perth and Lord George Murray to be lieutenant-generals, Lord Elcho colonel of the life-guards, the Earl of Kilmarnock colonel of the hussars, and Lord Pitsligo colonel of the Angus horse.

The army was at this time in the best possible condition, and provided with all the conveniences which could attend a deliberate campaign. The men were fresh, by their long rest at Edinburgh, well clothed and well appointed; they carried with them provisions for four days: and their baggage was promptly transported, by about 150 wains, and as many sumpter-horses,[2] carrying large baskets across their backs.

At the commencement of this singular march, the insurgents

---

1 Merchant's *Hist. Reb.*, p. 127.

2 They had pressed 800 horses into their service out of the county of Mid-Lothian alone.

amounted in gross numbers to 6000, 500 of whom were cavalry, and 3000 Highlanders. Thirteen regiments, many of them very small, were composed of the Highland clans; five regiments, generally more numerous, of Lowlanders; and besides the two troops of horse-guards, who wore a uniform, and were commanded by Lords Elcho and Balmerino, there were bodies of horse under the orders of Kilmarnock and Pitsligo, the first coarsely dressed and indifferently armed, and the last clothed in the ordinary fashion of country-gentlemen, each armed with such weapons as he pleased to carry, or could most readily command. A small body of the lighter horse was selected to scour the country for intelligence.[1]

The Highland regiments were commanded by their chiefs, and generally officered by the kinsmen of that dignitary, according as they were near of kin. Each regiment had two captains,

---

[1] The following list will convey a more distinct view of the Highland army, as constituted at this interesting period. It is from the *Life of the Duke of Cumberland*. 8vo. London, 1767.

CLAN REGIMENTS, AND THEIR COMMANDERS.

Locheil—Cameron of Locheil...700
Appin—Stuart of Ardshiel..200
Clanranald—Macdonald [younger] of Clanranald....................300
Keppoch—Macdonald of Keppoch.....................................200
Kinlochmoidart—Macdonald of Kinlochmoidart......................100
Glencoe—Macdonald of Glencoe.....................................120
Mackinnon—Mackinnon of Mackinnon................................120
Macpherson—Macpherson of Cluny..................................120
Glengarry—Macdonell of Glengarry.................................300
Glenbucket—Gordon of Glenbucket.................................300
Maclachlan—Maclachlan of that ilk................................260
Struan—Robertson of Struan.......................................200
Glenmorriston—Grant of Glenmorriston.............................100
                                                              ———
                                                              2960

LOWLAND REGIMENTS.

Athole—Lord George Murray..600
Ogilvie—Lord Ogilvie, Angus men..................................900
Perth—Duke of Perth...700
Nairn—Lord Nairn...200
Edinburgh—Roy Stuart...450

HORSE.

Lord Elcho and Lord Balmerino....................................120
Lord Pitsligo..80
Earl of Kilmarnock...60

two lieutenants, and two ensigns. The front rank of the regiments was filled by men of good birth, who in the Highlands, however poor in fortune, are styled gentlemen, and who had for pay one shilling a day, while that of the ordinary men was only sixpence. The pay of the captains was half-a-crown, of the lieutenants two shillings, of the ensigns one shilling and sixpence. Each of the gentlemen of the front rank was completely armed, in the fashion of the Highlanders, with a musket, a broadsword, a pair of pistols, a dirk at the belt, to which were also attached a knife and fork ; the left arm sustained a round target, made of wood and leather, and studded with nails ; and some who chose to be armed with extraordinary care, besides the dagger at the belt, carried a smaller one stuck into the garter of the right leg, which they could use in certain situations, when the other was beyond their reach. The undistinguished warriors of the rear ranks were in general armed in a much inferior manner, many of them wanting targets.

On the evening of Friday the 1st of November, a considerable portion of the army, under the command of Lord George Murray, took the road for Peebles, intending to proceed to Carlisle by Moffat. The remainder left Dalkeith on the 3d, the Prince walking at their head, with his target over his shoulder. He had previously lodged two nights in the palace of the Duke of Buccleuch. This party took a route more directly south, affecting a design of meeting and fighting Marshal Wade at Newcastle. On passing this morning by Prestonhall gate, the Prince found breakfast prepared for him there by order of the Duchess of Gordon, the lady of the neighbouring mansion ; for which act of hospitality her Grace lost a pension of £1000, which the government had bestowed upon her in consideration of her bringing up her family in the Protestant religion.[1] In like manner, as he passed Fala Dams, the ladies of Whitburgh, sisters of his valuable adherent Robert Anderson, gave him and his immediate attendants a refection in the open air ; after

---

* Tradition.

which, in compliance with their request for a keepsake, he cut for them a piece of velvet from the hilt of his sword. Passing over Soutra Hill, he concluded the first day's march at Lauder, where he took up his quarters in Thirlstane Castle, the seat of the Earl of Lauderdale. Next day, on account of a false report that there was a strong body of dragoons advancing in this direction to meet him, he fell back upon Channelkirk, in order to bring up the rear of his troops, who had lingered there during the night. He marched that day (the 4th) to Kelso, walking all the way on foot, in order to encourage the men. A third party assumed a middle course, by Galashiels, Selkirk, Hawick, and Mosspaul.

The western division, which had charge of the cannon and most of the baggage, arrived at Peebles on the evening of Saturday the 2d of November. The sun was setting as the first lines devolved from the hills which environ the place on every side, and, throwing back a thousand threatening glances from the arms of the moving band, caused alarm among the peaceful townsmen, who had only heard enough about the insurrection and its agents to make them fear the worst from such a visit. Contrary to expectation, the mountaineers neither attempted to cut the throats nor to violate the property of the inhabitants. They let it be known, wherever they went, that they required certain acts of obedience on the part of the people ; and that, if these were not willingly rendered, they had the will, as they possessed the power, of using force. The leader demanded payment of the cess, on pain of military execution ; and little parties, calling upon various householders within and without the town, requested such supplies of provisions as could be properly spared, with the alternative of having their houses given up to plunder. But scarcely any incivility was ever shewn in the outset.[1]

This division of the insurgents, after spending a day or two at Peebles, went up Tweedsmuir to Moffat, and then, directing their route down Annandale, entered England near Longtown.

[1] Tradition at Peebles.

Charles remained at Kelso from the Monday when he arrived till Wednesday, preserving the further direction of his march a secret. In order the better to perplex the army which awaited him at Newcastle, he sent orders to Wooler, a town upon the road to that city, commanding the preparation of quarters for his whole army. On Wednesday morning, however, he suddenly gave out orders for a march towards the opposite extremity of the Border.

During his brief residence at Kelso, he sent a party of about thirty men down the Tweed, to the place, not far distant, where that river becomes the boundary of the two kingdoms, with orders there to cross the water, and proclaim his father upon English ground. The party, after doing so, immediately returned to Kelso.

The Prince lodged this night in Jedburgh, whence he set out early next morning,[1] and, crossing the high grounds to the south-west, led his men up Rule Water, famed of old for its hardy warriors, and over the *Knot o' the Gate* into Liddesdale, equally noted in former times for its predatory bands, as in more recent times for its primitive yeomen and romantic minstrelsy. After a march of at least twenty-five miles, he slept that night at Haggiehaugh, upon Liddel Water, his men lodging upon the ground, or in the houses, barns, and byres of the neighbouring peasantry. Before going to rest, he purchased a small flock of sheep for provisions to his men, and had a person sent for to kill and dress them. Charles Scott, a neighbouring farmer, more commonly called, in the fashion of that country, *Charlie o' Kirnton*, was the man employed for this purpose. He was up all night killing sheep, and the Prince next morning

---

[1] When the author was at Jedburgh, in November 1826, he saw an ancient lady who had been seven years of age when the Highlanders passed her native town, and who distinctly remembered all the circumstances of the memorable pageant. According to her report, they had a great number of horses, which it was said they had taken from the dragoons at Preston. She saw some of them dressing these animals in a stable, and could mimic the strange uncouth jabber which they used in performing the duties of hostlers. In particular, she remembers hearing them call to the beasts: ' Stand about, Cope !' &c. As at many other places, Charles was here saluted with marks of homage by many of the people as he passed, all the women running out to get a kiss of his hand, &c.

gave him half a guinea for his trouble.   Two Highlanders, who
had observed Charlie receive this guerdon, followed him as he
was going home, and clapping their pistols to his breast,
demanded an instant surrender of ' ta hauf keenie ;' a command
which the yeoman was obliged to obey, for fear of the pistols,
though his strength and resolution, celebrated to this day as
far surpassing those of modern men, would have enabled him
to defy double the number of assailants unprovided with such
weapons.[1]

Next day, Friday the 8th of November, Charles proceeded
down Liddel Water; and the middle column, which had marched
by Selkirk, Hawick, and down Ewesdale, came up to him at
Gritmill Green, upon the banks of the Esk, four miles below
Langholm.   When the first division soon after entered England,
they raised a loud shout, and unsheathed their swords ; but
some grew pale when informed that Locheil, in drawing his
weapon, had cut his hand, this being looked on as an evil omen.
The Prince took up his quarters for the night at Reddings, in
Cumberland.   On the succeeding day he was joined by the
western column.

During this march the Highland army lost a great portion of
its numbers by desertion.   The eastern column, led by Charles
himself, suffered most from this cause.   The Lanarkshire and
Stirlingshire roads are described as having for some days
swarmed with the men who thus abandoned the standard ;[2] and
great quantities of arms were found lying in the fields adjacent
to the line of march, which the deserters had flung away.[3]

On the 9th of November, Charles, having concentrated his
forces, approached Carlisle—a city which could once boast of
being the bulwark of England against the Scots in this direction,
but whose fortifications were now antiquated, and not in the
best order.   Less pains had been taken on the present occasion
to fortify the cities in the west of England than those upon the
east ; and while Newcastle and Hull had been for many weeks

---

[1] Tradition in Liddesdale.   [2] *Edin. Courant* for the time.   [3] Tradition at Peebles.

prepared to resist the insurgents, Carlisle was invested only four or five days after having first apprehended danger. It was protected by an ancient castle, in which there was a company of invalids; and the city itself was surrounded by an old and somewhat dilapidated wall, manned on the present occasion by the citizens, assisted by a considerable body of militia, which had been raised in the counties of Cumberland and Westmoreland.

On the 9th, a party of the Prince's hussars appeared on Stanwix Bank, and began to survey the city through glasses: but a few shots being fired at them from the walls, they were obliged to retire. Next day the insurgent army having passed the river Eden by several fords, invested the city on all sides; and the Prince sent a letter to the mayor, requiring him to surrender peaceably, in order to spare the effusion of blood, which must be the inevitable consequence of a refusal. The mayor, who was very confident, and had published an advertisement informing the world that he was not Paterson, a Scotchman, but Pattison, a loyal-hearted Englishman, answered by a discharge of cannon at the besiegers. Intelligence soon after reaching the Prince that Marshal Wade was marching from Newcastle to relieve Carlisle, he judged it proper to advance against that general, in order to engage the royal army in the mountainous country which intervenes betwixt the two towns. Leaving a small portion of his army to annoy Carlisle, he reached Warwick Castle at ten o'clock in the forenoon of the 11th, and quartered next night at Brampton and the adjacent villages.[1] He then learned that the information regarding Wade was false, and sent back the Duke of Perth, with several regiments of foot and some troops of horse, to prosecute the siege of Carlisle with all possible vigour.

Having prepared a quantity of ladders, fascines, and carriages out of the wood in Corby and Warwick parks, the besieging party reappeared in full force before the city on the afternoon

---

[1] Home's *History*.

L

of the 13th, and broke ground for a battery within forty fathoms
of the walls, the Duke of Perth and Lord George Murray
working in the trenches without their coats, in order to encourage
the troops.   The garrison of the city kept up a continual firing
during these operations, but without doing much harm.   Next
day, intimidated by the formidable appearance of the enemy's
works, and fatigued almost beyond their natural strength by
several nights of ceaseless watching, they felt disposed to resign
the city ; and accordingly, on the first motion of the besiegers
towards an assault, Pattison the Englishman was fain to display
a white flag from the walls, and ask terms for the surrender of
the town.   A cessation of hostilities being then agreed upon,
an express was sent to Brampton, to learn the Prince's pleasure ;
who, remembering the example of Edinburgh, would assign no
terms for the city unless the castle were included.   This being
reported to the garrison, Colonel Durand, the commander of
that fortress, consented to surrender his charge along with the
city.   At ten o'clock in the morning of the 15th the gates of
Carlisle were thrown open, and many a brave man passed with
a rejoicing heart beneath the arches over which his head was
hereafter to be stationed in dismal sentinelship.   The Duke of
Perth, on receiving the submission of the garrison, shook them
by the hands, told them they were brave fellows, and asked
them to enlist in his service.   He secured all the arms of the
militia and garrison, besides about 1000 stand in the castle,
with 200 good horses.   A great quantity of valuables, which
had been deposited there for safety by the neighbouring gentry,
fell likewise into his hands ; but these are said to have been
returned to their owners.   Next day the old Chevalier and his
son were proclaimed at the cross, in presence of the mayor and
aldermen, and a new document was at the same time read, under
the title of a ' Declaration of the King's Majesty to his English
Subjects.'   Charles was not personally received with much
favour in Carlisle, but his taking a town of such consequence,
after so brief a siege, gave some lustre to his arms, and increased
the fears of the government.

The short time spent by the army at Carlisle was marked by some rather important dissensions among the principal officers.   According to Maxwell of Kirkconnel, the origin of these was with Secretary Murray, who aimed at exercising an exclusive influence over the Prince, and disliked Lord George Murray as the rival he had most reason to dread.   He had gained over Sheridan, O'Sullivan, and the Duke of Perth (the last from easy-judging good nature) to support him.   When Lord George, before the blockade of Carlisle, requested to be charged by the Prince with the terms he was inclined to grant to the town, Secretary Murray told him sharply that that was a matter within his province, and with which Lord George had no right to interfere.   When Lord George afterwards saw the Duke of Perth take the chief command at the siege, the measure of his dissatisfaction was filled.   He immediately (on the 15th) sent a resignation of his commission to the Prince, stating that he would henceforth act as a volunteer, and would that night take his place as such in the trenches.   In a letter of the same date to his brother Tullibardine, he assigns the causes above stated for his resolution, adding, in the spirit of a true partisan and genuine Highlander: ' I shall shew as a volunteer that no man wishes more success to the cause ; and I can be of more use charging in the first rank of your Athole men, than as a general, where I was constantly at a loss to know what was doing.'   The Duke of Perth no sooner heard of the step taken by Lord George, than he also sent in his resignation as lieutenant-general, avowing his intention thenceforward to serve at the head of his own regiment.   There might be fretfulness, or something worse, in Lord George's motives, but those of Perth, who was of prior appointment as a lieutenant-general, and therefore formally entitled to take the chief command at the siege, could not but be pure.   Yet the army, while generally liking the Duke of Perth, had a higher opinion of the talents and experience of Lord George Murray as a commander, and when they heard of his resignation of his commission, a very general wish was expressed that he should resume it, while no such feeling was avowed with respect to the duke. Most of them had, in fact, another and strong reason for desiring that Perth should not be conspicuous either in command of the army or at the Prince's councils. His being a Catholic was already the subject of much unfavourable remark in the public journals, and seemed calculated to injure their prospects very seriously in England. There were even ante-revolution laws which made him ineligible as a councillor. They therefore presented a petition to the Prince, with one breath requesting him to reinstate Lord George Murray, and to dismiss Roman Catholics from his councils. Charles instantly complied with the first request, but, from the spirit of courtesy and gratitude, hesitated about the second. Some difficulty seemed likely to arise on that point, when the duke himself, learning what was the opinion of the army, put all to rights by informing the Prince that he was quite happy, for the sake of what was thought the good of the cause, to serve without a general's commission. Henceforth, Lord George Murray held the chief command in the army.

On the day after the reduction of Carlisle, Marshal Wade commenced a march from Newcastle; but hearing of the success of the insurgents, and being unable to cross the country on account of a great fall of snow, his excellency found it necessary to return to that city on the 22d.

More effectual means were now taken by the king to suppress what was generally styled 'the unnatural rebellion.' Before the Scottish army set foot on English ground, the mass of the British troops had landed at London from Flanders; and while the Prince was residing in Carlisle, an army of 10,000 troops, chiefly veteran and experienced, was rendezvoused in Stafford-shire to oppose him. It seemed scarcely possible that he should either elude or vanquish so strong a force; and even the High-landers themselves, with all their valour, real and adventitious, had little hope of doing so. In order, moreover, that the fate of the empire should not be perilled on such a chance, another army was raised for the protection of London, which the king was resolved to command in person. Charles himself was not intimidated by these great preparations, which he trusted to overcome by the vigour of his measures, and by the assistance which he expected in England. But the greater part of his council viewed the government proceedings with alarm.

At a council of war held a few days after the surrender of Carlisle, various movements were proposed and taken under consideration. It was proposed to march to Newcastle, and bring Wade's army to an action. It was proposed to march directly to London, by the Lancashire road, at the hazard of encountering the superior force mustered in Staffordshire. A third proposal urged an immediate retreat to Scotland, as there seemed no appearance of either a French invasion or an English insurrection. Charles declared his wish to march to London at all hazards, and desired Lord George Murray to give his opinion of the various proposals. Lord George spoke at some length, compared the advantages and disadvantages of each of the proposals, and concluded that, if his Royal Highness chose to make a trial of what could be done by a march to the southward, he was persuaded that his army, small as it was, would follow him. Charles instantly decided for the march.

Before proceeding, Charles sent Maclachlan of Maclachlan back to Scotland with a letter to Lord Strathallan, whom he had left at Perth commander-in-chief of his forces in Scotland, ordering him to march, with all the troops he might have collected, after the army into England. Meanwhile, he received some discouraging intelligence from the north. No sooner had he vacated Edinburgh, than it had returned under Whig domination; and even at Dundee and Perth, where he had considerable bodies of troops stationed, there had been outbreaks of popular feeling in behalf of the government.

Thirty baggage-wagons, in which were the tents for the army, had been left behind at Lockerby, through the eagerness of those in charge to get forward to the siege of Carlisle. These were seized on the 14th by a large party of people from Dumfries, and carried in triumph to that town. Charles sent Locheil to reclaim the property, or £2000 in lieu of it; but before either object could be accomplished, he had to recall the party to join the army on its march to the south. Owing to the want of tents and the severity of the weather (the 20th of November, old style, was in reality the 1st of December), it was necessary to arrange the march in such a way as to get the army accommodated in the towns along the road. It was determined that one portion of the army should march a day's journey ahead of the other, the latter always occupying at night the quarters which the former had vacated in the morning; but that, where the country would admit of it, there should be only half a day's march betwixt the two bodies.[1]

The army, on being mustered at Carlisle, was found to amount to about 4500, a full thousand having dropped away in the march from Edinburgh. Yet Charles had no doubt that it would soon be largely increased by the accession of his English friends. On the 21st, the first detachment of the army, consisting of five of the Low-country regiments, with Elcho's life-guards, under Lord George Murray, marched to Penrith. Next day, while these went forward to Kendal, the clan regiments, and the remainder of the horse, under the Prince in person, proceeded to Penrith, leaving 150 men as a garrison in Carlisle. The cannon followed the second division, under the care of the Duke of Perth's regiment.[2] In both divisions, each regiment had the van by turns. Thus they advanced by Shap, Kendal, Lancaster, and Garstang, to Preston, where the two divisions joined on the 27th. To encourage his men, Charles generally went on foot beside them. As he passed over the desolate tract between Penrith and Shap, he was so much overcome by fatigue and want of sleep, that he found it necessary to take hold of one of the clan Ogilvie by the shoulder-belt, to prevent him from falling; and he thus walked several miles half asleep.[3] As yet, they had observed nothing but marks of aversion and

---

[1] Maxwell's *Narrative*.   [2] Home's *History*.
[3] Information by a Scottish bishop, who has conversed with the proud Ogilvie whose shoulder was thus honoured.

suspicion amongst the English people. Their political object seemed to excite no sympathy; their uncouth dress, language, and habits spread terror before their march. It is credibly affirmed that many of the women hid their children at their approach, under an impression that they were cannibals, fond, in particular, of the flesh of infants.[1] Everywhere there was great surprise that these men, so far from acting like savage robbers, expressed a polite gratitude for what refreshments were given them. The Highlanders every day began their painful march before daybreak, with no provisions but what they carried in the shape of oatmeal, in a long bag by their sides, and which they never cooked, but merely mixed, before eating, with a canteen full of cold water—trusting for any variety in this simple cheer to the accident of a bullock killed for their use, or to the hospitality of their landlords at night. The English were amazed to find that men could, upon this fare, walk from twenty to thirty miles in a winter day, exposed to bitter cold and tempestuous weather, with what appeared to them imperfect clothing, or rather rags; and that, though generally housed some hours after sunset, they invariably rose very early to prosecute their march, taking advantage of the moonlight, which then shone in the mornings before daybreak.

At Preston, for the first time, did a slight gleam of approbation rest on the cause. The bells were rung at their

---

[1] 'The terror of the English was truly inconceivable, and in many cases they seemed bereft of their senses. One evening, as Mr Cameron of Locheil entered the lodgings assigned him, his landlady, an old woman, threw herself at his feet, and with uplifted hands, and tears in her eyes, supplicated him to take her life, but to spare her two little children. He asked her if she was in her senses, and told her to explain herself; when she answered, that *everybody said the Highlanders ate children, and made them their common food.* Mr Cameron having assured her that they would not injure either her or her little children, or any person whatever, she looked at him for some moments with an air of surprise, and then opened a press, calling out with a loud voice: "Come out, children; the gentleman will not eat you." The children immediately left the press, where she had concealed them, and threw themselves at his feet.'—*Johnstone's Memoirs*, p. 101.

In a letter from Derby, which made the round of the journals, the writer describes the ferocity and filthiness of the troop which was quartered upon him, with extravagant expressions of disgust. He allows, however, that he was amused a good deal to see them, before meat, take off their bonnets, assume a reverent air, and say grace, 'as if they had been Christians.'

entry, probably by the intervention of the Catholics, who abounded in the town. Some huzzas attended the reading of the proclamations, and a few recruits were obtained. Mr Townley, a Catholic gentleman, here joined the standard, being the first man of distinction who had done so in England. A council of war was held, at which the Prince, ever eager, like his ancestor Bruce, to 'go on,' renewed his assurances of English and French assistance, and thereby prevailed on the chiefs to continue their southward march. The clansmen had a superstitious dread, in consequence of the misfortunes of their party at Preston in 1715, that they would never get beyond this town: to dispel the illusion, Lord George Murray crossed the Ribble, and quartered a number of men on the other side.

On the 28th, the whole army left Preston, and, quartering for the night at Wigan, advanced on the ensuing day to Manchester. This town, now so remarkable for a reforming spirit, contained, in 1745, a larger proportion of the adherents of legitimacy than perhaps any other in England. Here, therefore, it might be expected that Charles would have a good reception, and obtain large reinforcements, if he was anywhere to be so fortunate in his southward march.

One Dickson, a sergeant enlisted into the Highland army from the prisoners taken at Prestonpans, having got more than a day's march ahead of the rest, entered Manchester on the morning of the 28th, attended by his mistress and a drummer. The adventure was entirely an idea of his own, and even contrary to the orders of his superior officer. Within an hour of his arrival he began to beat up for recruits. The populace did not at first interrupt him, conceiving that the whole army was near the town; but when they learned that no part of it could be expected till the evening, they surrounded him in a tumultuous manner, with the intention of taking him prisoner. Dickson presented his blunderbuss, which was charged with slugs, threatening to blow out the brains of those who first dared to lay hands on himself or the two who accompanied him; and by turning round continually, facing in all directions, and behaving like a lion, he soon enlarged the circle which a crowd of people had formed around him. Having continued for some time to manœuvre in this way, those of the inhabitants of Manchester who were attached to the house of Stuart took arms, and flew to the assistance of Dickson, to rescue him from the fury of the mob; so that he had soon 500 or 600 men to aid him, who dispersed the crowd in a very short time. He now triumphed in his turn, and, putting himself at the head of his followers, proudly paraded, undisturbed, the whole day with his drummer, enlisting all who offered themselves. The number of his levies has been differently stated. The Chevalier Johnstone says he obtained 180 recruits; but another authority says only thirty, 'to each of whom a white cockade was given, and a bounty of five guineas promised.'[1]

About nine o'clock that night, the vanguard, consisting of about 100 horsemen, arrived in Manchester; and next day the whole army came up. The Prince entered at two in the afternoon, walking in the midst of a select band of Highlanders; his dress a light tartan plaid, belted with a blue sash, a gray wig, and a blue velvet bonnet, topped by a rose of white ribbons, the badge of his house. He took up his quarters in a handsome house in Market Street, belonging to a gentleman named Dickenson—afterwards, from that circumstance, called 'The Palace,' and long after used as an inn.[2] A local writer has given a sufficiently minute account of what happened at Manchester on this and the following day. 'In the course of the day [the 29th], the public crier was sent round the town to require that all persons who had any duties to pay, or any public money in their hands, should pay the amount into the hands of Secretary Murray, at the palace, taking the receipt of this officer as their discharge. As evening approached, the bellman was again despatched to announce that there would that night be an illumination in honour of the arrival of the Prince. The illumination accordingly took place, bonfires were made, and the

---

[1] *Manchester Gazette*, January 19, 1828.
[2] The house has for some years been replaced by a new building.

bells rung joyfully; but the treasury was not much replenished, till a peremptory demand was made upon the inhabitants. Many of the communications at the headquarters were made with the intervention of a green silk curtain, which was suspended in the room of audience, and through which, it is said, even the master of the house, from prudential motives, communicated with his guest without seeing him. The borough-reeve, James Waller of Ridgefield, Esq., was made the reluctant organ for communicating the proclamations of the rebel army to the people; but the Rev. Mr Clayton celebrated, in strains of eloquence, the arrival of the Prince in the collegiate church, for which act of disaffection to the reigning sovereign he was afterwards degraded. A young clergyman, of the name of Coppoch, lately from the university, received the appointment of chaplain to the Prince.[1]

On the 30th, the whole of the rebel army, with the artillery and baggage, consisting of sixteen pieces of cannon, a number of covered wagons, and about one hundred laden horses, were assembled in the town and neighbourhood of Manchester. The recruiting service went on briskly, and from 200 to 300 young men, chiefly of the lower class, were dignified with the name of the Manchester regiment, of which Francis Townley, Esq., was appointed commander. Thomas Theodorus Deacon, Charles Deacon, and Robert Deacon, the sons of a nonjuring minister, catching the contagion of disloyalty, became officers in this corps; and George Fletcher, a linendraper in Salford; James Dawson, of St John's College, Cambridge, son of Mr Dawson of Manchester; and John Beswick, a linendraper in Manchester, were placed in the rank of captains. Thomas Chadwick, bred a tallow-chandler, was appointed lieutenant; and Thomas Syddall, the son of the peruke-maker who was executed for taking part in the rebellion of 1715, was appointed adjutant. Both officers and men wore white cockades, and the authority of the colonel was indicated by the addition of a tartan sash.

---

[1] Common rumour represented this young man as the rebel Bishop of Carlisle, as if the Prince had nominated him to that see. No such appointment ever took place.

The other officers had each a broadsword by his side, and a brace of pistols in his girdle. Before the Manchester regiment entered upon their campaign, they had the honour to be reviewed by their Prince the young Chevalier; and Colonel Townley, as if foreseeing their destiny, selected the churchyard for the field of review. The contributions levied upon the town amounted to £3000, and many of the horses within reach were put into requisition either to mount the cavalry or to convey the baggage. The conduct of the Highlanders was in some instances rapacious, wasteful, and offensive; but in general the troops conducted themselves with moderation, and the behaviour of their officers was conciliatory, and even courteous.[1]

An impression had prevailed that the Highland army might march into Wales, a country in which they could act with advantage as irregular troops, and where their cause was understood to have many friends. The bridges over the Mersey, on the way to Chester, had therefore been broken down, to impede their progress. This precaution proved unnecessary.

On the 1st of December, the army left Manchester in two divisions, one of which took the road to Stockport, the other that to Knottesford, thus shewing that London was their object. The bridges had been broken down in this direction also; the army had therefore to cross the Mersey by other means.[2] At Knottesford, a temporary bridge was made of the trunks of

---

[1] From a paper entitled 'The Highland Army in Manchester in 1745,' which appeared in the *Manchester Gazette*, January 19, 1828.

[2] While at Manchester, Charles published the following curious proclamation, for a copy of which I have been indebted to the kindness of an inhabitant of that town. The sneer at good old *Grandmother Wade*, who, according to the Jacobite punster, could not *wade* through the snow, will scarcely fail to be relished:

'TO THE INHABITANTS OF MANCHESTER.

'His Royal Highness being informed that several bridges have been pulled down in this country, he has given orders to repair them forthwith, particularly that at Crossford, which is to be done this night by his own troops, though his Royal Highness does not propose to make use of it for his own army, but believes it will be of service to the country; and if any forces that were with General Wade be coming this road, *they may have the benefit of it.*

'MANCHESTER, *Nov.* 30, 1745.'

poplar-trees, laid lengthwise, with planks across. The horse and artillery passed at Cheadleford. The Prince, with the other detachment, crossed at Stockport, having the water up to his middle. Here a romantic circumstance is said to have taken place. A few gentlemen of Cheshire had drawn up on the south bank of the river to welcome the Prince on his crossing the river, and among them was a Mrs Skyring, a lady in extreme old age. 'As a child, she had been lifted up in her mother's arms to view the happy landing at Dover of Charles II. Her father, an old cavalier, had afterwards to undergo not merely neglect, but oppression, from that thankless monarch; still, however, he and his wife continued devoted to the royal cause, and their daughter grew up as devoted as they. After the expulsion of the Stuarts, all her thoughts, her hopes, her prayers, were directed to another restoration. Ever afterwards she had, with rigid punctuality, laid aside one-half of her yearly income, to remit for the exiled family abroad; concealing only, what she said was of no importance to them, the name of the giver. She had now parted with her jewels, her plate, and every little article of value she possessed, the price of which, in a purse, she laid at the feet of Prince Charles, while, straining her dim eyes to gaze on his features, and pressing his hand to her shrivelled lips, she exclaimed with affectionate rapture, in the words of Simeon: " Lord, now lettest thou thy servant depart in peace !" It is added that she did not survive the shock, when, a few days afterwards, she was informed of the retreat. Such, even when misdirected in its object, or exaggerated in its force, was the old spirit of loyalty in England !'[1]

In the evening (December 1), the two divisions joined at Macclesfield, where Charles received intelligence that the Duke of Cumberland had taken command of the army mustered in Staffordshire,[2] which was now on its march, and quartered at

---

[1] *History of Great Britain*, by Lord Mahon, who states that he derived the anecdote from the late Lord Keith.

[2] The Duke of Cumberland left London on the 25th, and superseded Sir John Ligonier in the command of the army.

Lichfield, Coventry, Stafford, and Newcastle-under-Lyne. It was resolved that the Highland army should march to Derby. To deceive the enemy as to this design, Lord George Murray proceeded with a column to Congleton, on the straight road to Lichfield, while the rest advanced to Derby. It was calculated that the English commander, hearing of a body on the march towards his present position, would concentrate his forces and his attention there, and thus allow the main body of the Highland forces to pass beyond him uninterrupted. As Lord George advanced to Congleton, the Duke of Kingston, in command of a body of horse, retired from that town to Newcastle-under-Lyne. An advanced party of Lord George's men, under Colonel Ker, went forward at night (December 2) towards Newcastle-under-Lyne, whence the dragoons broke up with great precipitation, some of them escaping through windows. This party seized one Weir, a noted spy, who was only saved from hanging by the clemency of the Prince.[1] The effect of these movements, and of the false intelligence given out, was exactly what had been expected. The duke, at Stafford (December 2), received intelligence that a large body of the insurgents were at Congleton, and that the rest were to be there at night. He therefore proceeded that night *at eleven o'clock* to Stone, thus allowing the main body of the Highlanders to get past him. Early in the morning of the 3d, having effected his design, Lord George left Congleton, and passing through Leek, reached Ashbourne in the evening.

Some hours after he had passed Leek, the Prince, with the main body of the army, arrived there, being on the straight road to Derby. At midnight, the latter party set out from Leek, and reached Ashbourne early in the morning, in order that any sudden attack from the Duke of Cumberland might find them all together. Early on the 4th, a portion of the army proceeded to Derby, which they entered at eleven in the forenoon. About three, Lord Elcho came in with the life-guards and some of the

---

[1] Maxwell of Kirkconnel.

principal officers on horseback, 'making a very respectable appearance.' The main body of the army continued to enter in small detachments during all the latter part of the day (to convey, as was supposed, an impression of the greatness of their numbers), with bagpipes playing and colours unfurled;[1] and in the evening the Prince arrived on foot, and took up his quarters in the house of the Earl of Exeter. During the day the bells were rung, and bonfires lighted, and there was an illumination (how far voluntary is not stated) at night. The magistrates were ordered to attend the proclamations in their official gowns; but when it was known that they had sent these away beforehand, their attendance was excused, and the proclamations were made by the common crier.

Charles was now within 127 miles—to him less than a week's march—of the capital of England. In consequence of the dexterous manœuvre of Lord George Murray, he could have advanced thither without fighting with the Duke of Cumberland, who was, on the 4th, returning from Stone to Stafford, where he was nine miles farther from London than the Chevalier, whom he could have had no hope of overtaking with infantry, supposing that Charles had been pleased to proceed immediately.[2] Two armies in succession had thus been eluded by the Highlanders—that of Wade, in consequence of the weather or the old marshal's inactivity,[3] and that of Cumberland, through the ingenuity of their own leaders. There remained yet a third army at Finchley Common; but it was not formidable in character or numbers, and probably might have failed to meet the clans in battle, if they had marched still onward. No invading band, since the days of the Saxon kings, had ever been allowed to advance so far and so threateningly into England; for though the Duke of Hamilton, in 1648, had got to Uttoxeter,

---

[1] Boyse, 104. Their colours were mostly white, with red crosses.

[2] The duke employed the 5th in marching to Lichfield, where he would have had some chance of intercepting the Highlanders, who had spent that day at Derby.

[3] Wade's army had now advanced from Newcastle into Yorkshire. It was at Wetherby on the 4th, and on the 5th was marching to Doncaster, the commander having then heard of the advance of the Highlanders into Derbyshire.

it was only with a small portion of an army broken to pieces a good way farther north.[1]

Hitherto the English people had entertained a very inadequate idea of the insurrection. If we are to judge from the tenor of the public journals, where the Highland army is invariably spoken of with contempt, both on physical and moral grounds, the English generally had not the most faint apprehension of the bold and generous spirit of self-devotion which prompted these men to leave their homes, and thus expose themselves not only to the perils of war, but the pains of treason, for the sake of a cause which, however mistakenly, they conceived to be that of justice and patriotism. The whole expedition of the Chevalier and his attendant bands seems to have been regarded as only an odd piece of mob-procedure, which a proper exertion of regular military force would put down. There even seems to have been some disposition to look upon it as a novel kind of show. The poet Gray writes from Cambridge : ' Here we had no more sense of danger than if it were the battle of Cannæ. I heard three sensible middle-aged men, when the Scotch were said to be at Stamford, and actually were at Derby, talking of hiring a chaise to go to Caxton, a place on the high-road [on the high-road, be it recollected, from Derby to London, from which it is only distant fifty miles], to see the Pretender and the Highlanders as they passed.' Much of the apprehension was no doubt owing to a line of policy assumed by the government party. It was thought equivalent to a profession of Jacobitism to speak in respectful terms of the Chevalier, his followers, or the strength of his army. This of course was a sword that cut two ways, for while it tended to keep down popular feeling in behalf of Charles, it also

[1] Swarkeston Bridge, six miles beyond Derby, on the road to London, was, in reality, the extreme point of this singular invasion, because the insurgents posted an advanced guard there, which kept possession of the pass till the retreat was determined on. No former host from Scotland penetrated beyond the Tees, or overran more than the frontier counties ; but this last, and, it may be added, *least*, of all the armies Scotland ever sent against the Southron, had thus reached the Trent, traversed five counties in succession, and insulted the very centre of England.

favoured a feeling of security in the highest degree useful to him.

Now, however, the metropolis at least became strongly impressed with a sense of danger. When intelligence reached it that the Highlanders were getting past the Duke of Cumberland's army, and had reached Derby, consternation took possession of the inhabitants. Fielding, in his *True Patriot*, describes the degree of terror which prevailed as beyond all belief. The Chevalier Johnstone, speaking from information which he procured a few months afterwards on the spot, says that the shops were shut, many people fled to the country, taking with them their most precious effects, and the Bank only escaped insolvency by paying in sixpences to persons in its confidence, who, going out at one door, and returning at another, received the same money over and over again, and thus kept back the *bonâ fide* holders of notes. The ministers were perplexed. It has been alleged that the Duke of Newcastle, then one of the secretaries of state, shut himself up in his house for a day, deliberating whether he should not at once declare for the Stuarts. King George was said to have ordered his yachts, in which he had embarked his most valuable effects, to remain at the Tower stairs, in readiness to sail at a moment's warning. Perhaps some of these allegations were mere popular rumour, but they shew at least a degree of fear which must have been thought sufficient to render them credible. And, in truth, the danger, if danger it is to be called, was by no means inconsiderable, for not only was the Highland army within a few days' march, with little to oppose its progress, but there was a party in the city, including, it now appears, one of the aldermen (a Mr Heathcote), who were expected to make a public appearance in the same cause, and a French army was expected to land on the coast. The day of all this consternation was afterwards remembered under the expressive appellation of *Black Friday*.

CHAPTER XVI.

RETREAT TO SCOTLAND.

'The games are done, and Cæsar is returning.'
Julius Cæsar.

INTELLIGENCE reached the Prince at Derby of the arrival of Lord John Drummond, brother of the Duke of Perth, at Montrose with a body of French troops. A treaty had been entered into at Fontainebleau, on the 23d of October, between the Marquis d'Argenson on the part of Louis XV., and Colonel O'Brien on the part of Charles, Prince Regent of Scotland, agreeing that there should be friendship and alliance between the parties; that the king should aid the Prince Regent in every practicable way against their common enemy the Elector of Hanover; and that the king should furnish the Prince with a body of troops from his Irish regiments, along with other troops, 'to defend the provinces which had submitted, or should submit, to the regency, to attack the common enemy, and to follow every movement which should be judged useful or necessary.'[1] In consequence of this agreement, Lord John Drummond, who was a subject of France, embarked 1000 men about the middle of November at Dunkirk, together with a considerable quantity of stores and ammunition. Excepting a few transports taken by English cruisers, containing one or two hundred of the men, this little armament arrived in good order at Montrose near the end of November; and Drummond, on the 2d of December, published the following manifesto: 'We, Lord John Drummond, commander-in-chief of his most Christian Majesty's forces in Scotland, do hereby declare that we are come to this kingdom with written orders to make war against

---

[1] The whole treaty is printed from the Stuart Papers in the Appendix to Browne's *History of the Highlands.*

M

the king of England, Elector of Hanover, and his adherents; and that the positive orders we have from his most Christian Majesty are, to attack all his enemies in this kingdom, whom he has declared to be those who will not immediately join and assist, as far as will lie in their power, the Prince of Wales, Regent in Scotland, &c., and his ally; and whom he is resolved, with the concurrence of the king of Spain, to support in taking possession of Scotland, England, and Ireland, if necessary, at the expense of all the men and money he is master of; to which three kingdoms the family of Stuart have so just and indisputable a title. And his most Christian Majesty's positive orders are, that his enemies should be used in this kingdom in proportion to the harm they do or intend to his Royal Highness's cause.' Lord John, according to instructions he had received, lost no time in sending a messenger to Count Nassau, commander of the Dutch auxiliaries called over into England, requiring him to observe a neutrality, agreeably to the capitulations of Tournay and Dendermonde, by which they had agreed for a certain time not to fight against the king of France and his allies.

Immediately after the departure of Lord John Drummond from France, the ministers made serious preparations for a much larger armament, which they designed to have landed on the south coast of England. Ten thousand troops were mustered for this purpose, and Prince Henry Stuart, Charles's younger brother, was brought to Paris to accompany the expedition. Every preparation had been made; the king had taken leave of the young Prince, telling him that he would ' dine quietly in London on the 9th of January ' (meaning the 29th of December, old style); and the plan was only abandoned when intelligence came of the retreat of the Highland army from Derby.[1] Had that army gone on, the French invasion would have taken place in time to support Charles in London, supposing that he had

[1] The concentration of the English fleet to oppose the intended invasion, allowed the French privateers to be unusually active. In the months of November and December, these marauders were calculated to have taken a hundred and sixty British vessels, valued at £660,000.

seized the government; and the Stuart dynasty must have been reinstated on the throne.

The morning of the 5th saw the Prince at Derby, eager to go forward on his march at all hazards, but hopeful that succours from France, and a rising of his English friends, would make it less dangerous than it appeared. The men in general were in high spirits, and very anxious to come to an engagement with the Duke of Cumberland's army. The common expectation was, that a battle was about to take place; and with this view there was a general sharpening of broadswords at the cutlers' shops, and some took the sacrament in the churches. Little was it thought that their leaders were about to resolve upon quite a contrary movement.

At a council of war held on the morning of the 5th, Lord George Murray and the other members gave it as their unanimous opinion that the army ought to return to Scotland. Lord George pointed out that they were about to be environed by three armies, amounting collectively to about 30,000 men, while their own forces were not above 5000, if so many. Supposing an unsuccessful engagement with any of those armies, it could not be expected that one man would escape, for the militia would beset every road. The Prince, if not slain in the battle, must fall into the enemy's hands. The whole world would blame them as fools for running into such a risk. Charles answered that he regarded not his own danger. He 'pressed with all the force of argument to go forward. He did not doubt,' he said, 'that the justice of his cause would prevail. He was hopeful there might be a defection in the enemy's army, and that many would declare for him. He was so very bent on putting all to the risk, that the Duke of Perth was for it, since his Royal Highness was. At last he proposed going to Wales, instead of returning to Carlisle; but every other officer declared his opinion for a retreat.' These are nearly the words of Lord George Murray;[1] we are elsewhere told that the Prince

---

[1] Narrative, *Jacobite Memoirs*.

condescended to use entreaties to induce his adherents to alter their resolution. 'Rather than go back,' he said, 'I could wish to be twenty feet underground!'[1] His chagrin, when he found his councillors obdurate, was beyond all bounds. The council broke up, in the understanding that the retreat was to commence next morning, Lord George volunteering to take the post of honour in the rear, provided only that he should not be troubled with the baggage.

In the course of the day Charles spoke of the intended movement to various officers, in such terms, that a few, particularly Secretary Murray and Sir Thomas Sheridan (from a desire of ingratiating themselves with him, as Lord George Murray suspected), expressed their regret for the resolution, saying that they had approved of it in the morning only from an idea that the soldiers would not go heartily into a battle when they knew that their officers were otherwise inclined. In the evening, when the whole of the officers were once more together, and were given to understand what these gentlemen had said, they told the Prince 'that they valued their lives as little as brave men ought to do, and if he inclined to go forward, they would do their duty to the last; but they desired that those who had advised his Royal Highness to march forward would sign their opinion, which would be a satisfaction to them.'[2] Murray and Sheridan were not disposed to do this, and the retreat was therefore determined upon.

During the earlier part of the march of the Prince into England, the leading Jacobites of that country had kept back, under an impression that, with so small a force, he was not likely to produce a general mustering of the party in his favour. Charles had therefore little or no communication of any kind with the party during his march.[3] Yet it appears that the very boldness of his onward movement, especially taken in connection with the expected descent from France, at length disposed

---

[1] Memoirs of Captain Daniel, a volunteer, MS , *apud* Lord Mahon's *History*.

[2] Lord George Murray's Narrative, *Jacobite Memoirs*.

[3] Examination of Secretary Murray, Appendix to Lord Mahon's *History*.

them to come out; and many were just on the point of declaring themselves, and marching to join his army, when the retreat from Derby was determined on. A Mr Barry arrived in Derby two days after the Prince left it, with a message from Sir Watkin William Wynne and Lord Barrymore, to assure him, in the name of many friends of the cause, that they were ready to join him in what manner he pleased, either in the capital, or every one to rise in his own county.[1] I have likewise been assured that many of the Welsh gentry had actually left their homes, and were on their way to join Charles, when intelligence of his retreat at once sent them all back peaceably, convinced that it was now too late to contribute their assistance. These men, from the power they had over their tenantry, could have added materially to his military force.[2] In fact, from all that appears, we must conclude that the insurgents had a very considerable chance of success from an onward movement—also, no doubt, a chance of destruction, and yet not worse than what ultimately befell many of them—while a retreat broke in a moment the spell which their gallantry had conjured up, and gave the enemy a great advantage over them.

The resolution of the council not being made known that night to the army at large, the common men, and many of the officers, on commencing their march next morning before daybreak, thought they were going to fight the Duke of Cumberland, and displayed the utmost cheerfulness and alacrity. But as soon as daylight allowed them to see the surrounding objects, and they found, from marks they had taken of the road, that they were retracing their steps, nothing was to be heard throughout the army but expressions of rage and lamentation. 'If we had been beaten,' says the Chevalier Johnstone, 'our grief could not have been greater.'

---

[1] The Prince mentions this in a letter to his father, February 12, 1747. Stuart Papers; Lord Mahon's *History*.

[2] My informant adds, that the Jacobite squires of Wales used afterwards, in their cups, to boast how far each had travelled on his way to join the Chevalier; a man who had gone fifty miles looking upon himself as twice as good a partisan as one who had gone only five-and-twenty; and so on.

The vexation of the army on this account was nothing to the bitter disappointment of its unhappy leader. *Vestigia nulla retrorsum* had been his motto from the beginning; and so long as he was going forward, no danger, and far less any privation or fatigue, had given him the least concern. But now, when at length compelled to turn back from the glittering prize which had almost been within his grasp, he lost all his former spirit, and, from being the leader of his hardy bands, became in appearance, as he was in reality, their reluctant follower. In the march forward, he had always been first up in the morning, had the men in motion before break of day, and generally walked, in dress and arms similar to their own, at the head of their body; but now, all his alacrity gone, and with hopes nearly blighted, he permitted the whole army to march before him (except a rearguard, whom he often compelled to wait for him a long time); and on coming out of his lodgings, dejectedly mounted a horse, and then rode on, without intercourse with his men, to the quarters assigned for him in the van.

The retreat of the army was concerted with so much secrecy, and conducted with so much skill, that it was two days' march ahead of the royal forces ere the Duke of Cumberland could make himself certain of the fact, or take measures for a pursuit. When he at length ascertained that they were retiring, he changed the defensive system which he had hitherto pursued for one of active annoyance. Putting himself at the head of his dragoons, and having mounted 1000 foot on horses provided by the gentlemen of Staffordshire, he started from Meriden Common, a position he had taken near Coventry, and, passing by very bad roads through Uttoxeter and Cheadle, came to Macclesfield on the evening of the 10th, full two days after the insurgents had reached the same point. He here received intelligence that, after retreating with wonderful expedition through Ashbourne, Leek, and Macclesfield, the enemy had just that morning left Manchester, and set forward to Wigan.

The Highlanders managed their retreat in such a manner as to unite expedition with perfect coolness, and never to allow the enemy to obtain a single advantage. Though on foot, and pursued by cavalry, they kept distinctly ahead of all danger or annoyance for twelve days, two of which they had spent in undisturbed rest at Preston and Lancaster.[1] The troops of the duke were reinforced on the 12th by a body of horse, which General Wade, now with the army in the centre of Yorkshire, sent with haste over Blackstone Edge to intercept the retiring host, but who only reached Preston after it had been several hours evacuated, and in time to join the pursuing force of the Duke of Cumberland. After a halt of one day, occasioned by the false alarm of an invasion on the southern coast, the pursuing army, amounting to 3000 or 4000 horse, continued their course from Preston, through roads which had been rendered almost impassable, partly by the weather, and partly by the exertions of men. Orders had been communicated by the duke to the country-people to break down bridges, destroy the roads, and use all means in their power to retard the insurgent army.[2] But while the hardy mountaineers found little inconvenience from either storm in the air or ruts in the ground, these very

1 At Wigan, some fanatic, intending to shoot the Prince, fired at O'Sullivan by mistake. Charles would not allow any harm to be done to the assassin. Captain Daniel, who mentions this fact, with a bitter comment on what he thought such injudicious clemency, also complains respecting a woman and her son who were brought before Charles, accused of murdering one of his volunteers at Manchester, and who confessed their crime, but whom he would not allow to be punished.

2 'The news of the retreat of the invading army had not reached Kendal, when, on the market-day, the Duke of Perth drove rapidly up the street, accompanied by an escort of horse. The town and country people instantly took it into their heads that the rebels had been defeated, and at once resolved on capturing the duke, in whose defence the escort fired on the populace, many of whom had armed themselves with guns. His Grace, putting his head out of the carriage window, with much humanity commanded his men to "fire high, it being useless to fire on a mob." This thoughtless procedure was not unattended with loss of life, and gave rise to a circumstance involved in future mystery. The duke's servant was knocked off his horse, upon which a countryman instantly leaped, and rode off. This was done in the heat of the rencontre, and no one had taken notice who the man was, nor was he ever discovered : on the horse was a portmanteau, containing a considerable sum of money. The servant died of his injuries, and was buried, along with some others of his countrymen, in that part of the churchyard next the river ; a flat stone, with a suitable inscription, was laid down, commemorative of their fate.'—*Communication in the Edinburgh Advertiser* (*newspaper*), *Nov.* 23, 1827. See also *Scots Magazine*, 1745, p. 577.

The duke was on this occasion endeavouring to reach Scotland with orders, preparatory to the arrival of the army. The resistance he met with at Kendal shewed that he could not detach himself far from the army with safety, and he therefore proceeded no farther.

circumstances served materially to impede the English dragoons, and to place the two armies upon what might be considered a more equal footing than they could otherwise have been.

The Prince, with the main body of his troops, was at Penrith on the evening of the 17th; but his rearguard, under the command of Lord George Murray, owing to the breaking down of some ammunition wagons, was this night with great difficulty brought only to Shap. The delay thus occasioned allowed the lightest of the duke's horse to overtake the rear of the retiring army. Early in the morning of the 18th, soon after it had commenced its march from Shap, some of the English chasseurs were seen hovering on the adjoining heights; and about mid-day, as the Highlanders were approaching the enclosures around Clifton Hall, a body of light horse seemed to be forming for attack upon an eminence a little way in front. Against these, who were merely volunteer militia of the district, Lord George Murray ordered the Glengarry clan to go forward; but, without waiting for an engagement, they immediately retreated.

The rearguard consisted of John Roy Stuart's regiment of 200 men, of the Glengarry clan, and a few companies which attended the ammunition wagons; but it was reinforced on the present occasion by the Stuarts of Appin and Cluny Macpherson's regiment, being about 1000 men in all. Lord George, under a deep sense of the importance of his trust, was the last man in the line. Anxious to check the pursuit, he despatched Stuart forward to Penrith, requesting that 1000 men might be sent to him from the main body there stationed. With this force he intended to have gained the flank of the duke's army, now approaching obliquely from the left, and to have attacked them under favour of the approaching night. But Charles returned Stuart with an order, requiring him to march with all speed forward to Penrith, without taking any offensive measures against the duke. This order, proceeding upon a general view of what was proper, would have been attended, as Lord George well perceived, with injurious effects; for the men could not have retired in the face of the enemy without being much exposed. He therefore desired Colonel Stuart not to mention the Prince's wishes to any one; and proceeded to make arrangements for giving the enemy the necessary check. At the bridge, a little to the south of the village of Clifton, where the road passed between a high stone-wall surrounding Lord Lonsdale's park and the hedge enclosures of Clifton Hall, he placed the Glengarry regiment and John Roy Stuart's along the wall—the latter being nearest the village—and the Appin and Macpherson regiments within the opposite enclosures. Soon after sunset, the main body of the duke's army, composed exclusively of cavalry, and said to be about 4000 in number, came up and formed in two lines on the moor about a mile behind.

In order to deceive the enemy as to his numbers, Lord George made some men pass behind the hedges with the colours, and returning secretly, again pass, displaying the colours once more, and this several times over. Full of anxiety about his critical situation, he passed backwards and forwards amongst the men, encouraging them to behave with firmness. He then placed himself at the head of the Macphersons, with Cluny by his side. In a narrative by Cluny,[1] it is stated that he did not ultimately give orders for action till he had asked the opinion of the chief, and found him willing to make the attack, if ordered. Daylight passed away, succeeded by a dark and cloudy night, with occasional bursts of moonlight. By one of these transient gleams, Lord George saw a body of men—dismounted dragoons, or infantry who had resumed their proper mode of warfare—coming forward upon the enclosures beyond the road. He ordered the two regiments near him to advance, in doing which they received a fire from the enemy. At this Lord George exclaimed: 'Claymore!' an ordinary war-cry among the Highlanders, and rushed on sword in hand. The whole left wing, then making a direct and spirited attack, forced the dismounted dragoons back to their main body with considerable slaughter, and shouted to let the right wing know

[1] Of which an extract is given by Scott as a note to a chapter of *Waverley*, in the edition of 1829.

of their success.   They then retired in order to their original
position; while the Macdonalds, with equal intrepidity, repulsed
the dragoons opposite to their body.   A check having thus
been given to the pursuing army, Lord George drew off his men
towards Penrith, where they rested and refreshed themselves.[1]
The English, in their accounts of this fight, allow that they had
forty private men killed and wounded, and four officers wounded;
they insinuate that the Highland army suffered a much greater
loss; but a letter by a person present speaks of only five found
dead on the field; while the gazette published by the Prince
at Glasgow admits the loss of twelve men, who had gone too
far forward on the moor, and who might have been taken
prisoners.   At an earlier period of the day, Lord George Murray
had taken the Duke of Cumberland's footman, whom the Prince
instantly sent back to his master.   A Mr Hamilton, an officer
in the Prince's hussars, had been taken, from want of caution,
before the skirmish by a straggling party.[2]

The whole of the Highland army spent the night of the 19th
of December at Carlisle, where it was thought necessary, on
evacuating the town next morning, to leave a garrison, consisting
of the Manchester regiment, some men from the Lowland
regiments, and a few French and Irish; in all 300.[3]   This small
garrison, animated with a greater share of courage and fidelity
to the cause they had embraced than of prudence or fore-
sight, resolved obstinately to defend the city, and took every

[1] A very minute account of the affair at Clifton is given by Lord George himself.   See
Jacobite Memoirs, 64—72.

[2] 'An inhabitant of the village of Clifton, named Thomas Savage, was very serviceable
in giving the English army timely notice of the disposition of the insurgents, who had hired
all the lodges and outhouses.   After the action, he joyfully entertained the Dukes of Cumberland, Richmond, and Kingston, besides 100 horse, in his own house.'—*Boyse*, 127.
'. . . . At the skirmish on Clifton Moor, General Honeywood fell covered with wounds.
On the retreat of the enemy, the general was carried in a mangled condition to Appleby,
where, to the surprise of all, he recovered.   He was afterwards so much respected there,
from the foregoing circumstances, and became so attached to the place, that he was elected
one of their members, and continued so to the day of his death.   Having a vote for the
county, it was there I had the honour of knowing him, of being shewn by him the scars of
those mouthed wounds he had received, and of hearing from himself the foregoing particulars.'—*Jackson's History of the Scottish Stage*, p. 80.

[3] He also left ten out of his thirteen pieces of cannon.

measure for that purpose which the time and season would allow.

Charles left Carlisle on the morning of the 20th, after having publicly thanked the garrison for their devoted loyalty, and promised to relieve them as soon as he could. The men, drawn up to hear his address, saw him depart with acclamations, and gazing from the walls, soon beheld their comrades draw near the beloved land to which *they* were never to return. The army reached the Esk, which forms the boundary of the two kingdoms, about two o'clock in the afternoon. The river, usually shallow, was swollen, by an incessant rain of several days, to the depth of four feet. Yet it was resolved to cross immediately, lest a continuation of the rain during the night should render the passage totally impracticable. A skilful arrangement was made, which almost obviated the dangers of the flood. The cavalry were stationed in the river, a few paces above the ford, to break the force of the current; and the infantry formed themselves in ranks of ten or twelve abreast, with their arms locked in such a manner as to support one another against the rapidity of the river, leaving sufficient intervals between the successive lines for the water to flow through. The whole passed over in perfect safety. Cavalry were placed farther down the river, to pick up all who might be carried away by the violence of the stream. None were lost, except a few girls. The transit of the river occupied an hour, during which, from the close numbers of the men, it appeared to be crossed by a paved street of heads and shoulders. When they got to the other side, and began to dry themselves at the fires lighted upon the bank for that purpose, they were overjoyed at once more finding their feet upon their native ground, and for a moment forgot the chagrin which had attended their retreat, with all depressing anticipations of the future.

An expedition was thus completed which, for boldness and address, is entitled to rank high amongst the most celebrated in ancient and modern times. It lasted six weeks, and was directed through a country decidedly hostile to the adventurers; it was done in the face of two armies, each capable of utterly annihilating it; and the weather was such as to add a thousand personal miseries to the general evils of the campaign. Yet such was the success which will sometimes attend the most desperate case, if conducted with resolution, that from the moment the inimical country was entered, to that in which it was abandoned, only forty men were lost, out of nearly 5000, by sickness, marauding, or the sword of the enemy. A magnanimity was preserved even in retreat beyond that of ordinary soldiers; and instead of flying in wild disorder, a prey to their pursuers, these desultory bands had turned against and smitten the superior army of their enemy, with a vigour which effectually checked it. They had carried the standard of Glenfinnin a hundred and fifty miles into a country full of foes; and now they brought it back unscathed, through the accumulated dangers of storm and war.

In their descent upon England, when, in the height of their expectations, private rapine had few charms, the Highlanders conducted themselves with tolerable propriety; and as the public money was everywhere raised, they had been able to pay for food with some degree of regularity. But in their retreat, when their pay was more precarious, private property was less respected, though not invaded or injured to nearly so great an extent as might have been expected.

The unhappy garrison of Carlisle saw their fortifications invested by the whole force of the Duke of Cumberland on the very day following the departure of their fellow-soldiers. They fired upon all who came within reach of their guns, and shewed an intention of holding out to the last extremity. But the duke, having procured cannon from Whitehaven, erected a battery on the 28th, and began to play upon the crazy walls of the town and castle. On the morning of the 30th a white flag appeared upon the walls, and the governor signified a wish to enter into a capitulation. The cannon then ceased, and a message was sent by Governor Hamilton to the duke, desiring to know what terms he would be pleased to give them. His royal highness replied that the only terms he would or could grant were, 'that they should not be put to the sword, but reserved for his majesty's pleasure.' These terms were accepted, and the royal army immediately took possession of the city and castle, placing all the garrison under a strong guard in the cathedral. The fate meted out to them will be described in the sequel.

It was now judged proper that, as the more immediate danger from the Highland army was past, the Duke of Cumberland should return to London, in order to be of service in repelling the invasion which was still dreaded from France on the south coast. He accordingly proceeded thither, leaving his troops under the command of General Wade and Lieutenant-general Hawley, the last of whom was ordered to conduct a portion of the army into Scotland, while Wade remained at Newcastle.

The Chevalier meanwhile pursued his march towards the north. On crossing the Esk, he divided his army into two parties, one of which went by Ecclefechan and Moffat, with Lord George Murray and Lords Ogilvie and Nairn. He himself led the other, with the Duke of Perth, Lords Elcho and Pitsligo, Locheil, Clanranald, Glengarry, and Keppoch. He lodged the first night at Annan. Next day, Lord Elcho advanced with 400 or 500 men to take possession of Dumfries. The rest went forward with himself on the day following. Dumfries had reason, on this occasion, for alarm, on account of the seizure of the baggage-wagons at Lockerby. The clans marched into it as into a town where they expected resistance, or at least no kindly reception; and on an idiot being observed with a gun in his hand behind a grave-stone in the churchyard, which they supposed he was about to fire upon them, it was with the greatest difficulty that the poor creature's life was spared.[1] The Prince took up his lodging in what was then the best house in the town, being that which is now the Commercial Inn, near the centre of the market-place. He had ordered the citizens to contribute the sum of £2000 for his use, with 1000 pair of shoes; some of his men adding, that they might consider it well

[1] Tradition at Dumfries.

that their town was not laid in ashes. So lately as 1836, an aged female lived in Edinburgh who recollected the occupation of Dumfries by the Highland army, being then seventeen years of age.[1] She lived opposite to the Prince's lodging, and frequently saw him. In her father's house several of the men were quartered, and it was her recollection that they greatly lamented the course which they had taken, and feared the issue of the expedition. The proprietor of the house occupied by the Prince was Mr Richard Lowthian, a nonjuror, and proprietor of Staffold Hall, in Cumberland. Though well affected to the Prince's cause, he judged it prudent not to come into his presence, and yet neither did he wish to offend him by the appearance of deliberately going out of his way. The expedient he adopted in this dilemma was one highly characteristic of the time—he got himself filled so extremely drunk, that his being kept back from the company of his guest was only a matter of decency. His wife, who could not well be taxed with treason, did the honours of the house without scruple ; and some other Jacobite ladies, particularly those of the attainted house of Carnwath,[2] came forward to grace his court. When the author was at Dumfries in 1838, he saw, in the possession of a private family, one of a set of table napkins, of the most beautiful damask, resembling the finest satin, which the ladies Dalzell of Carnwath had taken to grace the table of the Prince,[3] and which they had kept ever after with the care due to the most precious relics. The drawing-room in which Charles received company is a very handsome one, panelled all round with Corinthian pilasters, the capitals of which are touched with dim gold. He was sitting here at supper with his officers and other friends, when he was told that a messenger had arrived with intelligence respecting the enemy. One M'Ghie, a painter in Dumfries, and a friend of the insurgents, had been imposed upon at Annan with the

---

[1] Widow Blake was the name of this remarkable person, who died at fully the age of 108. She had been the wife of a dragoon in the reign of George II.

[2] Dalzell, Earl of Carnwath, attainted in 1716 ; restored in 1826, in the person of Robert Alexander Dalzell.

[3] It bore the initials J. D., and the date 1704.

false news that the Duke of Cumberland had already taken Carlisle, and was advancing to Dumfries. Charles received this intelligence in another room, and soon after returned to his friends with a countenance manifestly dejected. The consequence was, that he hurriedly left the town next day, with only £1100 of the £2000, but carrying the provost and another gentleman as security for the payment of the remainder. Mrs Lowthian received from him, as a token of regard, a pair of leather gloves, so extremely fine, that they could be drawn through her ring. These, as well as the bed he had slept on, were carefully preserved by the family, and are still in existence.[1]

On the morning of the 23d the Highland army directed its march up Nithsdale, and the Chevalier spent the night at Drumlanrig, the seat of the Duke of Queensberry. He occupied the state-bed, while a great number of his men lay upon straw in the great gallery. Before departing next day, it must be regretted that the Highlanders took that opportunity of expressing their love of King James by slashing with their swords a series of portraits representing King William, Queen Mary, and Queen Anne, which hung in the grand staircase—a present from the last of these sovereigns to James, Duke of Queensberry, in consideration of his services at the Union.

From Drumlanrig, Charles proceeded through the wild pass of Dalveen into Clydesdale, designing to march upon Glasgow, though still endeavouring to conceal his intentions from the members of government at Edinburgh. He spent the night in Douglas Castle, the residence of the Duke of Douglas. He next day proceeded along the uplands of Clydesdale towards the western capital, and halted at Hamilton, where he lodged in the palace of the Duke of Hamilton. He spent the next day in hunting through the princely parks attached to that house, shooting two pheasants, two partridges, and a deer. While there is ample evidence, from the account-book of his master-of-household,[2] that he was generally careful, during his march, to

[1] Information from Mr Lowthian Ross of Staffold Hall, and others.
[2] See *Jacobite Memoirs*.

make remuneration for his lodging and provision, it would
appear that at Drumlanrig and Douglas, the proprietors of
which were noted enemies of his family, he exacted free quarters.
At Hamilton, the master of which was understood to be well
affected, there were some small payments; but tradition avers
that both there and at Douglas the custom of giving vails to the
servants was neglected.

It was with great difficulty that, in this last day's march, his
men were prevented from sacking and burning the village of
Lesmahago.   During the absence of the army in England, the
people of this place, whose ancestors had distinguished themselves in resisting the house of Stuart when in power, committed
an act of hostility to Charles's cause, which was calculated to
excite the indignation of the whole army to no common degree.
The circumstances, as gathered from tradition, were as follow :
The youthful and gallant Kinlochmoidart, in a journey from the
Highlands, on his return from making a last appeal to Macleod
and Macdonald of Sleat, passed through Lesmahago on his way
to England, and was recognised by a young student of divinity,
named Linning, whose religious prepossessions led him to
regard the Prince's adherents with no friendly eye.   As the
insurgent gentleman was attended by only a single servant, this
zealot conceived a design of waylaying and capturing him, which
he immediately proceeded to put in execution.   Taking to
himself arms, and having roused the country-people, he set out
after the two travellers by a path which he knew would enable
him to intercept them as they proceeded along the road.   He
came up with them upon a waste called Brokencross Moor,
within two miles of the village, and shewing his arms, commanded them to surrender in the name of King George.
Kinlochmoidart's servant, on first seeing the rabble at a distance,
with their old guns and pitchforks, unslung his piece, and proposed to arrest their progress by a well-directed brace of bullets.
But the generous youth resolved rather to surrender at discretion,
than thus occasion an unnecessary effusion of blood.   He
accordingly gave himself up to the daring probationer, who

immediately conducted him, under a strong guard, to Edinburgh Castle, from which he was only removed some months afterwards to the shambles of Carlisle.[1]

The city of Glasgow, upon which Charles was now in full march, had much greater reason than Dumfries, or even Lesmahago, to expect severe treatment from the insurgents; while its wealth gave additional cause for alarm, without in the least degree supplying better means of defence. This city, newly sprung into importance, had never required nor received the means of defence, but was now lying, with its wide-spread modern streets and well-stored warehouses, fully exposed to the license of the invaders. It had distinguished itself, ever since the expulsion of the house of Stuart, by its attachment to the new government; and, since the Highlanders entered England, had, with gratuitous loyalty, raised a regiment of 1200 men, to aid in suppressing the insurrection. Obnoxious by its principles, and affording such prospects of easy and ample plunder, it was eagerly approached by the predatory bands of the Chevalier. By one of their most rapid marches, the first body entered Glasgow on Christmas-day, and on the following the Prince came up with the rest of the army. It has been calculated that, from their leaving Edinburgh, they had marched about 580 miles in fifty-six days, many of these being days of rest.

The necessities of the army are described as having been at this time greater than at any other period of the campaign. It was now two months since they had left the land of tartan; their clothes were of course in a dilapidated condition. The length and precipitancy of their late march had destroyed their brogues; and many of them were not only barefooted, but barelegged. Their hair hung wildly over their eyes; their beards were overgrown; and the exposed parts of their limbs were, in the language of Dougal Graham, tanned red with the weather. Altogether, they had a wayworn, savage appearance, and looked rather like a band of outlandish vagrants than a body of efficient

---

[1] Kinlochmoidart's captor was afterwards rewarded by government with an appointment to the pulpit of his native parish.

N

soldiery. The pressure of want compelled them to take every practicable measure for supplying themselves; and, in passing towards Glasgow, they had stripped such natives as they met of their shoes and other articles of dress.

Immediately upon his arrival, Charles took measures for the complete refitting of his army, by ordering the magistrates to provide 12,000 shirts, 6000 cloth coats, 6000 pair of stockings, and 6000 pair of shoes.[1]   He is also said to have sent for the provost (Buchanan), and sternly demanded the names of such as had subscribed for raising troops against him, threatening to hang the worthy magistrate in case of refusal.   The provost is said to have answered that he would name no person but himself, and that he was not afraid to die in such a cause.   He was forced to pay a fine of £500.[2]   From the town of Paisley the sum of £500 was exacted, and contributions were also raised in Renfrew and other towns near Glasgow.

Charles took up his residence in what was then considered the best house in the city, one belonging to a wealthy merchant named Glassford, which stood at the west end of the Trongate, and was afterwards taken down for the extension of that noble street.   At his arrival, he is said to have caused his men to enter this house by the front gate, go out by the back door, and then, making a circuit through some by-lanes, reappear in front of the mansion, as if they had been newly arrived.   But this *ruse*, practised in order to magnify the appearance of his army, was detected by the citizens of Glasgow, whose acute eyes recognised the botanical badges of the various clans, as they successively reappeared.   A careful estimate of his forces, made by the friends of government at Glasgow, represented them as about 3600 foot and 500 horse.   Of the latter, which were all much jaded, sixty were employed in carrying the sick; whilst about

[1] Inclusive of £5500 paid in September, the exactions from Glasgow amounted to £10,000, of which reimbursement was made by parliament in 1749.

[2] *Gentleman's Magazine*, January 1746, p. 43.   The various authentic anecdotes which shew the disinclination of the Prince to strong measures, throw a doubt on this tale of the day.

600 of the infantry neither had arms nor seemed able to use them.[1]

During his residence in Mr Glassford's house, Charles ate twice a day in public, though without ceremony, accompanied by a few of his officers, and waited upon by a small number of devoted Jacobite ladies. He also dressed much more elegantly here than he had done at any other place throughout the campaign.[2] But nothing could make the Whigs of Glasgow regard him with either respect or affection. Previously hostile to his cause, they were now incensed against him, by his severe exactions upon the public purse, and by the private depredations of his men. To such a height did this feeling arise, that an insane zealot snapped a pistol at him as he was riding along the Saltmarket.[3] He is said to have admired the regularity and beauty of the streets of Glasgow, but to have remarked, with bitterness, that nowhere had he found so few friends.[4] During the whole week he spent in the city, he procured no more than sixty recruits—a poor compensation for the numerous desertions which now began to take place, in consequence of the near approach of his men to their own country.

After having nearly succeeded in refitting his army, he held a grand review upon *the Green.* 'We marched out,' says Captain Daniel in his memoir of the campaign,[5] 'with drums beating, colours flying, bagpipes playing, and all the marks of a triumphant army, to the appointed ground, attended by multitudes of people, who had come from all parts to see us, and especially the ladies, who, though formerly much against us, were now charmed by the sight of the Prince into the most enthusiastic loyalty. I am somewhat at a loss,' continues this devoted cavalier, 'to give a description of the Prince as he appeared at the review. No object could be more charming, no personage more captivating, no deportment more agreeable, than his at

---

[1] *Scots Magazine,* viii. 29.
[2] James Gibb, in the Prince's Household Book, *Jacobite Memoirs.*
[3] Tradition.   [4] Boyse, 132.
[5] Preserved in the archives of Drummond Castle.

that time was; for, being well mounted and princely attired, having all the best endowments of both body and mind, he appeared to bear a sway above any comparison with the heroes of the last age; and the majesty and grandeur he displayed were truly noble and divine.'   It may be worth while to contrast with this flattering portraiture the description which has been given of Charles by a sober citizen of Glasgow.   'I managed,' says this person, quoting his memory after an interval of seventy years, 'to get so near him, as he passed homewards to his lodgings, that I could have touched him with my hand; and the impression which he made upon my mind shall never fade as long as I live.   He had a princely aspect, and its interest was much heightened by the dejection which appeared in his pale, fair countenance and downcast eye.   He evidently wanted confidence in his cause, and seemed to have a melancholy foreboding of that disaster which soon after ruined the hopes of his family for ever.'[1]

CHAPTER XVII.

PRELIMINARIES OF THE BATTLE OF FALKIRK.

> 'The Hielandmen cam owre the hill,
>   And owre the knowe, wi' richt gude will,
>   Now Geordie's men may brag their fill,
>   For wow but they were braw, man!
>   They had three generals o' the best,
>   Wi' lairds and lords, and a' the rest,
>   Chiels that were bred to stand the test,
>   And couldna rin awa, man!'
>   *Jacobite Song.*

HAVING recruited the spirits of his men, and improved their appointments, by eight days' residence in Glasgow, the Prince departed on the 3d of January, and sent forward his troops in

---

[1] *Attic Stories,* 290.

two detachments, one to Kilsyth, and the other to Cumbernauld. The inhabitants of Edinburgh, who, on the return of the Highland army from England, had apprehended a second visit, and who had resolved, in such a case, to defend the city, now set seriously about preparations for a siege. After Charles had left Edinburgh in the beginning of November, the Whig part of the community had gradually regained courage; and on the 13th of the month, when the insurgents were at the safe distance of Carlisle, the state officers had returned in a triumphant procession to their courts and chambers, saluted by a round of cannon from the castle, and a most valiant performance of Whig tunes upon the music-bells of St Giles's. Next day, Hamilton's and Gardiner's dragoons, with Price's and Ligonier's regiments of foot, boldly took possession of the city, probably assured of the safety of the measure by their avant-couriers the judges. It had been for some weeks the duty of these men, and of the Glasgow regiment of volunteers, to form posts at Stirling and other passes of the Forth, in order to prevent troops and stores passing southward to the Prince; but on the arrival of the Highland army at Glasgow, they retreated with great precipitation to Edinburgh (December 26), when it was determined, with the assistance of a number of rustic volunteers,[1] and the wreck of the Edinburgh regiment, to hold out the city at all hazards against the approaching insurgents. Their courage fortunately did not require to be put to so severe a proof; for, ere the Highlanders had left Glasgow, the English army, beginning to arrive, strengthened the city beyond all danger.

The command of the army, in the absence of the Duke of Cumberland, had been bestowed upon Lieutenant-general Henry Hawley, an officer of some standing, but ordinary abilities; who, having charged in the right wing of the king's army at

---

[1] Of these the congregations which had recently seceded from the Kirk of Scotland, and who were afterwards known by the name of the Associate Synod, formed a conspicuous portion—carrying colours on which was painted: 'For Religion, the Covenants, King, Kingdoms.'

Sheriffmuir, where the insurgents were repulsed with ease by the cavalry, entertained a confident notion that he would beat the whole of Prince Charles's army with a trifling force, and did not scruple to stigmatise the conduct of those who had hitherto been worsted by the Highlanders as rank pusillanimity.   It happened, in his approach to Edinburgh, that Hamilton's and Gardiner's dragoons, coming out to meet and congratulate him on his accession to the command, encountered him near Preston, the scene of their recent disgrace; which being pointed out to him, he sharply commanded the men to sheathe their swords, and see to use them better in the campaign about to ensue than they had hitherto done.[1]   Little did Hawley anticipate what a short week was to bring about.

The march of the English army was facilitated by the people of the Merse, Teviotdale, and Lothian, who brought horses to transport the baggage, and provisions to entertain the men.   At Dunbar, at Aberlady, and other places, they were feasted by the gentlemen of the district.[2]   The loyal part of the inhabitants of Edinburgh beheld the arrival of this army with satisfaction, and entered into an association to provide them with blankets.   The city was also illuminated in honour of the occasion; when a great number of windows belonging to recusant Jacobites, and to houses which happened to be unoccupied, were broken by the mob.

In his march from Glasgow, Prince Charles slept the first night at the mansion of Kilsyth, which belonged to a forfeited estate, and was now in the possession of Mr Campbell of Shawfield.   The steward had been previously ordered to provide for the Prince's reception, and told that all his expenses would be accounted for.   He had accordingly provided everything suitable for the entertainment of his Royal Highness and suite. Next morning, however, on presenting his bill, he was told that it should be allowed to him on his accounting (after the Restoration) for the rents of the estate, and that, in the meantime, he

---

[1] *Hist. Reb.* by an impartial hand, 134.   [2] *Scots Magazine*, viii. 32.

must be contented that the balance was not immediately struck and exacted.

On the succeeding day, Charles proceeded to Bannockburn House, where he was a welcome guest, this house being, as already mentioned, the residence of Sir Hugh Paterson, one of the most zealous of his friends. His troops lay this evening in the villages of Bannockburn, Denny, and St Ninians, while Lord George Murray occupied the town of Falkirk with the advanced guard of the army. In order to employ the time till he should be joined by his northern allies, Charles now resolved to reduce Stirling, which, commanding the principal avenue to the High-lands, had long been felt as an annoying barrier to his proceed-ings, and to subjugate which would have given an additional lustre to his arms.

Stirling, then a town of four or five thousand inhabitants, was imperfectly surrounded by a wall, and quite incapable of holding out against the insurgents; yet, by the instigation of the governor of the castle, who had resolved to die before surrendering his charge, an attempt was made to defend it. A small body of militia, consisting chiefly of the townsmen, was provided with arms from the castle; and the Reverend Ebenezer Erskine, founder of a well-known sect, and who was a clergyman in Stirling, did all he could to inspire them with courage, and even, it is said, assumed an active command in their ranks. By means of these men, the wretched defences of the town, which consisted on one entire side of only garden walls, were provided with a sort of guard, which Governor Blakeney endeavoured to animate by an assurance that, even in case of the worst, he would keep an open door for them in the castle.

On Sunday, the 5th of January, the town was invested by the insurgents, and about nine o'clock that evening a drummer approached the east gate, beating his instrument in the manner which indicates a message. The sentinels, ignorant of the forms of war, fired several shots at this messenger, upon which he found himself obliged to throw down his drum and take to his heels. The garrison then towed the deserted instrument in over the walls as a trophy.

On Monday, the insurgents having raised a battery within musket-shot of the town, and sent a more determined message to surrender, the magistrates implored a respite till next day at ten o'clock, which was granted. The whole of Tuesday was occupied in deliberations, and in adjusting the terms of surrender. The town, however, being stimulated that evening by the discharge of twenty-seven shots from the battery, a capitulation was concluded next morning, by which it was agreed to deliver up the town, under assurance of protection for the lives and property of the townsmen, whose arms, moreover, were permitted to be restored to the castle. The insurgents entered the town about three in the afternoon.

It now becomes necessary to advert to the transactions which had been taking place in the north of Scotland during the absence of the army in England. It will be recollected that Inverness was the point where President Forbes and the Earl of Loudoun proposed to rendezvous such of the Highlanders as they could induce to appear in arms for the government. Up to the middle of November, only five of the companies (which were to consist of 100 men each) had been mustered there. In the course of the few ensuing weeks, eighteen of the twenty which were contemplated had been assembled, four of them being the followers or tenants of the Laird of Macleod, two the Macdonalds of Sleat, two the Mackenzies of Kintail, two the Earl of Sutherland's men, two the Mackays, and of the Macleods of Assynt, the Rosses, the Grants, and Mackenzies of Lewis, one each, while one company had been raised in the town of Inverness. The primary cause of the mustering of these men for the government was simply that such was the will of their respective superiors. The men themselves, in general, were inclined to the other side, as indeed were the Highland people at large, with the exception only of a few chiefs, most of whom acted under reasons of mere policy. It was only by force of the clan-feeling of obedience to the chief, that the men in general were brought to serve King George. And even this powerful feeling did not in all instances prevail. For example, when the Laird of Macleod summoned his chief tacksmen or tenants to meet at Dunvegan, each with his quota of men, in order to go to the muster at Inverness, Macleod of Bernera, one of the principal men amongst them, wrote to him in the following, or similar terms: 'My dear laird, none of your clan would be more ready than I to attend your summons upon most occasions. I send you the men required, to whose service you are entitled; but, for myself, I go where a higher duty calls me.' And Bernera joined the Prince, with whom he continued to the end of the campaign, his own son being an officer in one of the laird's independent companies.[1]

As another illustration of the feeling which animated the dependants of the well-affected Highland proprietors, a body of Kintail Mackenzies were brought down by their chief, the Earl of Seaforth, to Brahan Castle, under pretence that his lordship's estates thereabouts were in danger from Lord Lovat, the real object being to draw them on to appear for the government, or at least to prevent them from joining the insurgent army. The men, at length penetrating the design, or at least thinking themselves deceived, went home, saying 'that they knew but one

---

[1] Information from Sir William Macleod Bannatyne, who, being cousin-german both to young Clanranald and Mr Macleod of Muiravonside (Charles's envoy to Skye), possessed much accurate knowledge respecting the transactions of this period, to which his own memory almost reached.* With reference to Bernera, Sir William added a curious anecdote, which was thus transcribed for me by my late amiable friend Mr Donald Gregory, author of a valuable historical work on the Highlands: 'Many years after the rebellion, an action was raised before the Court of Session, at the instance of the town of Paisley, against Secretary Murray, for the amount of a contribution imposed on the town, and received by the secretary on the Prince's behoof. While the judges were deliberating on this case, Bernera, in company with Sir W. M. B., entered the court. Lord Kames was speaking in his usual jocular way. "My lords," says he, "before proceeding to the merits of this cause, we should ascertain the proper designation of the defender. It appears to me that he should be styled Mr John Murray, secretary to Charles Edward Stuart, the leader of certain Highland banditti, who infested this country in 1745." It may be supposed that Bernera, who was himself one of the banditti, did not listen very patiently to this character of his comrades. Clenching his fist, he said to his companion: "If I had yon fellow anywhere than where he is now, I would teach him to call better men than himself banditti!"'

---

* Sir William died November 1833, aged above ninety.

king, and if they were not at liberty to fight for him, they would do it for no other.'[1]   It may thus be readily guessed that the troops gathered by Lord Loudoun were not likely, on a fair trial, to yield very hearty or effective service to the government. At the same time, it was of importance to the government that so many men should be engaged, however nominally, in its behalf, who might have otherwise been fighting under the insurgent standard.

The attention of Loudoun and the president was called chiefly to three points : the state of Fort Augustus under an investment by the Master of Lovat, the machinations of old Lovat himself, and some late proceedings in the counties of Aberdeen and Banff.   The earl marched with a party (December 3) to Fort Augustus, which he easily relieved.   He returned to Inverness on the 8th, after giving the people of Stratherrick (a district belonging to Lovat) a strong hint of what his troops would do to their country if they joined the insurgents.   Allowing his men a single day's rest, he set out on the 10th for Castle Downie or Beaufort, the residence of Lord Lovat, to obtain the best satisfaction he could for the peaceable behaviour of such of the Frasers as had not yet risen.   Lovat, still maintaining a fair face, promised to collect the arms of his clan for the earl, and, as a pledge for the fulfilment of his promise, agreed to accompany Lord Loudoun to Inverness.   There the earl waited with patience till the appointed day, when, finding that the old chief was dallying with him, he clapped a guard upon his lodgings. Lovat nevertheless escaped by a back door during the night, being carried off upon men's shoulders.   This was a perplexing event, for it obliged the earl to keep a large portion of his troops at Inverness, to watch the further proceedings of Lovat, while they were much needed in another quarter, to which our attention is now to be turned.

On the departure of the Highland army from Edinburgh,

---

[1] Paper by James Mackenzie, writer in Edinburgh (a native of Orkney), in Bishop Forbes's Papers (Lyon in Mourning, MS.), and attested by the bishop to be 'true and exact.'

Lord Lewis Gordon had returned to that district in Banff and Aberdeenshire over which his family had for centuries exercised almost unlimited control. There he busied himself for some weeks in raising men for the Prince's service, every landed proprietor being forced to furnish an able-bodied man, or £5 sterling, for every hundred Scots of his valued rent. He thus easily completed a regiment of two battalions, one of which he placed under the command of Gordon of Abbachy, the other under James Moir of Stoneywood. He also gathered a considerable sum of money. All this time his brother, the Duke of Gordon, kept up a fair appearance with the government. To put an end to the recruiting and exactions of Lord Lewis, the Laird of Macleod was despatched from Inverness on the 10th of December with his 500 clansmen, followed closely by 200 more under Major Monro of Culcairn, and soon after reinforced by 500 men under the Laird of Grant. An insurgent party, which had kept a post on the Spey, retired as he approached ; and Lord Lewis, falling back on Aberdeen, called forward to that place a number of men who had been raised in the counties of Forfar and Kincardine, together with some of Lord John Drummond's French troops recently landed at Montrose, and 300 Farquharsons under Farquharson of Monaltrie. In all, his lordship had about 1200 men. Meanwhile, the Laird of Grant, under some apprehension of danger to his own country, went home with his men. Culcairn, with his two companies, took post at Old Meldrum ; and Macleod, with only his 500 clansmen, advanced to Inverury, twelve miles from Aberdeen. Lord Lewis no sooner heard of this last incautious movement, than he marched from Aberdeen (December 23), and that afternoon, in the twilight, fell unexpectedly, with all his strength, upon the Macleods at Inverury. There being only 300 in the village against four times their number (for 200 were cantoned in the neighbourhood), and having had no preparation or warning, the Skye chief was in a situation of no small peril, more particularly as his men were not over-zealous in the cause. He quickly got them together, and, if we are to believe the government account, made a stand for about twenty minutes, fighting by moonlight. Their shot being at last expended, they retired with precipitation; nor did their retreat stop till they had got to Elgin.[1] Few were killed in this skirmish; but Lord Lewis took forty-one prisoners, among whom were Mr Gordon, younger of Ardoch, Forbes of Echt, Maitland of Pitrichie, and Mr John Chalmers, one of the professors of Aberdeen university, and remarkable as the first publisher of a newspaper north of the Forth.[2]

Lord Lewis thereafter conducted his forces to Perth, where Lord Strathallan already had a considerable body of troops assembled, including several hundreds of the Frasers, under the Master of Lovat, the Mackintoshes, 400 in number, a well-affected part of the clan Mackenzie, various recruits for the regiments in the south, some Low-country men, and the rest of the troops of Lord John Drummond. There was also a small party of Clanranald Macdonalds, who had come as a convoy with a considerable quantity of treasure, recently landed from a Spanish vessel in the island of Barra. The Mackintoshes had been raised under somewhat remarkable circumstances. The country of this clan was in Badenoch, not far from Inverness. The chief, or laird, usually called Mackintosh of Mackintosh, was, or affected to be, loyal to the existing sovereign, and personally appeared in arms on that side. At the same time his wife, a young woman of high spirit and resolution, raised the clan for the Chevalier, and adding to it the 300 Farquharsons just mentioned, formed a very good regiment, which was now ready for active service. The strange proceedings of this lady caused her to be distinguished by the jocular appellation of

---

[1] 'When he [Macleod] endeavoured to rally them at Elgin, they kept him in mind how he had already deceived them, by making them believe they were to serve the Young Man, when he first brought them out of the island; and afterwards how, to hold them together, at Inverness, he had dissembled with them, as if he always meant to let them follow their own inclinations; till at last, having led them to Inverury, a just dispersion (said they) had there befallen them for his perfidiousness to the Young Man. And yet (they told him), would he but still return to his duty, they would not so much as look home, for haste to go with him; whereas, if he continued obstinate, they would leave him to a man; which they did accordingly.'—*James Mackenzie's paper, as before quoted.*

[2] *The Aberdeen Journal,* which still exists under the charge of Mr Chalmers's descendant

Colonel Anne. It is said that, at a subsequent part of the campaign, Mackintosh himself, being taken in the capacity of a loyal militia captain by a party of the insurgents, was actually brought as a prisoner into the presence of his wife, who was then acting a semi-military part in the Chevalier's army.   She said, with military laconism : ' Your servant, captain !' to which he replied, with equal brevity : ' Your servant, colonel !'[1]   Into such strange relations are the various parts of society apt to be thrown by a civil war.

It will be recollected that Charles had sent Maclachlan of Maclachlan from Carlisle, to urge Lord Strathallan to forward to him all the men he had assembled at Perth.   His lordship, for what reason does not plainly appear, did not conceive it expedient to obey this order : perhaps he at first thought his forces too small, and afterwards the presence of a body of government troops at Stirling might seem a sufficient obstacle. The Highlanders, burning to be engaged in the active service of the Prince, urged him to allow them to march ; but in vain. They would have gone without his permission ; but they had no money, and many of those lately come down from the hills wanted arms.   Lord Strathallan had possession of money, arms, ammunition, and stores of all kinds ; and his views were supported by the Lowlanders and French.   The Highland officers formed various projects for getting at the money and arms, in order to proceed to the south, for, under the sense of so high a duty, they were not disposed to be very scrupulous.   Furious disputes had taken place between them and Lord Strathallan's supporters, and a battle seemed inevitable betwixt the two parties, when all was settled by the receipt of a letter from the Prince, dated at Dumfries, and conveyed by Rollo of Powhouse, commanding them to hold themselves in readiness to join the army, which was now marching to Glasgow, whence they should receive further orders.[2]   Charles was now joined at Stirling by

---

[1] Letter of the late Bishop Mackintosh, MS., in possession of the author.   Lady Mackintosh was a daughter of Farquharson of Invercauld, a friend of the government.
[2] Home, iii. 139.

these troops, who brought with them a great quantity of stores landed from France, and the Spanish money which had been debarked at the island of Barra.

The army, thus strengthened, broke ground before Stirling Castle on the 10th, and summoned Governor Blakeney to surrender. That officer gave for answer that he would defend his post to the last extremity, being determined to die, as he had lived, a man of honour. They first attempted to convert a large old building at the head of the town, called *Mar's Work*, into a battery; but finding themselves to be there peculiarly exposed to the fire of the garrison, they were soon obliged to look about for new ground.

On the day that Charles thus commenced the siege of Stirling, Hawley had been joined at Edinburgh by all the divisions of the army which he could immediately expect. As his force consisted of nearly eight thousand men, of whom thirteen hundred were cavalry, he considered himself fully a match for the insurgents, and now determined to offer them battle, though he knew that there were several other regiments on the march to Scotland, which would soon join him.[1] He was perhaps induced to take this step, partly by observing that the Highland force was every day increasing, and partly by a wish to relieve the garrison of Stirling; but a blind confidence in the powers of the army, especially the dragoons, and an ardent desire of distinguishing himself, must certainly be allowed to have chiefly instigated him to the measure. He had often been heard to reflect upon the misconduct of Cope (who, in his turn, had taken bets, it is said, to a large amount that this new commander would have no better success than himself). He therefore went on to battle under a kind of infatuation, of which the proper effects were soon seen.

On the morning of the 13th, five regiments, together with the Glasgow militia, and Hamilton's and Ligonier's (late Gardiner's)

---

1 Six thousand Hessians, who were compelled to serve the king of Great Britain in terms of a recent treaty, and who had embarked at Williamstadt on the 1st of January, were also at this time hourly expected to enter the Firth of Forth.

dragoons, left Edinburgh, under the command of Major-general Huske, and reached Linlithgow that evening.   A party of Highlanders under Lord George Murray, who had advanced thither, retired before them to Falkirk.   Next day three other regiments marched westwards to Borrowstounness, to be ready to support General Huske in case of an engagement; on the following morning, the remainder of the army, with the artillery, pursued the same route.   Hawley himself marched on the 16th, with Cobham's dragoons, who had just come up.   The army was accompanied by a north-of-England squire named Thornton, whose zealous loyalty had induced him to raise a band called the Yorkshire Blues, who were maintained and commanded by himself.

The whole of this well-disciplined and well-appointed force encamped to the north-west of Falkirk, upon the same field where, four centuries before, Sir John de Graham and Sir John Stewart of Bonkill, the friends of Wallace, had testified their patriotism in the arms of death.

On the morning of the 17th, Lieutenant-colonel John Campbell (afterwards Duke of Argyll), who had been hitherto exerting himself to keep the West Highlands quiet, joined the English camp with upwards of a thousand of his clan.

General Hawley was this morning spared the necessity of marching forward to raise the siege of Stirling, by intelligence that the Highlanders were in motion; for Prince Charles, learning the near approach of the English general, had resolved, with his usual ardour, to meet him half-way, and was now drawing out his men, as for a review, upon the Plean Moor, two miles to the east of Bannockburn, and about seven from Falkirk.   The English army did not, therefore, strike their camp, but judged it necessary to remain where they were till the intentions of the enemy should be revealed.

When the English lay upon the field of Falkirk, and the Highlanders were drawn up upon the Plean Moor, their respective camp lights were visible to each other over the level tract of country which intervened.   Betwixt the two armies lay the straggling remains of the once extensive Torwood, in whose gloomy recesses Wallace used to find a refuge suited to his depressed fortunes.

On this occasion, as on almost all others throughout the campaign, Charles found himself able to outgeneral the old and experienced officers whom the British government had sent against him. Though he had drawn out his men, and seemed ready for an immediate encounter with Hawley's army, he kept his real intentions a secret from even his own officers, making the main body believe that the evolutions in which they were engaged were only those of an ordinary review;[1] and it was not till mid-day that, having suddenly called a council of war, he announced his determination to march in the direction of the enemy.

The conduct of Hawley displayed as much of negligence on this occasion as that of Charles displayed calculation and alacrity. He was inspired, as already said, with a lofty contempt for the Highlanders, or 'Highland militia,' as he himself was pleased to call them. Having come to drive the wretched rabble from Stirling, he could not conceive the possibility of their coming to attack him at Falkirk. Being apprised, on the 16th, by a Mr Roger, who had passed through the Highland army, and conversed with some of the officers, that there was a proposal amongst them to march next day against him, he treated the informant with rudeness, and contented himself with giving vent to a vain expression of defiance.[2] On the morning of the day of battle, such was his continued security, that he obeyed an insidious invitation from the Countess of Kilmarnock, by retiring from the camp to breakfast with her at Callander House, although quite aware of that lady's relationship to an insurgent chief, and even perhaps of her own notorious attachment to the cause of Prince Charles. The *ruse* of the countess was attended with success. She was a woman of fine person and manners; and Hawley, completely fascinated,

---

[1] Chevalier Johnstone's *Memoirs*.
[2] MS. in possession of Mr David Constable.

spent the whole of this important forenoon in her company, without casting a thought upon his army.

Charles, observing the wind to come from the south-west, directed the march of his men towards a piece of ground considerably to the right of Hawley's camp, in order that, in the ensuing encounter, his troops might have that powerful ally to support them in rear.   He took care, at the same time, to despatch Lord John Drummond, with nearly all the horse, towards the other extremity of Hawley's lines, so as to distract and engage the attention of the enemy.   In order to produce still further uncertainty among the English regarding his intentions, he caused a body to retire to Stirling, with colours displayed in their sight; and upon the Plean Moor, which was thus entirely deserted, he left his great standard flying, as if that had still been his headquarters.

Perplexed by the various objects which they saw dispersed over the country, the English army remained in their camp, not altogether unapprehensive of an attack, but yet strongly disposed, like their commander, to scout the idea that the Highlanders would venture upon so daring a measure.   While they were still ignorant of the stealthy advance which Charles was making, a countryman, who had perceived it, came running into the camp, and exclaimed: 'Gentlemen, what are you about? The Highlanders will be immediately upon you!'   Some of the officers cried out: 'Seize that rascal—he is spreading a false alarm!'   But they were speedily assured of the truth of the report by two of their number, who had mounted a tree, and, through a telescope, discovered the Highlanders in motion. The alarm was immediately communicated to a commanding-officer, who, in his turn, lost no time in conveying it to Callander House.   Hawley received the intelligence with the utmost coolness, and contented himself with ordering that the men might put on their accoutrements, but said that they need not get under arms.   The troops obeyed the order, and proceeded to take their dinner.

It was between one and two o'clock that several gentlemen,

O

volunteer attendants on the camp, coming in upon the spur, gave final and decisive intelligence of the intention of the enemy.   They reported that they had seen the lines of the Highland infantry evolve from behind the Torwood, and cross the Carron by the *Steps* of Dunipace.   The drums instantly beat to arms; an urgent message was despatched for the recreant Hawley; and the lines were formed, in front of the camp, by officers on duty.   The negligence of their general was now bitterly reflected on by the men, many of whom seemed impressed with the idea that he had sold them to the enemy.

The last message which had been despatched to Callander succeeded in bringing Hawley to a sense of the exigency of his affairs, and he now came galloping up to his troops, with his head uncovered, and the appearance of one who has abruptly left a hospitable table.   The sky, which had hitherto been calm and cloudless, became at this moment overcast with heavy clouds, and a high wind beginning to blow from the south-west, foreboded a severe storm of rain.

While they stood in the position already mentioned, Charles was eagerly leading forward his desultory bands to a wild upland of irregular surface called Falkirk Muir, two miles south-west of the English camp.   In crossing the Carron at Dunipace Steps, and thus making for a rising ground where he could overlook Hawley's position, he precisely acted over again the course he had pursued four months before, in crossing the Esk at Mussel-burgh, and ascending the heights above Cope's station at Preston; and it may be added, that there is a remarkable resemblance in the corresponding localities.   Hawley, on learn-ing the direction Charles was taking, seems to have suspected that he was in danger of becoming the victim of a similar course of measures to that which occasioned the defeat of Cope; and having the bad effect of that general's caution before his eyes, he appears to have immediately adopted the resolution of dis-puting the high ground.   He therefore gave a hasty com-mand to the dragoons to march towards the top of the hill, in order, if possible, to anticipate the Highlanders; the foot he commanded to follow at quick pace, with their bayonets inserted in the musket.   To this precipitate measure, by which he placed his army on ground he had never seen, and which was extremely unfit for the movements of regular troops, while it was proportionately advantageous for the Highlanders, the disasters of the day are in a great measure to be attributed.

The dragoons galloped up a narrow way at the east end of Bantaskine Park ; the foot followed, with a show of promptitude and courage ; and the artillery, consisting of ten pieces, came last of all, driven by a band of Falkirk carters, who, with their horses, had been hastily pressed into King George's service that forenoon—for it was not till some time after this memorable campaign that the British artillery was drawn by horses and men regularly appointed for the purpose.   Whether from accident, or from the design of the drivers, who were ill affected to their duty, the artillery stuck in a swampy place at the end of the loan, beyond all power of extrication ; and the drivers then cut the traces of their horses, and scampered back to Falkirk.   The sullen south-west, against which the army was marching, now let forth its fury full in their faces, blinding them with rain, and rendering the ascent of the hill doubly painful. Still they struggled on, encouraged by the voice and gesture of their general, whose white uncovered head was everywhere conspicuous as he rode about, and who seemed ardently desirous to recover the effects of his negligence.

Before Hawley commenced this unlucky march, Charles had entered Falkirk Muir at another side, and was already ascending the hill.   His troops marched in two parallel columns, about two hundred paces asunder ; that which was nearest the king's army consisting of the clans which had been in England, and the other comprising all the late accessions, with some Low-country regiments.   The former was designed to become the front line in ranking up against the enemy.

A sort of race now commenced between the dragoons and clans towards the top of the moor ; each apparently esteeming the preoccupation of that ground as of the most essential importance to the event. The clans attained the eminence first, and the dragoons were obliged to take up somewhat lower ground, where they were prevented from coming into direct opposition with the Highlanders by a morass on their left.

The three Macdonald regiments, according to the right of the great Clan Colla to that distinguished position, marched at the head of the first column, with the intention of forming eventually the right wing of the army in battle-array; but, on the present occasion, Glencairnaig's minor regiment of Macgregors, exerting greater speed in the race with Hawley's dragoons, and being therefore the first to reach the top of the hill, took that post of honour, which they retained throughout the ensuing conflict. The first line of the insurgent army was therefore formed by the following regiments, reckoning from right to left: Macgregor, Keppoch, Clanranald, Glengarry, Appin, Cameron, the Frasers under the Master of Lovat, and the Macphersons under Cluny their chief. At the right extremity, Lord George Murray had the chief command, fighting, as usual, on foot. On the left, there was no general commander, unless it was Lord John Drummond, whose attention, however, was chiefly directed to his French regiment in the rear. The second line was chiefly composed of Low-country regiments, which stood in the following order: Athole, Ogilvie, Gordon, Farquharson, Cromarty, and the French. The Prince stood on an eminence [1] behind the second line, with the horse; having been implored by the army not to hazard his person by that active collision with the enemy for which, as at Preston, he had expressed his ardent desire.

Opposite to the Highland army thus disposed, but rather inclining to the north, on account of the morass and the declivity, the English foot were drawn up also in two lines, with the horse in front, and a reserve in the rear. The first line comprised the following regiments from right to left: Wolfe, Cholmondley, the Scots Royals, Price, and Ligonier; the second, Blakeney, Monro, Fleming, Barrel, and Battereau. The

---

[1] Still popularly termed *Charlie's Hill*, and now covered with wood.

reserve was composed of the Glasgow regiment, Howard's, and the Argyle militia.

Falkirk Muir, an upland now covered with thriving farms, and intersected by the Union Canal and Edinburgh and Glasgow Railway, was then a rough tract, irregular in its surface, without rising into peaks, and bearing no vegetation but heath. It was upon its broad ridge, at the top, that the two armies were disposed, the Highlanders extending more to the south, and occupying, as already stated, somewhat higher ground. The country was not encumbered by enclosures of any kind; but a sort of hollow, or *dean*, as it is called in Scotland, commenced nearly opposite to the centre of the Highland lines, and ran down between the two armies, gradually widening towards the plain below, and opening up at one place into a spacious basin. By this ravine, which was too deep to be easily passed from either side, two-thirds of the English were separated from about one-half of the Highland army. Owing to the convexity of the ground, the wings of both armies were invisible to each other.

To conclude this account of the disposition of the English, the Argyle Highlanders and Ligonier's regiment were stationed in the hollow just mentioned; the Glasgow regiment was posted at a farm-house behind the other extremity; and the horse stood a little in advance of the foot, opposite to the right wing of the Highlanders, without any portion of the ravine intervening. General Hawley commanded in the centre, Brigadier Cholmondley on the left, and Major-general Huske on the right. The horse were immediately under the command of Lieutenant-colonel Ligonier, who, stationed on the left with his own regiment (lately Gardiner's), had Cobham's and Hamilton's on his right, and personally stood almost opposite to Lord George Murray.

In numbers, the two armies were nearly equal, both amounting to about 8000; and as they were alike unsupplied by artillery (for the Highlanders had also left theirs behind), there could scarcely have been a better match, so far as strength was concerned.   But the English had disadvantages of another sort, such as the unfitness of the ground for their evolutions, the interruption given to so much of their lines by the ravine, the comparative lowness of their ground, and their having the wind and rain in their faces.

CHAPTER XVIII.

THE BATTLE OF FALKIRK.

'Says brave Locheil: " Pray have we won?
I see no troop, I hear no gun."
Says Drummond : " Faith, the battle's done,
I know not how or why, man."'
Jacobite Song.

It was near four o'clock, and the storm was rapidly bringing on premature darkness, when Hawley ordered his dragoons to advance, and commence the action.   As already mentioned, he had an idea that the Highlanders would not stand against the charge of a single troop of horse, much less did he expect them to resist three regiments, amounting to 1300 men.   The result shewed that he was mistaken.

These regiments, after making several feints to draw the fire of the Highlanders, in order then to rush in upon them, moved slowly forward; the Highland right wing, in like manner, advancing to meet them, under Lord George Murray, who made the most anxious efforts to keep it in line, and to restrain all firing till the proper moment.   There was the more reason for delay on the part of the Highland right wing, as the left was not yet fully formed.   After the two parties had confronted each other the better part of a quarter of an hour, the dragoons went on at a full trot, in good order, till within pistol-shot of the Highlanders.   Then Lord George gave orders to fire, which was done with such execution, that the dragoon regiments were instantly broken. Ligonier's and Hamilton's, the cravens of Preston, fled backwards right over the left wing of their own foot, who lay upon their faces; as they went, some were heard crying: 'Dear brethren, we shall all be massacred this day!'[1] Cobham's did little better, for it fled down the ravine, receiving a volley from the Highland line as it went along. The Highlanders had fired so near, and with such precision, as to bring many to the ground, including several officers of distinction. One small party of these dragoons acted with courage. It was kept together, and led to the charge, by Lieutenant-colonel Whitney, a brave officer, who had remained behind his retreating cavalry at Preston, though wounded in the sword-arm. As he was going forward at the head of his little troop to the attack, he recognised John Roy Stuart, a former friend, and cried out: 'Ha! are you there? We shall soon be up with you.' Stuart exclaimed in reply: 'You shall be welcome when you come—you shall have a warm reception!'[2] Almost at that moment the unfortunate leader received a shot, which tumbled him lifeless from the saddle. His party rushed resistlessly through the front line of the enemy, trampling down all that opposed them. But their bravery was unavailing. The Highlanders, taught to fight in all postures, and under every variety of circumstances, though thrown upon their backs beneath the feet of the cavalry, used their dirks in stabbing the horses under the belly, or, dragging down the men by their long-skirted coats, engaged with them in mortal struggles, during which they seldom failed to poniard their antagonists. The chief of Clanranald was thrown below a dead horse, from which he could not extricate himself, when one of his own clan tumbled down beside him in the arms of a dismounted dragoon. From his situation, the chief could not well make his condition known to any more

---

[1] *Life of John Metcalf*, a blind Englishman, who acted as musician to the Yorkshire Blues, and whose book contains many curious particulars regarding the battle of Falkirk, p. 89.

[2] Henderson's *Hist. Reb.* 266.

distant clansman, and it almost appeared that his existence depended upon the success which this man might have with the dragoon. After a brief and anxious interval, the Highlander contrived to stab his foeman, and then sprang to relieve his prostrate chief.[1]

This was but a trifling exception from the general fate of the dragoon charge. The mass retreated, doing great damage to the infantry of their own army. Lord George Murray was very anxious that the Macdonald regiments under his charge should keep their ranks, as the bulk of the English army was yet to engage, and the remainder of the Highland lines were as yet scarcely formed. But these regiments were too much elated by the repulse of the dragoons to obey any orders to that effect. Many of them broke off, sword in hand, and encountered the parties of militia stationed nearly opposite to them.

A few minutes after the dragoons had fled, the left wing, or rather moiety, of the Highland army, consisting of the Mackintoshes, Macphersons, Camerons, Stuarts of Appin, and others, were charged by the English regiments opposed to them, assisted by a party of horse. The Highlanders having met the horse with a good fire, advanced upon the foot sword in hand, their ranks thickened by a considerable number of individuals from the second line, who were too impatient for action to be restrained to that position. The Macdonalds were at the same moment rushing down in considerable numbers upon the left wing of the English army. Thus a simultaneous attack was made, by nearly the whole of the Highland front line, upon all the English regiments, except the three which outflanked the Prince's forces. Those regiments, half blinded and wholly disconcerted by the storm, and with their pieces rendered useless by the rain, gave way before the onset, and trooped off hurriedly in large parties towards Falkirk, bearing General Hawley along with them.

Some individuals who beheld the battle from the steeple of

----

[1] Chevalier Johnstone, 122.

Falkirk, used to describe these, its main events, as occupying a surprisingly brief space of time. They first saw the English army enter the misty and storm-covered moor at the top of the hill; then saw the dull atmosphere thickened by a fast-rolling smoke, and heard the pealing sounds of the discharge; immediately after they beheld the discomfited troops burst wildly from the cloud in which they had been involved, and rush, in far-spread disorder, over the face of the hill. From the commencement till what they styled 'the *break* of the battle,' there did not intervene more than ten minutes—so soon may an efficient body of men become, by one transient emotion of cowardice, a feeble and contemptible rabble.

The rout would have been total, but for the three outflanking regiments. These not having been opposed by any of the clans, having the ravine in front, and deriving some support from a small body of dragoons, stood their ground under the command of General Huske and Brigadier Cholmondley. When the Highlanders went past in pursuit, they received a volley from this part of the English army, which brought them to a pause, and caused them to draw back to their former ground, their impression being that some ambuscade was intended. This saved the English army from destruction. A pause took place, during which the bulk of the English infantry got back to Falkirk. It was not till Lord George Murray brought up the second line of his wing, and the pickets with some others on the other wing, that General Huske drew off his party, which he did in good order. There is some obscurity in the accounts of the action with respect to this particular juncture; but there can be no doubt that the English army retired into Falkirk without molestation from the Highlanders, and that the latter stayed for some time on the field of battle, or between it and the town, uncertain what to do further.

It would appear as if the very facility with which the Highlanders gained the earlier part of their victory, was a main cause of its being ultimately incomplete. When Lord John Drummond saw the Scots Royals fly, he cried: 'These men behaved admirably at Fontenoy—surely this is a feint.' It was impossible for even the Highlanders, humble as was their opinion of the British regiments, to believe that they would display so extreme a degree of cowardice; and when·they at length found no enemies before them, they could not help asking each other (in Gaelic): 'What is become of the men? Where are they?' Surprised, and apprehensive of some mysterious design, they remained for a considerable time irresolute.   Many of the officers were of opinion that they ought to retire for shelter to Dunipace and other villages in the rear; but Lord George Murray was decided for attempting to enter Falkirk immediately, lest the English army might post themselves advantageously in it. He was certain that at present they were in great confusion; but a little time might put them into a different condition. He concluded with Count Mercy's exclamation at the battle of Parma, that he would either lie in the town or in paradise. The Prince, when he came up, approved of the proposal to attempt the town; but he was himself advised to stay at some house on the face of the hill, till Lord George should inform him of the success of the attempt. The Master of Strathallan, and Mr Oliphant, younger of Gask, then disguised themselves as peasants, and went forward to Falkirk, where they learned that General Hawley, after giving orders to fire his tents, had retreated to the eastward, leaving the town vacant. On this fact being communicated to the army on the moor, three detachments, respectively under the command of Lord John Drummond, Locheil, and Lord George Murray, proceeded to the town, which they entered at three different points—Lord John's party by the west end, Locheil's by a lane near the centre, and Lord George's by another lane farther to the east. They found nothing but a few straggling parties in the streets. Nevertheless, considerable apprehensions of a renewed attack from the English army still prevailed. It was not till about seven o'clock that, the Earl of Kilmarnock having approached the Edinburgh road by byways through his own lands, and returned with intelligence that he had seen the English army hurrying along in full flight, the Prince at length thought proper to seek shelter in the town of Falkirk from the storm to which he had been exposed for five hours.

Charles was conducted, by torchlight, to a lodging which had been prepared for him in the house of a lady called Madam Graham, the widow of a physician, a Jacobite, and a woman whose intelligence and superior manners are still remembered with veneration at Falkirk. This house, which stands opposite to the steeple, was then the best in the town, and is still a tolerably handsome mansion, and occupied as the post-office; but, according to the fashion of times not very remote in Scotland, the best room, and that in which Charles was obliged to dine and hold his court, contains a bed concealed within folding-doors. Unexpected good fortune, however, reconciles the mind to trivial inconveniences; and it is not probable that the victor of Falkirk regretted to spend the evening of his triumph in an apartment about twelve feet square, lighted by one window, and which was at once his refectory and bed-chamber.

Only about 1500 of the Highland army rested that night in Falkirk. The remainder had scattered themselves to the west-ward, in search of shelter. A great deal of confusion had prevailed; some even retired, under the impression that their party had been defeated. Several chiefs, including Lord Lewis Gordon, met in the course of the evening at the house of Dunipace, in a state of uncertainty as to the general result of the battle, and ignorant even of the fate of their own regiments. At length, about eight o'clock, their minds were relieved by the arrival of Macdonald of Lochgarry, who had been sent from Falkirk to order the troops forward in the morning. The intelligence brought by this gentleman for the first time gave them reason to suppose that their army had had the best of the day.

The Falkirk party, with the exception of a few skirmishers sent off to harass the retreating enemy, employed themselves during this evening in securing the English camp and its contents, and in stripping the bodies of the slain. Hawley, in the brief interval between the rout and the pursuit, had made an attempt to strike his camp and take away his baggage; but, owing to the desertion of his wagoners, and the necessity of a speedy retreat, he was at last obliged to abandon the whole to the Highlanders, having only made an ineffectual attempt to set it on fire. Charles thus obtained possession of a vast quantity of military stores, while his men enriched themselves with such articles of value as the people of Falkirk had not previously abstracted. In addition to the tents, baggage, &c. which fell into his hands, he secured seven pieces of cannon, three mortars, 600 muskets, a large quantity of hand-grenades, and 4000 pounds-weight of powder, besides many standards and other trophies of victory. As for the slain, they were that night stripped so effectually, that a citizen of Falkirk, who next morning surveyed the field from a distance, and who lived till recent years to describe the scene, used to say that he could compare them to nothing but a large flock of white sheep at rest on the face of the hill.

Charles lost thirty-two men in the battle, including officers, and had 120 wounded. The loss on the English side is stated by the official returns to have been 280 in all, killed, wounded, and missing, but was probably much more considerable. The loss of officers was, in particular, very great. There were killed four captains and two lieutenants of Blakeney's, five captains and one lieutenant of Wolfe's, with no fewer than three lieutenant-colonels, Whitney, Bigger, and Powell. Colonel Ligonier, who had been under medical treatment for pleurisy, went to the battle contrary to advice, and formed the rearguard on the retreat to Linlithgow. The wetting he got that evening brought on a quinsy, of which he died on the 25th. It is worthy of note, though no more than was to have been expected, that the greatest loss took place in the regiments which soonest gave way. The most distinguished officer among the slain was Sir Robert Monro of Foulis, the chief of an ancient and honourable family in the Highlands, and whose regiment was chiefly composed, like those of the insurgent leaders, of his own clan.

Monro's had excited the admiration of Europe by its conduct at the battle of Fontenoy, where it had fought almost without intermission for a whole day; but on the present occasion it was seized with a panic, and fled at the first onset of the insurgents. Sir Robert alone, who was so corpulent a man that he had been obliged at Fontenoy to stand upon his feet when all the rest of his regiment lay down on their faces to avoid the enemy's fire, boldly faced the charging Highlanders. He was attacked at once by six antagonists, two of whom he laid dead at his feet with his half-pike, but a seventh came up, and discharged a shot into his body, by which he was mortally wounded.[1] His brother, an unarmed physician, at this juncture came to his relief, but shared in the indiscriminate slaughter which was then going on. Next day their bodies were found, stripped and defaced, in a little pool of water formed around them by the rain; and it was remarked in that of the brave Sir Robert, as an instance of the ruling passion strong in death, that his right hand still clenched the pommel of his sword, from which the whole blade had been broken off. The corpses were honourably interred in one grave in the parish churchyard,[2] near the tombs of Graham and Stewart, the heroes of the former battle of Falkirk.

The mass of Hawley's army spent that night at Linlithgow, about ten miles from the field. They next day continued the retreat to Edinburgh, where they arrived in the afternoon, in a state strikingly different from that order, freshness, and confidence in which they had left the city a few days before. The state officers, and other friends of the government, were more distressed by this affair than even by Preston, many of the

---

[1] 'Callum na Biobhaig—that is, Malcolm of the Small Lock of Hair—whose real name was Malcolm Macgregor, one of Glengyle's men, was the man that shot Sir Robert Monro at the battle of Falkirk, at the very first onset or beginning of the battle.'—*Letter of Bishop Mackintosh, MS., in possession of the author.*

[2] A monument has been erected over the grave of the two brothers, with a suitable inscription. There is a legend among the Jacobites, that on application being made to a gentleman in the neighbourhood of Falkirk for permission to take the necessary stones from his quarry, he answered, with the sly wit of his party: 'Monuments! an' ye like I'll gie ye monuments for them a'!'

troops employed on the occasion having been tried in several campaigns. Hawley's policy seems to have been to bluster through the disgrace. The accounts of the action published by him are full of gasconade. Any failure that he admits at all, he lays to the account of the bitter storm of wind and rain, which blew in the faces of his troops, and made their firelocks useless. While he makes some slight allusion to the retreat of the dragoons and part of his left wing of infantry, he lays great stress upon the gallant behaviour of his right wing, which, he says, repulsed the rebels, and drove them from the field. He represents this portion of his troops as staying *an hour* in the field, while the rebels durst not molest them. The whole retired *in good order* to Falkirk. He intended at first to occupy his camp ; but the weather proving extremely bad, and having advice that the enemy were pushing to get between him and Edinburgh, he resolved to march to Linlithgow. When the tents were to be struck, it was found that many of the drivers had ridden off with the horses ; he therefore ordered the tents to be burned. For the like reason, seven pieces of artillery had been left behind. He allowed of 280 men missing, but alleged that the enemy had lost many more. In short, the gazette accounts of the affair read remarkably well :[1] it only happens to be true that the general had mismanaged the march of his troops to the field, and their arrangement there ; that four-fifths of his army were disgracefully beaten and driven back ; that he

---

[1] A few days after, the following *jeu d'esprit*, ridiculing the terms of the government gazette, made the round of the journals : 'The Westminster chimney-sweeps, being in arms against the shoe-blackers of this neighbourhood (Whitehall), early yesterday morning were in motion to attack them. Our people had not at first any advice of the enemy's motions; and though scouts were sent out to Tothill Street, Milbank, and several other ways, they were not perceived till the front of them appeared at the bottom of King Street. Upon this the shoe-blackers formed with all expedition, and moved on to get advantage of the ground. But parties of the chimney-sweepers coming round by Channel Row and the Park, in spite of our teeth got to the windward of our friends, the wind being then north-east. Just as the armies engaged, a violent gust arose, which blew the soot from the chimney-sweepers so strongly in the eyes of our people, that they could not see at all, and thought proper to retreat in good order into the Mewse. The enemy's loss was judged to be very considerable ; but no particulars can be given, as it is believed they carried off their dead and wounded in their sacks. The battle was fought in the Broadway, just over against the Horse Guards. Our friends kept the field—especially the killed and wounded. We

lost his cannon, his camp, and most of its contents; and in less than twenty-four hours from the time of the action, had retired twenty-six miles from the field.

Hawley, before leaving Edinburgh, had erected two gibbets whereon to hang the Highlanders who should surrender to him in the victory he expected to achieve. After he returned in a state so different from that of a conqueror, he had to use these conspicuous monuments of his folly for the execution of some of his own men. He hanged no fewer than four in one day, permitting their bodies to remain on the gallows till sunset.[1] Such a sight had not been seen in Edinburgh since the day before the Duke of York opened the Scottish parliament in the year 1681, when five rebellious ministers were executed at once in the Grassmarket.[2] The captain of the artillery, who had deserted his charge at the beginning of the action, upon a horse which he cut from the train, was cashiered with infamy; and many of the private soldiers who had displayed extraordinary cowardice were severely whipped.

By a strange chance, Hawley carried along with him from Falkirk *one prisoner*. This was the gallant Major Macdonald of Tiendrish, cousin of Keppoch, and who had signalised himself by the attack upon the two companies of foot in Lochaber, at the beginning of the insurrection. Seeing the right wing of Hawley's army still keeping the field, and mistaking it for Lord John Drummond's regiment, he ran up to it, crying: ' Gentlemen, why do you stand here? Why don't you pursue the dogs?'

found, when we came to our quarters, that several stools, baskets, brushes, and blacking-pots were missing. This was owing to the behaviour of Jack Linklight and Tom Scrubit, who, being left in charge of the stores, abandoned them at the beginning of the action; but some accounts say that what they could not carry off they threw into the fire of a neighbouring gin-shop. The shoe-blackers are getting up a new set of tools, and design to attack the chimney-sweepers, who are now quiet in their cellars.'

[1] ' Both Hawley and his royal patron [the Duke of Cumberland] were signal exceptions to the rule that brave men are never cruel. Once, in Flanders, a deserter being hanged before Hawley's windows, the surgeons begged to have the body for dissection. But Hawley was reluctant to part with the pleasing spectacle: " At least," said he, " you shall give me the skeleton to hang up in the guard-room."'—Lord Mahon, quoting a letter of Horace Walpole, who added, that the soldiers' nickname for Hawley was 'the Lord Chief-justice.'

[2] Henderson's *History of the Rebellion*, ii. 77.

and he was in the midst of them before he discovered his error.
A cry was raised : ' Here is a rebel ! Here is a rebel !' He
attempted to pass for one of the loyal clan Campbell, trusting
that his white cockade was sufficiently blackened by the firing
and rain not to betray him.   But all in vain.   General Huske
was for shooting him on the spot, but was induced by Lord
Robert Kerr, an amiable officer, the son of the Marquis of
Lothian, to give him quarter.   He requested that he might be
allowed to surrender his arms to an officer, as he had the
honour to be one himself; and he advanced to Huske for that
purpose.   But the general had the usual contempt for the
Highland army, and swore he would do no rebel so much
honour.   The generous Kerr then stepped forward to take
Macdonald's arms.   Tiendrish could not perform even this act
of self-humiliation without a recollection of his dignity of blood
and station, and he drew forth his pistols from his belt with such
an air as impressed the English general with a dread of assas-
sination.   On his expressing this fear in his own vulgar language,
Macdonald drew himself up with still greater pride, and said he
could do nothing unbecoming a gentleman.   He was then
mounted on horseback, bound, and carried along with the
retreating army to Edinburgh.   The circumstances help to
shew that the English right wing retired from the field with
deliberation, though they did not perhaps linger a whole hour
upon it.

While the English industriously denied that they had lost the
battle, the insurgents made no very confident pretensions to
having gained it.   They were, in reality, mortified at having
taken so little advantage of the circumstances which fortune had
laid before them, and which, they were sensible, might never
occur again.   From Lord George Murray's narrative, it would
appear that, as to pre-arrangement and concert, there was as
remarkable a deficiency on the insurgent as on the government side.   If the bravery of the Macdonald regiments were
put out of view, it might be said that the storm had gained
them the battle.   The considerations which arose, from all the

circumstances, in the minds of the more reflecting officers, were not agreeable. They 'were convinced,' says Lord George Murray, ' that, *unless they could attack the enemy at very considerable advantage*, either by surprise or by some strong situation of ground, or a narrow pass, *they could not expect any great success*, especially if their numbers were noways equal; and that a body of regular troops was absolutely necessary to support them, when they should at any time go in, sword in hand; for they were sensible that, without more leisure and time than they could expect to have to discipline their own men, it would not be possible to make them keep their ranks, or rally soon enough upon any sudden emergency, so that any small body of the enemy either keeping in a body when they were in confusion, or rallying soon, would deprive them of a victory, even after they had done their best.' The significancy of these remarks will sufficiently appear, when we come to consider the next battle in which the clans were engaged.

The succeeding day, during which it continued to rain with little intermission, was spent at Falkirk by the insurgents in securing the spoils and burying the slain. They employed the country-people to dig a spacious pit upon the field of battle, into which they precipitated the naked corpses. The rustics who stood around easily distinguished the English soldiers from the Highlanders by their comparative nudity, and by the deep gashes which seamed their shoulders and breasts—the dreadful work of the broadsword. The number of slain inhumed in this pit was such, that some years after the surface sank down many feet, and there is still a considerable hollow at that part of the battle-field.

The Highland army lost more this day by an accident than it did on the preceding by the fire of the enemy. A private soldier of the Clanranald regiment had obtained a musket as part of his spoil upon the field of battle: finding it loaded, he was engaged at his lodgings in extracting the shot; the window was open, and nearly opposite there was a group of officers standing on the street. The man extracted a ball, and then fired off the piece, to clear it in the most expeditious manner of the powder; but, unfortunately, it had been double loaded, and the remaining ball pierced the body of young Glengarry, who was one of the group of bystanders. He soon after died in the arms of his clansmen, begging with his last breath that the man, of whose innocence he was satisfied, might not suffer; but nothing could restrain the indignation of his friends, who immediately seized the man, and loudly demanded life for life. Young Clanranald would have gladly protected his clansman; but, certain that any attempt he could make to that effect would only embroil his family in a feud with that of Glengarry, and, in the first place, cause that regiment to quit the Prince's service, he was reluctantly obliged to assent to their demand. The man was immediately taken out to the side of a park-wall near the town, and pierced with a volley of bullets. His own father put a shot into his body, from the desire to make his death as instantaneous as possible.

The Prince, who had most occasion to regret this accident, as it endangered the attachment of a valuable regiment, exerted himself, by shewing the most respectful attentions to the deceased, to console the clan for their loss. He caused the grave of Sir John Graham to be opened for the reception of the youthful soldier, as the only part of the churchyard of Falkirk which was worthy to be honoured with his corpse; and he himself attended the obsequies as chief mourner, holding the string which consigned his head to the grave. Charles's judicious kindness was not unappreciated by the grateful Highlanders; but, nevertheless, a considerable number yielded to their grief or rage so far as to desert his standard.

Another incident took place this day upon the street of Falkirk, which had almost become as tragical as the former, and which illustrates in a striking manner the peculiar ties of clanship. Lord Kilmarnock had brought up to the front of Charles's lodging a few prisoners whom he had taken the preceding night in the rear of the retreating army; and Charles was standing within the open window with a paper in his hand, conversing with Lord Kilmarnock, when a man was seen coming up the street in the uniform of an English regiment, with a musket and bayonet in his hand, and a black cockade upon his hat. A few captive volunteers, among whom Mr Home, the narrator of the incident, was one, beheld the man with surprise; and conceiving that he designed to assassinate the Prince, expected every moment to see him take aim and fire. Charles, observing the prisoners look all one way, turned his head in the same direction, and immediately comprehending the cause of their alarm, called in some surprise to Lord Kilmarnock, and pointed towards the soldier. The earl instantly descended to the street, and finding the man by that time just opposite to the window, went up to him, struck his hat off his head, and set his foot upon the black cockade. At that instant one of the numerous Highlanders who stood upon the pavement rushed forward, and violently pushed Lord Kilmarnock from his place. The earl pulled out a pistol, and presented it at the Highlander's head; the Highlander drew his dirk, and held it close to Kilmarnock's breast. In this posture they stood about half a minute, when a crowd of Highlanders rushed between the parties, and drove Kilmarnock away. The man with the dirk in his hand then took up the hat, put it on the soldier's head, and the Highlanders marched off with him in triumph.

This unaccountable pantomime astonished the prisoners, and they entreated an explanation from one of the insurgent officers who stood near. He answered that the soldier was not in reality what he seemed, but a Cameron, who had deserted his regiment (the Scots Royals) during the conflict, to join the company of his chief, when he had been permitted to retain his dress and arms till he could be provided with the uniform of the clan. The Highlander who interposed was his brother, and the crowd that had rushed in, his clansmen the Camerons. Lord Kilmarnock, in presuming to interfere, even through ignorance, in the affairs of a clan, had excited their high displeasure; 'nor, in my opinion,' continued the officer, 'can any person in the

Prince's army take that cockade out of the man's hat except Locheil himself.'

At this period of the campaign the mountaineers had become better acquainted than they were at first with the commodities of civilised life. Money had now become an object with them; and it is surprising what large sums some of them had amassed about their persons. At the battle of Falkirk, a private High-lander having pursued one of Barrel's regiment down the hill, and in his turn fled on the man turning about to oppose him, was shot through the head by Brigadier Cholmondley, and left to be rifled by the soldier. To the man's astonishment, no less a sum than sixteen guineas was found in the *sporran* or purse of the dead Highlander![1]

Prince Charles returned to Bannockburn on the evening of the 18th, leaving Lord George Murray, with a portion of the army, at Falkirk. Among other articles which the Prince had brought away with him from Glasgow was a printing-press, with its accompaniments of types and workmen. Sensible of the advantage which the other party had over him in their command of the public press, and no doubt incensed at the lies they were constantly propagating against him, he had employed his first leisure at Glasgow in publishing a journal of his march into England, which, if not free of a little gasconade, was certainly quite as faithful as the gazettes of government. He had brought the press along with him, in order to continue his publications

---

[1] During the stay of the Highlanders at Falkirk they treated the inhabitants with extra-ordinary lenity, on account of their connection with the Earl of Kilmarnock, and the readiness which they displayed in serving the cause of the Prince. An old woman, who lives (1827), at the age of ninety-seven, and was of course fifteen years of age at the time of the battle, informed the writer of these sheets that the Highlanders were considered a merciful enemy compared with the dragoons.

This general lenity was not without exceptions. A local correspondent states that a small party, on the day after the battle, laid violent hands on a flaming Jacobite named David Watt, then the principal innkeeper of Falkirk, brought him out to the street in front of his own door, and, setting him down squat upon the causeway, deliberately eased his feet of a pair of new shoes with silver buckles. He protested his Jacobitism to save them; but the spoliators, perhaps accustomed to such shallow excuses, disregarded his declaration; ironically observing: 'Sae muckle ta better—she'll no grumble to shange a progue for the Prince's guid.' It is added that David's principles were a good deal shaken by this unhappy incident.

occasionally; and he now issued from Bannockburn a quarto sheet, containing a well-penned and modest account of his victory at Falkirk. This, however, was destined to be the last of his gazettes, as the rapidity of his subsequent movements rendered it impossible to transport so large and complicated an engine.[1]

He now resumed the siege of Stirling Castle, having first sent a summons of surrender to General Blakeney, which that officer answered with his former firmness. He had been advised by an engineer of the name of Grant, who had conducted the siege of Carlisle, to open trenches in the churchyard, which lies between the castle and the town; but was induced to abandon that design by the citizens, who represented that it must insure the destruction of their houses. There were two other points from which the castle might be stormed, though not nearly so advantageous as that pointed out by Mr Grant—the Gowan Hill, an irregular eminence under the castle walls on the north side; and the Ladies' Hill, a small bare rock facing the south-east. The Prince, anxious to save the town, consulted with a French engineer, who had recently arrived in Scotland, if it would be possible to raise an effective battery upon either of these eminences. The person thus consulted was a Mr Gordon, styling himself Monsieur Mirabelle, a chevalier of the order of St Louis, but a man so whimsical both in his body and mind, that the Highlanders used to parody his *nom de guerre* into Mr Admirable.[2] It is the characteristic of ignorance never to think anything impossible; and this man at once undertook to open a battery upon the Gowan Hill, though there were not fifteen inches' depth of earth above the rock, and the walls of the castle overlooked it by at least fifty feet.

After many days of incessant labour, a sort of battery was constructed of bags of sand and wool, and a number of cannon brought to bear upon the fortress. General Blakeney had not

---

1 This printing-press existed, as a proof-press—that is, a press for printing proof-sheets— in Mr Duncan Stevenson's office, Edinburgh, so lately as 1824.

2 Chevalier Johnstone, 117.

taken all the advantage he might have done of his position to interrupt the works, conceiving that it was best to amuse the Highland army with the prospect of taking the castle, and thus give government time to concentrate its forces against them. But when the battery was opened, he thought proper to answer it in a suitable manner.   Such was the eminence of his situation, that it is said he could see the very shoe-buckles of the besiegers as they stood behind their intrenchments.   The cannon on this battery of course pointed upwards, and scarcely did the least harm either to his fortifications or his men.   The besieged, on the contrary, were able to destroy a great number of their opponents, including many French pickets, who were perhaps the best soldiers in their army.   The works were demolished at leisure, and the siege was then abandoned as a matter of course, after a considerable loss of men.

CHAPTER XIX.

ARRIVAL OF THE DUKE OF CUMBERLAND.

'The remnant of the royal blood
Comes pouring on me like a flood—
The princesses in number five—
Duke William, sweetest prince alive!'—SWIFT.

WHEN the news of Hawley's manœuvres at Falkirk reached the court of St James's, where a drawing-room happened to be held on that particular day, every countenance is said to have been marked with doubt and apprehension, excepting those only of the king himself, the Earl of Stair, and Sir John Cope.[1]   It was

---

[1] The face of this general is said to have been radiant with joy at the intelligence, which at once, in some measure, cleared his honour, and caused him to gain an immense sum of money.   But he was somewhat put out of countenance by an absent Scottish peer addressing him soon after by the title General Hawley, to the no small amusement of those who heard the *quid pro quo.—Quart. Rev.* xxxvi. 180.   As the reader may possibly feel some

now thought necessary to send a general against the insurgents, the best and most popular of whom the country could boast, and who, by one decisive effort, might at length be certain of success. The Duke of Cumberland, who, after tracking their course to Carlisle, had been recalled in apprehension of a French invasion, was now requested to resume the command which he then abandoned, and immediately to set out for the north. He lost no time in obeying his father's orders; and was so expeditious, as to arrive unexpectedly at Edinburgh early in the morning of the 30th of January, after a journey performed in the short space of four days.

This young general was of the same age as Charles—namely, twenty-five—but did not possess the same personal graces, being remarkably corpulent and unwieldy, while his manners were rough and unpleasing. As no Scotsman could be expected to describe him with impartiality, it may be as well here to use the words of Lord Mahon. ' His character,' says this writer, ' was adorned by considerable virtues—honesty of purpose, adherence to his promises, attachment to his friends. He was a dutiful son, and a liberal patron: as a soldier, he was enthusiastically fond of his profession; he had closely studied its details, and might even be lauded for capacity, in an age which, to England at least, was singularly barren of military merit. His unwearied activity and high personal courage would, however, at any period have justly claimed applause. But, as one of his own friends complains, " his judgment is too much guided by his passions, which are often violent and ungovernable." [1] Against his foreign

interest in the conduct of this unfortunate general, it may further be mentioned, upon the authority of the pamphlet ascribed to David Hume, that ' during the whole winter after the battle of Preston he was carried about London in his chair to escape the derision of the mob; till the news of the battle of Falkirk arrived, and then he pulled back the curtains, and shewed his face and his red ribbon to all the world. Thus,' adds the pamphleteer, ' the reputation of which the hero of Coltbridge [Fowkes, who was loudly and generally accused of cowardice] was the means of depriving him, was in a great measure restored to him by the hero of Falkirk.' Sir John Cope, of Brewern, Oxfordshire, Baronet—the hero, as we presume, of Preston—died March 28, 1765. Lieutenant-general Fowkes, who had been so prominent in the same military transactions, died on the ensuing day, having been sixty years an officer in the army.

[1] Lord Waldegrave's *Memoirs*, p. 23.

adversaries he displayed no undue asperity, and towards his soldiers he could sometimes shew compassion : thus, for instance, on arriving at Edinburgh, he immediately arrested the course of Hawley's savage executions : yet even his own army often murmured at his harshness and rigour ; and as to any rebel, he treated him with as little mercy as he might a wolf.   Never, perhaps, did any insurgents meet a more ungenerous enemy. From the deeds of blood in Scotland—committed by his own order in some cases, and connived at in many more—his contemporaries branded him with a disgraceful by-word—THE BUTCHER ; and the historian who cannot deny the guilt, must repeat and ratify the name.'

On arriving at Holyrood House, he immediately went to bed—occupying the same couch of state which Charles had used four months before.   After reposing two hours, he rose and proceeded to business.   Before eight o'clock, and before he had taken breakfast, he is said to have been busy with Generals Hawley and Huske, and other principal officers, whom he summoned so hastily that they appeared in their boots.   During the course of the forenoon he received visits from the state officers, the professors of the university, and the principal citizens, all of whom had the honour of kissing his hand. Meanwhile the music-bells were rung in his honour, and the magistrates prepared to present him with the freedom of the city.   In the midst of matters of state, he did not neglect those of war.   He descended to the large court in front of the palace, where a train of artillery had been collected, and made a careful and deliberate inspection of the pieces.   In the afternoon, according to appointment, a number of ladies, chiefly belonging to Whig families of distinction, paid their respects to him in the same hall where Charles had so lately entertained his fair adherents.[1]   He kissed them all round, made a short speech expressive of his satisfaction, and then retired to hold a council of war.

---

[1] They were dressed in splendid style ; and one of them, Miss Ker, did him the peculiar honour to appear with a *busk*, at the top of which was a crown, done in bugles, surrounded by the words : 'William, Duke of Cumberland, Britain's hero.'

The army had received various reinforcements since its retreat from Falkirk, and was prepared to march for some days before the duke's arrival.   Amongst other accessions, there was one of a very peculiar nature, which no Whig historian has as yet had the hardihood to record.   It will be remembered that the officers taken by the Prince at Preston had been allowed by him to go at large, on parole, and under an oath not to bear arms against the family of Stuart for a twelvemonth.   In the middle of January, some of these gentlemen, placed in little parties at Glammis, Cupar, and Leslie, had been 'delivered' by armed parties of the country-people, and brought, apparently by force, to Edinburgh.   Afterwards some others, who resided at St Andrews, Culross, and Pitfirran, were liberated by the same means, and also carried to Edinburgh.   The Edinburgh news-papers of the time describe them as at a loss how to act on this occasion; they did not appear in military dress or with their swords.   Now, however, the duke took it upon him to resolve the difficulty.   Incredible as it may appear, this prince, declaring their oath and parole to be dissolved, commanded them to return to duty in his army, and sent similar orders to all who still remained non-'delivered,' threatening them with the loss of their commissions if they refused.   A small number, including Sir Peter Halket, Mr Ross (son of Lord Ross), Captain Lucy Scott, and Lieutenants Farquharson and Cumming, refused com-pliance, remarking that the duke was master of their commis-sions, but not of their honour.   But the greater number rejoined their regiments, and served during the remainder of the campaign.

It was determined in the council that the army should set forward next morning towards the position of the insurgents, with his royal highness at its head.   So prompt a resolution gave new courage to the troops, and raised the hopes of the friends of government, hitherto very much depressed.

The duke set out from Holyrood House at nine o'clock in the morning of Friday the 31st of January, after having been only thirty hours in Edinburgh.

The army had departed early in the same morning, in two

columns; one by Borrowstounness, led by General Huske; the other by Linlithgow, of which the duke was to take the command in person. Ligonier's and Hamilton's dragoons patrolled the roads in advance, to prevent intelligence reaching the insurgents. The army comprised altogether fourteen battalions of infantry, four regiments of cavalry, the Argyle militia, and a train of artillery. The whole might amount to ten thousand men.

The Duke of Cumberland had been presented by the Earl of Hopetoun with a coach and twelve horses; and thinking it necessary to make his departure from Edinburgh with as much parade as possible, he used this equipage in passing through the town. As he passed up the Canongate and the High Street, he is said to have expressed great surprise at the number of broken windows which he saw; but when informed that this was the result of a recent illumination, and that a shattered casement only indicated the residence of a Jacobite, he laughed heartily. His coach was followed by a great number of persons of distinction, and by a vast mob. On reaching a place in the suburbs called Castlebarns, he left the coach, and mounted his horse. The state officers and others then crowded about him to take leave, and the mob gave him a hearty huzza. He took off his hat, and turning round, thanked the people for this expression of their regard; adding, that he had had but little time to cultivate their friendship, but would be well pleased when fortune gave him an opportunity of doing so. 'I am in great haste, my friends,' he cried; 'but I believe I shall soon be back to you with good news. Till then, adieu.' So saying, he shook hands with those nearest to him, paused a moment, and then exclaiming: 'Come, let us have a song before parting,' began to sing a ditty which had been composed in his own honour:

> 'Will ye play me fair,
>   Highland laddie, Highland laddie?'

Then stretching forth his hand, as if addressing the object of his hostility, he set forward at a gallop, to put himself at the head of the army.[1]

---

[1] Extract of a letter from Edinburgh, in Merchant's *History of the Rebellion,* 329.

He lodged this evening at Linlithgow, and it was the general expectation that he would engage the Highlanders next day. Straggling parties had been seen hovering on the hills between Falkirk and Linlithgow, which, on the morning of the 1st of February, had fallen back to the Torwood, giving out that they would there await the royal army. But as he proceeded towards Falkirk, stray Highlanders were brought before him, who reported that they were in reality conveying their baggage over the Forth, with the intention of retreating to the Highlands; and the intelligence seemed to be confirmed by the noise of a distant explosion, occasioned by the blowing up of their powder-magazine in the church of St Ninian's. The duke walked all the way from Linlithgow to Falkirk on foot, at the head of the Scots Royals, to encourage the men after the manner of his rival; but he now thought it unnecessary to pursue the march with extraordinary speed, and therefore rested this evening at Falkirk, where he found the soldiers who had been wounded in the late engagement deserted by their captors.

When his royal highness arrived in Falkirk, and it was debated what lodging he should choose, he is said to have inquired for the house which 'his cousin had occupied,' being sure, he said, that *that* would not only be the most comfortable in the town, but also the best provisioned. He accordingly passed the night in the same house and the same bed which have been already described as accommodating Charles on the evening of the battle. He next morning marched to Stirling, which he found evacuated by the insurgents, and where General Blakeney informed him that, but for his seasonable relief, he must have speedily surrendered the fortress for want of ammunition and provisions. A considerable number of straggling adherents of the Chevalier were here taken prisoners, and sent to Edinburgh Castle.[1]

[1] Amongst these was a Miss Jeany Cameron, whom popular report assigned to the Prince as a mistress. The mistake of Sophia Western for this lady at Gloucester, in Fielding's novel, would alone, if nothing else did, make her history interesting to us; yet it is one of the most obscure affairs connected with the insurrection. It has been already stated, on the authority of Mr Æneas Macdonald, that Mrs Jean Cameron witnessed the setting up of

The Highland army had in reality resolved to retire to the
north. For several days after the battle of Falkirk, Charles and
his chiefs contemplated fighting again, on nearly the same
ground, with the English army ; and with this design a review
of the troops was held on the field of Bannockburn. On the

the standard at Glenfinnin. The whole passage respecting her in Mr Macdonald's narrative is as follows : ' Here a considerable number of both *gentlemen* and *ladies* met to see
the ceremony ; among the rest the famous Miss Jeany Cameron, as she is commonly, but
very improperly called ; for she is a widow, nearer fifty than forty years of age. She is a
genteel, well-looked, handsome woman, with a pair of pretty eyes, and hair as black as jet.
She is of a very sprightly genius, and is very agreeable in conversation. She was so far
from accompanying the Prince's army, that she went off with the rest of the spectators as
soon as the army marched. Neither did she ever follow the camp, nor was ever with the
Prince but in public, when he had his court at Edinburgh.'—*Lyon in Mourning*, MS.
iii. 516.

Some years ago, a gentleman who knew the late Sir Ewen Cameron of Fassefern, nephew
of the Young Locheil of the '45, reported to the present writer the following particulars, as
well known to Sir Ewen, and altogether beyond question : ' The lady who made so much
noise in 1745-6 as Miss Jeany Cameron, was a daughter of Cameron of Glendessery. She
had married an Irish gentleman named O'Neal, with whom she lived several years in
Ireland, till obliged, by his brutal behaviour, to divorce him. She then returned to Inverness-shire, where her original name was given to her. At the time of the insurrection she
managed the estates of her brother, Cameron of Dungallon, who was *out*. She sent the
Prince a present of cattle at the time of his raising the standard, but *never saw him herself.*
She was a woman of beauty and fashion, of good manners and masculine understanding.
She died in 1774 [date wrong—see *postea*], at her house of Mount Cameron, in Lanarkshire.'

These various statements, though not quite consistent with each other, seem to be nearly
decisive that the Jean Cameron known in the Highlands as a lady of birth and breeding
was not connected with Charles in the way which has been alleged by popular rumour. On
the other hand, the lady taken at Stirling at the beginning of February, and conducted to
Edinburgh Castle, was kept there *till the 15th of November*, and then liberated along with
the Duchess of Perth, *on bail*. This fact, which the newspapers of the day make certain,
would seem to imply that the lady taken at Stirling was really a woman of figure, and some
political consequence. How this person came to be thought the same individual who had
been present at the raising of the standard, I must profess myself at a loss to conjecture.
Certainly, however, if there was a Jeany Cameron, or any person taking that name, in
attendance on Charles through his Lowland campaign, and subsequently taken at Stirling, it
was a different lady from Mrs Jean Cameron of the Glendessery family. The Jeany
Cameron tale altogether made such an impression on the public mind at the time, that a
Grub-Street novel was composed, of which it forms the groundwork. In Caulfield's
Portraits (4 vols. 4to), there is one of ' Miss Jeany Cameron,' accompanied by a professed
memoir, evidently in the main fictitious, and probably a mere abridgment of the novel. It
describes the lady as having been, in 1745, forty-six years of age, but still sufficiently handsome to charm the Prince.

The lady pointed to by Sir Ewen Cameron died on the 27th of June 1772. In the *Scots
Magazine*, where her death is recorded, she is described as ' Mrs Jean Cameron, sister to
Captain Allan Cameron of Glendessery.' Moreover, in the article ' Morven,' in Sir John
Sinclair's *Statistical Account of Scotland* (1794), it is mentioned that ' the session has
lately got £40, being the principal and interest of £20 bequeathed in the year 1772 to the
poor of Morven by Mrs Jean Cameron of Mount Cameron.'

28th, when he learned that the Duke of Cumberland was expected in a day or two to take the command of the army at Edinburgh, Charles continued of the same mind, and had a plan of the proposed battle drawn out by Lord George Murray. It was now, however, found that the army was greatly reduced in number, many being supposed to have gone home, though in reality some were only straggling over the country. Convinced that only 5000 men could now be brought into the field against the double numbers of the enemy, Lord George Murray, Locheil, Keppoch, Clanranald, Ardshiel, Lochgarry, Scothouse, and the Master of Lovat, drew up a paper at Falkirk on the 29th, representing this in strong terms to the Prince, and recommending that the army should retire to the north, where it could be usefully employed during the remainder of the winter in taking the forts, and could be at no loss to defend itself against superior forces till the spring, when, they were certain, an army of 10,000 men could easily be brought into the field, not to speak of the succours to be expected from abroad. Charles, on receiving this document at Bannockburn, sent Sir Thomas Sheridan to argue the matter with the chiefs: they in their turn sent Keppoch to argue with him. In the end, they succeeded in gaining his consent to the retreat.[1] For two days more, the appearance of an intention to fight the royal troops was kept up; but on the 31st, Lord George and the infantry posted at Falkirk marched to Bannockburn, leaving Pitsligo's, Elcho's, and Kilmarnock's horse to patrol before the English army.

It was agreed that night, at the Prince's quarters at Bannockburn, that the army should muster next morning at nine o'clock,

[1] His conduct on this occasion has been variously represented. Mr John Hay of Restalrig, who now acted as his secretary, and must have always been near his person, says that, on receiving the paper drawn up by the chiefs, he was transported with rage and vexation, and struck his head against the wall till he staggered, exclaiming loudly against Lord George Murray. On the other hand, Colonel Warren, who was some time after sent with despatches to France, writing to the old Chevalier from Paris, May 9, says that the Prince bore the proposition of the retreat to the north 'with that constancy and greatness he at once is master of: however severe and unnecessary it might appear to him, he generally,' adds this gentleman, 'waived his own opinion, and paid a deference to that of some of the chiefs as in reward of their services, and a mark of his condescension to what they judged for the good of your royal cause and their happiness,

and march with deliberation across the Forth. The men, however, had been struck with alarm respecting the approaching
army, and rising at daybreak of the 1st of February, they set
out in a straggling manner, without waiting for proper orders.
The movement was extremely discreditable, for the Prince and
other leaders were left behind, exposed to the risk of a sally
from Stirling Castle, and to all other hazards. Lord George
Murray seems inclined in his narrative to throw the blame of
the transaction on O'Sullivan, but without shewing any grounds
for his surmise. In the hurry of the occasion, the powder
belonging to the army, amounting to fifty barrels, was blown
up in the church of St Ninian's, killing ten country-people, and
also some of the Highlanders, besides endangering the person
of the Prince and some other persons of note who were passing
through the village at the time. It is not certain whether an
order had been given to destroy this powder; but certainly its
explosion at that particular moment must have been accidental,
when the preceding circumstances are considered. The heavy
cannon were at the same time spiked, and many other articles,
too bulky to be readily carried away, were thrown into the
Forth.

The Whig party papers represented the St Ninian's accident
in a light unfavourable to the Prince, alleging that he had
ordered the explosion for the purpose of destroying the
church and killing the unoffending villagers. So ridiculous a
charge is not worthy of notice. The opposite party were
perhaps equally unjust towards the royal army with reference to
another accident which befell on the same day. A portion of

which he gave proof was more to him than any other satisfaction he could propose, even to
life itself; so that they could not but admire his spirit, heart, and conduct. He has taught
them how to bear the inconveniences of adversity, or a mis-step, by looking forward, providing for the time to come, and taking lesson by what is past; and all this with such
prudence, dignity, caution, and dexterity, that really shew him to be born a general. I am
sure there never was one more universally beloved by his army, or more deserving it.' It
is possible that both accounts may be in some measure true. A new proposal for retreat to
one who had so set himself on going forward must have been extremely vexatious; momentary feeling might produce the conduct described by Mr Hay; but, the first gust having
expended itself, he might act the prudent and dignified part ascribed to him by Warren.

the troops quartered at Linlithgow had been lodged in the palace, upon straw laid along the halls. In the morning, about the time of their departure, the straw caught fire, and soon involved the palace in flames. The army left it in that state, and it soon became, what it now is, a blackened ruin. The impression of the people at the place was, and still is, that the affair was accidental, and I am disposed to believe that careless- ness in the management of their fires was the extent of guilt which can fairly be ascribed to the soldiery on this occasion.

CHAPTER XX.

MARCH TO THE NORTH.

'Now great Hawley leads on, with great Huske at his tail,
And the duke in the centre—this sure cannot fail.'

Jacobite Song.

THE last meal which Prince Charles partook of upon the Lowland territory, which he had now kept possession of for five months, was at Boquhan, on the 1st of February, immediately before crossing the Forth. He arrived here a little after mid-day, along with his principal officers, and sat down to a dinner which had been prepared for him. On the preceding evening, Captain Campbell, of the king's service, had come, with a party of soldiers, to the farm of Wester Frew, upon the north side of the river, and asked for a person who might shew him the fords. The farmer was a stanch Jacobite, and, suspecting no good to the Prince from the captain's inquiries, directed him, not to the regular and accustomed ford, but to one which was seldom used, a little farther up the river. Campbell then took from a cart several sackfuls of caltrops, which he threw into the stream. Having thus prepared, as he thought, for the annoyance of the insurgent army, he and his party withdrew. The farmer, secretly rejoicing at the service he had done to the Prince, crossed the water next day, along with his sons and servants, and remained near his royal highness all the time he was at dinner. When their meal was finished, the party took the proper ford, all except Charles, who, not thinking any information necessary regarding fords which he had used, rode through by one different from either of the above mentioned, and in which the farmer had seen one of Campbell's men deposit a single caltrop. The Prince's horse picked up this, and was wounded.[1]

The army spent the evening of that day (February 1) at Dunblane, while the Prince rode forward a few miles, and lodged at Drummond Castle, the princely seat of the Duke of Perth. The roads were now found so bad, that they were obliged to leave some of their baggage behind. They persisted, however, in a resolution which had been made, to take all their prisoners along with them to the north. These persons, after the battle, had been confined in the castle of Doune, near Dunblane, a strong old fortress, of which the Laird of Glengyle had been made governor, and they now joined the army in its retreat. Many of them took the earliest opportunity of making their escape, notwithstanding that they were treated with all possible civility, and had pledged their honour not to take advantage of any indulgences which might be shewn to them.

The Highland army reached Crieff next day, and the Prince slept at Lord John Drummond's house of Fairnton. On the 3d, the Prince reviewed his forces, and found that the decrease by desertion was much less than had been represented to him at Bannockburn, the number being only a thousand less than at the battle of Falkirk.[2] The enemies of Lord George Murray suspected him, and the others who had recommended the retreat, of deception; but it is probable that the army had been considerably increased during the last two days by the return of parties straggling in the country passed through. At a

---

[1] This information was derived from one of the farmer's sons, who survived till recent times.

[2] Maxwell of Kirkconnel's Narrative.

council now held some warm altercations took place. Lord George Murray had been incensed at the manner of the march from Bannockburn, and demanded to know who was blamable for it. Charles, to maintain peace, said he would take the blame of it upon himself.[1] It was determined that, for the sake of subsistence, the march to the north should be performed in two parties; one of which, consisting of the clans under Charles's command, should take the ordinary military road which General Cope had assumed in his northern expedition; while the Low-country regiments and horse should be conducted by Lord George Murray along the roads by the coast of Angus and Aberdeenshire. Inverness was to be the rendezvous. At the time this resolution was taken, the Duke of Cumberland was busy, thirty miles behind, in repairing the bridge of Stirling for the passage of his troops; one arch of that ancient and important structure having been destroyed, at an early period of the campaign, by Governor Blakeney, to prevent the transmission of supplies to Charles from the Highlands.

Nothing could more distinctly prove the individual superiority of the insurgent army over the king's troops, or rather, perhaps, the superiority of their desultory system over the formal rules of regular warfare, than the way in which they performed their retreat to the north. While the Duke of Cumberland had to wait a day for the repair of a bridge, and then could only drag his lumbering strength over the post-roads at the rate of twelve or fourteen miles in as many hours, Charles forded rivers, crossed over moors, and dared the winter dangers of a hilly country with alacrity and promptitude. A later generation saw the same system revived with effect by the great modern soldier of the continent; and it is impossible to give a better idea of the surprise with which the duke, on the present occasion, beheld the incalculable movements of his antagonist, than by recalling the perplexity of the old Austrian generals on observing the first movements of Bonaparte in Italy.

[1] Lord George Murray's Narrative.

At the commencement of the pursuit, the duke had been little more than a single day's march behind the retiring host, but on the sixth day he found this interval to have increased threefold. The Highland army had been passing through Perth, in straggling parties, during the whole of the 2d and 3d of February; he did not arrive there till the 6th, when he learned that one party had passed Blair in Athole, on the direct road to Inverness, while the other was just evacuating Montrose, on the route to Aberdeen. He then saw fit to discontinue the chase for the present; the weather being extremely unfit for the movements of his army, while the Highland hills which now rose to his view presented but few inducements for an advance. He contented himself with fishing up from the bottom of the Tay about fourteen guns which the insurgents had spiked and thrown into the bed of that river, and with sending out parties to plunder and harass the lands of the Perthshire insurgents. A vast quantity of cattle, horses, and even household goods, taken by the soldiers from the estates and houses of the disaffected, were publicly sold by the soldiers in Perth while the duke was present. The Duchess of Perth and Viscountess of Strathallan were seized in their respective houses and carried prisoners to Edinburgh Castle, whence they were not released till the ensuing November.

Before Cumberland had been many days in Perth, intelligence was brought to him that his brother-in-law, the Prince of Hesse, had entered the Firth of Forth with those auxiliary troops which, as already mentioned, his majesty had called over from the continent to aid in suppressing the insurrection. This armament cast anchor in Leith Roads on the 8th of February. The prince landed that night at Leith, and was immediately conducted to Holyrood House. He was attended by the Earl of Crawford, so famous in the wars of George II., by a son of the Duke of Wolfenbüttel, and by various other distinguished persons. The castle greeted his serene highness with a round of great guns; and next day, notwithstanding it was Sunday, the people flocked in great numbers to see and congratulate him. His troops, which amounted to five thousand in number, landed on that and the succeeding day, and were cantoned in the city.[1]

The Duke of Cumberland judged it necessary, on the 15th, to leave his camp at Perth and pay a hurried visit to the prince in Edinburgh. On his arrival, he was hailed with the loudest acclamations of the loyal inhabitants, as having already cleared the Low Country of its disturbers, and restored peace where he had lately found civil war. It was at this time the general impression that the insurgents, dismayed at his approach, had retired into the north only to disperse themselves, as Mar and his army had done in 1716 on the advance of the Duke of Argyll, and that, in imitation of his father's conduct at that time, Charles had left the country by one of the ports on the east coast.

On the evening of his arrival in Edinburgh, the duke and the prince held a council of war at the house of the Lord Justice-clerk, to determine their future operations. The generals who attended this meeting, imposed upon by the popular report, and disposed to flatter the duke, gave it unanimously as their opinion that the war was now at an end, and that his royal highness had nothing to do but send a few parties into the Highlands, as soon as the season would permit, who should exterminate all that remained of the insurgent force. When these persons had delivered their sentiments, the duke turned to Lord Milton, and desired to hear his opinion upon the present state of affairs. The judge begged to be excused from speaking in an assembly where his profession did not qualify

---

[1] The Hessian soldiers were remarkably handsome, good-looking men, with long fair hair, which they combed whenever they sat down. They acquired the affection and esteem of the people who had occasion to mix in their society during the ensuing campaign. Their good nature and pure manners were favourably compared with the coarse conversation and dissolute conduct of the British soldiery. It may be recorded, for the satisfaction of snuff-takers, that the Hessians were the first to introduce the use of *black rappee* into this country, in opposition to the original 'Scotch brown.' It may be added, on good authority, as a not less curious fact, that Edinburgh owes all the benefit which it derives from that useful institution, Gillespie's Hospital, to the same cause; the two brothers Gillespie, who founded that charity, having commenced the fortune which enabled them to do so by supplying the public with the new-fashioned species of snuff, in sufficient quantities, and of excellent quality, immediately on the Hessians introducing it.

him; but his royal highness insisted that he should speak, as he knew the Highlands and Highlanders better than any man present. His lordship then declared it as his opinion that the war was *not* at an end, but that the insurgents would again unite their scattered forces, and hazard a battle before abandoning the enterprise.[1] The duke, who had already seen the bad results of giving up the chase too soon, and of demitting the suppression of the insurrection to inferior hands, adopted this opinion; and immediately set out to rejoin his army, having previously given orders that the Hessian troops should follow him with all convenient speed.

The soundness of Lord Milton's opinion was proved by what followed. Notwithstanding the weather, and the desolation of the country, Charles succeeded in leading his force, without diminution, over the Grampians, to the shore of the Moray Firth; Lord George Murray reached the same point by the more circuitous route which he had adopted through Angus and Aberdeenshire. In his march through Badenoch the Prince reduced the small government fort of Ruthven; and Lord George, in passing Peterhead, was reinforced by some dismounted French pickets, who had just been landed at that port. The duke pursued Lord George's route at a leisurely pace, leaving the Hessians to guard the passes at Perth, and having sent on a body of troops under Sir Andrew Agnew to garrison the castle of Blair.

It was unfortunate that the commander of the royal army should have marched on this occasion through Angus and Aberdeenshire, because the symptoms of disaffection which he saw in these districts must have given him an extremely unfavourable impression of the kingdom in general, and had a strong effect in disposing him to treat it, after his victory, as a conquered country. Most of the gentlemen, throughout Angus at least, he found absent with the insurgent army; others paid him so little respect as to recruit almost before his eyes. In

---

[1] Home's Works, iii. 178.

the town of Forfar, a small party of Charles's forces beat up for new adherents on the day before he entered the town; and, being concealed by the inhabitants till he had gone past, continued to do the same immediately on his back being turned. When he lodged at the castle of Glammis,[1] on his troop preparing to depart in the morning, it was found that all the girths of his horses had been cut during the night, in order to retard his march. Afterwards, as he was slowly parading through the town of Brechin, hemmed closely in, and retarded by an immense crowd which had collected to see him, he observed a pretty girl standing on a *stair-head*, gazing, among others of her sex, at the unusual spectacle: it pleased him to honour this damsel with a low bow and an elevation of the hat. The object of his admiration returned the compliment by a contemptuous gesture which does not admit of description. Many will be disposed to think that, when he found the principles of rebellion revolutionising the female heart so far as to render it impervious to flattery, he was justifiable in considering the case desperate.

Having resolved, on reaching Aberdeen, to await the return of spring before proceeding farther, he marked his sense of the disaffection of this part of the country by subjecting part of it to the terrors of military law. A gentleman named Ferrier had raised about two hundred men for the service of the Chevalier throughout the braes of Angus, where, establishing a sort of camp, he laid the country under contribution even to the gates of Brechin. The duke despatched a party, which, not satisfied with expelling Ferrier, treated the country with excessive severity, mulcting all whom they could convict of Jacobitism, and burning the whole of the Episcopal meeting-houses. 'It cost some pains,' observes the *Scots Magazine* very gravely, 'to save Glenesk from being burned from end to end, being a nest of Jacobites.'

On Sunday the 16th of February, Charles reached Moy Hall,

---

[1] The Strathmore family, proprietors of this noble old seat, were Jacobites, though not engaged in the insurrection of 1745. So unwelcome a guest was the Duke of Cumberland, that orders were given, after he departed, to take down the bed in which he slept.

the seat of the Laird of Mackintosh, about sixteen miles from Inverness. The laird was absent on duty as a partisan of the government. The lady, who, as already mentioned, had raised the clan for the Prince, received him and his immediate attendants with great hospitality. Charles designed to rest here until his men should come up, before going nearer to Inverness, where the Earl of Loudoun had about seventeen hundred men in arms. Some one—suspected to be Grant of Dalrachny—sent information to Lord Loudoun that Charles was lodging at Moy Hall with a slender retinue; and the earl immediately formed the design of marching thither, in order to take him prisoner. Notwithstanding the exertions he made to keep the scheme a secret, it became known to the dowager Lady Mackintosh, who lived in Inverness, and who immediately despatched a messenger to put her daughter-in-law and the Prince on their guard. Meanwhile, in the evening, 1500 men had taken the road for Moy under the conduct of the earl. The messenger, a boy named Lachlan Mackintosh, tried to pass through the army on the road; but finding this difficult, and dreading that he might be arrested, he lay down in a ditch by the wayside till all had passed, and then bounded off by a circuitous road towards Moy. About five in the morning (Monday, 17th February) he reached the house 'in a top-sweat,' bearing information that the Earl of Loudoun's men were little more than a mile distant. The guard instantly awoke the Prince, who dressed quickly, and came down to the courtyard. Lady Mackintosh appeared there likewise, 'in her smock petticoat,' for it was no time for delicacy, and exerted herself to get the Prince and his guard sent to a place of safety, and all his valuable effects put out of the way. He went along the bank of Moy Loch to a place more than a mile off, where he met Locheil and a party of his troops, with whom he resolved to stand his ground in case of an attack. Meanwhile Lord Loudoun's expedition had experienced a strange interruption. Lady Mackintosh had, the night before, sent out a patrolling party, consisting of five men, armed with muskets, to keep guard on the road towards Inverness. The head of the party was a clever fellow named Fraser, the black-smith of Moy. When he became aware of the approach of a great body of men along the road, he instantly comprehended the design in view. Planting his men at intervals by the way-side, he fired his piece at the head of the approaching body, and by the shot killed the Laird of Macleod's piper, reputed the best of his time in the Highlands. The other men also fired, conveying the impression of a wide-spread body of opponents. The blacksmith was then heard crying upon the Camerons and Macdonalds to advance on the villains who designed to murder their Prince. The van of the advancing troops immediately fell into a panic, and, turning back with precipitation, they threw the rear into confusion, oversetting and trampling many as they went along. The whole army became inspired with the same terror, and fled amain to Inverness, where they arrived in a state of extreme distress from bruises, exhaustion, and mortification of mind. The Master of Ross, who was present as an officer, and afterwards passed through a long life as a soldier, subject to perils of all kinds, was heard in his latter days to declare that in all his career he had never known a situation so grievous as that in which he was at the *rout of Moy*. Information of the gallant exploit of the blacksmith soon reached Prince Charles, who immediately returned to Moy Hall.[1]

He this day gathered a sufficient number of his forces to enable him to advance on the next to Inverness. Meanwhile Lord Loudoun found it necessary to withdraw from that town. When the insurgents drew near (Tuesday, February 18), they found the Independent Companies making the best of their way across the Firth by the Kessock Ferry. The Highlanders entered a vacant town, and the earl's troops retired into Ross-shire.

Inverness, now a flourishing town of about twelve thousand inhabitants, where all the refinements and many of the elegancies of city life are to be met with, appears, from a publication of

---

[1] Home's *History*. *Jacobite Memoirs.*

the period,[1] to have been then only such a town as could be expected in the vicinity of a Highland and half-civilised territory —a royal burgh, yet not emancipated from feudal domination ; a seaport, but possessing only a slight local commerce ; confined in its dimensions, limited in population, and poor in its resources. A coach had never, at this time, been seen at Inverness ; nor was there a turnpike road within forty miles of its walls. The only advancement which it could be said to have made in civilisation was occasioned by the English garrison maintained in its fort by government, and by a few of the Highland gentry, who resided in it during the winter. It was in the town-house of one of these, Lady Drummuir, mother of the Lady Mackintosh—which, as appears, was then the only house in Inverness that had a room ungraced by a bed —that the young Chevalier took up his residence.

Though Charles thus easily obtained possession of Inverness, the fort still held out against him. Fort George, for such was its name, had been established at the Revolution upon the site of the ancient castle of Inverness—the scene of Duncan's murder in Shakspeare, if not in fact. A tall massive tower, reared upon an eminence, the sides of which were protected by bastions—commanding the town on one hand, and the bridge over the Ness on another—formed the whole of this place of strength, which had cost government altogether about £50,000 in its construction and maintenance. On the present occasion it was garrisoned by a company of Grants under the Laird of Rothiemurchus, a company of Macleods, and eighty regular troops, and had a sufficient store of ammunition and provisions.

The Highlanders, who had the greatest possible dislike to the government forts, were highly gratified when, after a siege of two days, this fell into their hands. Sixteen pieces of cannon and a hundred barrels of beef accompanied the rendition. The destruction of the fort, which was immediately ordered by the Prince, was not effected without loss. The French engineer

---

[1] Burt's *Letters from the North of Scotland.*

who was charged with this duty, thinking the match was extinguished, approached to examine it, when the explosion took place, and carried him up into the air along with the stones of the bastion.

Before the capture of Fort George, which took place on the 20th of February, Lord George Murray arrived with his column, after a very painful march through a country covered with snow. The army was now once more complete. The whole of the Lowland territory on the shore of the Moray Firth, besides all the adjacent Highlands, to the distance of a hundred miles from Inverness, was in the hands of the insurgents; but the duke interposed on one side, and the Hessians on another, to prevent all communication with the south; while Lord Loudoun hung with his native troops still nearer in a contrary direction.

CHAPTER XXI.

PROCEEDINGS IN THE NORTH.

'The north! what do they in the north?'
Richard III.

THOUGH their retreat before the face of the king's troops was virtually a confession of weakness, the Highland army was still determined to maintain the war with all possible vigour, hopeful that French succours would arrive in time to give them a victory. They determined that, while Cumberland waited at Aberdeen for the advance of spring, they should improve their position by a series of minor enterprises, such as the troops were fitted to perform in that country and in the existing state of the weather. These, in general, turned out in a manner remarkably creditable to the army.

Immediately after the capture of Fort George, Charles sent three hundred of the Irish pickets, under Brigadier Stapleton, to lay siege to Fort Augustus, thirty-two miles distant. This party, before their artillery could be brought through the snow, attacked the old barrack, and carried it immediately; the garrison, which consisted of three companies of Guise's regiment, retiring into the fort. A trench was opened on the 3d of March, and on the second day thereafter, the powder-magazine chancing to explode, the garrison was compelled to surrender. The party then proceeded to Fort William, where they were joined by the Camerons, Keppoch Macdonalds, and Stuarts of Appin, under Locheil; but, owing to delays occasioned by the difficulty of transporting the cannon, they were not ready to commence the siege of this more important fortress till the 20th of March. By the Irish and Highlanders united, the most vigorous attempts were made to obtain possession of the place, but without avail. On the 3d of April they were under the necessity of retiring, in order to join the army at Inverness, in anticipation of the approach of the royal army.

Early in March, the Prince despatched the Earl of Cromarty with a large detachment to beat up the quarters of Lord Loudoun in Ross-shire. The party consisted of the earl's own regiment of Mackenzies, the Mackintoshes, the small regiment of Mackinnons, the Macgregors, and the men commanded by Macdonald of Barrisdale. It was perhaps insufficient in point of numbers for the enterprise; but a greater deficiency seems to have been found in the commander, who left his men for a couple of days at Dingwall, while he went home to his own house. The Prince, hearing no good accounts of the detachment, sent Lord George Murray to take the command, who, immediately advancing with it to Tain, found, to his surprise, that Lord Loudoun's troops had passed the Firth of Dornoch into Sutherland two days before, without the Earl of Cromarty having obtained any intelligence of the fact, though he was in what the Highlanders emphatically called his own country. Lord George then consulted with the officers, and it was agreed that the enemy could not with propriety be followed by land, as, before it would be possible to turn the head of the Firth and attack Lord Loudoun, that nobleman might easily cross again into Ross-shire, leaving them in such a position with respect to Inverness that they might be unable to join the army before the expected engagement with the royal troops. It was at the same time agreed that, if they could procure boats to cross the Firth, they might attack Lord Loudoun, and the more effectively if they could cross before he was aware. With a view to such a movement, they determined not to advance to Tain, which would have the effect of keeping up his vigilance, but to retire to Dingwall, where they were within a day's march both of Tain and Inverness.

Lord George now returned to headquarters, and the further prosecution of the enterprise was intrusted to the Duke of Perth. As a preliminary step, a great number of fishing-boats were collected from the Morayshire coast, and brought to Findhorn ; and this with such secrecy, or so much under favour of the popular spirit of the district, that no friend of government had the least suspicion of the design. To avoid the government vessels cruising on the Moray Firth, Moir of Stoneywood carried this flotilla across to the shore near Tain in the course of a single night. The Duke of Perth had his party conducted to the spot, and immediately embarked a large portion of it, while the other proceeded to the head of the Firth, to intercept the enemy in that direction. A fog favoured the passage of the troops, who landed within a few miles of Dornoch, the position of the Earl of Loudoun's forces, without his lordship having the least suspicion of their approach. As they were advancing along the coast, they encountered a party of two hundred, some of whom fled back to the main body. Instead of falling upon this party at once, and pushing on for Dornoch, they entered into a tedious parley with it, ending in its capitulation, but destroying the opportunity of surprising Lord Loudoun's army. It is not improbable that this procedure was in consequence of an anxiety entertained by individuals in the detachment to avoid, if at all possible, a hostile collision with troops amongst whom were some of their own nearest relatives. The Chevalier

Johnstone informs us that at least Macdonald of Scothouse, the first cadet of the house of Clanranald, was under feelings of this kind, having a son who served as an officer under Lord Loudoun. Meanwhile this nobleman, accompanied by the Lord President Forbes, led off the main body of his army towards the central fastnesses of Sutherland, whither he was eagerly but vainly pursued by the Duke of Perth, who did not halt till he reached the head of Loch Shin.

By this event the Independent Companies, upon whom Forbes had expended so much zeal and exertion, were completely broken up. The Mackays now returned to their own country. The Macleods withdrew to Skye, where Loudoun and Forbes were glad to find a refuge. The Duke of Perth then returned with most of the insurgent troops to Inverness, leaving only the Earl of Cromarty, with a comparatively small detachment, to keep the loyalists of Sutherland in check.

Lord John Drummond was posted at Fochabers, on the east bank of the Spey, in command of a detachment of troops, some of which he placed at Cullen, others at Strathbogie. In this party was the well-disciplined regiment of John Roy Stuart, together with such of the native cavalry as had been kept together. Till the middle of March, these troops were not disturbed by the king's forces. At that time the Duke of Cumberland sent forward a large body of troops to take possession of a line of posts between the Dee and Spey. This had very nearly occasioned the destruction of the Strathbogie party. On the afternoon of the 17th, they were returning fatigued from a fruitless march against the young Laird of Grant, when they found the village on the point of falling into the hands of the enemy. The commanders were at first puzzled whether to retire immediately, leaving the stragglers to take their chance, or to pause and endeavour to concentrate their strength for a deliberate retreat. By adopting the latter plan, they gave confidence to their men. The whole party then made a skilful and safe retreat in the very face of the enemy, first to Keith, and afterwards to Fochabers.

Mr Maxwell of Kirkconnel, in noticing this affair, says: 'The intrepidity of the common men was very remarkable; they had seen themselves closely pursued by an enemy vastly superior; nevertheless, even after night came on, [when] a fresh alarm was given at Keith, they all repaired to their colours, and marched off in good order.' Lord John Drummond, now supposing that Cumberland was in full march towards the Spey, withdrew behind that river.

While posted there, Lord John sent detachments across the river every day to make demonstrations before the enemy, and patrol on the road between Fochabers and Keith. On the 20th, the detachment returned earlier than usual, apparently under an alarm from the appearance of a large body of the royal troops. This was in reality a feint to mislead the enemy, and with a view to surprising his advanced guard in the village of Keith during the ensuing night. Fifty picked men of Stuart's regiment, under Captain Robert Stewart, younger of Glenlivet, with some French troops, the whole commanded by Major Glasgow, crossed the Spey in the evening, and advancing stealthily, arrived about one in the morning at Keith, which they surrounded, without giving the least alarm. The troops posted there consisted of seventy Campbells and thirty of Kingston's dragoons. The sentinel, a Campbell, was seized and silenced; a Lieutenant Simpson swept round the place with a few horse; and Major Glasgow, with the remainder of the party, boldly entered the street. The French, finding a guard in the school, discharged upon them a platoon. At the same time a vigorous attack was made upon the main body of the Campbells, who were posted in the parish church. The dragoons fought in the street, but were soon overpowered. For some time the Campbells kept up a brisk fire from the church, but were also obliged to yield. No triumph on so small a scale could have been more complete. With the loss of one Frenchman, and at the expense of a few wounds, they secured the whole party, except five or six who escaped. On the government side there were nine killed, and a considerable number wounded. Before daybreak,

Major Glasgow had returned from this clever little affair to headquarters with eighty prisoners.

Of the transactions of this period, none was more brilliant than an expedition into Athole, executed by Lord George Murray. It has already been said that the Duke of Cumberland subjected Angus to military execution; his detachments in the upper part of Perthshire treated that country with even greater severity. As already mentioned, the mother of the Duke of Perth and the wife of Viscount Strathallan, for the crime of having relations in the insurgent army, were seized in their own houses, and hurried to Edinburgh Castle, where they remained prisoners for nine months in a small, unhealthy room. All the houses whose proprietors had gone with Prince Charles were burned, or retained for quarters to the military; the unhappy tenants being in either case expelled, to starve upon the snowy heath. When Lord George heard of this at Inverness, he resolved to succour his country from its oppressors. Having taken care to secure all the passes, so as to prevent his intentions from becoming known to the enemy, he set out about the middle of March with seven hundred men, none of whom knew the precise object of the expedition. On the evening of the 10th, having reached Dalnaspidal, upon the confines of Athole, a halt was called, and the whole body divided into a number of small parties. Lord George then informed them that he wished to surprise all the different posts of the royal troops before daylight, and as nearly as possible at the same time; for which purpose each party should select a post for whose strength it might be proportioned; and the general rendezvous, after all was done, was to be the Bridge of Bruar, two miles from Blair. The chief posts to be attacked were Bun-Rannoch, the house of Kynnachin, the house of Blairfettie, the house of Lude, the house of Faskally, and the inn of Blair; besides which, there were some of less strength and importance.

The parties set out immediately, each taking the shortest way to its respective post, and most of them reached the various points of attack before daybreak. At Bun-Rannoch, where there happened to be a late-wake[1] that night, the garrison (a party of Argyleshire men) were surprised in the midst of their enjoyment, and made prisoners without exchange of shot. The sentinel of Kynnachin being more vigilant, and having alarmed the party within, that house was not taken till after a short resistance, and the slaughter of one man. At Blairfettie the whole party was surprised, including the sentinel, and made prisoners after a brief but ineffectual resistance. The garrisons of Lude and Faskally were taken in the same manner; and only at the inn of Blair did the party attacked baffle the Highlanders, or succeed in making their escape.

This last party taking refuge in the castle of Blair, its governor, Sir Andrew Agnew, immediately got his men under arms, and marched out to see who they were that had attacked his posts. It was now nearly daybreak, and Lord George Murray stood at the place of rendezvous with only four-and-twenty men, anxiously waiting the return of the various parties. Fortunately, he received intelligence by a countryman of the approach of Sir Andrew. He hastily consulted with his attendants: some advised an immediate retreat along the road to Dalwhinnie; others were for crossing over the hills, and gaining a place of safety, by paths where they could not be pursued. By either of these plans the insurgent parties, as they returned, would have been successively cut off or made prisoners. Lord George therefore rejected them, and bethought him of a better expedient. Observing a long turf-wall in a field near the bridge, he ordered his men to ensconce themselves behind it, lying at a considerable distance from each other, and displaying the colours of the whole party at still greater intervals. Fortunately, he had with him all the pipers of the corps; these he ordered, as soon as they saw Sir Andrew's men appear, to strike up their most boisterous pibroch. The rest he commanded to brandish their swords over the wall.

The Blair garrison happened to appear just as the sun rose

---

[1] The festivity which attends the watching over a corpse.

above the horizon; and Lord George's orders being properly obeyed, the men stood still, seriously alarmed at the preparations which seemed to have been made for their reception. After listening half a minute to the tumult of bagpipes, and casting a brief glance at the glittering broadswords, they turned back (by order of their commander, however), and hastily sought shelter within the walls of the castle. The Highland leader, delighted with the success of his manœuvre, kept post at the bridge till about the half of his men had arrived, and then proceeded to invest Blair.

When rejoined by all his men, Lord George found that no fewer than thirty different posts had been surprised that morning, between the hours of three and five, without the loss of a single man. The same success, however, did not attend his deliberate siege, which he was obliged to raise on the 31st of March, after having only reduced the garrison to great distress for want of provisions.[1]

There is much truth in what a judicious observer has said regarding this portion of the Prince's expedition—that it is what most deserves the attention of reflecting persons. In military affairs, a victory dazzles common minds: the judicious inquire if the best use is made of means towards a desired end; and where they find this to be the case, whether with telling results or not, they give their approbation. Now, excepting at Fort William, the small army of the Prince was employed with remarkable skill, and to extremely good purpose, during the whole of this spring. He could not, however, create force which did not exist, or remedy the evils inflicted by fortune. During all this time he was embarrassed by want of money. Besides fifteen hundred pounds of Spanish money, which was found in the neighbourhood of Montrose, he had no foreign

[1] The British army never perhaps contained a man more insensible to fear than Sir Andrew Agnew. He possessed, at the same time, a sort of uncouth humour, which rendered him altogether a most remarkable person. During the siege of Blair, when Lord George was ineffectually battering the walls with two little cannon, he one day looked over the battlements, and observing the slight impression made by the balls, cried ironically: ' I daresay the man's mad—knocking down his own brother's house !'

supplies; and in the country itself his pecuniary resources were extremely narrow. Irregularities in the payment of his army tended of course to its disorganisation. He had hopes of supplies from France. At his retreat from Stirling, a gentleman had gone thither to direct the landing of friendly vessels in the district which he expected to possess between Inverness and Aberdeen. Several vessels, with both troops and money, were consequently conducted to that coast; but the difficulties of landing amongst the English cruisers proved insuperable. They either returned, or fell into the hands of the enemy. There was one particular vessel, the loss of which occurred in circumstances so galling, that a few details may be ventured upon.

In the latter part of November, the *Hazard* sloop of war, carrying sixteen guns, twenty-four swivels, and about eighty men, and commanded by Captain Hill, came into Montrose harbour, apparently for the purpose of punishing the town for its eminent services to the Prince, as a port for the reception of his French succours. The vessel, anchoring in the strait close by the town, fired upon it, although no troops of the Chevalier were present. The commander also seized three barks, of which he burned two, and put some guns into the other, that it might add to his powers of annoyance. Brechin was at this time occupied by a remarkably active and clever partisan of the Prince, the same David Ferrier who has been already mentioned as at a later period forming a camp on the Braes of Angus, and laying the whole country under contribution for the Stuart cause. Ferrier, and a Captain Erskine associated with him (a brother of Erskine of Dun), came down to Montrose with their men, and took post, one of them at the town, and the other on an island near the *Hazard*. Fortunately, a French vessel at this time appeared near the harbour, into which she was directed by signals from Captain Ferrier. She proved to have a hundred and fifty of Lord John Drummond's troops on board, with some cannon and stores. Ferrier landed six cannon, which he planted on convenient places commanding the *Hazard*. The vessel which had been taken and fortified by the *Hazard* had been left

R

at the quay, so that it fell into his hands. He took the cannon from that vessel, and planted it on an eminence called the Dial-hill. For a whole night he bombarded the English vessel, so that in the morning her captain was glad to send a flag of truce, requesting leave to go out to sea. This was refused, and the commander then gave her up to Ferrier, who immediately took possession of her in the name of Mr Carnegie of Balnamoon, governor of Forfarshire for the Prince.[1]

The *Hazard* was afterwards despatched to France as a *snow*, under the name of the *Prince Charles*, and was returning to Scotland with about £13,000 and other valuable supplies, when she was observed and chased by the *Sheerness* man-of-war. The place where the rencontre happened was near the northern extremity of Scotland, where a dangerous sea boils round a bold high coast, affording no port or place of shelter. The crew, unwilling to hazard their cargo by an action, made all sail to escape the guns of the *Sheerness*, which, however, kept so close, as to kill thirty-six of the men. After a day's chase, the *Prince Charles* ran in upon the sands of Melness, on the west side of Tongue Bay, where she was safe from the *Sheerness*, but not, as it soon appeared, from a more deadly enemy.

On the opposite side of this bay was the mansion of Lord Reay, where a considerable party of the troops of the Earl of Loudoun had taken refuge. On learning that the crew of the *Prince Charles* had landed with treasure, Lord Reay sent a boat across the bay to learn particulars ; and when he found that the French were not powerful in number, he resolved to attack them. Next day (March 26), as they were on their way to Inverness with their treasure, under the conduct of Mr Mackay, younger of Melness, they were beset by fifty Mackays under his lordship's steward, and as many of Lord Loudoun's troops ; and a fierce but brief conflict took place, during which a few of the French were killed, and some wounded. The foreign party then surrendered, consisting of twenty officers, and a hundred

---

and twenty soldiers and sailors. The treasure fell into the hands of the victors.

'Amidst all these misfortunes,' says Mr Maxwell, 'the Prince kept up his spirits wonderfully: he appeared gayer even than usual; he gave frequent balls to the ladies of Inverness, and danced himself, which he had declined doing at Edinburgh in the midst of his grandeur and prosperity.' He remained in this town the whole time between the 20th of February and the 10th of April, excepting eleven days in the middle of March, during which he visited Elgin and Gordon Castle. At the latter town he was ill, and in danger for two days; when, as Colonel Warren informs the old Chevalier in a letter, 'a timely bleeding hindered the cold turning into a fluxion *de poitrine*, and caused a joy in every heart not to be expressed.' Towards the end of this period, intelligence arrived that he was no longer to entertain any expectation of a regular armament from France, as not only the contemplated embarkation at Boulogne, but that more recently designed at Dunkirk, was now given up. It must have been a stunning blow to the little army, if anything can truly dishearten men of their order, ever the dupes of their wishes and their convictions.

The Duke of Cumberland remained from the 25th of February till the 8th of April at Aberdeen. In his letters he expressed the sentiments with which an acquaintance with Scotland had filled him. The people, he said, were almost to a man Jacobites. Even the loyalists were of little service to him. He could get no intelligence, and reckoned himself more in an enemy's country than when he was warring with the French in Flanders. Mild measures with such a country would not do. 'You will find,' says he to the Duke of Newcastle, 'that the whole of the laws of this ancient kingdom must be new-modelled. Were I to enumerate the villains and villainies this country abounds in, I should never have done.' It is a pity that he did not at least enumerate certain dubious acts committed by William, Duke of Cumberland, and Lieutenant-general Henry Hawley, of which the world wanted a right account for eighty

years. It appears that the former commander occupied the
house of a Mr Thomson, a legal practitioner, using all the
provisions it contained, with coal and candle, without making
the least compensation ; while Hawley took possession of that
belonging to Mrs Gordon of Halhead, and not only used the
lady's tea, linen, and china, without remuneration, but, on going
away, carried off all these articles, and everything else portable,
with, to all appearance, the concurrence of the commander-in-
chief—for the china was afterwards recognised in the shop of a
London broker, who mentioned that he had got it from an
infamous female, who stated that it had been given to her by
the Duke of Cumberland.[1]

The weather continued, till the beginning of April, to be
unfavourable for the march of regular troops. But about that
time a few days of dry cold wind, sweeping away the snow from
the hills, and drying the rivers, rendered it possible to proceed
without much difficulty, and the duke accordingly ordered a
march upon the 8th. He had been by this time supplied with
a fleet of victualling-ships, which were to sail along the coast,
and send provisions on shore as required by the army. His
host, comprising fifteen foot regiments, two of dragoons, with
Kingston's horse, a body of Argyleshire Highlanders, and a
detachment of Lord Loudoun's regiment, which had been
shipped over from Ross, amounted altogether to about nine
thousand men.

His royal highness reached Banff upon the 10th, encamping
in the neighbourhood of the town. Two Highland spies were
here seized, one of them in the act of notching the numbers of
the army upon a stick, according to a fashion which also obtains
among the North American Indians. They were both hanged.
On the 11th, the army moved forward to Cullen, where the Earl
of Findlater testified his loyalty by distributing two hundred
guineas among the troops. Strict orders were here issued to the
men not to stir out of the camp upon pain of death. During

---

[1] Full and well-authenticated particulars of these misdeeds are given in the *Jacobite
Memoirs*, from the papers of Bishop Forbes.

this day's march the army, keeping constantly upon the shore, were closely accompanied by the fleet. The weather was also good, and the men were cheered by the prospect of crossing the Spey without difficulty.

This great mountain-stream, so remarkable for its depth and rapidity, had hitherto been esteemed by Charles's army as almost a sufficient barrier between them and the Duke of Cumberland, and as, indeed, completely protecting their country upon the east. Charles had, several weeks before, instructed Lord John Drummond to defend the fords; and some batteries were raised, which it was expected might accomplish that object. But on the duke approaching with a quantity of cannon sufficient to force the passage, Lord John abandoned a position which he had not the power to maintain, and fell back upon Inverness. It is generally esteemed to have been a leading error in the commanders of the insurgent army to have so easily permitted the royal troops to surmount this grand barrier. But as the duke, with the assistance of his cannon, must have forced his way in spite of their efforts, it was perhaps best to permit him to pass without bloodshed. Lord George Murray was of this opinion, and is said to have urged it with the over-confident exclamation: 'The more of the elector's men come over, there will be the fewer to return!'

The royal army forded the Spey upon the afternoon of Saturday the 12th of April. For this purpose the troops were divided into three bodies, one of which crossed at Garmouth, another near Gordon Castle, and a third close by the church of Belly. The men had the water up to their waists; but such was the ease with which the operation was conducted, that only one dragoon and four women were swept away by the stream.

The duke encamped this evening upon the banks of the river, opposite to Fochabers, himself lodging in the manse of Belly. He marched next day (Sunday) through Elgin to the moor of Alves, where he was little more than thirty miles from Inverness. The march of next day brought him to Nairn, which was only sixteen miles from the position of the insurgents. On arriving at the bridge which gives entrance to this town from the east, the vanguard found it not yet evacuated by the rearguard of the party which had attempted to defend the Spey. Some firing took place from both ends of the bridge; but at last the insurgents retired, without much harm having been done on either side. The advancing party gave chase for several miles; but the Prince coming up unexpectedly with a reinforcement, the other in its turn retreated.

During the 15th, which was the duke's birthday, the army lay inactive in their camp at Nairn; and as each man had an allowance of brandy, cheese, and biscuit, at the duke's expense, the day was spent with appropriate festivity.

CHAPTER XXII.

PRELIMINARIES OF THE BATTLE OF CULLODEN.

'The day approached, when fortune should decide
The important enterprise.'   DRYDEN.

ON Monday the 14th, when intelligence reached Inverness of the royal army having crossed the Spey, Charles rode out towards Nairn to support his retiring party, but returned to Inverness before the evening. He then commanded the drums to be beat, and the pipes to be played through the town, in order to collect his men. When they had assembled in the streets, he walked backwards and forwards through their lines, and endeavoured to animate them for the action which seemed impending.

They hailed his appearance, and received his addresses with their usual enthusiasm; and, in the midst of the huzza which ensued, many voices exclaimed: 'We'll give Cumberland another Fontenoy!' He then mounted his horse, and, with colours flying and pipes playing, led them out to the parks around Culloden House, three or four miles from the town, where they prepared to bivouac for the night.

At six o'clock in the morning of the 15th, the army was led forward to Drummossie Moor (about a mile still farther from Inverness, in an easterly direction), and there drawn up in battle order to receive the Duke of Cumberland, who was expected to march this day from Nairn.   Charles's force at this time was much smaller than it had been at Falkirk, amounting to only about six thousand men.   He had issued orders some time before to the parties dispersed throughout the country, commanding them immediately to join ; but the Frasers, the Keppoch Macdonalds, Macphersons, Macgregors, some recruits of Glengarry, and the Mackenzies raised by the Earl of Cromarty, were still absent.   Under these circumstances, it was with some satisfaction that Charles learned the delay made by the enemy at Nairn, which seemed to promise time for the augmentation of his host.

The scarcity of provisions had now become so great, that the men were on this important day reduced to the miserable allowance of only one small loaf, and that of the worst kind.   Strange as the averment may appear, I have beheld and tasted a piece of the bread served out on this occasion ; being the remains of a loaf, or *bannock*, which had been carefully preserved for eighty-one years by the successive members of a Jacobite family.   It is impossible to imagine a composition of greater coarseness, or less likely either to please or satisfy the appetite ; and perhaps no recital, however eloquent, of the miseries to which Charles's army was reduced, could have impressed the reader with so strong an idea of the real extent of that misery as the sight of this singular relic.   Its ingredients appeared to be merely the husks of oats, and a coarse unclean species of dust, similar to what is found upon the floors of a mill.

During the afternoon of this day, many of the troops, unable to subsist upon provision at once so small in quantity and so wretched in quality, left their position, and either retired to Inverness, or roamed abroad through the country in search of more substantial food. Before the evening, those who remained had the mortification of seeing the victual-ships of the enemy enter the narrow arm of the sea which skirted their position, as if to tantalise them with the sight of a feast which it was not in their power to taste.

Drummossie Moor is a large heathy and mossy flat, two miles inland from the south shore of the Moray Firth, five miles distant from Inverness, and ten or twelve from Nairn. When the insurgents stood with their faces towards the Duke of Cumberland's camp at Nairn, they had Inverness behind them, a barrier of mountains, with the river Nairn intervening, on the right hand, and the sea, with the parks of Culloden, on the left.

Lord George Murray states, in his narrative,[1] that he greatly disapproved of the position assumed by the army—as many persons of military experience have done since his time, on visiting the ground, including in this number Marshal Macdonald, Duke of Tarentum. The surprise which most persons feel on visiting the ground becomes the greater, when it is observed that, in the immediate neighbourhood, on the south side of the river Nairn, there is a piece of ground, of an undulating and boggy character, where the Highlanders could have taken up a most favourable position, totally inaccessible to the enemy's horse and cannon. Lord George states that, on the 15th, at his desire, Brigadier Stapleton and Colonel Ker of Graden inspected this ground, and spoke favourably of it; but the dread lest the royal army might pass on and take possession of Inverness, prevented the proposal from being adopted. It has been insinuated that Charles was here guided by his tutor Sheridan and the French officers, who dreaded a hill campaign on their own account; but, in reality, the desire of covering Inverness appears to have been the chief reason for the step which was taken, Charles being, for his own part, inclined to it by his general anxiety for fighting, and the blind confidence he reposed

[1] *Jacobite Memoirs.*

in the prowess of his mountaineers.   It also appears that O'Sullivan, who selected the ground, had a good opinion of it, on account of the bogs and marshes by which it was interspersed.

There yet remained, before playing the great stake of a pitched battle, one chance of success by the irregular mode of warfare to which the army was accustomed, and Charles resolved to put it to trial.   This was a night-attack upon the camp of the Duke of Cumberland.   He rightly argued, that if his men could approach without being discovered, and make a simultaneous attack in more than one place, the royal forces, then probably either engaged in drinking their commander's health, or sleeping off the effects of the debauch, must be completely surprised and cut to pieces, or at least effectually routed.   The time appointed for setting out upon the march was eight in the evening, when daylight should have completely disappeared; and in the meantime great pains were taken to conceal the secret from the army.

This resolution was entered into at three in the afternoon, and orders were immediately given to collect the men who had gone off in search of provisions.   The officers dispersed themselves to Inverness and other places, and beseeched the stragglers to repair to the moor.   But, under the influence of hunger, they told their commanders to shoot them if they pleased, rather than compel them to starve any longer.   When the time came, therefore, little more than half of the army could be assembled.   Charles had previously declared, with his characteristic fervour, that though only a thousand of his men would accompany him, he would lead them on to the attack; and he was not now intimidated when he saw twice that number ready to assist in the enterprise; though some of his officers would willingly have made this deficiency of troops an excuse for abandoning what they esteemed at best a hazardous expedition.   Having given out for watchword the name of his father,[1]

1 ' King James the Eighth.'

he embraced Lord George Murray, who was to command the foremost column, and putting himself at the head of that which followed, gave the orders to march.

The greatest care had been taken to conceal the object of this expedition from the mass of the army, lest, being communicated by them to the country-people, it might reach the ears of the enemy. But the Duke of Cumberland having, like a prudent general, taken measures, ever since he approached the Highlanders, to watch their slightest motions, was by no means ignorant of their march towards his position, though he did not apprehend a nocturnal attack. He had commissioned various country-people, and some of his own Highland militiamen, to mingle with their columns, and inform him from time to time of the progress they were making ; and though he permitted his men to sleep, they were instructed to have their arms beside them. He did not suppose that the insurgents would be daring enough to fall upon his camp ; but he had taken measures to give them battle in its vicinity, as soon as they should demand it.

Among the instructions issued to the officers of Charles's army, to be communicated in proper time to the troops, one was, that no firearms should be used, but only sword, dirk, and bayonet. It was also enjoined that, on entering the camp, they should immediately set about cutting down or overturning the tents, and wherever a swelling or bulge was observed in the fallen canopy, ' there to strike and push vigorously.'[1] As the camp was only nine miles distant from their position, it was expected that they would reach it soon after midnight, and thus have sufficient time to execute the whole of their project before daylight. According to the plan of attack, the army was to march in a column along the north bank of the river Nairn till it reached a point about three miles from the duke's camp. It was there to be divided into two parties, one of which, comprehending about the third of the whole number, was to

---

[1] Lockhart Papers, ii. 508.

cross the river under the command of Lord George Murray, and march on till it was close to the camp. It was there to recross the river, and attack the camp on the east and south sides, while the other and large detachment should fall upon it from the west.

The night of the 15th of April chanced to be uncommonly dark. But this circumstance, so advantageous in one respect, was unfortunate in another, in as far as it impeded their progress. Their march lay, not in the public road, where their motions would have been so easily detected, but through waste and generally wet ground, considerably removed from both roads and houses, and where want of light was peculiarly disadvantageous. On this account their progress was very slow, and attended with much fatigue; and while many of the men dropped aside altogether, the rear column fell considerably behind the front. Lord George Murray, vexed at the slowness of the march, sent repeated requests, expressed in the most urgent terms, for the rear to join the van; but these were either disregarded or could not be executed.

It was two in the morning before the head of the first column had passed Kilravock, an ancient mansion three miles from the duke's camp; and Lord George then halted and called a council of officers, in which he declared it impossible for the army to reach the point of attack before daylight should expose them to the observation and fire of the enemy. Many officers, among whom was Mr Hepburn of Keith, spoke violently in favour of the original design; even asserting that the Highland broadsword would not be the worse of a little daylight to direct its operations. But Lord George, with more prudence, insisted upon the evils which must result to the whole army, and of course to the general cause, should their approach be observed and prepared for, as in all probability it would; and, hearing a drum beat in the distant camp, he expressed his conviction that the enemy were already alarmed. The urgency of the case demanding immediate determination, he took it upon his responsibility, as general, to turn back the men, Charles being so far in the rear that it would have required some time to procure his orders. As they were marching back, Charles, apprised of the resolution by his secretary, Mr John Hay, came galloping up, and had the mortification to find the army in full retreat. He was incensed in a high degree at Lord George, who, he said, had betrayed him. He was for still ordering the onward march; but when informed that Lord George was already far on his way back, he acquiesced in the retreat, saying: ''Tis no matter, then; we shall meet them, and behave like brave fellows.'[1] He appears to have afterwards been made fully sensible of the necessity of the measure.[2]

That the measure was indeed necessary, in opposition to those who afterwards continued to assert the contrary, seems to be put beyond dispute by the circumstance, that the day was fully dawned before the Highland army had proceeded *two* miles in the retreat, although they now marched by the straightest and best paths.

The Highlanders returned, fatigued and disconsolate, to their former position about seven o'clock in the morning, when they immediately addressed themselves to sleep, or went away in search of provisions. So scarce was food at this critical juncture, that the Prince himself, on retiring to Culloden House, could obtain no better refreshment than a little bread and whisky.[3] He felt the utmost anxiety regarding his men, among whom the pangs of hunger, upon bodies exhausted by fatigue, must have been working effects the most unpromising to his success; and he gave orders, before seeking any repose, that the whole country should now be mercilessly ransacked for the means of refreshment. His orders were not without effect. Considerable supplies were procured, and subjected to the cook's art at Inverness; but the poor famished clansmen were destined never to taste these provisions, the hour of battle arriving before they were prepared.

The moor of Culloden stretches away so far to the east, with

---

so little irregularity, and so few incumbent objects, that its
termination escapes the eyesight, and the horizon in that
direction resembles that of a shoreless sea.   It was about eleven
in the forenoon when the Highland guards first observed the
dim level outline of the plain to blacken with the marching
troops of the Duke of Cumberland, which seemed gradually to
rise above and occupy the horizon, like the darkness of a coming
storm dawning in the mariner's eye upon the distant waters.
Notice of their approach being carried to the Prince, he
instantly rose, and went out to the moor to put himself at the
head of his troops.[1] He there exerted himself to collect his
men from the various places to which they had straggled, ordering a cannon to be fired as a signal for their immediate assembling.   Macdonald of Keppoch and the Frasers had joined that
morning, to the great joy of the army ; and it was in something
like good spirits that they now prepared for battle.

When all had been collected that seemed within call, the
Prince found he had an army of about five thousand men, and
these in poor condition for fighting, to oppose to a force
reputed as numerous again, supported by superior horse and
artillery, and whose strength was unimpaired either by hunger
or fatigue.   It seemed scarcely possible that he should overcome
a host in every respect so much superior to his own ; and
various measures were proposed to him by his officers for
shunning battle in the meantime, and retiring to some position
where their peculiar mode of warfare would avail against a
regular army.   But Charles, for reasons already stated, insisted
upon immediate battle ; pointing out that the gross of the army
seemed in the highest degree anxious to come to blows, and
that they would probably fall off in ardour—perhaps altogether
disperse—if the present opportunity were not seized.

Active preparations were now, therefore, made for that conflict

[1] As he was quitting the house, the steward made up to him, with information that
dinner, ' consisting of a roasted side of lamb and two fowls,' was about to be laid upon the
table.   But he asked the man if he would have him to sit down to eat at such a moment,
and, hungry though he was, he immediately hurried out to the field.—*The Young
Chevalier*, 6.

upon which the issue of this singular national contest was finally to depend. The insurgents were drawn up by O'Sullivan (at once their adjutant and quartermaster-general) in two lines; the right protected by the turf-enclosures around a rude farm-stead, and their left extending towards a sort of morass in the direction of Culloden House. The front line consisted of the following clan regiments, reckoned from right to left: Athole, Cameron, Appin, Fraser, Mackintosh, Maclachlan and Maclean (forming one), John Roy Stuart, Farquharson, Clanranald, Keppoch, Glengarry. The second, for which it was with difficulty that enough of men were found, comprised the Low-country and foreign regiments, according to the following order: Lord Ogilvie, Lord Lewis Gordon, Glenbucket, the Duke of Perth, the Irish, the French. Four pieces of cannon were placed at each extremity of the front, and as many in the centre. Lord George Murray commanded the right wing, Lord John Drummond the left, General Stapleton the second line, Charles himself stood, with a small body of guards, upon a slight eminence in the rear.

While the insurgent army laboured under every kind of disadvantage, and were actuated by impulses of the most distracting and harassing nature, that of the Duke of Cumberland moved with all the deliberation and security proper to a superior and more confident force. They had struck their tents at five in the morning, when, the commanders of the various regiments having received their instructions in writing, the general orders of the day were read at the head of every company in the line. These bore, in allusion to the misbehaviour at Falkirk, that if any persons intrusted with the care of the train or baggage absconded or left their charge, they should be punished with immediate death, and that if any officer or soldier failed in his duty during the action, he should be *sentenced*. Another and more important order was then given to the army. The superiority of the broadsword over the bayonet at Preston and Falkirk had given rise to much discussion among military men, and during this winter many suggestions had been made and discussed in the public journals for putting the weapons of the regular troops upon a par with those of the insurgents. It was reserved for the Duke of Cumberland effectually to obviate the supposed superiority of the claymore and target. He had perceived that the greatest danger to which the regular troops were subjected in a charge of the Highlanders arose from the circumstance, that the latter received his antagonist's point in his target, swayed it aside, and then had the defenceless body of the soldier exposed to his own weapon. The duke conceived that if each man, on coming within the proper distance of the enemy, should direct his thrust, not at the man directly opposite to him, but against the one who fronted his right-hand comrade, the target would be rendered useless, and the Highlander would be wounded in the right side, under the sword-arm, ere he could ward off the thrust. Accordingly, he had instructed the men during the spring in this new exercise. When they had taken their morning meal, they were marched forward from the camp, arranged in three parallel divisions of four regiments each, headed by Huske, Sempill, and Mordaunt; having a column of artillery and baggage upon one hand, and a fifth of horse upon the other.

After a march of eight miles, through ground which appeared to the English soldiers very boggy and difficult, they came within sight of the insurgents, who were posted about a mile and a half in advance. The duke then commanded his lines to form, having learned that the Highlanders seemed inclined to make the attack. Soon after, on its being ascertained that no motion was perceptible in the Highland army, he ordered the lines to be restored to the form of columns, and to proceed in their march. Calling out, at the same time, to know if any man in the army was acquainted with the ground, he commanded the individual who presented himself to go a little way in advance, along with an officer of rank, to conduct the army, and especially the artillery, over the safest paths. When within a mile of the enemy, he ordered the army once more, and finally, to be formed in battle-array.

The royal army was disposed in three lines : the first containing, from left to right, the regiments of Barrel (now the 4th) and Munro (the 37th), the Scots Fusiliers (the 21st), Price's (the 14th), Cholmondley's (the 34th), and the Scots Royals (the 1st), under the command of the Earl of Albemarle; the second, in the same order, Wolfe's (the 8th), Sempill's (the 25th), Blyth's (the 20th), Ligonier's (the 48th), and Fleming's (the 35th), commanded by General Huske; the third, Blakeney's (the 27th), Battereau's,[1] Pulteney's (the 13th), and Howard's (the 3d), led by Brigadier Mordaunt.   The centres of all the regiments of the second line being behind the terminations of those of the first, and those of the third line occupying a similar position in regard to the second, the various bodies of which the army consisted were in a manner indented into each other.   Betwixt every two regiments of the first line were placed two cannon.   The left flank was protected by Kerr's dragoons (the 11th), under Colonel Lord Ancrum; the right by a bog; and Cobham's dragoons (the 10th) stood in two detachments beside the third line.   The Argyle Highlanders guarded the baggage.

The disposition thus made was allowed by the best military men of the period to have been altogether admirable, because it was impossible for the Highlanders to break one regiment without finding two ready to supply its place.   The arrangement of the insurgent army was also allowed to be very good, upon a supposition that they were to be attacked.

Duke William, full of anxiety for the event of the day, took the opportunity afforded by the halt to make a short speech to his soldiers.   The tenor of his harangue, which has been preserved in the note-book of an English officer, shews, in the most unequivocal manner, how apprehensive his royal highness was regarding the behaviour of his troops.   Without directly adverting to Preston or Falkirk, he implored them to be firm and collected—to dismiss all remembrance of former failures from their minds—to consider the great object for which they

---

[1] Broke in 1749.

were here, no less than to save the liberties of their country and the rights of their master.   Having read a letter to them, which he said had been found upon the person of a straggler, and in which sentiments of the most merciless nature were breathed against the English soldiery, he represented to them that, in their present circumstances, with marshy ways behind them, and surrounded by an enemy's country, their best, indeed their only chance of personal safety lay in hard fighting.   He was grieved, he said, to make the supposition that there could be a person reluctant to fight in the British army.   But if there were any here who would prefer to retire, whether from disinclination to the cause, or because they had relations in the rebel army, he begged them in the name of God to do so, as he would rather face the Highlanders with one thousand determined men at his back, than have ten thousand with a tithe who were lukewarm. The men, catching enthusiasm from his language, shouted, 'Flanders! Flanders!' and impatiently desired to be led forward to battle.

It was suggested to the duke at this juncture that he should permit the men to dine, as it was now nearly one o'clock, then the usual time for that meal, and as they would not probably have another opportunity of satisfying their hunger for several hours.   But he decidedly rejected the proposal.   'The men,' he said, 'will fight better and more actively otherwise ; and, moreover, it would be a bad omen.   You remember what a dessert they got to their dinner at Falkirk.'

The army now marched forward in complete battle-array, their fixed bayonets glittering in the sun, their colours flying, and the sound of a hundred drums rolling forward in defiance of the insurgents.   Lord Kilmarnock is said to have remarked, on seeing the army approach, that he felt a presentiment of defeat, from the cool, orderly, determined manner in which they marched.   When within 600 yards of the Highland lines, they found the ground so marshy as to take most of the regiments up to the ankles in water ; and the artillery horses then sinking in a bog, some of the soldiers slung their carabines, and dragged the carriages on to their proper position. Soon after, the bog was found to terminate upon the right, so as to leave that flank uncovered; which being perceived by the all-vigilant duke, he ordered Pulteney's regiment to take its place beside the Scots Royals, and a body of horse to cover the whole wing in the same manner with the left. The army finally halted at the distance of five hundred paces from the Highlanders.

The day, which had hitherto been fair and sunny, was now partially overcast, and a shower of snowy rain began to beat with violence from the north-east. The Highlanders, to whom the weather had been so favourable at Falkirk, were somewhat disconcerted on finding it against them at Culloden; the spirits of the regulars were proportionally raised. Charles saw and felt the disadvantage, and made some attempts, by manœuvring, to get to windward of the royal army; but Duke William, equally vigilant, contrived to counteract all his movements; so that, after half an hour spent in mutual endeavours to outflank each other, the two armies at last occupied nearly their original ground.

Whilst these vain manœuvres were going on, an incident took place which serves to shew the spirit of self-devotion which animated the Highlanders on this occasion. A poor mountaineer, resolving to sacrifice his life for his Prince and clan, approached the lines of the English, demanded quarter, and was sent to the rear. As he lounged backwards and forwards through the lines, apparently indifferent to what was going on, and even paying no attention to the ridicule with which the soldiers greeted his uncouth appearance, Lord Bury, son of the Earl of Albemarle, and aide-de-camp to the duke, happened to pass in the discharge of his duties, when all at once the Highlander seized one of the soldiers' muskets, and discharged it at that officer, receiving next moment, with perfect indifference, and as a matter of course, the shot with which another soldier immediately terminated his own existence. He had intended to shoot the Duke of Cumberland, but fired prematurely, and without effect, at an inferior officer, whose gaudy apparel seemed, in his simple eyes, to indicate the highest rank.

There is a print, executed at the time,[1] in which the beginning, middle, and end of the battle of Culloden are simultaneously represented. It is calculated to be of material service in portraying the various successive events of the action, and also in conveying a good idea of the ground, and of the positions and appearance of the armies. The spectator is supposed to stand within the enclosures so often mentioned, and to look northward along the lines, towards Culloden House and the Moray Firth. In the foreground, rather for the sake of giving

Battle of Culloden.

a portrait of the hero of the day, than because this was his position, the artist has represented the duke on horseback, with a walking-cane extended in his hand, a star upon the breast of his long gold-laced coat, and his head, with its close curls and tri-cocked hat, inclined towards an aide-de-camp, to whom he is giving orders. The long, compact lines of the British regiments, each three men deep, extend along the plain, with narrow intervals between; the two flags of each regiment rising from

[1] London; drawn by A. Heckel, engraved by L. S., and sold by Robert Wilkinson.

the centre; the officers standing at the extremities, with their spontoons in their hands, and the drummers a little in advance, beating their instruments. The men have tri-cocked hats, long coats resembling the modern surtout, sash-belts from which a sword depends, and long white gaiters buttoned up the sides. The dragoons exhibit still more cumbrous superfluity of attire; their long loose skirts flying behind them as they ride, whilst their trunk square-toed boots, their massive stirrup-leathers, their huge holster-pistols and carabines, give altogether an idea of dignity and strength, much in contrast with the light fantastic hussar uniforms of modern times.

The Highlanders, on the other hand, stand in lines equally compact, and, like the regular regiments, each three men deep. The only peculiarity in their dress, which is so well known as to require no general description, seems to be, that the philibeg, or kilt, is pulled through betwixt the legs in such a way as to shew more of the front of the thigh than is exhibited by the modern specimens of that peculiar garment. They have muskets over their left shoulders, basket-hilted broadswords by their left sides, pistols stuck into their girdles, and a small pouch hanging down upon the right loin, perhaps for holding their ammunition. By the right side of every piece of ordnance there is a cylindrical piece of wicker-work, for the protection of the artillerymen, all of whom appear to wear kilts like the rest.

The ground upon which the armies stand is the plain swelling moor already described, out of which Culloden House raises its erect form, without any of the plantations which now surround it. The spires of Inverness are seen upon the left, close to the sea-shore. Upon the Moray Firth, which stretches along the background of the picture, the victualling-ships ride at anchor, like witnesses of the scene about to ensue; and the magnificent hills of Ross raise their lofty forms in the remoter distance.

Such were the aspect and circumstances of the two armies, upon whose conduct, during the next little hour, the future interests of Britain might in some measure be considered to depend.

CHAPTER XXIII.

BATTLE OF CULLODEN.

'Fair lady, mourn the memory
    Of all our Scottish fame;
Fair lady, mourn the memory
    Even of the Scottish name!
How proud were we of our young Prince,
    And of his native sway!
But all our hopes are past and gone
    Upon Culloden day.

There was no lack of bravery there,
    No spare of blood or breath:
For, one to two, our foes we dared,
    For freedom or for death.
The bitterness of grief is past,
    Of terror and dismay;
The die was risked, and foully cast,
    Upon Culloden day.'

Jacobite Song.

THE action was commenced by the Highlanders, who fired their cannon for a few minutes without being answered by the royal artillery. They had brought their guns to bear upon a point where, by means of glasses, they thought they could perceive the duke. But the shot went clear over the heads of the king's troops, and for a long time did no other mischief than carrying off a leg from one of Blyth's regiment.

A few minutes after one o'clock, soon after the Highlanders had opened up their battery, Colonel Belford got orders to commence a cannonade, chiefly with a view to provoke the enemy to advance. The colonel, who was an excellent engineer, performed his duty with such effect as to make whole lanes through the ranks of the insurgents. He fired two pieces at a body of horse amongst whom it was believed the Prince was stationed; and with such precision did he take his aim, that that personage was bespattered with dirt raised by the balls, and a man holding a led-horse by his side was killed.

Meanwhile the duke rode about, calling upon his men to be firm in their ranks—to permit the Highlanders to mingle with them—to let them feel the force of the bayonet—to 'make them know what men they had to do with.' He also ordered Wolfe's regiment to form *en potence* at the extremity of the left wing—that is, to take a position perpendicular to the general line, so as to be ready to fall in upon and enclose the Highlanders as soon as they should attack that division of his army. He also ordered two regiments of the rear line, or reserve, to advance to the second. Finally, he himself took his position between the first and second lines, opposite to the centre of Howard's regiment, and of course a little nearer the left than the right wing.

Prince Charles, before the commencement of the battle, had ridden along the lines of his little army, endeavouring, by the animation of his gestures, countenance, and language, to excite the Highlanders to their highest pitch of courage. They answered him with cheers, and with many an expression of devotion, which he could only understand by the look with which it was uttered. He then again retired to the eminence which he originally occupied, and prepared with an anxious mind to await the fortune of the day.

The great object of both parties at the battle of Culloden seems to have been, which should force the other to leave its position, and make the attack. Charles for a long time expected that the duke would do this, because he was favoured with the wind and weather. But the duke, finding his cannon rapidly thinning the Highland ranks, without experiencing any loss in return, felt no occasion to make such a motion, and it therefore became incumbent upon Charles to take that course himself.

The victory of Preston, where the Highlanders experienced little or no annoyance from cannon, had done away with a great deal of the fear in which they originally held these engines of destruction; and it seems to have been a capital error on Charles's part to have restrained them, on the present occasion, to a position where that terror got some reason and leisure to return. He ought to have, on the contrary, rushed up, at the very first, to the lines of his enemy, and endeavoured to silence their artillery, as he had done at Preston, by a *coup de main.* Had he done so, a great number of lives might have been saved, and the attack would have been made with lines less broken, and a more uniform and simultaneous impulse.

It was not till the cannonade had continued nearly half an hour, and the Highlanders had seen many of their kindred stretched upon the heath, that Charles at last gave way to the necessity of ordering a charge. The aide-de-camp intrusted to carry his message to the lieutenant-general—a youth of the name of Maclauchlan—was killed by a cannon-ball before he reached the first line; but the general sentiment of the army, as reported to Lord George Murray, supplied the want; and that general took it upon him to order an attack, without Charles's permission having been communicated.

Lord George had scarcely determined upon ordering a general movement, when the Mackintoshes—a brave and devoted clan —though not before engaged in action [1]—unable any longer to brook the unavenged slaughter made by the cannon, broke from the centre of the line, and rushed forward through smoke and snow to mingle with the enemy. The Athole-men, Camerons, Stuarts, Frasers, and Macleans also went on, Lord George Murray heading them with that rash bravery befitting the commander of such forces. Thus, in the course of one or two

---

[1] One of this corps, though not of the clan name—old John Grant, long keeper of the inn at Aviemore—used to tell that the first thing he saw of the enemy was the long line of white gaiters belonging to an English regiment, which was suddenly revealed, when about twenty yards from him, by a blast of wind which blew aside the smoke. According to the report of this veteran, the mode of drilling used by his leader upon Culloden Moor was very simple, being directed by the following string of orders, expressed in Gaelic: 'Come, my lads—fall in, with your faces to Fortrose, and your backs to the Green of Muirtown—load your firelocks—good—make ready—present—now take good aim—fire—be sure to do execution—that's the point.'—*Information by the editor of the Culloden Papers.*

minutes, the charge was general along the whole line, except at the left extremity, where the Macdonalds, dissatisfied with their position, hesitated to engage.

It was the custom of the Highlanders, before an onset, to *scrug their bonnets*—that is, to pull their little blue caps down over their brows—so as to insure them against falling off in the ensuing *mêlée*. Never, perhaps, was this motion performed with so much emphasis as on the present occasion, when every man's forehead burned with the desire to revenge some dear friend who had fallen a victim to the murderous artillery. A Lowland gentleman, who was in the line, and who survived till a late period, used always, in relating the events of Culloden, to comment, with a feeling of something like awe, upon the more than natural expression of rage which glowed on every face and gleamed in every eye as he surveyed the extended line at this moment.

The action and event of the onset were, throughout, quite as dreadful as the mental emotion which urged it. Notwithstanding that the three files of the front line of English poured forth their incessant fire of musketry—notwithstanding that the cannon, now loaded with grape-shot, swept the field as with a hail-storm—notwithstanding the flank fire of Wolfe's regiment— onward, onward went the headlong Highlanders, flinging themselves into, rather than rushing upon, the lines of the enemy, which, indeed, they did not see for smoke till involved among their weapons. All that courage, all that despair could do, was done. It was a moment of dreadful and agonising suspense, but only a moment—for the whirlwind does not reap the forest with greater rapidity than the Highlanders cleared the line. Nevertheless, almost every man in their front rank, chief and gentleman, fell before the deadly weapons which they had braved; and although the enemy gave way, it was not till every bayonet was bent and bloody with the strife.

When the first line had been thus swept aside, the assailants continued their impetuous advance till they came near the second, when, being almost annihilated by a profuse and well-directed fire, the shattered remains of what had been but an hour before a numerous and confident force, began to give way. Still a few rushed on, resolved rather to die than forfeit their well-acquired and dearly estimated honour. They rushed on; but not a man ever came in contact with the enemy. The last survivor perished as he reached the points of the bayonets.[1]

The persevering and desperate valour displayed by the Highlanders on this occasion, is proved by the circumstance, that at one part of the plain, where a very vigorous attack had been made, their bodies were afterwards found *in layers three and four deep;* so many, it would appear, having in succession mounted over a prostrate friend, to share in the same certain fate. The slaughter was particularly great among the brave Mackintoshes; insomuch, that the heroic lady who sent them to the field afterwards told the party by whom she was taken prisoner that only three of her officers had escaped.

While the rest of the clans were performing this brilliant though fatal charge, the Macdonalds, as already stated, withheld themselves, on account of their removal to the left wing. According to the report of one of their officers,[2] the clan not only resented this indignity, but considered it as omening evil fortune to the day; their clan never having fought elsewhere than on the right wing since the auspicious battle of Bannockburn. The Duke of Perth, who was stationed amongst them, endeavoured to appease their anger by telling them that, if they fought with their characteristic bravery, they would make the left wing a right, in which case he would assume for ever after the honourable surname of Macdonald. But the insult was not to be expiated by this appeal to clanship. Though induced to discharge their muskets, and even to advance some way, they never made an onset. They endured the fire of the English regiments

---

[1] 'The late Mr Macdonald of Glenaladale told me, some years ago, that he saw John Mor Macgilvra, major of the Mackintoshes, a *gun-shot past the enemy's cannon,* and that he was surrounded by the reinforcements sent against the Mackintoshes; that he killed a dozen men with his broadsword, while some of the halberts were run into his body. When Cumberland heard of it, he said he would have given a great sum of money to have saved his life.'—*Letter of Bishop Mackintosh, MS.* 1810.

[2] Lockhart Papers, ii. 510.

without flinching; only expressing their rage by hewing up the heath with their swords; but they at last fled when they saw the other clans give way. From this conduct there was a brilliant exception in the chieftain of Keppoch, a man of chivalrous character, and noted for great private worth. When the rest of his clan retreated, Keppoch exclaimed, with feelings not to be appreciated in modern society: 'My God, have the children of my tribe forsaken me!'—he then advanced, with a pistol in one hand and a drawn sword in the other, resolved apparently to sacrifice his life to the offended genius of his name. He had got but a little way from his regiment, when a musket-shot brought him to the ground. A clansman of more than ordinary devotedness, who followed him, and with tears and prayers conjured him not to throw his life away, raised him, with the cheering assurance that his wound was not mortal, and that he might still quit the field with life. Keppoch desired his faithful follower to take care of himself, and again rushing forward, received another shot, and fell to rise no more.

When the whole front line of Charles's host had been thus repulsed, there only remained to him the hope that his Lowland and foreign troops, upon whom the wreck of the clans had fallen back, might yet make head against the English infantry, and he eagerly sought to put himself at their head. But though a troop of the Irish pickets, by a spirited fire, checked the pursuit which a body of dragoons commenced after the Macdonalds, and one of Lord Lewis Gordon's regiments did similar service in regard to another troop which now began to break through the enclosures on the right,[1] the whole body gave way at once on observing the English regiments advancing to charge them. Their hearts were broken with despair rather than with terror; and they could only reply to his animating exclamations: 'Prions—ochon! ochon!'[2]—the ejaculation by which Highlanders express the bitterest grief. As they said this, they fled;

[1] These enclosures had been broken down for their passage by the Argyle Highlanders.
[2] *The Young Chevalier*, p. 7.

nor could all his entreaties, or those of his officers, prevail upon them to stand.

It was indeed a complete rout. The mountaineers had done all that their system of warfare taught them, and all that their natural strength had enabled them to perform : they had found this vain ; and all that then remained was to reserve their lives, if possible, for some future effort. Charles lingered late on the field, in the hope that all was not lost. He even moved to charge the enemy, and it required the utmost efforts of his attendants to make him withdraw. He at last only left the field, when to have remained would have but added his own destruction to that of the many brave men who had already spilled their heart's blood in his cause.[1]

The pursuit of the royal forces did not immediately follow. After the insurgents had withdrawn their shattered strength, the English regiments, some of which had suffered severely, were ordered to resume the ground where they had stood, and to dress their ranks. The dragoon regiments, with which the duke had calculated to enclose the charging Highlanders as in a trap, were checked, as already stated, by the flanks of the Prince's second line ; and they had altogether been so handled by the insurgents,[2] that it was some time ere they recovered breath or courage sufficient to commence or sustain a general pursuit.

The English dragoons at length *did* break forward, and join,

---

[1] It required all the eloquence, and indeed all the active exertions of O'Sullivan to make Charles quit the field. A cornet in his service, when questioned upon this subject at the point of death, declared he saw O'Sullivan, after using entreaties in vain, turn the head of the Prince's horse, and drag him away.—*See Quart. Rev.* No. 71. An anecdote at issue with this statement was often related by the late Sir James Steuart of Coltness. Lord Elcho (who was uncle to Sir James) was said to have gone up to the Prince, and entreated him to put himself at the head of the broken troops, and renew the charge. On the Prince refusing, Elcho was represented as addressing him in violently discourteous language, which concluded with a vow that he would never again see his face. There are reasons for disbelieving this tale—particularly the fact, that Elcho rode for several miles from the field in the immediate company of the Prince, and afterwards kept up a correspondence with him.

[2] The Rev. Donald Mackintosh, usually called Bishop Mackintosh, writing in 1810, says: ' John Miln, an old bellman in Edinburgh, is still alive : he is one of *the fifteen men* whom our Clan Chattan left of Barrel's regiment at Culloden.'—*MS. in my possession.*

as intended, in the centre of the field, so as to make a vigorous and united charge upon the rear of the fugitives. Charles's army then broke into two bodies of unequal magnitude; one of which took the open road for Inverness, while the other turned off towards the south-west, crossed the water of Nairn, and found refuge among the hills.

The fate of the first of these divisions was the most disastrous, their route admitting of the easiest pursuit. It lay along an open moor, which the light horse of the enemy could bound over without obstruction. A dreadful slaughter took place, involving many of the inhabitants of Inverness, who had approached the battle-ground from curiosity, and whose dress subjected them to the undiscriminating vengeance of the soldiery. Some of the French, who fled early, reached Inverness in safety; but scarcely any who wore the Highland dress escaped. A broad pavement of carnage marked four out of the five miles intervening betwixt the battle-field and that city; the last of the slain being found at a place called Millburn, about a mile from the extremity of the suburbs.[1]

Some other portions of the retiring army displayed a self-protecting coolness and resolution.[2] The right wing, in its way

[1] Tradition at Inverness, confirmed by Mr Home. 'The battle was witnessed by many gentlemen (amateurs), who rode from Inverness for that purpose—among the rest, my grandfather, Mr —— of ——, and Mr Evan Baillie of Aberiachan. They took post upon a small hill, not far from where the Prince and his suite were stationed, and there remained till dislodged by the cannon-balls falling about them. In their retreat they passed through Inverness, and at the bridge-end met the Frasers, under the Master of Lovat. These had not been in time for the battle; but the Master seemed very anxious to defend the passage of the bridge, and spoke much of fighting there. Mr Baillie, who was a warm Jacobite, and rather testy in his way, sternly addressed the Master in these words: " Fighting ! by G—, Master, you were not in the way when fighting might have been of service. You had better now say nothing about it !"'—*From information contributed in writing by the editor of the Culloden Papers.*

[2] A strange instance of their cunning is commemorated by Mr Ray, a volunteer, who wrote an account of the insurrection. 'In the flight,' says he, 'I came up with a pretty young Highlander, who called out to me: "Hold your hand—I am a Campbell." On which I asked him : "Where 's your bonnet?" "Somebody has snatched it off my head." I mention this to shew how we distinguished our loyal clans from the rebels, they being dressed and equipped all in one way, except the bonnet ; ours having a red or yellow cross or ribbon, theirs a white cockade. He having neither of these distinctions, I desired him, if he was a Campbell, to follow me, which he promised ; but on the first opportunity he gave me the slip.'

to cross the river Nairn, met a large party of English dragoons which had been despatched to intercept them. Such was the desperate fury of their appearance, that the troopers opened their ranks in respectful silence to permit them to pass. Only one man attempted to annoy the fugitives. He was an officer, and dearly did he pay for his temerity. Advancing to seize a Highlander, the man cut him down with one blow of his claymore. Not content with this, the Highlander stooped down, and, with the greatest deliberation, possessed himself of his victim's gold watch. He then joined the retreat, whilst the commander of the party could only look on in silence, astonished at the coolness of the mountaineer.[1]

Another Highlander signalised himself in a still more remarkable manner. He was a man of prodigious bodily strength; his name Golice Macbane. When all his companions had fled, Golice, singled out and wounded, set his back against a wall, and, with his target and claymore, bore singly the onset of a party of dragoons. Pushed to desperation, he made resistless strokes at his enemies, who crowded and encumbered themselves to have each the glory of slaying him. 'Save that brave fellow!' was the unregarded cry of some officers. Poor Macbane was cut to pieces, though not, it is said, till thirteen of his enemies lay dead around him.[2]

The battle of Culloden is said to have lasted little more than forty minutes, most of which brief space of time was spent in distant firing, and very little in the active struggle. It was as complete a victory as possible on the part of the royal army, and any other result would surely have been very discreditable to the English army. Their numbers and condition for fighting were so superior, their artillery did so much for them, and the plan of the battle was so much in their favour, that to have lost the day would have argued a degree of misbehaviour for which even Preston and Falkirk had not prepared us. Great praise

---

[1] Chevalier Johnstone's *Memoirs*.

[2] Cromek's *Remains of Nithsdale and Galloway Song*, p. 200. This man, according to Henderson's *History*, was six feet four inches and a quarter high. He had several bayonet-stabs, a large cut in his head, and his thigh-bone broken through.

was awarded afterwards to Barrel's, Munro's, and some other regiments, for their fortitude in bearing the attack of the High-landers, and for their killing so many; but these battalions were in reality completely beat aside, and the whole front line shaken so much, that, had the Macdonald regiments made a simul-taneous charge along with the other clans, the day might have had a different issue.

CHAPTER XXIV.

TRANSACTIONS IMMEDIATELY AFTER THE BATTLE OF CULLODEN.

'The target is torn from the arms of the just,
  The helmet is cleft on the brow of the brave;
The claymore for ever in darkness must rust,
  But red is the sword of the stranger and slave.
The hoof of the horse, and the foot of the proud,
  Have trod o'er the plumes on the bonnet of blue:
Why slept the red bolt in the breast of the cloud,
  When tyranny revelled in blood of the true?
Farewell, my young hero, the gallant and good!
  The crown of thy fathers is torn from thy brow.'
                                        JAMES HOGG.

THE reader has seen that after the battles of Preston and Falkirk the party left in possession of the field treated the wounded of the enemy with humanity—that the same party acted with liberal kindness towards their prisoners—and that the leader, in particular, manifested on various occasions a degree of clemency and forbearance with which even his own officers sometimes found fault, as being carried to what they thought a dangerous extreme. We are now to see how the Duke of Cumberland and his army are to conduct themselves under the first triumph which their party had achieved during the campaign.

It has already been stated that, in the pursuit towards Inverness, no quarter was given. To excuse this afterwards, a regimental order was produced, as having been found on the person of 'a rebel,' and signed by Lord George Murray, commanding the insurgent army to give no quarter to the king's troops. It is well known that no such order was given out to the insurgent army, and as it was not alluded to in the official accounts of the battle prepared under the duke's care, there seems much, though perhaps not conclusive evidence that it was a forgery, made up after the fact, in order to palliate butcheries which had their sole origin in the vengeance of fear or native barbarity.

Immediately after the conclusion of the battle, the men, under the command of their officers, traversed the field, stabbing with their bayonets, or cutting down with their swords, such of the wounded of the defeated party as came under their notice. This was done as much in sport as in rage, and as the work went on, the men at length began to amuse themselves by splashing and dabbling each other with blood. They at length looked, as one of themselves has reported, 'more like so many butchers than an army of Christian soldiers.'[1] It was under such circumstances that it became the duty of the chaplains to read the morning service of the day, in which (being the 16th of the month) the 79th psalm occurs as the first to be read : 'O God, the heathen are come into thine inheritance : thy holy temple have they defiled : they have laid Jerusalem on heaps. *The dead bodies of thy servants have they given to be meat unto the fowls of heaven*, the flesh of thy saints unto the beasts of the earth. *Their blood have they shed like water* round about Jerusalem : and *there was none to bury them.* We are become a reproach to our neighbours. . . . *They have devoured Jacob, and laid waste his dwelling-place.* . . . *Let the sighing of the prisoner come before thee :* according to the greatness of thy power, preserve those that are appointed to die ;' &c. It has been said, and the fact would be by no means surprising, that an order to substitute another psalm was immediately given.[1]

In the sycophant publications of the time, it is stated that, after the duke had refreshed himself, he took 'a serious walk' over the field, 'followed by some of his attendants, who observed him to be in deep meditation. He laid his hand upon his breast, and with his eyes lifted up to heaven, was heard to say: " Lord, what am I that I should be spared, when so many brave men lie dead upon the spot!"—an expression of such deep humility towards God, and compassion towards his fellow-creatures, as is truly worthy a Christian hero.' There is a better authenticated anecdote, which stands in fine contrast with this piece of cant. Riding over the field, attended by some of his officers, the duke observed a young wounded Highlander resting on his elbow and staring at the royal party. He asked the man to whom he belonged, and received for answer: 'To the Prince.' He instantly called to an officer to shoot 'that insolent scoundrel.' The officer, Major Wolfe, declined the task, saying that his commission was at the disposal of his royal highness, but he could never consent to become an executioner. The duke asked several other officers in succession to 'pistol' the wounded man, but with the like result. Then seeing a common soldier, he asked him if he had a charge in his piece; and the man answering in the affirmative, he commanded him to do the required duty, which was immediately performed. The youth thus slain was Mr Charles Fraser, younger of Inverallachy, lieutenant-colonel of the Master of Lovat's regiment. The officer who first refused was afterwards observed to decline in favour with his commander.[2]

As already stated, the English dragoons pursued the chase till within a mile of Inverness. The duke, leaving the infantry at dinner on the battle-field, soon after marched forward to take possession of the town. As he proceeded, a drummer came out

---

[1] It is proper to mention that this anecdote rests on Jacobite tradition.

[2] Critique upon Home's *Hist. Reb.* in *Anti-Jacobin Review*, vol. xiii., by the late Sir Henry Steuart of Allanton, Bart.

with a letter from General Stapleton, soliciting quarter for him-self and the French and Irish regiments under his charge.   The duke commanded Sir Joseph Yorke to alight from his horse, and with his pencil write a note to the general, assuring him and the others in whose behalf he wrote, of fair quarter and honourable treatment.   He then sent forward Captain Campbell of Sempill's regiment, with his company of grenadiers, to take possession of the town.

Already Inverness had been the scene of several of those wild acts which war brings to the doors of peaceful men.   A sick gentleman of the insurgent army, named James Aberdeen, lay in the house of one widow Davidson, and being this afternoon at the height of a fever, he was unable to make his escape.   Of this fact some soldiers chanced to become aware through the imprudence of a maid-servant.   They immediately rushed into the sick-chamber and cut the throat of the unfortunate man where he lay.   Two Low-countrymen, flying from the field of battle without arms, were followed hotly by a Cumberland volunteer on horseback.   Having entered the town, they went into the well-house to conceal themselves, but were observed by their pursuer, who, having given his horse to a girl on the street to be held for him, went into the place, and notwithstanding the piteous cries of the two men, cut them down with his sword. The monster who acted thus was one Ray, who afterwards pub-lished a coarsely written narrative of the insurrection.[1]

The duke, while knowing no mercy towards 'rebels,' was not without a proper regard for the welfare of his own men.   On entering Inverness, he lost no time in going to the tolbooth and church, in which the prisoners taken at former periods by the insurgents were confined.   As they joyfully descended into the street, he clapped them on the back with expressions of kind-ness, and immediately after ordered them food, new clothes, and their arrears of pay.   It was alleged that they had not been well used by the insurgent officers; but for this no evidence has

[1] See the proper authorities for these facts in *Jacobite Memoirs*.

T

ever been adduced.   One officer, indeed, who had a newly raised corps, being anxious to obtain clothes for his men, took it upon him, without the least authority, to strip the prisoners of their coats; but the Prince was immediately made aware of what was going on, and commanded the clothes of the men to be restored to them.   This happened about a week before the battle.

Several of the Jacobite ladies who had attended their husbands during the campaign with so much fortitude, were made prisoners at Inverness.   It is reported, in one of the vulgar party productions of the time, that they had just drunk tea, and were preparing for a ball, at which the Prince and his officers were to be entertained after his expected victory, when the entrance of the fugitives informed them of the fatal reverse their friends had met with.   The duke's soldiers found a considerable quantity of provision which had been preparing for the Highlanders.[1]

The royal army marched in the evening to Inverness, and there formed a camp.   One of the duke's first duties at headquarters was to select from the prisoners those who had deserted from the royal army, to subject them to a brief military trial, and then to consign them to the death of traitors.   No fewer than thirty-six suffered this punishment, including a sergeant named Dunbar, who was found dressed in a suit of laced clothes he had taken from Major Lockhart at the battle of Falkirk, and

---

[1] As at Holyrood House, Falkirk, and various other places, the duke took up his lodgings in the same house, the same room, and the same bed which his precursor Charles had just vacated. It may be safely conjectured that Lady Drummuir, whose daughter, Lady Mackintosh, had here acted as the presiding divinity of Charles's household for two months before,* would by no means relish the presence of her new tenant, but that *he*, on the contrary, would be esteemed as an intruder, where his predecessor had been a welcome and honoured guest. The comment which she afterwards passed upon this eventful period in the history of her household is still a tradition in her family. ‘I've had twa kings' bairns living wi' me in my time, and to tell you the truth, *I wish I may never hae another.*’

---

* Lady Mackintosh was taken prisoner after the battle of Culloden, and carried up to London, but was soon set at liberty. Cumberland, it is said, gave a ball, to which he invited this lady. The first tune played was, *Up and waur them a', Willie*, to which he requested her to dance. Having consented, she asked him, when they were done, if, since she had danced to his tune, he would dance to hers. He could not refuse to a lady, and ‘Colonel Ann’ asked for *The auld Stuarts back again!* To this tune our singularly associated couple also danced.—*Letter of Bishop Mackintosh, MS.*

who, on that account, was exposed upon the gibbet for forty-eight hours. This melancholy list is said to have included a youthful cadet of the noble family of Forbes, whose zeal in behalf of the house of Stuart, overcoming his regard for the military oath, had caused him to desert an English regiment, in which he was a cadet, for the purpose of joining Charles's standard. While this youth was yet suspended upon the gibbet, an English officer, unable to restrain his indignation at the delinquency of the culprit, ran up to the scarce inanimate corpse and stabbed it with his sword, exclaiming at the same time, with a gross execration, that 'all his countrymen were traitors and rebels like himself.' At this time there was a jealousy respecting our national honour, which more just treatment on the part of England has long since lulled asleep. It was not, therefore, wonderful that the language of this rude man, being overheard by a Scottish officer of the king's army, provoked him to draw his sword and demand satisfaction for the insult. The two men were presently engaged in combat on the open street. Others coming up, and learning the cause of the quarrel, also drew and joined in, according to their respective prepossessions. The men then beat to arms, and joined the ranks of their respective officers. In short, it seemed likely that the victorious army would soon be involved in a new war within itself, when the duke, hearing of the tumult, hurried to the scene, and exerted himself to restore peace. He found the two parties about to make a general charge against each other, and it was not without using some eloquence to soothe the wounded feelings of the Scottish officers, that he succeeded in putting an end to the dispute.

It being reported to the commander next day that a considerable number of the wounded 'rebels' lying on Culloden Moor were still in life, he ordered a party to proceed to the spot, avowedly for the humane purpose of putting them out of pain ! The order was obeyed with military punctuality. About seventy poor wretches were gathered amongst the heaps of slain, and carried to pieces of rising ground, where, being properly

ranged, they were despatched by platoons of musketry. On the
ensuing day (Friday), when it was understood that some others
of the wounded had found shelter in the neighbouring houses,
other parties were sent to search for them, and subject them to
the same treatment. Many were accordingly dragged forth, and
of these all, except a very few, were coolly murdered. The
young Laird of Macleod was afterwards heard to declare that on
this day he saw seventy-two persons killed in cold blood. In one
instance the sheltering hut was set fire to, and burned under a
guard, by whom any one attempting to escape was instantly
bayoneted. Amidst the ashes, thirty-two blackened corpses
were found. Nineteen wounded officers of the Highland army
had been carried from a wood in which they at first found
shelter, to the courtyard of Culloden House, where the steward,
though at considerable risk to himself, administered to them
some little comforts. These men were now discovered by the
royal troops, who immediately had them carried out on carts to
a park wall near by, where, being all ranged up, they were told
to prepare for instant death. Such as were able threw themselves on their knees to ask for mercy at the only tribunal where
they could now hope for it, and while they were thus engaged, a
platoon of musketry put an end to the lives of nearly all. To
complete the work, the soldiers were ordered to club their
muskets, and beat out the brains of such as shewed any
symptoms of life. This order was obeyed with full effect in all
except one surprising instance. A person named John Alexander Fraser, or familiarly Maciver, who had been an officer in
the Master of Lovat's regiment, was amongst those who did not
perish by the shot. A soldier struck him on the face with the
butt of his musket, broke the upper part of his nose and cheek-
bone, and dashed out one of his eyes. He was left for dead,
yet still retained some remains of life. A young officer of the
British army—said to have been Lord Boyd—riding by some
time after, observed him stir, and had the humanity to cause his
servant to carry the mutilated wretch to a neighbouring kiln,
where he remained for three months, and was cured of his

wounds. He lived many years after, a dismal memorial of the cruelties of Culloden.[1]

Notwithstanding the mercilessness of the pursuit, a considerable number of the Prince's men were made prisoners,[2] and placed in confinement in the church and tolbooth of Inverness. There they were treated with the greatest inhumanity. Many were stripped of their clothes, and allowed to remain for a long time with scarcely a rag upon their bodies. For food they were allowed only a little meal, not more than half of what is necessary for subsistence. The wounded received no attention or succour of any kind from their captors, and were even forbidden to receive any from two surgeons of their own party, named Lauder and Rattray, who had been taken at the same time. The humane citizens of Inverness beheld these cruelties with horror; but for several days it was dangerous for any one to attempt to send clothes or food to the prisoners, or to make any effort in behalf of such as were wounded. The unfortunate men were at length put on board vessels to be sent to London, that they might there be at the pleasure of the government. No provision was made for their comfort in these vessels. They were huddled in their naked or half-naked state into holds, where they sat or lay upon stones, with an allowance of one bottle of cold water, and from half a pound to twelve ounces of oatmeal, or rather the shealings of oats, a day. In one vessel no fewer than a hundred and fifty-seven were thus stowed away: a survivor reported that they had to burrow amidst the earth

1 All the above facts are amply authenticated in the papers collected by Bishop Forbes, and published by the present writer in the volume entitled *Jacobite Memoirs*.

2 The Earl of Kilmarnock became a prisoner on the field. During the confusion of the flight, being half-blinded by smoke and snow, he mistook a party of dragoons for Fitzjames's horse, and was accordingly taken. He was soon after led along the lines of the British infantry, in which his eldest son, then a very young man, held the commission of an ensign. The earl had lost his hat in the strife, and his long hair was flying in disorder around his head and over his face. The soldiers stood mute in their lines, beholding the unfortunate nobleman. Among the rest stood Lord Boyd, compelled by his situation to witness, without the power of alleviating, the humiliation of his father. When the earl came past the place where his son stood, the youth, unable to bear any longer that his father's head should be exposed to the storm, stepped out of the ranks, without regard to discipline, and taking off his own hat, placed it over his father's disordered and windbeaten locks. He then returned to his place, without having uttered a word.

and stones forming the ballast, as the only resource to keep themselves warm. In this state of unheard-of misery many fell grievously sick, but yet received no care at the hands of those who guarded them. It would be only painful to detail their condition more minutely. Some general idea of the atrocious treatment they met with may be formed from the fact, that of the number above stated as being pent up in one vessel, only forty-nine were in life at the end of the eight months during which they were kept at sea.[1]

The number of Highlanders slain upon the field of Culloden was never well ascertained, but it could not be much less than a thousand; that is, a fifth of their army. The list comprised many important men; for in this, as in all the former battles, the chiefs and gentlemen, as the best armed, and to shew an example of bravery, went foremost into the strife, and were of course most exposed. Out of the five regiments which charged the English—the Camerons, Stuarts, Frasers, Mackintoshes, and Macleans—almost all the leaders and front-rank men were killed. Maclachlan, colonel of the regiment last mentioned, which included a body of his own name, was killed in the onset. His lieutenant-colonel, Maclean of Drimnin, who then assumed the command, was bringing off his shattered forces, when he observed two of his sons, who had fought by his side, severely wounded, and heard that a third had been left dead on the field. Exclaiming: 'It shall not be for nought!' this brave old gentleman, without bonnet or wig, rushed back into the fight, attacked two dragoons, killed one, and wounded the other, but was at last cut down by other three, who came up to the assistance of their comrades. Macgillivray of Drumnaglass, colonel of the Mackintosh regiment, was killed in the attack, with the lieutenant-colonel, the major, and all the other officers of the regiment, with the exception, as already stated, of three. Charles Fraser, younger of Inverallachy, who was lieutenant-colonel of the Fraser

1 These facts are from the reports of eye-witnesses and sufferers, printed in *Jacobite Memoirs*.

regiment, and commanded it on this occasion,[1] was killed under the extraordinary circumstances already related.   Seventeen officers and gentlemen of the Appin regiment were slain, and ten wounded; but Stuart of Ardshiel, who commanded it, escaped; as did Locheil, the chief and leader of the Camerons. No distinguished persons fell among the Lowland regiments except the Viscount Strathallan[2] and the Laird of Aldie.[3]

The field yet bears witness to the carnage of which it was the scene.   In the midst of its dark heath various little eminences are to be seen, displaying a lively verdure but too unequivocally expressive of the dreadful tale.   These are so distinct and well defined, that the eye may almost, by their means, trace the positions of the armies, or at least discover where the fight was most warmly contested.   The way towards Inverness is fringed with many such doleful memorials of the dead.   Modern curiosity has, in some cases, violated these sanctuaries, for the purpose of procuring some relic of the ill-fated warriors; and the Gael, with nobler sentiment, were long in the habit of pilgrimising to the spot, in order to translate the bones of their friends to consecrated ground, afar in their own western glens.

The duke employed the few days immediately following the battle in securing and disposing of the spoil, which was very considerable.   He had taken thirty pieces of cannon, 2320 firelocks, 190 broadswords, thirty-seven barrels of powder, and

[1] The Master of Lovat, as intimated in a preceding note, was not present at the battle of Culloden.   He was marching towards the field with a large body of his clan, when, meeting the fugitives, he judged it expedient to turn along with them, and retire to his own country.   In performing this retrograde motion the colours were still kept flying, and the bagpipes continued to play.

[2] An officer, being afterwards examined, in a proof which was led in order to prove the viscount's death before the act of attainder, and being questioned as to his reasons for knowing that that nobleman died on the field of Culloden, gave for answer that he had thrust his spontoon through the viscount's body on that day.   It appears, however, that his lordship did not die immediately after his wound.   He lived to receive the *viaticum* from a Catholic priest who happened to be upon the field.   The sacred morsel was hastily composed of oatmeal and water, which the clergyman procured at a neighbouring cottage. This clergyman went to France, became an abbé, but revisiting his native country, mentioned the circumstance to one of my informants—the Scottish bishop so often quoted.

[3] The Laird of Aldie was killed at Culloden at the head of his battalion.   Neither his own body, nor that of one of his sons who accompanied him, was ever found.—*Letter of his grandson, General Robertson of Lude*, 1810, MS.

twenty-two carts of ammunition. The soldiers were allowed half-a-crown for every musket, and a shilling for every broadsword, which they could bring into quarters; it being the anxious wish of government to keep as many arms as possible out of the hands of the natives. In order, moreover, to put a great public indignity upon the insurgents, the sum of sixteen guineas was allowed for each stand of their colours; and fourteen of these melancholy emblems of departed glory being thus procured, they were, on the 4th of June, carried by a procession of chimney-sweeps from the castle to the cross of Edinburgh, and there burned by the hands of the common hangman, with many suitable marks of contempt.

The victory of Culloden was cheaply purchased by the British army. The whole amount of killed, wounded, and missing was 310, including few officers, and but one man of any distinction. This last was Lord Robert Kerr, second son of the Marquis of Lothian, a captain of grenadiers in Barrel's regiment, a young man remarkable for his handsome person and great promise. Standing at the head of his company when the Highlanders made the charge, he received the first man upon his spontoon, but was instantly slain with many wounds. Although the victory was mainly attributable to the cannon and musketry, some portions of the royal army behaved with a degree of courage highly honourable to them. There was scarcely an officer or soldier in Barrel's regiment, and that part of Munro's which was engaged, who did not kill one or two Highlanders with his spontoon or bayonet, before giving way to their irresistible violence.

The spreading intelligence of the battle was received, of course, with opposite feelings by the two parties. To the Jacobites, it came as a total overthrow of the hopes of sixty years, and the signal for a letting loose of vengeance against Scotland and many of her best and bravest sons. An Aberdeenshire gentleman has told the writer of this history that his parents, for a month after the battle of Culloden, never rose any morning without leaving their pillows soaked with tears. It has also been stated that some very aged female members of the party, after this time, never rose again from bed, though previously accustomed to mingle in society. To the nation in general, the news seemed highly acceptable. The victory was celebrated in most towns of the south of Scotland, and throughout England, with bonfires and ringing of bells. The joy of the high personages of the state was in proportion to their late fears. The duke received the thanks of parliament, and an addition of £25,000 to his annual income.

CHAPTER XXV.

SUPPRESSION OF THE INSURRECTION.

'Whilst the warm blood bedews my veins,
 And unimpaired remembrance reigns,
 Resentment of my country's fate
 Within my filial breast shall beat ;
 And, spite of her insulting foe,
 My sympathising verse shall flow ;
 Mourn, hapless Caledonia, mourn,
 Thy banished peace, thy laurels torn !'
                                        SMOLLETT.

WHEN at last forced off the field, Charles fled with a large party of horse, including his chief counsellors and friends. His flight was protected by the foot, who followed closely behind. The party crossed the Nairn at the ford of Falie, about four miles from the battle-field, and there a hurried council was held respecting further proceedings. Notwithstanding their severe defeat, there can be no doubt that the general inclination of the insurgent chiefs was for a continuance of the war. They conceived that, if they kept together within the Highland frontier, they might protect their territories from the vengeance of the royal troops, until possibly some succours might arrive from

France, so as to enable them to act on the offensive, or at least until the government, worn out by their resistance, might grant them favourable terms.   On the other hand, Charles appears to have formed a plan for his own conduct, in which the views of the Highland gentlemen were not regarded.   His wish was to make his way as quickly as possible to France, in order to use personal exertions in procuring those powerful supplies which had been so much, but so vainly, wished for.   He expected to find French vessels hovering on the west coast, in one of which he might obtain a quick passage to that country.   He therefore had determined to proceed in this direction without loss of time.

Without announcing his intentions, he desired that the remains of the army should rendezvous at Ruthven in Badenoch, and there wait for further orders ; after which he took his leave of those accompanying him, and set out upon his westerly course, attended only by those who had been his immediate counsellors and friends during the campaign—namely, Sir Thomas Sheridan, Mr O'Sullivan, Captain O'Neal, and Mr John Hay, with a few individuals of inferior note.   The bulk of the army proceeded towards Ruthven by the *Highland road*, and on their way meeting Cluny and his men hastening to the field, took them back along with them to swell their numbers at the rendezvous.

Charles had been led out of the field of Culloden, and guided on his route hitherto, by one Edward Burke, a poor Highlander, who usually acted as a sedan-carrier in Edinburgh, but was now servant to Mr Alexander Macleod of Muiravonside.   By the same person the party was now guided to Tordarroch, 'where they got no access [the house being deserted and shut up], and from Tordarroch to Aberarder, where likewise they got no access, and from Aberarder to Faroline, and from Faroline to Gortuleg.'[1] This last place was the seat of Mr Thomas Fraser, chamberlain and confidential agent of Lord Lovat, and the same gentleman who had executed a somewhat remarkable mission for his lordship at an early period of the campaign.[2]   Lovat was at this

[1] Burke's Narrative, *Jacobite Memoirs.*   [2] See Chapter v.

time residing at Gortuleg, and the house had that day been the
scene of extensive culinary operations, for the purpose of cele-
brating by a feast the victory which it was expected the Prince
would gain over his enemies. A girl of ten years of age, who
lived in the house at the time, reported to the late Mrs Grant
of Laggan, that in the confusion arising from these proceedings
she had been shut up in a little closet, to be out of the way, and
there sat for some time an unwilling prisoner, contemplating a
marsh in the plain below, which was supposed to be a haunt of
the fairies. Suddenly the tumultuous noise that had filled the
house all day was succeeded by a deep silence. She ventured
out, and saw no creature in the house but Lovat, sitting in his
great chair in deep thought. On venturing to the door, she
found the rest of the inmates standing in a group, regarding
with the keenest anxiety a party of horsemen who had entered
the vale below the house. The whole circumstances impressed
her with the idea that she was looking upon a band of those
supernatural beings whom she understood to haunt the vale
occasionally. Having heard that the fairies only remain visible
at any time between one winking of the eyelids and another,
she strove to keep her eyes open as long as possible, in order to
prolong the vision. She was soon undeceived, for, on the troop
approaching, the fatal reverse of the Prince's cause was understood; and the women, breaking into mournful cries, began
to tear off their handkerchiefs to make bandages for the wounded.
The viands prepared for the feast were seized and distributed
without ceremony by the party, many of whom then proceeded
on their course. Charles, with his immediate attendants,
entered the house, and received the first personal greetings of
Lord Lovat at the sad moment which informed the aged chief of
the utter ruin of himself and his family. One account represents
his lordship as running about the house in a state of distraction,
crying out to his attendants : ' Chop off my head ! chop off my
head !' But the report of the young person above mentioned
was, that Lovat received the Prince with expressions of attachment, but reproached him with great asperity when he heard him

declare his intention to abandon the enterprise. 'Remember,' he said fiercely, 'your great ancestor Robert Bruce, who lost eleven battles and won Scotland by the twelfth.' The Prince made little answer, but, after taking some refreshment, and drinking a few glasses of wine, set out towards Fort Augustus. Lord Lovat was soon after carried off in his litter to a place of safety.[1]

Charles and his little party were seen, at two o'clock in the morning, riding rapidly past the ruins of that fort; and about two hours before daybreak they arrived at Invergarry, the seat of Macdonell of Glengarry, which was, on the present occasion, deserted of its tenants, and in a condition very ill calculated to support the hospitable character of a Highland mansion. Destitute at once of furniture and provisions, and attended by only a single domestic, however easily a party of natives might have accommodated themselves within its walls, it was particularly unfit to entertain a prince and a stranger. This was the first day of Charles's wanderings, and its privations but too truly omened those of the succeeding five months.

The Prince and his party were so much fatigued with their ride, which was one of little less than forty miles, that they gladly stretched themselves upon the floor in their clothes. They slept till mid-day, when Edward Burke having fortunately caught two salmon in the water of Garry, they had a better dinner than they expected, though the only drink they could procure was the pure element from which their meat had been taken. All the company here took leave of Charles except O'Sullivan, O'Neal, and Edward Burke, who was left to be the Prince's guide, and whose clothes his royal highness now assumed. This small party set out at two o'clock for Loch Arkaig, where they arrived about nine at night, and lodged in the house of Donald Cameron of Glenpean. Charles was so excessively fatigued, that he fell asleep as Edward Burke was unbuttoning

---

[1] I derive the recollections of the young inmate of Gortuleg House from a letter of Mrs Grant, MS. The particulars given by the young lady respecting the meeting of the Prince and Lovat are, in my opinion, likely to be true.

his spatterdashes. Next morning, Friday the 18th, they held their route still farther westward to Mewboll, a farm-house near the extremity of Locheil's country, where they were well entertained. A considerable part of the following day was spent in waiting for intelligence of their friends, which not arriving, they at last set out, for fear of being discovered and taken. There being no longer any road, they were here obliged to abandon their horses, and begin to walk on foot. They came in the evening to a place called Oban, near the head of Loch Morar, where they took up their lodging in a wretched little *sheiling* or hovel used for shearing sheep, near the corner of a wood.

Next day, Sunday the 20th of April, Charles and his three attendants crossed, with inconceivable pain and difficulty, one of those ranges of lofty and rugged hills which, alternately with lochs or arms of the sea, penetrate the country at this part of the West Highlands. Their lodging-place this evening was at Glenbiasdale, in Arisaig, a small village near the place where the Prince had first landed. Here several fugitives joined the dejected little party.

From Ruthven, the day after the battle, Lord George Murray wrote a long letter to the Prince, giving in very plain terms his opinion of his royal highness's chief advisers, to whom he attributed the defeat, and resigning his own command, but at the same time manifesting anything but a supposition that the war was now to be abandoned. One or two thousand men had here assembled, not in the highest spirits, but resolute to defend themselves and the territories of the insurgent clans as long as they could. We have an affecting anecdote from Bishop Mackintosh,[1] of the standard-bearer of the Duke of Perth arriving this day, and presenting the colours to his superior, who said: 'Poor as I am, I would rather than a thousand guineas that they are safe.' They lingered at the spot for a few days, but were at length dispersed, in consequence of the receipt of a letter which the Prince addressed to them from Glenbiasdale. In this, after some professions of devotion to them and

---

[1] Letter, MS.

their interests, he informed them that, seeing he could do nothing for them on this side of the water, he intended instantly to proceed to France, there to ' engage the court either to assist us effectually and powerfully, or at least to procure you such terms as you would not obtain otherwise.' In the measures they would take for defending themselves, he recommended them to confide in the Duke of Perth and Lord George Murray. He desired that they would endeavour to keep his departure as long concealed as possible. Finally, he called on the Almighty to bless and direct them. Although he did not here direct them to disperse, but, on the contrary, implied an expectation that they would maintain the struggle, they seem to have considered the letter as the death-note of the war. Accordingly, taking a melancholy leave of each other, they dispersed—the gentlemen to seek concealment in, or escape from, the country, and the common men to return to their homes.[1]

At Glenbiasdale, Charles was joined by young Clanranald, Mr Lockhart younger of Carnwath, Mr Æneas Macdonald, and some others, by whom it was reported that the western seas were much beset by English vessels, so that the Prince could scarcely hope to make an immediate escape in that direction without incurring considerable risk. This was staggering intelligence, and caused Charles to consider if it would not yet be the best course to remain at the head of as many men as he could assemble. He also thought of trusting himself amongst the Macleods in the Isle of Skye. Clanranald suggested that he might remain where he was ; and for his accommodation and concealment a few summer sheilings or cots could be fitted up amongst the hills, where he would be tolerably safe until a trusty person should take a trip to the Isles and look out for

---

[1] The Earl of Cromarty had been left with a party in Sutherland to overawe the loyalists there ; but on the 15th of April he allowed himself to be surprised at Dunrobin Castle, apart from his men, by a party of the Earl of Sutherland's militia. His men, attacked by an inferior force, were defeated, when many were killed, and 178 taken prisoners. The earl himself, his son, and several friends, were seized that evening by stratagem, while conferring with a party of the assailants respecting terms of surrender. The whole were brought in a sloop-of-war to Inverness the second day after the battle of Culloden.

a ship in which to convey away his royal highness from the country.

Mr Æneas Macdonald had at this time recently landed from the Isles, in charge of a large sum of French money which had been debarked in Barra; and he was attended by a faithful old man, Donald Macleod of Gualtergill, in the Isle of Skye, who had been of great use in piloting him through very considerable dangers. A message was sent to Kinlochmoidart, where Donald now was, pressingly desiring him to come to meet the Prince at Borodale. Donald immediately set out, and, in passing through the forest of Glenbiasdale, he encountered a stranger walking by himself, who, making up to him, asked if he was Donald Macleod of Gualtergill. Donald, instantly recognising him, notwithstanding his mean attire, said: 'I am the same man, please your highness, at your service.' 'Then,' said the Prince, 'you see, Donald, I am in distress: I therefore throw myself into your bosom, and let you do with me what you like. I hear you are an honest man, and fit to be trusted.' When the old man, a year after, related these particulars to the individual who has reported them, the tears were streaming along his cheeks like rain.

Charles desired Donald to go with letters from him to Sir Alexander Macdonald and the Laird of Macleod, requesting their protection; but the old man positively refused, saying that such a course would be attended with certain ruin, for, so far from being well inclined to him, they were at this moment employed with their men in searching for him at a place not above ten or twelve miles distant. Charles then asked if he would undertake to pilot him to the Isles, where he thought he would be in more safety than in his present situation. Macleod answered that he was ready to do anything in the world for him, and undergo any risk in his behalf, except only that of communicating with the two apostate chiefs of Skye.

Accordingly, on the evening of the 24th, Charles, along with O'Sullivan, O'Neal, Burke, and seven other persons, set sail in an open eight-oared boat from Lochnanuagh, the bay where he first landed.   Donald Macleod, acting as pilot, sat at the stern, with Charles betwixt his knees.   This aged person, being an experienced mariner, was certain, from the appearance of the sky, that a storm was about to ensue, and entreated the Prince to defer his voyage till next day.   But Charles insisted upon immediately leaving the continent, where he apprehended so much danger.   In the boat there were four pecks of oatmeal, and a pot in which they could boil meat when they landed.

As old Macleod had foretold, they had scarcely got fairly out to sea when a storm arose.   The wind blew a tempest; the waves of the Atlantic rose with tumultuous fury; and it was altogether a night surpassing in danger any that Macleod, an experienced boatman, had ever before seen upon that wild sea. To add to their distress, the rain poured down in torrents, and they had neither pump nor compass.   In the darkness of the night, none of the crew knew where they were, and serious apprehensions were entertained lest the boat should either founder or be driven upon Skye, where the person of the Prince would be apt to become a prey to the militia, who were roaming about that island in great numbers.   At length a period was put at once to their danger from the sea, and their apprehensions from the militia, by the approach of daylight, which shewed them to be on the coast of the Long Island, the storm having carried the boat upwards of sixty miles in nine or ten hours. They landed at Rossinish, the south-east angle of the isle of Benbecula, and, having drawn their boat upon dry land, prepared a humble entertainment with meal and the flesh of a cow which they had seized and killed.

The first consideration with the Duke of Cumberland, after securing the immediate fruits of his victory, was to disarm the ill-affected clans, and thus deprive them of all power of creating further disturbance.   It has been represented by his friends 'that he was at first disposed to take mild methods with them, and promised his protection to all who should come to his camp, deliver their arms, and submit to the king's mercy, before a certain day; that some complied, and were dismissed in peace, with protections; but that great numbers, especially the Camerons, Macdonalds, Grants, and Frasers, were perfidious, often promising to surrender at a certain time, and as often breaking their promises; that others equivocated, pretending to surrender their arms, by bringing in old useless guns and swords, while they concealed their best arms at home; and that his royal highness was then obliged to lay the rod more heavily upon them.'[1] On the other hand, the invitation to submit and give up their arms was not such as could have been expected to go far with men like the Highlanders under the existing circumstances. No guarantee of ultimate safety for life or property was held out. The protections were only for six weeks, at the end of which time, if disarmed, they might have become an unresisting prey to the vengeance of the government. The fears which they no doubt entertained were confirmed by an unfortunate act of the duke at Inverness. Sixty-nine men of Glenmorriston, and twelve from the vale of Urquhart, in all eighty-one, having been induced by the Laird of Grant to come to Inverness to surrender, were, upon some trifling demur, seized and put with the other prisoners into the king's vessels, where they were subjected to the horrible treatment already described.[2] An act of this kind might well deter the disaffected clans from throwing themselves unarmed upon the royal clemency, even if there had been no general reasons, as undoubtedly there were, for hesitating to take such a step.

Besides, it does not appear to be quite true that the duke waited for the alleged instances of perfidiousness before wreaking vengeance on the insurgents. So early as the 18th of April, two days after the battle, he sent Brigadier Mordaunt with a detachment to the Aird—a district belonging to Lord Lovat, a short day's march from Inverness—in order to subject it to military execution. Beaufort Castle, the seat of Lovat, was

---

[1] *Scots Magazine*, 1746, p. 287.
[2] Narrative of the Rev. James Hay of Inverness, *Jacobite Memoirs*. Those who did not die on shipboard were sent to Barbadoes, where, three years after, out of the eighty-one who surrendered only eighteen were living.

burned, and the whole of the horses, cows, sheep, meal, and other provisions found in the district were brought away, for the use of the army. The aged chief, from a distant mountain top, beheld the house of his ancestors given to the flames.

The duke took vigorous measures to surround the disaffected districts, in order to prevent the insurgents who had retired thither from making their escape. Cobham's and Mark Kerr's regiments of dragoons were posted along the east coast of Scotland; the passes from the Highlands into the Low Country were guarded by militia; Lord Fortrose, son of the Earl of Seaforth, raised the Mackenzies to guard the passages to the Isles; and the Monroes, Mackays, and Earl of Sutherland's men took care of the more remote northern counties. British cruisers at the same time hovered on both coasts, to intercept any French or other vessels in which the insurgents might be attempting to leave the country. These measures were very effectual for the end in view, and in the course of a few weeks most of the jails north of the Forth were filled with prisoners. Lord Balmerino was one of the first persons of any eminence taken. He was brought by the Grants to Inverness on the 21st of April, and soon after sent, with the Earls of Cromarty and Kilmarnock, by a vessel to London. It has been said that his lordship voluntarily delivered himself, at the recommendation of Mr Grant younger of Rothiemurchus. The Marquis of Tullibardine was one of those who rendezvoused at Ruthven. When the dispersion took place, he travelled southward in company with an Italian named Mitchell, an old servant of the Chevalier St George; and, being in a bad state of health, he was tempted to seek refuge in the mansion of Drummakill, near Loch Lomond, the lady of the house being related to him. Mr Buchanan of Drummakill was, however, a zealous loyalist and officer of militia, and deemed it his duty to deliver up the marquis. On the 27th of April his lordship was conducted as a prisoner to Dumbarton Castle, and thence to Leith, where he embarked in a war-vessel, by which he was carried to London. It is stated that Drummakill was so much despised for this action, that no gentleman of his neighbourhood would after-wards be seen in his company.[1] Early in May, the government had also secured Sir James Kinloch, Colonel Ker of Graden, the Honourable William Murray, brother of the Earl of Dun-more, Mr Stirling of Kier, Mr Stirling of Craigbarnet, and some others. A party, in which were included Lord Ogilvie, Mr Hunter of Burnside, Mr Fletcher of Benshie, David Graham of Duntroon, and David Fotheringham, who had been governor of Dundee for Prince Charles, got on board a vessel riding off the Lights of Tay, and reached Norway in safety. The British government had enjoined all friendly powers to aid in appre-hending the unfortunate adherents of the Prince. The king of Denmark had consequently ordered all vessels landing in his ports to be examined, and all persons not possessing passports to be apprehended. These gentlemen were accordingly seized and put into prison in the castle of Bergen, but were soon after allowed to make their escape to France. It may be added, that Mr Hunter was one of the five exiles whom Smollett describes in such touching terms in his novel of *Peregrine Pickle,* as living at Boulogne, and going every day to the sea-side ' in order to indulge their longing eyes with a prospect of the white cliffs of Albion, which they must never more approach.'

Secretary Murray was sick at the time of the battle of Cul-loden. When the conflict was pending, he was carried in a litter to Foyers, on Loch Ness side. At first, the bad issue of the battle was concealed from him, and he was carried across the lake to the house of Glenmorriston for safety, but without the reason being disclosed to him. Dr Cameron there told him of the defeat. After sundry removes, he was carried to Invergarry, where he hoped to hear that a stand had been made by the remains of the army. Here he met the Duke of Perth ' quite worn out with fatigue,' and learned that, most of the chiefs being dispersed, there was no chance of a prolongation of the war. He then went to Locheil's country, and meeting

1 *Jacobite Memoirs,* p. 3, note.

that chief, devised with him, Stuart of Ardshiel, and some others, the raising of a small body of men, with whom they would 'keep the hills, till such time as they could be satisfied that the French either were or were not in earnest to support them.' At the same time they took measures to bring other chiefs into their scheme, and to detain the Prince on the mainland; but in the latter object they were not successful, the Prince having sailed before they could reach him with a message. Meanwhile, two French ships arrived at Borrodale with six casks of gold, which were secured by the secretary. These vessels, after beating off some British cruisers in the loch, departed with the Duke of Perth, 'then in a dying condition,' Lord John Drummond, Lord Elcho, Sir Thomas Sheridan, Mr Lockhart younger of Carnwath, Mr Hay, and several others. The money was carried to Loch Arkaig by Dr Cameron.[1]

For three weeks after the battle of Culloden, no attempt was made to penetrate that tract of the central and west Highlands which formed the chief stronghold of the Jacobite clans. There a considerable number of the insurgents were still disposed to offer armed resistance to the government. On the 8th of May, a meeting of leaders and men of consequence took place at Muirlaggan, near the head of Loch Arkaig, for the purpose of concerting measures for a new rising. The chief person present was young Locheil, who, after being wounded in both ankles at the battle, had been conducted away on horseback by his faithful clansmen, and was now a cripple, unable to travel on foot. Accident had brought Lord Lovat to the spot, and there were also present Clanranald, Glenbucket, John Roy Stuart, Major Kennedy, Secretary Murray, Macdonald of Barrisdale, Mr Alexander Macleod, and a nephew of Keppoch.[2] These gentlemen were greatly encouraged in their project by the landing of the six casks of gold, which amounted to no less

---

1 Narrative by Murray, MS. in possession (1847) of Mr W. H. Murray of Edinburgh.
2 Narrative of John Cameron, Presbyterian minister at Fort William (an actor on the Prince's side), *Lyon in Mourning*, MS. i. 162.

than £38,000.   It was agreed that the Camerons, Macdonells
of Glengarry, Keppoch, and Clanranald, the Stuarts of Appin,
the Mackinnons and Macleods, should rendezvous on the 15th
at Auchnacarry, in the braes of Lochaber; while the Frasers,
Mackintoshes, Macphersons, and the Atholemen should be
apprised of the resolution, that they might take measures to
rise on the same day, and join the rest.   These resolutions and
others were written down, and the document has been preserved and printed;[1] but no signed copy has ever been found.
To enable the chiefs to raise their men, Mr Murray distributed
600 louis-d'ors amongst them, and further gave forty to the
Laird of Mackinnon, and sent twenty to Macleod of Raasay
and Macdonald younger of Scothouse.

This attempt to renew the war came to nothing.   If we are
to believe Mr Murray, the conduct of Lovat on this occasion
was marked by his usual duplicity, cunning, and treachery:
'He complained that the order he had required to empower
him to seize upon the person of Mr Forbes of Culloden had not
been granted in the terms he required—namely, dead or alive.
From which he endeavoured to shew *how easy it would have
been to accomplish his death,* and thereby have prevented the
junction of Macleod with the other northern clans, who had
done so much hurt to the Prince's affairs; and that, provided
the order had been in these terms, the attempt upon his house
would not have been abortive; but, as they had not sufficient
power, they were obliged to make a shameful retreat, inconsistent
with the honour of his clan!'   Lovat played them altogether
false as to the sending of his clan to the rendezvous, and Mr
Murray also accuses Lochgarry of shewing indifference to the
interest of the party on that occasion.   'Clanranald disappointed
them not only of his quota of men, but of the ammunition he
had engaged for.'   On the day that the resolutions were entered
into, the Earl of Loudoun left Inverness at the head of 1700
militia, to take possession of Lochaber and the adjoining

----

[1] In Mr Home's appendix.

districts.   Locheil had got about 300 Camerons together, and Glengarry and Barrisdale 150 men each; cattle were purchased by Mr Murray to supply the gathering troops with food, and ammunition for their use was about to be sent by Clanranald from Arisaig, when the advance of the Earl of Loudoun obliged them all to disperse.   Locheil was nearly surprised by a body of troops, whom he mistook at a distance for Barrisdale's men, and who would have taken him, if some faithful follower had not given him timely intelligence of the red crosses which they wore in their bonnets.[1]   He escaped by crossing the loch in a boat which he kept on purpose.   Immediately before the dispersion of the party, Mr Murray had the greater part of his French money buried in secret places, £15,000 being sunk in a rivulet near the head of Loch Arkaig, and £12,000 near the foot of the same lake, '£5000 being reserved for necessary expenses.'[2]

The Earl of Loudoun executed his mission in Lochaber with mercy, and induced a considerable number of the people to deliver up their arms.   General Campbell, at the head of his clan militia, was equally successful in Appin and Glencoe.   But the duke was already exasperated by the delay, and had now resolved to take very severe measures to reduce the disaffected to obedience.   On the 23d of May he marched from Inverness, with Kingston's horse and eleven battalions of foot, and encamped at Fort Augustus.   It is said that, in the well connected with this ruined fort, the bodies of eleven of the late garrison were found; and it was supposed that these men had been drowned by the insurgent troops after the taking of the place in March.   There was no proof that such was the case, and indeed it was extremely unlikely : the more obvious supposition is, that the bodies were those of the men killed in the

---

[1] John Cameron's Narrative, as before.

[2] The particulars here given respecting the money possessed by Mr Murray are from a well-authenticated copy, which the author possesses, of an account which the secretary seems to have drawn up from memory of the moneys which he received and disbursed at this time.   As this document relates some curious circumstances, it is printed at the close of the present narrative.

siege. The discovery, however, and the supposition, inflamed the rancour borne by many of the officers and soldiers against the disaffected clans, and probably had no small effect in hardening their minds to the duty now imposed upon them. Meanwhile, many of the Macphersons had surrendered to a party of troops marching from Perth to Inverness, and the men of Strontian, Morven, and Ardnamurchan had also submitted.

From Fort Augustus the duke despatched parties in all directions around, to disarm and desolate the various disaffected districts. The cruelties practised by these parties were such as, if not perfectly well authenticated, we could scarcely believe to have been practised only a century ago in our comparatively civilised land. Not only were the mansions of the chiefs Locheil, Glengarry, Cluny, Keppoch, Kinlochmoidart, Glengyle, Ardshiel, and many others plundered and burned, but those of many inferior gentlemen, and even the huts of the common people, were in like manner destroyed. The cattle, sheep, and provisions of all kinds were carried off to Fort Augustus. In many instances the women and children were stripped naked, and left exposed : in some, the females were subjected to even more horrible treatment. A great number of men, unarmed and inoffensive, including some aged beggars, were shot in the fields and on the mountain-side, rather in the spirit of wantonness than for any definite object. Many hapless people perished of cold and hunger amongst the hills. Others followed, in abject herds, their departing cattle, and at Fort Augustus begged, for the support of a wretched existence, to get the offal, or even to be allowed to lick up the blood, of those which were killed for the use of the army. Before the 10th of June the task of desolation was complete throughout all the western parts of Inverness-shire ; and the curse which had been denounced upon Scotland by the religious enthusiasts of the preceding century was at length so entirely fulfilled in this remote region, that it would have been literally possible to travel for days through the depopulated glens *without seeing a chimney smoke, or hearing a cock crow.*

It is generally allowed that the duke himself, though the instigator of these cruelties, did not shew so much open or active cruelty as some of the more immediate instruments of the royal vengeance.   General Hawley was one of the most remorseless of all the commanding-officers; apparently thinking no extent of cruelty a sufficient compensation for his loss of honour at Falkirk.   The names of Lieutenant-colonel Howard, Captain Caroline Scott, and Major Lockhart are also to be handed down as worthy of everlasting execration.   The last, in particular, did not even respect the protections which Lord Loudoun had extended (by virtue of a commission from the duke) to those who had taken an early opportunity of submitting, but used only to observe to the unhappy individuals who expected to be saved on that account, as he ordered them to execution and their houses to the flames, that ' *though they were to shew him a protection from Heaven, it should not prevent him from doing his duty!*'

It reflects great credit upon the Highlanders that, in the midst of these calamities, they displayed no disposition to take mean or insidious modes of avenging them, though, with arms in their hands, and acquainted as they were with the country, they might have often done so both easily and securely.   Only one soldier is said to have perished by the hand of an assassin during the whole of the frightful campaign.   A domestic belonging to the house of Glengarry, on reaching his home after a short expedition, found that, during his absence, his property had been destroyed, his wife violated, and his home rendered desolate.   In the bitterness of the moment he vowed deadly revenge.   Learning that the officer who had commanded the spoliators, and who had been the ravisher of his wife, rode upon a white horse, he rushed abroad with his musket, determined never to rest till he had accomplished his vow.   After wandering several weeks without discovering the offender, he one day observed an officer approaching at the head of a party mounted upon the white horse he had heard described.   This was not the real perpetrator of his wrongs, but Major Monro of Culcairn (a younger brother of the late Sir Robert Monro of Foulis), who had, unfortunately for himself, borrowed the animal on which he rode. The infuriated Highlander took aim from behind some craggy banks which overlooked the road, and shot the major dead. He then fled through the rugged country, and was soon beyond pursuit. On afterwards learning that he had killed an innocent man, he burst his gun, and renounced the vow which had bound him to vengeance.

Whilst the natives and the fugitive Prince were enduring every species of hardship, Duke William and his myrmidons at Fort Augustus spent their time in a round of festivities. Enriched by the sale of their spoils, the soldiers could purchase all the luxuries which the Lowlands could supply, or which could be conveniently transported over the Grampians; and for several weeks their camp exhibited all the coarse and obstreperous revelries of an English fair. In order to amuse them, the duke instituted races, which were run by the trulls of the camp, with circumstances of indecency forbidding description. General Hawley also ran a race with the infamous Howard, and, probably rendered a proficient in that exercise by his practice at Falkirk, gained it by four inches.

Not content with laying waste the country of the active insurgents, they extended their ravages, before the end of the season, over peaceful districts, to the very gates of the capital; and for some time Scotland might be said to have been treated throughout its whole bounds as a conquered country subjected to military law. The voice of Lord President Forbes was occasionally heard amidst these outrages, like that of Pity described in the allegory as interposing in some barbarous scene; but on this amiable man remonstrating with the duke, by a representation that his soldiers were breaking the laws of the land, his royal highness is said to have answered with scorn: 'The laws, my lord! By G—, I'll make a brigade give laws!' He was afterwards heard at Inverness to allude to the President as 'that old woman who talked to me about humanity.' No form of trial was adopted with the insurgents, even within a few miles of the seat of the Court of Session; nor did the soldiers ever appeal to the neighbouring justices for warrants when about to plunder their houses. The lawful creditors of unfortunate individuals were, in innumerable instances, mortified at seeing a lawless band seize the property to which they looked for payment, and unceremoniously expose it to public sale for their own behalf.

Besides the measures already described as having been taken for the capture of the Chevalier and his friends, others were adopted of a nature which shewed the anxiety of government to attain that object. The General Assembly of the church, about the end of May, was required to command all the Established clergymen throughout the country to read a proclamation from their pulpits, in which the duke ordered every minister and every loyal subject to exert themselves in discovering and seizing the rebels; and the General Assembly complied with the requisition. Many of the individual clergymen, with a better spirit, refused to read this paper, or left it to be read by their precentors; in consequence of which, the duke sent another order to the church, commanding every minister to give in a list of the rebels belonging to his parish. With this last still fewer complied, the clergymen of Edinburgh ranking among the recusants; and the duke, having then used individual applications, and even personal entreaties, in vain, troubled them with no more.

It is not observable in any authentic documents that those who gave food or shelter to the fugitives were punished with death; but it is at least certain that a proclamation was read in the churches of Perth and its vicinity, by order of the Duke of Cumberland, threatening with that punishment all who concealed them, or even their arms. Rewards were also offered in Ireland and the Isle of Man for the apprehension of any who might land in those territories; and the British ministers at foreign courts in alliance with his majesty were ordered to secure all who might take refuge there. No means, in short, were omitted which might tend to the great object of exterminating these unhappy objects of state resentment.

Macdonald of Barrisdale, having surrendered with his adherents, was immediately liberated—an instance of mercy so extraordinary, as to give rise to a rumour that he had undertaken to aid in seizing the fugitive Prince. About the beginning of May, as already mentioned, the Duke of Perth and some others got off in the two French ships which had landed the large sum of money in Moidart; but the duke, completely exhausted by fatigue, died at sea a few days after going on board. Locheil remained for several months in concealment, and ultimately sailed in the same vessel with the Prince. Early in June, Lord Lovat was discovered and taken prisoner in a small island in Loch Morrar, where he had lived for twelve days on oatmeal and water. Lord George Murray escaped to the south, where, late in the year, he embarked in disguise for France; but Mr Murray of Broughton, after making his way through the passes, was seized at the house of his brother-in-law, Mr Hunter of Polmood, in Peeblesshire.[1] He and Lovat were immediately sent to London.

---

[1] Murray, in his narrative, gives a minute account of his journey to the Lowlands, and of the separate journey of his wife, who was at this time in a peculiarly delicate state. While the lady lay in Locheil's country, a message was sent to an English commanding-officer explaining her condition, and requesting a pass for her, that she might travel to Edinburgh; but this being refused, she had to make the best of her way thither in disguise, which she succeeded in doing, and was, in the ensuing September, while residing there in concealment, delivered of a son, who was baptised Charles, but did not long survive.

Mrs Murray went abroad at her husband's request, but did not remain faithful to him. A few years after the insurrection, the ex-secretary married a young Quaker lady named Webb, whom he found in a provincial English boarding-school. She had six children to him, the eldest being Mr Charles Murray, afterwards a well-known comedian. The ex-secretary sold his estate of Broughton, in 1764, to Dickson of Havana, whose agent in the transaction was Mr Walter Scott, W.S., father of Sir Walter. This circumstance seems to have been what occasioned the remarkable visit of Murray to that gentleman, which Mr Lockhart has related in his *Life of Sir Walter Scott.*

Mr Charles Murray, who was born in 1754, was a little boy playing about the room in which his father sat in their house in London, when a tall, stout, red-faced gentleman came in, and remained for some time conversing with his father. Some weeks after, the father said to the son: 'Charles, do you remember that stout gentleman who called upon me some time ago?' 'Yes, sir.' 'Well, boy, remember you have seen your Prince.'

CHAPTER XXVI.

CHARLES'S WANDERINGS—THE LONG ISLAND.

'He might put on a hat, a muffler, and a kerchief, and so escape.'
SHAKSPEARE.

CHARLES was left in the remote and desolate island of Benbecula, where he had arrived after a night-voyage of no ordinary danger. His accommodations in this place were of the humblest description. A cow-house, destitute of a door, was his palace; his couch of state was formed of filthy straw and a sailcloth; and the regal banquet, composed of oatmeal and boiled flesh, was served up in the homely pot in which it had been prepared. The storm continued for fourteen hours; and it was not till the third day after (Tuesday, the 29th of April) that he could leave the island. They set sail for Stornoway, the chief port in the Isle of Lewis, where Donald Macleod entertained hopes of procuring a vessel to convey the Prince to France. A storm, however, coming on, as on the former occasion, their little vessel was driven upon the small isle of Glass, about forty miles northward of Benbecula, and fully as far distant from Stornoway. They disembarked about two hours before daybreak, and, finding the inhabitants engaged in the hostile interest under the Laird of Macleod, were obliged to assume the character of merchantmen who had been shipwrecked in a voyage to Orkney; O'Sullivan and the Prince calling themselves Sinclair, as father and son; the rest of the crew taking other names. They were entertained here by Donald Campbell, tacksman or leaseholder of the island, who was so kind as to lend his own boat to Donald Macleod, that he might go to Stornoway in order to hire a vessel for the Prince's service. Donald set out next day, leaving the Prince in Campbell's house.

A message came from the faithful Macleod on the 3d of May, intimating his having succeeded in his object, and requesting the Prince immediately to set forward. Another boat, therefore, being manned, Charles set sail next day for Stornoway. The wind proving contrary, he was obliged to land in Loch Sheffort, at the distance of above twenty miles from Stornoway. All this way he had to walk on foot over a pathless moor, which, in addition to all other disadvantages, was extremely wet. Being misled by the ignorance of their guide, the disconsolate little party did not get near Stornoway till the 5th at noon; when, stopping at the Point of Arynish, about half a mile from the town, they sent forward their guide to Donald Macleod, imploring him to bring them out some refreshment. Donald soon came with provisions, and took them to the house of Mrs Mackenzie of Kildun, where the Prince went to sleep. Returning to Stornoway, Donald was confounded to observe the people all rising in commotion. His servant, having become tipsy, blabbed for whom the vessel was designed, at the same time hinting that the Prince was in a condition to take it by force, if he could not obtain it by good-will. This intimation was confirmed by a chain of alarms, communicated from a clergyman in South Uist to his father in the Harris, and thence to another minister in the Lewis. Donald exerted his eloquence to shew them the absurdity of their fears, representing the inability of the Prince, with so small a band, to do them the least injury, and finally threatening that, if they should hurt but a hair of his head, it would be amply and fearfully revenged upon them, in this their lonely situation, by his royal highness's foreign friends. By working alternately upon their pity and their fears, he succeeded in pacifying them; and all they at last desired was, that he should leave their country. Donald requested to have a pilot, but nobody could be persuaded to perform that service. He then returned to the house in which the Prince was reposing, and informed him of the disagreeable aspect of his affairs. Some proposed to fly instantly to the moors; but Charles resolved to stand his ground, lest such a measure should encourage his enemies to pursue. They soon after learned that the boat in which they came to Lewis had been taken out to sea by two of the crew, while the other two had fled to the country, from fear of the people of Stornoway. They were therefore obliged to spend the afternoon, in a state of painful alarm, at Mrs Mackenzie's house.

The Prince, O'Sullivan, and O'Neal had at this time only six shirts amongst them. During their residence at Kildun, they killed a cow, for which the lady refused to take payment, till compelled by his royal highness. They also procured two pecks of meal, with plenty of brandy and sugar. With these provisions, the whole party set sail next morning in the boat, which had returned ashore during the night. They thought at first of going to Orkney, but the crew, now only two in number, would not undertake so long a voyage. The Prince wished to go to Bollein in Kintail; but this also the men refused, on account of the length of the voyage. A resolution was then taken to steer southward, as the only other course open to them. Soon after, four large vessels appearing at a distance, they put into the small desert isle of Eiurn or Iffurt, near Harris, a little way north of Glass, where they had been a few days before.

The island was temporarily occupied by only a few fishermen, all of whom fled to the interior at the approach of the boat, which they believed to be sent with a pressgang from the vessels within sight. They left their fish in large quantities drying upon the shore, to the great satisfaction of the wanderers, who made a hearty meal upon it. Their lodging here was a miserable hovel, the roof of which was so imperfect, that it had to be covered with a sailcloth. They lay upon the floor, keeping watch by turns. The things given to them by Mrs Mackenzie of Kildun added much to their comfort. Out of the brains of her cow the Prince baked a cake, which they ate with relish. They were also able to make a little hot punch, which cheered them greatly. Generally, Ned Burke acted as cook and baker; but the Prince, when he lent his hand to that work, usually excelled his humble follower.   One day, while the rest were asleep, the Prince and Burke employed themselves socially in preparing a dish of fish, when the latter remembering a piece of butter which Lady Kildun had given them, went for it to the boat, but found it jammed into a mass of crumbled bread.   He thought it useless ; but the Prince, saying that bread could never spoil butter, took it, melted it, and presented it with the fish, which it greatly improved.   While thus humbling himself, he and the gentlemen of his party took their food apart from the boatmen, though both parties had no better knives and forks than their fingers, and no table or chairs but the bare rock. When about to leave the island, the Prince was going to leave money upon the place where they had got the fish, but Donald Macleod prevented him, by representing the necessity of acting up to their supposed character of a pressgang ; adding, according to the report of Dougal Graham :

> ' Is it not the man-of-war-men's way
> To take all things, but not to pay ? '

Charles yielded to the suggestions of his sagacious counsellor, though not without reluctance.

After a residence of four days upon this little island, the party once more set sail (May 10), and, cruising along the shores of the Long Island, touched at Glass (where they had been before), with the intention of paying Donald Campbell for the hire of his boat.   Before they had got time to land, four men came up, and it was thought necessary to send Edward Burke ashore to confer with them, before the Prince should hazard his person on the island.   These fellows manifesting a desire of seizing the boat, Burke, to escape their clutches, was under the necessity of hastily jumping back into it and pushing off from the shore. On account of the calm, they had to row all night, although excessively faint for want of food.   About daybreak they hoisted their sail to catch the wind, which then began to rise.   Not having any fresh water, they were obliged, during this miserable day, to subsist upon meal stirred into brine.   Charles himself is said to have partaken of this nauseous food with some degree of satisfaction, observing that, if ever he mounted a throne, he should not fail to remember ' those who dined with him to-day.' They considered themselves fortunate, however, in being able to qualify the *salt-water drammock*, as it was called, with a dram of brandy.

As they proceeded in their boat, they suddenly found themselves near an English man-of-war, which immediately gave them chase. The Prince called the men to row with their utmost speed, saying : ' If we escape this danger, you shall have a handsome reward ; if not, I 'll be sunk rather than be taken.' The ship, after a pursuit of three leagues, found itself becalmed. The Prince's light skiff soon got out of sight, and went in amongst the rocks at the Point of Roundil, in the Harris. Soon after, on stealing out to pursue his course, the boat was espied and pursued by another ship; and it was with the greatest difficulty the crew got ashore at Loch-wiskaway in Benbecula. Scarcely had he landed when a storm arose, and blew his pursuers off the coast. Charles, elated at the double escape he had made, could not help exclaiming to his companions that he believed he was not designed to die by either weapon or water.

Soon after landing upon Benbecula, one of the boatmen began to search among the rocks for shell-fish, and had the good fortune to catch a crab, which he held up to the Prince with a joyful exclamation. Charles instantly took a pail or bucket, which they carried with them, and ran to receive the prize from the man's hands. They soon filled this vessel with crabs, and then directed their steps to a hut about two miles inland, Charles insisting upon carrying the bucket. On reaching the hovel, it was found to be one of the very meanest and most primitive description, the door being so low, that they were obliged to enter upon their hands and knees. Resolving to remain here for some time, Charles ordered his faithful servant Burke to improve the hovel by lowering the threshold. He also sent a message to the old Laird of Clanranald, the father of his youthful adherent, acquainting him of his arrival, and of his present hapless condition.

Clanranald, who had lived in the Long Island during the whole progress of the war, came immediately, bringing with him some Spanish wines, provisions, shoes, and stockings. He found the youth who had recently agitated Britain in so extraordinary a manner, and whose pretensions to a throne he considered indubitable, reclining in a hovel little larger than an English hog-sty, and perhaps more filthy; his face haggard with disease, hunger, and exposure to the weather; and his shirt, to use the expressive language of Dougal Graham, as dingy as a dish-clout. He procured him six good shirts from Lady Clanranald, with a supply of every other convenience which was attainable; and after spending a day or two in the hut, it was determined that he should remove to a more sequestered and secure place of hiding near the centre of South Uist.

Before removing, the Prince despatched Donald Macleod to the mainland with letters to Locheil and Secretary Murray, desiring to know the state of affairs in the country, and requesting from the secretary a supply of cash. Donald made his way to these two gentlemen, who were still at the head of Loch Arkaig, though all hope of continued resistance to the government had been given up. He got letters from both gentlemen, informing the Prince of the utter ruin of his affairs on the mainland, but he did not obtain the desired supply of cash. According to his own account,[1] the secretary said he had only sixty louis-d'ors, which was little enough for his own necessities: but it is not easy to reconcile this with what we have seen regarding the large sum landed from the French vessel. The most feasible explanation is, that the money had by this time been secreted, and the country where it lay was so much possessed by the king's troops as to prevent its being approached. Donald returned to the Prince after an absence of eighteen days.[2] He

[1] *Jacobite Memoirs.*
[2] It appears from the manuscript of Secretary Murray that the two messengers who came from the Prince to see Locheil and Murray did not speak of money while they were at the head of Loch Arkaig, and not till the party was on the west coast two days after, Murray having gone thither with the design of sailing to Uist and bringing Charles back to the

found the royal fugitive in a better hut than that in which he had left him, having two cow-hides stretched out upon four sticks, as an awning to cover him when asleep. His habitation was called the Forest-house of Glencoridale, being situated in a lonely and secluded vale, with a convenient access either to the hills or to the sea in case of a visit from the enemy. South Uist is remarkable above all the Hebrides for abundance of game, and Charles had here amused himself with field-sports. He shewed himself remarkably expert in shooting fowl upon the wing. Sometimes he also went out in a boat upon the creek near his residence, and with hand-lines caught a species of fish called lyths. Most of his faithful boatmen still remained with him, and he was provided by Clanranald with a dozen of stout gillies to act as watchmen and couriers. The old gentleman, as well as his brother Boisdale, often attended him, to cheer his solitude and administer to his comforts.

In order to give the reader a proper idea of the danger which the Prince ran at this time, it is necessary to remind him that the reward of £30,000, which had been offered by the government for his apprehension at the beginning of the campaign, still hung over his head, and indeed was now more ostentatiously offered than before. The magnitude of the sum was such as seemed calculated to overcome every scruple on the part of at least his inferior adherents; and it was daily expected throughout the country that he would be given up by one or other of those to whom he intrusted his person. That no means for the accomplishment of such an end might be omitted, parties of

mainland, although extremely sick at the time, and little prepared for such an expedition. The design of sailing to Uist for this purpose was prevented, and the two messengers returned by themselves. Murray states that, on their asking money from him for the Prince, he answered 'that he was surprised they had not mentioned that when at the head of Loch Arkaig, when it was in his power to have given them any sum they could demand, but that now he had none alongst with him, save a little for common necessaries on the road.' This seems sufficient to defend the secretary from the charge brought by Donald Macleod; for in such circumstances it could have been no easy matter to command a supply of money from the hoard buried beside Lock Arkaig. Had it been possible, there could be no reason for Murray refusing to send a supply out of so large a sum, unless, indeed, as he insinuates, he had reason to doubt the faith of the messengers, who, he says, shewed him no written authority from the Prince.

soldiers were sent out in every direction, full of eagerness to secure the prize. The duke's instructions to these emissaries were invariably expressed in the simple words: 'No prisoners, gentlemen—you understand me.' Among all who were employed in this duty, no man seems to have been more zealous than John Campbell of Mamore (afterwards fourth Duke of Argyll), who had some months before been invested with a command over the troops and garrisons of the West Highlands. On a report arising that the Chevalier had taken refuge in St Kilda, General Campbell instantly repaired to the island with a large fleet. St Kilda 'placed far amidst the melancholy main,' is the remotest of all the Western Islands, and is peopled by only a few aboriginal families, who subsist chiefly on fish and sea-fowl, paying a rent to the Laird of Macleod, whose factor, sent once a year to collect their dues, was the only visitor whom they ever saw. On Campbell's fleet coming within sight, the people fled in terror to caves and the tops of mountains, and it was not without considerable difficulty that the general could procure a hearing amongst them. His men asked those whom they found 'what had become of the Pretender?' expecting to discover their guilt by their confusion, or perhaps to get a candid confession. But the only answer they could obtain from the simple islanders was, 'that they had never heard of such a person.' All that they could tell about the late troubles was, that they heard a report, probably communicated by some stray fishermen, that their laird (Macleod) had been at war with a woman a great way abroad, and that he had got the better of her.

Charles spent several weeks in comparative comfort at Glencoridale. One day he shot a deer, which was brought to their retreat. As they were preparing some collops from it, a poor starved boy came in amongst them, and seeing the dish, thrust his hand into it to satisfy his hunger. Burke, who acted as cook, reproved the act with a stroke of the back of his hand, when the Prince interfered, saying: 'Ned, you don't remember the Scriptures, which enjoin us to feed the hungry and clothe

the naked. You ought rather to give him meat than a stripe.'
The Prince then ordered some clothes for the boy, and paid for
them, adding : ' I cannot see any one perish for lack of food
or raiment, having it in my power to preserve him.'   This kindness met an ungrateful return ; for the boy, after being fed and
clothed, having detected the quality of the Prince, and hearing
of the approach of 1500 Campbells, Macleods, and Macdonalds,
went to inform them where they might find the object of their
search.   Fortunately, they did not believe his tale, and only
treated him with ridicule.   It may here be remarked, that
upwards of a hundred people were aware of Charles being
lodged in Glencoridale, and not one, besides this boy, was ever
known to give the slightest hint on the subject to parties
unfriendly to him.

During his residence in Glencoridale, Lady Margaret Macdonald, wife of Sir Alexander Macdonald of Sleat, sent the
newspapers of the day on various occasions to the Prince, in
whose behalf she felt deeply, notwithstanding that her husband
had remained loyal to the government.   The medium employed
by Lady Margaret for this purpose was Hugh Macdonald of
Balshair, in North Uist, an honest gentleman, well affected to
the Prince's cause, though he had not been in his army.   The
time at length arrived when the military authorities became
aware that Charles was in the Long Island, and a resolution
was taken to land several large bodies of militia and regulars in
that range, in the hope of capturing him.   When Lady Margaret
learned this resolution, she sent intelligence of it to Balshair,
with a request that he would seek out the royal fugitive, and,
communicating it to him, concert measures with other friends
for his safety.   Balshair accordingly proceeded to Glencoridale,
after making an appointment with Boisdale to meet him at the
same place, but to go to it by a different route, in order that
their going might attract less attention.   We have a curious
account of the visit from Balshair himself :

' Being a misty day, I came near them before they discovered
me, which surprised them.   One of them, namely, Lieutenant-

colonel O'Sullivan, on my approach, bespoke the Young Gentleman [the Prince] in French : accordingly, he ran into the house. One Captain Allan Macdonald, in their company, who knew me, advised them not to be concerned, as they were in no danger from me. O'Sullivan introduces me to the hut. He [the Prince] saluted me very kindly, and told me he was heartily glad to see the face of an honest man in such a remote corner. His dress was then a tartan short-coat and vest of the same, got from Lady Clanranald; his nightcap all patched with soot-drops; his shirt, hands, and face, patched with the same; a short kilt, tartan hose, and Highland brogues; his upper coat being English cloth. He called a dram, being the first article of a Highland entertainment; which being over, he called for meat. There was about a half-stone of butter laid on a timber plate, and near a leg of beef laid on a chest before us, all patched with soot-drops, notwithstanding its being washed *toties quoties*. As we had done, who entered the hut but Boisdale, who seemed to be a very welcome guest to the Young Gentleman, as they had been together above once before. Boisdale then told him there was a party come to Barra in suit of him. He asked what they were. Boisdale said they were Macdonalds and Macleods. He then said he was not the least concerned, as they were Highlanders, and more especially such. I spoke to Boisdale about leaving Glencoridale, as our stay there would be of dangerous consequence, and of no advantage to him. The Young Gentleman told us, as it was but seldom he met with friends he could enjoy himself with, he would not on any account part with us that night. Boisdale says to me, we could not, in good manners, part with him that night. I replied, if he would risk staying himself—all this in Highlands [Gaelic]—that I would for my part. The Young Gentleman advises Edward Burke to fill the bowl; but before we'd begin with our bowl, Boisdale insisted on his being shaved first, and then putting on a clean shirt, which he was importuned to do; and Burke shaved him. Then we began with our bowl, frank and free. As we were turning merry, we were turning more free. At last

I starts the question if his highness would take it amiss if I should tell him the greatest objections against him in Great Britain. He said not. I told that popery and arbitrary government were the two chiefest. He said it was only bad constructions his enemies put on 't. " Do you know, Mr Macdonald," he says, " what religion are all the princes in Europe of?" I told him I imagined they were of the same established religion of the nation they lived in. He told me then they had little or no religion at all. Boisdale then told him that his predecessor, Donald Clanranald, had fought seven set battles for his; yet, after the Restoration, he was not owned by King Charles at court. The Prince said: " Boisdale, don't be rubbing up old sores, for if I came home, the case would be otherwise with me." I then says to him that, notwithstanding of what freedom we enjoyed there with him, we could have no access to him if he was settled at London; and [he] told us then, if he had never so much ado, he 'd be one night merry with his Highland friends. We continued this drinking for *three days and three nights*. He still had the better of us, and even of Boisdale himself, notwithstanding his being as able a bowlsman, I daresay, as any in Scotland.'[1]

Charles, though he at first spoke lightly of the approaching militia, soon became aware that his position in South Uist was one of considerable danger. It became necessary for him to shift his quarters; yet he and his friends could scarcely tell in what direction he ought to fly. They went, however, into the barge (June 14), and proceeded to Wiay island, between South Uist and Benbecula, where they remained four nights. On the 18th, the Prince, O'Neal, and Burke went to Rossinish, leaving O'Sullivan and Macleod in Wiay. Charles passed two nights at Rossinish; when, being informed that some militia were approaching Benbecula, he thought it would be best to return to Coridale. How to do so, was the question; for the militia-boats were already hovering between Wiay, where his boat was, and his present position.   However, Macleod and O'Sullivan, setting out in the night, came in the boat to Rossinish, and took him off.   The entire party was at sea in the barge on their way back to Coridale, when they saw two men-of-war, one of which proved to contain the notorious Captain Caroline Scott, on his way with a party to direct and stimulate the search of the militia, and with orders to explore the Long Island from end to end rather than not seize the Wanderer.   The fugitive party put into a place called Aikersideallich, near Uishnish, where they spent the night, the Prince sleeping in the cleft of a rock, with his bonnet drawn over his eyes.   Afterwards they took boat again, and rowed to the south part of South Uist, designing to go into Loch Boisdale, where they hoped to have Mr Macdonald of Boisdale for their friend.   On the way, seeing some ships, they had to take refuge for the day in a creek, and it was not till night that they succeeded in reaching the place for which they were bound.   Coming on shore much exhausted, they took up their quarters in an old tower, where preparations were making for food and rest, when Donald Macleod espied two sail, which they knew to be English.   Charles, with three of the company, immediately fled to the mountains, while the rest took the boat farther into the loch.   The ships passed away to seaward, and they were then enabled to meet again.   For two nights more they stayed in the open fields, with the sails of the boat covering them.   Their hopes of assistance from Boisdale were here cruelly frustrated by intelligence that that gentleman had been taken into custody, notwithstanding his apparent neutrality.   Nevertheless, Lady Boisdale sent them four bottles of brandy, and contributed every other comfort in her power. On the third night they went farther into the loch, and there rested for two nights more.   But here they were astounded by the information that the ferocious Scott had landed near them, and that they were nearly environed by their enemies.   Charles no sooner learned this, than, 'taking a couple of shirts under his arm,' he set off towards Benbecula, allowing none to follow him but O'Neal.   According to the recollection of Donald

Macleod, it was on the 24th of June that he thus parted, as it proved finally, with the three or four men who for nearly two months had followed him under every danger and every hardship. Of this parting the faithful boatman could not speak to the reporter of his memoirs without 'greeting sore.'[1] Before going away, the Prince caused the rowers to be paid a shilling a day for their services, and gave Donald Macleod a draught on Mr John Hay for sixty pistoles; which, however, Donald never found an opportunity of presenting.

It was at this time of peculiar difficulty that Charles was to be indebted for his preservation to the gallantry and generous self-devotion of a young female—the celebrated Flora Macdonald. This lady, daughter of the deceased Mr Macdonald of Milton, in South Uist, usually resided in the Isle of Skye with her mother, who was now married to Hugh Macdonald of Armadale, in that island. For the present, Flora lived in Uist, on a visit to her brother, and was on very intimate terms with the Clanranald family, whose mansion of Ormaclade was only three or four miles distant from her brother's house. The circumstances under which this lady was brought to aid the Chevalier have been obscurely related. According to her own narrative,[2] she had undertaken the task before Saturday the 21st of June, which, however, does not well consist with the accounts given by the other parties. O'Neal's relation, of which at this place Bishop Forbes approves as being consonant to what he had heard from Miss Macdonald's own mouth, gives the following particulars as occurring during the night on which the Prince left Loch Boisdale. 'At midnight we came to a hut [belonging to Macdonald of Milton], where, by good fortune, we met with Miss Flora Macdonald, whom I formerly knew. I quitted the Prince at some distance from the hut, and went with a design to inform myself if the Independent Companies were to pass that way next day, as we had been informed. The young lady answered me, not, and said that they were not to pass till the

day after. Then I told her I had brought a friend to see her ;
and she, with some emotion, asked me if it was the Prince.   I
answered her it was, and instantly brought her in.   We then
consulted on the imminent danger the Prince was in, and could
think of no more proper and safe expedient than to propose to
Miss Flora to convey him to the Isle of Skye, where her mother
lived.   This seemed the more feasible, as the young lady's
[step]father, being captain of an Independent Company, would
accord her a pass for herself and a servant, to go to visit her
mother.   The Prince assented, and immediately proposed it to
the young lady ; to which she answered with the greatest respect
and loyalty, but declined it, saying Sir Alexander Macdonald
was too much her friend [for her] to be the instrument of his
ruin.   I endeavoured to obviate this, by assuring her Sir
Alexander was not in the country, and that she could, with the
greatest facility, convey the Prince to her mother's, as she lived
close by the water-side.   I then demonstrated to her the honour
and immortality that would redound to her by such a glorious
action ; and she at length acquiesced, after the Prince had told
her the sense he would always retain of so conspicuous a service.
She promised to acquaint us next day, when things were ripe
for execution, and we parted for the mountains of Coridale.'
It seems probable that one fact only of any importance is
omitted here—namely, that Miss Macdonald had been brought
to the hut by some previous concert, and expected there to meet
with the Prince.   It also appears that the hut where Charles
and Miss Macdonald met was in Benbecula, to which the Prince
had gone after leaving Loch Boisdale.

Miss Macdonald now set out for Clanranald's house, in order
to prepare for her expedition.   In crossing the sea-ford between
Benbecula and South Uist, she and her servant, having no
passports, were made prisoners by a party of militia.   Desiring
to see the officer in command, she was told he would not be
there till next morning.   She then asked his name, and upon
their mentioning Mr Macdonald of Armadale (her stepfather),
she chose rather to stay all night in their guard-house than

answer any more questions. Next day (Sunday the 22d) Mr Macdonald arrived, and was greatly surprised to find his step-daughter in custody; but being, as there is good reason to believe, well disposed to the unfortunate Prince, he readily entered into Miss Flora's views, and not only liberated her, but furnished her with a passport for herself, her servant, and a female named Betty Burke—under which character Prince Charles was to be concealed—as also a letter to her mother, recommending this Betty Burke as an Irish girl who could spin well, and would therefore suit the lady exactly, as he knew she was at present in want of such an assistant in her domestic duties.

Thus furnished, Flora and Lady Clanranald, with some attendants, came, on the 27th, to the royal wanderer, with the disguise necessary for the character which he was to assume. On entering the hut, they found his royal highness engaged in roasting the heart and liver of a sheep upon a wooden spit; a sight at which some of the party could not help shedding tears. Charles, always the least concerned at his distressing circumstances, though never forgetting the hopes inspired by his birth, jocularly observed that it would be well perhaps for all kings if they had to come through such a fiery ordeal as he was now enduring. They soon after sat down to dinner, Miss Macdonald on his right hand, and Lady Clanranald on his left. A small shallop had been previously made ready, and was now floating near the shore.

While thus sitting, the party was informed by a messenger that General Campbell, with a great number of soldiers, had arrived at Benbecula; and soon after another messenger came with the intelligence that Captain Ferguson, with an advanced party, was come to Ormaclade. Lady Clanranald judged it proper to go home to amuse them. Ferguson examined her very strictly; but she readily excused herself by the pretext that she had been visiting a sick child. She was afterwards taken into custody, along with her husband, and both paid for their kindness to the Prince by a long confinement in London.

The Prince was now obliged to part with his last remaining companion, O'Neal. The poor fellow made an earnest request to be allowed to accompany him on his further wanderings, but Miss Macdonald could not be prevailed upon to agree to the proposal. In the forenoon (Saturday, June 28), it being resolved to proceed to sea, Miss Macdonald desired Charles to dress himself in the disguise, which consisted of ' a flowered linen gown, a light-coloured quilted petticoat, a white apron, and a mantle of dun camlet made after the Irish fashion with a hood;' and the party soon after set out for the beach. On this occasion Miss Macdonald was attended by one Neil Macdonald, commonly called Neil Mackechan, a sort of preceptor in the Clanranald family, and who may have some interest in the eyes of the readers of modern European history, as having become the father of Marshal Macdonald, Duke of Tarentum. They arrived at the beach very wet and very much fatigued, and made a fire upon a rock, to keep themselves warm till night. They were soon greatly alarmed by seeing four wherries full of armed men apparently making towards the shore, which made them extinguish their fire and conceal themselves. The wherries, however, sailed by to the southward without stopping, though within a gunshot of the place where our little party were lying concealed amongst the heath.

About eight o'clock in the evening, the party got safely away from Benbecula, and directed their course to the Isle of Skye. It may here be remarked that generally throughout the extraordinary wanderings of the Prince, after he himself had made the most surprising escapes from his enemies, most of those who aided him fell almost immediately after into the hands of those who had been in search of him. Two or three days after he left the Long Island, a French cutter, containing 120 men, arrived at South Uist for the purpose of carrying him off. O'Sullivan, who was much reduced by his late style of living, immediately went on board. O'Neal, anxious to serve the Prince, made an appointment to be taken up by the vessel at Loch Seaforth, near the Isle of Raasay, and set out in pursuit of the Prince, that he might bring him to that place, and so get him carried away to France. The plan misgave; the vessel sailed for its own country, carrying O'Sullivan into safety; and O'Neal, after some wanderings in Skye and elsewhere, was apprehended in Benbecula, and sent prisoner to London. The journal of this person shews a somewhat confused intellect, but he certainly possessed a generous heart. Donald Macleod wandered about for some time, enduring great hardships, which must have been severe on a man who had seen sixty-seven years: he was at length taken (July 5) in Skye, and also sent to London as a prisoner. Edward Burke was more fortunate. He obtained concealment in a lonely part of the Isle of Harris till after the Act of Indemnity passed in 1747, when, being safe, he returned to Edinburgh, purchased (probably by Jacobite contributions) a sedan-chair, and contentedly spent the remainder of his days in his original occupation.

CHAPTER XXVII.

CHARLES'S WANDERINGS—SKYE.

'Far over yon hills of the heather so green,
    And down by the Corrie that sings to the sea,
The lovely young Flora sat sighing her lane,
    The dew on her plaid, and the tear in her e'e.
She looked at a boat with the breezes that swung
    Away on the wave like a bird of the main;
And aye as it lessened, she sighed and she sung:
    "Fareweel to the lad I shall ne'er see again!
Fareweel to my hero, the gallant and young;
    Fareweel to the lad I shall ne'er see again!"'

Jacobite Song.

THE weather continued fair till the boat containing the Prince had got several leagues from shore, when it became somewhat stormy. Exposed in such a vessel to the cold night-air, at the

mercy of a raging sea, and at the same time haunted by the
fear of man's more deadly hostility, the sensations of the
little party cannot be supposed to have been very agreeable.
Charles could not help perceiving the uneasiness of his
attendants, and anxious to compensate, by all the means in
his power, for the pain which he occasioned to them, he
endeavoured to sustain their spirits by singing and talking.
He sang the lively old song entitled *The Restoration;* and
told a few playful stories, which yielded them some amusement.

When day dawned, they found themselves out of sight of
land, without any means of determining in what part of the
Hebrides they were. They sailed, however, but a little way
farther, when they perceived the lofty mountains and dark bold
headlands of Skye. Making with all speed towards that coast,
they soon approached Waternish, one of the western points of
the island. They had no sooner drawn near to the shore than
they perceived a body of militia stationed at the place. These
men had a boat, but no oars. The men in Miss Macdonald's
boat no sooner perceived them, than they began to pull heartily
in the contrary direction. The soldiers called upon them to
land, upon peril of being shot at; but it was resolved to escape
at all risks, and they exerted their utmost energies in pulling off
their little vessel. The soldiers then put their threat in execution by firing, but fortunately without hitting the boat or any
of its crew. Charles called upon the boatmen 'not to mind
the villains;' and they assured him that, if they cared at all, it
was only for him; to which he replied, with undaunted lightness
of demeanour: 'Oh, no fear of me!' He then entreated Miss
Macdonald to lie down at the bottom of the boat, in order to
avoid the bullets, as nothing, he said, could give him at that
moment greater pain than if any accident were to befall her.
She refused, however, to do as he desired, unless he also took
the same measure for his safety, which, she told him, was of
much more importance than hers. It was not till after some
altercation that they agreed to ensconce themselves together in

the bottom of the boat. The rowers soon pulled them out of all further danger.

When once more fairly out to sea, and in some measure recovered from this alarm, Miss Macdonald, overcome with the watchfulness and anxiety of the night, fell asleep upon the bottom of the boat. Charles had previously rendered the kindest attentions to his amiable preserver, refusing to partake of a small quantity of wine which Lady Clanranald had brought to him before embarking, upon the plea that it should be reserved for her, both on account of her sex and the extraordinary hardships she was undergoing. He now sat down beside her, and watched with tender and anxious regard, lest the boatmen should happen to disturb her in the course of their awkward movements.

In the eagerness of Duke William's emissaries to take Charles upon the Long Island, where they had certain information he was, Skye, on which the Prince was now about to land, was left comparatively unwatched. The island was, however, chiefly possessed by two clans—the Sleat Macdonalds and Macleods—whose superiors had proved renegade to the Stuart cause, and even raised men on the opposite side. Macleod went so far in his hostility as to exert himself personally, and with real eagerness, to effect the capture of the Prince. Parties of their militia were posted throughout the island, one of which had nearly taken the boat with its important charge when it was off Waternish. At the same time the people of the island did not in general sympathise in the views of their chiefs, and there were some gentlemen of both clans who were well affected to the Prince, and had even been in arms on his behalf.

Proceeding on their voyage a few miles to the northward, the little party in the boat put into a creek, or cleft, to rest and refresh the fatigued rowers; but the alarm which their appearance occasioned in a neighbouring village quickly obliged them to put off again. At length they landed safely at a place within the parish of Kilmuir, about twelve miles from Waternish, and very near Sir Alexander Macdonald's seat of Mugstat.

Sir Alexander was at this time at Fort Augustus, in attendance on the Duke of Cumberland; but his spouse, Lady Margaret Macdonald—one of the beautiful daughters of Alexander and Susanna, Earl and Countess of Eglintoune, a lady in the bloom of life, of elegant manners, and one who was accustomed to figure in the fashionable scenes of the metropolis—now resided at Mugstat. Well affected from education to the house of Stuart, and possessed of humane feelings, she had pitied the condition of the Prince in the Long Island, of which she was made aware, and had sent him, as has been already stated, the newspapers of the day, which he had regarded as a great obligation. Mr Macdonald of Balshair, who served as a medium for this intercourse, had recently transmitted a letter of thanks, written by the Prince to Lady Margaret, enclosed in one to his brother Donald Roy Macdonald, one of the Prince's captains, who was now residing, for the cure of a wound in his foot (got at Culloden), in the house of Mr John Maclean, surgeon in Trotternish. Donald Roy, a well-bred Highland gentleman,[1] delivered the Prince's letter to Lady Margaret with his own hand, and immediately after, as he had been ordered, desired her ladyship to burn it, for the sake of her own safety, as well as that of the Prince. But, kissing it, she said: ' No, I will not burn it—I will preserve it for the sake of him who sent it to me. Although King George's forces should come to the house, I hope I shall find a way to secure the letter.'[2] She hid it in a closet. The purport of Balshair's letter to Donald Roy was, that the Prince (the escape with Flora Macdonald not being then projected) designed to leave the Long Island and take refuge in a small solitary isle named Fladdachuan, six miles from Trotternish, and inhabited by only one family, tenants under Sir Alexander Macdonald. Donald was desired to keep

[1] He was one of the only two gentlemen of Sir Alexander Macdonald's following who went out. Mr Forbes preserves several Latin verses by him, bearing out the representation made by General Stewart, in his work on the Highland Regiments, respecting the learned education given in those days to the gentlemen of the Western Islands.

[2] When some troops afterwards came to the house in quest of the Prince, she deemed it prudent to destroy this document which she did with great regret.

a look-out, and be ready to assist the Prince with necessaries in that island. At the interview which Donald had with Lady Margaret, she entered heartily into the scheme, and gave him six shirts, and twenty broad pieces of gold, for the Prince's use. She offered blankets, which Donald refused, as he could not get them carried without the risk of exciting suspicion. During the interval between the receipt of these letters and the arrival of the Prince in Skye, Donald had gone to Fladdachuan to look out for the expected stranger, but of course in vain. Lady Margaret had also more recently received, by a Mrs Macdonald of Kirkibost in North Uist, a letter informing her of the altered scheme, and of the concern which Miss Flora was taking in the matter. She was therefore in some measure prepared for the arrival of the Prince in Skye, but not for his coming so near her residence.

When the boat containing the Wanderer had landed, Miss Macdonald, attended by Neil Mackechan, proceeded to the house, leaving Charles, in his female dress, sitting on her trunk upon the beach.[1] On arriving at the house, she desired a servant to inform Lady Margaret that she had called on her way home from the Long Island.[2] She was immediately introduced to the family apartment, where she found, besides Mrs Macdonald of Kirkibost, a Lieutenant Macleod,[3] the commander of a band of militia stationed near by, three or four of whom were also in the house. There was also present Mr Alexander Macdonald of Kingsburgh, a gentleman of the neighbourhood, who acted as chamberlain or factor to Sir Alexander, and who was, she knew, a sound Jacobite. Miss Macdonald entered easily into conversation with the officer, who asked her a number of questions—as, where she had come from, where she was going, and so forth—all of which she answered without manifesting the least trace of that confusion

---

[1] Narrative (MS.) in my possession, by Colonel Macalister of Barr and Cour, in Argyleshire.

[2] Flora Macdonald's Narrative, *Jacobite Memoirs.*

[3] Son of Donald Macleod of Balmeanagh.

which might have been expected from a young lady under such circumstances. The same man had been in the custom of examining every boat which landed from the Long Island : that, for instance, in which Mrs Macdonald of Kirkibost arrived had been so examined ; and I can only account for his allowing that of Miss Flora to pass, by the circumstance of his meeting her under the imposing courtesies of the drawing-room of a lady of rank. Miss Macdonald, with the same self-possession, dined in Lieutenant Macleod's company. Seizing a proper opportunity, she apprised Kingsburgh of the circumstances of the Prince, and he immediately proceeded to another room, and sent for Lady Margaret, that he might break the intelligence to her in private. She was greatly alarmed, insomuch as to scream, and exclaim aloud that she and her family were undone; but Kingsburgh, who was a cool, sensible man, soon calmed her fears in some degree, assuring her that, if necessary, he would take the Prince to his own house. He was now, he said, an old man, and it made little difference to him whether he should immediately die with a halter about his neck, or await a natural death, which could not be far distant.[1] It was then agreed to send an express to Donald Roy, requesting his immediate attendance on business of the utmost importance. It does not appear to have been thought that Donald was in any danger from Lieutenant Macleod; and indeed the reverse of this appears, for he tells us himself[2] that he at this time used to meet the militiamen and jest with them on his late career as a rebel officer. For the protection, however, of Lady Margaret, the letter was directed by Mrs Macdonald of Kirkibost, and put into the messenger's hands, as from her.

When Donald soon after approached the house, he saw Lady Margaret and Kingsburgh walking together in the garden, as in deep consultation. Her ladyship's first address to him was : ' Oh, Donald, we are ruined for ever ! '[3] The three now held an anxious council as to the best means of disposing of the

[1] Colonel Macalister's Narrative.
[2] Narrative printed in *Jacobite Memoirs.*   [3] Donald Roy's Narrative.

W

Prince, whose resting-place for the meantime was at the bottom
of the garden in which they were walking. It was suggested
that he might proceed in the boat to the island of Raasay;
but this was seen to be dangerous, as he would require to pass
a military party in sailing along the coast in that direction. It
was at last determined that he should be sent overland to
Portree, the principal port in Skye, and thence transported to
Raasay. What made this island seem so fitting a refuge was,
that the proprietor, a principal man of the clan Macleod, had
been in the Prince's army with his 'following,' his eldest son
alone remaining loyal, to save the estate in case of the worst.
It was arranged that Donald Roy should be at Portree on the
arrival of the Prince, after having in the meantime sought out
the young laird of Raasay, in order to consult about putting his
royal highness under his father's charge. It was further contemplated that Raasay and Donald Roy might conduct the
Prince to Seaforth's country on the mainland, and place him
amongst the Mackenzies; but afterwards it was found that
Charles objected to this part of the scheme, thinking that to go
from place to place was safer than to stay in any one district.

Donald Roy now set out in quest of young Raasay, who, he
understood, was at Tottrome near Portree. Soon after, while
Miss Flora still carried on conversation in the dining-room,
Kingsburgh took his leave, as to go home; provided himself
with a bottle of wine, a tumbler, and some biscuits; and went
to introduce himself to the fugitive Prince. Charles was not
now so near Mugstat House as at first. Mackechan had in the
meantime gone to inform him that Kingsburgh was to come
and take charge of him, and also to conduct him to a more
secluded spot at a greater distance. Kingsburgh had some
difficulty at first in finding the place : at length, seeing a few
sheep run off in alarm, and cross a dry-stone enclosure, and
calculating that they must have been startled by a human being,
he went to the spot, and there found Charles in his female
disguise. The Prince, on seeing him, rose up and came forward
threateningly, with a large knotted stick in his hand. 'Are

you Mr Macdonald of Kingsburgh?' he demanded; which being answered in the affirmative, he instantly changed his demeanour, and said: 'Then let us be going.' Kingsburgh requested him to delay a little while, in order to take some refreshment; and spreading out his wine, tumbler, and biscuits upon the top of a rock, enabled the famished Prince to make a hearty meal, in the course of which he drank familiarly to his future conductor. They then proceeded on their journey, the first object of which was Kingsburgh House, situated at some miles' distance on the north shore of Loch Snizort. As they walked along, Mr Macdonald remarked, in high spirits, how fortunate it was that he had been at Mugstat that day. He had come, he said, without any reason of either business or duty which he could remember. 'I 'll tell you the cause,' said Charles; 'Providence sent you there to take care of me.' He evinced on other occasions an inclination to suppose himself under the protection of a special Providence; and he certainly had as much cause for forming such a notion as the most of those who have fallen into the same belief.

Some time after, when it might have been supposed that Kingsburgh and the Prince would be a little way advanced on their journey, Flora Macdonald rose from table to take her departure. Lady Margaret affected great concern at her short stay, and entreated that she would prolong it at least till next day; reminding her that, when last at Mugstat, she had promised a much longer visit. Flora, on the other hand, pleaded the necessity of getting immediately home to attend her mother, who was unwell, and entirely alone in these troublesome times. After a proper reciprocation of entreaties and refusals, Lady Margaret, with great apparent reluctance, permitted her young friend to depart.

Miss Macdonald and Mackechan were accompanied in their journey by Mrs Macdonald of Kirkibost, and by that lady's male and female servants, all the five riding on horseback. They soon came up with Kingsburgh and the Prince, who had walked thus far on the public road, but were soon after to turn off upon an unfrequented path across the wild country. Flora, anxious that her fellow-traveller's servants, who were uninitiated in the secret, should not see the route which Kingsburgh and the Prince were about to take, called upon the party to ride faster; and they passed the two pedestrians at a trot. Mrs Macdonald's girl, however, could not help observing the extraordinary appearance of the female with whom Kingsburgh was walking, and exclaimed that she 'had never seen such a tall, impudent-looking woman in her life! See!' she continued, addressing Flora, 'what long strides the jade takes! I daresay she's an Irishwoman, or else a man in woman's clothes.' Flora confirmed her in the former supposition, and soon after parted with her fellow-travellers, in order to rejoin Kingsburgh and the Prince.

These individuals, in walking along the road, were at first a good deal annoyed by the number of country-people whom they met returning from church, and who all expressed wonder at the uncommon height and awkwardness of the apparent female. The opportunity of talking to their landlord's factotum being too precious to be despised, these people fastened themselves on Kingsburgh, who, under the particular circumstances, felt a good deal annoyed by them, but at last bethought himself of saying: 'Oh, sirs! cannot you let alone talking of your worldly affairs on Sabbath, and have patience till another day?' They took the pious hint, and moved off.[1] In crossing a stream which traversed the road, Charles held up his petticoats indelicately high, to save them from being wet. Kingsburgh pointed out that, by doing so, he must excite strange suspicions among those who should happen to see him; and his royal highness promised to take better care on the next occasion. Accordingly, in crossing another stream, he permitted his skirts to hang down and float upon the water. Kingsburgh again represented that this mode was as likely as the other to attract observation; and the Prince could not help laughing at the difficulty of

---

[1] 'Account of the P——'s Escape,' *Scots Magazine*, 1749.

adjusting this trifling and yet important matter. His conductor further observed that, instead of returning the obeisance which the country-people made to them in passing by a courtesy, his royal highness made a bow; and also that, in some other gestures and attitudes of person, he completely forgot the woman, and resumed the man. 'Your enemies,' remarked Kingsburgh, 'call you a pretender; but if you be, I can tell you you are the worst at your trade I ever saw.' 'Why,' replied Charles, laughing, 'I believe my enemies do me as much injustice in this as in some other and more important particulars. I have all my life despised assumed characters, and am perhaps the worst dissimulator in the world.' The whole party—Charles, Kingsburgh, and Miss Macdonald—arrived in safety at Kingsburgh House about eleven at night.

The house of Kingsburgh was not at this time in the best possible case for entertaining guests of distinction; and, to add to the distress of the occasion, all the inmates had long been gone to bed. The old gentleman, however, lost no time in putting matters in proper trim for affording a supper to the party. He introduced Charles into the hall, and sent a servant up-stairs to rouse his lady. Lady Kingsburgh, on being informed of her husband's arrival, with guests, did not choose to rise, but contented herself with sending down an apology for her non-appearance, and a request that they would help themselves to whatever was in the house. She had scarcely despatched the servant, when her daughter, a girl of seven years, came running up to her bedside, and informed her, with many expressions of childish surprise, that her father had brought home the most 'odd, muckle, ill-shaken-up wife she had ever seen—and brought her into the hall too!' Kingsburgh himself immediately came up, and desired her to lose no time in rising, as her presence was absolutely necessary for the entertainment of his fellow-travellers. She was now truly roused, and even alarmed; the mysterious sententiousness of her husband suggesting to her that he had taken under his protection some of the proscribed fugitives who were then known to be skulking in the country.

As she was putting on her clothes, she sent her daughter down-stairs for her keys, which she remembered to have left in the hall. The girl, however, came back immediately, declaring, with marks of the greatest alarm, that she could not go into the hall for fear of the tall woman, who was walking backwards and forwards through it in a manner, she said, perfectly frightful. Lady Kingsburgh then went down herself, but could not help hesitating, when she came to the door, at sight of this mysterious stranger. Kingsburgh coming up, she desired him to go in for the keys; but he bade her go in herself; and, after some further demur, in at last she went.

On her entering, Charles rose up from a seat which he had taken at the end of the hall, and advanced to salute her. Her apprehensions were now confirmed beyond a doubt; for, in performing the ceremony of the salute, she felt the roughness of a male cheek, and such were her feelings at the discovery, that she almost fainted away. Not a word passed between her and the unfortunate stranger. When she got out of the hall, she eagerly made up to Kingsburgh, and disclosed to him all her suspicions. She did not upbraid her husband for having been so imprudent, but, on the contrary, asked if he thought the stranger would know anything regarding the Prince. Kingsburgh then took his wife's hands into his own, and said seriously: 'My dear, this is the Prince himself.'

She could not restrain her alarm when he pronounced these emphatic words, but exclaimed: 'The Prince! then we'll be all hanged!'

Kingsburgh replied: 'We can die but once—could we ever die in a better cause? We are only doing an act of humanity, which anybody might do. Go,' he added, 'and make haste with supper. Bring us eggs, butter, cheese, and whatever else you can quickly make ready.'

'Eggs, butter, and cheese!' repeated Mrs Macdonald, alarmed upon a new but scarcely less interesting score—the honour of her housewifeship; 'what a supper is that for a prince—he'll never look at it!'

'Ah, my good wife,' replied Kingsburgh, 'you little know how this poor Prince has fared of late! Our supper will be a treat to him. Besides, to make a formal supper would cause the servants to suspect something. Make haste, and come to supper yourself.'

Lady Kingsburgh was almost as much alarmed at her husband's last expression as she had been about her provisions. '*Me* come to supper!' she exclaimed; 'I know not how to behave before majesty!'

'But you must come,' Kingsburgh replied; 'the Prince would not eat a bit without you; and you'll find it no difficult matter to behave before him—he is so easy and obliging in conversation.'

Supper being accordingly soon after prepared, and Miss Flora Macdonald introduced, Charles, who had always paid the most respectful attentions to his preserver, placed her upon his right hand, and Lady Kingsburgh on his left. He ate very heartily, and afterwards drank a bumper of brandy to the health and prosperity of his landlord. When his repast was finished, and the ladies had retired, he took out a little black stunted tobacco-pipe which he carried with him, and which, among his companions, went by the name of '*the cutty*,' and proceeded to take a smoke, informing Kingsburgh that he had been obliged to have recourse to that exercise during his wanderings, on account of a toothache which occasionally afflicted him. Kingsburgh then produced a small china punch-bowl, and, in Scottish fashion, made up, with usquebaugh, hot water, and sugar, the celebrated composition called toddy, dealing it out to Charles and himself in glasses. The Prince was pleased to express himself greatly delighted with this beverage, and soon, with Kingsburgh's assistance, emptied the little bowl, after which it was again filled. The two friends, unequal in rank, but united in common feelings, talked over their glasses in a style so familiar, so kindly, and so much to the satisfaction of each other, that they did not observe the lapse of time, and it was an hour not the earliest in the morning ere either thought of retiring. It might have been expected that Charles, from fatigue, and from a wish to enjoy once more the comforts of a good bed, to which he had been so long a stranger, would have been the first to propose this measure. On the contrary, Kingsburgh had to perform the disagreeable duty of breaking up the company. After they had emptied the bowl several times, and when he himself had become anxious for repose, he thought it necessary to hint to the Prince that, as he would require to be up and away as soon as possible on the morrow, he had better now go to bed, in order that he might enjoy a proper term of sleep. To his surprise, Charles was by no means anxious for rest. On the contrary, he insisted upon 'another bowl,' that they might, as he said, finish their conversation. Kingsburgh violated his feelings as a host so far as to refuse this request, urging that it was absolutely necessary that his royal highness should retire, for the reason he had stated. Charles as eagerly pressed the necessity of more drink; and, after some good-humoured altercation, when Kingsburgh took away the bowl to put it by, his royal highness rose to detain it, and a struggle ensued, in which the little vessel broke into two pieces, Charles retaining one in his hands, and Kingsburgh holding the other.[1] The strife was thus brought to an end, and the Prince no longer objected to go to bed.

After having retired from the supper-table, Lady Kingsburgh desired Miss Flora to relate the adventures in which she had been concerned with his royal highness. At the termination of the recital, the hostess inquired what had been done with the boatmen who brought them to Skye. Miss Macdonald said they had been sent back to South Uist. Lady Kingsburgh observed that they ought not to have been permitted to return immediately, lest, falling into the hands of the Prince's enemies in that island, they might divulge the secret of his route. Her conjecture, which turned out to have been correct, though

---

[1] This bowl, and the tumbler which Kingsburgh took from Mugstat, that the Prince might drink his wine from it, were, in 1827, in the possession of Colonel Macalister of Barr and Cour.

happily without being attended with evil consequences to the Prince, determined Flora to change the Prince's clothes next day.

So much did Charles enjoy the novel pleasure of a good bed, that though he seldom, during his distresses, slept above four hours, he on this occasion slept about ten, not awaking till roused, at one o'clock next day, by his kind landlord. Kingsburgh inquiring, like a good host, how he had reposed, the Prince answered that he had never enjoyed a more agreeable or a longer sleep in his life. He had almost forgot, he said, what a good bed was. Kingsburgh begged leave to tell his guest that it was full time to think of another march. It would be proper, he continued, for him to go away in the same dress which he wore when he entered the house, in order to avoid raising suspicions among the servants; but as the rumour of his disguise might have taken air, it would be advisable to assume another garb at the earliest opportunity. The only reformation he thought it would be allowable to make in his habiliments at present was a change of shoes, those which the Prince had brought with him being worn so much that his toes protruded through them. Kingsburgh happened to have a pair in the house which he had never worn, and those he provided for the accommodation of his friend. When Charles had shifted the old for the new, Kingsburgh took up the former, tied them together, and hung them up in a corner of his house, observing that they might yet stand him in good stead. Charles asked him what he meant by that, and the old man replied: 'Why, when you are fairly settled at St James's, I shall introduce myself by shaking these shoes at you, to put you in mind of your night's entertainment and protection under my roof.' Charles smiled at the conceit of the good old gentleman, and bade him be as good as his word. Kingsburgh accordingly kept these strange relics, or the greater portion of them, as long as he lived. After his death, and when all prospect of Charles's restoration to St James's was gone, his family permitted the remainder to be cut to pieces, and dispersed among their friends. It is the recollection of one of his descendants that Jacobite ladies often took away the pieces they got in their bosoms.[1]

When Charles was to dress, Mrs Macdonald caused her daughter to act as his handmaid, for, as she afterwards told Bishop Forbes, 'the deil a preen he could put in.' While Miss Macdonald[2] was dressing him, he was like to fall over with laughing. After the pinners, gown, hood, and mantle were put on, he said: 'Oh, Miss, you have forgot my apron. Where is my apron? Get me my apron here, for it is a principal part of my dress.' Kingsburgh and his lady informed their friends afterwards that at this time he behaved not like one that was in danger, but as mirthfully as if he had been putting on women's clothes merely for a frolic. Lady Kingsburgh having asked a lock of his hair, to preserve as a keepsake, he laid down his head upon Flora's lap, and told her to cut off as much as she chose. Flora severed a lock, the half of which she gave to Lady Kingsburgh, and the other half retained for herself.

In the evening, after having taken another hearty meal, Charles addressed himself to his departure. He had observed that Mrs Macdonald, like most ladies of birth and fashion of her time, took snuff; and on approaching her to take his leave, he asked to have 'a pinch from her mull.' The good lady took that opportunity of presenting the box to his royal highness as 'a keepsake.' He accepted it with many thanks, rendering at the same time his warmest acknowledgments of the kindness with which he had been treated under her roof. After he had taken a tender farewell, she went up-stairs to his bedroom, and folded the sheets in which he had lain, declaring that they

---

[1] Within the second board of the fifth volume of Bishop Forbes's collection of papers entitled *The Lyon in Mourning*, now in my possession, are two small pieces of leather, carefully sealed down, with the following note: 'The above are pieces of one of the lugs of those identical brogues which the Prince wore, when disguised in the female dress, under the name of Betty Burke, as handmaid to Miss Flora Macdonald.' It appears, from the contents of the volume, that Mr Forbes had written to Kingsburgh requesting these fragments, and received them, along with a letter from that gentleman, dated July 15, 1748.

[2] This lady afterwards became Mrs Macalister, and was, I presume, mother of Colonel Macalister, who, in 1827, obligingly wrote for me the manuscript which has been quoted.

should never again be washed or used till her death, when they should be employed as her winding-sheet. She was afterwards induced to divide this valuable memorial of her distinguished guest with the amiable Flora, who, it may be mentioned, many years afterwards carried her moiety of it to America. In the course of her strangely adventurous life, and though often reduced to situations of the greatest distress by the republican insurgents, she never parted with it till the day of her death, when her body was wrapped in its precious folds, and consigned with it to the grave.

Charles now set out from Kingsburgh, with the intention of walking to Portree, about fourteen miles distant, where he had the cheerful prospect of finding a boat ready to convey him to Raasay. He was attended by his faithful friends Flora and Kingsburgh, the last carrying under his arm a suit of male Highland attire for his royal highness's use. When they had got to a considerable distance from the house, Kingsburgh conducted the Prince into a wood, and assisted him in changing his clothes. The suit which he now put on consisted, as usual, of a short coat and waistcoat, a philibeg and short hose, a plaid, a wig, and a bonnet. Kingsburgh and the Prince then took a parting embrace, in doing which tears fell from the eyes of both, and a few drops of blood from the Prince's nose. The former being alarmed at sight of the blood, the Prince told him that it was usually so with him when he parted from dear friends. He then set out with Mackechan [1] on his journey, a little herd-boy

---

[1] At a meeting of Mr and Mrs Macdonald of Kingsburgh, and some other persons, in Lady Bruce's house, citadel of Leith, July 11, 1747, the conversation turned on a small work descriptive of the Prince's wanderings, entitled *Alexis, or the Young Adventurer; a Novel.* (London: T. Cooper, 1746.) In the report of the conversation which has been preserved by Bishop Forbes, one of the persons present, the following passage occurs with respect to that pamphlet : as relating to the father of a historical personage of no small note, it seems worthy of being preserved.

' It was represented to Kingsburgh that his lady, during his confinement, had been telling some folks that, upon conversing with him (her husband) about the pamphlet *Alexis,* he should have said that he knew nobody who could be the author of it but Neil Mackechan, so pointed and exact it was in giving the narrative. Kingsburgh, looking to his lady, said : " Goodwife, you may remember I said that I knew nobody who could be the author of that pamphlet but Neil Mackechan or myself."'

When it was suggested that Neil Mackechan (a low man) could not be thought capable acting as their guide, and Miss Flora proceeding to the same place by a different way.   Kingsburgh hid the cast-off garments of Betty Burke in a bush, where they lay for some time; but at length, from fear of the military, he carried them home, and burned the whole except the gown.   The preservation of the gown was owing to his daughter, who insisted upon keeping it as a relic of their Prince, and because it was a pretty print.   A Jacobite manufacturer of the name of Carmichael, at Leith, afterwards used it as a pattern, and sold an immense quantity of cloth, precisely similar in appearance, to the 'loyal' ladies of Scotland.[1]

When Donald Roy made application to young Raasay, he was mortified by the information that old Raasay had left his hiding-place upon the island, and gone to Knoidart, a part of Glengarry's estate upon the mainland.   The young gentleman, however, though he had been reserved from the insurrection for the purpose of saving the estate, was as well affected to the Chevalier as either his father or his younger brothers, who led out the clan, and instantly proposed to conduct the Wanderer to Raasay, where he could at least remain concealed till the old gentleman's advice might be obtained for farther procedure. Donald approved of the plan; but the difficulty was how to get

of drawing up anything of that sort, Kingsburgh and his lady informed the company that Mackechan had been educated in the Scots College in Paris, with the view of commencing clergyman; but that, after getting his education, he had dropped the design; that therefore he was capable enough, and that he had proved a great comfort to the Prince in his wanderings, by talking to him in the French language about matters of importance in their difficulties, when perhaps it was not so prudent or convenient that those who were present should know what they were conversing about.   They told likewise that they had never been so much afraid of any person's conduct as that of Mackechan; because he was a good-natured man, and very timorous in his temper.   But they frankly owned they had done him great injustice, by entertaining any suspicions about him, for that he had behaved to admiration, and had got abroad with the Prince, the great wish of his soul, for he could never think of parting with him at any time, but upon condition of meeting again, which Mackechan was so lucky as frequently to accomplish, even when at parting they could scarce condescend upon a time or place when and where to meet.

[1] Bishop Forbes has also preserved a fragment of the '*identical gown*,' which, he says, was sent to him by Mrs Macdonald of Kingsburgh.   Beneath it he has fastened a piece of the *apron-string*, which he says he got from Miss Flora Macdonald, November 5, 1747, 'when I saw the apron, and had it about me.'   The two fragments do not seem in the least to have suffered from time.

a boat. They could not trust a Portree crew, and all the Raasay boats had been destroyed or carried off by the military, except two belonging to Malcolm Macleod, a cousin of young Raasay, which he had somewhere concealed.

There was at that time in the same house with young Raasay a younger brother, named Murdoch Macleod, who had been wounded at the battle of Culloden, and was now slowly recovering. Murdoch, being informed of the business in hand, said he would once more risk his life for Prince Charles; and it having occurred that there was a little boat upon a fresh-water lake in the neighbourhood, he, with his brother and some women, brought it to the sea, by extraordinary exertion, across a Highland mile of land, one-half of which was bog, and the other a steep precipice. The gallant brothers, with the assistance of a little boy, rowed this to Raasay, where they hoped to find Malcolm Macleod, and get one of his good boats, with which they might return to Portree and receive the Wanderer; or, in case of not finding him, they were to make the small boat serve, though the danger was considerable.

Malcolm Macleod, who was soon to act a conspicuous part in the deliverance of the Prince, had been a captain in his service, and fought at the battle of Culloden. Being easily found by his cousins, he lost no time in producing one of his boats, which he succeeded in manning with two stout boatmen, named John Mackenzie and Donald Macfriar, who had also been in the Prince's army. Malcolm, being the oldest and most cautious man of the party, suggested that, as young Raasay was hitherto a clear man, he should not on the present occasion run any risk; but that he himself and Murdoch, who were already 'as black as they could be,' should alone conduct the expedition. Young Raasay answered, with an oath, that he would go, 'though it should cost him the estate and the head.' 'In God's name, then,' said Malcolm, 'let us proceed!' The two boatmen, however, now stopped short, and refused to move, till they should be informed of their destination. They were sworn to secrecy, and made acquainted with not only the extent of their voyage, but also its object; after which, they expressed the utmost eagerness to proceed.

The boat soon crossed the narrow sound which divides Raasay from Skye, and being landed about half a mile from the harbour of Portree, Malcolm and Macfriar were despatched to look for Prince Charles, while young Raasay and Murdoch remained on the shore.

Donald Roy and Malcolm Macleod now met at a little public-house, the only one in the village, and soon after Miss Flora joined them, and gave information of the approach of the Prince and his two attendants. Immediately thereafter, the boy who had attended Charles as his guide came to the door, and asking for Donald Roy, informed him that a gentleman wished to see him at a little distance. He went in the direction indicated, and found the Prince, who embraced him kindly, putting his head first over one shoulder and then over the other, and desiring him to be equally unceremonious, for, night though it was, there might still be sufficient light to enable any lurking bystander to observe their motions, and who could not, of course, fail to suspect the real state of the case if he saw one gentleman treating another with the etiquette due to a prince. It had been a rainy evening, and Charles was thoroughly wet. On Donald expressing his regret for this circumstance, the Prince said: 'I am more sorry that *our lady*'—for so he used to name Miss Macdonald—'should be exposed to such an evening.' They now went into the inn, Donald going first; but no ceremony seems to have passed on meeting Miss Macdonald and Malcolm Macleod. The Prince called for a dram in the first place, of which he seemed in much need, as the rain was streaming down from his plaid, and he had no trews or philibeg.[1] The company joined in urging him to shift and put on a dry shirt, Donald Roy offering him his philibeg. He at first refused, from delicacy towards Miss Macdonald; but he was at length prevailed on to disregard ceremony. When he had

[1] Such is Donald Roy's statement, though another narrator describes the Prince as getting a full Highland suit from Kingsburgh.

put on the fresh shirt, some food was brought in, and he fell to it as he was, his long walk having furnished him with a ravenous appetite. Donald Roy, notwithstanding the anxiety of the moment, fell a-laughing at the strange figure he now cut; when, seeing the Prince looking at him, he said: 'Sir, I believe that is the English fashion.'

'What fashion do you mean?'

'Why, they say the English, when they intend to eat very heartily, cast off their clothes.'

'They are right,' said Charles, 'lest anything should incommode their hands when they are at work.'

He now asked for a drink; but there being no fermented liquor in Skye except in gentlemen's houses, he was obliged to slake his thirst with water from a dirty-looking wooden and rough-edged vessel, which the landlord employed to bale his boat. Donald Roy took a draught from this unpleasant cup, and handed it to the Prince, with a whispered assurance that it was tolerably clean, and that prudence required him to drink from it without hesitation, lest he should raise suspicions among the people of the house. Charles then put it to his lips, and took a hearty draught, after which he put on his philibeg and other clothes.

Donald Roy urged him to make haste to leave the house, as, there being but one room for all comers, he ran a considerable risk of being detected. Though anxious to stay all night, on account of the rain, he now prepared to set out for the boat, but first made an endeavour to prevail on Donald to accompany him, for he said he had experienced so much fidelity and kindness from the Macdonalds, that he thought he should feel himself safe if he still had one of that clan with him. Donald excused himself, on account of his wound, which forbade his travelling except on horseback, and also because, by remaining in Skye, he might be of greater service to him than by accompanying him. It was agreed, however, that young Raasay should return in the boat on the ensuing Thursday, and, meeting Donald at a particular place which they appointed, carry him over to join the Prince in Raasay. Charles now called for some tobacco, that he might smoke a pipe before departing, and the landlord brought a quarter of a pound of a very coarse kind in the scales, for which Charles gave him sixpence. Donald Roy desired the man to bring the change. The Prince smiled at his exactness, and was for refusing the three-halfpence; but Donald insisted on his taking this little sum, as 'the bawbees,' he said, 'might in his present situation be useful to him.' Donald then shewed him a separate pocket in his sporran, or Highland purse, into which he slipped them.

The little party had drunk a whole bottle of whisky. In paying the reckoning, the Prince got change for a guinea. He then desired to have change for another guinea; but the landlord had only eleven shillings more. Charles was for taking this sum in lieu of his guinea, as likely to be more useful to him than the piece of gold; but Donald Roy prevented him, on the plea that such an appearance of indifference to money was calculated to raise suspicion of his quality. He now took farewell of Miss Flora Macdonald and Mackechan. Approaching the young lady, he said: 'I believe, madam, I owe you a crown of borrowed money.' She told him it was but half-a-crown; which he accordingly paid her, with thanks. He then saluted her, saying: 'For all that has happened, I hope, madam, we shall meet in St James's yet.' Before leaving the house, he tied a bottle of whisky to his belt at one side, and a bottle of brandy, with some shirts (which had been brought from Kingsburgh), and a cold fowl in a napkin, at the other. As the party were leaving the door, they observed the landlord looking after them: to deceive him, they took a different way from that intended, and approached the boat by a circuitous route. When Donald afterwards returned to the house to take some rest, this man, whose name was Charles Macnab, was very inquisitive about the stranger, who he was, and where he had parted with him. Donald said, with affected indifference, that he was only a brother rebel, a Sir John Macdonald, an Irishman, who had been skulking among his friends in Skye, but was now gone for the continent. Macnab said he had entertained a strong notion that the gentleman might happen to be the Prince in disguise, 'for he had something about him that looked very noble.'[1] Donald afterwards went to Kingsburgh, to tell the good people there of the Prince's safe departure, and next to Mugstat, to give the like information to Lady Margaret Macdonald. At the latter place, he met and spent a pleasant evening with Lieutenant Macleod, the gentleman whom Miss Flora had amused to such good purpose.[2]

[1] Donald Roy's Narrative.

[2] 'About six or eight days after the Prince left Skye, Captain Ferguson followed him in hot pursuit; and having extorted from the boatmen, at or in their return to South Uist, an exact description of the gown and dress the Prince had worn, he first went to Sir Alexander Macdonald's, where, after a strict search, hearing only of Miss Flora Macdonald, he thence proceeded in all haste to Kingsburgh, where he examined every person with the utmost exactness. He asked Kingsburgh where Miss Macdonald, and the person who was with her in woman's clothes, had lain? Kingsburgh answered, he knew where Miss Flora had lain; but as for servants, he never asked any questions about them. The captain then asked Lady Kingsburgh whether she had laid the young Pretender and Miss Flora in one bed? To which she answered: "Whom you mean by the *young Pretender* I do not pretend to guess; but I can assure you it is not the fashion in Skye to lay mistress and maid in one bed." Upon visiting the rooms wherein each had lain, the captain could not but remark that the room the supposed maid had possessed was better than that of the mistress.

'Kingsburgh was made a prisoner, and, by General Campbell's order, he went on parole, without any guard, to Fort Augustus, where he was plundered of everything, thrown into a dungeon, and loaded with irons. When Sir Everard Fawkener examined him, he put him in mind how noble an opportunity he had lost of making himself and his family for ever. To which Kingsburgh replied: "Had I gold and silver piled heaps upon heaps to the bulk of yon huge mountain, that mass could not afford me half the satisfaction I find in my own breast from doing what I have done." While Kingsburgh was prisoner at Fort Augustus, an officer of distinction came and asked him if he would know the young Pretender's head if he saw it? Kingsburgh said he would know the head very well if it were on the shoulders. "But what if the head be not on the shoulders—do you think you should know it in that case?" "In that case," answered Kingsburgh, "I will not pretend to know anything about it." So no head was brought him.

'Kingsburgh was removed hence to Edinburgh Castle, under a strong guard of Kingston's light horse. He was at first put into a room with some other gentlemen, and afterwards removed into one by himself, without being allowed to go over the threshold, or to see any person, except the officer upon guard, the sergeant, and the keeper; which last was appointed to attend him as a servant. And here he was kept till, by the act of grace, he was set at liberty on the 4th of July 1747; having thus, as an author observes, got a whole year's safe lodging for affording that of one night.'—*Scots Magazine*, 1749.

Alexander Macdonald, Esq. of Kingsburgh, died February 13, 1772, aged eighty-three.

In the diary of Sir James Mackintosh (see his Memoirs by his son) is an interesting anecdote of Kingsburgh, which one might wish to be true, if it is not. 'The excellent President Forbes represented to the Duke of Cumberland, that to execute so popular a man as Kingsburgh would excite a new rebellion. But he was so deeply involved in the escape of Charles, that his destruction seemed to be certain. At Fort Augustus, while he was a

When the Prince entered the boat, and the names of all the individuals composing the crew, including young Raasay, were

prisoner, an order came to the officer on guard for the release of some prisoners. Amongst others, the officer called the name of Alexander Macdonald, asking Kingsburgh if that was not he. He answered: "That is my name; but I suspect there must be some mistake." The officer said: "D—— you! what mistake? Is not your name Alexander Macdonald?" Kingsburgh said it was, but repeated his warning twice or thrice. He at last went out and met a friend, who advised him instantly to go out and leave the fort. Kingsburgh said: "No; I must wait at the opposite alehouse till I see whether the officer gets into a scrape." He waited. In two hours an officer came with a body of soldiers, and made the subaltern on guard prisoner for having set at large so dangerous a rebel. Kingsburgh immediately ran across the street, and saying to the officer: "I told you there was a mistake," surrendered himself.'

Miss Macdonald, having taken leave of the Prince, left Portree immediately, and proceeded to her mother's house of Armadale in the district of Sleat. She never told her mother, or any one else, what she had done. Eight or ten days after her arrival, she received a message from Donald Macdonald of Castleton, a neighbouring gentleman, requesting her to come to him, and stating that he sent the message at the instigation of an officer of an independent company, who proved to be Macleod of Talisker. Somewhat suspicious of what might happen, she consulted her friends, who unanimously advised her not to go: but 'go she would.'* On her way, she met her stepfather returning home, and had not gone much farther, when she was seized by an officer and a party of soldiers, and hurried on board Captain Ferguson's vessel. General Campbell, who was on board, ordered that she should be well treated; and finding her story had been blabbed by the boatmen, she confessed all to that officer.

She was soon after transferred from the ship commanded by Ferguson to one commanded by Commodore Smith, a humane person, capable of appreciating her noble conduct. By the permission of General Campbell, she was now allowed to land at Armadale and take leave of her mother: her stepfather was by this time in hiding, from fear lest his concern in the Prince's escape should bring him into trouble. Flora, who had hitherto been without a change of clothes, here obtained all she required, and engaged as her attendant an honest good girl, named Kate Macdowall, who could not speak a word of any language but Gaelic. She then returned on board the vessel, and was in time carried to the south. It chanced that she here had for one of her fellow-prisoners the worthy Captain O'Neal, who had engaged her to undertake the charge of the Prince—and who, by the way, had made her the offer on that occasion of his hand in marriage, as a protection to her good fame. When she first met him on board, she went playfully up, and slapping him gently on the cheek with the palm of her hand, said: 'To that black face do I owe all my misfortune!' O'Neal told her that, instead of being her misfortune, it was her highest honour, and that if she continued to act up to the character she had already shewn, not pretending to repent of what she had done, or to be ashamed of it, it would yet redound greatly to her happiness.

The vessel in which she was having put into Leith Road early in September, and remained there till November, many of the well-affected in Edinburgh had an opportunity of paying her in person the homage due to her character. Amongst these was the Rev. Mr Forbes, the Episcopal minister of the port, whose pen was fortunately active on the occasion. I extract the following from his memoranda:

'In the journal taken, &c. Miss Macdonald has omitted several things which she particularly mentioned to those who conversed with her when she was lying in the Road of Leith,

---

* The words of her own narrative, *Jacobite Memoirs*.

announced to him, he would not permit the usual ceremonies of respect, but saluted them as his equals. It was nearly

on board the *Eltham* and the *Bridgewater* ships-of-war. She told that when the Prince put on women's clothes, he proposed carrying a pistol under one of his petticoats, for making some small defence in case of an attack; but Miss declared against it, alleging that if any persons should happen to search them, the pistol would only serve to make a discovery. . . . . The Prince was obliged to content himself with only a short heavy cudgel, with which he designed to do his best to knock down any single person that should attack him.

'She used likewise to tell that, in their passage to the Isle of Skye, a heavy rain fell upon them, which, with former fatigues, distressed her much. To divert her, the Prince sang several pretty songs. She fell asleep, and to keep her so, the Prince still continued to sing. Happening to awake with some little bustle in the boat, she found the Prince leaning over her with his hands spread about her head. She asked what was the matter. The Prince told her that one of the rowers, being obliged to do somewhat about the sail, behoved to step over her body (the boat was so small); and lest he should have done her hurt, either by stumbling or trampling upon her in the dark, he had been doing his best to preserve his guardian from harm. When Miss Macdonald was telling this particular part of the adventure to some ladies that were paying their respects to her, some of them with rapture cried out: "Oh, Miss! what a happy creature are you, who had that dear Prince to lull you asleep, and to take such care of you with his hands spread about your head when you was sleeping! You are surely the happiest woman in the world!" "I could," says one of them [Miss Mary Clerk *], "wipe your shoes with pleasure, and think it my honour so to do, when I reflect that you had the honour to have the Prince for your handmaid. We all envy you greatly." Much about the same time, a lady of rank and dignity [Lady Mary Cochrane†] being on board with Miss Macdonald, a brisk gale began to blow and make the sea rough, and not so easy for a small boat to row to Leith. The lady whispered to Miss Macdonald that she would with pleasure stay on board all night, that she might have it to say that she had the honour of lying in the same bed with that person who had been so happy as to be guardian to her Prince. Accordingly, they did sleep in one bed that night. Several ladies [my Lady Bruce,‡ Lady Mary Cochrane, Mrs Rattray,§ Mrs Cheap, Miss Peggie Forbes, Miss Susie Graham, Miss Magdalen Clerk, Miss Mary Clerk, Miss Rachie Houston, Miss Peggie Callander] made valuable presents to Miss Macdonald; namely, gowns, shirts, head-suits, shoes, stockings, &c. &c. Commodore Smith made her a present when she was in Leith Road of a handsome suit of riding-clothes, with plain mounting, and some fine linen for riding-shirts, as also a gown to her woman Kate Macdowall, and some linen to be shifts for poor Kate, who [had] generously offered herself to Miss Macdonald, when she could get not one that would venture to go with her. . . . .

'When Miss Macdonald was on board the *Bridgewater* in Leith Road, accounts had come that the Prince was taken prisoner, and one of the officers had brought the news of this report on board. She got an opportunity of talking privately to some who were then visiting her, and said, with tears in her eyes: "Alas! I am afraid that now all is in vain that I have done! The Prince at last is in the hands of his enemies!" Though at that

---

* One of the daughters of Mr Hugh Clerk, merchant in Leith, a son of Robert Clerk of Listonshiels, a cadet of the Penicuik family.

† Probably a daughter of Thomas, sixth Earl of Dundonald.

‡ Widow of Sir William Bruce of Kinross. In her house, in the citadel of Leith, Mr Forbes at this time lived.

§ The wife of Mr Rattray, surgeon in Edinburgh, the same who had been for a short time a prisoner at Inverness.

daylight (July 1) when he left Portree.   'As they were rowing along in the boat, the Prince conversed to and fro, and fre-

time great fear was entertained about the truth of this account, yet those that were with Miss Macdonald endeavoured all they could to cheer her up, and to dissuade her from believing any such thing; but still fears haunted her mind, till the matter was cleared up, and the contrary appeared. . . . .

'One day, in the Road of Leith, a lady [Miss Rachie Houston] asking Miss if she had any books on board, she said she had only a prayer-book, but regretted much the want of a Bible, which that lady soon furnished her with in a present, in two pretty pocket volumes handsomely bound. That she might have some innocent and useful employment for her time, care was taken by a lady [Lady Bruce] to send her a thimble, needles, white thread

FLORA MACDONALD.

of different sorts, &c. with some linen and cambric, cut and shaped according to the newest fashions. This piece of friendship Miss Flora admired as much as any instance of kindness and regard that had been shewn her, because all the time she had been in custody she was quite idle, having no work to do, and thereby time passed very dully on.

'While she was in the Road of Leith, she never was allowed to set her foot once on shore; though in other respects the officers were extremely civil and complaisant to her, and took it exceedingly well when any persons came to visit her. Sometimes they were so obliging as to come ashore for good company to attend her, and frequently declared that if they knew any person to come on board out of curiosity, and not out of respect for Miss

quently said that friends who shewed their friendship in distress were the real friends, and that he hoped his friends would not

Macdonald, that person should not have access to her. This genteel behaviour makes it to be presumed that their orders were so exceedingly strict, that they could not dare to bring her ashore. Commodore Smith, commander of the *Eltham*, behaved like a father to her, and tendered her many good advices as to her behaviour in her ticklish situation: and Captain Knowler of the *Bridgewater* used her with the utmost decency and politeness. When company came to her, she was indulged the privilege, by both these humane and well-bred gentlemen, to call for anything on board, as if she had been at her own fireside: and the servants of the cabin were obliged to give her all manner of attendance; and she had the liberty to invite any of her friends to dine with her when she pleased. Her behaviour in company was so easy, modest, and well adjusted, that every visitant was much surprised; for she had never been out of the islands of South Uist and Skye till about a year before the Prince's arrival, that she had been in the family of Macdonald of Largoe, in Argyleshire, for the space of ten or eleven months.

'Some that went on board to pay their respects to her used to take a dance in the cabin, and to press her much to share with them in the diversion; but with all their importunity, they could not prevail with her to take a trip. She told them that at present her dancing days were done, and she would not readily entertain a thought of that diversion till she should be assured of her Prince's safety, and perhaps not till she should be blessed with the happiness of seeing him again. Although she was easy and cheerful, yet she had a certain mixture of gravity in all her behaviour, which became her situation exceedingly well, and set her off to great advantage. She is of a low stature, of a fair complexion, and well enough shaped. One would not discern by her conversation that she had spent all her former days in the Highlands; for she talks English (or rather Scots) easily, and not at all through the Erse tone. She has a sweet voice, and sings well, and no lady, Edinburgh-bred, can acquit herself better at the tea-table than what she did when in Leith Road. Her wise conduct in one of the most perplexing scenes that can happen in life, her fortitude and good sense, are memorable instances of the strength of a female mind, even in those years that are tender and inexperienced.'

The ship in which Miss Macdonald was confined left Leith Road on the 7th of November, and carried her straightway to London, where she was kept in a not less honourable captivity in the house of a private family, till the passing of the act of indemnity in July 1747, when she was discharged without being asked a single question. Her story had by this time excited not less interest in the metropolis than it had done in Scotland. Being received after her liberation into the house of the dowager Lady Primrose of Dunipace, she was there visited by crowds of the fashionable world, who paid her such homage as would have turned the heads of ninety-nine of a hundred women of any age, country, or condition. On her mind they produced no effect but that of surprise: she had only, she thought, performed an act of common humanity, and she had never thought of it in any other light till she found the world making so much ado about it. Lord Mahon mentions, I do not know upon what authority, that a subscription to the amount of £1500 was raised for her in London. Mr Robert Cole of London possesses an original letter of hers, addressed to Innes and Clerk, merchants of that city, and dated at Kingsburgh, April 23, 1751, in which she makes mention of £627 lodged in their hands for her behoof by Lady Primrose, and that she understood that more would follow from the same quarter.

Soon after returning to her own country, Flora was married (November 6, 1750) to Mr Alexander Macdonald, younger of Kingsburgh, to whom she bore a large family of sons and daughters. When Dr Johnson and Mr Boswell visited Skye, they were entertained by Mr and Mrs Macdonald at Kingsburgh. Johnson, in his *Journey to the Western Islands*, introduces her well-known maiden name, which he says is one ' that will be mentioned in

have reason to repent for the services done him, and that he would happily yet end what he had begun, or die in the attempt.'[1]   He slept a little on the passage to Raasay, and, after a voyage of ten miles, they landed at a place called Glam. As almost all the houses in the island had been burned by the soldiery, and as some were not eligible as places of conceal-

history, and, if courage and fidelity be virtues, mentioned with honour.' He adds: ' She is a woman of middle stature, soft features, gentle manners, and elegant presence.' Soon after this period, under the influence of the passion for emigration which was then raging in the Highlands, Kingsburgh and his lady went to North Carolina, where they purchased and settled upon an estate. She bore with her across the Atlantic the sheet in which the Prince had lain, that it might serve as her shroud, wherever it should be her fate to lay down her bones. Mr Macdonald had scarcely been settled on his property, when the unfortunate contest between the colonists and the mother-country involved him in trouble. Like most of his countrymen in America, he sided with the British government, and the consequence was that he was imprisoned as a dangerous person. On being liberated, he took arms against the colonists, as captain in a regiment called the North Carolina Highlanders, and he and his wife met with many strange adventures in the course of the contest. At the conclusion of the war, they found it necessary to leave the country of their adoption, and return to Skye. In the voyage homeward, the vessel encountered a French ship of war, and an action ensued. While the other ladies were confined below, Flora insisted upon remaining on deck, where she endeavoured, by her voice and example, to animate the sailors. She was unfortunately thrown down in the bustle, and broke her arm ; which caused her afterwards to observe, in the spirit of poor Mercutio, that she had now perilled her life in behalf of both the house of Stuart and that of Brunswick, and got very little for her pains.

She spent the remainder of her life in Skye, and at her death, which took place March 5, 1790, when she had attained the age of seventy, was actually buried in the shroud which she had so strangely selected for that purpose in her youth, and carried with her through so many adventures and migrations. She retained to the last that vivacity and vigour of character which has procured her so much historical distinction. Her husband, who survived her a few years, died on the half-pay list as a British officer ; and no fewer than five of her sons served their king in a military capacity. Charles, the eldest son, was a captain in the Queen's Rangers. He was a most accomplished man : Lord Macdonald, on seeing him lowered into the grave, said : ' There lies the most finished gentleman of my family and name.' Alexander, the second son, was also an officer : he was lost at sea. The third son, Ranald, was a captain of marines, of high professional character, and remarkable for the elegance of his appearance. James, the fourth son, served in Tarleton's British Legion, and was a brave and experienced officer. Lieutenant-colonel John Macdonald of Exeter was the last survivor of these gallant soldiers. There were, moreover, two daughters, one of whom, Mrs Major Macleod of Lochbay, in the Isle of Skye, survived to give information to the author of this work, at the time of its first publication in 1827. Flora lies buried in a mausoleum of the Kingsburgh family in the churchyard of Kilmuir, without a stone to mark her grave.

Donald Roy Macdonald, who had taken such an important interest in the Prince's progress through Skye, skulked in caves, where he was supplied with necessaries by Lady Margaret Macdonald, till the passing of the act of indemnity in 1747, when he was enabled to go at large.

[1] Narrative by Murdoch Macleod, *Lyon in Mourning*, MS. iv. 862.

ment, it was not without difficulty that the Prince was accommodated. A resolution was at length made that the whole company should lodge in a little hovel which some shepherds had lately built, though it could afford them absolutely nothing but shelter from the open air. When they had settled here, young Raasay went away, and in about two hours returned with a young kid, which they immediately proceeded to roast, and ate with butter, cream, and oaten bread, the Prince preferring the last to a wheaten loaf, and calling it his own country bread. ' After their little repast was over, he began to inquire narrowly about the damages done in the island. Upon his being told of all the houses burned, and of the other great depredations in the island, to which the houses were but a trifle, he seemed much affected, but at the same time said that, instead of the huts burned, he would yet build houses of stone. Afterwards, walking on a narrow green near the cottage, he said that this was a bitter hard life, but he would rather live ten years in that way than be taken by his enemies, and seemed a little surprised himself how he did bear such fatigues; " for," says he, " since the battle of Culloden, I have endured more than would kill a hundred : sure Providence does not design this for nothing. I'm thus certainly yet reserved for some good." Thus they passed the day, and after having taken some supper, he went to rest with as great pleasure, and in outward appearance as little concerned, as if in the greatest prosperity.' [1]

Though there were no parties of military upon Raasay, and although all the inhabitants were well affected, it was thought proper by Charles's attendants to use the utmost caution. Watches were established upon the tops of all the neighbouring heights, and no one of the party appeared in public except young Raasay, who was, as already mentioned, a clear man. Donald Roy being stationed upon Skye, to give intelligence in case of any annoyance from that quarter, the Prince might have almost considered himself secure upon this wild and secluded

[1] Murdoch Macleod's Narrative.

island. Laying aside the wretchedness of his lodging, he might also be esteemed as not in the worst possible predicament as to living. Young Raasay was in the midst of his own flocks, and had only to use insidious means to procure for his royal highness and the whole party plenty of fresh provisions.

The Prince's bed of state here was one made, in the primitive Highland fashion, of heather, with the stalks upright, and the bloom uppermost. He enjoyed long, but not unbroken slumbers, often starting, and giving unconscious expression to the feelings and imagery of his dreams. Malcolm Macleod, who watched him on these occasions, informed Mr Boswell that his half-suppressed exclamations were sometimes in French, some-times in Italian, and occasionally in English; though the ingenious tourist could not help questioning Malcolm's ability to distinguish at least two of these tongues. One of his expres-sions in English was: 'O God, poor Scotland!' his mind having probably been then engaged in lamenting the military tyranny by which, in consequence of his unfortunate enterprise, a great part of the nation was so bitterly agonised.

The only stranger, besides the Prince, then known to be upon the island of Raasay, and of course the only person from whom they apprehended particular danger, was a man who had come about a fortnight before for the ostensible purpose of selling a roll of tobacco. The tobacco had been long sold, and yet the man wandered about, apparently reluctant to quit the island. Nobody knew anything about him, and he was suspected to be a spy. One day John Mackenzie came running down from the place where he had been watching with the alarming intelligence that this mysterious individual was approaching the hut. The three gentlemen who attended the Prince—young Raasay, Murdoch Macleod, and Malcolm—immediately held a council of war upon the subject, the result of which was, that the man should be put to death without ceremony. The mind of Charles shrunk with horror from the proposal, and assuming a grave and even severe countenance, he said: 'God forbid that we should take away a man's life who may be innocent, while we can preserve our own.' The gentlemen, however, persisted in their resolution, while he as strenuously continued to take the merciful side. In the midst of the debate, John Mackenzie, the watchman, who sat at the door of the hut, said in Erse: 'He must be shot: you are the king, but we are the parliament, and will do what we choose.' Charles, seeing his friends smile, asked what the man had said, which being reported to him in English, he observed that he was a clever fellow; and, notwithstanding the perilous situation he was in, he could not help laughing.[1] Fortunately the unknown person walked past, without perceiving that there were people in the hut. Malcolm Macleod afterwards declared that, had he stopped or come forward, they were resolved to despatch him; that he would have done so himself, although the victim had been his own brother! Dougal Graham, indeed, reports that young Raasay had his pistol ready cocked for the purpose.

After a residence of two days and a half upon the island of Raasay, Charles expressed a strong wish to leave it, alleging that it was too narrow to afford good room for skulking, and also professing an anxiety to meet with Donald Roy Macdonald in Skye. His attendants combated his wishes, but he insisted on the point so earnestly, that they at last gave way. The whole party accordingly set sail, on the evening of the 3d of July, in the same open boat which had brought them over to Raasay. Before they had proceeded far, the wind began to blow hard, and to drive so much sea-water into their vessel, that they begged to return and wait a more favourable opportunity. But the Prince insisted upon proceeding, in spite of every danger, exclaiming that Providence had not brought him through so many perilous chances to end his life in this simple manner at last. To encourage them, he sang a lively Erse song, although very little acquainted with that language. They continued their voyage, notwithstanding that the water came into

---

[1] Mr Boswell, by conversing with this man, discovered that, in reality, he had no intention of amusing Prince Charles by an allusion to the power which the British parliament had exercised over the fortunes of his family, but spoke only from the simple idea that many voices were better than one.—See Boswell's *Tour*, 2d edition, p. 228.

the boat in such quantities as to require the utmost exertions of Malcolm to keep it from sinking. 'Gentlemen,' he said, 'I hope to thank you for this trouble yet at St James's.' After a rough voyage of about fifteen miles, they landed safe, about eleven o'clock at night, at a place called Nicholson's Great Rock, near Scorobreck in Trotternish, the northern limb or peninsula of the Isle of Skye. There being no convenient landing-place, the party had to jump out into the surf, and haul the boat ashore. Charles, who was already drenched to the skin, and encumbered with a large greatcoat, was the third man to fling himself into the sea for this purpose. After landing, he eagerly assisted in hauling the boat ashore.

The only lodging which the party could find to solace them for all the fatigues and discomforts of their voyage, was a lonely cow-house belonging to Mr Nicholson of Scorobreck, a mansion about two miles distant. Lest there might be some people in this hovel, young Raasay went forward to inspect it, while the rest walked slowly behind. 'What must become of your royal highness,' said Murdoch, 'if there be people in the house, for certainly you must perish, if long exposed to such weather?' 'I care nothing for it,' replied the Prince, 'for I have been abroad in a hundred such nights.' Young Raasay having come back reporting that the byre was empty, they entered, kindled a fire, and lying down around it, partook of some bread and cheese, their only provisions. At an early hour in the morning, young Raasay went away to meet Donald Roy, according to the appointment which had been made with him. The Prince, who had stretched himself beside the fire, slept till noon, when he rose and went out with Murdoch to a little hill near by, where Malcolm Macleod and the two boatmen had been standing sentry. He ordered them to go in and take some sleep, of which, he said, they had much need, and he himself should meanwhile keep watch. He here expressed to Murdoch great anxiety for the return of his elder brother, saying he would wait for him till eight o'clock, but no longer. He then asked Murdoch if he could travel well, to which the youth replied in the negative, his wound being still unhealed. The Prince then asked if he knew his cousin Malcolm well, and if he was a discreet man, who might be safely trusted. Murdoch gave a strong testimony to both the discretion and fidelity of Malcolm; which seems to have determined the Prince as to his next movements. He told Murdoch that he expected to get a boat on the other side of Skye to carry him to the island of Rum. In case this expectation should not be fulfilled, he wished Murdoch to be within two days at a particular point a few miles off with his own six-oared boat, which he understood to be an excellent sailer, in order to take him off if necessary. Lest, however, it should be judged unsafe for him to sail in that boat through the strait between Skye and the mainland, on account of the guards there posted, he wished Donald Roy to go to Sleat and have another boat ready for him in that district. 'All this,' said he to Murdoch, 'you must endeavour to manage aright, for it is a matter of the utmost consequence. It will be a piece of great friendship, which I shall never forget.' He also expressed a strong wish that the concern of young Raasay in aiding his concealment should be kept a profound secret, adding that he, for one, would never say a word about it.[1]

The Prince now returned with Murdoch to the byre, designing to wait there till eight o'clock; but the sight of a stranger at a distance determined him to set out sooner. After presenting Murdoch with his silver spoon, knife, and fork, and desiring him to keep them till he saw him again, he left the hovel, with Malcolm Macleod alone in his company. When they had walked about a mile, Malcolm made bold to ask his royal highness where he intended to go. 'Malcolm,' answered the Prince impressively, 'I commit myself entirely to you; carry me to Mackinnon's bounds in Skye;' meaning that portion of the island which belonged to the chief of Mackinnon, the only one of the three great proprietors of Skye who had been concerned in his late enterprise. Malcolm objected that such a journey would be dangerous, on account of the militia who patrolled the island; but Charles answered that there was nothing now to be done without danger. 'You, Malcolm,' he continued, 'must now act the master, and I the man.' Accordingly, taking the bag which contained his linen, and strapping it over his shoulders, he desired his faithful companion to go in advance as a gentleman, while he trudged behind in the character of a servant. Malcolm acquiesced in the plan; and it was also agreed that the Prince should pass for one Lewie Caw, the son of a surgeon in Crieff, and lately in the Highland army in a medical capacity, but who was now known to be skulking in Skye amongst some relations. They set forward in this fashion towards Mackinnon's country, which was distant twenty-four Highland miles, and could only be reached from this point by traversing a very wild and mountainous tract.[1]

Malcolm, though himself an excellent pedestrian, as most of his countrymen were, used afterwards to own that, in this long and painful journey, he found himself far excelled by Prince Charles, whose rapidity of motion was such, that it was with the greatest difficulty he could be restrained to his proper place in the rear. His royal highness informed Malcolm that, trusting to his speed of foot, he felt little apprehension on the score of being chased by a party of English soldiers, provided he got out of musket-shot; though he owned he was not just so confident of escaping any of the Highland militia who might fall in with him. Malcolm asked him what they should do if surprised before getting to the proper distance. 'Fight, to be sure,' was the Prince's reply. 'I think,' rejoined Malcolm, 'if there were no more than four of them, I would engage to manage two.' 'And I,' added Charles, 'would engage to do for the other two.'

In walking over the mountains, they kept as much as possible out of sight of houses; but they occasionally met a few country-

---

[1] A list of the things carried by Charles on this occasion has been preserved—'two shirts, one pair of stockings, one pair of brogues, a bottle of brandy, some scraps of mouldy bread and cheese, a three-pint stone bottle for water.'—*Lyon in Mourning*, i. 141.

people wandering about. On these occasions Charles took care to display the demeanour of a servant; touching his bonnet when spoken to by his apparent master, and also when addressing him. As they went along, it occurred to the Prince that the waistcoat he wore, being a scarlet tartan with a gold twist button, was too fine for a servant, and he proposed to exchange it for that worn by Mr Macleod. While he was putting on his companion's vest, he said: 'I hope, Macleod, to give you a much better vest for this yet.' On approaching Mackinnon's country, in which many of the people, having been in the Highland army, might be presumed to know the Prince, it was thought proper still further to deepen his disguise. Taking off his periwig, and putting it into his pocket, he took out a dirty white napkin, and desired Malcolm to tie that about his head, bringing it down upon his eyes and nose. Over this he put his bonnet. He then tore the ruffles from his shirt, and took the buckles out of his shoes, putting strings in their place. He desired his friend to look at him, and say if he was yet sufficiently disguised. Macleod told him that he thought he might yet be recognised. Charles said: 'This is an odd, remarkable face I have got, that nothing can disguise it.' Macleod, however, did not think the risk of detection lay alone in the face. He used to say that Charles could dissemble everything but his *air*. 'There is not a person,' said he, 'that knows what the air of a noble or great man is, but, upon seeing the Prince in any disguise he could put on, would see something about him that was not ordinary, something of the stately and grand.'

In the course of their walk, Malcolm informed him of the many barbarities committed by the Duke of Cumberland after the battle of Culloden. The Prince was amazed, as he might well be, at the recital, and said he could scarcely believe what he heard. Macleod, in the narrative he afterwards communicated to the Rev. Mr Forbes, states some particulars respecting the personal condition of the Prince at this time which modern ears might dislike to hear. To put the matter into the most delicate form, the reader must be asked to imagine the worst

feature of the squalor of a wayside beggar. ' This serves,' says
Malcolm, ' to shew that he was reduced to the very lowest ebb
of misery and distress, and is a certain indication of that greatness of soul which could rise above all misfortunes, and bear up,
with a cheerfulness not to be equalled in history, under all the
scenes of woe that could happen. He used to say that the
fatigues and distresses he underwent signified nothing at all,
because he was only a single person ; but when he reflected on
the many brave fellows who suffered in his cause, that, he
behoved to own, did strike him to the heart, and did sink very
deep into him.' [1]

The principal support which the two pedestrians had during
their long walk was derived from a bottle of brandy carried by
Malcolm, with the assistance of the wayside springs. This
source of comfort became exhausted before the end of their
journey, all except a single glass, which the Prince insisted that
his companion should drink, protesting that he could better
endure to want it. When the bottle was fairly drained, Malcolm
hid it in the ground, where he afterwards found and resumed
possession of it in quieter times.

After a journey of more than thirty English miles, they arrived
in the morning at Ellagol, near Kilmaree, in the country of
Mackinnon, where they happened to meet two of that clan who
had been engaged in the insurrection. The men stared at the
Prince for a little, and soon recognising him, fairly lifted up their
voices and wept. Malcolm immediately put them on their
guard, lest such an expression of sympathy, though honourable
to them, should discover their Prince to his enemies. He also
swore them to secrecy upon his naked dirk, after the fashion of
the Highlanders, and requested them to go away, without taking
further notice of his royal highness. It is barely necessary to
say that they kept their word.

Being now near Mackinnon's house, Malcolm asked the
Prince if he wished to see the laird. Charles answered that,
with the highest respect for the worth and fidelity of old

[1] *Jacobite Memoirs*, 476.

Mackinnon, he did not think him the person precisely fitted for his present purpose; and he wished rather to be conducted to the house of some other gentleman. Malcolm then determined that the Prince should go to the house of his brother-in-law, Mr John Mackinnon, who had been a captain in the insurgent army.

Leaving Charles at a little distance, till he should reconnoitre, Malcolm entered the house himself, and saw his sister, who informed him that her husband had gone out, but was expected back very soon. He intended, he said, to spend a day or two in her house, provided there were no soldiers in the neighbourhood. She assured him he would be perfectly safe. Then he informed her that he had brought a brother in distress along with him, one Lewie Caw, whom he had engaged, from pity, as his servant, and who had fallen sick during their journey. Mrs Mackinnon desired that Caw might be instantly brought in and entertained.

Charles being immediately introduced, the lady of the house could not help saying, as he entered: 'Poor man! I pity him. At the same time, my heart warms to a man of his appearance.' She provided the two with a plentiful meal, during which Charles sat at a respectful distance from the table, with his bonnet off, partaking only of the inferior articles. Malcolm, moved by the Prince's humility, requested him to draw near the table and eat along with him, as there was no company in the house. But Charles answered, he knew better what became a servant; and it was only after an earnest entreaty, that, making a profound bow, he at length permitted himself to take advantage of the offer. When their meal was concluded, a serving-girl came in with warm water, after the mode of ancient Highland hospitality, to wash Malcolm's feet. This was a ceremony much needed in the present case by the Prince, for, in the course of the journey, he had fallen into a bog, and bemired himself up to the middle. When the woman had washed Malcolm's feet, he said: 'You see that poor sick man there; I hope you will wash his feet too; it will be a great charity, for he has as much need as I have.'

'No such thing,' said she in Gaelic, her only language; 'although I wash the master's feet, I am not obliged to wash the servant's. What! he's but a low country-woman's son; I will not wash his feet indeed.' After some entreaties, he prevailed on her to wash the Prince's feet; but she performed the office so roughly, that Charles had to entreat Macleod to intercede with her for somewhat gentler usage.

The two travellers afterwards went to sleep, while Mrs Mackinnon took her station on the top of a neighbouring hill, to watch the approach of the least danger. Charles only slept two hours, but Malcolm, having suffered more from fatigue, continued in bed a good while longer. On rising, he was astonished to find his indefatigable companion dandling and singing to Mrs Mackinnon's infant, with an appearance of as much cheerfulness and alacrity as if he had endured neither danger nor fatigue. An old woman sat near him looking on. Malcolm could not help expressing his surprise at so extraordinary a sight, when the Prince exclaimed with gaiety, and half-forgetting his assumed character: 'Who knows but this little fellow may be a captain in my service yet?' 'Or you rather an old sergeant in his company,' said the old woman.

Malcolm, now hearing that his brother-in-law was approaching the house, went out to meet him, in order to sound his disposition in regard to Prince Charles. After the usual salutations, pointing to some ships of war which lay at a distance, he said: 'What, Mackinnon, if the Prince be on board one of those?'

'God forbid!' was Mackinnon's devout answer.

Malcolm, then assured that he might be trusted, asked: 'What if he were here, John? Do you think he would be safe?'

'That he would,' answered Mackinnon; 'we should take care of him.'

'Then, John,' said Malcolm, 'he is in your house.'

Mackinnon, in a transport, was for running in immediately and paying his obeisance; but Malcolm stopped him, till he should compose himself, and be tutored to preserve his royal highness's incognito. When he was fairly instructed as to his behaviour, Malcolm permitted him to enter; but no sooner had the warm-hearted Highlander set his eyes upon the unfortunate Prince, than he burst into tears, and had to leave the room.

During the course of the day, a consultation being held as to the best means of transporting Charles to the mainland, it was agreed that John Mackinnon should go to his chief and hire a boat for that purpose. He was enjoined to keep the secret from the old gentleman, and to pretend that the boat was intended for the use of his brother-in-law alone. He went accordingly; but the force of clanship proved too much for his discretion, and he disclosed the fact of the Prince being in his house. The chief, delighted with the intelligence, at once got ready his own boat, and, with his lady, set out to pay his respects to the Wanderer. On John returning to the house, and confessing what he had done, Charles felt somewhat uneasy, but resolved to make the best of the circumstances. He went out and received the old chief, and the whole party then partook of an entertainment of cold meat and wine, which Lady Mackinnon laid out in a neighbouring cave upon the shore.

It was now determined that Charles should be conducted by the old laird and John Mackinnon to the mainland, while Malcolm should remain in Skye, lest he should be missed, and thus create suspicion, and also to interrupt or distract the pursuit which would probably be made after the Prince. It was about eight o'clock at night when the party repaired to the water's edge, where the boat was lying ready to sail. At that moment two English men-of-war hove in sight, apparently bearing towards them; and Malcolm, in high alarm, counselled the Prince to delay his voyage till next morning, more especially as the wind was favourable to the enemy, which it would not be to his boat. Charles, however, would not listen to his suggestions, urging, with enthusiastic vehemence, the result of former good fortune, and that he felt confident the wind would change in his favour the moment that he required its good services.

He then remembered the two contingent appointments he had made with Murdoch Macleod, for a meeting with that gentleman or with Donald Roy Macdonald, and bethought him of the duty under which he lay in civility to apprise them of the step he was now taking. Malcolm said it was no matter, and offered to make the apology himself. 'That's not enough,' said the Prince. 'Have you paper, pen, and ink? I'll write a few lines; I'm obliged to do so in good manners.' Writing materials being presented, he penned a letter in something like the following terms :

'SIR—I have parted (thank God) as intended. Remember me to all friends, and thank them for the trouble they have been at. I am, sir, your humble servant,   JAMES THOMSON.
ELLIGHUIL, *July* 4, 1746.'

To this letter he affixed no address : it is stated by Malcolm Macleod, in his narrative, to have been designed by the Prince for Murdoch ; on the other hand, Donald Roy affirms that it was meant for him, and that to him Malcolm sent it.[1] The dispute does not seem to be one of much consequence.

The Prince next took out his purse, and desired Malcolm's acceptance of ten guineas, along with a silver stock-buckle. The generous Highlander refused to take the money, which he saw, from the slenderness of the Prince's purse, could ill be spared ; but Charles at length prevailed upon him to accept the gift, asserting that he would have need of it in the skulking life he was now leading, and at the same time expressing a confidence that he would get his own exchequer supplied on reaching the mainland. 'Malcolm,' he then said, 'let us smoke a pipe together before we part.' A light was instantly procured from the flint of Malcolm's musket, and the two fond though unequal companions took a last parting smoke from the stumped pipe or *cutty* which Charles had hitherto used in his wanderings. Malcolm obtained, and for a long time preserved this fragment

---

[1] There is an angry letter on this point by Donald in Bishop Forbes's collection. He accuses Malcolm of lying and vain-glory—I would hope without any just cause.

of pipe, which he afterwards was induced to present to Dr Burton of York, a devout Jacobite, who was at the pains to get a handsome case made in which to keep it.

After a tender and long-protracted adieu, the Prince went into the boat, which, with the chief and Mr John Mackinnon, immediately put out to sea, under the management of a few stout rowers. The affectionate Malcolm sat down upon the side of a hill, partly to watch the proceedings of the two tenders, and partly that he might see his dearly beloved Prince as long as distance and eyesight would permit. He afterwards used to tell, with the true superstitious reverence of a stickler for the *jus divinum*, that, precisely as the Prince predicted, he had not gone far out to sea when the wind shifted in such a manner as to part him effectually from the inimical vessels.

Malcolm returned home next day by the way of Kingsburgh, where he related the Prince's late adventures to a grateful and admiring audience. He had to inform Lady Kingsburgh of one circumstance, which must have given her unqualified pleasure. During his travels with the Prince, his royal highness had expressed a high sense of the value of her ladyship's present— the snuff-box already mentioned. He had asked the meaning of the device which adorned the lid—a pair of clasped hands, with the words 'Rob Gib'—which Malcolm explained as emblematic of sincere friendship, and as alluding to a circumstance in which an ancestor of the Prince was concerned. Rob Gib was the court-fool of Scotland in the reign of James V.; it was a saying of his that all the official courtiers served his majesty for selfish ends, except himself, who, for his part, had no other contract with the king than 'stark love and kindness.' The Prince expressed himself an ardent admirer of the principle symbolised by the device, and declared he would endeavour to keep the box as long as he lived.

Malcolm being asked his opinion of the Prince, as one who had seen him in the extremes of both prosperous and adverse fortune, replied that 'he was the most cautious man he ever saw, not to be a coward ; and the bravest, not to be rash.'

About ten days after he had parted with the Prince, Malcolm was apprehended, put aboard a ship, and conveyed to London, where he was kept in confinement the same space of time as Miss Flora Macdonald. On being discharged from jail, Miss Macdonald was provided with a postchaise, to convey her back to Scotland, by a Jacobite lady of quality resident in London; and being desired to choose a person who might accompany her, she named her fellow-sufferer Malcolm. 'And so,' Malcolm used afterwards to observe triumphantly, 'I went up to London to be hanged, and returned in a braw postchaise with Miss Flora Macdonald.'[1]

CHAPTER XXVIII.

CHARLES'S WANDERINGS—THE MAINLAND.

> 'On hills that are by right his ain,
>   He roams a lonely stranger ;
> On ilka hand he 's pressed by want,
>   On ilka side by danger.
> Yestreen I met him in a glen,
>   My heart near bursted fairly,
> For sadly changed indeed was he—
>   Oh, waes me for Prince Charlie !'
>   *Jacobite Song.*

THAT part of the mainland to which the Prince was now directing his course, might be considered as well qualified

---

[1] Boswell's *Tour to the Hebrides ;* where a vivid portraiture has been preserved of this excellent specimen of the Highland gentleman, as he appeared in 1773. 'He was now,' says Mr Boswell, 'sixty-two years of age, hale and well proportioned, with a manly countenance, tanned by the weather, yet having a ruddiness in his cheeks, over a great part of which his rough beard extended. His eye was quick and lively, yet his look was not fierce; but he appeared at once firm and good-humoured. He wore a pair of brogues— tartan hose which came up only near to his knees—a purple camlet kilt—a black waistcoat —a short green cloth coat, bound with gold cord—a yellowish bushy wig—a large blue bonnet, with a gold thread button. I never saw a figure which gave a more perfect representation of a Highland gentleman. I wished much to have a picture of him just as he was. I found him frank and *polite*, in the true sense of the word.'

to afford him shelter, as far as the physical character of the country and the dispositions of its inhabitants were concerned. It was the same well-affected district which he had selected for his first landing, and in which he had reared the standard of his enterprise. Consisting of ranges of rough mountains, alternating with long narrow arms of the sea and fresh-water lakes, it was very suitable for a skulking life. On the other hand, it had been visited and laid waste by the barbarous soldiery, whose post at Fort William was not far distant, and some of whom were scattered in parties over the country.

After a rough night-voyage of thirty miles, during which they passed and exchanged a few words with a boat containing armed militia, but which could not stop to inspect their company, on account of the storm, Charles and his friends landed at four in the morning (July 5) at a place called Little Mallack, on the south side of Loch Nevis, one of the estuaries mentioned. Knowing that there were military in the neighbourhood, they were afraid to leave this place, and accordingly remained in it for three days and three nights, sleeping in the open air. The Laird of Mackinnon having on the fourth day gone with one of the boatmen to seek a cave for a lodging, the Prince, with John Mackinnon and the other three rowers, took to the boat, and proceeded up the loch. As they turned a point, they suddenly struck their oars upon a boat tied to a rock, and saw five men with red crosses over their bonnets standing on the shore. These men, who were government militia, immediately called out, demanding whence they came. The boatmen answered from Sleat. The militiamen ordered them to come ashore, intending, of course, to inspect the boat, and finding their order not complied with, they instantly jumped into their own boat and gave chase. At the time when the boat containing the Prince came in sight of these men, Charles was sitting in the bottom, between Mackinnon's knees, and covered by Mackinnon's plaid, in order to be out of sight, in case of any such misadventure occurring. On being hailed by the men, he was for jumping ashore; but Mackinnon would not allow him to do so, and constrained him, though with some difficulty, to remain in his present situation. Now that the hostile party were in pursuit, Charles was constantly inquiring of Mackinnon if they were gaining upon them. Mackinnon replied in the negative, but nevertheless gave his men directions to have their muskets ready, in case of their being overtaken, and when they fired, to be sure to take good aim. The Prince, hearing these orders, entreated that no life might be taken without absolute necessity; to which John heartily agreed, but nevertheless said that, if forced to come to blows, he would make it his endeavour that not a man escaped to tell the tidings. Presently they approached a part of the shore where the hill was wooded down to the very beach. 'Here,' said he to the Prince, 'it may be quite safe to land, for, if once we be on shore, the red crosses will be obliged to sheer off, for fear of our firing at them from behind the trees.' The boat had no sooner touched the shore, than the Prince, with Mackinnon and one of the men, leaped out, and nimbly ascended the hill, from the top of which they beheld the adverse party, as predicted by John, returning from their fruitless pursuit. Mackinnon, congratulating the Prince on his escape, asked his pardon for thwarting his wishes in the boat, which Charles, it may be imagined, readily granted. His reason, he said, for wishing to jump ashore was, 'that he would rather fight for his life than be taken prisoner; but he hoped that God would never so far afflict the king his father, or the duke his brother, as that he should fall alive into the hands of his enemies.'[1]

On this eminence the Prince slept three hours, and then returning to the boat, he re-embarked, and crossed the loch to a little island near the seat of Macdonald of Scothouse. Here Charles remained, while John Mackinnon went to Scothouse with a message to Clanranald, who was residing there. As John was drawing near the house, he saw Clanranald walking by himself, who no sooner spied the approaching stranger, than he hastened to get within doors. John overtook him, and seized him by the skirts just as he was entering the door. The old chief, turning round in alarm, was reassured when he found himself addressed by John Mackinnon. They went to the back of the garden to converse, and there John informed him that he had come to apprise him of the Prince being in the neighbourhood, and that it was the wish of his royal highness that Clanranald should advise as to his future course, and point out some one into whose hands he might now with safety be put. Clanranald, although he had befriended Charles in South Uist, was not now disposed to do so, probably in consequence of the trouble which had in the interim befallen others who had concerned themselves in his behalf. He therefore treated Mackinnon's message with coldness, saying that he did not know of any one who could take charge of the Prince, and that the only course he could advise him to take, was to return to whence he came, and remain in the island of Rona—this being a small grass island evidently unfit to shelter the royal fugitive. Mackinnon took leave of him in great indignation, and returned to report his mission to the Prince, who heard the recital with tranquillity, only remarking: ' Well, Mr Mackinnon, there is no help for it; we must do the best we can for ourselves.' [1]

They now returned across the loch to Little Mallack, where they had first landed from Skye, and where they were rejoined by the old Laird of Mackinnon and the other boatman. Having resolved to apply to Macdonald of Morar, they set out for the house of that gentleman, which was situated on the fresh-water lake, Loch Morar, about seven or eight Highland miles distant. As they passed a cottage on their way, they observed some people coming down towards the road, whereupon the Prince caused John Mackinnon to fold his plaid for him, and throw it over his shoulder, with his knapsack upon it, tying a handkerchief about his head, to complete the disguise. As they went

---

[1] The particulars of this interview were obtained by the Rev. Mr Forbes from the mouth of John Mackinnon, as that gentleman lay confined with lameness in the Royal Infirmary of Edinburgh, April 25, 1761. They are recorded more at large in the *Lyon in Mourning*, viii. 1831.

along, a stranger asked John if that was his servant, to which he answered in the affirmative, adding that, as the poor fellow was not well, he intended to leave him at Morar's house.

On their way, they received at a sheiling a draught of milk from the hand of Archibald Macdonnell, a grandson of Scothouse. At another cottage belonging to Scothouse they bought another draught of milk, and obtained a guide to conduct them to Morar, the night being dark, and the road bad. At the ford near Morar's house, which was pretty deep, Mr Mackinnon desired the guide to take that poor sick young fellow (pointing to the Prince) upon his back and carry him across. The man said, in the true Highland spirit, of which the maid-servant at John Mackinnon's house had afforded another specimen: 'The deil be on the back where he comes, or any fellow of a servant like him; but I 'll take you on my back, sir, if you please, and carry you safely through the ford.' Mackinnon declined the proposal, saying that, if the lad must wade, he would wade too, to help him, and take care lest any harm should happen to him. He then took hold of the Prince's arm, and they went through the ford together. The man's refusal in reality pleased the Prince and his friends very much, as it proved that his person was pretty well disguised.

At an early hour in the morning they reached Morar, which they found to have been burned, in consequence of its owner being in the insurrection. Mr Macdonald and his family were accommodated in a bothy or hut near the ruins of the house. Mackinnon entered this small mansion by himself, and roused the family, when Morar hastily rose from bed, and came to the door to greet the Prince. Having dismissed his children and servants, he introduced Charles into the house, where his lady, a sister of Locheil, no sooner beheld that sad spectacle of fallen royalty, than she burst into a flood of tears. The only refreshment she could set before the party was some cold salmon warmed again, without bread. The Prince and his friends were then conducted by Morar to a cave near by, where they slept ten hours.

Morar now went to seek for young Clanranald, whose aid or advice might, he thought, be of service to the Prince. Returning next day to the party, he appeared, to their great surprise and regret, in quite a different humour from what he had manifested at their first arrival. When he told the Prince that he had been unable to find young Clanranald, Charles said to him: 'Well, Morar, there is no help for that; you must do the best you can yourself.' He answered that he could do nothing for his royal highness, and as little did he know of any person to whose care he could recommend him. 'This is very hard,' said the Prince; 'you were very kind yesternight, Morar, and said you could find out a hiding-place proof against all the search of the enemy's forces, and now you say you can do nothing at all for me. You can travel to no place but what I will travel to; no eatables or drinkables can you take but what I can take a share along with you, and be well content with them, and even pay handsomely for them. When fortune smiled on me, and I had pay to give, I found some people ready enough to serve me; but now that fortune frowns on me, and I have no pay to give, they forsake me in my necessity.'

Morar's conduct highly incensed John Mackinnon, who said: 'I am persuaded, Morar, though you deny it, you have met with your betters, and got bad counsel, otherwise you would not have changed your mind so much as you have done in so short a time.' Morar persisted in denying that he had seen young Clanranald, or received any bad counsel; but he was as firm in continuing to refuse all further aid to the Prince.

Charles, completely overcome by his feelings, now broke out with: 'O God Almighty! look down upon my circumstances, and pity me, for I am in a most melancholy situation. Some of those who joined me at first, and appeared to be my fast friends, now turn their backs upon me in my greatest need; and some of those again who refused to join me, and stood at a distance, are now among my best friends; for it is remarkable that those of Sir Alexander Macdonald's following have been most faithful to me in my distress, and contributed greatly to my preservation.'

Then he added : ' I hope, Mr Mackinnon, you will not desert me too, but do all for my preservation that you can.'

The aged chief, supposing himself to be here addressed, declared, while the tears gushed from his eyes : ' I never will leave your royal highness in the day of danger, but will, under God, do all I can for you, and go with you wherever you order me.'

' O no,' said the Prince, ' that is too much for a person of your advanced years, sir. I heartily thank you for your readiness to take care of me ; but one of your age cannot well hold out with the dangers and fatigues I must undergo. It was to your friend John here, a stout young man, I was addressing myself.'

' Well, then,' said John, ' with the help of God, I will go through the wide world with your royal highness.'

The old laird here accordingly parted with them, and the Prince and John Mackinnon proceeded, with a son of Morar's for guide, to Borodale, the residence of Mr Angus Macdonald, and the place where Charles had first lodged after his landing from France. He said he was sure that honest old Angus Macdonald would do all he could for him. In the course of the night the little party had crossed into Arisaig, and before day they arrived at Borodale, where they found the house burned, and the proprietor lodging, like Morar, in a bothy or hut. John Mackinnon went in abruptly, desiring Angus to rise. He was at first a little alarmed, but soon recognising Mackinnon's voice, rose in his blankets, and came to the door. John asked him if he had heard anything of the Prince, to which he answered : ' No.'

' What,' said John, ' would you give for a sight of him ?'

' Time was,' replied the old gentleman, ' that I would have given a hearty bottle to see him safe ; but since I see you, I expect to hear some news of him.'

' Well, then,' said Mackinnon, ' I have brought him here, and will commit him to your charge. I have done my duty ; do you yours.'

'I am glad of it,' said Angus, 'and shall not fail to take care of him. I shall lodge him so securely, that all the forces in Britain shall not find him out.'[1]

According to the tradition of Angus Macdonald's family, the Prince did not enter this humble bothy without reluctance, remembering that one of his sons had never been heard of since the day of Culloden. He felt distressed at the idea of meeting a mother who had suffered this sad loss on his account. When he did enter, he approached the lady with tears in his eyes, and asked if she could endure the sight of one who had been the cause of so much distress to her and her family. Yes, she said, she would be glad to serve her Prince, though *all* her sons had perished in his service, for in doing so they had only done their duty.[2]

John Mackinnon now left the Prince, and returned to his house in Skye, where he no sooner arrived, than he and two of his rowers were taken by a party of militia, who conveyed them to Kilvory, and placed them in the cruel hands of Captain Ferguson. Being required by this monster to disclose the place of the Prince's retreat, and giving a positive refusal to the demand, Ferguson caused one of the men to be stripped, tied to a tree, and lashed till the blood gushed from both his sides; he also threatened Mackinnon with the same treatment. Nothing could extort a confession from these faithful men. Mackinnon was then sent on board the *Furnace* sloop-of-war, where he met with civil treatment from General Campbell. He was afterwards sent to London, and confined there till July 1747.[3]

---

[1] John Mackinnon's Narrative, *Jacobite Memoirs*, 496.

[2] Communicated to me in 1827 by the late Mr Macdonald of Glenaladale (originally of Borodale), grandson of the lady. It only seems doubtful whether the incident took place now, or at the end of April, when the Prince embarked at Borodale for the Long Island.

[3] Mr Mackinnon came to Edinburgh at the beginning of the year 1761, afflicted by a severe lameness from the top of his thighs downwards. He was then in necessitous circumstances, and had left a wife and four children in Skye poorly provided for. From an independence of spirit, he chose rather to go into the public infirmary than be a burden to particular friends; but after a residence there of six months, he was dismissed uncured, and with no hope of relief except from the waters at Bath. Carried thither by the generosity of a *faithful few* residing in Edinburgh, he received every kindness suited to his circumstances from Thomas Bowdler of Ashley, Dr Haviland, and some other Jacobite gentlemen;

Angus Macdonald kept the Prince for three days in a hut in the neighbouring wood, and in the meantime his youngest son, John Macdonald, went with a letter from Charles to Mr Macdonald of Glenaladale, lately major of the Clanranald regiment, whom he expected to befriend him in the present exigency. During the absence of this messenger, intelligence was received of the capture of the old Laird of Mackinnon in Morar's bothy;[1] and it being then judged unsafe for Charles to stay any longer so near Borodale, he was conducted, by Angus and another son named Ranald, to a more secure place of retreat, at the distance of four miles along the shore to the eastward. The coast there consists of a steep precipice: in the cleft between two rocks a hut had been artfully constructed, with the grassy side of the turf outwards, so that it exactly resembled a natural green bank. This hut formed the new hiding-place of the royal fugitive. The vessel in which John Mackinnon was kept after his capture having come into Lochnanuagh, lay for some time at anchor close to this retreat, without any one on board having the slightest suspicion that it was a place of concealment.

The Prince remained secure in this place for several days. Two days after he had despatched John Macdonald to Glenaladale—namely, on the 15th of July—the letter was delivered

but here also he steadily insisted, against their wishes, upon going into the public hospital. His disorder defied all remedy, and he died on the 11th of May 1762, aged forty-eight. Dr Haviland then gave his body a place in the same grave in which he designed to be buried himself. An inscription intended for a monument over his grave (never executed) appeared in the *Scots Magazine* for that year.

[1] This gentleman was sent to London in the vessel commanded by the atrocious Ferguson, in which also were Donald and Malcolm Macleod. Though subjected to the same severe privations and cruel usage with the rest, and nearly seventy years of age, he maintained rather better health than any of his companions. After lying for a long time in the Thames, he was put into the New Jail in Southwark, whence he was liberated in July 1747. Bishop Forbes thus notices the death of this old gentleman:

'*May* 7, 1756.—Died at his house of Kilmaine, in the Isle of Skye, John Mackinnon of that ilk, *i. e.* the old Laird of Mackinnon, in the 75th year of his age, leaving issue two sons and a daughter, Charles, Lachlan, and Margaret, all born after the 71st year of his age. He used to say he hoped God would not take him off the earth but on the field of battle, when fighting for his king and country. He frequently retired to the cave in which the Prince, and he himself and his lady, dined just before the Prince's leaving Skye in his skulking, and there he would have entertained himself with laying down a plan for the Restoration, and with the execution thereof in theory, and then came home extremely well pleased.'

into the hands of that gentleman, who immediately came to Borodale, and paid the Prince a visit. Next day Angus Macdonald received a letter from his son-in-law, Angus Mackechan, residing in the Glen of Morar, informing him that a rumour was beginning to be whispered about of the Prince being concealed at Borodale, and offering for the acceptance of his royal highness a more secure asylum which he had prepared in Morar. The Prince sent Ranald Macdonald to survey and report upon the nature of this asylum, and next day sent out John to watch the motions of the military. The latter soon returned, with the alarming intelligence that a government ship had entered Lochnanuagh, being, it would appear, the same in which John Mackinnon was confined. Charles, without waiting for Ranald's return, set out with Glenaladale, Angus and John Macdonald, to Glen Morar; and on the way, at a place called Corry-bincabir, met Angus Mackechan, who informed them that young Clanranald had come to a place a few miles off, in order to conduct his royal highness to a retreat which he had prepared for him. Charles would gladly have gone immediately to put himself under the protection of young Clanranald, but the lateness of the hour determined him to prefer the Glen Morar asylum for that night, and go to the other place next day.

Borodale, who had gone on before as an advanced guard, learning, in the course of the night, that General Campbell, with several men-of-war and a considerable body of troops, had anchored near Loch Nevis, while Captain Scott had brought another party into the lower part of Arisaig, waited upon the Prince next morning (the 23d) with that alarming intelligence. The situation of the Prince was now in the highest degree critical. He seemed in a great measure surrounded by his enemies; for they, having become aware of his landing amongst the estuaries formerly mentioned, had drawn a cordon of troops along from the head of Loch Hourn, the most northerly, to the head of Loch Shiel, the most southerly, so as to leave him scarcely any chance of escape on the land side. The cordon consisted of single sentinels, planted within sight of each other, who permitted no one to pass unchallenged. By night, large fires were lighted, between which the men continually passed to and fro, so as to leave no place for more than a few minutes at a time unvisited. It was now impossible for the Prince to join young Clanranald, for the troops were interposed. To remain where he was seemed equally dangerous, as the enemy might be expected gradually to close in upon him, and make his capture almost a matter of certainty.

Feeling the necessity of using great caution, he now parted with Angus Macdonald and Angus Mackechan, and taking with him only Glenaladale, Lieutenant John Macdonald (Glenaladale's brother), and the other John Macdonald, son of Angus of Borodale, that the party might be as little conspicuous as was consistent with his safety, he set out at eleven in the forenoon, and by mid-day reached the top of a hill called Scoorveig, at the eastern extremity of Arisaig, where he stopped to take some refreshment, while one of his attendants (John Macdonald, brother to Glenaladale) went to Glenfinnin for intelligence, and to appoint two men stationed there to join the Prince that evening on the top of a hill called Swerninck Corrichan, above Loch Arkaig, in Locheil's country. The Prince soon afterwards set out, with his two remaining friends, and about two o'clock came to the top of a hill called Fruighvain. Here, observing some men driving cattle, Glenaladale walked forward to inquire the reason, and soon after returned with the intelligence that they were his tenants flying before the approach of a strong body of troops, who had come to the head of Loch Arkaig, to prevent the Prince from escaping in that direction. It was of course unadvisable to pursue that route, and the wanderers immediately despatched a messenger to Glenfinnin, which was only about a mile off, to recall Glenaladale's brother and the two men who were to have gone to Loch Arkaig. Glenaladale likewise sent a man to a neighbouring hill for Donald Cameron of Glenpean, an honest farmer, who had removed thither with his effects on the approach of the soldiers, and who, from his acquaintance with the country, promised to be an excellent guide. While they waited the return of these messengers, one of the tenants' wives, pitying the condition of her landlord, came up the hill with some new milk for his refreshment. The Prince, perceiving her approach, covered his head with a handkerchief, and assumed the appearance of a servant who had got a headache. The day was excessively warm, and the milk, of course, grateful to the palate of a wayworn traveller; but Glenaladale used afterwards to confess that he could as well have spared the officious kindness of the good woman. It was with some difficulty, moreover, that he could get her dismissed without the pail in which she had brought the milk, so as to enable him with safety to give the Prince a share more suitable to his real than his supposed rank.

The messenger who had been sent to Glenfinnin soon after returned, without having found Glenaladale's brother or the two men (they having run off towards the place where they expected to find the party), but brought intelligence that a hundred of the Argyle militia were approaching the very hill on which the Prince was stationed. On this alarming news, the terrified party dislodged, without waiting for Glenpean, and set forward on their perilous journey. About eleven at night, as they were passing through a hollow way between two hills, they observed a man coming down one of the hills towards them; upon which Charles and young Macdonald stepped aside, while Glenaladale advanced to discover whether he was friend or foe. This person turned out to be the very individual they were most anxious to see, Donald Cameron of Glenpean, who had made all haste to overtake them after receiving their message. Glenaladale immediately brought him to the Prince, who had lodged one night in his house soon after the battle of Culloden, and to whom he now recounted all he knew regarding the position of the king's troops. As desired by the messenger, Donald had brought all the provisions he could gather; but the whole consisted of only a few handfuls of oatmeal and about a pound of butter. Miserable as this fare was in quality and amount, it proved of great service during the next few days, while the party were passing through the guards.   The Prince no sooner saw it, than, having been previously almost famished, he ate heartily of it: for four days he got nothing but a little of the oatmeal and butter.[1]   It was probably to this period of his career that he alluded when, some weeks after, in passing into Badenoch to meet Locheil, he told a gentleman of the Keppoch tribe that he had come to know what a quarter of a peck of meal was, having once subsisted upon such a quantity for the better part of a week.[2]

Donald Cameron, assuming the character of their guide, now set forward with them through a road so wild and rugged, as to be almost impervious even in daylight.   Travelling all night with untiring diligence, they arrived next morning (July 24) at the top of a hill in the braes of Loch Arkaig, called Mamnan-Callum, from whence they could perceive their enemy's camp, distant about a mile.   Cameron knew that this hill had been searched the day before, and therefore conjecturing that it would not be again searched that day, he counselled that they should take up their abode there till the evening, and endeavour in the meantime to procure the refreshment of sleep. They reposed for two hours, after which the whole party, except the Prince, got up to keep sentry.   They had not been long awake, when they were alarmed by the appearance of a man at a little distance.   Cameron, on account of his acquaintance with the country and its people, was selected to approach and accost this person, who, to the great joy of the whole party, turned out to be Glenaladale's brother.   This gentleman had no sooner discovered, on the preceding day, that the Prince did not keep his appointment, than he began to wander, in a state of extreme alarm, through the country in search of either his royal highness or of intelligence regarding his fate.   The same apprehensions which he had entertained regarding the party, they had entertained regarding him; and it was now with sensations of the utmost pleasure that these unfortunate gentlemen

---

[1] Statement taken down from Donald Cameron by Bishop Forbes: *Lyon in Mourning.*
[2] *Lyon in Mourning*, viii. 1828.

mutually congratulated each other upon a meeting which they had so little reason to expect.

Charles remained with his trusty little band upon the hill Mam-nan-Callum all that day, without experiencing any disturbance from the soldiers. They set out about nine in the evening towards the south, and at one in the morning (July 25) came to Corrinangaul, on the confines of Knoidart and Loch Arkaig. Here Cameron hoped to fall in with and procure provisions from some of the people who had fled before the face of the encroaching soldiery. During this harassing and perilous march, the party had had no food but a little of Donald Cameron's oatmeal and butter, eaten without any form of cooking.

For two days the Prince had now been skirting along the interior of that chain of sentries which has been described as extending from Loch Hourn to Loch Shiel. In his dreary and stealthy night-journeys he could distinctly see the fires which marked the posts of the enemy, and even hear the stated cries of the sentinels, as they slowly crossed backwards and forwards. These fires were placed at brief intervals, and every quarter of an hour a patrolling party passed along to see that the sentinels were upon the alert. It seemed scarcely possible that the forlorn little party should evade or break from a toil whose meshes were at once so strong and so closely set. Yet the want of provisions, and the fear of being soon inextricably environed, rendered it imperatively necessary that they should make the attempt, though it were only to anticipate their fate.

This desperate enterprise being fixed for the succeeding night, Glenaladale and Glenpean ventured down to some sheilings in search of provisions, while the Prince and the other two Macdonalds remained upon the hill. The sheilings were found to have been abandoned, and the two commissaries returned without their errand. It was then judged proper to shift from their present situation to a secret place upon the brow of a hill at the head of Lochnaig, which was about a mile from the position of the troops, and where they might expect to spend the intervening day in greater security. Here they slept for some time.   After awaking, Glenpean and Glenaladale's brother were sent off to the hill above them in quest of food, while Glenaladale and the younger Macdonald watched over the Prince, who still remained asleep.   The commissaries did not return till the afternoon, when two small cheeses proved all that they had been able to procure throughout the country. This was very dry food; and as they did not know when they might get more, they were obliged to use it very sparingly.   To increase the mortification of the unhappy Prince, the commissaries reported that a troop of a hundred men were coming up the opposite side of the hill in search of the fugitive country-people, and that they possibly might light upon their place of concealment.

Under these distressing circumstances, it was Charles's wisest, or rather his only policy, to remain as closely concealed as possible.   Notwithstanding, therefore, that the soldiers searched very narrowly, and all round him, he kept perfectly close, with his company, till eight in the evening, when, the search being done, they set out at a quick pace towards the steep hill called Drumachosi.   In ascending this hill, immediately after passing the small camp in the valley, the Prince met a nearly fatal accident.   The night was very dark, the hill very steep, and the gentlemen went in a line, Donald Cameron first, the Prince next, after him Glenaladale, behind whom came the two John Macdonalds.   In crossing a small rivulet which gushed out of the hill, and glided over a precipice, Charles slipped a foot, and fell, and he would certainly have tumbled over the rock, and been dashed to pieces below, if Cameron had not seized him by one arm, and Glenaladale by the other, and so recovered him.[1]   On reaching the top of the hill, they discerned the fires of a camp directly in their front, which they thought they could scarcely shun.   Resolved, however, to make the attempt at all hazards, they approached the dreaded object till they could

---

[1] These particulars are given in a letter addressed by Glenaladale to Bishop Forbes, and which the bishop received in December 1749; a copy of which document is preserved in his collection in my possession.

actually hear the soldiers talking to each other. Then creeping up the next hill, they spied the fires of another camp, which also seemed to lie directly in their path. Here they at last determined to make the attempt.

Cameron at this juncture, with the true generosity of a High-lander, proposed to go forward himself, and *prove* the possibility of escape, before permitting the Prince to hazard his more precious person. 'If I get safe through,' he remarked, 'and also return safe, then you may venture with greater security, and I shall be all the better fitted to conduct you.' Be it remarked, he made this courageous proposal in the face of an omen which, though ridiculous enough, was perhaps sufficient to have unmanned a person who, with equal superstition, had not so noble or so exciting a cause to brace his nerves. He began to complain that his nose was *itchy*, a clear sign, he averred, that they had great dangers to go through. Charles, notwithstanding his perilous circumstances, could not help laughing at this fantastic alarm, though he must have been at the same time deeply impressed with admiration of the devoted-ness and real bravery of the Highlander.

Glenpean having put the passage to the proof, and, to the great joy of the company, returned in safety, the whole set forward, headed by him as guide. It was now about two o'clock in the morning, and the brilliancy of the fires was beginning to fade before the advancing lights of day. Betwixt the two posts which they intended to cross there was a small mountain stream, whose winter torrents had, in the course of ages, worn a deep channel among the rocks. Up this deep and narrow defile, at the moment when the sentinels were returning to the fires, and had their backs turned towards the place, the party crept upon all-fours, with the stealthy caution and quiet of a party of Indian savages. A few minutes sufficed to carry them to a place where they were completely screened from the observation of the enemy.

Having thus escaped from one of the greatest dangers which had yet environed him, Charles, whose spirits always displayed great elasticity, gaily addressed Glenpean with an inquiry about his nose. The good gentleman confessed it was a great deal better since they had passed the sentries, but that it was still 'a wee yeuky.' 'What! Donald,' cried the Prince gaily, 'have we still more guards to pass?'

After walking about two miles, they came to a place on the Glenelg side of the head of Loch Hourn called Corriscorridale, where, finding what they considered a well-concealed spot, they called a halt, and partook of some refreshments. As already mentioned, the commissariat was in a miserable state. Animal spirits, however, compensated every privation to Charles. Cutting a slice of cheese, which he covered with oatmeal, and seasoning that dry fare with a drink from the neighbouring spring, he contentedly stretched the form upon the cold ground, whose home, in the words of the old song, 'should have been a palace.' He passed the whole of the succeeding day in this place, without any improvement in his food.

It was now resolved, as the West Highlands had become so unsafe a place of residence, to repair northwards to a portion of the Mackenzies' country, which, on account of the loyalty of the inhabitants, had not been subjected to a military police. They decamped for this purpose about eight o'clock at night, when, to their indescribable alarm, they discovered that they had spent the day within cannon-shot of two of the enemy's posts, and that at this moment a company of soldiers was employed in their immediate neighbourhood in driving some sheep into a hut for slaughter. This, however, only hastened their march; and about three o'clock in the morning (July 27) they reached Glenshiel, a wild vale in the estate of the Earl of Seaforth. The little provision they had had being now entirely exhausted, Glenaladale and John Macdonald (Borodale's son) were sent out in search of supplies, while Charles remained behind, with Cameron and the elder Lieutenant Macdonald, Glenaladale's brother. While Glenaladale was inquiring among some country-people about a guide to conduct them to Poole-Ewe, where he understood that some French vessels had lately been

seen, a Glengarry man came running up, having been chased
by soldiers out of his own country, where they had killed his
father the day before.   Glenaladale knew this man at first sight,
and being aware that he had served in the Prince's army, and
was a trustworthy person, resolved to keep him in reserve as a
guide to Glengarry's country, in case he should not succeed
in his present quest.   Having then furnished himself with some
provisions, he returned to the Prince; and as soon as they had
refreshed themselves, the whole party retired to a secure place
on the face of an adjacent hill, in order to sleep.   Getting up
about four in the afternoon, they dismissed their faithful guide,
Cameron, who could no longer be of any service.   Soon after,
Glenaladale, observing the Glengarry fugitive passing in his way
back to his own country, slipped out of his den, and, without
disclosing his purpose, used arguments with the man to induce
him to remain in a by-place till such time as he could be sure
of a guide to Poole-Ewe.   He then returned to the Prince, who
approved of his precaution.   About seven o'clock, the man whom
he had employed to procure a guide to Poole-Ewe, brought
intelligence that the only French vessel which had been there
was gone, and that a guide could not have been procured, even
though that had not been the case.   Glenaladale immediately
dismissed the messenger, and brought this intelligence to the
Prince, whose course it was now resolved to change in the way
proposed.   Accordingly, the Glengarry man being introduced
to his royal highness, and having undertaken the office, the
whole party set out late at night towards the south, designing
to form a junction, if possible, with Locheil and some other
chiefs, who, it was understood, still remained secure even in the
vicinity of the enemy's forts.

Charles experienced at this juncture one of those remarkable
deliverances which induced so many of his adherents to believe
that his life was under the immediate and constant care of
Heaven.   Before proceeding very far on this night's journey,
Glenaladale, clapping his hands upon his side, declared he had
lost his purse.   As this contained forty guineas, which the

Prince had confided to him for the purchase of provisions, and which was the sole stock of the company, Glenaladale was extremely perplexed at the loss, and proposed to return to the place from whence they had just set out, in order to search for it. Charles opposed this measure, and used many entreaties to prevent it; but Glenaladale insisted upon the necessity of recovering what was so important to them, and accordingly went back along with the younger lieutenant, while the Prince, with Glenaladale's brother and the guide, remained behind to await their return. While Glenaladale was absent, Charles spied an officer and two private soldiers advancing under arms along the path which they had just left. Trembling with joy at so signal a deliverance, he and his friends retired behind a rock, where they could see the motions of the soldiers, without being seen by them. The men passed by, unconscious of the prize which had so nearly fallen into their hands. Though rejoicing in their own preservation, Charles and his two companions remained in a state of great anxiety for the safety of Glenaladale and his companion, who might chance to meet the enemy in their turn. On coming to their last resting-place, these two gentlemen found the purse, but, upon opening it, discovered, to their mortification, that the gold was gone. 'Reflecting,' continues Glenaladale's journal, 'that it might have been taken away by a little boy whom their landlord had sent with a present of milk to Glenaladale, and whom they had left at the place where the purse was forgotten, they went back a mile farther to their landlord's house, whose name was Gilchrist Macrath,[1] and through his means got the boy to restore all

---

[1] Glenaladale speaks only of having obtained provisions from this Macrath, while the Prince remained in hiding at a distance. In Mr Home's History, a somewhat different account is given, I know not on what authority. The whole passage in that work is as follows: 'After having crossed the line of posts, Glenaladale, thinking the West Highlands a very unsafe place for Charles, resolved to conduct him to the Ross-shire Highlands, amongst those Mackenzies who had remained loyal, and therefore were not visited with troops. These Mackenzies, Glenaladale thought, would not betray Charles; and the person whom he pitched upon to confide in was Sir Alexander Mackenzie of Coul. Charles and his attendants, setting out for Ross-shire on foot, suffered greatly in their journey from want of provisions; and when they came to the Braes of Kintail, inhabited by the Macraws, a barbarous people, among whom there were but few gentlemen, necessity obliged them to

back, which he did to a trifle.' Fortunately, in returning to
the Prince, they took a different route, and thus escaped the
little party of soldiers, who must otherwise have met them.
When the company was once more reunited, they joined heartily
in returning thanks to God for their safety. Charles was now
so thoroughly impressed with a belief of his immunity from
danger, that he said he 'scarcely believed he could be taken
though he had a mind to it.'

They travelled all the remainder of the night, till they came
to a hill-side above Strathcluanie, where, choosing a secret place,
they rested till three o'clock in the succeeding afternoon
(July 28). Then setting out again, they had not walked above
a mile along the hill-side, when they were alarmed by hearing
several shots fired on the top of the hill, which they rightly
judged to be occasioned by the soldiers chasing and murdering

call at the house of one Christopher Macraw. Glenaladale, leaving Charles with the
French officer at some distance, went to Macraw's house, and told him that he and two
of his friends were likely to perish for want of food, and desired him to furnish them with
some victuals, for which they would pay. Macraw insisted upon knowing who his two
friends were, which Glenaladale seemed unwilling to tell. Macraw still insisted; and
Glenaladale told him at last that it was young Clanranald and a relation of his. Notwithstanding the consequence of the persons, Macraw, though rich for an ordinary Highlander,
made Glenaladale pay very dear for some provisions he gave him. Having received the
money, he grew better humoured, and desired Glenaladale and the other two to pass the
night in his house; which they did. In the course of the conversation they talked of the
times, and Macraw exclaimed against the Highlanders who had taken arms with Charles,
and said that they and those who still protected him were fools and madmen; that they
ought to deliver themselves and the country from distress, by giving him up, and taking the
reward which government had offered. That night a Macdonald, who had been in the
rebel army, came to Macraw's house: at first sight he knew Charles, and took an opportunity of warning Glenaladale to take care that Christopher should not discover the quality
of his guest. Glenaladale desired this man, who seemed so friendly and so prudent, to
give him his opinion, as he had traversed the country, what he thought was the safest place
for Charles, mentioning at the same time his scheme of carrying him to the country of
the Mackenzies; which Macdonald did not approve, saying that there were some troops
got among the Mackenzies, and that he thought their country by no means safe; but that
he had passed the former night in the great hill of Corado, which lies between Kintail and
Glenmorriston; that in the most remote part of that hill, called Corambian, there lived
seven men upon whom the Prince might absolutely depend, for they were brave and faithful, and most of them had been in his army. As Charles wished to get nearer Lochaber
and Badenoch, where Locheil and Cluny were, he resolved to go to Corambian. Next
morning he and his attendants set out, taking Macdonald for their guide;' &c. It is
possible that Glenaladale omitted or slurred over this circumstance, out of delicacy to
Macraw, or Macrath, who seems to have behaved on the occasion in a manner very
uncharacteristic of the genuine Highlander.

the poor people who had fled thither with their cattle! They now steered their course northward, and late at night reached the top of a high hill betwixt the Braes of Glenmorriston and Strathglass, where they lodged all night, the Prince reposing in an open cave, so narrow as not to permit him to stretch himself. This was one of the most uncomfortable nights he had as yet spent. The rain had fallen heavily and incessantly during the whole of the preceding day, and he was of course wet to the skin. No fire could be had to dry him. Without food, and deprived of sleep by the narrowness and hardness of his bed, the only comfort he could obtain was the miserable one of smoking a pipe.

The Glengarry man now informed the party of a band of skulkers who, he knew, haunted this neighbourhood, and were, he thought, likely to prove efficient friends to the Prince, in whose army they had served. These were the famous *Seven Men of Glenmorriston,* usually represented as robbers, but who only were so in a modified sense. As persons engaged in the Rebellion, they had seen their little possessions given as a prey to the spoiler; they had also seen seventy of their fellow-dalesmen recompensed for surrendering, by being sent as slaves to the colonies. Rendered desperate, they had entered into an association of offence and defence against the duke and his army, binding themselves by solemn oath never to yield, but to fight on any particular emergency to the last drop of their blood, and never, till the day of their death, to give up their arms. At first they were seven in number—namely, Patrick Grant, a farmer, commonly called Black Peter of Craskie; John Macdonnell, *alias* Campbell; Alexander Macdonnell; Alexander, Donald, and Hugh Chisholm, brothers; and Grigor Macgregor. Afterwards, in the course of their marches with the Prince, an eighth, Hugh Macmillan, joined them, and took their oath.[1] They lived at this time a wild life amongst the

[1] The adventures in connection with the Glenmorriston men are here for the first time minutely and faithfully described, the information being derived from the Rev. Mr Forbes's reports of conversations he had, in 1751, with Patrick Grant, the chief of the party (*Lyon in Mourning,* from p. 1660 to p. 1703).

mountains, supplying themselves with necessaries chiefly by bold attacks upon the military parties, from whom they often retrieved cattle and other spoil.

As some specimens of the doings of these men—About twenty days before the Prince joined them, seven private soldiers, journeying from Fort Augustus to Glenelg with some provisions, particularly wine and wheaten bread, which were carried on the backs of two horses, were, at a rough part of the way, attacked by four of the Glenmorriston men, the two Macdonnells and Alexander and Donald Chisholm, who, firing, shot two of the men dead. The others ran off, leaving their guide to shift for himself; and the assailants then buried the slain men, let loose the horses, and carried the hampers to their cave. Some days after, meeting one Robert Grant, a native of Strathspey, who went about for the purpose of informing on all the men he could discover to have been in the Rebellion, they shot him dead, and cutting off his head, placed it upon a tree in a little wood near the high-road in Glenmorriston, where it long remained as a terror to similar evil-doers. Three days after this violent act, they met a herd-boy, who informed them that the cattle belonging to an uncle of Patrick Grant had been driven off by a large party of soldiers; and the tale was soon confirmed by their observing the cattle moving along a part of the road from Fort Augustus to Glenelg, about eight miles from the former place, and near the hill of Lundy. The seven men made all speed to over-take the military party, and on getting within hearing, called out to them, in the most threatening manner they could assume, not to advance one step farther, but to leave the cattle to them, and be gone. The officers, three in number, drew up their party as for resistance, and sent one Donald Fraser, a militia-man, to learn what they wanted, and to order them to surrender, and take advantage of the royal protection. To this Patrick Grant answered, that nothing but the cattle would satisfy them, and that they would fight to their last breath rather than surrender. They also hinted at friends whom they had in the rear.   The officers, apparently staggered at their boldness, and knowing how dangerous a few enemies were amidst the neighbouring rocks, did not attempt to fight with them, but ordered the cattle to be driven forward.   The seven men then made a lateral movement, and commenced a running fire, two by two, with some effect.   Still, the cattle and the soldiers moved on.   The assailants then went forward to a narrow and dangerous pass, where, taking up a strong position, they gave their fire with such effect, that the men, terrified at this unusual kind of warfare, fell into confusion, and many fled.   The officers then sent a second message, but with the same result, and strange to say, the affair ended by the men being allowed to carry off the cattle, together with a horse laden with provisions.[1]

It was into the hands of such men that the Prince was now to pass.   The proposal of the Glengarry man being acceded to, he set out at three in the morning of the 29th, with Glenaladale's brother, to seek for them, and, if possible, negotiate for their receiving the distressed party under their care, without the Prince being mentioned.   The two messengers were successful.   The Glenmorriston men agreed to receive the party (the chief of whom they understood to be Glenaladale), and it was arranged that the fugitives should repair to a cave called Coiraghoth, in the Braes of Glenmorriston, where the men engaged to meet them by a particular hour.   Charles accordingly set out with his attendants for this place, where they found, at the time of their arrival, only three of the men —namely, the two Macdonnells and Alexander Chisholm. Glenaladale went forward to converse with them, and hinted that he had young Clanranald in his company.   They professed that they would be very glad to see young Clanranald, and take all possible care of him.   They were then brought out to meet the party; but they had no sooner set eyes upon the person who was to pass for young Clanranald, than they knew

---

[1] This story, as well as the two preceding, was reported by Patrick Grant himself to the Rev. Mr Forbes in 1751; and its truth was attested by the Donald Fraser mentioned in it, who happened to be in Edinburgh at the same time.

him to be the Prince. He was received by them with the greatest demonstrations of fidelity and kindness, and conducted to their cave, where, at Charles's request, they took an oath, administered by Glenaladale, in the dreadful terms then customary among the Highlanders—'that their backs should be to God, and their faces to the devil, that all the curses the Scriptures did pronounce might come upon them and all their posterity, if they did not stand firm to the Prince in the greatest dangers, and if they should discover to any person, man, woman, or child, that the Prince was in their keeping, till once his person should be out of danger.' This oath they kept so well, that not one of them spoke of the Prince having been in their company till a twelvemonth after he had sailed to France. Charles proposed that he and Glenaladale should take a like oath of fidelity to the men—namely, that if danger should come, they should stand by one another to the last drop of their blood; but the men refused to take this pledge from the Prince and Glenaladale.

Charles now broke a fast of about forty-eight hours by a refreshment of mutton, butter, and cheese, with some whisky. Next day, the other four, who had been absent in search of provisions, returned with a dead deer and a live ox. These men also knew the Prince at first sight, and took the same oath with the rest. They killed the ox in his presence. They still wanted bread, and only had a little salt; but fresh water was supplied to them in abundance by a spring which glided through the cave.

On his arrival at the cave, Charles, who was always anxious to limit the number of those to whom he trusted himself, said he was perfectly well satisfied with the three men as a guard, and hinted that, in case he should wish to shift his quarters, it might not be necessary to wait for the return of the other four. On this being communicated to the three men, they (being unable to speak a word of English) desired Glenaladale to inform his royal highness that they could not comply with such a proposal, in consequence of the oath they had taken

to keep by each other, and that if the Prince wanted them
to be useful to him, which they would gladly be with all their
heart, he behoved to trust himself to the other four as well as
to them. In this there was not only high principle towards
their comrades, but a prudential consideration of what was
best for the Prince; for, by remaining together, they could
better keep watch around their position, and allow of the
detachments necessary for obtaining provisions.

When the four men had taken the oath, Charles told the
whole seven that they were the first privy council he had had
sworn to him since the battle of Culloden, and that he should
never forget them or theirs 'if ever he came to his own.'
Hereupon one of them hinted to him that a priest who used
to come amongst them in Glenmorriston frequently had told
them that King Charles II., after his restoration, was not very
mindful of his friends. Their guest said he was heartily sorry
for that, and hoped he should act differently: for this he gave
them his word, the word of a Prince.

Three days of repose and good nourishment in Coiraghoth
recruited the Prince considerably, and being afraid to stay
too long in any one place, he and his attendants shifted their
quarters (August 2) to another and equally romantic cave
about two miles off, named Coirskreaoch. Here, after taking
some food, and planting sentries at proper points of outlook,
they made up a bed of heath for the Prince in a small recess
resembling a closet opening from the cave. He remained in
this cave four days; when, hearing that one Campbell, a captain
of militia, and factor to the Earl of Seaforth, was encamped
within four miles of him, he thought proper to remove. On
the evening of the 6th, he and his attendants set out in a
northerly direction, and by break of day on the 7th, they had
passed the height of the country, and come in upon Strathglass,
a district belonging to 'The Chisholm.'[1] In the evening, two
of the men who had been left as scouts brought intelligence

[1] The chief of this small clan, whose residence is at Erchless Castle in Strathglass, is so
styled in the Highlands.

that they need be in no apprehension from the factor Campbell for that night; and they then repaired to a neighbouring sheiling, or hut, where, after kindling a fire, and taking some refreshment, they prepared a bed for the Prince, composed of sods with the grass uppermost, on which he slept soundly the whole night.

He remained in this place two days. During that time he despatched a messenger to Poole-Ewe, to learn with greater certainty if any French vessels had touched at Poole-Ewe, and if they were still there. That he might be ready to take advantage of these vessels, if any such should be at Poole-Ewe, he resolved to draw somewhat nearer to the west coast. His messenger, before setting out, had been appointed to bring him intelligence to a particular place judged convenient for the purpose. Early in the morning of the 9th, he and his friends and attendants, about a dozen persons in all, set out to the northward by an unfrequented moor-road, and came that night to a sheiling, where they halted for a few hours. At two o'clock in the morning of the 10th, they once more addressed themselves to their journey, and at noon came to Glencannich, where they passed the remainder of the day in a wood, and at night repaired to a neighbouring hamlet. At two o'clock in the morning they left this place, and climbed a hill called Peina-cherine, on the north side of Glencannich, where they passed the day, and sent off two of their party to obtain a fresh supply of provisions. This place, which is about forty Highland miles from Poole-Ewe, is the most northerly point which the Prince reached on the mainland.[1] At night they repaired to a sheiling, in which they remained two days, waiting for the return of the messenger. At the end of that time[2] the man rejoined them,

[1] So says Patrick Grant, in his report to the Rev. Robert Forbes. A cave is shewn in Glenstrathfarrar, to the north of Glencannich, as having been used by the Prince; but if Grant be correct, the Prince never was in Glenstrathfarrar, nor within the distance from it of seven miles.

[2] 'In Glencanna, upon Lammas day,' said Patrick Grant, 'the Prince spoke much to the praise of one of the daughters of the king of France, and drank her health, and made all the company do so likewise. Patrick does not remember her name; but the Prince told them that her hair was as black as a raven, and that she was a mighty fine agreeable lady,

with intelligence that the only vessel which had ever touched at Poole-Ewe had sailed again, leaving a couple of men, who had set out for Locheil's country in quest of the Prince. Anxious to know if these men had any despatches for him, he resolved to return towards Locheil's country, in order, if possible, to meet them.

They set out at night (August 13), and recrossing the Water of Cannich, and passing near young Chisholm's house, arrived about two in the morning at a place called Fassanacoill in Strathglass. Here it was thought proper to tarry, until scouts should bring back intelligence of the state of the country to the south, and if the search for him was over in that quarter, and the troops returned to Fort Augustus. While the scouts were absent, the party remained in a dense wood, completely concealed from the neighbouring people. They were supplied with provisions by one John Chisholm, a farmer, who had been in the insurgent army, but to whom they did not at first confide the secret of the Prince being of the party. Charles having at length expressed a wish to see Chisholm, Patrick Grant and another were despatched to bring him. They desired him to come along with them to see 'a friend whom they knew he would like well to see.' Apprehending from this that they had a person of some consequence with them, he said he had a bottle of wine which a priest had left with him, and he should be glad to take it along with him. 'What, John,' said Grant, ' have you had a bottle of wine all this time, and not given it to us before?' On coming into the presence of the Prince, John knew him at first sight. Patrick Grant, according to his own simple recital, put the bottle of wine into the Prince's hands,

being sweet-natured and humble; that he (the Prince) could not fail to love her, as he was sure she entertained a great regard for him, as did likewise the dauphin, whom the Prince commended much. Upon this John Macdonnell said : " As that lady is so good-natured, agreeable, and humble, would to God we had her here, for we would take the best care of her in our power, and, if possible, be kinder to her than to your royal highness." This made them all laugh heartily, and the Prince answered : " God forbid, for, were she here, and seized, to ransom her person would make peace upon any terms the Elector of Hanover would propose." They spoke upon this lady a whole hour without intermission.'—*From Reports of Conversations with Patrick Grant, by the Rev. R. Forbes*, 1752.

and requested him to drink to him, 'for,' said he, 'I do not remember that your royal highness has drunk to me since you came among our hands.' 'Accordingly, the Prince put the bottle of wine to his mouth, and drank a health to Patrick Grant and all friends. John Chisholm having received good payment for any provisions he had furnished, and finding that they had been purchased for the use of his Prince, immediately offered to return the whole price, and pressed the thing much; but the Prince would not hear of it at all, and ordered him to keep the money.' Chisholm took the same oath as the Glenmorriston men.

Some traits of the Prince's personal condition and conduct while with the Glenmorriston men, as reported by Patrick Grant, may be appreciated by those who still regard with a feeling of melancholy interest the tale of the last Stuart. His clothes, which were of the Highland fashion, were coarse, tattered, and squalid almost beyond description, and he constantly slept in them, seldom getting a clean shirt above once a fortnight. He continued, accordingly, to suffer from the annoyance which Malcolm Macleod described him as suffering from in Skye. He was also afflicted with a very distressing ailment of the bowels. Nevertheless, 'he bore up under all his misfortunes with great resolution and cheerfulness, never murmuring or complaining of the hardness and severity of his condition.' He was observed to make a practice of withdrawing himself every morning and evening to perform his devotions. 'Glenaladale,' said Patrick Grant, 'was interpreter between the Prince and us, and it was agreed upon that we should say nothing but what the Prince should be made to understand, and that the Prince should say nothing but what we likewise should be made to understand. By this means the Prince discovered that we were much addicted to common swearing in our conversation, for which he caused Glenaladale to reprove us in his [the Prince's] name; and at last the Prince, by his repeated reproofs, prevailed on us so far, that we gave that custom of swearing quite up.' Patrick Grant stated that the Prince walked so nimbly in the daytime, that few persons could hold out with him; but he did not travel so well by night, when, being unaccustomed to the rough and boggy ground on the Highland hills, he was constantly getting himself immersed in some deep hole, from which his companions had to draw him out. All the time he was with the Glenmorriston men, his appetite was observed to be good. When the party were at their meals, they sat in a circle, each having his morsel on his knee. The Prince would never allow them to keep off their bonnets when in his company—probably a precaution against his rank being detected, in the event of any hostile party approaching them before they were aware. He used to give directions about their homely cookery, and sometimes tended a roast himself.

It would appear that not exactly everything said by the men was interpreted to the royal wanderer. After he had parted with them, and got into new hands, conversing about these faithful adherents, he remarked that he had often heard them use the expression *Ho Sian*, which he supposed to be the name of one of them, and that certainly that person was the chief amongst them, since they addressed him so often. In reality, this expression was *Aos Ian*—'Hark you, John!'—which they often had occasion to use to John Macdonnell, one of the cleverest of their number, and to whose judgment they usually deferred in all important matters. It will amuse the reader to learn that Bishop Forbes, with true Jacobite feeling, adopted the mistaken phrase of the Prince, and applied it afterwards as a name to John Macdonnell, and wished him to hand it down to his children.

'Patrick Grant said that the Prince, when with them, used to declare that he had great confidence in the king of France as a true and fast friend; and that the king his father, and his own brother Henry, would risk all to save him. He used to say much in praise of Prince Henry, as one preferable to himself in all respects, and as one of the greatest spirits and activity.'

In due time the spies returned with intelligence that the troops had returned to their camp at Fort Augustus, and that there was consequently a prospect of the Prince being able to execute his design of crossing the Great Glen, and joining Locheil in Badenoch. They therefore set out at six in the morning of the 17th, and, travelling by an unfrequented road, at ten in the forenoon reached the Braes of Glenmorriston. Having passed the day on the top of a hill, they set out at night, but had not travelled above a mile, when they learned that a strong military party had been sent to the Braes of Glengarry in quest of the Prince. Upon this it was resolved to proceed no farther, until the motions of the enemy should be farther known; and they repaired to a neighbouring sheiling, where they passed the remainder of the night. In the morning of the 18th, three men were sent off towards Loch Arkaig, in Locheil's country, two of whom were to seek out, and, if possible, form an appointment for the Prince with Cameron of Clunes, while the other was to turn at Glengarry, and bring back intelligence of the movements of the party said to be in that district, so that Charles might perhaps be able to proceed, even while the meeting with Clunes was in the way of being arranged.

We have here a remarkable anecdote of the Prince, which may be best related in the language in which Mr Forbes has reported it from the mouth of Patrick Grant. When returned to Glenmorriston Braes, 'the Prince was pretty positive to proceed forwards sooner than the Glenmorriston men thought it safe for him, and they would by no means allow him to go, till they should think it safe for him so to do. In a word, the kind contention ran so high, that they threatened to turn their backs upon him, and to leave him, if he did not listen to their counsel, as they knew the country best, and what dangers might happen to him in it; and immediately insisted upon his taking some little refreshment and rest, and staying there as long as they judged it safe for him. But the Prince refused to eat or to drink, because they would not do as he desired. Upon this they plainly told him, that if he did not eat and drink heartily, he could not well hold out with the fatigues he was obliged to undergo in his present situation; that if he

2A

should happen to turn faintish by abstaining from meat and drink too long, and then danger should come nigh them, he would not be in a condition either to get away from it, or to act his part in any shape so well as he would wish to do; and therefore they urged him more than ever (as being absolutely necessary for him) to take some refreshment and rest; which accordingly he did. The Prince said: "I find kings and princes must be ruled by their privy council, but I believe there is not in all the world a more absolute privy council than what I have at present;" &c. They added, they had rather tie him than comply with him, so well did they know his danger. The Prince was at last obliged to yield the point, as he found them positive to the last degree, and as they assured him, if he complied with their requests in behalf of his safety, the enemy should not get within two miles of him without being discovered. This was the only time (said Patrick Grant) that we ever differed with the Prince in any one thing, and we were very sorry for it.' It is distressing to think that, on the very day when Charles was acting thus unreasonably with his humble but faithful followers on the Braes of Glenmorriston, the brave Balmerino and the gentle Kilmarnock were laying down their lives in his cause on the scaffold of Tower-hill.

While the party rested at this place, Patrick Grant and Alexander Chisholm went out to forage for provisions, and in the course of their walk met the Laird of Glenmorriston (Grant), who had been in the Prince's army, and had had his house burned and his lands pillaged in consequence. Glenmorriston asked them where they now lived, as they were seldom seen— what they were doing—and how did they obtain the means of subsistence. 'What is become,' said he, 'of the Prince? I have heard that he has passed the Braes of Knoidart.' Even to this gentleman, whom habit had trained them to regard with the greatest respect, they would not disclose any of their secrets, merely remarking, that as the enemy were plundering the country, it were a pity not to share in the spoil; and that they accordingly did so, and made a shift to live upon it. On their return to the Prince, they informed him of this interview, and said that, if his royal highness pleased, they would bring Glenmorriston to see him, he being a faithful and trusty friend. 'The Prince said he was so well pleased with his present guard, that he wanted none other; and that *he had experienced poor folks to be as faithful and firm as any men, rich or high, could be.*'[1]

On the 19th, the man who was to bring intelligence from Glengarry came back, reporting that that district was clear of troops. The Prince, therefore, with his party, now ten in number, set out in the afternoon, under the benefit of a fog, and

---

[1] Bishop Forbes's report of conversations with Patrick Grant. Some less authentic anecdotes of the Glenmorriston men have been circulated. It is stated that at the first introduction of the Prince to their fraternity, as they were sitting at dinner, one of them, with great tact, exclaimed: 'Ha, Dougal M'Cullony, I'm glad to see thee!' and welcomed him as an old acquaintance of his own order, being then uncertain if his rank could be safely confided to the rest. This story does not appear to be true, though it is certain that the men generally called the Prince by the name Dougal, for safety. It has also been stated that, to supply him with linen, they attacked some officers' servants travelling behind a military detachment, killed one of them, and seizing a portmanteau, brought it home to their cave. A still more questionable tale represents them as going in disguise to Fort Augustus, and bringing back newspapers for the Prince.

Another dubious tale, referring to nearly this period, may here be adverted to. A young man named Roderick Mackenzie, the son of a jeweller in Edinburgh, and who had been in the Prince's Life-guards, resembled him much in person. While skulking in the Braes of Glenmorriston, he was beset by a military party, and finding escape impossible, he assumed a bold air, faced the soldiers, and as they poured the shot into his body, exclaimed: 'Villains, you have killed your Prince!' The men, believing that they had secured the grand prize, cut off the head of the unfortunate youth, and brought it to Fort Augustus, where we have already seen that application was made to Macdonald of Kingsburgh to ascertain if he thought he could distinguish the head of the Prince detached from his body. It is said that the head was generally looked on as the head of the Prince, and that Duke William carried it to London along with him, in order to ascertain the fact with more precision. One Richard Morison, who had been the Prince's valet, now lay a prisoner in Carlisle; he was hastily summoned to London, and promised pardon on condition that he would truly declare if the head was that of his late master. Morison having fallen sick on his arrival, an interval ensued, during which the head became so putrid as to make recognition impossible, but Morison nevertheless secured his pardon. That there is some truth in this story we can scarcely doubt, yet it is suspiciously deficient in locality and date. I find that the Rev. Mr Forbes made inquiry respecting the circumstances, but never could obtain any certain particulars. A lady, however, informs me that she remembers, when a child, visiting, in their house at the head of Gray's Close, in the High Street of Edinburgh, two old ladies who were understood to be the sisters of this Mackenzie, and who enjoyed a small pension on that account. The effects of the incident in allaying the heat of the search for the Prince have obviously been much exaggerated; for it is within the ten days after the duke's departure from Fort Augustus, that we find the exertions made to capture him in Arisaig by means of the chain of posts.

passing through Glenmorriston and the minor vale of Glenluing, arrived late at night on the Braes of Glengarry. When they came to the Garry Water, it was found breast-deep with the rain ; nevertheless, they crossed it in safety, and ascending the hill for about a mile, tarried there for the remainder of the night in the open air, notwithstanding that it rained heavily. Early in the morning (August 20), the heavy rain still continuing, they advanced six Highland miles across hills and moors, and about ten in the forenoon came to the hill above Auchnasual, where the two messengers had been appointed to meet them on their return from Cameron of Clunes. They passed the day in a most inconvenient habitation, 'it raining as heavy within as without.'[1] Towards the afternoon, after they had begun to despair of the return of their messengers, and were deliberating what should be done, the two men came in, bringing a message from Clunes to Glenaladale, to the effect that he could not wait upon him immediately, but had directed that the party should lodge for that night in a certain wood two miles off, where he would meet them in the morning.

Two of the men, Patrick Grant and Alexander Macdonnell, were now despatched to reconnoitre their proposed lodging-place, and finding it suitable, they quickly returned to bring forward the party. Their provisions were now reduced to half a peck of meal, and they had starvation staring them in the face. By the greatest good fortune, Patrick shot a large hart at the place where they were to pass the night; so that when the Prince and the rest arrived, they had one of the finest meals they had as yet enjoyed.

They were this evening joined by Macdonnell of Lochgarry, who had been the commander of a regiment in the insurgent army; and early next day, as appointed, Cameron of Clunes came to them : both of these gentlemen lived in concealment in the neighbouring mountains. By them the Prince was conducted that afternoon (August 21) to a wood at the foot of Loch

Arkaig, where he and his party lay that night.   Here the Glen-morriston men left him, and returned to their own glen, all except Patrick Grant, who stayed behind, that the Prince might be enabled, when he should get a supply of money, to make, through him, a pecuniary acknowledgment of the services of the fraternity.   Grant accordingly waited for some days, and ultimately carried home with him twenty-four guineas, being at the rate of three guineas for each man.[1]

---

[1] The public may be anxious to know the subsequent history of these men.   How long they kept together, or pursued their wild mode of life, I have not ascertained: probably it was not later than July 1747, when the act of indemnity permitted all the less distinguished rebels to shew their faces once more in society.   In 1751, Grant informed Mr Forbes that Alexander Macdonnell and Alexander Chisholm were then dead.   Grigor Macgregor was taken some time after 'the troubles,' and imprisoned in Inverness, but had the good fortune to make his escape, and in 1751 was 'alive and in good health, and as ready for a good ploy as ever.'   The attack upon the soldiers and seizure of the cattle having excited much notice, Chisholm of Strathglass, on whose ground it had taken place, was incited to attempt to capture the Glenmorriston men, who were suspected of being the actors in that strange adventure; and accordingly, in November 1746, John Macdonnell was taken in his bed, and carried to Inverness.   He was kept there for many months, but at length liberated, there being no evidence against him, and the act of indemnity being then passed.

Patrick Grant, when Mr Forbes saw him in 1751, had come from the Highlands in a state of poverty, and ignorant of English, but determined on going abroad, and seeking out the Prince.   'If he be on the face of the earth,' said he, 'I 'll find him out, and, meet when we will, he and I shall never part again.'   It was with great difficulty that some rational people, into whose hands he fell, prevailed on him to give up this mad project.   While lingering in Edinburgh, he fell into company with the same Donald Fraser who had acted as a messenger between the officers and the Glenmorriston men.   Fraser reminded him jocularly that on that occasion Grant had taken from him a quarter of a pound of tobacco, which, he said, Patrick should now replace or pay.   'What!' said Patrick, 'repay you that!   No; you were an enemy then, and the tobacco was lawful spoil; I will never pay you for that.'   The company, all of them Jacobites, enjoyed this conversation very much.   Patrick Grant was pressed into the army in 1759, and served in North America.   At the peace of 1763, he returned to Glenmorriston with a Chelsea pension.

John Macdonnell, who had been one of the leaders of the outlawed fraternity, and whom the Prince had supposed to be called Os Ean, lived for many years after in the Braes of Glenmorriston.   In May 1754, 'John Macewan Vic-William, *alias* Macdonnell, some time residenter in Ballado in Glenmorriston,' was sentenced at Inverary to be hanged for theft and robbery; which sentence was carried into effect at Inverlochy on the 31st of the month (*Scots Magazine*, 1754, p. 202).   This man, on being apprehended, had given himself out as one of the Glenmorriston men who had protected the Prince, thinking that the identity of his name and locality would favour the imposture, and that the imposture would operate in his favour, in the event of his being brought to trial.   It had, in reality, that effect, for many gentlemen in the Highlands exerted themselves, after his condemnation, to save his life.   The rumour thenceforth became general in the north of Scotland that one of the Glenmorriston men, who had scorned the bribe of £30,000, was hanged for stealing a cow !   The tale has often been repeated, and lastly in the *Tales of a Grandfather*, published in 1830—so difficult is it to overtake any false allegation with a contradiction.   The real state

Charles now once more turned his thoughts to Cluny and Locheil, who, he understood, were living in a comparatively agreeable concealment in Badenoch, far to the south of the Great Glen of Albyn—that profound valley, filled with a chain of lakes and rivers, which has since become the bed of the Caledonian Canal. Clunes, however, informed him that it would not be safe for him to attempt to cross this water-pervaded glen, as every isthmus and ferry along its whole extent was guarded by the military. It was judged prudent that he should remain for the present near Loch Arkaig, and only send a messenger to apprise Locheil where he was, and to request him, if possible, to join him in his present retreat. One John Macpherson, or Maccoilveen, a tenant of Locheil, was accordingly engaged, and sent on this errand.

of the case, as above stated, appears in Mr Forbes's papers, being the result of a conversation in 1756 with Patrick Grant. It is added in the same place, that the real John Macdonnell was a Campbell, who, on removing to the property of Macdonnell of Glengarry, had, as was customary, taken the name of that chief. John was supported for some years by Mr Macdonald of Glenaladale; but at the death of that gentleman, he fell into poverty.

In 1762, we find Mr Macnab of Inchewen making an endeavour to raise some money amongst his Jacobite friends for John, whom he represents as then above sixty years of age, unable to work, and burdened with a sickly wife and a young family. Of the condition of the man at that time, we have an affecting picture in the following letter addressed by a Mr Mackenzie, teacher in Tain, to Mr Forbes: 'I happened to be two weeks ago in Strathglass, at the young Chisholm's house, and on the 25th ult., as I was walking alone by the river's side, I met an aged man, who saluted me, as is ordinary in the Highlands, and asked if I had snuff; which I answered by giving him my box, which introduced a parley. I inquired whence and who he was. He answered from Glenmorriston, and that his name is John Maccoilvee Eandue, or, if I pleased, John Macdonnell. I inquired if he knew Patrick Grant. He said very well, and that he had shared in the cause of Patrick's reputation; that he frequently attended, *summa fide*, his r——l master, ministering sometimes to his relief, and that the P——e called him often by the name of Os Ean. I told him, if he could find good credentials for what he advanced, his fidelity at the critical juncture might yet avail him. He declared that Patrick Grant and others of repute could vouch for what he asserted; that he was now reduced to great want. He had one of his sons, a pretty boy, with him, seeking service for him, having kept him a little time at a charity school. After giving him a mite to buy his supper, we bade good-night.' It appears that more than one sum of five pounds was raised in the south, and sent to this poor man, whose history is ultimately summed up in the following passage of a letter by Bishop Forbes, dated June 8, 1775: 'Poor Os Ean, upon failing of his usual moiety, joined the emigrants in August last, to seek a grave in a foreign land, where his merit is not known, and would be little regarded.'

Hugh Chisholm long survived this period. He was in Edinburgh for a considerable time between the years 1780 and 1790, and gave some account of the Prince's adventures with the Glenmorriston men to Mr Home. At this time he fell under the notice of Sir Walter

Locheil had about the same time learned that Charles was on the mainland, and not far to the north of the Great Glen, and from his fastness in Badenoch he sent his brothers, Dr Archibald and the Rev. John Cameron, by different roads, to obtain information respecting him.   The doctor had not travelled far when he met Maccoilveen, whom he eagerly questioned, but in vain. The faithful Highlander having been ordered to say not a word of the Prince to any but Locheil, would tell nothing but that he was going to that chief with intelligence of great consequence. Dr Cameron about the same time met with the two French officers who had landed in June from a vessel at Poole-Ewe, and had since then been wandering about in quest of the Prince. They had come from Dunkirk, with sixty other young men, who, with the gallantry of their nation, had formed themselves into a company of volunteers for the purpose of rescuing the commander of an enterprise which had excited their admiration. Four officers had landed, but two were immediately taken, and of these two, one named Fitzgerald was hanged at Fort William,

Scott, who gives the following particulars respecting him in the *Tales of a Grandfather:* 'Another, by name Hugh Chisholm, resided in Edinburgh, and was well known to your grandfather, then a young man at college, who subscribed with others to a small annuity, which was sufficient to render him comfortable.   He returned to his native country, and died in Strathglass some time subsequent to 1812.   He was a noble commanding figure, of six feet and upwards; had a very stately demeanour, and always wore the Highland garb. The author often questioned him about this remarkable period of his life.   He always spoke as a high-minded man, who thought he had done no more than his duty, but was happy that it had fallen to his individual lot to discharge it. . . . .   Hugh had some particular notions and customs.   He kept his right hand usually in his bosom, as if worthy of more care than the rest of his person, because Charles Edward had shaken hands with him when they separated.   When he received his little dole (I am ashamed of the small amount, but I had not much to give), which he always did with the dignity of one collecting tribute rather than receiving alms, he extended his left hand with great courtesy, making an excuse for not offering the other, "that it was sick."   But the true reason was, that he would not contaminate with a meaner touch the hand that had been grasped by his rightful Prince.   If pressed on this topic, or offered money to employ the right hand, he would answer with passion that, if your hand were full of gold, and he might be owner of it all for touching it with his right hand, he would not comply with your request.   He remained to the last day of his life a believer in the restoration of the Stuart family in the person of Charles Edward, as the Jews confide in the advent of the Messiah; nor could he ever be convinced of the death of his favourite Prince.   A scheme, he believed, was formed by which every fifth man in the Highlands was to rise—if that number was insufficient, every third man was to be called—" if that be not enough," said the old man, raising himself and waving his hand, " we will all gather and go together."   Such delusions amused his last years, but when I knew him he was perfectly sane in his intellects.'

on the charge of having been a spy in Flanders. After the
other two had wandered for some time about Seaforth's country,
Lochgarry, hearing that they had letters for the Prince, sent
Captain Macraw and his own servant for them, that they might
be sent to Locheil, since the Prince was not to be found. It
seems to have been in consequence of what Lochgarry did, that
they were now on their way to visit Locheil; though how two
such men could travel unharmed through such a country, it
seems difficult to understand.

Dr Cameron, with the two officers and the Prince's messenger,
returned to Locheil. The two gentlemen told the chief that
they had left their papers with Mr Alexander Macleod, one of
the Prince's aides-de-camp, whom they had met in Seaforth's
country—a story which proved quite true, but which now only
raised a suspicion of their being spies in the mind of Locheil,
more particularly as they had not mentioned any such thing
to Lochgarry. Locheil committed them to the charge
of a friend near by, that they might wait for further
orders.[1]

Dr Cameron once more set out in quest of the Prince, and at
Auchnacarry, the ruined seat of his family, he met his brother,
the Rev. John Cameron, who had gone before, by a different
way, on the same errand. The two joined, and, attended by
four servants, set out in a boat along Loch Arkaig. The Prince
at this time lived in a small hut, which had been built for his
accommodation in the wood betwixt Auchnasual and the end of
Loch Arkaig. The two gentlemen, seeing some men in arms
by the water-side, sent two of Clunes's children to learn who
they were, and finding they belonged to Clunes, sent the boat
for them. When they came, the two gentlemen dismissed their
own servants, under the pretence that they were going to skulk
for a few days in the wood, and feared lest a retinue should
attract observation. They then crossed the river, and proceeded
towards the hut in which they were informed the Prince resided.

[1] For these facts, and for the materials of this part of the narrative generally, I am
indebted to a journal by the Rev. John Cameron, transcribed in the *Lyon in Mourning*.

According to one account, Clunes joined their party as they were proceeding.

The approach of this party was the cause of a dreadful alarm to Prince Charles. He was at this time asleep, with one of Clunes's sons, while Patrick Grant kept watch. Patrick, usually so prompt and trusty, nodded at his post, and did not observe the approaching party till it was near at hand. Conceiving them to be a party of militia, he roused the Prince, to whom he proposed that they should instantly fly to the mountains. Charles refused to do this, and said it was much the safer course to remain in ambuscade, fire at the men when they came near, and take their chance for the rest. He and Grant, with young Cameron, therefore laid their pieces along the stones, and were preparing to fire, when, recognising the figure of Clunes, they became aware that there was no danger. Alarm was succeeded by great joy when Charles received two brothers of his beloved Locheil, and learned that that chief, though not yet quite cured of the wounds in his ankles, was in good health. He thrice audibly thanked God for the welfare of his friend. John Cameron describes his appearance and manners. 'He was barefooted, had an old black kilt coat on, philibeg, and waistcoat, a dirty shirt, and a long red beard, a gun in his hand, a pistol and dirk by his side. He was very cheerful, and in good health, and, in my opinion, fatter than when he was at Inverness. They had killed a cow the day before, and the servants were roasting some of it with spits. The Prince knew their names, spoke in a familiar way to them, and some Erse. He ate very heartily of the roasted beef and some bread we had from Fort Augustus, and no man could sleep sounder in the night than he.'

Next day (August 26) the party removed to a wood called Torvuilt, near Auchnacarry. Here Charles now expressed a wish to cross the Great Glen and join Locheil; but this measure was considered premature by his attendants, on account of a statement having recently appeared in the newspapers that he had gone over Corriearrack with Locheil and thirty men, which would undoubtedly occasion a vigilant search in those parts. He was advised to remain where he was, as in all probability the attention of the troops would be withdrawn from the north of the Great Glen, while it was directed with proportionate closeness to the south.   In the meantime, Dr Cameron ventured into Lochaber to procure intelligence, and Lochgarry posted himself upon the isthmus betwixt the east end of Loch Lochy and the west end of Loch Linnhe, to watch the motions of the troops.   The Prince at the same time despatched his faithful attendant Glenaladale, who had shared every privation with him for a month past, to await the arrival of any French vessels on the west coast, and to apprise him of such an event whenever it should take place.

Charles remained for some days in the neighbourhood of Auchnacarry.   Having heard from Archibald and John Cameron of the two French officers having had an interview with Locheil, he expressed a strong wish to see them ; but John Cameron represented the suspicions entertained of them by his brother, and recommended caution.   The Prince agreed that caution was necessary.   It was surprising, he said, that two men, strangers, without one word of Erse, could escape from the troops, who were always in motion in quest of himself and his followers.   Yet, as they might be true men, and have something of importance to communicate, he thought it proper that he should see them, only taking care that, if treacherous, they should have no advantage over him.   He therefore penned a letter to them, stating that he had retired to a remote country, where he had none in his company but one Captain Drummond and a servant ; as he could not come to see them without danger, he had sent Drummond, to whom, he said, they might communicate whatever they had to say to himself.   The officers were then sent for, and brought to a place near his retreat.   He went himself, as Captain Drummond, and delivered the letter. They had previously informed Locheil that they had never seen the Prince, and they now seemed to confirm the truth of what they had said, by not appearing to recognise him under the assumed character.   They communicated to him all their intelligence, which, however, was of little importance to him in his present situation.   They asked many questions regarding the Prince's manner of living, and heard his answers with great surprise.   After staying two days, they returned to Locheil. Charles afterwards sent to Mr Macleod for their papers, but found them to be of no use, being in cipher, addressed to the French ambassador, and unintelligible for want of the key.

Towards the end of August, they were disturbed in their retreat at Auchnacarry by intelligence of the approach of a large military party.   This proved to be a detachment of two hundred men, which had been sent from Fort Augustus, under the command of Captain Grant of Knockando, in consequence of intelligence that the Prince was skulking in that district. Charles was that day in a hut near the Water of Kiaig, a mile from Clunes.   It was eight in the morning when Mr John Cameron, who had fortunately gone out for intelligence, returned to give the alarm.   'I wakened the Prince,' says he, 'and desired him not to be surprised, for that a body of the enemy was in sight.   He, with the utmost composure, got up, called for his gun, sent for Captain Macraw, and Sandy, Clunes's son, who, with a servant, were doing duty as sentries about the wood.' The party mustered eight, and all made the resolution, if escape was impossible, to die fighting bravely with their arms in their hands.   They were fortunately able to get to the top of the mountain unobserved, by the cover of the wood.   That night they travelled to another hill called Mullantagart, which is prodigiously steep, high, and craggy.   On the top of that eminence they remained all day without a morsel of food.   In the evening one of Clunes's sons came, and told them that his father would meet them at a certain place in the hills somewhat distant with provisions.   Charles set out for this spot, which was only to be reached by the most difficult paths.   Toiling along amongst rocks and stumps of trees, which tore their clothes and limbs, they at length proposed to halt and rest all night.   But Charles, though the most exhausted of the party, insisted upon keeping their appointment with Clunes. After proceeding some way farther, Charles had to acknowledge himself utterly incapable of further exertion, when the generous Highlanders took hold of his arms and supported him along, though themselves tottering under their unparalleled fatigue. Almost perishing with hunger, and sinking under the dreadful exertions of the night, they at last reached their destination ; where, to their great relief, they found Clunes and his son, with a cow which they had killed and partly dressed. Here they remained for a day or two, till Lochgarry and Dr Cameron arrived with the welcome intelligence that the passes were not now so strictly guarded, and that the Prince might safely venture at least a stage nearer to Locheil.

The Prince now crossed Loch Arkaig, and was conducted to a fastness in the fir-wood of Auchnacarry, belonging to Locheil. Here he received a message from that chieftain and Macpherson of Cluny, informing him of their retreat in Badenoch, and that the latter gentleman would meet him on a certain day at the place where he was, in order to conduct him to their habitation, which they judged the safest place for him. Impatient to see these dear friends, he would not wait for the arrival of Cluny at Auchnacarry, but set out for Badenoch immediately, trusting to meet the coming chief by the way, and take him back. Of the journey into Badenoch, a long and dangerous one, no particulars have been preserved, excepting that, as the Prince was entering the district, he received from Mr Macdonald of Tullochcroam (a place on the side of Loch Laggan) a coarse brown short coat, a shirt, and a pair of shoes—articles of which he stood in great need.[1] It was on this occasion, and to this gentleman, that he said he had come to know what a quarter of a peck of meal was, as he had once lived on such a quantity for nearly a week. He arrived in Badenoch on the 29th of August, and spent the first night at a place called Corineuir, at the foot of the great mountain Benalder. This is a point considerably to the east of any

---

[1] *Lyon in Mourning*, MS., viii. 1828.

district he had as yet haunted. On the opposite side of Benalder, Loch Ericht divides Badenoch from Athole. It is one of the roughest and wildest parts of the Highlands, and therefore little apt to be intruded upon, although the great road between Edinburgh and Inverness passes at the distance of a few miles. The country was destitute of wood; but it made up for this deficiency as a place of concealment by the rockiness of its hills and glens. The country was part of the estate of Macpherson of Cluny, and was used in summer for grazing his cattle; but it was considered as the remotest of his *grassings*.

Cluny and Locheil, who were cousins-german, and much attached to each other, had lived here in sequestered huts or sheilings for several months with various friends, and attended by servants, being chiefly supplied with provisions by Macpherson younger of Breakachie, who was married to a sister of Cluny.[1] Their residence in the district was known to many persons, whose fidelity, however, was such, that the Earl of Loudoun, who had a military post at Sherowmore, not many miles distant, never all the time had the slightest knowledge or suspicion of the fact. The Highlanders did, indeed, during this summer exemplify the virtue of secrecy in an extraordinary manner. Many of the principal persons concerned in the

---

[1] After the breaking up of the scheme of resistance in May, and the occupation of Lochaber by the troops, Locheil was very anxious to get into Badenoch, 'not only,' says Mr Forbes, reporting the conversation of young Breakachie, 'for ease and safety to his own person, but likewise because he was not able to stand the melancholy accounts that were ever reaching his ears about the cruelties and severities committed by the military upon the people round about him in Lochaber. And even when Locheil was in Badenoch, such moving narratives were told him of the sufferings of his own people and others in Lochaber, as bore very hard upon him. One day, when accounts were brought to Locheil in Badenoch that the poor people in Lochaber had been so pillaged and harassed that they had not really necessaries to keep in their lives, Locheil took out his purse and gave all the money he could well spare to be distributed among such in Lochaber. "And," said Breakachie, "I remember nothing better than that Sir Stewart Threipland at that time took out his purse and gave five guineas, expressing himself in these words: 'I am sure,' said Sir Stewart, 'I have not so much to myself; but then, if I be spared, I know where to get more, whereas these poor people know not where to get the smallest assistance.'"'—*Lyon in Mourning*, vii. 1480.

The conversation, of which the above is a part, occurred in February 1750. Breakachie then assured Mr Forbes that he believed the Clan Cameron must have lost in all about three hundred men in the affair of 1745-6, having suffered considerably in all the three battles, as well as in the outrages committed by the military after Culloden.

insurrection had been concealed and supported ever since Culloden in those very districts which were the most thoroughly beset with troops, and which had been most ravaged and plundered.   After the escape of the Prince through the cordon between Loch Hourn and Loch Shiel in the latter part of July, the military powers at Fort Augustus seem to have scarcely ever got a ray of genuine intelligence respecting his motions.   His friends, all except the very few who attended him, were equally at a loss to imagine where he was, or how he contrived to keep himself concealed.   His enemies 'sometimes thought he had got himself removed to the east coast through the hills of Athole, and laid an embargo upon all the shipping from that quarter.   At other times they had information that he lurked in the shires of Angus or Mearns, and a search was made for him in the most suspected places of those shires; and particularly the house of Mr Barclay of Urie in Mearns, whose lady was aunt to Locheil by the father, and to Cluny by the mother, was most narrowly searched; while he was quite safe and unconcerned in Benalder.'[1]

Next day, August 30, Charles was conducted to a place called Mellaneuir, also on Benalder, where Locheil was now living in a small hut with Macpherson younger of Breakachie, his principal servant Allan Cameron, and two servants of Cluny.   When Locheil saw five men approaching under arms—namely, the Prince, Lochgarry, Dr Archibald Cameron, and two servants— he imagined that they must be a military party, who, learning his retreat, had come to seize him.   It was in vain to think of flying, even though the supposed military party had been more numerous, for he was still a cripple, in consequence of the wounds in his ankles.   He therefore resolved to defend himself as well as circumstances would permit.   Twelve firelocks and some pistols were prepared; the chief and his four companions had taken up positions, and levelled each his piece, and all was ready for saluting the approaching party with a carefully aimed

---

[1] Narrative written by Donald Macpherson, youngest brother of Cluny; preserved in Rev. Mr Forbes's collections, MS., in my possession.

volley, when Locheil distinguished the figures of his friends. Then, hobbling out as well as he could, he received the Prince with an enthusiastic welcome, and attempted to pay his duty to him on his knees. This ceremony Charles forbade. ' My dear Locheil,' said he, ' you don't know who may be looking from the tops of yonder hills; if any be there, and if they see such motions, they will conclude that I am here, which may prove of bad consequence.' Locheil then ushered him into his hovel, which, though small, was well furnished with viands and liquors. Young Breakachie had helped his friends to a sufficiency of newly killed mutton, some cured beef sausages, plenty of butter and cheese, a large well-cured bacon ham, and an anker of whisky. The Prince, ' upon his entry, took a hearty dram, which he pretty often called for thereafter, to drink his friends' healths ; and when there were some minced collops dressed with butter for him in a large saucepan that Locheil and Cluny carried always about with them, and which was the only fire-vessel they had, he ate heartily, and said, with a very cheerful and lively countenance : " Now, gentlemen, I live like a prince," though at the same time he was no otherwise served than by eating the collops out of the saucepan, only that he had a silver spoon. After dinner, he asked Locheil if he had still lived, during his skulking in that place, in such a good way; to which Locheil answered : " Yes, sir, I have, for now near three months that I have been here with my cousin Cluny and Breakachie, who has so provided for me, that I have still had plenty of such as you see, and I thank Heaven that your royal highness has come safe through so many dangers to take a part."'

Cluny, on reaching Auchnacarry, and finding Charles gone, immediately returned to Badenoch, and he arrived at Mellaneuir two days after the Prince. On entering the hut, he would have knelt; but Charles prevented him, and taking him in his arms, kissed him affectionately. He soon after said : ' I'm sorry, Cluny, that you and your regiment were not at Culloden ; I did not hear till lately that you were so near us that day.'

Cluny, finding that the Prince had not a change of linen,

caused his three sisters [1] to set about making some shirts for
him. They did so with good-will, and soon furnished him with
what was wanted. The gentlemen whom Charles here met for
the first time in his wanderings were, like all those he had met
previously, astonished at the elasticity of mind which he displayed in circumstances of so much discomfort and danger, and
under prospects, to say the least of them, so much less brilliant
than what had recently been before him.[2]

The day after Cluny's arrival, it was thought expedient that
there should be a change of quarters. They therefore removed
two Highland miles farther into the recesses of Benalder, to a
sheiling called Uiskchilra, 'superlatively bad and smoky,' as
Donald Macpherson has described it, but which the Prince
never once complained of. It may here be remarked, that the
precautions which Locheil and Cluny had formerly taken for
their safety, were much increased after the Prince had joined

[1] Isabel, widow of Mackintosh of Aberardar; Christian, wife of Breakachie; and Anne,
then unmarried, but afterwards the wife of Macpherson of Dalrady.

[2] The Rev. Mr Forbes appears to have taken down the following anecdote, illustrative of
the cheerfulness of the Prince under his distresses, from the mouth of Captain O'Neal, while
a prisoner in Edinburgh Castle, July 1747.

'O'Neal frankly owned that, in place of his being useful to the Prince, by endeavouring
to comfort and support him when dangers thickened upon them, the Prince had the like
good offices to perform to him, and that he frequently exerted himself, in different shapes,
to raise his spirits. One time, having nothing to eat for about two days but some mouldy
dirty crumbs in O'Neal's pocket, they luckily happened at last to come to a very mean
cottage, where they found only an old poor woman, who received them kindly, and gave
each of them two eggs and a piece of bear-bannock, but having not so much in her hut as a
cup of cold water to give them to put down their morsel, she told them that some lasses had
lately gone up the hill to milk the goats, &c., and that, if they would follow them, probably
they might have a drink of milk from them. The advice was very seasonable, and away
they went, the honest old woman directing them the way they should go. The Prince skipped
so speedily up the hill, that O'Neal could not keep up with him. The lasses gave them
plenty of milk, and poor O'Neal lay along upon the grass, being quite undone with fatigue
and fear. The Prince did all he could to rouse him up, but all to no purpose. At last the
Prince, turning from him, said : " Come, my lasses, what would you think to dance a
Highland reel with me ? We cannot have a bagpipe just now, but I shall sing you a
strathspey reel !" The dance went merrily on, and the Prince skipped so nimbly,
knacking his thumbs and clapping his hands, that O'Neal was soon surprised out of his
thoughtful mood, being ashamed to remain any longer in the dumps when his Prince had
been at so much pains to divert his melancholy. He was sure, he said, that the Prince
entered into this frolic merely on his account, for that there could be no dancing at his
heart, seeing at that time they knew not where to move one foot.'—*Lyon in Mourning*,
MS., i. 191.

them. Breakachie had formerly been intrusted with the power of bringing any one to them in whom he could trust; but no one was now introduced till after a council had been held, and formal permission given. Trusty watchmen were planted on the neighbouring hills, to give notice of the approach of any strangers or military; and Cluny even contrived to have spies in the Earl of Loudoun's camp.

After spending two or three uncomfortable days in the smoky sheiling, they removed to 'a very romantic and comical habitation, made by Cluny, at two miles' farther distance into Benalder, called the *Cage*. It was really a curiosity,' says Donald Macpherson, 'and can scarcely be described to perfection. It was situate in the face of a very rough, high, rocky mountain called Letternilichk, which is still a part of Benalder, full of great stones and crevices, and some scattered wood interspersed. The habitation called the Cage, in the face of that mountain, was within a small thick bush of wood. There were first some rows of trees laid down, in order to level a floor for the habitation, and as the place was steep, this raised the lower side to equal height with the other, and these trees, in the way of joists or planks, were entirely well levelled with earth and gravel. There were betwixt the trees, growing naturally on their own roots, some stakes fixed in the earth, which, with the trees, were interwoven with ropes made of heath and birch twigs all to the top of the Cage, it being of a round, or rather oval shape, and the whole thatched and covered over with fog. This whole fabric hung, as it were, by a large tree which reclined from the one end all along the roof to the other, and which gave it the name of the Cage; and by chance there happened to be two stones, at a small distance from [each] other, next the precipice, resembling the pillars of a bosom chimney, and here was the fire placed. The smoke had its vent out there, all along a very stony part of the rock, which and the smoke were so much of a colour, that no one could have distinguished the one from the other in the clearest day. The Cage was only large enough to contain six or seven persons, four of which number were frequently employed in playing at cards, one idle looking on, one baking, and another firing bread and cooking.'[1]

The hopes of the Prince for an escape from the country were still resting in the prospect of the arrival of some French vessel in the lonely estuaries of the west coast of Inverness-shire. He knew that Colonel Warren was exerting himself to fit out a small armament for this purpose; but still many accidents might occur to mar the consummation of the design. It would appear that two other plans were formed for getting him shipped away from Scotland. The Rev. John Cameron was despatched by his brother to Edinburgh, there to exert himself to get a vessel hired, to come to some appointed station on the east coast, and there lie in readiness to take the party on board. Such a vessel actually was provided; it went to the station; and Mr Cameron returned to Benalder to bring away the party, but found them gone.[2] Breakachie was also sent from Uiskchilra to find out John Roy Stuart, who was skulking somewhere in the country, with orders to go in company with John directly to the east coast, and there hire a vessel. Lest both schemes should fail, and the Prince be obliged to spend the winter in the Highlands, Cluny, who seems to have had a constructive genius, fitted up a subterranean retreat, boarded thickly all round, and otherwise provided against the severity of the season. But all of these precautions, though wisely taken, proved useless, in consequence of the arrival of Colonel Warren's expedition.

Two vessels of force, *L'Hereux* and *La Princesse de Conti*, had been fitted out by the exertions of this gentleman, who was promised a baronetcy by the old Chevalier in the event of his

---

[1] 'All about his royal highness, during his abode in Benalder of Badenoch, were Locheil, Cluny, Lochgarry, Dr Cameron, and Breakachie; one Allan Cameron, a young genteel lad of Calard's family, who was principal servant to Locheil; and four servants belonging to Cluny, particularly James Macpherson, his piper, Paul Macpherson, his horse-keeper, Murdoch and Duncan Macphersons. This Murdoch the Prince generally called *Murick*, who, and Paul, could speak no English, and were commonly employed in carrying provisions from Breakachie.'—*Donald Macpherson's Narrative*, MS.

[2] This gentleman, being now left to shift for himself, made his way back to Edinburgh in disguise, and at last got off in the same coach with Lady Locheil and her children for London, on which occasion the lady passed for a Mrs Campbell. They all got safely to France.

bringing off the Prince. Setting sail from St Malo in the
latter part of August, they arrived in Lochnanuagh on the 6th
of September. Next day four gentlemen, including Captain
Sheridan, son of Sir Thomas, and a Mr O'Beirne, a lieutenant
in the French service, landed to make inquiry about the Prince,
and were received by Macdonald of Glenaladale, who had taken
his station in that part of the country for the purpose of communicating to Charles any intelligence of the arrival of French
vessels. He now lost no time in setting out to the neighbourhood of Auchnacarry, expecting there to find Cameron of
Clunes, who was appointed to be a medium for forwarding the
intelligence to the Prince wherever he might then be. When
Glenaladale arrived at the place where he expected to see
Clunes, he found that gentleman removed he knew not whither,
in consequence of some alarm from the military, who had
destroyed his hut. Being himself altogether ignorant of Charles's
present hiding-place, Glenaladale was thrown by this accident
into a state of great perplexity and distress, for he reflected that,
if the Prince did not quickly come to Lochnanuagh, the vessels
might be obliged to sail without him. He was wandering about
in this state of mind when he encountered an old woman, who
chanced to know the place to which Clunes had withdrawn.
Having obtained from her this information, he immediately
communicated with Clunes, who instantly despatched the faithful Maccoilveen to convey the intelligence to Cluny, that it
might be by him imparted to the Prince. Glenaladale then
returned to inform the French officers that they might expect
ere long to be joined by the royal wanderer.

Charles, meanwhile, had despatched Cluny and Dr Cameron
on some private business to Loch Arkaig. Travelling in a very
dark night through the outskirts of Badenoch, these two gentlemen, by great good-fortune, met and recognised Maccoilveen,
as he was proceeding with his message. Had they missed him,
they would have gone on to Loch Arkaig, and as Maccoilveen
would have communicated with none but Cluny, it would not
have been till after their return, and probably then too late,

that Charles would have heard of the arrival of the vessels.   It thus appears that he was favoured by two remarkable chances in obtaining this important information, without either of which the design of his embarkation would have probably been defeated.

Cluny, though he now turned back with Dr Cameron, was so anxious to forward the good news to the Prince, that he immediately procured a trusty man, one Alexander Macpherson, son of Benjamin Macpherson in Gallovie, to run express with it to the Cage.   He and Cameron arrived there about one in the morning, September 13, when they found the Prince already prepared to start on his journey.   They immediately started, and before daylight, had reached their former habitation in Uiskchilra.

From the place where he met Maccoilveen, Cluny had also sent off a messenger, one Murdoch Macpherson, a near relation of Macpherson of Invereshie, to stop young Breakachie on his mission to the east coast, and to desire him to return to the Prince's quarters.   'The said Murdoch came to Breakachie when going to bed;[1] and then Breakachie's lady, one of Cluny's sisters, finding out the matter, began to talk of her dismal situation, of having so many children, and being then big with child.   Upon which Breakachie said: "I put no value upon you or your bairns, unless you can bring me forth immediately thirty thousand men in arms ready to serve my master!"

'Instantly Breakachie set out on his return to the Prince, and took along with him John Roy Stuart (whom the Prince used to call the *Body*), but did not allow John Roy to know that the Prince was in Badenoch, but only that they were going to see Locheil, &c.   When the Prince heard that Breakachie and John Roy Stuart were coming near the hut Uiskchilra, he wrapped himself up in a plaid and lay down, in order to surprise John Roy the more when he should enter the hut.   In the door of the hut there was a pool or puddle, and when John Roy

---

[1] The original language of the narrative by Donald Macpherson (*Lyon in Mourning*, vii.) is here used.

Stuart just was entering, the Prince peeped out of the plaid, which so surprised John Roy, that he cried out : " O Lord ! my master ! " and fell down in the puddle in a faint.

' Breakachie likewise brought along with him to Uiskchilra three fusees, one mounted with gold, a second with silver, and the third half-mounted, all belonging to the Prince himself, who had desired Breakachie to fetch him these pieces at some convenient time. When the Prince saw the fusees, he expressed great joy, saying : " It is remarkable that my enemies have not discovered one farthing of my money, a rag of my clothes, or one piece of my arms ; " an event which the Prince himself did not know till he came to Benalder, where he was particularly informed that all the above things were still preserved from the hands of his enemies.

' The Prince (as is already observed) arrived at his old quarters in Uiskchilra, in his way to the ships, against daylight, on the morning of September 13, where he remained till near night, and then set off, and was by daylight, the 14th, at Corvoy, where he slept some time. Upon his being refreshed with sleep, he, being at a sufficient distance from any country,[1] did spend the day by diverting himself and his company with throwing up of bonnets in the air, and shooting at them, to try the three foresaid favourite fusees, and to try who was the best marksman ; in which diversion his royal highness by far exceeded. In the evening of the 14th he set forward, and went on as far as Uisknifichit, on the confines of Glenroy, which marches with a part of the Braes of Badenoch, in which last place he refreshed himself some hours with sleep ; and, before it was daylight, got over Glenroy, the 15th, and kept themselves private all day. As they were approaching towards Locheil's seat, Auchnacarry, they came to the river Lochy at night, being fine moonshine. The difficulty was how to get over. Upon this Clunes Cameron met them on the water-side, at whom Locheil asked how they would get over the river. He

---

[1] Meaning any inhabited district.

said : " Very well ; for I have an old boat carried from Loch Arkaig, that the enemy left unburned of all the boats you had, Locheil." Locheil asked to see the boat. Upon seeing it, he said : " I am afraid we will not be safe with it." Quoth Clunes : " I shall cross first, and shew you the way." The matter was agreed upon. Clunes, upon reflection, said : " I have six bottles of brandy, and I believe all of you will be the better of a dram." This brandy was brought from Fort Augustus, where the enemy lay in garrison, about nine miles from that part of Lochy where they were about to cross. Locheil went to the Prince, and said : " Will your royal highness take a dram ?" " Oh," said the Prince, " can you have a dram here ?" " Yes," replied Locheil, " and that from Fort Augustus too ;" which pleased the Prince much, that he should have provisions from his enemies. He said : " Come, let us have it." Upon this three of the bottles were drunk. Then they passed the river Lochy by three crossings : Clunes Cameron in the first with so many ; then the Prince in the second with so many ; and in the last Locheil with so many. In the third and last ferrying, the crazy boat leaked so much, that there would be four or five pints of water in the bottom, and in hurrying over, the three remaining bottles of brandy were all broken. When the Prince called for a dram, he was told that the bottles were broken, and that the common fellows had drunk all that was in the bottom of the boat, as being good punch, which had made the fellows so merry, that they made great diversion to the company as they marched along.

' After the morning of the 16th, the Prince arrived in Auchnacarry, Locheil's seat, where he was as ill off as anywhere else for accommodation, as the enemy had burned and demolished the place. All the 16th he stayed there, and set out at night, and arrived, the 17th, at a place called Glencamger, in the head of Loch Arkaig, where he found Cluny and Dr Cameron, who had prepared for him, expecting him. By a very great good chance, Cluny, understanding that he himself and others of them would be necessarily obliged to travel often betwixt

Badenoch and Locheil's country, and knowing that it was scarce possible for people travelling that way—even those that could be seen, and much less they that could not—to find provisions in their passage, as all was rummaged and plundered by the enemy, planted a small store of meal, carried from Badenoch, in the house of one Murdoch Macpherson, in Coilerig of Glenroy, a trusty man, and tenant to Keppoch, in the road and about half way, to be still a ready supply in case of need; from which secret small magazine he and Mr Cameron brought some with them as they went forward from Benalder, and had it made into bannocks against the Prince's coming to Glencamger; and when he and his company arrived, there was a cow killed; on which bannocks and beef, his royal highness, with his whole retinue, were regaled and feasted plentifully [1] that night. On the 18th, he set out from Glencamger with daylight, and upon the 19th arrived at the shipping; what was extant of the Glencamger bannocks and beef having been all the provisions till then.'

Cluny and Breakachie now took leave of the Prince, and returned to Badenoch, for it was the inclination of this chief to remain concealed in his own fastnesses, rather than seek a refuge on a foreign soil.

Before the arrival of the Prince, a considerable number of skulking gentlemen and others had assembled, in order to proceed in the vessels to France. Amongst these were young Clanranald, Glenaladale, Macdonald of Dalely and his two brothers. They had seized Macdonald of Barrisdale on the

---

[1] At this place the Prince gave the following letter to Cluny, acknowledging his services, and promising reward. Sir Walter Scott, who possessed the original, was good enough to communicate a copy in 1827. The Prince appears to have used *new style* in his date.

'Mr M'PHERSON of Clunie—

'As we are sensible of your and clan's fidelity and integrity to us during our adventures in Scotland and England in the years 1745 and 1746, in recovering our just rights from the Elector of Hanover, by which you have suffered very great losses in your interest and person, I therefore promise, when it shall please God to put it in my power, to make a grateful return suitable to your sufferings.   CHARLES, P. R.

'DIRALAGICH IN GLENCAMGIER OF LOCHARKAIG,
     8th September 1746.'

suspicion of his having made a paction with the enemy to deliver up the Prince; and this gentleman was actually carried to France, and there kept for a considerable time as a prisoner. Charles waited upwards of a day, to allow of a few more assembling, and he then (Saturday, September 20) went on board *L'Hereux*, accompanied by Locheil, Lochgarry, John Roy Stuart, and Dr Cameron.   From the vessel he wrote a letter to Cluny, informing him of his embarkation, and of the excellent state in which he found the vessels.   Twenty-three gentlemen, and a hundred and seven men of common rank, are said to have sailed with him in the two ships.   ' The gentlemen, as well as commons, *were seen to weep*, though they boasted of being soon back with an irresistible force.' [1]

The unparalleled tale of the Prince's wanderings is now concluded.   For upwards of five months he had skulked as a proscribed fugitive through the mountains and seas of the West Highlands, often in the most imminent danger of being taken, and generally exposed to very severe personal hardships; yet he eluded all search, and never lost his health or spirits in any fatal degree.   The narrowness of his own escapes is shewn strikingly in the circumstance of so many persons being taken immediately after having contributed to his safety.   The reader must have already accorded all due praise to the people who, by their kindness and fidelity, had been the chief means of working out his deliverance.   Scarcely any gentlemen to whom he applied for protection, or to aid in effecting his movements, refused to peril their own safety on his account; hundreds, many of whom were in the humblest walks of life, had been intrusted with his secret, or had become aware of it; yet, if we overlook the beggar-boy in South Uist, and the dubious case of Barrisdale, none had attempted to give him up to his enemies.[2]   Thirty thousand pounds had been offered in vain

---

[1] Newspaper report of the day.

[2] Much as we must admire the fidelity of the Highlanders on this occasion, it would not be just to human nature to say that it is without parallel. M. Berryer, the eloquent partisan of the fallen dynasty of France, at his trial, October 16, 1832, mentioned that, in

for the life of one human being, in a country where the sum
would have purchased a princely estate.   The conduct of the
Prince himself under his extraordinary dangers and hardships is
allowed by all who gave their personal recollections of it to
have been marked by great caution and prudence, as well as by
a high degree of fortitude, and a cheerfulness which no misery
could extinguish.   Perhaps the testimonies to his cheerfulness
are only too strong, and might lead to a conclusion different
from that intended by the witnesses—namely, that he was
scarcely considerate enough of the wretchedness which his
ambition had occasioned to others.   Here, however, we are met
by the strong expressions of sympathy for those injured in his
cause which he uttered in Raasay and Skye.   It is also expressly
stated by several of his fellow-adventurers that he put on
appearances of cheerfulness, on various occasions, to keep up
the spirits of those around him.   His conduct throughout his
wanderings appears, upon the whole, creditable to him, whatever
shades may have settled upon his character at a later period.
That it entirely pleased the gentlemen who associated with him,
is abundantly evident.   All of these, in their various narratives,
speak of him with the greatest admiration.   The Rev. John
Cameron, in particular, sums up with the following panegyric :
' He submitted with patience to his adverse fortune ; was
cheerful ; and frequently desired those who were with him to
be so.   He was cautious when in the greatest danger ; never
at a loss in resolving what to do.   He regretted more the
distress of those who suffered for adhering to his interest, than
the hardships and dangers he was hourly exposed to.   To
conclude, he possesses all the virtues that form the character
of *a true hero and a great prince.*'   The interest he bore in the
eyes of his followers could not be entirely the offspring of the
fascination of birth and rank.   I have a letter of Bishop

the Vendéan campaign of that year, the Duchesse de Berri changed her abode not less than
three or four times a week, that every change was known to eight or ten persons at least,
and yet, in the course of six months, not a single person betrayed the honourable confidence
reposed in him.

Mackintosh before me, in which that venerable person mentions that he had known many individuals who had gone out to fight for Prince Charles, but he never knew one who regretted having fought for him, or did not seem as if he would have gladly perilled life in his cause once more.

CHAPTER XXIX.

TRIALS AND EXECUTIONS.

'And statutes reap the refuse of the sword.'—JOHNSON.

LONG before Charles's escape, a multitude of his followers, less fortunate, had met a cruel and bloody death upon the scaffolds of England.   The necessity of terrifying the friends of the house of Stuart from all future attempts on its behalf, had reconciled the meek to a policy which there can be no doubt sprang immediately from the vengeful spirit of certain leading men, and particularly the Duke of Cumberland, who had only left the Highlands in order to seek new victims in the south.[1] Few, probably, would deny that the late attempt to disturb a settlement in which the bulk of the nation acquiesced, called for some exercise of the law's severity; but I would hope that, in the present age, there are still fewer who can behold unmoved a cruel death falling as a punishment upon men who, so far from being actuated by the spirit of crime, had been prompted by nearly as high a sense of duty as the mind of man ever experiences.   The conduct of the men themselves in their last moments, and the declarations they left behind them, form a most affecting commentary on the laws which dictate death and ignominy for offences of sentiment and opinion.

---

[1] The duke, after his return to London, continued to 'press for measures of the utmost severity.'—*H. Walpole to H. Mann.*

The officers of the English regiment taken at Carlisle were the first victims. Eighteen of these unfortunate gentlemen, at the head of whom was Mr Francis Townley, the colonel of the Manchester regiment, were tried before a grand jury at the court-house on St Margaret's Hill, Southwark, in the county of Surrey, on the 15th of July and four following days. All were condemned to death except one, and on the 29th of the month, four days after the arrival of the Duke of Cumberland at St James's, an order came to their place of confinement, ordering the execution, on the succeeding day, of nine who were judged to be most guilty—namely, Francis Townley, George Fletcher, Thomas Chadwick, James Dawson, Thomas Deacon, John Beswick, Andrew Blood, Thomas Syddall, and David Morgan; the other eight being reprieved for three weeks.

These ill-fated persons were roused from sleep at six o'clock in the morning of July 30, to prepare for death. The firmness which they displayed throughout the whole scene was very remarkable. Only Syddall was observed to tremble when the halter was put about his neck. When their irons had been knocked off, their arms pinioned, and the ropes adjusted about their necks, they were put into three sledges.

Kennington Common was the place appointed for their execution; and as the spectacle was expected to be attended with all those circumstances of barbarity awarded by the English law of treason, the London mob had assembled in extraordinary numbers to witness it. A pile of fagots and a block were placed near the gallows, and while the prisoners were removing from the sledges into the cart from which they were to be turned off, the fagots were set on fire, and the guards formed a circle round the place of execution. The prisoners were not attended by clergymen of any persuasion; but Morgan, who had been a barrister-at-law, read prayers and other pious meditations from a book of devotion, to which the rest seemed very attentive, joining in all the responses and ejaculations with great fervour. Half an hour was spent in these exercises, during which they betrayed no symptoms of irresolution, though their deportment was said to be perfectly suitable, at the same time, to their unhappy circumstances.   On concluding prayers, they took some written papers from their books and threw them among the spectators.   These were found to contain declarations to the effect that they died in a just cause, that they did not repent of what they had done, and that they doubted not but their deaths would be avenged, together with some expressions which were considered treasonable.   They likewise delivered papers severally to the sheriff, and then threw away their hats, which were found to contain other treasonable documents.   According to the atrocious treason law of Edward III., the culprits were only allowed to hang three minutes.   Then, with life scarcely extinct, their bodies were placed on a block, disembowelled and beheaded, the viscera being thrown into a fire.   The mutilated remains were conveyed back to prison on the sledges, and the heads of Townley and Fletcher were, three days after, affixed upon Temple Bar, while those of Deacon, Beswick, Chadwick, and Syddall were preserved in spirits, in order to be disposed in the same way at Carlisle and Manchester.

The mob of London had hooted these ill-fated gentlemen on their passage to and from their trials ; but at the execution they looked on with faces betokening at least pity for their misfortunes, if not also admiration of their courage.   A circumstance observed at the time excited much commiseration amongst the crowd. This was the appearance at the place of execution of Charles Deacon, a very youthful brother of one of the culprits, himself a culprit, and under sentence of death for the same offence, but who had been permitted to attend the last scene of his brother's life in a coach, along with a guard.   Another circumstance still more affecting came afterwards to the knowledge of the public. James Dawson, the son of a gentleman of Lancashire, and who had not completed his studies at St John's College, Cambridge, was attached to a young lady, of good family and fortune, at the time when some youthful excesses induced him to run away from college and join the insurgents.   Had he been acquitted, or if he could have obtained the royal mercy, the day of his enlargement was fixed by the parents of both parties to have been that of their marriage. When it was ascertained that he was to suffer the cruel death which has just been described, the inconsolable young lady determined, notwithstanding the remonstrances of her friends, to witness the execution; and she accordingly followed the sledges in a hackney-coach, accompanied by a gentleman nearly related to her, and one female friend. She got near enough to see the fire which was to consume her lover's heart, besides all the other dreadful preparations for his fate, without betraying any extravagant emotions. She also succeeded in restraining her feelings during the progress of the bloody tragedy. But when all was over, and the shouts of the multitude rang in her ears, she drew her head back into the coach, and crying: 'My dear, I follow thee, I follow thee—sweet Jesus, receive both our souls together!' fell upon the neck of her companion, and expired in the moment she was speaking.[1]

Bills of indictment having been found by the grand-jury of Surrey against the Earls of Kilmarnock and Cromarty, and Lord Balmerino, these three noblemen[2] were tried by the House of Peers on the 28th of July. This high solemnity was conducted with great state, a hundred and thirty-five peers being present. Lord Chancellor Hardwicke acted on the occasion as lord high steward, or president of the assembly. Westminster Hall was fitted up in a most magnificent manner for the purpose. Mr George Ross was appointed solicitor for Kilmarnock and Balmerino, and Mr Adam Gordon for Cromarty, at their own request.

When reciprocal compliments had passed between the prisoners and their peers, the indictments were read; to which Kilmarnock and Cromarty successively pleaded 'Guilty,' recommending themselves to the king's mercy. Balmerino, before *pleading* to his indictment—that is to say, before avowing himself guilty or not guilty—asked the lord high steward if it

---

[1] This incident became, in the hands of Shenstone, the subject of a well-known ballad.

[2] The Marquis of Tullibardine had died in the Tower, June 9, of an illness which had affected him throughout the whole time of the campaign.

would avail him anything to prove that he was not at the siege of Carlisle, as specified in the indictment, but ten miles distant. His grace answered that it might or might not be of service, according to the circumstances: but he begged to remind his lordship that it was contrary to form to allow the prisoner to ask any questions before pleading, and he therefore desired his lordship to plead. 'Plead!' cried Balmerino, who knew nothing of the technicalities of an English court, and whose bold blunt mind stood in no awe of this august assembly—'why, I am pleading as fast as I can.' The steward explained what was technically meant by pleading, and his lordship then pleaded 'Not guilty.' The court immediately proceeded to his trial, which was soon despatched. King's counsel were heard in the first place, and five or six witnesses were then examined in succession, by whom it was proved that his lordship entered Carlisle, though not on the day specified, at the head of a cavalry regiment, called, from his name, Elphinstone's Horse, with his sword drawn. The prisoners had no counsel, but Balmerino himself made an exception, which was overruled. The lord high steward then asked if he had anything further to offer in his defence, to which his lordship answered that he was sorry he had given the court so much trouble, and had nothing more to say. On this the lords retired to the House of Peers, and the opinion of the judges being asked touching the overt act, they declared that it was not material, as other facts were proved beyond contradiction. They then returned to the hall, where the steward, according to ancient usage, asking them one by one, beginning with the youngest baron: 'My Lord of ——, is Arthur, Lord Balmerino, guilty of high treason?' each answered, laying his right hand upon his left breast: 'Guilty, upon my honour, my lord.' The prisoners were afterwards recalled to the bar, informed of the verdict of the court, and remanded to the Tower till the day after next, when they were again to appear, in order to receive sentence. The House immediately broke up, and the prisoners were conveyed back to prison, with the edge of the axe turned towards them.

When the court met again on the 30th, the lord high steward made a speech to the prisoners, and asked each of them 'if he had anything to offer why judgment of death should not pass against them?' To this question Kilmarnock replied in a speech expressive of deep contrition for his conduct, and imploring the court to intercede with the king in his behalf. He represented that he had been educated in Revolution principles, and even appeared in arms in behalf of the present royal family; that having joined the insurgents in a rash moment, he had immediately repented the step, and resolved to take the first opportunity of putting himself into the hands of government; for this purpose he had separated himself from his corps at the battle of Culloden, and surrendered himself a prisoner, though he might easily have escaped. He, moreover, endeavoured to make merit with the court for having employed himself solicitously, during the progress of the insurrection, in softening the horrors which the war had occasioned in his country, and in protecting the royalist prisoners from the abuse of their captors. Finally, he made a declaration of affection for the reigning family, not more incredible from his past actions than it was humiliating in his present condition, and concluded with an asseveration that, even if condemned to death, he would employ his last moments in 'praying for the preservation of the illustrious House of Hanover.' The Earl of Cromarty pronounced a speech of nearly the same complexion, but concluding with a more eloquent appeal to the clemency of his majesty. 'Nothing remains, my lords,' he said, 'but to throw myself, my life, and fortune upon your lordships' compassion. But of these, my lords, as to myself is the least part of my sufferings. I have involved an affectionate wife, with an unborn infant, as parties of my guilt, to share its penalties; I have involved my eldest son, whose infancy and regard for his parents hurried him down the stream of rebellion; I have involved also eight innocent children, who must feel their parent's punishment before they know his guilt. Let them, my lords, be pledges to his majesty, let them be pledges to your lordships, let them be pledges to my

country, for mercy; let the silent eloquence of their grief and
tears, let the powerful language of innocent nature, supply my
want of eloquence and persuasion; let me enjoy mercy, but no
longer than I deserve it; and let me no longer enjoy life than I
shall use it to efface the crime I have been guilty of. Whilst I
thus intercede to his majesty, through the medium of your lordships, let the remorse of my guilt as a subject, let the sorrow of
my heart as a husband, let the anguish of my mind as a father,
speak the rest of my misery. As your lordships are men, feel
as men; but may none of you ever suffer the smallest part of
my anguish. But if, after all, my lords, my safety shall be found
inconsistent with that of the public, and nothing but my blood
can atone for my unhappy crime; if the sacrifice of my life,
my fortune, and family is judged indispensably necessary for
stopping the loud demands of public justice, and if the bitter
cup is not to pass from me, not mine, but thy will, O God, be
done!'

The mind of Balmerino was superior to such humiliation.
When the question was put to him, he pleaded that an indictment could not be found in the county of Surrey for a crime
laid to be committed at Carlisle in December last, in regard
that the act ordaining the rebels to be tried in such counties as
the king should appoint, which was not passed till March, could
not have a retrospective effect; and he desired to be allowed
counsel. On this the Earl of Bath asked if the noble lord at the
bar had had any counsel allowed him, and was answered that he
had never desired any. Balmerino replied that all the defences
which had occurred to him or his solicitor having been laid
before a counsellor, and by him judged to be trifling, he had
not chosen to give the court needless trouble; and that the
above objection had only been hinted to him an hour or two
before he was brought into court. After some altercation, the
court assigned Messrs Wilbraham and Forrester as counsel to
his lordship, and adjourned till the 1st of August.

Being again brought to the bar on that day, the Earls of
Kilmarnock and Cromarty were again asked if they had

anything to propose why judgment of death should not pass upon them, and answered in the negative. The lord high steward informed Balmerino, that having started an objection, desired counsel, and had their assistance, he was now to make use of it if he thought fit. His lordship answered that his counsel having satisfied him there was nothing in the objection that could do him service, he declined having them heard; that he would not have made the objection, if he had not been persuaded there was ground for it; and that he was sorry for the trouble he had given his grace and the peers. All the prisoners having thus submitted to the court, the lord high steward made a long and pathetic speech, which he concluded by pronouncing sentence of death. The prisoners were then withdrawn from the bar.

The Earl of Kilmarnock, who was only in his forty-second year, and extremely anxious for life, presented a petition for mercy to the king, and others to the Prince of Wales and the Duke of Cumberland, entreating them to intercede in his behalf with their royal father. The tenor of these petitions was much the same with that of his speech, equally penitential and humble. That to the duke contained a vindication of himself from some aspersions which had reached his royal highness, and which he understood had prejudiced that personage against him. It had been whispered that the earl was concerned in the order said to have been found in the pocket of a prisoner after the battle of Culloden, and that, moreover, he had exercised sundry other cruelties upon the prisoners in the hands of the insurgents. Both of these charges he distinctly denied, and probably with truth—though the assertion that he had voluntarily surrendered himself to government, contained in his speech and in the petition to the king, was afterwards confessed by himself to have been made only with the view of moving his majesty to mercy.

The Earl of Cromarty, whose share in the insurrection had been much less conspicuous, made similar efforts to obtain the royal grace. The countess went about, after the sentence had been pronounced, delivering petitions in person to all the lords of the cabinet council; and on the following Sunday she went in mourning to Kensington Palace to petition majesty itself. When the interesting condition of this lady is considered, it must be allowed that a more powerful mode of intercession could not have been adopted. She waylaid the king as he was going to chapel, fell upon her knees before him, seized the hem of his coat, and presenting a petition, fainted away at his feet. His majesty raised her up with his own hand, received her petition, and gave it to the Duke of Grafton, who was in attendance, desiring Lady Stair, who accompanied Lady Cromarty, to conduct her to an apartment where care might be taken of her. A day or two after, the Dukes of Hamilton and Montrose, the Earl of Stair, and several other courtiers, interceded with his majesty in the unfortunate earl's behalf.

Balmerino made no effort to save his life, but behaved after this period as one who had resigned himself to death, and who despises those who are to inflict it. On learning that his two brothers in affliction had made their applications for mercy, he said sneeringly, that as they had such great interest at court, they might have squeezed his name in with their own. A gentleman calling upon him a week after his sentence, and apologising for intruding upon the few hours which his lordship had to live, he replied: 'O sir, no intrusion at all—I have done nothing to make my conscience uneasy. I shall die with a true heart, and undaunted; for I think no man fit to live who is not fit to die; nor am I anyways concerned at what I have done.'

The Earl of Cromarty received a pardon on the 9th of August, and on the 11th an order was signed in council for the execution of Lords Kilmarnock and Balmerino. Cromarty and Kilmarnock had both alike hoped for pardon, and most persons expected that Balmerino would be the only victim. But the unfavourable impression which the Duke of Cumberland had received of the character of Kilmarnock, together with the prevarications upon which he had grounded his claims for mercy, determined, it was supposed, that he should also perish.[1]

Nothing could mark more strongly the different characters of these two unfortunate noblemen, than the way in which each respectively received intelligence of this final order. It was communicated to Kilmarnock by Mr Foster, a dissenting or Presbyterian clergyman, who had spent some time before with his lordship in religious exercises, and in some measure prepared his mind for the announcement. When the words of doom fell upon the ear of the culprit, their force was softened by the religious consolations with which they were accompanied, and Kilmarnock received them with tranquillity and resignation. Balmerino, on the contrary, heard the news with all the unconcern and levity with which he might have some months before received an order for some military movement. He was sitting at dinner with his lady when the warrant arrived; and on her starting up distractedly and swooning away, he coolly proceeded to recover her by the usual means, and then remarking that it should not make him lose his dinner, sat down again to table as if nothing had happened. He could even scarcely help chiding her for the concern she had displayed in his behalf, requesting her to resume her seat at table, and laughing outright when she declared her inability to eat.

On the Saturday preceding the Monday when the execution was to take place, General Williamson thought proper to give Kilmarnock an account of all the circumstances of solemnity

---

[1] The pardon of Lord Cromarty was accompanied by the condition that he should spend the remainder of his days at a particular spot in Devonshire. One of his daughters became Lady Elibank, and was an elegant and admired woman. One day, in company, when some discussion arose about the beauty of the long gloves she wore on her hands and arms, a lady sitting beside her said, that if her ladyship would excuse the remark, she would say that the hands and arms were sufficient to make any gloves look well. 'Ah! madam,' replied Lady Elibank, 'let us never be vain of such things; these hands and arms at one time washed the clothes and prepared the food of a father, mother, and seven other children.'

The child unborn at the time of the earl's condemnation became the wife of Sir William Murray of Ochtertyre. It is alleged, by all who remember Lady Augusta Murray, that she had the natural mark of an axe upon her neck, which was supposed to have been impressed by the labouring imagination of her mother.

and outward terror which would accompany it. Being informed that an executioner was provided, who, besides being expert, was *a very good sort of man*, he exclaimed : 'General, this is one of the worst circumstances that you have mentioned. I cannot thoroughly like, for a work of this kind, your good sort of men. One of that character must be tender-hearted and compassionate; and a rougher and less sensible person would be much more fit for the office.' Throughout this trying conversation, his lordship is said to have maintained as much composure as the least compassionate reader can do in perusing a mere report of it.

When the day arrived, and the general went to inform the earl that the sheriffs were waiting for the prisoners, his lordship, having completely prepared himself for the announcement, was not in the least agitated, but said calmly: 'General, I am ready, and will follow you.' In going down-stairs he met Balmerino at the first landing-place, who embraced him affectionately, and said: 'My lord, I am heartily sorry to have your company in this expedition.' The two unfortunate noblemen were then conducted to the Tower-gate, and delivered over to the sheriffs. As they were leaving the Tower, the deputy-lieutenant, according to custom, cried : 'God bless King George !' to which Kilmarnock made a bow, while the inflexible Balmerino exclaimed : '*God bless King James!*' The procession moved in a slow and solemn manner towards the house prepared for the reception of the lords. In their progress, some person was heard to exclaim from the surrounding crowd : 'Which is Balmerino?' when that nobleman instantly turned half round and politely said : 'I am Balmerino.'

The two lords were conducted to separate apartments, where they remained for some time in retirement with their friends. Kilmarnock received a message from Balmerino requesting an interview, which being consented to, Balmerino was introduced into Kilmarnock's apartment. The conversation which took place is reported by Mr Foster to have been precisely as follows:

Balmerino. My lord, I beg leave to ask your lordship one question.

Kilmarnock. To any question, my lord, that you shall think it proper to ask, I believe I shall see no reason to decline giving an answer.

Bal. Why, then, my lord, did you ever see or know of any order, signed by the Prince, to give no quarter at Culloden?

Kil. No, my lord.

Bal. Nor I neither; and therefore it seems to be an invention to justify their own murders.

Kil. No, my lord, I do not think that inference can be drawn from it; because, while I was at Inverness, I was informed by several officers that there was such an order signed 'George Murray,' and that it was in the duke's custody.

Bal. Lord George Murray! Why, then, they should not charge it upon the Prince.

His lordship then took his leave, embracing his fellow-prisoner with great tenderness, and saying to him: 'My dear Lord Kilmarnock, I am only sorry that I cannot pay all this reckoning alone. Once more, farewell for ever!'

Lord Kilmarnock spent nearly an hour after this conversation in devotion with Mr Foster and the gentleman attending him, and in making declarations that he sincerely repented of his crime, and had resumed at this last hour his former attachment to the reigning family. His rank giving him a precedence in what was to ensue, he was led first to the scaffold. Before leaving the room, he took a tender farewell of all the friends who attended him. When he stepped upon the scaffold, not-withstanding all his previous attempts to familiarise his mind with the idea of the scene, he could not help being somewhat appalled at the sight of so many dreadful objects, and he muttered in the ear of one of the attendant clergymen: 'Home, this is terrible!' He was habited in doleful black, and bore a countenance which, though quite composed, wore the deepest hue of melancholy. The sight of his careworn but still hand-some figure, and of his pale, resigned countenance, produced a great impression upon the spectators, many of whom burst into tears. The executioner himself was so much affected, that he was obliged to drink several glasses of spirits, to brace his nerves for the work before him.

From a rare contemporary print of the execution of Lord Kilmarnock, it appears that the scaffold was very small, and that there were not above six or seven persons upon it at the time his lordship submitted to the block. The block—which is still preserved and shewn in the Tower—is a piece of wood, considerably higher than may be generally supposed; the culprit only requiring to kneel and bend a little forward, in order to bring his neck over it. The cloth which originally covered the surrounding rails is turned up in such a manner as to give the spectators below an uninterrupted view of the scene. The culprit appears kneeling at the block, without his coat and waistcoat, and the frill of his shirt hanging down. The figures upon the scaffold, all except one of fearfully important character, are dressed in full dark suits of the fashion of King George II.'s reign, and most of them have white handkerchiefs at their eyes, and express, by their attitudes, a violent degree of grief.

It was a little after mid-day when the unhappy Kilmarnock approached the scene of his last sufferings. After mounting the scaffold, and taking leave of Mr Foster, who chose to retire, he proceeded to arrange his dress for the occasion. He informed the executioner, to whom he gave a purse containing five guineas, that he should give the signal for the descent of the axe about two minutes after he should lay his neck upon the block, by dropping a handkerchief. Then he went forward and knelt upon a black cushion, which was placed for the purpose before the block. Whether to support himself, or as a more convenient posture for devotion, he happened to lay his hands upon the surface of the block, along with his neck, and the executioner was obliged to desire him to let them fall down, lest they should be mangled or break the blow. Being informed that the neck of his waistcoat was in the way, he rose once more upon his feet, and with the help of one of his friends, Mr Walkingshaw of Scotstoun, had that garment taken off. This done, and the neck being made completely bare to the shoulder, he again knelt down as before. Mr Home's servant, who held a corner of the cloth to receive his head, heard him at this moment remind the executioner that he would give the signal in about two minutes. That interval he spent in fervent devotion, as appeared by the motion of his hands, and now and then of his head. Having then fixed his neck down close upon the block, he gave the signal, and his body remained without the least motion till the descent of the axe, which went so far through the neck at the first blow, that only a little piece of skin remained to be severed by the second.[1]

The head, which immediately dropped into the cloth, was not exposed in the usual manner by the executioner, in consequence of the prisoner's express request, but deposited with his body in the coffin, which was then delivered to his friends, and placed in the hearse. The scaffold was then cleaned, and strewed with fresh sawdust, so that no appearance of a former execution might remain to offend the feelings of Lord Balmerino ; and the executioner, who was dressed in white, changed such of his clothes as were bloody.

The under-sheriff then went to the apartment of Balmerino, who, upon his entrance, said that he supposed Lord Kilmarnock was now no more, and asked how the executioner had performed his duty. Being informed upon this point, he remarked that it was well done. He had previously maintained before his friends a show of resolution and indifference which astonished them, twice taking wine, with a little bread, and desiring them to drink him ' ain degrae ta haiven.' He now said : ' Gentlemen, I will detain you no longer, for I desire not to protract my life ;' saluted them with an air of cheerfulness, which drew tears from every eye but his own, and hastened to the scaffold.

The appearance of Balmerino upon this fatal stage produced

[1] Colonel Craufurd of Craufurdland in Ayrshire, next neighbour to the Earl of Kilmarnock at his seat of Dean Castle, thought it his duty to attend his lordship as a friend on this occasion ; for which simple act of courtesy and humanity he was, it is said, immediately cashiered.

a very different sensation among the spectators from that occasioned by Kilmarnock. His firm step, his bold and manly, though rough figure, but above all, his dress—the same regimental suit of blue, turned up with red, which he had worn throughout the late campaign—excited admiration rather than any emotion of pity. So far from expressing any concern about his approaching death, he even reproved the tenderness of such of his friends as were about him. Walking round the scaffold, he bowed to the people, and inspected the inscription upon his coffin, which he declared to be correct. He also asked which was his hearse, and ordered the man to drive near. Then looking with an air of satisfaction at the block, which he designated as his '*pillow of rest*,' he took out a paper, and putting on his spectacles, read it to the few about him. It contained a declaration of his unshaken adherence to the house of Stuart, and of his regret for ever having served in the armies of their enemies, Queen Anne and George I., which he considered the only faults of his life tending to justify his present fate.

Finally, he called for the executioner, who immediately appeared, and was about to ask his forgiveness, when Balmerino stopped him by saying : ' Friend, you need not ask forgiveness ; the execution of your duty is commendable.' Presenting the man with three guineas, he added : ' Friend, I never had much money ; this is all I now have ; I wish it were more for your sake, and I am sorry I can add nothing to it but my coat and waistcoat.' He took off these garments, and laid them upon his coffin for the executioner.

In his immediate preparations for death, this singular man displayed the same wonderful coolness and intrepidity. Having put on a flannel vest which had been made on purpose, together with a cap of tartan, to denote, he said, that he died a Scotsman, he approached the block, and kneeling down, went through a sort of rehearsal of the execution for the instruction of the executioner, shewing him how he should give the signal for the blow by dropping his arms. He then returned to his friends, took a tender farewell of them, and looking round upon the crowd, said : ' I am afraid there are some who may think my behaviour bold; but' (addressing a gentleman near him) 'remember, sir, what I tell you—it arises from a confidence in God, and a clear conscience.'

At this moment he observed the executioner standing with the axe, and going up to him, took the weapon into his own hand and felt its edge. On returning it, he shewed the man where to strike his neck, and animated him to do it with vigour and resolution ; adding, ' for in that, friend, will consist your mercy.' With a countenance of the utmost cheerfulness he then knelt down at the block, and uttering the following words—' O Lord, reward my friends, forgive my enemies, bless the Prince and the Duke, and receive my soul '—dropped his arms for the blow. The executioner, recollecting the deliberation of Lord Kilmarnock, was thrown out by the suddenness with which the signal was made in the present case, and gave his blow without taking accurate aim at the proper place. He hit the unfortunate nobleman between the shoulders, depriving him in a great measure, it was supposed, of sensation, but not producing death. It has been said by some who were present that Balmerino turned his head half round and gnashed his teeth in the face of the executioner. If this was the case, it fortunately did not prevent the man from recovering his presence of mind ; for he immediately brought down another blow, which went through two-thirds of the neck. Death attended this stroke, and the body fell away from the block. It was presently replaced by some of the bystanders, and a third blow completed the work.[1]

The fate of these unfortunate noblemen excited more public interest than perhaps any other transaction connected with the insurrection. The Jacobites, together with all such as were of a

[1] The day before his death, Balmerino penned a letter for the old Chevalier, reciting some of his services, stating that he was about to die ' with great satisfaction and peace of mind ' in the best of causes, and entreating that he would provide for his wife, ' so that she should not want bread, which otherwise she must do, my brother having left more debt on the estate than it was worth, and [I] having nothing in the world to give her.' The Chevalier attended to this request, by sending Lady Balmerino £60 in May 1747. Her ladyship survived, in straitened circumstances, for a few years.

bold temperament, applauded the behaviour of Balmerino ; while the Whigs, and all persons of a pious disposition, admired the placid and devout resignation of Kilmarnock. Every member of the community seemed to have chosen his favourite noble- man, in whose behalf he was prepared to talk, dispute, and even to fight. Innumerable publications appeared regarding them, informing the public of their history, and discussing their respective and very opposite characters.

James Nicholson, Walter Ogilvie, and Donald Macdonald, forming a selection from the Scottish officers taken at Carlisle, were the next victims of the offended state. They were con- demned at St Margaret's Hill on the 2d of August (along with Alexander Macgrowther, who was afterwards reprieved), and executed at Kennington Common on the 22d. Nicholson had kept a coffee-house at Leith, and was a man in middle life ; but Macdonald and Ogilvie were both young men of good families, the first a cadet of the family of Keppoch, and the other a native of the county of Banff. They were conducted to the place of execution in a sledge, guarded by a party of horse grenadiers and a detachment of the foot-guards. Macdonald and Nicholson appeared at the last solemn scene in their Highland dress. They spent an hour in devotion upon the scaffold, and were then executed in precisely the same manner with Francis Townley and his companions, except that they were permitted to hang fifteen minutes before being dismembered.

During the course of the two ensuing months many trials took place at St Margaret's Hill, without any of the prisoners receiving sentence of death. But on the 15th of November, judgment was pronounced upon no fewer than twenty-two persons, who had been convicted singly at different times ; and out of these, five were ordered for execution on the 28th of November. The names of the unfortunate persons were John Hamilton, Alexander Leith, Sir John Wedderburn, Andrew Wood, and James Bradshaw. Hamilton had been governor of Carlisle, and signed its capitulation ; Leith was an aged and infirm man, who had distinguished himself by his activity as a captain in the Duke of Perth's regiment; Sir John Wedderburn had acted as receiver of the excise duties and cess raised by the insurgents; Andrew Wood was a youth of little more than two-and-twenty, who had displayed great courage and zeal in the regiment of John Roy Stuart; and Bradshaw was a respectable and wealthy merchant of Manchester, who had abandoned his business, and spent his fortune in the cause for which he was now to lay down his life.

The execution of these gentlemen, which took place on the 28th of November, was attended with some affecting circumstances. Before nine o'clock in the morning, the servants of the keeper unlocked the rooms in which Sir John Wedderburn, Mr Hamilton, and James Bradshaw were confined, and uttering the awful announcement that they were to die, desired them to prepare themselves for the sheriff, who would immediately come to demand their persons. Although this was the first certain intelligence they had of their fate, they received it with calmness, and said they would soon be ready to obey the sheriff's request. They then took a melancholy farewell of a fellow-officer of the name of Farquharson, who had been respited, and was confined on the same side of the prison. The keeper's servants proceeded to rouse the rest of the doomed men, besides one of the name of Lindsay, who was as yet expected to share their fate. When they were told to prepare for the sheriff, Wood inquired if Governor Hamilton had been finally consigned to execution; and being answered in the affirmative, remarked 'that he was sorry for that poor old gentleman.' They were led into the fore-part of the prison, and provided with a slight refreshment. On account of the policy of government in granting reprieves at the last hour, Bradshaw still hoped to be pardoned, and endeavoured on this occasion to display a confident cheerfulness of manner. Wood, entertaining no such expectations, called for wine, and drank the health of his political idols, boldly assigning to each his treasonable title. Lindsay's reprieve arrived at the moment when he was submitting to have his hands tied, and produced such an effect upon his feelings as almost to deprive him of the life which it was designed to save. The sanguine Bradshaw, whose halter was just then thrown over his head, eagerly inquired 'if there was any news for him.' The answer was: 'The sheriff is come, and waits for you!'

They were drawn to the place of execution in two sledges, Bradshaw shedding tears of disappointment and wretchedness. They arrived at the foot of the fatal tree a little after noon, and the execution immediately took place in the midst of a vast crowd of spectators. The whole prayed for King James, and declared they did not fear death.

In the meantime, this bloody work had been proceeding with still greater energy at Carlisle and York, where it was thought necessary to try most of the insurgents who had been taken at Culloden by the forms of an English court of Oyer and Terminer, instead of placing them at the mercy of their countrymen, who were now too generally suspected of disaffection to be intrusted with a commission so important. Carlisle, the principal scene of their misdeeds in England, was selected for the trial of most of the prisoners, as a place more likely than any other to produce a jury of the stamp required by government. The result proved that, however much the Scottish people might labour under the imputation of humanity, their Cumbrian neighbours were not much tinged with that disloyal vice.

About the beginning of August, a herd—for such it might be termed—of these ill-fated persons was impelled, like one of their own *droves* of black-cattle from the Highlands, towards Carlisle,[1] where, on being imprisoned, they were found to amount to no less than three hundred and eighty-five. To try

---

[1] One Maclaren, a Balquhidder man, who had been concerned in cattle-dealing, and had often travelled this road before in more peaceful style, contrived to make his escape amongst the hills at the head of Dumfriesshire. There is in that district a deep hollow called the Marquis of Annandale's Beef-tub, because the Border thieves used to keep their stolen cattle in it. The road skirted along the top of the steep-down sides of this pit. Seizing a lucky moment, Maclaren enveloped himself in his plaid, and rolled down into the hollow, regardless of the shot which the soldiers sent after him. Being received into the mist which lay at the bottom, he was instantly lost to pursuit; and it is said that he spent that night in the *Crook Inn*, where the party had been the night before, and where he obtained concealment, although there was another party of soldiers in the house.

so many individuals, with the certainty of finding almost all of them guilty, would have looked something like premeditated massacre, and might have had an effect upon the nation very different from what was intended. It was therefore determined that, while all the officers, and others who had distinguished themselves by zeal in the insurrection, should be tried, the great mass should be permitted to cast lots, one in twenty to be tried, and the rest to be transported. Several individuals refused this extrajudicial proffer of grace, and chose rather to take their chance upon a fair trial. The evidences were chiefly drawn from the ranks of the king's army. Bills of indictment were found against a hundred and nineteen individuals.

The time which intervened between the indictment and trial of the Carlisle prisoners was occupied by the judges at York, where the grand-jury found bills of indictment against seventy-five insurgents there confined. In this city, not long before, the high-sheriff's chaplain had preached a sermon upon a very significant text (Numbers, xxv. 5) : 'And Moses said unto the judges of Israel, Slay ye every one his men that were joined unto Baal-peor.'

The judges again sat at Carlisle on the 9th of September, on which, and the two following days, most of the hundred and nineteen prisoners were arraigned. On the 12th, the grand-jury sat again, and found bills against fifteen more. Out of the *hundred and thirty-three* persons in all thus brought to the bar at Carlisle, *one* obtained delay on account of an allegation that he was a peer, *eleven* pled guilty when arraigned, *thirty-two* pled guilty when brought to trial, *thirty-seven* were found guilty, *eleven* found guilty, but recommended to mercy, *thirty-six* acquitted, and *five* remanded to prison to wait for further evidence.

The trials at York commenced on the 2d of October, and ended on the 7th, when, out of the seventy-five persons indicted, *two* pled guilty when arraigned, and *fifty-two* when brought to trial, *twelve* were found guilty, *four* found guilty, but recommended to mercy, and *five* acquitted. Seventy in all received sentence of death. The process of all these trials appears to have been extremely simple. Most of the prisoners endeavoured to take advantage of the notorious slavery in which the clans were held by their chiefs, by pleading that they had been forced into the insurgent army against their will; but their defence was in every case easily repelled.

Before the middle of October, an order was sent to Carlisle for the execution of *thirty* out of the ninety-one persons there imprisoned under sentence; *ten* at Carlisle on the 18th (October), *ten* at Brampton on the 21st, and *ten* at Penrith on the 28th. Of the first ten, one was afterwards reprieved. The names of the remaining nine were Thomas Coppock,[1] Edward Roper, Francis Buchanan of Arnprior,[2] Donald Macdonald of Kinlochmoidart,[3] Donald Macdonald of Tiendrish,[4] John Henderson,

---

[1] This person seems to have been a young student of theology, of indifferent character. He joined the Prince at Manchester, and was one of those left behind at Carlisle. There was a ridiculous report that the Prince, at Carlisle, on the return of the army, made him bishop of that see. One of the witnesses on his trial, improving on the story, said he had received that appointment from Hamilton, the governor of the town for the Prince. Yet this man is seriously spoken of in the contemporary journals as 'the titular bishop of Carlisle.' When condemned, seeing some of his companions weeping, he told them, with some exclamations not very appropriate to the clerical character, to cheer up—they would not be tried by a Cumberland jury in the other world.

[2] This is the gentleman alluded to at page 80 of this History. According to documents in the Rev. Mr Forbes's collection, he had not been concerned in the enterprise in any way, although undoubtedly in his private sentiments he was well affected to the house of Stuart. He was taken prisoner at his own house of Leny in Perthshire a short while before the battle of Culloden, and carried to Stirling Castle. There, and on his subsequent journey to Carlisle, he was treated by the military as a man who was a prisoner by mistake. Often, on the road, he was allowed to ride on in front, to order dinner at the inns for the party. At Carlisle, he was, to his own great surprise, put in irons in a dungeon; and when a friend remonstrated with the solicitor-general in his behalf, that officer said: 'Give yourself no trouble about that gentleman. I shall take care of him. I have particular orders about him; for he *must* suffer.' At his trial, nothing could be proved against him but that he had written an unsubscribed letter to the Highland army. An application was made in his favour at court, but without success. He died lamenting the neutral course which caution had induced him to take in the late civil war.

[3] This gentleman, the only Highland chieftain brought to the scaffold on this occasion, had been taken prisoner at Lesmahago, under circumstances narrated at page 208. He had never once drawn his sword in the insurrection, but had entertained the Prince at his house (immediately before the raising of the standard), and had afterwards gone on an embassy from him to the Laird of Macleod and Sir Alexander Macdonald of Sleat.

[4] This was the individual who had commanded the party at High Bridge at the beginning of the insurrection (see page 45), and who had afterwards been taken prisoner in such remarkable circumstances at Falkirk (page 239). The Rev. Mr Forbes, who was confined in the same room with him in Edinburgh Castle, speaks highly of him (*Lyon in Mourning*). 'He was,' says Forbes, 'a brave, undaunted, honest man, of a good countenance, and of a

John Macnaughton, James Brand, and Hugh Cameron. They were executed, according to order, with all those circumstances of barbarity which had already attended the former executions. Out of the ten who were appointed to die at Brampton, only six eventually suffered—James Innes, Patrick Lindsay, Ronald

strong robust make. He was much given to pious acts of devotion [being a Roman Catholic], and *was remarkably a gentleman of excellent good manners.* He bore all his sufferings with great submission and cheerfulness of temper.' In the course of the summer (1746), he was removed to Carlisle to undergo his trial ; and on the 24th of August we find him writing to his friend Forbes as follows : ' Dear sir, you have no doubt heard before now that our trials come on on the 9th of September ; may God stand with the righteous ! The whole gentlemen who came from Scotland are all together in one floor, with upwards of one hundred private men, so that we are much thronged. They have not all got irons as yet ; but they have not forgot me, nor the rest of most distinction ; and the whole will soon be provided. You 'll make my compliments to Lady Bruce and Mr Clerk's family, but especially to Miss Mally Clerk, and tell her that, notwithstanding my irons, I could dance a Highland reel with her. Mr Patrick Murray makes offer of his compliments to you, and I hope we 'll meet soon.'

The hope under which this letter was written was soon extinguished by the result of his trial. He was there found guilty, though, as happened in too many similar cases, upon evidence altogether false, and with reference to facts in which he had had no concern. His friends and legal agents had all entreated him to plead guilty, as the only chance of escape ; but he was too zealous a partisan of the house of Stuart to make the submission which that would have implied to the Hanover dynasty. On their pressing the advice with some importunity, he declared, in a tone which precluded all further argument, that rather than do so, he would submit to be taken and hanged at the bar before the face of those judges by whom he was soon to be tried.

It would appear that some effort was made by his wife and other friends to intercede in his behalf with the government. On the 28th of September, he writes that he is ' in good health, heart, and spirits.' ' If it is my fate,' says he, ' to go to the scaffold, I daresay that I 'll go as a Christian and a man of honour ought to do. But it is possible that a broken ill-used major may be a colonel before he dies.' All hope of pardon was soon proved to be vain : the government could not forgive one who had acted so remarkable a part in the late contest, and who had been taken with the blood of its servants still streaming from his sword. On the 17th of October, he addressed the following farewell letter to one of his friends in Edinburgh : ' My dear sir, I received yours yesterday, and as I am to die to-morrow, this is my last farewell to you. May God reward you for your services to me from time to time, and may God restore my dear Prince, and receive my soul at the hour of death. You 'll manage what money Mr Stewart is due me as you see proper ; for my poor wife will want money much, to pay her rents and other debts. I conclude with my blessings to yourself and to all the honourable honest ladies of my acquaintance in Edinburgh, and to all other friends in general, and in particular those of the Castle, and I am with love and affection, my dear sir, yours till death.   DONALD MACDONALD.'

It is impossible to contemplate the fate of a man like Tiendrish without a feeling of interest. In a speech which he delivered on the scaffold, he declared : ' It was principle, and a thorough conviction of its being my duty to God, my injured king, and oppressed country, which engaged me to take up arms under the standard and magnanimous conduct of his Royal Highness Charles, Prince of Wales : I solemnly declare I had no by-views in drawing my sword in that just and honourable cause.'

Macdonald, Thomas Park, Peter Taylor, and Michael Delard—one having died in prison, and the remaining three having been reprieved. Mercy was also extended to three of the ten who were designed for execution at Penrith. The names of those who suffered at the latter place were Robert Lyon,[1] David Home, Andrew Swan, James Harvie, John Robottom, Philip Hunt, and Valentine Holt.

In addition to the twenty-two persons thus executed in the west of England, other twenty-two suffered at the city of York —namely, on the 1st of November, Captain George Hamilton, Daniel Fraser, Edward Clavering, Charles Gordon, Benjamin Mason, James Main, William Collony, William Dempsy, Angus Macdonald, and James Sparks; on the 8th of the same month, David Roe, William Hunter, John Endsworth, John Maclean, John Macgregor, Simon Mackenzie, Alexander Parker, Thomas Macginnes, Archibald Kennedy, James Thomson, and Michael Brady; and on the 15th, James Reid. Eleven more were executed at Carlisle on the 15th of November—namely, Sir Archibald Primrose of Dunipace,[2] Charles Gordon of Terperse,

---

1 Mr Lyon was a young presbyter of the Episcopal Church of Scotland, and apparently connected with Perthshire. Under a strong religious sense of duty, particularly with regard to the suffering church to which he belonged, he had joined the expedition, in which he had borne all his own charges. The speech pronounced by him on the scaffold was reprinted in the 25th number of *Blackwood's Edinburgh Magazine*, on account of the well-expressed and well-reasoned view which it gives of the opinions by which a large portion of Prince Charles's adherents were actuated. In Mr Forbes's collection, besides a copy of this able document, there is one of a tenderer kind, a letter written to his mother and sister in contemplation of death—not seeking, but giving consolation. Mr Forbes has also bound up amongst his papers a copy of ' the Communion Office for the use of the Church of Scotland,' as ' authorised by K. Charles I., anno 1636,' being, as Mr Forbes takes care to note, ' the identical copy which the Rev. Mr Robert Lyon made use of in consecrating the Holy Eucharist in Carlisle Castle,' where ' he had the happiness to communicate above fifty of his fellow-prisoners, amongst whom were Mr Thomas Coppock, the English clergyman, and Arnprior.'

2 In Mr Forbes's collections is a letter written by Sir Archibald on the day of his death to his sister, commending to her care his wife and children, and regretting nothing but their condition and his own giving way so far to bad advice as to have pleaded guilty in the hope of pardon. ' This day,' he says, ' I am to suffer for my religion, my Prince, and my country: for each of these I wish I had a thousand lives to spend.' There is also a letter to the same lady, from Mr James Wright, writer in Edinburgh, enclosing the above, and dated ' Carlisle, November 15, four o'clock in the afternoon,' being a very short while after the death of Sir Archibald. ' Madam,' he says, ' your brother, who is no more, delivered me this immediately before he suffered. I waited on him to the last, and with

Patrick Murray, goldsmith in Stirling, Patrick Keir, Alexander Stevenson, Robert Reid, John Wallace, James Mitchell, Molineux Eaton, Thomas Hays, and Barnaby Matthews.

All these unhappy individuals are said to have behaved, throughout the last trying scene, with a degree of decent firmness which surprised the beholders. Every one of them continued till his last moment to justify the cause which had brought him to the scaffold, and some even declared that, if set at liberty, they would act in the same way as they had done. They all prayed in their last moments for the exiled royal family, particularly for Prince Charles, whom they concurred in representing as a pattern of all manly excellence, and as a person calculated to render the nation happy, should it ever have the good fortune to see him restored.

The lives of nearly eighty persons had now been destroyed, in atonement of the terror into which the state had been thrown by the insurrection. There yet remained, however, a few individuals, who, having excited the displeasure of government in a peculiar degree, were marked as unfit for pardon. The first of these was Charles Ratcliffe, younger brother to the Earl of Derwentwater who had been executed in 1716; he had himself only evaded the same fate, at that time, by making his escape from Newgate. This gentleman, taking upon himself the title of Earl of Derwentwater, was made prisoner, in November 1745, on board a French vessel on its way to Scotland with supplies for Prince Charles. After lying a year in confinement, he was brought up to the bar of the King's Bench (November 21, 1746), when the sentence which had been passed thirty years before was again read to him. He endeavoured to perplex the court regarding his identity, but it was established satisfactorily, it is said, by the barber who had shaved him when in the Tower in 1716, and he was condemned to be executed on the 8th of December. That day he came upon the scaffold in a handsome

some other friends witnessed his interment in St Cuthbert's churchyard. He lies on the north side of the church, within four yards of the second window from the steeple. Mr Gordon of Terperse, and Patrick Murray, goldsmith, lie just by him. God Almighty support his disconsolate lady and all his relations.'

dress, and conducted himself throughout the dreadful scene with a manly courage and proud bearing, which seemed to indicate that he held the malice of his enemies and the stroke of death in equal scorn.

The last of all *the martyrs*, as they were styled by their own party, was Lord Lovat. This singular old man was impeached by the House of Commons on the 11th of December; and his trial took place before the House of Peers on the 9th of March 1747 and several successive days. On this momentous occasion he seems to have exerted all the talents for dissimulation and chicanery which had, up to this time, served him so well. But the evidence produced against him was of that kind which no artifice could invalidate. He was confronted with a prodigious number of letters which he had written to the exiled family, and in particular to the young Chevalier, promising them his assistance, and negotiating the proposed elevation of his family to a dukedom. These had been procured from Murray of Broughton, who, preferring to live the life of a dog to dying the death of a man, had engaged with government to make all the discoveries in his power for his own pardon.[1] Lovat could make no effective stand against such documents, and although he uttered an exculpatory and palliative speech of some eloquence, he was condemned to die.

During the space of a week which intervened between his sentence and its execution, he maintained, without the least interruption, that flow of animal spirits and lively conversation for which he had been so remarkable throughout his life. He talked to the people about him of his approaching death as he would have talked of a journey which he designed to take, and

[1] The Rev. Mr Forbes relates that Dr Burton of York informed him that, in September 1746, he (Dr Burton) asked Mr Æneas Macdonald, then in confinement in London, 'his opinion of Mr John Murray of Broughton, particularly whether he entertained any fears about his turning evidence, as the common talk in London gave it out. Mr Macdonald's answer was, that he believed Mr Murray to be so honest between man and man, that in private ,life he would not be guilty of a dirty or dishonest action; but then (he said) he knew him to be such a coward, and to be possessed with such a fear of death, that (for his own part) he was much afraid Mr Murray might be brought the length of doing anything to save a wretched life.'—*Lyon in Mourning*, iii. 522.

he made the circumstances which were to attend it the subject
of innumerable witticisms and playful remarks. When informed,
in the forenoon before he left the prison, that a scaffold had
fallen near the place of execution, by which many persons were
killed and maimed, he only remarked : ' The mair mischief, the
better sport.' Though so weak as to require the assistance of
two persons in mounting the scaffold, he there maintained a
show of indifference to death. He felt the edge of the axe, and
expressed himself satisfied with its sharpness. He called the
executioner, gave him ten guineas, and told him to do his duty
with firmness and accuracy ; adding, that he would be very
angry with him if he should hack and mangle his shoulders.
He professed to die in the Roman Catholic faith, and spent
some time in devotion. As if to be in character to the very
last, he resigned his breath with the almost sacred words upon
his lips : ' *Dulce et decorum est pro patriâ mori.*'

CHAPTER XXX.

PRINCE CHARLES IN FRANCE.

' Come, poor remains of friends, rest on this rock.'
SHAKSPEARE.

THE vessels which had taken the Prince and his friends on
board at Lochnanuagh on the 20th of September, made a
prosperous voyage to the coast of France. It was the Prince's
original intention to proceed to Nantes ; and if he had done so,
he would probably have encountered a British squadron under
Admiral Lestock, then cruising off the coast of Bretagne.
Having altered his course, and been chased by two English
sloops of war, from which he escaped in a thick fog, he landed,
on Monday the 29th of September (10th October, new style),
at Roscoff, near Morlaix, whence he immediately wrote letters
to his brother and father, informing them of his safety.

He arrived in France full of the ideas which had possessed him immediately after the battle of Culloden respecting a new and effectual expedition to be fitted out in his behalf by the French government. It was his wish immediately to see the king, in order to use his influence with him to obtain a proper armament. He therefore stopped only two days at Morlaix for rest, and then set out for Paris. Near the city he was met by a band of young noblemen, headed by his brother, who, on meeting him, did not at first know him, on account of the change his person had undergone, being now 'broader and fatter' than formerly; but, on recognising him, fell on his neck and welcomed him in the most affectionate manner. The government had ordered the castle of St Antoine to be fitted up for his reception, but they were not disposed to receive him openly as the Prince Regent of Great Britain; and when he formally applied for an interview with the king, then at Fontainebleau, he was not favoured with a public audience, but permitted to come in only a comparatively private or incognito fashion. The truth is, the French had been unfortunate in the war, particularly by sea, and already the necessity of suing for peace with Great Britain was beginning to be apprehended. Louis was anxious to give the British court as little further cause of offence as possible. At the same time, it was not in his nature not to admire the singular career of the Prince, and to wish him well.

Charles, since he was not allowed a nominally public reception in his assumed character, resolved to make his visit, to appearance, as public as possible. He therefore went to Fontainebleau in a splendid equipage and magnificent dress, attended by other carriages, in which were the Lords Elcho and Ogilvie, Mr Kelly his secretary, the elder Locheil, and others of his principal friends. The king, who now saw him for the first time in his life, met him with a warm embrace, and a complimentary speech worthy of the nation most remarkable for such addresses: 'Mon très cher Prince, je rends grâce au ciel, qui me donne le plaisir extrême de vous voir arrivé en bonne santé, après tant de fatigues et de dangers. Vous avez fait voir que toutes les grandes qualités des héros et des philosophes se trouvent unies en vous ; et j'espère qu'un de ces jours vous recev'rez la récompense d'un mérite si extraordinaire.'[1] After staying a little while with the king, the Prince passed to the apartment of the queen, who also gave him a kind reception. The whole court flocked about him to pay their congratulations, and he and his friends that evening supped in the palace.

The government had already taken into consideration the sad state of the Scottish officers who had landed in France, and had ordered the sum of thirty-four thousand livres to be distributed amongst them according to their rank. Afterwards the further sum of twenty-eight thousand nine hundred was given to those officers who had landed with the Prince, young Locheil getting four thousand, his father three thousand, Lochgarry three thousand, John Roy Stuart three thousand, and others in proportion to their rank. The command of a regiment was also conferred on Lord Ogilvie. But when Charles made advances with respect to a new expedition, he found himself treated with coldness. After two interviews with the king, he (November 10) presented a memorial, earnestly calling his majesty's attention to the wish nearest his heart. Scotland, he said, was on the brink of ruin, and the severity of the government had occasioned such discontent, that if he were again to land in it with a proper armament, the number of his adherents would be tripled. He had become convinced, from his late campaign, that only a moderate army of regular troops was required to enable the people of Great Britain to shake off the yoke under which they groaned ; eighteen or twenty thousand men were sufficient, and these he requested from the French government. No attention seems to have been paid to his demand, which the government probably found itself in no condition to comply with. It is to be remarked, that the idea of a renewal of the late war was

---

[1] ' My dearest Prince, I thank Heaven for the extreme pleasure it gives me to see you returned in safety, after so many fatigues and dangers. You have proved that all the great qualities of the heroes and philosophers are united in you ; and I hope that one day you will receive the reward of such extraordinary merit.'

not confined to his own ambitious mind, but was greatly encouraged by his Scottish friends, and by none more eagerly than by young Locheil, who for some time refused to take a French regiment which was offered to him, lest his doing so might propagate a notion that the Prince had little hopes of renewed aid from France. Charles also wrote at this juncture to the king of Spain, condoling with him on the death of his lately deceased father, Philip V., and expressing a strong hope that the friendship he had enjoyed from that monarch would be continued by his successor.

As the reluctance of the French court to befriend him actively became more apparent to Charles, he lost his former tone of moderation. Every high passion, on being thwarted in its object, raises irritation, and it is from this time that we are to date a revolution in Charles's character which has made it almost impossible to recognise, in his middle life and age, the manly, clement, and heroic youth who led the Highland army in 1745. His father earnestly remonstrated against the manner in which he acted towards the court of France, but in vain. Neither did he take any counsel from the many able and high-principled Scottish officers who were now in Paris: almost his sole adviser was his secretary Kelly, who seems to have been eminently unworthy of the confidence reposed in him.

About the end of January (1747) he left Paris, and retired to Avignon, much against the will of his friends, who regarded the step as an admission that his cause was hopeless. But in reality he contemplated a secret journey to Madrid, in order to try if Ferdinand VI. would give those supplies which he could not obtain in France. Travelling very privately, he reached the Spanish capital early in March, and met with a civil reception from the new monarch, of whom he asked aid in men, arms, and ships with provisions, towards a new expedition. He was informed in answer that Spain could at present spare no ships: the other demands were spoken of in a manner which led him to suppose that they would be granted; but ultimately he found his application unavailing. He returned to Paris on the 24th of March.

He now renewed his applications to the French court, but still without success. Within twenty days from his return to Paris, he is found deliberating on the propriety of proposing marriage to the Czarina[1] of Russia, with a view to her giving him the required aid—a project from which his father dissuaded him, as not in the least likely to be successful. All this procedure shews the extreme eagerness which possessed him to be again at the head of an expedition in Britain, and the sense he had of the value of the present crisis. Two things he dreaded above all as likely to preclude a new attempt—a peace between France and England, which the French people eagerly desired, and the completion of the subjugation and disarmament of the Scottish Highlanders by the British government—an event certain to give great discouragement to his English friends, as they depended much on the warlike character of that people for the means of bringing about a restoration. It is no wonder, then, that Charles chafed and groaned under the difficulties which beset him. He saw what he thought the last opportunity of regaining the British crown passing before him, and was unable to take advantage of it, because, as he thought, a few selfish ministers were indifferent to his interests in common with those of their own countries. These views were not his own only. We find young Locheil, in February 1747, eagerly urging a new expedition, on however small a scale, to Scotland, on the ground that, if undertaken now, it would find the people unsubdued and still armed, as well as eager to save their country from the slavery to which the existing government seemed to have doomed it.

The spring passed, and summer arrived, and still there was no appearance of a grant of troops or arms on the part of France. The government pressed a large pension on the Prince, but he refused to accept it. It was with difficulty they could even

---

1 Elizabeth I., daughter of Peter the Great. She was eleven years the senior of Prince Charles.

induce young Locheil to take the command of a regiment. It was at this particular time (June 1747), when he was suffering all the ills attending on those who wait for the favour of courts, that his brother Henry, with his father's full consent, became an ecclesiastic, and accepted a cardinal's hat from the pope. Charles heard with frenzy of a proceeding by which he knew that his cause would be deeply injured in Britain, and which, moreover, was sure to be received everywhere as a tacit acknowledgment on the part of the family that his views on the crown were now hopeless. He had previously regarded his brother with great affection, but he now cast him from his bosom. Even his father he could scarcely forgive for his share in so fatal a step. Lord George Murray at this time came to Paris to pay his respects to him; but the Prince, though in his wanderings he had spoken mildly of Lord George, was now imbittered against him; and this honourable man, who had sacrificed his country and family prospects in his cause, was obliged to retire from France not only without seeing him, but under some dread lest the Prince should cause him to be arrested.[1]

Months passed on, during which the proceedings of the

---

[1] It was probably about the time when the hopes of renewed assistance from France were declining, that Mr William Hamilton of Bangour wrote the following imitation of the Scottish version of the 137th psalm—a composition of much more than his usual energy, and concluding with an almost prophetic malediction:

'On Gallia's shore we sat and wept,
    When Scotland we thought on,
Robbed of her bravest sons, and all
    Her ancient spirit gone.

"Revenge," the sons of Gallia said,
    "Revenge your native land:
Already your insulting foes
    Crowd the Batavian strand."

How shall the sons of freedom e'er
    For foreign conquest fight?
For power how wield the sword, unsheathed
    For liberty and right?

If thee, O Scotland, I forget,
    Even with my latest breath,

Prince came little to the knowledge of his father or the public. That secretiveness which he had shewn in the Highlands when passing from one retreat and one set of friends to another, now reappeared, and it marked much of his future career. It has been said that he rejoiced in the victories gained by the British in the course of the war, rather than in those gained by the French; but this must be taken with limitation. There is extant a letter in which he congratulated Louis XV. on the victory of Lafelt. While trusting only to obscure, and, it has been said, worthless counsellors, there is indubitable evidence that he freely gave from his means to relieve and support the other gentlemen of his party who had taken refuge in France. In an account current with his banker, Mr George Waters, junior, we find repeated disbursements of large sums to Clanranald, Ardshiel, Gordon of Glenbucket, Lord Nairn, and others of equal or less note.[1] The unfortunate propensity to drinking, by which his last years were so much clouded, is first

> May foul dishonour stain my name,
>   And bring a coward's death !
>
> May sad remorse of fancied guilt
>   My future days employ,
> If all thy sacred rights are not
>   Above my chiefest joy.
>
> Remember England's children, Lord,
>   Who on Drummossie * day,
> Deaf to the voice of kindred love,
>   " Rase, rase it quite," did say.
>
> And thou, proud Gallia, faithless friend,
>   Whose ruin is not far,
> Just Heaven on thy devoted head
>   Pour all the woes of war.
>
> When thou thy slaughtered little ones
>   And ravished dames shalt see,
> Such help, such pity, mayst thou have
>   As Scotland had from thee !'

[1] In a letter to his father, Paris, December 19, 1746, he says : 'I suppose O'Brien has already given an account to you of what pains I am at, and what has been done concerning the poor Scotch. I told Marquis d'Argenson t'other day how sensible I was at the king's goodness for what he has done for them, and that I would go, if necessary, upon my knees for them, but that I would never ask anything for myself; for I came only into this country to do what I could for my poor country, and not for myself.'

* Drummossie, another name for the moor of Culloden.

noticed in 1747, in an unsigned letter to Mr William Murray
(titular Lord Dunbar); but the reader has seen proof that this
taste was awakened in the course of his Highland adventures,
being probably attributable in part to the hardships he then
suffered, and partly to the effect of the evil customs of the
country working upon one previously unaccustomed to liquor,
and unprepared to indulge in it, particularly under such
circumstances, without contracting an uncontrollable liking
for it.[1]

In the spring of 1748, the inclination of France for peace
assumed a definite form, and proposals being in the first place
submitted by the king, it was agreed by the powers at war to
hold a congress at Aix-la-Chapelle.   Charles beheld this transaction as the death-warrant of all his immediate hopes; but,
blinded by passionate violence, he had not the prudence to
submit with resignation to a turn of affairs altogether beyond his

---

[1] Besides the various notices of his liking for ardent spirits given in the chapters descriptive of his wanderings, one or two more may here be noted from the manuscript collections
of the Rev. Mr Forbes. In a journal by young Clanranald, Glenaladale, &c. (*Lyon in
Mourning*, iii. 589), it is stated that, when in the forest-house of Glencoridale in South
Uist, 'he would step into a by-chamber, which served as a pantry, and, when he stood in
need of it, put the bottle of brandy to his head without ceremony.' In the Rev. Mr
Forbes's report of conversations which he had with Kingsburgh and his wife (*Lyon*, ii. 209),
there is a passage referring to the night which Charles spent in their house : 'The Prince
ate four roasted eggs, some collops, plenty of bread and butter, and—to use the words of
Mrs Macdonald—"the deil a drap did he want of twa bottles of sma' beer; God do him
good o't ; for weel I wat he had my blessing to gae doun wi't." After he had made a
plentiful supper, he called for a dram, and when the bottle of brandy was brought, he said
he would fill the glass for himself, "for," said he, "*I have learned in my skulking to take
a hearty dram.*" He filled up a bumper, and drank it off to the happiness and prosperity
of his landlord and landlady.' These and other like circumstances are mentioned by the
reporters, without apparently the remotest idea that the habits of the Prince were in danger
of being permanently affected ; but their value as testimony is not the worse on that
account. I introduce them here in a spirit far from that of blame. Charles had previously,
like most natives of southern Europe, been unaccustomed to liquor. On such a person the
drinking customs of the people amongst whom he fell were calculated to have a fatal effect.
It would also appear, from what we every day see amongst the miserably poor, that there
is a condition of defective physical comfort in which alcohol presents itself as a remedy and
compensation, and in that character is scarcely to be resisted by human weakness. This
law is of course as ready to operate upon a prince, suddenly reduced to personal misery,
as upon a wretch who has long known it, and perhaps even more so. Probably the habits
originally contracted under physical discomfort were, in the Prince's case, revived and
confirmed afterwards under the anguish of a disappointed and exasperated spirit, which had
unfortunately not been trained to look for superior consolations.

control. During the summer, while the negotiations were going
on, it was expected that he would quietly retire from France, as
there could be no doubt that one of the stipulations would bind
the king to afford him no longer an asylum. On the contrary,
he hired a handsome house on the Quai Théatin, and ordered
such furnishings for it as marked a determination to remain in
Paris. When any one spoke of the treaty, he affected indifference, and changed the subject. Nor was this all. He caused a
medal to be struck, with his head on one side, and on the other
a quantity of shipping, with the words: *Amor et spes Britanniæ*
('The love and hope of Britain')—a deliberate insult to the
French government, which had suffered so much from the
British marine force. The ministers deeply resented this act,
and urged the king to take notice of it; but he declined doing
so, apparently from a wish not to exasperate the Prince any
further. The Prince of Conti, a very proud noble, soon after
meeting Charles in the Luxembourg gardens, addressed him
with an air of pleasantry, but with a latent sneer, on this subject.
The device, he said, was not very applicable, for the British
navy had not proved very friendly to him. 'Cela est vrai,
prince,' said Charles; 'mais je suis nonobstant l'ami de la
flotte contre tous ses ennemis, comme je regarderai toujours la
gloire d'Angleterre comme la mienne, et sa gloire est dans sa
flotte !'[1] He appears in a more respectable light in the protest
for a reservation of his rights which he caused to be presented
to the representatives of the various powers met at Aix-la-
Chapelle. This document, dated at Paris, July 16, after
alluding to the wrongs suffered by his house, and stating the
powers granted him by his father, protests 'against all which
may be said, done, or stipulated in the assembly to the prejudice and diminution of the lawful rights of our most honoured
father and lord, of our own, of the princes or princesses that
are or will be born of our royal house.' 'We declare,' it

---

[1] 'That is very true, prince; but nevertheless I am a friend to the navy against all
enemies whatever, as I shall always look upon the glory of England as my own, and her
glory is in her navy.'

proceeds, 'that we regard, and always will regard, as null, void, and of no effect, everything that may be statuted or stipulated which may tend to the acknowledgment of any other person whatsoever as sovereign of the kingdoms of Great Britain, besides the person of the most high and most excellent prince, James the Third, our most honoured lord and father, and, in default of him, the person of the nearest heir, agreeably to the fundamental laws of Great Britain.' Finally, 'we declare to all the subjects of our most honoured lord and father, and more particularly to those who have given us recently shining proofs of their attachment to the interests of our royal family, and to the primitive constitution of their country, that nothing shall ever alter the lively and sincere love which our birth inspires us with for them; and that the just gratitude which we have for their fidelity, zeal, and courage, shall never be effaced from our heart. That, so far from listening to any proposition that tends to destroy or weaken the indissoluble ties which unite us, we look, and always will look, upon ourselves as under the most intimate and indispensable obligation to be constantly attentive to all that may contribute to their happiness; and that we shall always be ready to spill the very last drop of our blood to deliver them from a foreign yoke.'[1]   M. Montesquieu, to whom Charles submitted a copy of this protest, complimented him on it, as written with simplicity, with dignity, and even with eloquence.

He enclosed a copy of the paper to the king of France, assuring him that, while obliged thus to defend his rights, he entertained the greatest respect for his majesty's sacred person, and hoped never to forfeit his friendship.

The treaty, meanwhile, was known to contain a clause stipulating that Charles should no longer reside in France. His voluntary retirement from the kingdom was every day looked for, but in vain. When the king perceived that Charles made no motion to leave his dominions, he despatched the Cardinal

---

[1] These extracts are from a translation of the French original in the Rev. Mr Forbes's collection of papers.

de Tencin with instructions to hint to him, in as delicate a manner as possible, the necessity of his taking that step. The cardinal performed his office with the greatest discretion, and endeavoured with all his eloquence to palliate the conduct of his master. But Charles treated him only with evasive answers, and he was obliged to withdraw without having obtained any satisfactory avowal of his royal highness's intentions. The king waited for some days, in the hope that Charles would depart, but was then obliged to despatch another messenger with still more urgent entreaties. The person selected for this purpose was the Duke de Gesvres, governor of Paris, who, besides instructions to urge his departure, carried a *carte blanche*, which the Prince was requested to fill up with any sum he might please to demand as a pension, in consideration of his obeying the king's wishes. When this ambassador disclosed his proposals to Charles, he is said to have treated them with unequivocal marks of contempt, saying that ' pensions were quite out of the question in the present case, and that he only wished the king to keep his word.' The duke pointed out the necessity of the negotiations which required his departure from France ; but Charles, on the other hand, insisted upon the previous treaty between his most Christian majesty and himself, by which they had become mutual allies. The Duke de Gesvres being thus unsuccessful, the Count de Maurepas and the pope's nuncio were one after another sent upon the same errand, and the king even wrote a letter to him with his own hand ; but all without effect.

As no attempt was made by either party to conceal these strange proceedings, they soon became known over Europe. In Paris they excited a degree of interest such as no public event was ever before known to occasion. For a person in such peculiar circumstances to thwart the intentions, and disregard the power, of the Grand Monarch, was esteemed in that region a most extraordinary instance of daring. His exploits in Scotland, and the fascinating graces of his person, had previously disposed the Parisians to an extravagant degree of admiration, and it was completed when to these charms was added that arising from his unmerited distresses. He now became an object of even more attraction than the king himself. Whenever he appeared upon the public walks, the whole company followed him. When he entered the theatre, he became the sole spectacle of the place. On all occasions he seemed the only person who was insensible to the sorrows of his fate; and while he talked with his usual gaiety to the young noblemen who surrounded him, no one could speak of him without admiration, and some could not behold him without tears.

The public feeling so liberally excited in his favour was by no means agreeable to the king, and far less to the ministry. There were other personages whom it yet further offended. These were the Earl of Sussex and Lord Cathcart, two British noblemen, then residing in Paris as hostages to guarantee the restoration of Cape Breton to its original proprietors the French, in terms of the treaty. Charles was known to have commented with bitterness upon the meanness of the British government in giving hostages to France; and the two noblemen could not help, moreover, feeling personally piqued at the respect which was everywhere shewn to the public enemy of their country, while they themselves were treated with ill-suppressed contempt. They therefore complained to the French monarch that there was one important article of the treaty which he had not fulfilled. His majesty gave them for answer that he only waited the return of a messenger from Rome, with an answer to a letter which he had written to the old Pretender, demanding that Charles should be withdrawn, by paternal authority, from the kingdom, before taking active measures to that effect.

The messenger mentioned by the king returned on the 9th of December (1748) with a letter from the old Chevalier, enclosing another, under a flying seal, addressed to his son, in which he commanded the Prince to obey the king's wishes. His majesty, after having read the last epistle, sent it to Charles, by way of giving him a last chance of declaring his submission to the royal authority; but the inflexible Prince thought proper to hold out even against his father's commands. He declared openly that no pensions, promises, or advantages whatever should induce him to renounce his just rights; that, on the contrary, he was resolved to consecrate the last moments of his life to their recovery. The king no sooner learned that he was still unwilling to depart, than he called a council of state, where it was determined to arrest him, and carry him out of the kingdom by force. Louis was still so averse to treat his unfortunate ally with disrespect, and still entertained so much regard for him, that when the order for his arrest was presented for signature, he exclaimed, with sorrow which we may hope was not affected: 'Ah, pauvre prince! qu'il est difficile pour un roi d'être un véritable ami!' The order was signed at three o'clock in the afternoon, but it was blazed all over Paris before the evening. A person of the Prince's retinue heard and carried him the intelligence, but he affected not to believe it. Next day (December 10), as he was walking in the Tuileries, a person of condition informed him that he would certainly be seized that very day if he did not prevent it by an immediate departure; but, resolved to put the government to the last extremity, he treated the intelligence as chimerical, and turning to one of his followers, ordered a box to be hired for him that night at the opera.

The preparations made for his arrest were upon a scale proportioned to the importance of his character, or rather were dictated by the extent of public favour which he was supposed to enjoy. No fewer than twelve hundred of the guards were drawn out and posted in the court of the Palais-Royal; a great number of sergeants and grenadiers, armed in cuirasses and helmets, filled the passage of the opera-house; the *guet*, or city police, were stationed in the streets to stop all carriages. The sergeants of the grenadiers, as the most intrepid, were selected to seize the Prince. Two companies of grenadiers took post in the courtyard of the kitchens, where the Duke de Biron, commander of the French guards, and who was commissioned to superintend, waited in a coach, disguised, to see the issue of the enterprise. The mousquetaires had orders to be ready to mount on horseback; troops were posted upon the road from the

Palais-Royal to the state-prison of Vincennes, in which the
Prince was to be disposed.   Hatchets and scaling-ladders were
prepared, and locksmiths directed to attend, in order to take his
royal highness by escalade, in case he should throw himself into
some house, and there attempt to stand a siege.   A physician
and three surgeons, moreover, were ordered to be in readiness
to dress whoever might be wounded.

Into this well-prepared and formidable trap Charles entered
with all the unthinking boldness of a desperate man.   Scorning
the repeated warnings he had received, and disregarding a
friendly voice which told him, as he passed along in his carriage,
that the opera-house was beset, he drove up as usual to that
place; where he no sooner alighted on the ground, than he was
surrounded by six sergeants dressed in plain clothes, who seized
his person; one taking care of each limb, while other two
crossed their arms, and bore him off the street into the courtyard of the Palais-Royal; the soldiers in the meantime keeping
off the crowd with fixed bayonets, and seizing the few persons
who attended him.   When he was brought into the courtyard,
Major de Vaudreuil, who had been deputed to act by the Duke
de Biron, approached his royal highness and said: 'Prince,
your arms: I arrest you in the name of the king.'   Charles
immediately presented his sword; but that not satisfying his
captors, they searched his person, and found a pair of pistols
and a poniard, together with a penknife and a book, all of
which they removed.   They then bound him with silk cord, of
which the duke had provided ten ells on purpose, and hurried
him into a hired coach, which was immediately driven off,
attended by a strong guard.   Another party in the meantime
entered his palace, and arrested all his followers and servants,
who were immediately conveyed to the Bastile, though soon
afterwards liberated.   Charles was conveyed to the castle of
Vincennes, and thrust into an upper room of narrow dimensions,[1]

1 The account of the Prince's seizure is from *An Authentic Account of the Young
Chevalier in France* (London, 1749). It is supported by a letter amongst the Stuart Papers,
Browne's Appendix, No. clxviii.

where he was left to seek repose, attended by only a single friend—the faithful Neil Mackechan, who, with Flora Macdonald, had accompanied him in his journey through Skye.[1] So long as he was in the presence of the soldiers, or any officers of the French government, he had maintained a lofty air, and spoken in a haughty tone, as if to shew that he was superior to his misfortunes; but when finally left in this desolate chamber, with only a friend to observe him, he gave way to the tumult of painful feeling which agitated his breast. Throwing himself upon a chair, according to the report of Mackechan, as afterwards communicated to a family in Skye, he clasped his hands together, and bursting into tears, exclaimed: 'Ah, my faithful mountaineers! you would never have treated me thus! Would I were still with you!'—his mind apparently reverting at this moment of peculiar distress to the transient glories of his late brilliant though unhappy enterprise.

Charles was kept in confinement till the 15th, when, having given his parole that he would not return to the French dominions, he was taken from Vincennes, and carried by easy stages, under a guard, to Avignon.

CHAPTER XXXI.

MEASURES FOR PREVENTION OF FURTHER DISTURBANCES.

' Sir, I have heard another story—
He was a most confounded Tory,
And grew, or he is much belied,
Extremely dull before he died.'

IN the parliamentary session of 1747, several measures were brought forward and passed, for the purpose of preventing future disturbance on account of the succession.

---

[1] Neil Mackechan or Macdonald had been, at the Prince's desire, appointed a lieutenant in Lord Ogilvie's regiment of the Scotch Brigade in the service of France. He subsequently had a pension of 300 livres per annum.—*Letter of Colonel John Macdonald (son of Flora), MS., in possession of the author.*

The first was one of mercy, an act of indemnity granting pardon to all who still survived of the late offenders, excepting about eighty persons mentioned by name, these being generally individuals of some note in the insurrection, or who had been connected with it.[1]   At the same time that this act was passed

[1] Of noblemen excepted, there were the Earls of Traquair and Clancarty ; of baronets, Sir James Steuart, Sir John Douglas, Sir James Harrington, Sir James Campbell, Sir William Dunbar, and Sir Alexander Bannerman ; of Highland chiefs and gentlemen of note, Macdonnell of Glengarry, Macleod of Raasay, Macgregor of Glengyle, Grant of Glenmorriston, Robertson of Struan, Chisholm of Comar, Drummond of Bochaldy, Fraser of Foyers, Fraser of Gortuleg, Fraser of Browick, Æneas and James Macdonald, brothers to the late Kinlochmoidart, Stuart of Kynnachin, Robertson of Blairfetty, Robertson of Faskally, and Robert Murray (originally Macgregor) of Glencarnock ; of Lowland gentlemen of note, Archibald Stewart, late Lord Provost of Edinburgh, Thomas Blair of Glasclune, James Carnegy of Boysack, Charles Cumming of Kinninmond, John Fullerton younger of Dudwick, Alexander Gordon of Carnousie, John Gordon of Avachie, Robert Gordon younger of Logie, James Gordon of Glastyrum, David Hunter of Burnside, John Halden of Lanrick, Andrew Hay younger of Rannes, Alexander Irvine of Drum, James Moir of Stoneywood, Thomas Ogilvie of East Mill, Thomas Ogilvie of Coul, James Stirling of Craigbarnet, John Turner younger of Turnerhall, and Andrew Wauchope of Niddry.   The act also excepted those who had formerly been specified in what was called the Act of Attainder.   That act, which had been passed in the month of May 1746, after reciting that on or before April 18, certain persons named had traitorously levied war against the king, and were now fled from justice, enacted that the said persons should be held guilty of high treason, and stand attainted, if they did not surrender themselves to justice before the 12th of July.   The persons named in this act were : Alexander, Earl of Kellie ; William, Viscount of Strathallan ; Alexander, Lord Pitsligo ; David Wemyss, Esq., commonly called Lord Elcho, eldest son and heir-apparent of James, Earl of Wemyss ; James Drummond, Esq., eldest son and heir-apparent of William, Viscount of Strathallan ; Simon Fraser, Esq., eldest son and heir-apparent of Simon, Lord Lovat ; George Murray, Esq., commonly called Lord George Murray, brother to James, Duke of Athole ; Lewis Gordon, Esq., commonly called Lord Lewis Gordon, brother to Cosmo George, Duke of Gordon ; James Drummond, taking upon himself the title of Duke of Perth ; James Graham, late of Duntroon, taking on himself the title of Viscount of Dundee ; John Nairn, taking upon himself the title or style of Lord Nairn ; David Ogilvie, taking upon himself the title of Lord Ogilvie ; John Drummond, taking upon himself the style or title of Lord John Drummond, brother to James Drummond, taking on himself the title of Duke of Perth ; Robert Mercer, Esq., otherwise Nairn of Aldie ; Sir William Gordon of Park ; John Murray of Broughton, Esq. ; John Gordon the elder of Glenbucket ; Donald Cameron the younger of Locheil ; Dr Archibald Cameron, brother to Donald Cameron the younger of Locheil ; Ludovick Cameron of Tor Castle ; Alexander Cameron of Dungallon ; Donald Macdonald of Clanranald, junior, son to Ronald Macdonald of Clanranald ; Donald Macdonald of Lochgarry ; Alexander Macdonald of Keppoch ; Archibald Macdonald, son of Colonel Macdonald of Barrisdale ; Alexander Macdonald of Glencoe ; Evan Macpherson of Cluny ; Lachlan Maclachlan of Castle Lachlan ; John Mackinnon of Mackinnon ; Charles Stuart of Ardshiel ; George Lockhart, eldest son and heir-apparent of George Lockhart of Carnwath ; Lawrence Oliphant the elder of Gask ; Lawrence Oliphant the younger of Gask ; James Graham the younger of Airth ; John Stuart, commonly called John Roy Stuart ; Francis Farquharson of Monalterye ; Alexander Macgilivrae of Drumaglash ; Lachlan Mackintosh, merchant at Inverness ; Malcolm Ross, son of Alexander Ross of

(June 1747), a considerable number of persons, including those who had been apprehended for their concern in the Prince's escape, were liberated.

An act was passed for enforcing those already in existence for disarming the Highlanders. It was now ordained that if any man residing within the Highland line should fail to deliver up his arms before the 1st of August 1747, or if any man should attempt to conceal arms either in his house or in the fields, he was to be for the first offence fined in fifteen pounds, and imprisoned without bail till payment. If payment was not made within one month, he was to be transported to America as a common soldier, if able to serve; if not able to serve, he was to be imprisoned for six months, and then only liberated on finding security for his good behaviour during the next ten years. If the offender was a woman, she was to be fined in the same sum, imprisoned till payment, and afterwards confined for six months. A second offence against this law was to be visited with no less a punishment than transportation for seven years.

Not only were the Highlanders deprived of their arms, but their very dress was proscribed, and by still severer penalties. The same act ordained that, after the 1st of August 1747, if any person, whether man or boy, within the same tract of country, were found wearing the clothes commonly called 'the Highland clothes;' that is, the plaid, philibeg, trews, shoulder-belts, or any part whatsoever of the Highland garb, or if any person were found to wear a dress composed of tartan or party-coloured cloth, he should be imprisoned six months without bail for the first offence, and on its repetition be transported for seven years.

It was thus hoped that not only would the Highlanders be incapable of again levying war against the state, but that, their distinction as a nation being destroyed, they would with all haste become obedient servants to government, like the rest of

Pitcalny: Alexander Macleod, son to Mr John Macleod, advocate; John Hay, portioner of Restalrig, writer to the signet; Andrew Lumsdale, otherwise Lumsdain, son to William Lumsdale, otherwise Lumsdain, writer in Edinburgh; and William Fidler, clerk in the auditor's office in the Exchequer of Scotland.

the community. As might have been expected, the result was very different. The clans were, it is true, effectually prevented from ever again going to the field against the House of Hanover, but they were not induced to regard that family or their government with any additional degree of favour. On the contrary, their previous disaffection was exasperated by these harsh measures into absolute hatred. ' Even the loyal clans,' says Dr Johnson, ' murmured with an appearance of justice, that after having defended the king, they were forbidden for the future to defend themselves, and that the sword should be forfeited which had been legally employed.' But if the loss of their arms occasioned discontent, the change of their dress produced feelings still less favourable to the existing government. Had the whole race been decimated, as their historian General Stewart remarks, more violent grief, indignation, and shame could not have been excited among them than by this encroachment upon their dearest national prejudices. It may be said, in conclusion, that if the Highlanders have eventually become good servants to the state, and undistinguishable in dress and demeanour from the rest of the population, no part of the blessing is to be ascribed to this enactment.

The next act of the legislature was the celebrated one for abolishing heritable jurisdictions in Scotland. It was supposed that, by putting an end to the power which all land-proprietors had hitherto possessed of judging in civil and criminal cases among their dependants, the spirit of clanship would receive a mortal blow. Accordingly, it was resolved to buy up all these petty jurisdictions from the proprietors, and to vest them in sheriffs, who should be appointed by the king. It was also resolved that the hereditary justiciarship of Scotland, vested in the family of Argyll, should be purchased, and transferred to the High Court and Circuit-courts of Justiciary, and that all constabularies should be abolished, except the office of high constable. The whole sum granted by parliament in exchange for the heritable jurisdictions was £152,000 — one of the cheapest purchases of patronage and power ever made.   A companion act abolished the right of ward-holding, by which landlords commanded the military services of their tenants. By these means the last conspicuous features of the feudal system were brought to an end in Scotland. Another act bore reference to the religious body styled the Scottish Episcopalians. The Episcopal Church had ceased to be the established religion of the country, when its supporters, the Stuarts, ceased to reign over Britain. Previously to that period, it had been unpopular among the lower orders of people—originally, on account of a prejudice which they had against bishops, and latterly, on account of the injudicious persecutions which this church was the occasion of bringing upon the Presbyterians. Want of popular favour joined at the Revolution with another circumstance to procure its downfall. King William, before leaving Holland, had promised, in a declaration, to maintain it in all its privileges; and when he had settled himself at London, he was prepared to keep his promise. On proceeding, however, to sound the bishops as to their affection to his government, he found them obstinate in their adherence to the former monarch, alleging that, as they had already sworn to be faithful to James and his heirs—for such was then the tenor of the oath of allegiance—they could not in conscience transfer their fealty to him. William then saw fit to establish the Presbyterian Church, the members of which, he understood, had already testified their abhorrence of the late government by desecrating the fanes of Episcopacy, and rabbling out its clergy. From this time Episcopacy was marked as the religion of the Jacobites, and subjected to a variety of restrictions and persecutions, not more at the hands of the reformed government, than at those of the Presbyterian clergy and common people. In the reign of Queen Anne, when the Earl of Strathmore endeavoured to obtain an act of parliament 'for the toleration of all Protestants in the exercise of religious worship,' a strong representation was offered against it by the General Assembly, concluding in these words: 'That they were persuaded that to enact a toleration for those in the Episcopal way—*which God in*

His infinite mercy avert!—would be to establish iniquity by a law, and would bring upon the promoters thereof, and their families, the dreadful guilt of all those sins and pernicious effects that might ensue thereupon.'[1] The Episcopal forms continued, nevertheless, to be adhered to by the greater part of the wealth and rank, and no mean portion of the intelligence of the country, down to the year 1745, when, as already mentioned, its chapels sent forth not a few enthusiasts to join the standard of Prince Charles, and it of course attracted the determined hostility of the existing government. Duke William, in his march to the north, finding it identified beyond all doubt with the disaffection of the district of Angus, had thought proper to visit it with the terrors of military law; and the battle of Culloden had only been gained one week, when he succeeded in closing up every place of worship throughout the country in which a nonjuring clergyman officiated. On this occasion, the Bibles, prayer-books, and other furniture of many of the chapels, were taken out by the soldiers and openly burned, and even the buildings were in some instances destroyed. It was now resolved to subject the Episcopalian body to a system of persecution which might have the colour of law. An act was accordingly passed, less than three months after the conclusion of the war, by which it was ordained that any Episcopal clergyman officiating after the 1st of September 1746, without having taken the oaths of allegiance, abjuration, and assurance, or without praying once, during the performance of worship, for the king, his heirs and successors, and for all the royal family, should, for the first offence, suffer six months' imprisonment; for the second (upon conviction before the High Court of Justiciary), be transported to the American plantations for life, and, in case of returning from banishment, be subjected to perpetual imprisonment. It was also ordained that no proprietor of a closed Episcopal meeting-house should regain possession of it till he gave security for £100 that he would not again permit it to be occupied by a

---

[1] Belsham's *History of England*, i. 293.

nonjuring clergyman. In order to prevent these unfortunate ministers from officiating even in private, it was also enacted that every house in which five or more persons met to hear them perform service, should be considered a meeting-house within the meaning of the act. With a purpose still more malevolent—that of entirely destroying the apostolical ordination which the clergy of the Scottish Episcopal Church had continued to transmit from one to another since the Revolution—it was decreed that no letters of orders should be registered after the 1st of September, except such as had been given by the Church of England or the Church of Ireland.

Cruel as this persecution was, it might not eventually have injured the church so much, if it had not also extended to the laity. The act declared that if, after the 1st of September 1746, any person should resort to an illegal Episcopal meeting-house, and not give notice within five days of such illegal meeting to some proper magistrate, he should be subjected to fine or imprisonment. It declared further that no peer of Scotland should be capable of being elected one of the sixteen peers of parliament, or of voting at such election; and that no person should be capable of being elected a member of parliament for any shire or burgh who should, within the compass of any future year, be twice present at divine service in an Episcopal meeting in Scotland not held according to law.

In this state of things,[1] some of the clergy, who, though steady and zealous Episcopalians, had always professed themselves not Jacobites, feeling it their duty to render their chapels legal meeting-houses, repaired to the proper magistrates, took the oaths to government required by the act, and got their letters of orders registered before the 1st of September. But this compliance availed them nothing. In May 1748, the act of 1746 was amended, and an enactment made that no letters of orders not granted by some bishop of the Church of England or of Ireland should be sufficient to qualify any Scottish Episcopal

---

[1] Keith's Catalogue, with Appendix, by the Rev. Dr Russell, p. 511.

pastor, whether the same had been registered before or since the 1st of September 1746; and that every such registration, whether made before or since, should now be null and void. This act was directed against the very religion of the Scottish Episcopalians, for it precluded them from the privileges of political repentance. As such it was felt by the English bishops, not one of whom ventured to support the bill, while some spoke strenuously against it, as a flagrant attack on the leading principles of Christian liberty.

That these statutes were not mere matters of form, but that the penalties were rigorously put in execution, could be proved by numerous instances. One clergyman, not more distinguished by his well-known poetical genius than by his piety and private worth, the Rev. John Skinner of Longmay in Aberdeenshire, was imprisoned, in terms of the second act, for six months, in the public jail of the county town, although he had previously taken all the loyal oaths, and for two years prayed for the king by name. Other clergymen who did not pray for the king by name, suffered similar imprisonments; and a few were obliged to take refuge in England and elsewhere from the penalties with which they were threatened.

The general result of the two statutes was simply to annihilate the conscientious portion of the church. It was now impossible for a lay member of it to continue in the faith of his forefathers and that of his own youth, without incurring disqualifications of the most grievous sort. Altogether, the persecutions to which the church was subjected were of a nature even more severe than those with which the Presbyterians were visited in the reign of Charles II. In what are considered the hottest periods of that persecution, the clergymen were permitted to retain parish churches, upon the simple condition of yielding verbal obedience to the government, and not one individual suffered punishment who was not also a rebel against the state. But in this persecution of a later and milder time, the whole clergy were deprived of even the privileges of dissenters, and exposed to the severest punishment, except death, for simply withholding their allegiance. The Presbyterians could at any time have saved themselves by pronouncing the Scriptural phrase : 'God save the king;' but the Episcopalians could not escape, without actually perjuring themselves—without swearing (by the oath of abjuration) that they believed, what no unprejudiced man could believe, that the Pretender was a supposititious child.

If the persecution of the Episcopalians surpassed that of the Presbyterians in severity, it is not less true that the members of the former church displayed fully as much constancy under their afflictions. Instead of fomenting civil rebellion, or declaiming in their private assemblies against the government which treated them with so much cruelty, they submitted with meekness to a fate which they could not controvert. Instead of flying to the fields and publishing their grievances at conventicles, they sought to administer those ordinances to private families which they were prevented from dispensing to a congregation. Individual clergymen have thus been known to perform worship no less than sixteen times in one day.[1]

[1] The shifts to which the Jacobite Episcopalians were put, in order to perform the ceremonies of religion without incurring legal vengeance, were quite as distressing as those of the nonconformists of King Charles's time. In the Episcopal Register of Muthill in Perthshire there is the following entry, under date of March 20, 1750, in the handwriting of the Rev. William Erskine, Episcopal minister there (father of the late William Erskine, Esq., advocate, better known by his senatorial title of Lord Kinedder):

'*N.B.*—With such excessive severity were the penal laws executed at this time, that Andrew Moir having neglected to keep his appointment with me at my own house this morning, and following me to Lord Rollo's house of Duncrub, we could not take the child into a house, but I was obliged to go under the cover of trees in one of Lord Rollo's parks, to prevent our being discovered, and baptise the child there—namely, Helen, lawful daughter of Andrew Moir and Anne Grey, in Crofthead of Fairnton, born the 18th, and was baptised the 20th of March 1750.'

The following anecdote may be related as illustrative of the magnanimity which these unfortunate clergymen occasionally displayed under their afflicting circumstances. It refers to an old lady who died lately (1827) in Edinburgh, and who related it to my informant. This person was born at Dundee, and had the fortune to be the grand-daughter, paternally, of a minister of the established church, while her grandfather by the mother's side was a bishop of the Episcopal communion. Her mother wished ardently that she should be baptised by her father the bishop, while her husband's father, on the other hand, was determined to perform that office himself. Such was the state of the times, that the bishop could not act in the way proposed without great danger, nor was he sure that the paternal grandfather of the child might not be so much exasperated as to inform upon him. Firmly edified, however, in the certainty that his conduct was worthy in the eyes of God,

However much the historian of this period may be disposed to condemn the cruelty displayed in these statutes, he must certainly acknowledge that they were attended eventually with the desired effect of disabling the malcontent part of the community. By the first, the Highlanders were deprived of the means of carrying on an active warfare, and put in a fair way of becoming amalgamated with the rest of the community. By the second, the whole people of Scotland were emancipated from their obligations to the aristocracy, and enabled to prosecute commercial and agricultural enterprise with increased effect. By the third, a religious community which had formerly cherished unfailing affection for the House of Stuart was completely broken up, and in a manner compelled to transfer their allegiance to the existing government.

The spirit of Jacobitism, during its period of decay, was something very different from what it had been in the year 1745. It had till that period been the spirit of young as well as old people, and possessed sufficient strength to excite its votaries into active warfare. But as the Stuarts then ceased to acquire fresh adherents, and their claims became daily more and more obsolete, it was now left entirely to the generation which had witnessed its glories; in other words, became dependent upon the existence of a few old enthusiasts, more generally of the female than the male sex. After this period, indeed, Jacobitism became identified with the weakness of old age, and ceased to have the power of moving any heart, except one which might have throbbed with love for Prince Charles, or heaved to the stern music of Gladsmuir and Culloden.

---

whatever might be its merits in those of men, he resolved to brave every contingency. So firmly, indeed, was he determined to perform his duty, that on reaching his daughter's room, he made this remarkable declaration : ' If there were a gibbet,' he said, ' in one corner of the room, and the child in the other corner, and if I were informed that the said gibbet was to be the certain and immediate penalty of my conduct, still would I baptise the child !' He had just concluded the ceremony when the paternal grandfather arrived to perform the rite in his peculiar way, but as there were no hostile witnesses to prove what had been done, it was impossible to punish the celebrator.

CHAPTER XXXII.

SUBSEQUENT LIFE OF PRINCE CHARLES.

' Last scene of all,
That ends this strange eventful history.'

PRINCE CHARLES was left at the end of 1748 in Avignon, immediately after having been liberated from the castle of Vincennes. He had not been two months in that city, when suddenly he disappeared, and for a long time little was known of his motions. It is now ascertained that he privately returned into France, attended only by a Colonel Goring, and that in May he visited Paris. About this time he is supposed to have contemplated a match with a princess of the house of Hesse-Darmstadt; but no serious negotiation seems ever to have been entered upon. For more than a year he was lost sight of by his friends, and even by his father and brother. Morbid feeling, acting upon a character naturally secretive, seems to have been the cause of this strange conduct. During this time his father occasionally addressed letters to him, complaining of his capricious behaviour, but in terms of affecting mildness. He first reappears when, according to Dr King, he visited London. ' September . . , 1750,' says that gentleman,[1] ' I received a note from my Lady Primrose, who desired to see me immediately. As soon as I waited on her, she led me into her dressing-room, and presented me to ———.[2] If I was surprised

---

[1] *Political and Literary Anecdotes of his own Times,* by Dr William King, Principal of St Mary's Hall, Oxon. Second edition, 1819. Dr King had been a keen Jacobite, and was one of the ablest literary men of the party in 1745. He lived to see the prudence of reconciling himself to the reigning family, and being then of course much reviled by his former party, seems to have contracted a furious antipathy to the Prince and all who still adhered to him. I have no doubt that much of what he has written respecting Charles is untrue, and that the rest is grossly exaggerated. The evidence of a party deserter respecting his late friends should obviously be received with caution.

[2] The Prince.

to find him there, I was still more astonished when he acquainted me with the motives which had induced him to hazard a journey to England at this juncture. The impatience of his friends who were in exile had formed a scheme which was impracticable; but although it had been as feasible as they had represented it to him, yet no preparation had been made, nor was anything ready to carry it into execution. He was soon convinced that he had been deceived, and therefore, after a stay in London of five days only, he returned to the place from whence he came.' The writer adds in a note : ' He came one evening to my lodgings and drank tea with me : my servant, after he was gone, said to me " that he thought my new visitor very like Prince Charles." " Why," said I, " have you ever seen Prince Charles ?" " No, sir," replied the fellow; " but this gentleman, whoever he may be, exactly resembles the busts of him which are sold in Red Lion Street, and are said to be the busts of Prince Charles." The truth is, these busts were taken in plaster of Paris from his face.' It would appear that something of importance was contemplated on this occasion by the Prince, as he obtained, with a view to it, a renewal of his powers from his father.

Obscurity again settles upon him for a period. Where he travelled, or where he stayed, what name and character he assumed, and by whom he was attended, were unknown to his friends in Britain, and even to those abroad who might have been expected to be most in his confidence. One gentleman who knew him, found him, in April 1752, for a few days at Campvere, in the island of Walcheren. He appears, from published papers, to have trafficked a little with the Swedish court, with a view to aid towards a new enterprise; and I have been informed that at Stockholm there are traces of his having once resided there, particularly the insignia he wore in some high masonic character, which are still preserved in one of the lodges established in that city. A letter, of date 12th November 1753, signed with his incognito name John Douglas, but without place, informs Colonel Goring that he had written to Avignon to pay off all his Roman Catholic servants, and his mistress, who was also a Roman Catholic, and had behaved insolently, but that he still retained two gentlemen and all the Protestant servants.[1] Another letter adds the reason for dismissing his servants, 'as I am not able to maintain them any more,' and further expresses his hope that if they go to Rome his father will maintain them. The preference of the Protestant to the Catholic servants would seem to indicate attachment for the former religion, which he is said to have about this time embraced. In a letter to his father's secretary, Edgar, 24th March 1754,[2] we have some revelations shewing a decidedly morbid state of mind. 'I am grieved to think that

---

[1] Browne's Appendix.

[2] This Mr Edgar acted as private secretary to the old Chevalier for nearly fifty years. He was a fine specimen of the high-minded, warm-hearted, old Scottish gentleman—a character at no time difficult to find in the Jacobite party, whatever may be thought of the judgment shewn by it in its general aims and purposes. To a great-grandniece of Mr Edgar I am indebted for the following particulars :

'Some considerable time after the '15, the British government had reason to believe that another attempt was to be made for the exiled family. Sir Robert Walpole directed his spies to learn who was most in King James's confidence, and what were the character and circumstances of the individual. He was told that the king's private secretary was the younger son of a Scotch laird of small fortune ; that he was of a generous, hospitable turn, fond of entertaining his countrymen when in Rome ; and that he had but a small salary. This was just what Sir Robert wanted, and he wrote to Edgar, offering a handsome sum if he would betray the intentions of his master. Edgar put the letter into the fire, and returned no answer. Several other epistles, bearing advancing offers, met the same fate. Sir Robert, thinking that he had not yet come up to the secretary's price, then wrote (and this time without making any conditions) that he had placed ten thousand pounds in the Bank of Venice in the name of Mr Edgar. The secretary then consulted his master, and after a brief interval, returned for answer that he had received Sir Robert's letter. He thanked him for the ten thousand pounds, which he had lost no time in drawing from the bank, and had just laid at the feet of his royal master, who had the best title to gold that came, as this had done, from England.

'My mother, when in her teens, during her first visit to Edinburgh, heard this story told at a dinner-party in the house of Dr Webster, amongst a company consisting chiefly of Jacobites, by Mr Andrew Lumisden, who had succeeded her granduncle as secretary during the few years in which King James survived his faithful servant. She was delighted with the anecdote, but had doubts of its truth, as she had never heard her father mention it. On retiring from the party, she wrote to her father begging to know if it was true, and if so, why he had never told her of it. The reply was—it was perfectly true, but that *she need not wonder that he had not boasted of his uncle being an honest man.*

'My mother has several private letters from her granduncle to his nephew (her father), written after the return of the latter from his ten years' exile, consequent on his joining the Prince in '45. They exhibit the amiable character of the dear old man in the most engaging light. His warm affection for his friends, his native land, and the home of his childhood, continued to the last, though he lived and died far away from all.'

our master [his father] should think that my silence was either neglect or want of duty; but in reality my situation is such, that I have nothing to say but *imprecations against the fatality of being born in such a detestable age.* There are only two things that, with all due respect that I have, and shall always have, for my master, who is so great a lover of justice that he will never exact from me, and that I can never be capable to do. These are such things as may be either against my interest or honour. My interest does not imply any human views, but only such steps as can conduct to the prosperity and happiness of our country. The unworthy behaviour of certain ministers of 10th December 1748, has put it out of my power to settle anywhere without honour or interest being at stake; and were it even possible for me to find a place of abode, I think our family have had sufferings enough, that will always hinder me to marry as long as in misfortune, for that would only conduce to increase misery, or subject any of the family that would have the spirit of their father to be tied neck and heel rather than yield to a vile ministry.' Amongst other distresses, he seems about this time to have been troubled by creditors. In September 1754, he writes to Cluny Macpherson, who had remained till now in hiding in Scotland, requiring him to come over with all the money which had been left under his care in Scotland, 'for I happen to be at present in great straits.' He made anxious application to the Earl Marischal for his services; but his lordship was too little disposed to approve of his conduct to commit himself personally even as an adviser.

In 1755, a gentleman whose name is given as D——s (perhaps Dawkins) communicated to some of the Jacobite party in Britain a very unfavourable account of the Prince's conduct, representing him as one abandoned to a debauched life, insomuch as to bring his health, and even his life, into danger—that in his excesses he had no guard on his conduct or expressions, and was in some degree void of reason—that he was always too precipitate in taking his resolutions, and was then obstinate and deaf to the most solid advice—that he put no value on, and was ungrateful for, the very best services, and was unforgiving and revengeful for the very smallest offence—in short, that he united in his single person all the vices and faults that had ever been in his family, without one of their virtues. In consequence of this representation, certain individuals, whose names have not become known, commissioned a gentleman to carry over from them a memorial, reciting all which had been said, and pointing out the great injury it was calculated to give to his prospects in Britain; entreating him at the same time to live with circumspection and decency, and proposing to send to him some person entirely trusted by them, who might act as his counsellor. It seems likely that a threat to break with him, in the event of his not listening to their remonstrance, was carried by the messenger. The Prince, only enraged by the charges brought against him, replied in scornful terms. 'Gentlemen,' he says, 'I some time ago received a very surprising message, delivered in a still more surprising manner. Reason may, and I hope always shall, prevail; but my heart deceives me if threats or promises ever can. I had always determined to await events in silence or patience, and believed the advances which to your knowledge I have already made, were as great as could be reasonably expected on my part. Yet the influence of well-wishers, of whose sincerity I am satisfied, has made me put pen to paper in vindication of my character, which I understand by them some unworthy people have had the insolence to attack, very possibly to serve some mean purpose of their own. Conscious of my conduct, I despise their low malice; and I consider it to be below my dignity to treat them in the terms they merit.'[1] Immediately after (September 16), we find him writing in melancholy terms to Mr Edgar: 'My sentiments, my honour, my real interest, joined with the unworthy behaviour of some people, has reduced me these several years past to great

[1] The remonstrance, and the Prince's answer, are given in Browne's Appendix. Dr King seems to allude to this remonstrance when he states that a Colonel Macnamara went to the Prince, as a commissioner from the British Jacobites, to request him to dismiss his mistress, Miss Walkingshaw; which the Prince, he says, refused to do. There is no word of a mistress in the documents above quoted.

straits, but *now more than ever*, which obliges me with concern to dismiss the most part of my family. I send you here a list of them, hoping that, when you lay it before the king, he will, out of his good heart, have compassion on such poor distressed subjects.' For some time after we altogether lose sight of this unhappy Prince, but it is believed that he chiefly resided in great privacy at Avignon. How affecting a scrap of his writing about 1760, which has been preserved : ' De vivre et pas vivre est beaucoup plus que de mourir !'

The papers of Bishop Forbes contain a number of particulars respecting the latter life of the Prince. It appears very decisively from these papers that Charles embraced the religion of the Church of England. The bishop preserves a copy of a letter dictated by him to his friends in Britain, under date August 12, 1762, and to the following effect : ' Assure my friends in Britain that I am in perfect health ; that I hope it will come like a thunderbolt ; and that I shall not neglect to recompense every worthy subject as soon as it shall be in my power. They may be assured I shall live and die in the religion of the Church of England, which I have embraced ; and that no kind thing can be said, but what I wish to all my dear friends, for whose good I wish more to be amongst them, than for any advantage it would be to myself, as I have no great ambition except for their welfare.' In June 1763, the first trace appears, in the bishop's memoranda, of a desire on the part of the British Jacobites that the Prince should marry ; and it is amusing to observe with what piety they hope that such an event may be brought about, and that it may be productive of future pretenders to the throne. Mrs Oliphant of Gask, in Perthshire, or, as she is here called, Lady Gask, appears as the moving person in the affair—and the Prince is shadowed forth as a female cousin of that gentlewoman under the designation of Cousin Peggy. A gentleman in London, writing to Forbes, 8th August 1763, mentions that Lady Gask had arrived amongst her friends—the Chevalier's court in Italy—and found them all well ; that Cousin Peggy thanked the bishop for a pot of marmalade he had sent her ;

and that she only waited for a convenient opportunity to visit her friends in Britain.   Another letter, unsubscribed, of date October 27, 1763, mentions that Cousin Peggy had enjoyed a hearty laugh on being informed recently that ' a certain friend sacredly preserved the favourite brogues, and made friends drink out of them '—alluding evidently to the Highland shoes worn by the Prince while travelling through Skye in a female dress, and which had been preserved by Macdonald of Kingsburgh, his guide and host on that occasion.

' The 1st of January 1766 '—so runs a paragraph entered by the bishop—' (about a quarter after nine o'clock) put a period to the troubles and disappointments of good old Mr JAMES MISFORTUNATE '—meaning the old Chevalier, who, we learn, had long been confined to bed with general weakness.   Charles, who now considered himself king of England, had the mortification, as is well known, to find his pretensions acknowledged by no European court, not even by the pope, for the sake of whose faith his grandfather had forfeited his throne.   About a year before the death of the old Chevalier, Charles had renewed his correspondence with his brother, who acted towards him in the most forgiving and generous manner, and made the most strenuous exertions to prepare the way for the pope acknowledging his royal character, after their father should have departed this life.   When James died, Charles was on his way to Rome, and was met on the road, two posts beyond Florence, by Mr Andrew Lumisden, with accounts of the sad event, and of his accession to the nominal dignity of king.   Arriving in Rome, he was received by the immediate attendants of his father as king, but the pope positively refused to acknowledge his title.[1]   In

1 In a letter from John Farquharson of Ardlerg, a refugee Jacobite residing at Dunkirk, to Bishop Forbes, of date May 20, 1767, occurs the following passage : ' The gentleman [that is, the Prince] is positive that he is the peculiar care of Heaven, as passing through so many dangers, and that he is designed for some great end.   He takes all his misfortunes (if you believe those about him) like the true Christian hero.   His answer to the pope, when he sent him word that he would not allow him to take on any titles there, was somewhat good.   He told the nuncio that the loss of Culloden gave him more real concern than any loss he could suffer by any orders from his holiness, and that whatever titles he would take, neither pope nor conclave could nor had any right to take from him.   This I had from a gentleman who was present.'—Lyon in Mourning, x. 1901.

these circumstances, no one being able to visit him, he was left quite alone : Mr Lumisden compared him and his immediate attendants, isolated in Roman society, to the crew of a vessel at sea. Even the heads of the English, Scotch, and Irish colleges were sent from Rome in disgrace for receiving him as king within their own walls. To these distresses was added that of limited income, for the revenues which his father had derived from the courts of France and Spain were not continued to him. He had not more than 15,000 crowns per annum, including an allowance of 10,000 from the pope, which his brother had made over to him. He now withdrew to his late father's seat at Albano, where he lived for some years under the modest title of Count of Albany, but still without abandoning his pretensions. In the *Pleasures of Hope*, Campbell has omitted one remarkable exemplification of that passion—namely, its tenacity and intensity in the breasts of an expiring party. We find Bishop Forbes in the ensuing September congratulating himself on the information communicated by a ' Mr O.,' probably Oliphant, that ' some great and principal persons were beginning to turn their views to my Favourite Lady, as the only one to extricate them out of their difficulties, and set to rights their disjointed affairs '—meaning, probably, the troubles occasioned by the reception of the Stamp Act in America.

Throughout this and the ensuing year, great anxiety is expressed by the bishop and his correspondents respecting the equivocal conduct of the Chevalier in continuing Roman Catholic clergymen in his household, and attending Roman Catholic places of worship, though they are from time to time requested, by persons in his confidence, not to judge too hastily from appearances. Much anxiety is expressed that he should leave Italy, and thoughts seem to have been entertained of his visiting his friends in Scotland—of course incognito. Early, however, in 1769, the worthy beings who looked to him as their legitimate sovereign, and made a religion of their attachment to him, are shocked still more grievously by hearing of his habit of tippling, and that in a drunken fit he had dismissed all his

Scottish attendants, and supplied their places with Italians. Much difficulty is experienced by Bishop Forbes in obtaining correct information on this subject; but at length he receives full particulars from two individuals who had been at the Chevalier's court, and whom he distinguishes only by the appellation of the Fellow-travellers. At a meeting on the 8th of this month with Bishop Gordon,[1] at Moffat, he communicates these particulars, most curiously glossed by party prepossession, in the following terms:

'That John Hay,[2] Andrew Lumisden,[3] and Captain Urquhart had been dismissed for a real act of disobedience. It was true, indeed, that the k—— had been in use, for some time past, to call frequently for t'other glass of wine at dinner and supper, not from any liking to liquor, but like one absent in mind, when he met with things that vexed him, as too often was the case. One day at dinner he had done so till he was somewhat intoxicated, and in that condition proposed going to an oratorio in the afternoon; but they absolutely refused to attend him. Yea, he went into his coach, and they would by no means go into it; upon which he returned to his apartments and dismissed them. In a day or two he sent for them to return to their duty; but they happening to consult with the Cardinal York, he advised them absolutely not to return; which counsel they followed; and he took care to have four Italians put into their places, as persons more fit for his purposes and designs. The cardinal would have been well enough pleased had John Stewart, a constant and faithful attendant, been likewise dismissed; but that could not

1 Minister of a London congregation of nonjurors. This gentleman had baptised the Prince's eldest child by Miss Walkingshaw.
2 John Hay, who had been a writer to the signet in Edinburgh, and was designed 'portioner of Restalrig,' acted as vice-chamberlain or treasurer to the Prince during the latter part of the campaign of 1745-6. He is described, in a memoir by Sir Thomas Strange (MS.), as brother to Lord Huntingdon, one of the judges of the Court of Session. Charles, after the death of his father, knighted him. Subsequently to his dismissal, he returned to Britain on a writ of nolle prosequi, and visited his Scotch friends, including Sir Thomas Miller of Glenlee, then Lord Justice-clerk.
3 Lumisden was brother-in-law to the celebrated engraver, Sir Robert Strange, and published a respectable work on the Antiquities of Rome. He soon after made his peace with the government, and returned to his native country.

take place, as both master and servant, an Athole-man, were not willing to part.   Therefore there are still two Britons with him—Mr Wagstaffe, an Englishman,[1] and John Stewart, a Scotsman.   He now enjoys more ease and quiet than formerly, and has never been seen concerned in the least with liquor since that event, which had been happily attended with one good effect, to make him think more seriously upon what had happened ; and no man could be of a more firm and determined resolution than he was known to be.   Not a blot, nor so much as a pimple, was in his face, though maliciously given out by some as if it were all over blotted ; but he is jolly and plump, though not to excess, being still agile, and fit for undergoing toil.'   With respect to his religion, the bishop stated that his informants had been empowered to give out that any demonstrations he might make in favour of the Roman Catholic faith were owing to the difficulty of his situation, as, even between eleven and twelve years of age, he had made up his mind against the truth of its doctrines, and determined on the change that had subsequently taken place in his professions.   It is also stated that he only remained at Rome in the hope of obtaining a recognition of his titles, and a pension from the new pope. We also have the following note : ' That Mrs Forbes had given the two Fellow-travellers a piece of seed-cake, which they took entire to the k——, making a present of it to him, and withal telling him from whom they had it.   " Ay," said he, " a piece of seed-cake from Scotland, and from Edinburgh too !"   Then rising from his seat, and opening a drawer : " There," said he, " you see me deposit it, and no tooth shall go upon it but my own." '   Charles had further sent a memorandum for a copy of the bishop's narrative of his escape, and a *cookery-book of English pastry puddings;* and we are afterwards informed that the former work, when sent, was translated into Italian, and published at Rome.

Soon after, intelligence of a more cheerful nature visits these

---

[1] The Chevalier's Protestant chaplain.

zealous votaries of divine right.   A friend recently at Rome
informs Forbes that Charles ' is a great economist, and pays all
accounts once a month at furthest, and that he gets up in the
morning about four o'clock, takes breakfast about seven, dines
at twelve on the plainest dishes, drinks tea at four, sups betwixt
seven and eight, and is in his bedchamber by nine, or before it '
—habits, it must be allowed, very different from those of most
professed tipplers.   ' I heard lately,' says another correspondent
of the bishop in 1770, ' that Cousin Peggy was well, much in
company now with the great folks, and received all the honours
from them she could desire.'   It is also curious to observe what
hopes were inspired into the breasts of the Jacobites by the
Wilkes tumults and the commercial difficulties of this era.   In
November of the year just quoted, Bishop Gordon writes
that ' Cousin Peggy is still lively and active, and ready for
employment ; and, now troubles seem to be rising in the
world more and more, I think it not improbable but she
may again find occasion for the exercise of her talents.'   In
April of the ensuing year, John Farquharson of Ardlerg writes
that the king had been using his divine right in a medical way.
' He is now fairly turned physician, and has made this year
several wonderful cures, particularly one of a princess, looked
upon [as] incurable.   This has been of service to him, adds
greatly to his character, and has given him the name of the
Miraculous Doctor.'

In the beginning of 1772 the Chevalier made a journey *incog.*
to Paris, travelling a thousand miles in seven days, without
being affected by it in his appearance.   The movement may be
surmised to have been connected with a negotiation for his
marriage to Louisa, Princess of Stolberg, which the French and
Spanish monarchs had concocted.   The nuptials, which took
place in the ensuing April, seem to have kindled up great joy
amongst the Scottish Jacobites.   Louisa immediately becomes
the subject of loyal toasts, some of them by no means over-
delicate in the turn of their allusions.   An engraving of her
portrait is handed about.   She is celebrated in stiff but

thoroughly cordial verses; and all is satisfaction and happy expectation. Charles and his wife were privately presented to Louis XVI. in the spring of 1775. They did not on that occasion make any public appearance in Paris, whence they went to Bayonne, on their way to visit the king of Spain. In the ensuing May, a letter from Florence appeared in the English newspapers, stating that he lived there in great poverty, barely able to keep a carriage, on which he was not allowed to put any armorial bearings. He is described as extremely corpulent, owing to a total disuse of exercise, and much pimpled in the face, in consequence of drinking.

In a work entitled *Letters from Italy, by a Lady,* published in 1776, the authoress (Mrs Miller) gives an account of two meetings she had with Charles at Rome, probably in the preceding year. While she was passing the evening at the Duchess of Bracciano's, one of the gentlemen in waiting announced *Il Re* (The King), the title by which he was known at Rome. She was anxious, from motives of prudence, to avoid speaking to him, but on entering, he made her a particular bow, sat down on the same sofa, and began a conversation with her and the duchess. ' At last he addressed me in particular, and asked me how many days since my arrival in Rome, how long I should stay, and several such questions. . . . . At my departure, I took leave of the Duchess of Bracciano (agreeable to the custom), and the Chevalier, officiously civil, rose up and wished me a good-night. He is naturally above the middle size, but stoops excessively : he appears bloated and red in the face, his countenance heavy and sleepy, which is attributed to his having given into excess of drinking ; but when a young man, he must have been esteemed handsome. His complexion is of the fair tint, his eyes blue, his hair light-brown, and the contour of his face a long oval. He is by no means thin, has a noble presence and a graceful manner ; his dress was scarlet, laced with a broad gold lace ; he wears his blue ribbon outside of his coat, from which depends a cameo (antique) as large as the palm of my hand ; and wears the same garter and motto as those of the order of St George in England : upon the whole, he has a melancholic, mortified appearance.'

There can be no room to doubt that about this time the habits of the unfortunate Prince were undergoing a rapid change for the worse, and that he soon after began to render his wife extremely unhappy. About the year 1778, the poet Alfieri, then under thirty years of age, and the most enthusiastic and passionate of mortals, became acquainted with this princess, whose character is universally allowed to have been as amiable as her person was beautiful. He first saw her in the great gallery of Florence, and hearing her say, in reference to a portrait of Charles XII. of Sweden, that she thought the dress becoming, he astonished the inhabitants of the city by, two days after, appearing in the streets in an exact copy of that extraordinary uniform. A sonnet which he afterwards composed upon her, under the title of *Ritratto della ma Donna* (' Description of my Mistress '), has been thus translated :

> ' Bright are the dark locks of her braided hair ;
>   Grecian her brow ; its silken eyebrows brown ;
> Her eyes—O lover, to describe forbear !—
>   Life can their glance impart, and death their frown !
> Her mouth no rosebud, and no rose her cheek,
>   May emulate in freshness, fragrance, hue :
> A voice so soft and sweet, to hear her speak
>   Inspires delight and pleasures ever new :
> A smile to soothe all passions save despair ;
>   A slight and graceful form ; a neck of snow ;
> A soft white hand, and polished arm as fair ;
>   A foot whose traces Love delights to shew.
> And with these outward charms, which all adoie,
>   A mind and heart more pure and perfect given ;
> For thee thy lover can desire no more,
>   Adorned by every grace and gift of Heaven.'

Unable at length to endure any longer the harshness of her husband, the princess employed the services of Alfieri in enabling her to escape from his influence. According to a plan arranged by the poet, Charles and his wife walked one morning to a neighbouring convent, for the ostensible purpose of inspecting the work of the nuns. The princess, moving smartly in advance, entered the convent, where it had been agreed that she was to receive protection. When Charles came up, he was refused admittance, and he never saw his wife again. The princess soon after removed to Rome, where she was received with brotherly kindness by Cardinal York, and finally she proceeded to Paris. All this was accomplished without her having in the least compromised her reputation. She ultimately formed a secret alliance, as was supposed, with Alfieri, with whom she lived till his death in 1803. She afterwards resided at Florence, where she died in January 1824, aged seventy-two, having long enjoyed a pension of £2000 per annum from the British crown.[1]

Even when sunk in the absolute sottishness which is so apt to befall greatly disappointed men, there were not wanting in Charles Edward gleams of that natural spirit which led him to a hostile shore with seven men, and carried him into the midst of three armies, each his superior : the light of a better day still gleamed fitfully on the dishonoured head of the Last Stuart. When the late venerable primus of the Scottish episcopate (Walker) was at Rome in the early years of the present century, he received from the lips of Cardinal York the following anecdote : 'Mr Greathead, a personal friend of Mr Fox, succeeded, when at Rome in 1782 or 1783, in obtaining an interview with Charles Edward ; and being alone with him for some time, studiously led the conversation to his enterprise in Scotland, and to the occurrences which succeeded the failure of that attempt. The Prince manifested some reluctance to enter upon these topics, appearing at the same time to undergo so much mental suffering, that his guest regretted the freedom he had used in calling up the remembrance of his misfortunes. At length, however, the Prince

---

[1] It is said that this lady, after the death of Alfieri, made a left-handed marriage with his friend, Francis Xavier Fabre, a French historical painter, whom she appointed her universal executor.

seemed to shake off the load which oppressed him; his eye brightened, his face assumed unwonted animation, and he entered upon the narrative of his Scottish campaigns with a distinct but somewhat vehement energy of manner—recounted his marches, his battles, his victories, his retreats, and his defeats—detailed his hair-breadth escapes in the Western Isles, the inviolable and devoted attachment of his Highland friends, and at length proceeded to allude to the dreadful penalties with which the chiefs among them had been visited. But here the tide of emotion rose too high to allow him to go on—his voice faltered, his eye became fixed, and he fell convulsed on the floor. The noise brought into the room his daughter, the Duchess of Albany, who happened to be in an adjoining apartment. "Sir," she exclaimed, "what is this? You have been speaking to my father about Scotland and the High-landers! No one dares to mention these subjects in his presence." [1]

It is also an affecting, and, I may surely add, redeeming circumstance in the life of this ill-fated Prince, that amongst the amusements of his last and lonely hours was that of playing on the bagpipe those airs which, in his brighter days, soothed him in the bivouac, or led him to victory. [2] Domenico Corri, the musician, in his Life of himself, gives some interesting particulars of the Prince's latter years. After stating that some fortunate connections had raised him to the honour of con-ducting the concert parties given at Rome by the English and native nobility, he adds: 'This period was the pontificate of Ganganelli, who was the friend of Prince Charles the Pretender, brother of Cardinal York. That prince frequently gave enter-tainments and concerts to the nobility, the conducting of which was also assigned to me. With Prince Charles I had, previously to this period, lived two years, during which time he had kept

---

[1] The above anecdote was published in the *Episcopal Magazine*, a work conducted by Bishop Russell.

[2] A beautiful set of pipes, which belonged to him, having the joints bound with silver, was purchased from his servant early in this century by Mr Skene of Rubislaw, who still (1846) possesses them.

entirely private, not seeing any one whatever, it being in the
reign of the preceding pope, who had refused to acknowledge
the title he assumed.   In his retired life Prince Charles
employed his hours in exercise and music, of which he was
remarkably fond.   I usually remained alone with him every
evening, the Prince playing the violoncello, and I the harpsi-
chord, also composing together little pieces of music; yet these
tête-à-têtes were of a sombre cast.   The apartment in which we
sat was hung with old red damask, with two candles only, and
on the table a pair of loaded pistols (instruments not at all
congenial to my fancy), which he would often take up, examine,
and again replace on the table; yet the manners of this Prince
were always mild, affable, and pleasing.'   In September 1787,
in the prospect of an early dissolution, Charles legitimated,
by a deed recorded in the parliament of Paris, his natural
daughter, created her Duchess of Albany, and constituted her
his sole heir.[1]   He latterly lived constantly at Florence, in a
palace in the Via Bastino, which belonged in 1818 to the
Duchess San Clemente, when the Scottish gentleman who
communicates this circumstance temporarily occupied it—the
rooms still bearing at that time many of the crowns, mottoes,
and devices with which it had been decorated to suit its former
inhabitant.   On the 30th of January 1788,[2] Charles Stuart sank
under an attack of palsy and apoplexy, expiring in the arms
of his faithful attendant, Mr Nairn, son of the attainted Lord
Nairn.   His death occasioned a paragraph in the papers, but
made little noise in the general world.   In Scotland, however,
where his name was associated with romantic achievement and
historical recollections, there were still a few faithful hearts to

[1] The Duchess of Albany was the Prince's daughter by Miss Walkingshaw. She is said
to have received an excellent education, and to have been an elegant and amiable woman.
It is also said that Charles long refused to legitimate her, and that she was for a long time
supported by the Cardinal York, who gave her 6000 crowns per annum. She died in 1789,
of an abscess in her side, the consequence of a fall from a horse, being then about forty
years of age.

[2] The 31st was the date given out at the time; but Lord Mahon ascertained that the 30th
was the true date. His attendants appear to have practised a small deception, to avoid
raising any feeling among the remnant of the party respecting his dying on a day deemed
fatal to the house of Stuart.

bleed at the intelligence that this last of a lofty line was no more. Sir Walter Scott recollected a gentleman named Stuart, a friend of his father's family, calling one day in mourning, when, being asked if he had suffered any family loss, he answered: 'My poor Chief!'—a brief answer, but sufficient for those to whom it was addressed. Charles was buried with due ceremony in the cathedral of Frascati, where his brother resided.[1] An urn containing his heart was deposited in the

[1] Henry Stuart, Cardinal de York, was not a favourite with the Jacobites during his middle life, probably on account solely of his having accepted honours in the Romish church. His character in latter life appeared that of a mild and inoffensive man. In 1784, when Charles was believed to be dying, Cardinal York presented to the pope, the foreign ministers at Rome, and others, a paper declaring the title which he should have to the British crown, in the event of his brother's decease. On the death of his brother in 1788, he took no other steps than to cause this declaration to be read, and to strike a medal bearing his name as 'Henricus IX. Angliæ Rex,' with the addition 'Dei gratia, sed non voluntate hominum.' He was Bishop of Frascati, and had two rich livings in France, the abbeys of Anchin and St Amand, besides a considerable pension from Spain. The abbeys were lost to him at the time of the French Revolution. On the successful invasion of Italy by Bonaparte, his revenues as cardinal and bishop were also lost, and about the same time he appears to have been deprived of his Spanish pension. To aid the pope in making up the sum required by the French general, the cardinal disposed of his family jewels, including a ruby, esteemed the largest and most perfect known, and valued at £50,000. In the reduced state in which he was now left, he remained in retirement at his villa near Rome till 1798, when the revolutionary troops attacked and plundered his palace, and forced him to fly for his life. He went first to Padua, and afterwards to Venice, supporting himself by the sale of a small quantity of silver plate, which was soon exhausted, and he was then quite destitute. Some time after, Sir John Hippesley Coxe, who had been acquainted with Cardinal Borgia in Italy, received from that prelate an account of the condition of the unfortunate Cardinal York. This he communicated to Mr Andrew Stuart, who drew up a memorial of the case, which was carried by Mr Secretary Dundas to the throne. George III. immediately ordered the Earl of Minto, then ambassador at Vienna, to offer the cardinal, in the most delicate terms possible, a pension of £4000 per annum. The earl, in a letter of February 9, 1800, dated from Vienna, thus addressed the object of the royal bounty: 'I have received the orders of his majesty the king of Great Britain to remit to your eminence the sum of £2000, and to assure your eminence that, in accepting this mark of the interest and esteem of his majesty, you will give him sensible pleasure. I am at the same time ordered to acquaint your eminence with his majesty's intention to transmit a similar sum in the month of July, if the circumstances remain such that your eminence continues disposed to accept it. . . . . In executing the orders of the king my master, your eminence will do me the justice to believe that I am deeply sensible of the honour of being the organ of the noble and touching sentiments with which his majesty has condescended to charge me, and which have been inspired into him on the one hand by his own virtues, and on the other by the eminent qualities of the august person in whom he wishes to repair, as far as possible, the disasters into which the universal scourge of our times has dragged, in a special manner, all who are most worthy of veneration and respect.' It is not unworthy of remark, that Charles and his brother Henry had a legal claim on the English government for the arrears of the parliamentary settlement made upon their

same church, inscribed with a few expressive lines by the
Abbate Felicé.   A Scottish periodical work soon after presented
the following lines as a proposed epitaph for his monument
at Rome :

> ' Remote from Britain, in this foreign shrine,
>   Ends the last hope of Stuart's ancient line—
>   Reflection must excite the generous tear,
>   And royalty, secure, will learn to fear.
>   O ye of Britain's isle—no more unjust,
>   Your hearts acknowledge here your Charles' dust.
>   The virtuous in the tomb their rights maintain ;
>   Alive his virtues challenged them in vain.'

Many whose destiny has never subjected them to severe
trials, will call the habits of this unhappy Prince a proof
that he never possessed a magnanimous character, as he must
have otherwise scorned so wretched a solacement for his
misfortunes.   Let these persons pray that they may never be
reduced to analogous circumstances, or placed in similar
temptations.   To be born with disputable pretensions is one
of the greatest of misfortunes.   Even in the middle walks of
life, how often do we see industry, worth, and ability wrecked
in their course, in consequence of the inheritance of some
claims of property, which the law cannot be brought to sanction
till it has worn out all that could have enjoyed the boon !   How
much severer the calamity of being born to the prospect of the
highest object of human ambition—ever in view, and ever
denied—to be born, in short, as Cardinal York expressed it, a
king by the grace of God, but not by the will of man !   It has

grandmother, the queen-consort of James II.   Charles had empowered his natural daughter
to take some steps respecting this claim, and the good offices of Louis XVI. were sought,
for the purpose of representing the case to the British sovereign.   Louis declined the
task, remarking, with little anticipation of the fate of his own race : ' C'est une famille
malheureuse ; dont je ne veux plus entendre parler.'

The cardinal returned in 1801 to Rome, where he continued to enjoy the pension till his
death in June 1807.   He bequeathed to the Prince of Wales the order of the Garter which
belonged to his ancestor Charles I., and a ring which had been anciently worn by the
kings of Scotland at their coronation.   The Prince afterwards caused a monument to be
raised to the memory of the old Chevalier and his two sons in St Peter's at Rome.

always appeared to me that, in the case of Prince Charles
Edward, the agony of hope deferred and severe disappointment, and the degradations ultimately put upon him by
individuals who, by birth, were no more than his equals, wore
out a spirit originally vigorous, and from which, in happier
circumstances, good fruits might have been expected.

The subsequent history of a few of the more remarkable
individuals who had been concerned in the affair of 1745, and
survived it, may here be given.

The Duke of Perth died on the 11th of May 1746, in his
voyage to France, his constitution having been completely worn
out by about three weeks of skulking in the Highlands.   His
brother, Lord John Drummond, made his escape in the same
vessel, and died next year in the French service at Bergen-
op-Zoom.   Two elegantly expressed Latin epitaphs for these
two unfortunate noblemen, as inscribed in the chapel of the
English nuns at Antwerp, and narrating the above circumstances, are copied in the Rev. Mr Forbes's papers.[1]

Lord George Murray, after a long concealment in the Highlands, got on board a vessel in the Firth of Forth, and obtained
a passage to Holland.   The reader has seen the ill success of
an attempt he made to see the Prince at Paris.   The justice
denied to him by Charles, and by many other individuals who
had been associated with him in the late enterprise, was done
to him by the old Chevalier, who gave him an apartment in his
palace, and treated him with much distinction.   Lord George,
under the assumed name of De Valignie, wrote a letter to Mr
Hamilton of Bangour, dated Emerich, August 5, 1749, giving an
account of the last few days of the campaign of 1745.   He also
composed a complete memoir of the campaign, which was
published in the *Jacobite Memoirs*, 1834.   Lord George died at

---

[1] I mention this circumstance as an addition to the proof that the Duke of Perth really
died at sea in May 1746, this fact having of late years been challenged by a claimant of
the Perth titles and estates, who asserts that the duke did not embark for France, but,
withdrawing to an obscure place in the county of Durham, there sank into the condition
of a shoemaker, married a humble woman, and died in 1782, after becoming the father of
several children, the eldest of whom was father to the claimant.

Medenblinck, in Holland, in 1760. On the death of James, second Duke of Athole, in 1764, John, the eldest son of Lord George, who had married the only daughter and child of the late duke, would have succeeded to the title in course of law, but for the attainder of his father. A petition to the king, on which the House of Lords gave a favourable report, overcame the objection, and the lineal posterity of Lord George have accordingly enjoyed, since 1764, this princely name, and all the great demesnes connected with it.

Young Locheil obtained, as we have seen, a regiment in the French service. He did not, however, enjoy this long; for while on duty at Borgue, he was carried off by an inflammation of the brain, October 26, 1748. The death of this amiable and truly respectable man was bewailed by both parties. In the *Scots Magazine* of the time, there was inserted a very honourable poetical tribute to his memory, evidently the composition of one who did not sympathise in his political opinions : it ends with the singular thought, that the gentle Locheil is now 'a Whig in heaven.' The elder Locheil died in the same year. The territories of the family were restored to it in 1784, in consequence of an act then passed for giving back the forfeited estates to the heirs, under certain restrictions.

Macpherson of Cluny remained in hiding on what had been his estate for nine years after the insurrection, chiefly residing in a cave near the site of his destroyed house, and supported by his faithful adherents. He had the charge of the large sum of money which had been secreted in the neighbourhood of Loch Arkaig, and probably kept himself in readiness, on a fitting occasion, once more to appear in arms with his clan for the house of Stuart. Cluny withdrew to France in 1755, and died there in the ensuing year. His estate, which also was restored to his family, is now enjoyed by his posterity.

Lord Ogilvie rose to the rank of lieutenant-general in the French service. In 1778 he procured from George III. a free pardon and reversal of his attainder, and was thereafter enabled to live upon his family estates in Scotland, where he died in

1803, at the age of seventy-nine. His lady, who had been actively concerned in raising men for the enterprise, and who accompanied her husband on the expedition to England, was taken prisoner after the battle of Culloden, and imprisoned in Edinburgh Castle, whence she escaped in the November following. Having made her way to France, she died there in 1757, at the age of thirty-three. It would appear that Lord and Lady Ogilvie were each only about twenty years of age when they entered upon the campaign of 1745. It may be mentioned, to the honour of Lord Ogilvie, that after the death of Louis XVI., he refused any longer to draw his pension as a French officer, and even declined to accept its arrears when these were offered by Bonaparte.

Sir James Steuart, being in France at the time of the battle of Culloden, escaped the dangers which beset so many of his friends, but, excepted from the act of indemnity, he could not return to his native country. For eighteen years he resided abroad with his wife, and during that time, turning his mind to the subject of finance, became one of the most accomplished political economists of his day. Being pardoned and restored to his property in 1763, he published in England, four years thereafter, *An Inquiry into the Principles of Political Economy*, which was followed by several smaller works. Sir James died at Coltness in 1780.

Mr Hamilton of Bangour, after the battle of Culloden, skulked for some time in the Highlands, and then escaped to France. By the intercession of a number of powerful friends, he soon obtained a pardon, and returned home; but his constitution being irremediably shattered by the hardships he had suffered in hiding, he died of a slow consumption at Lyon in 1754. Some of the poetry of this gentleman retains popularity, and his name can never be altogether forgotten while that of Wordsworth exists, for it was in consequence of a ballad of Bangour's that the great bard of the lakes wrote his various poems on Yarrow.

Sir Alexander Macdonald died in 1747, but the Laird of

Macleod survived till 1772, an object of general dislike in the Highlands, not so much on account of his apostacy from the Stuart cause, as for the active part he was believed to have taken in the attempts to seize the fugitive Prince. Prosperity did not smile upon him, and when he died, he left his estate almost hopelessly encumbered. The fortunes of the Siol Tormod were, however, redeemed by his son, the brave, prudent, and generous General Macleod—the man described by Burns as

'a chieftain worth gowd,
Though bred amang mountains of snaw.'

Mr Murray of Broughton, being taken into custody at Polmood in Peeblesshire, and removed to London, entered into an arrangement with government to give information and evidence, for the purpose of saving his own life. His evidence was the means of destroying Lord Lovat; but the information he gave against the Duke of Beaufort, Sir Watkyn William Wynne, and other English Jacobites, was of no avail, for want of the second witness required in English law. After this dismal surrender of honour, the secretary dragged out a wretched life upon a pension of £200 a year. On the death of his brother, Sir Charles Murray of Stanhope, baronet, he assumed the family title, and died in December 1777, leaving three sons, David, Robert, and Thomas, the eldest of whom, an officer in the navy, took up the title after his death. The secretary employed his leisure in his latter days in writing a memoir of the transactions of 1745, including a very minute account of the negotiations and other circumstances which preceded it, and in which he had himself been much concerned.[1]

Dr Archibald Cameron escaped to France in the same vessel with the Prince, to whom he had been of important service during his wanderings. A letter of Glengarry to the old Chevalier's secretary, Mr Edgar, of date 'Boulogne-sur-Mer, 16th January 1750,' and extant in the Stuart Papers, gives an

---

[1] This memoir, I believe, exists in manuscript in the possession of the family of the late William H. Murray, Esq., of the Theatre Royal, Edinburgh.

account of a visit which Dr Cameron had then recently paid to
the Highlands; when he gave out that all might shift for themselves, as the king and Prince had given up hopes of restoration.
The letter further states that Dr Cameron took into his possession six thousand louis-d'ors, out of the large sum which he had
assisted to conceal near Loch Arkaig; Cluny Macpherson being
unable to prevent his doing so, though he obliged the doctor to
give a receipt for the sum.   With this money, it was said Dr
Cameron designed to enter into a mercantile copartnery at
Dunkirk.   In a letter of Lochgarry (cousin of Glengarry) to
Prince Charles, dated at Paris, June 22, 1750, the writer relates
that he had lately been in Scotland, and saw Cluny, who gave
him an account of the money left in his charge, much of which
had been 'torn from him,' so that the sum now in his hands
was only sixteen thousand louis.   Lochgarry expresses an
anxious wish to be commissioned *with Dr Cameron* to go to
Scotland and bring over the remaining sum.   It is scarcely
possible to make out from these notices any clear idea of
Dr Cameron's procedure, more especially as we afterwards find
his widow communicating intelligence which had reached her
of a proposal having been made by Glengarry to sell himself
to the government as an informer.   It is, however, certain that
Dr Cameron revisited Scotland in 1753, and was then taken
prisoner in the house of Stewart of Glenbuckie, by a party of
soldiers from the garrison of Inversnaid.   Being carried to
London, and there arraigned upon the act of attainder, in which
his name was included, he was sentenced to die the death of a
traitor.   His wife, then residing with seven children at Lille in
Flanders, came to London, and presented petitions in his behalf,
but without avail.   He was executed on the 7th of June, con-
ducting himself on the occasion with a degree of firmness and
cheerfulness scarcely less than that manifested by Balmerino.[1]

[1] In the burial register of the old chapel of the Savoy occurs the following entry: '1753,
Dr Archd. Cameron drawn on a sledge from the Tower, and executed at Tyburn for high
treason, on Thursday the 7th June, and buried as above in the chancel vault.   Vault fee
not paid, J. W.'   This entry being discovered some years ago, a few gentlemen combined
to put up a small tablet to Dr Cameron near the supposed site of his sepulture.

The government was greatly blamed for this act of severity, which then appeared needless; but it is probable that they had secret information of certain dangerous traffickings which the agents of the House of Stuart were still carrying on in the Highlands, and acted under the belief that the sacrifice of Dr Cameron was necessary to prevent further attempts on the throne.

APPENDIX.

ACCOUNT OF CHARGE AND DISCHARGE, BY MR MURRAY
OF BROUGHTON, RESPECTING SUMS OF THE PRINCE'S
MONEY IN HIS POSSESSION AFTER THE BATTLE OF
CULLODEN.[1]

CHARGE.

Received from Sir Thomas Sherridan in the wood upon the side of Locharkik, opposite to a place called Callich, about ten days after the battle of Culloden, 1000 guineas..	£1,050	0
From Do. more, and, so far as Mr Murray can remember, at the same time with the above, in Spainish coin, 700 pistoles, valued at 17s. 6d. each	612	10
Six casks of French gold landed at Burradale, containing louis-d'ores........	35,000	0
Mr M. thinking it unreasonable that the louis should be given at the value of 20 shillings, as formerly, paid away about 2250 of them as guineas..	112	10
From a French officer who had landed upon the East Coast with 2000 guineas...	1,000	0

N.B.—This French officer was charged with 2000 guineas, but
said he had 1000 taken from him as he passed thro' the
Mackenzies' country, and gave in an account of deductions
from the other thousand ; but as Mr M. cannot charge his
memory with the extent of the sum, he has charged himself
with one thousand pounds, tho' he still thinks he did not
receive quite so much.

Total charge.............................	£37,775	0

---

[1] *Note in the handwriting of Bishop Forbes.*—' N.B.   This is a rare and curious paper,
taken from the handwriting of John Murray of Broughton, Esq., Secretary to C. P. R.,
being charge and discharge of money matters upon, and by, the said Mr Murray.'

DISCHARGE.

VOUCHERS.

1. This article may be vouched by Mr M'Donald of Clanronald, younger, Mr Stewart of Ardsheill, Mr Cammeron of Torcastle, Doctor Cameron, Charles Stewart, one of Mr Murray's clerks, and by all the surviving people of Lochaber, Morar, Knoydart, Ariseg, and Moydart.

    1. It being judged proper to give some money toward the support of the wounded and the widows of those who died at Culloden, it was agreed to give half a guinea to the former, and a guinea to each of the latter ; and according to the lists given in by those who had an opportunity, the sum amounted to 500 lowis, valued as guineas.. £525   0

2. This sum was paid by Charles Stuart, in presence of L—d Lovit, Locheil, Clanronald younger, M'Leod you^{r.} of Neuck, Do^{d.} Cameron, M'Donald, nephew to Cappoch, Mackinnon, Barisdale, Lochgary, Glenbucket, Major Kennedy, and Captn. Alex^{r.} M'Nabb, with some others.

    2. At a meeting at a place called Callich, upon the side of Locharkik, where it was proposed to raise a body of men to continue the war. To enable the several commanders to make their compliments, there was distributed among them 600 lowis, valued as guineas.......... 630   0

3 and 4. This gentleman is still alive, and Mr M. is ready to believe is a person of veracity, and will acknowledge it.

    3. To the Laird of M'Kinnan, the same day and place........ 40   0

    4. Sent by d^{o.} to M'Leod of Raza, and M'Donald yor. of Scotus, being all that remained of the sum Mr M. then had carried with him... 20   0

£1,215   0

5. This money was paid by Charles Stuart according to the acco^{ts.} given in to him, except what was due to Barisdale's regiment, which Mr M. paid to Mr Colin M'Kenzie, his adjutant and paymaster, at Doct^{r.} Cameron's house in Glendesherie, and amounted to about £300. Mr M'Kenzie is now in London.

Carry over,................£1,215   0

Brought over.................. £1,215 0

5. To arrears due the troops, from the beginning of March
till the 16th day of April inclusive, according to the
musters of such regiments as had an opportunity to give
them in, about 1500 lowis at a guinea each.............. 1,575 0

6 and 7. Mr M'Leod you'. of Neuck may remember this.
Raza having wrote with a little too much warmth, Mr M'Leod
made an apology to Mr M. for him, and beg'd that it might not
prevent him from sending a supply ; and he will likewise remember that it was by his uncle Bernera that it was sent, and that
Mr M. told him that he had given that gentleman £50. Mr M.
is informed that Bernera is still alive.

6. Sent from the wood on the side of Locharkik by M'Leod
of Bernèra to M'Leod of Raza, upon the receipt of a
letter from him complaining that the former sum was
too small.. 40 0
7. To M'Leod of Bernera at the same time..................... 50 0

8. Mr M. paid Mrs Cameron above £40 for part of these
cattle in the Doct's. presence ; the others he cannot call to mind,
being country people.

8. To cattle bought from Doct'. Cameron and others, to
supply the men rendezvouzed at Glenmely.................. 80 0

9. Doct'. Cameron was the person Mr M. chiefly imployed to
procure these horses, and some of them were bought from a
tenant of Lochiells in Glenpayen.

9. To horses to carry the ammunition ingaged to be sent by
Mr M'Donald yo'. of Clanronald, from the coast of
Ariseg to the head of Lochsheill............................. 45 0

10. Mr M. has no other voucher for this article save that the
man is alive ; he was one of Col. Baggot's troop, and remarkably
well known all over the Highlands.

10. To Evan Uisile Cameron on the side of Locharkik....... 3 3
                                                            ————
                                                       £3,008 3

11 and 12. As this gentleman is dead, Mr M. can bring no
proof, as the confusion and hurry was very great at the time, tho'
if he delivered the £20 to his father, he is still alive, and it will
be a presumption of his having at the same time received the
£100.

Carry over.................. £3,008 3

Brought over.................. £3,008 3

11. To Mr M'Donald of Barisdale, at the head of Locharkik,
   on the evening we were obliged to disperse...............   100 0

12. To his father by him...   20 0

13. This gentleman is now alive; he received his money in a
small cottage, in presence of Lochiell his nephew, Cammeron of
Torcastle, and many others.

13. To Mr Campbell of Ardslignish at the same time.........   40 0

14. Of this no proof can be brought, unless Sʳ Stewart Threpland, who was so kind as to attend him, remembers that he had
Spainish coin; but the great intimacy that alwise subsisted betwixt
Locheil and Mr M. would seem to confirm it; and what makes
him remember it the better, was his chiding him for being too
easy to give money to whoever asked it; and that by giving him
that sum, he had but a few remaining pistoles in his own pocket.

14. To Cameron of Lochiel the same evening in Spanish
   gold, he being then on horseback, ready to set out, and
   told Mr M. that he had not one farthing left, having
   given all among his own people about.....................   40 0

15. It is impossible to give any other proof of this charge than
that everybody present can say how much Mr M. was harassed
at that time by demands, insomuch that he was glad to get away,
and to send the money that remained in casks along with Lochiel
for protection.

15. To several people at the same time and place in small
   sums about..   100 0

16. Mr M'Leod will remember that it was with difficulty Mr
M. could prevail upon him to take it, he saying that he had got
enough of his own.

16. To Mr Alexʳ M'Leod yoʳ of Neuck that evening... .....   50 0
                                                          ─────
                                                        £3,358 3

17. This article Major Kennedy will remember to have seen
Mr M. pay in Morar, upon the receipt of a letter and message
from his lordship, when we were together with Clanronald on our
way to meet Mr Allan M'Donald, a churchman, and ── M'Leod,
going to the Isle of Uist.

17. To Lord Lovat, to pay his guard..............................   20 0

Carry over.................. £3,378 3

Brought over.................. £3,378 3

18. Major Kennedy and Charles Stewart made this journey with Mr Murray.

 18. To expences and small gratuitys in passing thro' Moydart and Arrisaig, with a view to have gone over to the Isle of Uist to the Prince...   10 0

19. This gentleman is now in Scotland.

 19. To Cameron of Dungallon in Gleneurich....................   100 0

20. There were there several of the Cameron officers all in want of money, to whom Mr M. gave each a small sum.

 20. To several officers, and others of the same name, and at the same place, about.....................................   50 0

21. This gentleman wrote a letter to Mr M., saying that he had got intelligence from one M'Kenzie that a body of 300 French were landed in the north near to Caithness, and begging him to prevail with Lochiell to raise some men and march north, but the intelligence was laugh'd at.

 21. To some M'Donalds who were sent with a letter from Barrisdale...   5 5

22. This Cameron of Torcastle may remember, he being present when Cameron came to ask Lochiell's advice about his surrendering to Gen[l.] Campbell.

 22. To Donald Moir Cameron, adjutant to Lochiel's regiment, in a wood upon the side of Lochsheill..............   5 5

23. There were likewise in company Torcastle and his son, and Mr M. imagines none of the surviving gentlemen can have forgot it.

 23. To guides, &c., when Locheill, Major Kennedy, Sir David Murray, Sir Stewart Threpland, and others, went over to Appin..   10 0

£3,558 13

24 and 25. This gentleman is living, and Mr M. flatters himself will be ready to acknowledge it.

 24. To Mr Stewart of Ardsheil, in the wood above Ballaheulish, where Locheill, Sir Stewart Threpland, Sir

Carry over.................. £3,558 13

Brought over.................. £3,558 13

David Murray, Major Kennedy, &c. were with him for
some days..   100 0

25. To him as arrears due to his regiment till then not paid,
Mr M. thinks more than 100 0

26. This will not admit of a voucher, but it is reasonable to
believe that Mr M. could give them no less.

26. To the boatmen who carried us over into Appin...........   5 0

27. The major is still living; he seem'd very sensible of the
favour, and said it was just one year's pay.

27. To Major Kennedy, in the wood of Ballaheulish, when
he went to surrender himself at Fort-William............   150 0

28 and 29. Ardsheil will be able to call both these articles to
mind, having applyed to him to employ people to look for it, and
when found, he sent his servant with it.

28. To recovering a pocket-book, dropt by Mr M. in the
above-mentioned wood......................... ....   5 0

29. To the express, one Donald Stewart, a servant of Ardsheil's, who was sent with the pocket-book to Glenlyon.   3 3

30. This gentleman is now in Scotland.   Mr M. is only doubt-
full whether it was £150 or only 100 louis-dores, but thinks it was
100 louis's & 50 guineas; if he has overcharged him, he hopes it
will be forgiven, as it is not done with a view to exhaust the
sum.

30. To Sir Stewart Threpland, in the wood near to Kinlochleven..   150 0

31. Mr Cameron cannot have forgot this, for M. M. insisted
upon his conveying of it to his wife, and probably Sir Stewart
Threpland, then present, may remember the conversation.

31. To Doctr. Cameron at the same time and place............   100 0

32. This sum was given at the same time with the two former,
it having been agreed upon betwixt Locheill and Mr M. that he
M. should go to Glenlyon, where he expected to meet his sister
Mrs M'Dougal, and send her back to Edinburgh to procure a ship

Carry over.................. £4,171 16

Brought over................. £4,171 16

for them; and in case she did not come, he was to proceed himself south to procure one and bring her to the east coast of Fyffe,
it being then reported that the P. was sailed in a meal ship from
the island of Uist for France. This Sir Stewart Threpland and
Doct^r. Cameron cannot have forgot, there being no access at that
time to raise any of the money that was buried.

32. To Cameron of Lochiell, at the same place, to enable
   him to supply the P——, in case of his returning to the
   main land—

   Louis... 1,000 0
   Guineas, 500.. 525 0

33. This article may easily be imagined. We were seven in
company, and obliged to send out scouts every night, the enemy
being on all quarters.

33. To expences when in Rannoch and Glenlyon, together
   with Dr Cameron and Dr Murray......................... 20 0

£5,716 16

34. This gentleman is now in Scotland. He met Mr M. in
Rannoch, and conducted him south so far as Monteith. Mr M.
believes him to be a man of candor and veracity, and that he
will acknowledge it.

34. To Alexander M'Nabb, captain in Kappoch's regiment,
   as arrears due his company.................................. 30 0
N.B.—It is to be observed that Capt M'Nabb was no follower of Kappoch's, but brought his company from Brodalbin.
So was not included in the arrears paid to Kappoch regm^t.

35. Mr M. gave this money to Mrs Menzies of Culdairs in her
own house, she having informed him of their being in that
country.

35. To Mr Norval Hume and other three gentlemen then
   skulking in Glenlyon... 25 0

36. This money was given to him upon the south side of Glenlyon, among the rocks—where Sir D. Murray, Dr Cameron, Mr
John Cameron the minister, now an officer in Lord Ogilvie's
regiment, and M. M., had slept that night—to buy whiskie and
snuff for Lochiell, with a fair wig, and other things to disguise
Mr M. when he went south.

Carry over................. £5,771 16

Brought over.................. £5,771 16

36. To John M'Naughton to purchase necessarys when in
   Glenlyon...   5 5

37. This must alone hang upon her and Mr M.'s assertion.
   37. To Mrs Macdougal to carry her south...........................   42 0

38. This money Mr M. gave her at her own house of M., to be
taken care of by her husband, and two days after he received a
message by his former servant, Robert Buchannan, that the
money was buried in the garden. The pistols, tho Mr M.'s property, and often demanded, have always been refused.

   38. Deposited in Mrs Menzies of Culdairs's hands —— louis-
      dores..   3,500 0
      guineas 351..   368 11
                                                                           ———————
                                                                           £9,687 12

Likewise a pair of pistols inlaid with gold, which Mr M. had
   given him by the P——e.

39. This money Mr M. gave in Brodalbine, Capt. M'Nab
being present.

   39. To Robert Buchanan, when he brought the account of
      the moneys being buried.....................................   5 5

40. This affair is too remarkable to have escaped the memory
of any present. A court-martial having sit upon two men who
were suspected, and the circumstances appearing so strong, that
the members were ready to condemn them, about 11 o'clock at
night, Mr Harrison came to Mr M., then in bed in the next room,
and told him that he had discovered the cask, and would deliver
it next morning. Mr M. desired the court-martial to break up,
and set the men at liberty. Next day there was a meeting about
it, when Mr Harrison refused to name the persons, as the discovery had been made to him in confession. But the thing being
strongly insisted on, Bishop M'Donald agreed that he should
describe them, which, together with other circumstances, made
it plain that D——l and this Irishman were the persons concerned. There were present at this meeting at the foot of Loch-
morar, Bishop M'Donald, Mr Harrison, M'Donald of Clan
Ronald yor., Alexander M'Leod of Neuck yor., Barrisdale, Major
Kennedy, M'Donald yor. of Scotus, and several others.

                                                        Carry over.................. £9,692 17

Brought over.................. £9,692 17

N.B.—Mr M. is informed that the above-named D——l is now an officer in Lord Ogilvie's regiment.

40. When the French ships were attacked at Burradale, the money was landed, and secreted in a wood, lest the enemy had prevailed and made a descent, and whilst it was there, one of the casks was carried off by an Irishman, whose name Mr M. has forgot, and one D——l, a Lancashire man, now an officer abroad; but, finding that they could not convey away the whole, D——l asked one Harrison, a churchman, if he would hear his own companion's confession, which Harrison having agreed to, the Irishman carried him in to the wood, and discovered the cask, but at the same time broke it open, and took one bag, which, upon reckoning the whole sum in the wood upon the side of Locharkik, was found to have contained 700 louis-d'ores... 700 0

————

£10,392 17

41. This sum of 15,000 louis-dores, 1000 in each bag, counted over exactly, was divided into three parcels, 5000 in each, one parcel put under a rock in a small rivulet, the other two parcels in the ground at a little distance, the holes made and the money deposited by Sir Stewart Threpland,[1] Mr Alexander M'Leod yor. of Neuck, Major Kennedy, and Dr Cameron.

————

Carry over..............£10,392 17

[1] This gentleman, so frequently mentioned in Mr Murray's paper, and also alluded to in several parts of the preceding narrative, was a younger brother of the young gentleman slain in the pursuit at Preston, both being the children of Sir David Threipland, Bart., of Fingask, in Perthshire. Sir David, who had been engaged in the insurrection of 1715-16, when he entertained the old Chevalier for a night in his house, was, in 1745, only the tenant of estates which had once been his property. Being then old and infirm, he was unable to go out, but he sent to the field all his sons who were then of an age to bear arms. After the battle of Culloden, Stewart Threipland remained in company with Locheil, to whom, in his then wounded condition, he was of considerable service, having been bred to the medical profession. An anecdote, reflecting the highest credit on his benevolence, is related in a note at page 429. Sometime in the month of July he left Locheil in his concealment, and went to Edinburgh in the disguise of a Presbyterian probationer. From the Scottish he made his way to the English capital, in the company of Mr William Gordon, a bookseller of good repute in those days, whose apprentice he appeared to be. Afterwards he escaped abroad, where he remained a considerable time, living in intimacy with Mr Hamilton of Bangour, Sir James Steuart, and Mr Andrew Lumisden. In time he found himself at liberty to return home and live in peace. Having an estate by his wife, he was enabled to succour many of the unfortunate men of his party—at one time he

Brought over..................£10,392 17

41. Buried near to the head of Locharkik, opposite to
    Callich, lowis-dores... 15,000 0

42. This money was buried in two parcels, 6000 in each, all in
bags of 1000 each, the night before we were obliged to retire
from Lochiell's house of Achnacarry, by Doctor Cameron and
Mr Alexander M'Leod, who carried it upon their shoulders from
the above-mentioned house.

42. Buried near the foot of the above-mentioned lake,
    lowis-d'ores 12,000 0

43. About 90 guineas of this sum he had in his pocket when
he was taken.

43. Mr M. carried in his pocket from Glenlyon................. 110 10

44. Mr M. bought this horse from a gentleman in Balwhidder,

                              Carry over.................. £37,503 7

had no fewer than twenty depending upon him. Not long before the act of 1784, for restoring
the forfeited estates, Sir Stewart, as he was called by courtesy, bought back Fingask.
The title of the family was formally restored in 1824, and is now enjoyed by his grandson,
Sir Peter Murray Threipland of Fingask, Bart.

It may here be not improper to introduce an anecdote connected with the birth of Sir
Stewart Threipland, which appears highly characteristic of the Jacobite party. It is
related in the language of the late Mr Moncrieff Threipland of Middleton, younger son
of Sir Stewart. ' . . . . When the troops of the government had possession of Fingask in
1716, and some of the soldiers were quartered in the house, the good lady [Sir David's lady]
became alarmingly ill; and in the midst of much anxiety and care—her husband and sons
at a distance—uncertain of their fate, and the cause in which they were embarked giving
way on every side—my father was born. It was thought that, under all the distressing
circumstances of her situation, she could not survive, and a clergyman of the Episcopal
church in Perth was sent for privately (the clergy of that persuasion being marked men at
that period, as known adherents of the Jacobite cause). He, having administered the
sacrament, proposed, as so favourable an opportunity might not occur again, to baptise the
child. This suggestion, communicated in a whisper to the nurse, and others who were in
attendance, was at once assented to by them; but the difficulty consisted in knowing by
what name the infant should be called, his father having left no directions, and his poor
mother being thought much too weak to be consulted on the subject. The good lady,
however, had heard a little of what was passing near her bed, and drawing back the
curtain, she called out in a faint voice: " Stewart, Stewart !" This was enough, and
by that name accordingly was my father christened before the clergyman left the house.'

It may also be not unworthy of notice that this heroine was a member of the family
of Smythe of Methven, and probably a descendant of the high-spirited lady who, in the
reign of Charles II., took such bold measures to put down the conventicles in her neighbourhood. For some notice of that lady and her anti-Covenanting proceedings, see *Tales
of a Grandfather.*

Brought over.................. £37,503 7

to carry him south, in presence of Capt. M'Nab and —— Murray, brother to the Laird of Glencairnock.

44. To a horse.. 5 5

Total discharge..£37,508 12
Total charge....................................£37,775 0
Balance... 266 8

£37,775 0 £37,775 0

N.B.—Mr M. gave twenty guineas to his nephew, Sir David Murray, in Glenlyon; but as he has since been informed that the young gentleman says he returned it, his pockets being tore, it is not charged.

There was a small sum given to some few M'Leans at Glenmaly, but as Mr M. don't remember the exact sum, he has not charged it.

There was a small sum given to Charles Stewart when sent from Appin to Morar, to procure intelligence of the Prince.

And at the same time, some money given to a son of Cameron of Cluns, who left Appin together with Stewart, both paid in the wood above Balloheullish.

A triffile given to John Bain, Mr Murray's servant, when sent from Glenlyon to Lochiell.

A small sum to John Cameron, uncle to John Cameron of Kinlochleven, at the head of that lake.

And Mr M. likewise thinks there was some money paid to the troops at Glenmaley; but as they were few in number, the sum must have been inconsiderable.

A triffile to the boatmen who carried Lochiell, Sir Stewart Threpland, Sir David Murray, Doctor Cameron, and Mr M. up Lochleven.

Q[n.] 1. Has as honest an account been made of the 27,000 louis-dores?

2. Has the person to whose care it was committed applyed as little of it to his own use?

INDEX.

THE END.

Edinburgh: Printed by W. & R. Chambers, Limited.

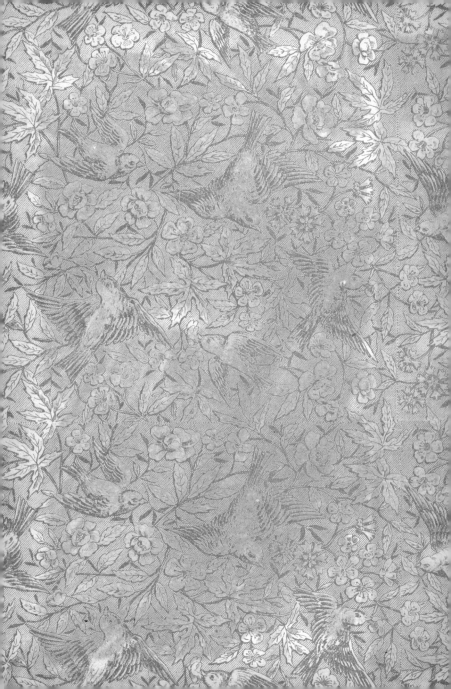